# Culture and Psychology

*To our descendants. May we learn to treat our cultural differences as sources of strength and find peace in our shared identity as one species inhabiting this tiny blue marble spinning through space.*

# Culture and Psychology

**Stephen Fox**
*University of Hawai'i*

Los Angeles | London | New Delhi
Singapore | Washington DC | Melbourne

FOR INFORMATION:

SAGE Publications, Inc.
2455 Teller Road
Thousand Oaks, California 91320
E-mail: order@sagepub.com

SAGE Publications Ltd.
1 Oliver's Yard
55 City Road
London EC1Y 1SP
United Kingdom

SAGE Publications India Pvt. Ltd.
B 1/I 1 Mohan Cooperative Industrial Area
Mathura Road, New Delhi 110 044
India

SAGE Publications Asia-Pacific Pte. Ltd.
18 Cross Street #10-10/11/12
China Square Central
Singapore 048423

Printed in the United States of America

Library of Congress Cataloging-in-Publication Data

Names: Fox, Stephen, author.

Title: Culture and psychology / Stephen Fox.

Description: Los Angeles : SAGE, [2020] | Includes bibliographical references and index.

Identifiers: LCCN 2019007214 | ISBN 9781506364421 (pbk. : alk. paper)

Subjects: LCSH: Ethnopsychology. | Culture.

Classification: LCC GN270 .F69 2020 | DDC 155.8/2—dc23
LC record available at https://lccn.loc.gov/2019007214

This book is printed on acid-free paper.

SUSTAINABLE FORESTRY INITIATIVE

Certified Chain of Custody
Promoting Sustainable Forestry
www.sfiprogram.org
SFI-01268

SFI label applies to text stock

Senior Acquisitions Editor: Lara Parra
Senior Content Development Editor: Emma Newsom
Editorial Assistant: Elizabeth Cruz
Production Editor: Jane Martinez
Copy Editor: Diana Breti
Typesetter: C&M Digitals (P) Ltd.
Proofreader: Jeff Bryant
Indexer: Wendy Allex
Cover Designer: Candice Harman
Marketing Manager: Katherine Hepburn

19 20 21 22 23 10 9 8 7 6 5 4 3 2 1

# BRIEF CONTENTS

# DETAILED CONTENTS

# PREFACE

*Kia ora, e komo mai, Namaste, selamat, welcome.* Each of those greetings reflects concepts, histories, and life-ways of its original language and culture. This book will guide you on a journey toward understanding thoughts, behaviors, and beliefs different from your own—perhaps the hardest mental challenge a human can undertake.

I began this book as a supplement to the text I had been assigned for my cultural psychology classes at my first teaching position following my PhD. That book lacked information on acculturation—the processes that occur when people must live in conjunction with other cultures—something my students faced daily on a campus at the edge of Honolulu's bustling Chinatown. Constant intercultural contact affects life in most countries now, impacting personal, political, and professional domains via trade, travel, migration, media, and the internet. Our survival depends, to no small degree, on intercultural and international understanding and cooperation. The initial chapter, written as a supplement for my students, grew into the present book, with examples and explanations drawn from my teaching adventures.

I chose to include arts examples as a theme for the book because, in my experience, they convey beautifully how people think and why they act in certain ways, teaching us morals in folk tales, connecting us to each other in hymns and anthems, inspiring us with symbols, and soothing us in our sorrows. Our arts and stories encapsulate beliefs and norms of cultures in their most transmittable, memorable forms, which is, in fact, why they serve their primary cultural functions so well.

A Chinese love story can serve as an example of love relationships in another culture, but it also contains information about social order and hierarchy, behavioral norms and prohibitions, and worldview. From long before written history, folk tales and myths have entertained people, whether gathered around a fire or sitting at a table, but they do more. Stories provide models and prototypes of ways to be and not to be. To find out how people live and think, one can listen to these tales and analyze their arts, revealing the meanings and priorities underpinning their existence. We humans do deceive ourselves in many ways, but our artistic expression tends to be very authentic.

The book grew from that foundation into its present form. My students responded well to the added material and said (in anonymous surveys, of course) that the artistic examples and stories I included held their interest and helped them understand concepts better. For examples, I drew on the knowledge of arts and culture I developed as a professional musician, artist, and journalist prior to entering psychology. I played with musicians of many cultures, sometimes with hurdles and misunderstandings to negotiate arising from cultural differences. During my time as a journalist, I interviewed and wrote about hundreds of musicians, visual artists, theatrical performers, and dancers from a wide array of cultures. I did this as a resident of Hawai'i, which is arguably the most openly embracing multicultural environment in the world. Hawai'i is not without prejudice and occasional intercultural conflict, but on a day-to-day basis, cultures coexist in a relatively tolerant atmosphere. Those experiences informed my academic study of culture as I came to view it through a psychological lens.

This textbook introduces students to the study of the individual mind in cultural context from the viewpoint of psychological science, rigorously researched and yet accessible in style. We begin by discussing ways culture can be defined, followed by an overview of evidence of how human culture evolved over many millennia of migration and cultural diversification. We then turn to processes by which humans shape, maintain, and transmit culture, followed by a discussion of primary approaches and methodologies for studying the interactions of psychological factors and culture. The remaining chapters provide a survey of current and seminal research in the field, with chapters on self, development, relationships, cognition and perception, emotion, and well-being. The text closes with a chapter on life in our increasingly multicultural world, including challenges and benefits for organizations and business, the military, and education.

Learning objectives include the following:

- Understanding of current research in cultural, indigenous, and cross-cultural psychology

- Insight into how culture shapes human cognition, behavior, and beliefs

- Introspective awareness of how cultural origin has shaped the student's own mind

- Appreciation of diversity in our communities and workplaces

- Greater skill at negotiating multicultural and intercultural situations

- Awareness of how cultural factors may influence mental health and treatment

This material is designed to be used by a wide audience, including psychology students as an upper division requirement; undergraduates as part of diversity and cultural competence degree outcomes; business students preparing to manage diverse workforces; educators addressing student needs in diverse populations; graduate students preparing for professions involving intercultural contact; and medical personnel, clinicians, counselors, and social workers serving diverse clientele.

Our job as educators is to convey information to students successfully, and if we are very lucky or highly skilled, they may also become better thinkers and global citizens as we go. A strong basis in research and thorough explanations of relevant theories are crucial, of course. We also need student engagement. No rule says we cannot have fun while we learn. I suggest we should. This book is a tool to transmit psychology's understanding of how culture shapes the human mind and experience in an inspiring and enjoyable way. Hopefully you feel engaged and informed as you read and share the excitement I feel for teaching this topic.

## LEARNING FEATURES

The novel approach of this text is the use of cultural materials and processes such as art, literature, and music to exemplify and explain psychological mechanisms and processes related to culture and cultural differences. The accessible examples have inherent utility in discussions and activities *because* they are so engaging.

As with most cultural psychology texts, chapters follow a survey format, covering a broad range of topics including methodology, cognition, relationships, and so on. Concepts build chapter by chapter, leading to practical cultural considerations for business, clinical application, and education in the final chapters.

The book includes tools designed to stimulate active engagement in the learning process. Each chapter begins and ends with questions designed to facilitate linkage of concepts for long-term retention. An **opening vignette** asks students to imagine a situation relevant to the topic. **Learning objectives** for each section facilitate outcome assessment at every step. Tied to learning objectives, **Spotlight** examples elaborate on concepts, and **Why It Matters** features explain the relevance of the chapter topics. Each chapter ends with a **Summary** and **Glossary**.

The tone of the book is slightly relaxed, to make difficult concepts more approachable without sacrificing scientific rigor. I conducted efficacy testing of these chapters with my students over several years to assure their effectiveness in achieving student learning outcomes. The use of artistic, literary, and musical examples provides a built-in method to make material relevant and enjoyable for students.

## INSTRUCTOR RESOURCES

SAGE offers instructor resources on the password-protected resource site. Please visit https://study.sagepub.com/foxculturepsychology.

Those assets include the following:

**Test Bank:** A test bank in MS Word format that contains multiple choice, true/false, and short answer questions for each chapter. The test bank provides a diverse range of prewritten options, as well as the opportunity to edit any question and insert personalized questions, to assess student progress and understanding.

**PowerPoints:** Editable chapter-specific MS PowerPoint slides offer complete flexibility in easily creating a multimedia presentation for your course.

# ACKNOWLEDGMENTS

Enormous thanks go to acquisitions editor Lara Parra for providing a home for this book at SAGE. Many thanks also to developmental editor Emma Newsom, who shepherded the work to completion, to Diana Breti for her incredible attention to detail in copy editing, and to the rest of the SAGE publishing team.

I also want to acknowledge the people who trained me in the ways of psychology and its approach to culture, principally Anthony Marsella, my master's adviser. I accidentally heard him give a speech on the need to make psychology international, intercultural, and interdisciplinary that was so superbly inspiring that I switched from ethnomusicology to the Community and Cultural Psychology program. Colleen Ward, adviser for my PhD at Victoria University of Wellington, NZ, along with Marc Wilson, who was my second adviser, completed the arduous task of reshaping a musician into a qualified psychological researcher. Committee members and examiners included Cliff O'Donnell and Ashley Maynard at UH Manoa, and Kenneth Strongman, Ronald Fisher, and Nan Sussman for the VUW doctoral degree. My thanks to you all.

Along the way, I also had the good fortune to meet and spend time with some amazing figures. Paul Pedersen and Ype Poortinga shared meals with me during my grad student days, greatly expanding my depth of understanding of the field. Others I met more briefly at conferences or as visiting scholars included Geert Hofstede, Harry Triandis, John Berry, and Patricia Greenfield, seminal figures in the field. You will find their work cited generously throughout the book.

A number of friends and colleagues assisted in shaping the book from design through peer review. Notable among those is Sammyh Khan, from my cohort at Victoria University, now at Keele University, who reviewed numerous chapters and provided advice throughout the process. Christine Karper, now of the University of Florida Health Cancer Center, also provided ongoing feedback on the project and reviewed many chapters. Thanks also to Tavis Ryan King for his service as a reviewer and for his insight on coverage of LGBTQ+ topics. Mickey Weems helped greatly with editing and advice in the final stages of writing. Warm thanks also to esteemed researcher and author Elaine Hatfield, who offered wise counsel as one of the first set of peer reviewers when the project began and whose social psych class, co-taught with her husband Richard Rapson, shaped my understanding of love and intimacy across cultures.

I appreciate the reviewers who devoted time and energy to reviewing and critiquing initial drafts of the chapters:

Eliane M. Boucher, Providence College

Paul F. Cunningham, Rivier University

Jill S. Haarsch, Elizabeth City State University

Carol R. Huckaby, Albertus Magnus College

Tavis Ryan King, Surrey Adult Learning

Aya Shigeto, Nova Southeastern University

Lona Whitmarsh, Fairleigh Dickinson University

Deborah L. Wiese, Miami University, Ohio

Most notably, Nani Azman deserves a medal for exceptional service as grammar maven and concept checker, having read and edited copy for every chapter, sometimes at multiple stages. She and our daughter Zoë, who already have my undying love and appreciation, also put up with the travails of a sometimes grumpy author over the six years of this writing process.

# ABOUT THE AUTHOR

**Stephen Fox** received his doctorate from Victoria University of Wellington, NZ, at the Centre for Applied Cross-Cultural Research. He earned his MA in community and cultural psychology at the University of Hawai'i at Manoa. In addition to his academic life, he has been a lifelong professional musician and composer with more than 20 film score credits, along with collaborations and concert performances with musicians from Hawai'i, Japan, West Africa, Indonesia, and other cultures. He has three decades of journalism experience writing about culture and entertainment for a number of publications. He currently lives on Maui, where he works as an independent researcher consulting on distance education, program evaluation, and grant support for a variety of organizations. He lectures in psychology and music in the University of Hawai'i system.

Sara Miller McCune founded SAGE Publishing in 1965 to support the dissemination of usable knowledge and educate a global community. SAGE publishes more than 1000 journals and over 600 new books each year, spanning a wide range of subject areas. Our growing selection of library products includes archives, data, case studies and video. SAGE remains majority owned by our founder and after her lifetime will become owned by a charitable trust that secures the company's continued independence.

Los Angeles | London | New Delhi | Singapore | Washington DC | Melbourne

# INTRODUCTION TO THE PSYCHOLOGICAL STUDY OF CULTURE

## Chapter 1 Outline

## Learning Objectives

LO 1.1 Explain the relevance of culture to psychological research.

LO 1.2 Evaluate existing definitions of culture and their relevance for cultural research.

LO 1.3 Describe evidence of factors that made human culture possible.

LO 1.4 Identify brain structures that enable human thought and communication and relevant theories about human social interaction.

LO 1.5 Describe configurations of basic human groups.

LO 1.6 Discuss the rise of symbolic thought and communication and its effect on rate of innovation in human culture.

LO 1.7 Explain how cultural products and processes provide evidence of basic psychological parameters of culture.

# PREPARING TO READ

- What comes to mind when you think of the word *culture*?

- What is/are your culture(s)?

- Have you ever had to interact with someone whose actions seemed strange or difficult to understand because he or she came from another culture?

*If you were moving from island to island around the Pacific a few thousand years ago, during the Great Pacific Migration, you would have traveled by* waka *(Māori), also called* wa'a *(Hawaiian) or* canoe *(English). These were not simple carved logs; they were durable and sophisticated ocean-voyaging vessels that had sails and outriggers for speed and stability and were capable of journeys covering thousands of miles. The risks and planning required were as daunting as a journey to Mars, perhaps with less chance of surviving or returning. The navigators steered by stars and currents in ways still never mastered in the West. They eventually settled the largest maritime expanse in the world, from the Maldives in the Indian Ocean to Rapa Nui (Easter Island) in the east, to Hawai'i in the*

**Figure 1.1  Canoe From New Zealand at a Gathering of Traditional Deep-Sea Voyaging Canoes From Across the Polynesian Triangle at Keehi Lagoon**

*Source:* tropicalpixsingapore/istockphoto.com

north, to Aotearoa (New Zealand) in the south. One such vessel, the Hōkūleʻa, recently circumnavigated the globe with the crew using only traditional navigation by stars and currents (see Figure 1.1).

Waka were crucial in the lives of Polynesians and, as such, held metaphorical and practical meanings that filled Polynesians' explanations of life and the world. Waka provide conveyance from one place to another. Something that takes you from one way of knowing to different understanding is a metaphorical waka. A teacher is like a navigator who guides your journey of learning. A textbook is a language vessel that carries knowledge from one person to another. This text is a vessel to help you reach greater understanding of how people live and think in cultures unlike your own and how culture has shaped you as you live in your culture.

# WHY IT MATTERS

This text will challenge your ideas of how people think and feel and why they believe and act as they do. One frequent assumption is that Western culture, that of Europe and its colonial descendants, is the pinnacle of human thought and achievement. How do you feel about the idea that a few people could set out on a hand-crafted vessel without even a compass to sail around the whole earth? People from Polynesian traditions hold continuing bodies of knowledge stretching back thousands of years before Europe developed civilization. Did your upbringing prepare you for challenges like that?

## 1.1 THE JOURNEY OF CULTURE

### LO 1.1: Explain the relevance of culture to psychological research.

ʻIke Pono *speaks to clear and certain comprehension and understanding; to recognize and understand completely and with a feeling and sense of righteousness.*

*Native Hawaiian Hospitality Association, 2013*

Humans have explored and settled the entire earth, with every land mass and stretch of water mapped and catalogued, so that even those who cannot navigate by stars and currents have GPS to draw upon. As we spread around the planet, though, we forgot our common origins. We now speak thousands of different languages and, more important, we approach life from different perspectives. We have branched into completely disparate, often conflicting, ways of viewing life, nature, the universe, and our fellow humans.

As we expanded, we developed different technological abilities, including the capacity to blow up the entire planet. Because we have forgotten our common origins, violence erupts with alarming frequency on local to international levels, ranging from military attack to less obvious violence done by embargos and inequitable distribution of resources. These factors claim millions of lives each year. Ultimately, our survival as a planet and species depends upon intercultural understanding and cooperation. We may be able to observe and describe the many lights in the night sky, but we can only live on one tiny planet so far.

This book intends to convey you to greater understanding of how people learn to feel and think as members and products of cultures. All humans share formative and functional processes, even if the resulting person ends up very unlike you, but understanding how culture shapes the person can help us to appreciate the vast diversity of human culture. Hopefully, those who read this text will end up able to empathize a bit with even the most different person because we all share the same DNA and we all have to survive on this one little marble spinning across the vastness of space. The better we know our fellow passengers on this planetary *waka*, the more we can accommodate varied points of view, the better we are equipped to negotiate solutions, and the less likely we are to use lethal violence to achieve our goals.

## Psychology and Culture

*A culturally sensitive psychology . . . is and must be based not only upon what people actually do, but what they say they do and what they say caused them to do what they did.*

*Bruner, 1990, p. 16*

Humans are unquestionably social creatures. People require parents, at least for biological reproduction, and someone must nurture us for our first couple of years. Our food, shelter, and clothing must be made, and even if we learn to make all of that ourselves, the knowledge we need is socially transmitted to us from those who came before. Humans exist, according to Caporael and Brewer (1995), in an unavoidable state of **obligatory interdependence**: human life is the product of thousands of years of cumulative and continuing social cooperation (Richerson & Boyd, 2008). The accumulations of habits, knowledge, and beliefs we have collected along the way form building blocks of culture.

Our lives are full of interactions with other people—parents, siblings, friends, or employers, along with the tellers, cashiers, bus drivers, and physicians who are occasionally encountered in our **social convoy** (see Figure 1.2), a concept that includes all those who accompany us through our daily journeys (Kahn & Antonucci, 1980). In all cultures, there are things people are encouraged to do and activities that are discouraged, either by laws, morals, or community pressures. Our interactions are governed by these rules, in the form of norms and customs that are culturally determined. We have certain bodies of knowledge instilled in us as we grow, so that we are toilet trained and can read textbooks or tend a flock of goats. We know what to eat and what is going to make us sick; this is a very important body of knowledge. We learn our collections of knowledge

**Figure 1.2    Social Convoy Elements of Common Social Interactions**

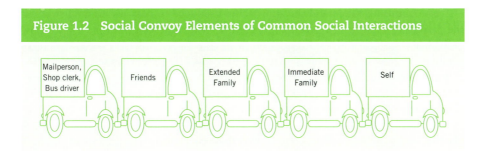

in particular ways, whether in a school, on a farm, or in a hunting party. We share these broad categories of learning and acting, yet we differ in the details of every one of them.

For our purposes, the general goal of psychological science is to explain the laws by which individual minds work, and we will explore aspects of this study throughout the book. Bringing culture to the study adds inevitable overlapping of interests with disciplines such as anthropology, cultural geography, and sociology, for instance when we examine the ways different cultures approach mealtime (see Figure 1.3). Does the family eat together at one time? Are they separated by gender? Are members served in order of age, rank, gender, or hunger level? A cultural psychologist might look at how meal sharing affects an adolescent's senses of connectedness and well-being (Crespo, Jose, Kielpikowski, & Pryor 2013).

**Figure 1.3    Venn Diagram of Mealtime as a Topic of Study**

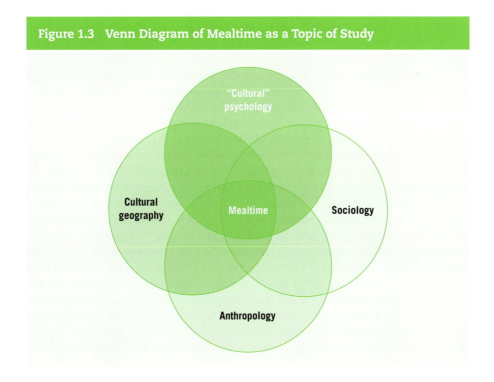

The questions asked and the approaches used lead to very different answers in the various disciplines. In psychology, culture ultimately can illuminate both how individual cognition and resulting action shapes our larger collective social structures and how cultures simultaneously shape the individual (Schaller, Conway, & Crandall, 2004). Gelfand and Kashima (2016) propose that "culture is essential to human psychology" (p. iv), such that no real understanding of humans is possible without inclusion of these cultural forces.

Obviously, there are differences between cultures. The question for psychology is whether culture makes a difference in areas that are normally the domain of psychology, such as cognition, emotion, or development. As shall be discussed, the science of psychology emerged primarily from Europe and America, and the overwhelming body of research has been conducted by researchers from those cultures, with people (mostly students) from those cultures as participants in their studies. Given psychology's broad goal of finding universal laws to describe and explain behavior, the discipline's laws, theories, and assumptions should hold true for all humans, but differences continue to emerge. Psychology programs can now be found in most countries, from Afghanistan (Kabul University) to Zimbabwe (University of Zimbabwe), providing more perspectives and diversity of data. In cultural research from all over the world, effects of culture are being observed scientifically, and a culturally informed body of literature is growing.

To illuminate the relationship between mind and culture, this text will use past and current research and real-life examples, along with creative expressions found in the arts, music, and literature of different cultures. Perhaps we take our shoes off at the door of a house when we enter, or perhaps our host gets profoundly uncomfortable upon seeing our unshod feet, and that may constitute a droll difference we can laugh about at parties. Behind that slight difference in custom may lie hundreds of generations of thought, transmitted and modified across the centuries, and reflecting very sound hygienic practice or spiritual wisdom shaping our preferences. Particular customs are fascinating in their many forms, but how do they come to be, and why are they so very different? How are they expressed, transmitted, and enforced and why? What do they mean to us and to others? These questions, regarding underlying beliefs and motivations and not simply whether or not someone wears shoes inside the house, are what we will study.

As Bruner (1990) proposes, a culturally sensitive psychology asks why we do particular things and why we think we do them. Unlike behaviorist John Watson (1913), who was only concerned with observable behavior, we are concerned with the cognition behind the action. Subtleties of culture are often so deeply ingrained that we are unaware of them unless we encounter something that runs contrary to our norms, such as bumping into someone while walking down a sidewalk in a country that passes on the opposite side from our accustomed norm. Humans have a common genetic propensity for right-handedness, but norms of passing another pedestrian or car are learned and then automated beneath our active level of consciousness. Culture forms the canvas and palette with which we paint our lives in frameworks passed down for generations, and consciousness of the rationale may be lost to history; few people are aware that Americans drive on the right because Napoleon changed traffic flow so that habit would unmask British spies in France, and America adopted his scheme. Eras and situations color our individual lives, set against shifting sociocultural backgrounds as history marches on. Within our inherited cognitive frame, each human helps to create relationships and interactions with others, our systems of learning and bodies of knowledge, and our philosophical and moral systems. The different ways these common parameters are flavored by culture and circumstance make our collective creation of life on earth a fascinating tapestry of diversity.

## REALITY CHECK

*Have you encountered people from other cultures this week?*

*Was there anything about their actions that seemed unusual to you?*

*How have cultural differences shaped events in the news this week?*

## 1.2 WHAT IS CULTURE?

### LO 1.2: Evaluate existing definitions of culture and their relevance for cultural research.

### The Problem of Defining Culture

Culture is our topic of study, but what is it? We use the term *culture* without much thought, and everyone seems to know what we mean, at least in casual conversation. Anyone speaking a language with a word for *culture* might answer that, yes, of course, they know what culture is. When you ask for a clear definition, though, the topic may become quite murky. In English, *culture* may refer to ballet, a group of people, or a Petri dish of growing bacteria. *Culture* can refer to the products and processes of a group or to the group itself. Is it the things we make, such as our paintings, sculptures, or symphonies? Is it how we behave? We see culture constantly all around us; everything humans make or do is a product of culture. The manifestations of culture are, however, the metaphorical tip of the iceberg (Hanley, 1999). Those outward expressions of culture and identity are products of behaviors, directed by belief systems, arising from worldviews and ways of thinking. It is obvious to anyone reading a newspaper or newsfeed that we have different opinions about how to live and what is right and proper to do. Is culture the behavior or the belief system that directs those behaviors? We share belief systems with some people, and yet others hold beliefs so different from ours that they are in irreconcilable conflict. Those belief systems underlie how we make decisions as individuals and nations.

Culture becomes most important when someone from a different culture does something we cannot fathom. Sitting at home alone, we are not consciously aware of culture; only when we run into something exotic or inexplicable do we suddenly take note of culture. Perhaps a person is oddly quiet or loud, or eats food that smells funny, or they bash your brains in when you arrive in their village, as happened to many 1960s missionaries attempting to convert the previously uncontacted Yanomamo of the Amazon (Chagnon, 1988, 1974). Then culture matters a lot. Hofstede (1980) reminds us that a fish does not understand water until it is on dry land, and we become aware of culture only in the face of the unfamiliar.

Definition of culture evades easy confinement; it shifts depending upon one's perspective and priorities. Ultimately, the concept of culture is itself a product of culture, which makes definition a dangerously circular piece of logic: culture can only be defined within the terms and understanding of a culture in which someone feels obliged to define culture. This endless loop is one reason culture is troubling to many psychologists. To study something, Western science says we need an **operational definition** of the concept; in other words, we need a way to specify what we will study and how it can be quantified. Usually, that process begins by examining previous research on the topic.

## Defining Culture in the Social Sciences

An erstwhile definition of culture in social sciences came from an early anthropologist, Edward Burnett Tylor (Kashima & Gelfand, 2012). In his 1871 work *Culture or Civilization, Taken in Its Wide Ethnographic Sense,* Tylor defines culture as "that complex whole which includes knowledge, belief, art, morals, law, custom, and any other capabilities and habits acquired by man as a member of society" (p. 1). By 1952, Kroeber and Kluckholn found 164 definitions of culture in use (Shteynberg, 2010). Psychologists studying culture have described it more narrowly in recent years, for instance as unique patterns of behaviors and beliefs that distinguish one group from another (e.g., Keefe, 1992; Phinney, 1990). Geert Hofstede (1980), one of the pioneers of cultural psychology, described culture as "the collective programming of the mind which distinguishes the members of one group from another" (p. 21), using a computer analogy to distinguish cultural components, which would be software, from the neural structures of our brains that would be analogous to the hardware. We will see, however, that even our neurons are pruned and shaped by culture, optimizing them for a particular set of stimuli. Yoshihisa Kashima (2008), a social psychologist from Japan, describes culture more abstractly as "an enduring and shared system of meaning" (p. 107). He continues, "Clearly, people coordinate their activities in their daily living with their shared understandings about institutions, practices, symbols, and concepts" (pp. 107–108). Ultimately, human life is a shared process, however one approaches the description.

## Our Operational Definition

The preceding definitions vary in focus and emphasis, depending upon the authors' backgrounds, training, research interests, and audiences. Each was influenced by the origins, perspectives, and purposes of the writers themselves, as is this text, and together,

# SPOTLIGHT

## BEHIND CUSTOMS: SHOES INSIDE OR OUTSIDE?

In cultures from India to China to Aotearoa (New Zealand), you will be expected to remove your footwear when you enter a home or a sacred space. If you are from an Asian or Polynesian culture, this is completely normal and you are wondering why the textbook is wasting space on the topic. In Europe and its former colonies, people wear shoes into churches and homes without thinking twice.

Spending time with Māori friends in Aotearoa, I was told that the shoe prohibition there is part of the *tapu* system—called *kapu* in Hawaiian—which I knew also included some dietary rules and ideas about not trespassing on sacred ground. Westerners misheard the word as "taboo" and thought it meant "forbidden," though it is more broadly a system for enhancing health and well-being and maintaining social order. *Tapu* practice also forbids defecation in waterways above where people drink and even sitting on a table where food would be served. The Māori were fantastically healthy when the Europeans arrived. John Liddiard Nicholas reported in 1817, "I never thought it likely they could be so fine a race of people as I now found them."

The Māori *tapu* system, I came to understand, formed a public health doctrine on both mental and physical levels. During my time in Aotearoa, I went to a conference in the Malaysian portion of Borneo, and at night on my way back from the conference or the *pasar malam* (night market) I would see creatures scurrying about with six and four legs that told me I did not want my shoes anywhere near my sleeping space (see Figure 1.4). Shortly after returning from Borneo, I visited my sister's farm and was reminded that shoe removal is a marvelous idea in most places, for health reasons (see Figure 1.5). The additional effect of shoe removal in Māori culture and in Asian temples is to establish a clear division between the mundane and the sacred, the world and the divine, so that, upon entering temple or the

**Figure 1.4  Market Stall, Kota Kinabalu, Malaysia**

**Figure 1.5  Woman and Children With Goat, Florida**

*(Continued)*

*wharenui* (meeting house) of a *marae*, the turbulence of the world is left at the door. Similarly, our homes remain free of the turbulence pathogens bring if we leave shoes outside. *Tapu* is about physical, mental, and spiritual hygiene, resolving our conflicts and maintaining harmony.

### Why It Matters

Customs are among the most visible examples of culture and cultural difference. Although some customs reflect superficial practices, others arise from differences in belief or moral systems or from worldviews crucial to culture and cultural difference. Customs and norms are often obeyed without conscious awareness, but people may react strongly when presented with violations. As such, the study of customs may provide insight into or explanations of cultural differences, which can be useful, for instance, in prevention or resolution of conflict.

they provide context to understand how psychology has accommodated the idea of culture. To those we may add Kashima and Gelfand's (2012) more recent explanation: "By culture, we mean a set of meanings or information that is nongenetically transmitted from one individual to another, which is more or less shared within a population (or a group), and endures for some generations" (p. 500). The component of *nongenetic* transmission differentiates culture from biology and instinct, without excluding epigenetic effects to be discussed later. The generational component separates culture from momentary phenomena or fads that are not repeated or sustained. Mesoudi (2009) cautions that overly specific definitions may rely too much on the perspective of a particular discipline or philosophical stance and thereby discourage avenues of inquiry, but operational definitions require clarity and specificity. For this text, we will distill our operational definition of **culture** from psychologists like Hofstede, Kashima, and Phinney, acknowledging the anthropologists and others from whom they drew inspiration: **Cultures are constellations of thought and behavior characteristic of a particular group of people that are transmitted nongenetically and survive for an extended period of time, and by which meanings and identities are created and shared.**

In order to understand how our psyches end up similar and/or different depending on our cultural origins and experiences, this text will explore concepts and phenomena including how human culture came to be; how we share, maintain, and transmit its elements; and how culture shapes the ways we live, think, and interact.

## REALITY CHECK

*Why is culture difficult to define?*

*How has cultural psychology attempted to define culture?*

*What components of human life might relate to culture and psychology?*

*Explain our operational definition of culture.*

# 1.3 A VERY BRIEF PREHISTORY OF HUMAN CULTURE

## LO 1.3: Describe evidence of factors that made human culture possible.

### Earliest Evidence of Modern Human Origin

According to recent genetic analysis, human beings—all of us—originated around 70,000 years ago on a windswept seashore of what is now South Africa (Henn et al., 2011; Soares et al., 2011; Underhill et al., 2000; Vigilant, Stoneking, Harpending, Hawkes, & Wilson, 1991). The continent had been devastated for centuries by a gargantuan drought, but a fortunate few hundred souls lived in a milder region around what South Africans now call the Blombos Caves, and they gradually procreated and prospered. The climate was a little more hospitable, but something else was afoot, some difference in these people—and they were, indeed, people, genetically virtually identical to us now. There was something about how this group thought or learned or cooperated (or all of these) that enabled them to survive while most of their hominid cousins across Africa faded from existence.

In those distant days, we already lived in communities, and we probably survived because of our aptitude for working together. As our hearty forbearers spread, they encountered different environments and obstacles and found myriad solutions to the difficulties they faced across the eons. We adapted and adopted different attitudes and ideas. Successive generations moved farther and farther across the planet, until their descendants had spread from desert to swamp to Alpine forest, reaching the proverbial four corners of the globe. We owe our existence today to something about those particular Blombos people, about *us*, because *we* (their descendants) have become wildly successful as a subspecies, despite being weaker, smaller-brained, smaller-toothed, and slower than many of our hominid cousins. Those other hominids roamed the world for hundreds of thousands of years, but only *Homo sapiens sapiens* have developed high heels, computers, and nuclear bombs. Those things are products of culture, and they came to exist via processes of the mind in cultural context over time. Everything we have and use exists only because billions of our ancestors have lived and learned and passed on what they knew to their descendants in the grand procession of culture. Eventually, we developed reading skills and books, and now we can communicate across time and space with digital technologies. This book is really an ode to that epic journey from the Blombos Caves to the present and a guide to navigating the different ways of being and thinking that developed along the way.

### Accelerating Cultural Complexity

To appreciate what culture is, we must dig briefly into the dim recesses of time to see its origins. We cannot know when people began to think like we do; we can, however, skim rapidly over the evidence from paleontology and anthropology to see when the seeds of certain behaviors and abilities were sown. Much as life on Earth began as nucleotides, eventually forming single-celled organisms and gradually becoming complex organisms consisting of trillions of cells, the earlier, simpler neural structures and abilities set the patterns for what we have become, from simple creatures to mammals to primates to humans. The accelerating development of biological complexity parallels the story of cultural progress, how we developed and maintain culture, and how culture may progress into the future.

*Homo sapiens sapiens*, in particular, are unique, extremely complex organisms who move around and do things on a little bauble in a remote corner of the known universe. The term *known* reflects part of the uniqueness: we can *think* about concepts not connected to momentary need for sustenance or shelter; hence, we say we are *sapient*, and we develop collections of thought that form *what* we know and *how* we know. We have words to describe ways of knowing, referred to as **epistemology**, in English. We think and act in predictable ways, systematically, and yet these systems may differ markedly from human to human depending upon our cultures of origin and individual proclivities. Ralph Waldo Emerson said, "The ancestor of every action is a thought." From our thinking, we constructed our lives and cultures, including the concept of uniqueness and the ability to map our location among the stars.

We have no way to ascertain for certain whether there are similar organisms in the billions of star systems surrounding our planet. We have developed highly detailed categories to classify creatures with whom we share the planet, but we cannot yet find ways to communicate with other creatures on our own planet sufficiently to know with certainty that our thought processes are not similar. We have no comparison group of creatures on other planets, and despite having no real idea of how the creatures who share our own planet might think and feel, we seem quite convinced of human superiority. We can observe living earthly creatures, however, and we have fossil evidence of what we share and when we diverged as we evolved. In that sweeping history of our planetary existence, we can find what we have in common with our fellow animals and how human culture may actually be unique.

Humanity has existed for a brief moment in the 13-billion-year history of the universe. Our whole solar system only coalesced two thirds of the way through the story, and modern humans have been around for a mere 120,000 years, or less than 1/1,000 of one percent of the great universal span. Shirov and Gordon (2013) applied **Moore's Law**, that computers double in complexity every two years, to the complexity of life, and estimated that it would have taken 9.7 billion years, plus or minus 2.5 billion, to reach the current level of complexity of organisms on Earth. The article is highly hypothetical but may illuminate parallels in the increasing complexity of human culture. Our particular type of hominid may have only been around for a brief time in the cosmic scale, but the fact that we can conceive of such immensity seems amazing for creatures so recently evolved. Most of our fellow creatures appear to be aware only of the present and recent past and confine their activities to immediate needs (your dog or cat, for instance). Lenski and Lenski (1987) studied our rate of technological innovation and reached similar conclusions that we are in the midst of a rapidly accelerating explosion of complexity in which culture is a predictable development. Whether the process is, indeed, linear or we are part of some great cycle is unknown, but certainly, we can look at the evidence of evolution in human culture and see that there are trends that lead from sticks and stones to airplanes and internet at an amazing rate.

## Is Culture Uniquely Human?

As discussed earlier, the funny thing about culture is that we have a hard time saying exactly what it is, so saying whether humans are the only ones who can claim it becomes difficult. We share the most fundamental needs and activities with all of our primate relatives and, to varying degrees, with many of the other creatures of Earth. In terms of basics, living creatures all eat, interact, and procreate. Sociality, the tendency to associate in groups, is characteristic of creatures from bees to bison, with forces of evolution shaping the specific ways social species cooperate and communicate to promote their survival. Bees and ants perform highly organized, cooperative behaviors: ants communicate via chemicals released (van Wilgenburg, Sulc, Shea, & Tsutsui, 2010), and bees actually dance the distance and trajectory information they need to convey food locations (Dyer, 2002; von Frisch, 1953). Mammals and birds generally have a variety of sounds and movements that communicate information of varying complexity. Members of family Canidae, which includes dogs and wolves, express themselves using a wide range of vocal sounds and postural cues (Anton, Tedford, & Wang, 2008; Bekoff, 1977; Robbins, 2000). Whales and porpoises use highly complex patterns of sound to communicate with each other (May-Collado, Agnarsson, & Wartzok, 2007; Tyack, 1981). Some species come together only to mate. Others live together in herds, flocks, or packs, deliberately coordinating protection from predators or organizing their predatory hunting.

In cognitive ability, more variation appears. Insects appear capable only of instinctive behavior, with adaptations appearing very slowly over countless generations. Other creatures may learn more readily and engage in complex processes. Dogs and rhesus monkeys are capable of simple numerism and can count and add up to about four items. New Zealand robins have been observed to remember and differentiate larger numbers of up to 64 food items (Garland, Low, & Burns, 2012). Creatures enjoy the company of their fellows to greater and lesser degrees and in different intensities. Many creatures appear to love their young and each other, and a great many play, especially when they are young. The basics are shared while more complex activities are less and less common across species. We humans like to think we are the pinnacle of this tapering pyramid of uniqueness, but we do have commonalities with other creatures, and these commonalities can illuminate how humans came to be such social creatures, as we rewind toward the roots of our global family tree.

Other than humans, creatures create few things, other than perhaps nests, honey, or tools for a specific task, so they have little to show for their efforts other than millions of years of survival. They also learn new ways to do new things as a species slowly, compared to humans. Does this mean they lack culture? Are there meaningful ways we can differentiate between culture and other organized systems of cooperation and communication? From an evolutionary perspective, there should be a patterned progression from slime to symbolic reasoning, and we should see shared physiological structures dating back to our common ancestors along the way (called *homology*). Homology predicts it is more likely that species share common features because they are descended from a common ancestor with that feature than that both developed the feature independently (Stone, 2006).

## 1.4 STRUCTURAL COMPONENTS OF HUMAN THOUGHT

### LO 1.4: Identify brain structures that enable human thought and communication and relevant theories about human social interaction.

Humans share a number of characteristics with the other living things in our world, and yet somehow we are unlike any other creature. We will focus on two major theories to examine aspects of how we have arrived at our current level and diversity of cultures: the *social brain hypothesis* and *theory of mind*, looking at what we share with our evolutionary cousins for homologic support along the way.

### Bigger Brains: The Social Brain Hypothesis

In the 1930's, anthropologists and other scientists began to notice that creatures' brains varied in relation to their body size, and creatures with more brain proportionate to their size tended to be capable of more complex behaviors (Jerison, 1975). The basic idea is that brain size should be fairly consistent from one mammal to the next, and a bigger creature has a proportionately bigger brain. Some creatures have brains that are bigger than average, compared to creatures of similar size. This is the case with humans. Figure 1.6, for example, is a photo of my sister and her dog, who weigh roughly the same amount. If brains are consistently sized, then sister and dog should have the same sized brain, but in fact, one has a larger brain than the other, and I am hoping it is my sister.

All of our closer primate relatives—orangutan, gorillas, bonobos, and chimpanzees—share a few social activities with us. We all live and eat together, sleeping in nests, either crafted from branches and trees or in

**Figure 1.6 Encephalization Quotient of Human and Dog**

EQ 7.39
Brain weight 1228g

EQ 1.2
Brain weight 460 g

beds and houses. The mystery has been why some of these bigger primate brains were more successful in the evolutionary process, allowing certain creatures to spread across the planet and invent automobiles while others are decreasing in range. The developing human brains did not simply increase in size uniformly, but rather added the mass primarily in the neocortex, the forebrain, where our executive and reasoning functions are found (Dunbar, 2003).

Early research assumed that the greater capacity supported development and use of tools, but it is not simply that tool use enabled human advancement. Jerison (1975) viewed the creativity of the bigger brain as coming first, stating that the most meaningful evidence

> is not in the behavior of making and using tools but in the associated cognitive activity: planning the tool, judging its quality, and applying culturally transmitted information to its construction. . . . From this hypothesis one can argue that fossil tools and other artifacts provide evidence about the evolution of human brain:behavior relations. The syllogism is simple. Since living humans make tools by using human cognitive (and other) skills . . . obviously worked "fossil" tools indicate the evolution of "homologous" cognitive skills. (p. 28)

In other words, we can assume a certain amount and type of thinking, learning, and transmission goes into the making of tools, whether they are made of stone or printed in 3D from complex polymers. If a creature was making tools of some sort, the tools themselves provide evidence of cognitive mechanisms. It is the thinking, not the tools themselves, that is important. Jerison (1975) would say that cooperative hunting and tool-making are *products* of these larger brains rather than precursors. The larger brain enabled us to do these things, and do them together, rather than the advantages provided by these products leading to selection for increased brain. Stated differently, brains had to develop for some other reason first, and complex tools are a byproduct.

In this line of research, the other change that coincided with larger brains, perhaps the most important one, is the increasing size and complexity of group interaction and cooperation among primates. The primary evolutionary advantages that allowed hominids and humans to flourish, according to one line of research, were our growing social skills and our increased ability to act together, facilitated by specific developments in our brain capacity and structure, and hence it is termed the **social brain hypothesis** (Byrne & Whiten, 1988; Dunbar, 1998, 2003). The making of a simple tool can be an individual act. What truly distinguishes humans from other primates is our ability to make tools cooperatively, then pass on and enhance the process, eventually reaching a point where we can cooperate in the building of cities, pyramids, and spaceships.

Our neocortex relates at about 4:1 to the rest of the brain, a size that appeared when our optimal group size reached about 150 individuals, which is the number of people of whom we can comfortably be aware—our cognitive group size (Dunbar, 1998). We are, first and foremost, social creatures, but we did not suddenly go from small bands of monkeys to complex communities. It took millions of years, adding skills and growing our cultural complexity along the way. The social brain hypothesis suggests there were evolving structures bringing capacities to facilitate social complexity, including regions associated with creating and understanding language. Recent fMRI studies show that speech activates similar regions in the brains of dogs (Andics, Gácsi, Faragó, Kis, & Miklósi, 2014), which may be part of why humans and dogs have developed such a close coexistence. This means that the capacity for vocalizing had already begun to evolve when our lineages split 80 to 100 million years ago (mya). Humans evolved more complex forms of language, allowing more communication and cooperation, and eventually facilitating transmission of knowledge via print and digital media.

Humans cooperate incredibly well, despite our periodic aggressions and wars. By and large, most humans awake each day and go about their tasks helping more than they hurt each other. In the debates of nature versus nurture, Field (2001) and others propose that our altruism selfishly favors our own genetics, but this idea is contradicted by the many ways we enthusiastically help others and mix our genes as we migrate and move about. Hodgson (2013) proposes that cooperation may be rooted in genetics but that culture has been the greater force in transmission and reinforcement, enabling our greater success as a species. The social complexity allowed by our big brains gives us the ability to make abstract and shifting social alliances, leading to more options for success. Despite opportunities presented by digital communication, however, our functional group size in modern electronic social networks remains usually limited to a maximum group of about 150 people, with only extraverts interacting regularly and intensively with more people (Pollet, Roberts, & Dunbar, 2011). The story of becoming human twines our physical development of brain hardware with our improved thinking abilities (software), and our resulting ability to coordinate life with larger social groups.

A criticism of the social brain hypothesis is that the theory is based on analysis of historical and anthropological data from extinct creatures of bygone epochs rather than existing structures that can be tested now. If our brains evolved advanced cognitive skills specifically and solely for purposes of social cooperation, this does not explain the multiple other purposes of these systems. The forebrain's executive functions are useful in memory, language, social cognition, and tool manufacture and extend beyond simply helping in the social domain (Stone, 2006). We will next examine theory of mind, which may be more directly linked by homology to functions we share with other living cousins.

## Theory of Mind

Our cognitive awareness of our individual selves and others relates to what psychologists call **theory of mind** (ToM). Beginning in infancy, we learn the shocking fact that others are unaware of our internal thoughts. A baby may know she is hungry or has a wet diaper, but her mother may not know. In a few short months, we are brutally thrust from utter inseparable oneness within our mother's womb to irrevocable awareness that there are others who are *not* ourselves, and our thoughts are walled within our heads unless we can communicate them. Hunger and discomfort quickly motivate children to let others know their needs and wants. We also naturally begin to develop theories about what is going on in other people's minds, hence the term *theory of mind*. Stone (2006) explains that, "Humans make inferences about and interpret others' behavior in terms of their mental states, meaning their emotions, desires, goals, intentions, attention, knowledge, and beliefs" (p. 106). Full-blown, highest level ToM is uniquely human, we think, and is achieved in adulthood.

## Components of ToM

Stone (2006) suggests that the contribution of ToM to human existence can best be understood by looking at its components. Unlike the social brain hypothesis, ToM can be tested by examining a number of living evolutionary relatives for evidence of its components and of parallel brain structures that may be active in the processes. As a child develops, it retraces this evolutionary journey, each component marking a branching in our ancestral family tree:

- Inferring goals and intentions

- Joint attention

- Pretend play

- Mentalism: Understanding and acting based on others' mental states

  ○ Desire

  ○ Belief and knowledge

- Metarepresentation

The most basic skill of ToM is the ability to **infer goals and intentions** of another, to see the direction of another's behavior and the outcome toward which he or she is moving. Construed broadly, we share this ability with many mammals and other creatures, depending on where one draws the line differentiating instinct. A penguin must perceive that its mate is ready to go find some food and cooperate carefully when transferring the egg they gestate from one's feet to the other's or the egg will freeze. A wolf must be able to infer goals and intentions of both pack members and prey, in order to hunt. These abilities may be ascribed to instinct, or they may be rudimentary versions of what will become ToM in humans.

By between 5 and 9 months of age, a child can distinguish between intentional action and accidents, an ability that definitely requires inference of intentions that may not be shown overtly. This ability is shared by chimpanzees and orangutan, firmly dating the ability to our common ancestors 14 mya (Stone, 2006). Jellema, Baker, Wicker, and Perrett, (2000) recorded specific activity in the superior temporal sulcus (a brain area associated with ToM) when Japanese macaques (*macaca fuscata*) observed another monkey both looking at and reaching for an object. To monitor intent, the macaques used a brain structure employed by humans in another ToM function: joint attention.

In **joint attention**, eye gaze direction and finger pointing provide information to an observer about the focus of attention. In children, eye monitoring happens between

1 and 2 years of age. As with the macaques inferring goals, we use the superior temporal sulcus to synchronize our attention. The Japanese macaque can be trained by researchers to use pointing, but it does not do so in the wild. Chimps and apes also readily use pointing in captivity but less often in the wild. It is notable that monkeys walk on all fours and apes use a knuckle-dragging walk, so their hands are not free to gesture, and other means of communication must be employed.

**Pretend play** or pretense means that we can adopt a shared fiction, such as pretending that a doll is a baby, and share that play with another. Here, we get into murky water in distinguishing between play and instinctive behavior and in determining what a child knows about someone else's idea of what is going on. We do know that animals play and that young carnivores go through motions of hunting together. Young bonobo females are more likely than males to play with rudimentary dolls, providing evidence of both pretend play and of gender differences in that play (Kahlenberg & Wrangham, 2010). We know that a small human may tell you earnestly that the ragged stuffed bear is her baby, but it is more difficult to identify whether she accurately perceives your ideas about the play process, which would complete the full circle of shared pretending.

Between 18 and 24 months, children develop the ability to understand what other people want and desire, termed *mentalism*. They can understand that Daddy drinks coffee that smells really bad, but it seems to make him happy in the morning. They can verbalize what other people might like and want to do, which means they are demonstrably able to perceive the mental states of others and to interact with them via language. We know a great deal about ToM because we are developing language skills at the same time ToM is developing, so we can simply ask children about what they are thinking. We use symbolic systems (words) to transmit our wants and needs, and we use them to pass on the knowledge and ideas in our heads to those around us.

What we say, and what others say to us, helps us eventually to develop an ability called metarepresentation, in which we can think about the thoughts of others: "Billy thinks that doughnuts are tasty." We can recognize that Billy thinks something and identify what he is thinking. Metarepresentation is the penultimate level of ToM. We know that we have thoughts and that others have their thoughts, and we can consider the content of other people's minds. We can further contemplate ways to convey our own knowledge and beliefs and to use the beliefs of others to our advantage.

We can survive eating leaves, fruits, and grubs. We can cooperate on a hunt with a few grunts and gestures. We have chosen as a species, however, to do many more things than required for simple survival. Moving beyond survival, language becomes crucial for virtually everything that follows for the rest of our lives. Our use of symbolic thought, our communication of those ideas, and our skill in making our ideas into reality marks the end of our commonality with any creature we know that came before (Stone, 2006).

## The Last Hominid Standing

About 6 million years ago, we split from our nearest surviving relatives, bonobos and chimpanzees. All of the hominids that evolved on our side of the split are extinct except us. We have a lot in common with the bonobos and chimps, if you look at the big picture.

They use simple tools like twigs to access foods, and our tools have merely progressed to greater refinement (van Schaik, 2004; Pontzer, 2012). Primates show affection for each other and want to make friends. In a recent study of the bonobos at the Lola Ya Bonobo Sanctuary in the Democratic Republic of Congo, Tan and Hare (2013) placed bonobos in adjacent cages with the opportunity to share food with two other bonobos, one they knew and one they did not already know. The bonobo with the food would most often share first with the one it did not yet know, thereby making a new friend. The new friend would then let in the other, previously known bonobo, and they would all eat together. Getting to know someone over a meal is an ancient part of our behavioral repertoire, and it remains a way we bond at holidays, or international State dinners, or when meeting future in-laws. The bonobo understand intentions and how to shape the thoughts of other bonobos to achieve an intended amicable outcome. They are quite human in some ways, but in these past six million years, humans have achieved many things bonobos have not, for better or worse.

The big differences began to arise around the time our Australopithecine ancestors started walking upright, about 3 to 4 million years ago. Then we began making the big strides that led to what we consider human culture. It was a long, slow process, with sometimes a million years passing before each new innovation arose, but we advanced (Heine, 2013; Lenski & Lenski, 1987). The first relative we grant the name *Homo*, from the Latin for "man," was *Homo habilis*, who came on the scene about 2.3 million years ago. Jerison (1975) credits *Homo habilis* as the first big-brained hominid, and paleontologists have found animal bones that *Homo habilis* butchered with sharpened stone tools (Pontzer, 2012). They eventually began to cook food, which was probably their bigger contribution because it provided easily digested fuel for our growing brains.

The next known hominid was *Homo erectus*, who survived from 1.9 million years ago until 100,000 years ago, by which point *Homo sapiens sapiens* had already developed into our current form. *Homo erectus* was exceptionally adaptable, spreading across Africa, Europe, and Asia, with their larger brains approaching 1,250 cc (Anton, 2003). They certainly used fire, with evidence of regular cooking dating to 790,000 years ago (Goren-Inbar et al., 2004). These were people, not with great technological knowledge, perhaps, but with the heart, spunk, and savvy to evade extinction for eight times as long as we modern humans have lived so far. They may have spawned a number of offspring, notably *Homo heidelbergensis*, who survived for about a half million years.

*Homo heidelbergensis* first appeared 700 thousand years ago, and by 400 thousand years ago, they had fire well under control, losing their larger canine teeth to a softer, brain-friendly diet. They were well aware of their mortality, honoring the dead with simple burials for the first time in the archaeological record (Carbonell & Mosquera, 2006). Burial and some amount of ritual suggest that they were thinking in ways that extended well beyond immediate survival. Fossil evidence of healed injuries and chronic disability indicate they cared for injured and disabled individuals, demonstrating that they had compassion (Hublin, 2009; Pontzer, 2012). *Homo heidelbergensis* probably evolved into both *Homo sapiens neanderthalensis* (the Neanderthal "cave people") and eventually *Homo sapiens sapiens*. With the early *Homo sapiens*, the rate of innovation increased to one every 20,000 years or so, judging by material culture left behind (c.f. Lenski & Lenski, 1987).

The *Neanderthal* were tough folk, adapted to cold climates and willing to hunt down a mastodon for food. That required spears and a high level of cooperation, as well as serious strategic planning, even with their stocky, well-muscled build. They also left evidence of the biggest leap: abstract thought. They made bone and shell ornaments for personal adornment more than 50,000 years ago (Zilhao, 2012; see Figure 1.7). It takes tools and serious effort to make holes in teeth, shells, and rocks, but it also takes motivation. The items must have meaning and aesthetic rationale to be worth making and wearing. The artifacts were significant to those people, representing something to the maker and wearer, and therefore, they suggest a certain level of cognition.

These early people were not as primitive as we suppose, and surprising archaeological evidence such as stone artifacts on the southern Ionian Islands hint at pre-human sites there as early as 110,000 years ago. The places in question are off the coast of Greece, and Crete is about 100 miles (160 kilometers) from the mainland. Investigators have recovered quartz hand-axes, three-sided picks and stone cleavers from Crete that may date to about 170,000 years ago. The exceedingly old age of these artefacts suggests the seafarers who made them were not modern humans, who originated between 100,000 and 200,000 years ago and had not reached the Mediterranean at that time. Instead, they might have been Neanderthals or perhaps even *Homo erectus* (Choi, 2012). We tend to rate members of our own groups as more capable in the present day, and by discounting the intelligence of our hominid ancestors and relatives, we miss some of the story of how we became who we are. The traditional empirical stance of psychology has focused upon a separation of nature and culture, assuming that humans are different from creatures like primates who exist in a natural world distinct from our world of human thought and technical innovation (Kashima, 2000). It is more likely that intelligence and thought have been developing in humans for hundreds of centuries, and they made amazing

## Figure 1.7 Neanderthal Personal Adornments

*Source:* Zilhão (2012). Image courtesy of João Zilhão.

leaps in ideas and innovations long ago. Far from needing a "missing link" that connects primates to humans, we need to look at the evidence without ethnocentrism to see a rich and detailed story of how we became creatures of cultural groups.

## REALITY CHECK

*Explain theory of mind.*

*How did group size affect the development of culture?*

*How does human culture differ from the culture of other creatures, if it does?*

*Explain the social brain hypothesis.*

*What was added in terms of culture as we evolved?*

## 1.5 HUMAN GROUPS

### LO 1.5: Describe configurations of basic human groups.

In social psychology, a **group** is a set of two or more people who are doing or being something in common. Our doing and being happens together with parents, lovers, extended family, friends, schools, communities, regions, ethnicities, religions, and nations, all sharing one small planet. Our family forms our first set of relationships and our most basic group, whoever constitutes family in a given culture. A functional childhood prepares us for an adaptive adulthood, and as we grow, our group will nurture us toward the specific roles and behavioral norms of our culture.

### Evolution of Groups

> *A tribe including many members who, from possessing in a high degree the spirit of patriotism, fidelity, obedience, courage, and sympathy, were always ready to aid one another, and to sacrifice themselves for the common good, would be victorious over most other tribes; and this would be natural selection.*
>
> *Darwin, 1871, p. 132*

For their 40 million years of being, primates have lived in groups that grew in size and complexity until the present day. As Darwin suggests, it was probably increasing ability to cooperate and collaborate that enabled evolving humanity to flourish. The size of groups changed over time: Our brains arrived at modern dimensions around 250,000 years ago, when we also reached the *Dunbar's number* group size of about 150 individuals comfortably coexisting. Although 150 is the upper limit before village groups tended to split, Dunbar (1992, 1998) noted that the Pleistocene anthropological record indicates three sizes of groups: 30 to 50 members in bands, 100 to 200 in lineage groups, and 500 to 2,500 in tribes. We humans made our march toward modernity in these growing units, eventually combining these small units into larger composite groups as greater cooperation was required.

## Core Group Configurations

The development of human sociality revolves around basic patterns of social interaction repeated throughout human evolution. We interact with essentially the same generic sets of others—family, friends, and community—that our ancestors did hundreds of thousands of years ago. In a slightly different approach from Dunbar's, Linnda Caporael (1997, 2007) proposes four core configurations of social relationships: *dyad, task group, band,* and *macroband*. Dyads include hunter/prey, sexual partners, and mother/child, communicating intimately and often wordlessly. The task group is based on the hunting or gathering party that shares specific socially transmitted knowledge to complete tasks, prototypically food acquisition. The band is the tribal group who live together, including the dyads and task groups who depend on that larger group for security and survival. Until recent centuries, bands connected by language and lineage would gather seasonally as macrobands to share knowledge and enact rituals that enhanced cohesion, as seen in the Native American powwow. European macroband rituals are still reflected in Christmas and New Year's, marking midwinter, and Easter, marking the Vernal Equinox. During All Hallows Eve, *Día de los Muertos*, and the *Obon* Festivals of Japan and Okinawa, the living groups also interact ritually with departed ancestors, lending the larger groups a sense of cohesion and permanence across generations (see Figure 1.8).

**Figure 1.8  The *Obon* Festival**

These social structures are theoretically analogous to those underlying our modern, more complex social organizations. *Demos* is an ancient Greek term for geopolitical divisions, and it is used in biology to describe local populations of organisms living in close enough proximity to breed. David Hull (1988) used *demic structure* to describe modern scientific communities who exchange ideas and researchers. Applying the concept to contemporary societies, Caporael (2007) replaces *band* with the term **deme** and *macroband* with **macrodeme**. Academic departments or corporate regional offices equate to the deme. Caporael likens annual academic conferences to macrodeme gatherings, where ideas are exchanged and graduate students move to other academic demes, or where engineers move between tech corporations, exchanging young members between their intellectual tribes to spawn new ideas and knowledge.

We gain our socially transmitted knowledge *from* these groups and we contribute our own efforts and learning *to* those groups, which then develop into new forms over time. This model bears similarity to the inner rings of Bronfenbrenner's (1979, 1994) ecological systems model and to Vygotsky's (1978) emphasis on the cultural context of development, both of which will be discussed in later chapters. We are born into a family that is part of a clan, village, or community that exists within context of a region, a tribe, or a state. Some of us grow up to enter dyads of romance and/or marriage; some cultures have other forms of relationship for procreating the next generation. We all interact with and educate our young, passing along our patterns of relationship, within a region, ethnicity, religion, nation, and ultimately, as part of humanity as a whole. Membership is common to us all, in groups from core family outward, differing in the meanings we give to our relationships; how we interact with others; and how our memberships, roles, and responsibilities influence our behaviors and beliefs. Our cultural origins, memberships, and identities shape our similarities and differences in how we relate to others around us and in the people we become.

## REALITY CHECK

*Of what groups are you a member?*

*Do any of your groups fit the description of demes or macrodemes?*

*When do your groups gather? Holidays? Conferences? Sports events?*

## 1.6 COMMUNICATION AND INNOVATION

### LO 1.6: Discuss the rise of symbolic thought and communication and its effect on rate of innovation in human culture.

We are now undeniably different from our ancestors. A principle difference lies in the complexity of our communication. Our surviving ape relatives do demonstrate facility in learning and using gestures (de Waal, 2002), but the topics they can address are limited to their immediate physical and emotional situation. Humans systematically communicate highly complex and abstract concepts, a unique skill (Penn, Holyoak, & Povinelli, 2008). Somewhere along the way, we developed speech. Our mouths and throats evolved for eating, drinking, and breathing, but sounds emerged in reptilian days as a sort of bonus function, and gradually the structures adapted to more refined sound production. Our heads changed shape over millions of years, and the changes in our craniums coincided with development of the language centers in our brains. These include Broca's and Wernicke's areas, named for the scientists who identified them when they observed loss of language skills in people who had damage to those regions. We split from rhesus and macaque monkeys about 25 million years ago. In neural imaging studies, macaques, humans, and dogs show similar brain activation when they hear calls of their own kind (Andics et al., 2014; Gil-da-Costa, Martin, Lopes, Muñoz, Fritz, & Braun, 2006). Though they developed similar brain structures to process specific sounds from their cohorts, other primates lack larynx structures for speech. Fossil records do not show clearly when hominids acquired the correct physiology to create words, but we do know that humans are the only surviving members of the primate line with that ability, and for some reason, only humans compose sonnets and sing arias.

Speech enabled us to develop efficient ways to transmit our thoughts, and our enhanced frontal lobes enabled us to think increasingly profound thoughts to pass on. Language is a system of symbols by which we can facilitate transfer of subtle concepts represented by words and pictures. Once theory of mind processes began to inform us that others do not know our thoughts, we were compelled to find better ways to communicate our inner mental states. We represent the items, feelings, and concepts linguistically. The metarepresentation level of ToM depends upon being able to create conditional clauses about someone-thinking-something, which is a linguistic skill in itself. Whenever speech really came about, the ability certainly contributed to our more recent acceleration in technological innovation. The ability to reason about higher order concepts and to convey these concepts to others defines humans as something quite different from the other creatures of our planet.

## Life and the Art of Creating Culture

Once the first *Homo sapiens* departed the shores and caves of Blombos, they began to develop different skills and ideas. What we make and how we make it has obviously varied over the millennia, depending on environmental demands, materials available, and the technologies we shared at the time. This is why an anthropologist can identify the origin of an item by era and locale with a high degree of accuracy: the artifacts we leave and even our bones tell stories of how we lived and what we knew. We can look at evidence from an extinct civilization and know what they ate, how they got the food, what shelter they used, and, to some extent, what was on their minds. Arts convey our mental states in great detail, even at a distance of thousands of years. We can look at paintings on the walls of caves at Chauvet and Lascaux and we know that the artists were keen observers and superb at drafting; they saw as we see. We also know that the scenes had meaning as symbols of something important in life. We can suppose that the many rotund "Venus" figurines such as the Willendorf Venus were popular because they reminded their owners of the mysterious power of women to give us life.

ToM lets us know that the *other* is distinct from us to some degree, from those in our immediate family to the fringes of our extended family and friends, to our community. Beyond that limit, the *other* becomes increasingly alien and threatening because after a few short millennia, we no longer recognized our shared origins and began to compete violently for resources. The Yanomamo will battle with and steal from neighboring groups from whom they split only a few generations before (Chagnon, 1988b), and Americans went to war in 1776 while still politically aligned with their British land of origin. In our repertoire of non-survival skills and practices, we had to develop ways to maintain connectedness and cohesion with those close to us in order to stand against other groups of humans, now no longer family. Arts provided symbols and rituals, flags and pledges, to demonstrate shared identity and mark differences.

We may also have been developing musical skills at the same time we learned to use language, or perhaps our refining of perception of musical patterns from the noises around us allowed us to develop both language and music. It is a chicken-or-the-egg question, but somehow, we now have language, music, and visual arts, with symbolic content conveyed through all these means. They allow us to create common ground and shared experience and to develop and convey highly complex thoughts across generations. Think about how you learned the alphabet, which was probably via song. We have the ability to live in large, organized groups, in no small way because of our ability to share our thoughts in very creative ways. Cross (2001) explains,

> it could be that the emergence of proto-musical behaviour and their cultural actualization as music were crucial in precipitating the emergence of the cognitive and social flexibility that marks the appearance of *Homo sapiens sapiens*. (p. 100)

Actually, early language and music may not be solely the domain of modern humans. An artifact from Divje Babe in Slovenia may prove to be a 60,000 year old flute (Lau, Blackwell, Schwarcz, Turk, & Blickstein, 1997; see Fig. 1.9), though this is a topic of contention in the archaeological world. At that time, modern humans had probably not yet arrived in Europe, so if it is a flute, it was made by *Homo neanderthalensis* or some other relative.

## Rapid Change and the Advent of Humanity

About 200,000 years ago, humans who were morphologically very much like us appeared in Africa. By 100,000 years ago, mutations and selections had occurred, bringing our brains to their current 1,400 cc size (Pontzer, 2012). Soon afterward, we encountered the centuries of African drought and the stalwart survivors of Blombos on the South African coast. In this time period, we reached our optimal group size of about 150 people living and cooperating together, a number that has held throughout our subsequent migrations and adventures into new lands and on into digital realms (Dunbar, 1992; Roberts & Dunbar, 2011).

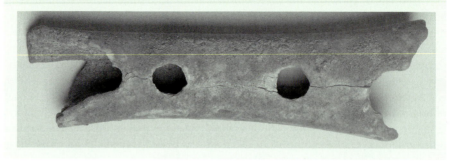

Source: Kunej & Turk (2000). Image courtesy of National Museum of Slovenia; photo by Tomaz Lauko.

Somewhere around 70,000 years ago, the Blombos people struck out for new territories and began to populate the world, facilitated, the social brain hypothesis would say, by our ability to cooperate as we go. Our rate of innovation skyrocketed. From 40,000 to 12,000 years ago, an innovation came along every couple of thousand years. Then we kicked into high gear when agriculture developed, with 5.2 innovations per thousand years. At 9,000 years ago, the rate began to compound exponentially, though genetically and neurologically, we were still essentially the same creatures we were before, and we still functioned best in direct contact with relatively small groups.

The innovations were not uniform across all groups of humans, and even now, we are not adapting perfectly to all of our newfound abilities and creations. Humans are paradoxical, capable of thoughts spanning beyond the present into the remote past and unimaginable future. We live increasingly well and make ever more efficient ways to die. We kill each other by the millions in arguments and conflicts over resources and over the ideas our thinking minds have created. We consume too much of our resources and foods in increasingly less healthy ways. We have also, conversely, created ideas and artworks that transcend meager existence into the mystical, from songs and symphonies to Stonehenge and the pyramids. Tools, tunes, and technology are creations of humanity that make our lives better and more meaningful on this little rock in the sky. All of these, good and bad, are acts of culture.

Tens of thousands of years ago, our ancestors had certainly begun to think in abstract terms of numbers and ideas. They buried their dead, which suggests that they were aware in each moment that people lived and died, perhaps more intimately than modern humans, who rarely see a dead person and probably will die in a hospital at an old age with few people they know around them. They told stories, made jewelry, painted pictures, and played music, which means they had complex thoughts and reasons to wear an adornment, express something they imagined, or create a soundtrack of musical background for their lives. These creative products, from language to painting to music, formed the repositories of our evolving cultures and provided the means to transmit them to future generations. Evidently, it worked well because we have inherited language and technologies and textbooks.

straightforward enough, until you start sorting out its components. Psychology as a formal discipline is less than two centuries of age, and we have only just developed the tools to see patterns of thought in the closed box of the brain via fMRI and other imaging techniques. Further, the discipline only began seriously to explore beyond its home base of Western culture in the last 60 years. We may be years from universals that can cross all cultural boundaries. We can, however, use current research to understand better those around us, near and far.

## Parameters of Culture

As we will see, psychological study of culture balances investigation of similarities and differences across cultures. Over the past few decades, researchers have proposed a number of ways to describe parameters of relevance in the study of culture: what comprises a culture, how cultures form and change, how cultures structure and order themselves, how they view the world and reality, and what the identifiable psychological components needed to predict behavior across culture might be.

In common parlance, culture has been equated with nationality, society, race, and ethnicity, which overlap and blur boundaries. Modern nations often include dozens of ethnic or racial groups who share the larger identity of "country." Terminologies change, and "race" is now considered outdated if not prejudiced, given that we are genetically virtually identical even if our skin colors differ. Major research has been done on *inter*-national levels, such as Hofstede's (1980) seminal study of dimensions of "cultural" variability, to be discussed later. Anthropology indicates that ethnocultural groups should probably be considered separately, even within national borders. While acknowledging the groundbreaking nation-level research that forms much of the psychological literature regarding culture, the need to understand processes and conflicts within multicultural environments suggests that we should use self-identified ethno-cultural groups, such as African American, Kosovar, Pashtun, or Māori, as our primary focus. Altogether, these are **levels of analysis**, which extend from individual to familial, to national, to global.

Broadly, cultures are shaped by ecological, social, and biological factors: the natural environment, the density and dispersion of people and their genetic propensities, and our interaction with germs and with other large organisms (think bison, mastodons, or horses). Eons of pressures from these forces have led to the identifiable groups seen today. Additionally, cultures interact with each other, currently in unprecedented domains such as electronic communities. These changes and forces are **extrinsic factors** that underlie many of the topics of difference addressed throughout the text.

Roots of social order *within* cultures and shared worldview extend back centuries. A social order described by Kung Fu-tse (Confucius) organized life in China and surrounding countries for more than two millennia, and a similarly rigid hierarchic structure remains central to the modern Chinese government. European culture traces its origins back to Mesopotamia and Greece, spread around the Mediterranean and beyond through trade and conquest, especially during the Roman era. These influences shape our beliefs about what is right and wrong and what and how we teach our children. The values, beliefs, and related stories we have inherited, passed on, and refined through generations form the historical contexts shaping our decision processes about how we act and interact on a daily basis.

Environmental, political, historical, and social forces have shaped our current set of nations and cultures, and although life is always in some state of flux, the present set has definable and observable characteristics. Culture composes our beliefs and values, the symbols that represent them, and the ways we express them in our lives and relationships. It is the cause of our most dangerous conflicts. Culture is inseparable from shared human existence, but our focus here is the individual and how the mind is shaped by culture. If cultures are relevant to psychology, there should be predictably in how they shape behaviors and beliefs, both in similarities and differences across cultures. This text discusses what are essentially normal topics of psychology examined from the viewpoint of cultural forces and contexts.

This first chapter began by defining culture because psychology is a science built on belief in definition and measurement, and it discussed evidence of factors that enabled human culture to evolve, including our mental and communication capacities and how these may have enabled us to succeed in cooperative groups. Chapter 2 looks at how culture is transmitted, maintained, and changed; ways we identify as members of larger groups like ethnicities and nationalities; and some observed dimensions of variation between cultures. Chapter 3 examines the history of culture in psychology and special methods required to deal with cultural and cross-cultural factors in psychological research.

The text then will discuss usual topics of introductory psychology: development, self and relations with others, cognition and perception, emotional expression, motivation, and morality. Finally, we turn to well-being and the effects of life in a multicultural world, concluding with the practical applications of culture in organizational and educational psychology and what psychology can contribute to greater peace and well-being in our future.

## Arts, Culture, and the Human Mind

*This line of research concerns the compartmentalization of culture for research purposes. Culture . . . is a conglomeration of many aspects of life, including food, clothing, music . . . it is easy to lose perspective, thinking that these scores become culture.*

*Matsumoto, Wessman, Preston, Brown, & Kuppersbusch, 1997*

Psychologies of culture have not yet widely examined those elements most commonly perceived as "cultural," such as art, music, ritual, customs, and food (Matsumoto et al., 1997). Arts are viewed as an affective rather than a cognitive set of processes and products, and the widespread attitude is that arts lie outside the realm of objective science (Bresler, 2006). In fairness, artists do deal in intangibles that are not easily quantified, but they are a rich source of information on the ways people live and think in every culture.

Roughly 5,000 distinct cultures remain on Earth (Marsella & Pedersen, 2004), and all are unique constellations of beliefs, behaviors, values, and worldviews: each one is the current product of thousands of years of adaptation to the situations they faced. The collected knowledge of any given culture—its ways of interacting, thinking, and being—form a tool kit contained and transmitted in its arts. In the songs, stories, and symbols of a culture—the domains of arts, artists, and cultural processes—one may find, neatly arrayed, the systems of meaning, concepts, and shared understandings of a culture, packaged within the actual institutions, practices, and symbols of that culture as they have been habitually shared and transmitted across the millennia (Burke, 1989; Frith, 1996; Geertz, 1973; Hargreave & North, 1999; Kashima, 2000, 2008; Turino, 1999).

Our challenge is to understand the various ways people live, act, believe, and think. Perhaps, if we really want to understand the ways people believe and think in cultures, we might find clues in the products they make to represent their beliefs and ideas, the vehicles by which cultural values and meanings are lived and transmitted across generations. W. E. Percy stated, "It is not enough that one is conscious of something; one is also conscious of something being something" (in Geertz, 1964, p. 61). Arts tell our stories; in short, they convey the meaning that makes something into something.

The objects and melodies we make are shaped by our thoughts, which have been shaped by the stories and languages we learned as children. Arts have been crafted over generations of historical contexts and events. It is a cyclic process that, in turn, shapes what our children learn, value, create, and pass on. A sculpture from ancient Rome, China, or Mesopotamia normally depicted a character from a myth or legend or an important person of the time. That particular image was important enough to represent in tangible form because it had particular meaning. Styles and subjects change, but across the eons, arts arise from the ideas we think and believe with enough conviction to pass the thought or belief onward into the future.

## Taonga Tuku Iho

> "Taonga" embraces the notion that there are things in the world, either naturally occurring, people, entities, or things made that are very precious—because what they do, they have very strong symbolic value as a carrier of identity. A carving can be taonga, but the art of carving is also taonga. "Tuku iho" is that which is passed down, or that which is passed on. So taonga tuku iho are those treasures or precious things that are passed on. "Taonga tuku iho," as a concept, is that we value the notion that we will pass on our treasures, and one of our greatest treasures is knowledge itself, knowledge about the culture, about the world.
>
> Ross Hemera, in Fox, 2010, p. 233

Thirty thousand years ago, the most popular image to create was a rotund female figure, probably representing the mysterious feminine creative force that brings us life through birth. Many have been found around the world, and regardless of the meaning of the image, an incredible amount of effort went into carving that figure using only sticks and stones. We have reasons for making the particular things and images we create, whether a crucifix, a Chinese Taoist *ba-gua*, or a fertility symbol. We developed our symbols over generations as shorthand to convey and reinforce complex sets of ideas, especially those that are central to our culture and worldview, because we are essentially lazy thinkers (Fiske & Taylor, 1984). We need efficiency so we can process new information amidst an overwhelming stream of experience, while retaining all that we have already learned.

Right now, you are probably sitting on something—a chair, bus seat, or the ground—but you do not feel it. You do not even notice the tip of your nose, though it is plainly in your view (take a look). This is called sensory adaptation, and what we tune out depends on our normal environment. We might tune out the chirping of birds and sound of wind in the leaves, or we might ignore the air conditioner and voices from the next classroom. What we ignore depends on what is usual and what may constitute a threat, such as a charging mastodon or an electrical burning smell, depending on your situation. With normal, nonthreatening stimuli, whatever those may be in your environs, we habituate to them so that we can pay attention to other tasks and ideas. This has been crucial to our survival because if you were constantly aware of every sensory input, you would go mad. We use **heuristics**—mental shortcuts—to make decisions swiftly so we do not freak out when the house cat comes by, but we react swiftly to a saber-toothed tiger outside the cave.

We synopsize our cultural ideas and ideals to reduce the workload of thinking and making decisions. The heuristic models that seem to work best become **conventional wisdom**, which social psychology has shown to be correct maybe half the time, but which provides a sense of organization and control in our world. Mental shortcuts underlie our skill sets and moral systems that assist our survival, along with our prejudices and stereotypes, and all of these definitely vary across cultures. We develop bodies of knowledge and corresponding ways of thinking using our marvelous brains. Some aspects are effective and some are not, but we generally seem to have benefited from having the systems of thought available. We learn and grow as individuals, cultures, and the species, and we pass on what we think is the best of what we learn from those who come before. Those are our intellectual *taonga*, the treasures of knowing and thinking.

We developed the ability to use images and symbols to represent our concepts of the ways we do things, the ways we live among others, and the ways we teach others. These elements of culture are transmitted with amazing fidelity and efficiency using our words and visual tools, now including printed or digitized words. These collections of words and symbols and the meanings we attach to them represent our ways of knowing and understanding the world. They are the treasures of culture we pass from generation to generation. In *te reo Māori* (Māori language), the things, ideas, and processes collectively are called *taonga tuku iho*. *Taonga* is treasure, a marvelous thing someone makes, a process that allows us to live better, or a way of thinking and perceiving reality that helps us flourish. *Taonga tuku iho* describes an indigenous epistemology—a way of knowing and of transmitting and maintaining culture across time and generations.

Humanity today benefits from hundreds of generations of treasures lovingly passed on and improved, developed in our minds, disseminated by communication processes, and shaping how we live, think, believe, and interact each day. Culture has been both the vehicle and the product of human culture. As a vehicle, it allows us to grow and live within a cohesive group and to pass that particular culture's way of being on to our children. In terms of product, what we make, whether image or song, contains evidence of what and how we think as a unique group in a particular time and place.

## Why We Will Use Arts as a Theme Throughout the Text

At Victoria University of Wellington, New Zealand, there is a *marae*, which is the sacred meeting and ceremonial compound of the Māori culture. That particular *marae* is named *Te Tumu Herenga Waka*, which is the term for the mooring posts of the great ocean-sailing *waka*, the canoes of ancient times (Taonui, 2012). The name was chosen because Māori from many different *iwi*, or tribes, attend VUW, and the *marae* was built as a connecting point for all of them, even if their *iwi* were at war in the past. In learning, we seek to anchor our knowledge so it becomes a part of us, and our knowledge, in turn, anchors us in our world. It is my sincere hope that this book will be useful to people of many cultures. As such, we need common ground, a common mooring point where we can have our meeting of minds. All cultures have artistic expression, through stories and images, songs and dances. Arts are, literally and figuratively, a common ground shared by all cultures.

Earlier, we discussed that the practical parameters of culture are our relationships and interactions with others, methods of learning and teaching, our bodies of knowledge, and our systems of morality and motivation. The making and the sharing of arts are both common to all cultures as processes and unique to the culture of origin in their forms. Arts provide a safe platform to view the differences between cultures because although we have very different rules about behavior, what we can do or say and how we can and cannot connect with others, these differences are expressed directly but safely in our poetry, songs, dramas, music, and visual arts. When Homer retold the *Iliad*, his recounting of the Trojan War also conveyed the Greek understanding of life in a world symbolically ruled by capricious gods who personify the unpredictable motivations and fates of mortal humans. The foibles of the gods and the mortal heroes exemplify moral and behavioral codes that were the highest and best ways the Greeks knew to systematize civil society, and the epic sagas conveyed this rationale across generations as surely as the great *waka* bore the Polynesians across the Pacific.

Every culture has a body of treasured works concealing its history, worldview, and belief system. The *Mahābhārata* encapsulates the collected wisdom of ancient India within the epic telling of the Kurukshetra War. By Bach's time, Protestantism was the norm in Germany, holding that humans could be redeemed on their own merit. His musical genius reflected a quest to elevate the spirit through the beauty of music into divine realms. Johannes Brahms's *A German Requiem*, from more than a century after Bach, was a work to aid the living in bereavement from a perspective reflecting the growing popularity of Humanistic values. Our folk stories, myths, and legends convey mundane and divine lessons about living day to day. Our cultural products, the songs, stories, and sculptures provide our most direct evidence of specific ways of thinking and being and their similarities and differences across time and cultures. Arts do not fully explain why our minds work as they do, but they tell us what a culture holds dear at a given point in history. For our text, they provide a common mooring point and a wealth of examples as we explore the domains of the mind across cultures.

## REALITY CHECK

*What can arts show us that is of value to psychology?*

*Why are heuristics important in our lives?*

## REFLECTING ON YOUR READING

- Has this chapter changed how you think about culture?

- As you go through your day, can you see any of the ways of being and interacting we share with our primate ancestors? What are they?

- Listen to a piece of music from another culture. What can you tell about that culture from the music?

## CHAPTER 1 SUMMARY

### 1.1  The Journey of Culture

Humans have spread around the entire globe, diversifying and learning as we went. People are unquestionably social, living in a state of obligatory interdependence that we share with our social convoy. Psychology seeks to understand laws governing the mind, and the addition of culture to that study adds elements of other social sciences to understand how people and cultures shape each other. Customs can illustrate way of thinking underlying cultures if we seek to understand why they exist.

### 1.2  What Is Culture?

Culture seems easy to define, but pinning down a definition is difficult. We see culture most clearly when faced with difference. A general definition of culture cannot really be created independent of culture. Social sciences view culture as patterns of beliefs and behaviors that distinguish one group from another, but there is no universally accepted definition and no encompassing explanation for cultural differences and effects.

Our lives include social relations and ways of interacting. We have bodies of knowledge for how to live that we learn in particular ways. We share these general parameters but differ in the contents, and we are largely unaware of the differences. Culture provides the context for creation of our unique lives. Culture is described as nongenetic components of being that are shared by groups of people, including the totality of their ways of life, transmitted across generations. We will also consider processes of shorter-term subcultures.

## 1.3 A Very Brief Prehistory of Human Culture

Genetic evidence suggests all modern humans descend from a group living at Blombos Caves in South Africa 70,000 years ago. We then spread across the globe, diversifying as we went.

Life in general has become more complex in a process theorized to have begun with the formation of the universe, and human culture is becoming more complex at an increasing rate. Humans have developed thought, including epistemology, or ways of knowing what we know. We have categorized the creatures of Earth and decided that we are unique and most advanced, despite having come into existence relatively recently. Our level of technology has increased in predictable ways, only reaching its current complexity in the past few centuries.

Humans do seem unique among living creatures, but we share common evolutionary origins with others, and these commonalities provide information about what we have become. Many creatures engage in social activity, including communication. Creatures vary more in their cognitive capacities. Some animals use rudimentary numbers and make simple tools. Homology predicts that ways of thinking we have in common may be due to shared brain structures, and this can be observed by studying evolutionary developments.

## 1.4 Structural Components of Human Thought

Two major theories relate to the differences between humans and other animals, the social brain hypothesis and theory of mind.

The size of an animal's brain relative to body size correlates with cultural complexity and, among primates, with group size. Social cooperation rather than ability to create tools probably enabled our success as a species. We can make social alliances beyond simple kinship groups, which has resulted in greater flexibility in adapting to different conditions. New fMRI studies show correspondence between areas of brain activity and social abilities. Despite this new evidence, the social brain hypothesis depends mostly on post-hoc examination of historic evidence.

Theory of mind (ToM) is a way of thinking we begin to develop in childhood. We learn that other people have different ideas from us, and we develop theories to understand how they think. Components of ToM are shared by other animals in ways that parallel the evolutionary processes leading to modern humans. The components are inferring goals and intentions; joint attention; pretend play; mentalism: understanding and acting based on others' mental states; desire belief and knowledge; and metarepresentation.

Children perceive intention as early as 5 months, a skill shared by primate relatives. The other components come into play as the child develops, leading to the ability to make metarepresentations, which are ideas about what others think.

Increasing differences began to arise about 6 mya when we split from chimpanzees and bonobos, beginning with the ability to walk upright, then the ability to make spears and more complex stone tools. *Homo erectus* began to use fire and *Homo heidelbergensis* disposed of their dead in ritual ways. Neanderthals showed signs of abstract thought and created art.

## 1.5 Human Groups

Groups are some number of people being or doing something in common. Morphologically modern humans seem to be most comfortable at the *Dunbar's number* group size of about 150 individuals, though we do join in larger groups for certain purposes. Core group configurations include *dyad, task group, band,* and *macroband,* allowing close interaction, collaboration on tasks, sharing of resources and protection, and larger gatherings for exchange of information and mates. These are reflected in Bronfenbrenner's ecological systems model.

## 1.6  Communication and Innovation

Humans are different from other animals in the complexity of our communication, though we share neural structures with dogs and apes among others. We have found increasingly effective ways to communicate and to enhance the range of thoughts we convey. Our topics and how we represent ideas evolved over time in ways identifiably specific to eras and regions. Over many millennia, musical ability emerged in parallel to verbal ability. Our rate of innovation increased over time, accelerating rapidly after the advent of agriculture.

## 1.7  Elements of Culture: Putting the Pieces Together

We share commonalities across cultures in the ways we socialize, learn, and think. These are studied in social, developmental, and cognitive psychology. Cultural psychologies study how culture has led to our different ways of thinking and acting. We have accumulated vast differences in language and ways of thinking. We have ongoing intercultural conflicts, but we also share artistic and creative processes by which we share and transmit our greatest cultural legacies.

The psychological study of culture balances investigating similarities and differences. A number of parameters have emerged in this study, describing what is important for understanding humans across cultures. Levels of analysis must be considered, because what is true for one ethnic group may not be shared across a nation and vice versa. Extrinsic factors of ecology and environment, as well as intra-cultural historical contexts, can inform us about what led to current cultural situations and can inform us about present day psychological states. As sciences, psychologies of culture seek measurable and predictable dimensions of stability and variation.

Arts are not usually discussed as a part of cultural psychology, though they contain the most complete picture of the beliefs, thoughts, and symbols of any culture. More than knowing simply what the components of culture are, understanding requires that we know *why* they are important. What we do and make is shaped by what we have learned from childhood, which in turn shapes what our children learn and do.

Humans have developed symbols as shorthand for concepts, especially those that are central to our cultures. We develop heuristics—easily accessible rules for decisions—so that we can make swift decisions, including generalizations considered conventional wisdom. *Taonga tuku iho* describes concepts of an indigenous epistemological system from Māori culture that includes valuation of knowledge and acknowledges intergenerational transmission of that knowledge. Arts provide a well-developed record of concepts and symbols found in all cultures. In this text, they provide an anchoring point and collection of examples as we explore culture and the mind.

## GLOSSARY

**Conventional wisdom:** A generally accepted viewpoint that a condition or series of events will happen in a particular way and/or lead to a particular outcome, whether or not this is factual.

**Cultures:** Constellations of thought and behavior characteristic of a particular group of people that are transmitted nongenetically and survive for an extended period of time, and by which meanings and identities are created and shared.

**Deme:** In ancient Greece, a local affiliative political division; in biology, a breeding group within a species.

**Epistemology:** The study of the origins and nature of knowledge.

**Extrinsic factors:** In this text, relevant issues outside of the domain of culture, or of a particular culture, that affect current situations in a culture.

**Group:** A set of two or more people who are being or doing something shared in time or locale.

**Heuristic:** A strategy for evaluating evidence quickly and with low effort used to reach decisions and/or conclusions based on minimal information.

**Historical contexts:** The constellation of events leading to current awareness and cognition in a culture.

**Homology:** Similarity in form or function to a different type of origin due to shared heritage from a common ancestor.

**Infer goals and intentions:** To see the direction of another's behavior and the outcome toward which he or she is moving.

**Joint attention:** A ToM function in which eye gaze direction and finger pointing provide information to an observer about the focus of attention.

**Levels of analysis:** Definition of exactly what population is being studied.

**Macrodeme:** A superordinate set of related tribal or social groups, related by language and custom and usually exchanging youths to mate.

**Metarepresentation:** The ability to formulate mental cognitions about the mental cognitions of others.

**Moore's Law:** An axiom originated by George E. Moore that the number of transistors in a computer (later, integrated circuits) would double every two years due to technological advances, thereby doubling computing power.

**Numerism:** The ability to understand and calculate numerical quanta.

**Obligatory interdependence**: The unavoidable state in which humans exist that is the product of thousands of years of cumulative and continuing social cooperation.

**Operational definition:** A clear specification of the phenomenon to be studied and the parameters by which it can be measured.

**Pretend play:** Fantasy activities in which objects, actions, or ideas are imagined to represent something else, such as a littermate substituting for prey in simulated attack or a box representing a boat to a child.

**Social brain hypothesis:** A theory that we developed larger brains with particular features, such as the prefrontal cortex, to facilitate cooperation in large, complex groups.

**Social convoy:** A network of close relationships, narrowly defined as those maintained for life, but more broadly construed as people we encounter on a daily basis for an extended period.

**Sociality:** The tendency to associate in groups.

**Theory of mind:** A normal development that begins during infancy when a child comprehends that he or she has thoughts and that other people have thoughts that are different from the child's.

# CULTURAL PROCESSES

## Chapter 2 Outline

## Learning Objectives

LO 2.1 Identify and differentiate concepts and components of social learning and transmission.

LO 2.2 Explain how social intelligence facilitates cumulative culture as humans adapt and learn as groups.

LO 2.3 Describe the characteristics and processes of cultural dynamic theories.

LO 2.4 Assess ways people share and use cultural information to cooperate as they construct their sense of reality and identity.

LO 2.5 Discuss the reasons and ways cultures change.

LO 2.6 Evaluate the utility of arts practices and products as avenues for understanding cultural processes.

# PREPARING TO READ

- What changes have you seen in your lifetime?
- Is there something you used to like that is now out of style?
- What do you think your country will be like in 5 years? 20 years?

*One day in 2010, Julie put a piece of grass in her ear and left it there. Evidently, she liked it because she repeated this behavior daily, leaving the straw-like grass hanging there as she went about her business. If the behavior seems a bit unusual compared to the behavior of your friends and neighbors, consider that Julie is a chimpanzee at the Chimfunshi Wildlife Orphanage Trust in Zambia. The scientists observing her have no idea why she adopted the grass-in-the-ear practice, but evidently she was a trendsetter; 8 of the 12 chimps in her group began to copy her, despite there being no survival benefit or other discernable reason why they did it (see Figure 2.1). Humans also adorn their ears and also receive no direct survival benefit from doing so (see Figure 2.2).*

**Figure 2.1   Julie With the Grass in Her Ear**

*Source:* van Leeuwen, Cronin, & Haun (2014). Image courtesy of E. J. van Leeuwen.

*Does Julie's action constitute a cultural act? Think of our operational definition of culture from Chapter 1: a culture includes (a) thoughts and behaviors, (b) of a group, (c) transmitted nongenetically, (d) surviving over time, (e) by which meanings and identities are shared and created. Julie behaved in a particular way, and she had to think about it in order to repeat the behavior, so she meets criterion (a). It was shared within her group, meeting criterion (b). It was transmitted to the others through observation, so she meets (c), nongenetic transmission, at least in the*

**Figure 2.2   Woman Wearing Earrings**

*Source:* **CoffeeAndMilk/istockphoto**

short term. We have no evidence for (d), survival over time, and without being able to ask the chimps, we do not know how grass-in-the-ear affects their identity. We can say that grass-in-the-ear meets some criteria of culture and provides a telling, if whimsical, parallel to earrings and other ornaments of human fashion.

*Humans are not the only creatures who create cultural phenomena, as Julie demonstrates. These cultural situations do not reach the complexity or scope of human culture, but, for example, killer whales have local dialects (Filatova, Ivkovich, Guzeev, Burdin, & Hoyt, 2017), and a certain group of bottlenose dolphins have a tradition, evidently passed from mother to daughter, of using sponges to assist in foraging (Bacher, Allen, Lindholm, Bejder, & Krützen, 2010). In the early 1950s, a group of Japanese researchers famously observed a macaque who washed her food, then later began to season her sweet potatoes by dipping them in ocean water. Others copied her, and it became a custom that survives in her band to this day (Hirata, Watanabe, & Masao, 2008). These are examples of behaviors evidently being passed onward in a social process whereby one creature sees another doing something and copies it. Whether these examples provide evidence of non-human culture is hotly debated, but they at least indicate some level of social transmission. This process of social learning underlies the foundations of human culture.*

## WHY IT MATTERS

Psychology seeks evidence to substantiate theories. In this case, we can understand processes of social learning better by looking at our evolutionary relatives for comparison. By seeing how transmission processes work among those creatures, we gain a clearer picture of how they work among humans.

## 2.1. SOCIAL LEARNING

### LO 2.1 Identify and differentiate concepts and components of social learning and transmission.

E hō mai (i) ka ʻike mai luna mai ē

ʻO nā mea huna noʻeau o nā mele ē

E hō mai, e hō mai, e hō mai ē (a)

*Give forth knowledge from above*

*Every little bit of wisdom contained in song*

*Give forth, give forth, oh give forth*

*Hawaiian chant by Edith Kanakaole*

*The struggle to maintain existence was carried on, not individually, but in groups. Each profited by the other's experience, hence there was concurrence toward that which proved most expedient. All at last adopted the same way for the same purpose; hence the ways turned into customs and became mass phenomena.*

*Sumner, 1906, p. 2*

The previous chapter discussed definitions of culture and evidence of how humans evolved into such cultural creatures. This chapter will look more closely at the processes of cultural formation, maintenance, transmission, and alteration. Throughout this text, we will discuss many areas of difference, but there are also areas of commonality that are fundamental to all human experience. Although the outcomes of the processes in this chapter differ, the processes themselves are shared across cultures. Our cultures include things we make and do, our beliefs and ideas, and organizing social structures. For culture to continue, these ideas and ways of being must be passed on with some degree of accuracy. Social transmission is repeated learning by new individuals from generation to generation, and it fuels both continuity and change. Social transmission involves two phases: learning, during which a new individual stores a process in memory, and reproduction, when the learned pattern is replicated by the learner (Tamariz & Kirby, 2014).

Social learning describes the acquisition of information or skill by new individuals, typically transmitted between related individuals of the same species (Box & Gibson, 1999). An unknown number of species share information socially—for instance, teaching their young how to find sustenance or to avoid becoming food for another creature. Some creatures, including otters, chimps, and humans, share information about using tools such as rocks to open shells or nuts. Others train their young to hunt or to hide. Broadly, social learning helps species adapt to environmental requirements and opportunities and has allowed humans to spread into ecosystems around the world. Social transmissions and learning across generations is fundamental to the existence of human culture, so this chapter will begin by discussing basic information transfer processes and will progress to more complex topics particular to human culture.

## Basics of Social Learning

With social learning apparently widespread across a great many species, why are humans so different? Why do other species, especially our primate cousins, not exhibit greater accumulation of knowledge, skills, or material artefacts? As discussed earlier, the social brain hypothesis provides one explanation, but even if one accepts that theory without question (something no scientist will do), evolution of our neural structures, languages, complex sociality, and our cultural accumulations happened simultaneously. We need more information to understand how and why humans ended up so uniquely complex. To fill these gaps, researchers in a number of fields have turned to comparisons across species for answers.

Chimpanzees (*Pan troglodytes*) have long been known to display tool use and problem-solving ability. Wolfgang Köhler (1927) spent part of World War I stuck at a primate research lab on Tenerife, in the Canary Islands. There he watched chimps stack boxes to reach food and use various tools to achieve goals. He even watched a chimp assemble a longer stick out of shorter sticks to reach food. Jane Goodall (1964) spent years living with primates in Africa, where she observed common tool use among the groups—for instance, using sticks to fish ants out of a hill. The nagging question was about causation; would apes simply reach similar solutions to obstacles by coincidence, given materials at hand and shared innate abilities, which would imply an instinctive or genetic origin of the ability? If, instead, they could pass on what they learned, this would imply rudimentary cultural capacities, and apes would provide comparison for understanding of human cultural processes.

Köhler (1927) observed compelling evidence of intelligence in primates, if problem-solving equates to intelligence, but not of social learning. In the 1980s, Tomasello and his colleagues (e.g., Tomasello, Davis-Dasilva, Cama & Bard, 1987) undertook several studies of social learning processes with primates. Chimpanzees in the studies learned use of a tool by seeing it used by a human—in this case, using a T-shaped bar to retrieve food placed out of reach. The chimpanzees learned the relation of tool to food, and they each used the tool in an approximately similar way to assist in getting the food. Tomasello (1990) termed this inexact copying **emulation**, one of the three important terms differentiating processes of social learning: imitation, emulation, and teaching.

In **imitation**, the learner copies the actions of the demonstrator as exactly as possible, whether each action is relevant or not. In emulation, it is actions leading to a consequential result that are reproduced, with less accurate replication of specific motions. Nielsen (2006) demonstrated that humans emulate outcome achievement at 12 months and progress to exact imitation by 24 months. Imitation and emulation can happen with or without the awareness or participation of the individual providing the model behavior. New parents learn this quickly when toddlers reach for hot pans or use naughty words they heard the parents say. **Teaching**, on the other hand, happens when a more experienced actor intentionally conveys knowledge or skill to a less experienced one. Teaching requires conscious participation of the teacher in transmission (Acerbi, Tennie, & Nunn, 2011).

All three forms of social learning involve **mirror neurons**, a special class of neurons found in primates, including humans, that fire in sympathy to observed actions. When one monkey (or human) observes another taking a purposeful action, neural activity of the observer/learner reflects the neural activity involved in actually doing the task. Mirror neurons provide a basic mechanism for understanding actions of others because action and perception are connected at the cortical level. Visual input activates corresponding neural connections in the observer, so the brain of the observer has essentially experienced doing the action already and seen the outcome. Before ever doing the task, the observer has already experienced a neural link between action, goal, and result (de Waal & Ferrari, 2012; Whiten & van de Waal, 2016).

Evolutionary development of these mirror neural structures probably facilitated the appearance of more complex imitation abilities, leading to human language and culture (Arbib, 2011). The ability to coordinate socially via **mimesis** (imitation, copying, or reproduction), including imitation of actions and replication of meaning, forms a likely mechanism for the rapid advancement of hominids that began about two million years ago (Donald, 2005). Further, these same mechanisms may underlie empathy and be crucial to processes by which humans understand the minds of others (Iacoboni, 2009).

Later studies compared the social learning processes of chimpanzees and human children (e.g., Nagell, Olguin, & Tomasello, 1993). In those studies, a human model would provide the example to be copied, adding a difference not necessary for achieving the goal, such as using a T-shaped rake with perpendicular tines, but turning the tines up, making the task more difficult. The chimps would learn to use the rake, but they would use it the more effective way, whereas the human children would perform the behavior exactly, even though it meant they sometimes failed. These results were later replicated using human and orangutan subjects (Call & Tomasello, 1995). The researchers proposed that the tendency to imitate behaviors exactly would relate to ability to replicate more complex behaviors. Did exact imitation improve the accuracy of transmission, and would this faithful imitation by humans provide the key to the rise of humanity's more elaborate cultures?

Andrew Whiten and colleagues later demonstrated that chimpanzees can accurately imitate behaviors (Whiten & van de Waal, 2016) and switch between imitation and emulation, depending on the situation and who models the behavior. Horner and Whiten (2005) found that young chimpanzees (average age 4 years) would imitate an entire action if they could not see how the result was achieved, but they would emulate only relevant actions when they knew what caused the desired outcome. Three- to 4-year-old human children, on the other hand, always employed imitation, including the irrelevant actions, at the expense of efficiency. Put more simply, apes are more willing to take shortcuts to a goal. Although it would seem that the apes are winning the contest, learning more quickly and achieving faster results, at least when compared to toddlers, they have not accumulated the cultural complexity of humans. Drive to imitate may be a key factor explaining why.

## Social Diffusion

More recent research looks beyond transfer between one individual and another, investigating how information and skills move within and between groups. Social transmission occurs on group levels among several primate species, providing data for comparison with humans. In the wild, primates have been observed to develop new behaviors that are then transmitted to other individuals and to other groups, including food washing by Japanese macaques, mentioned above. Whiten and van de Waal (2016) reviewed 19 studies that looked at diffusion of behavior in primate groups, with multiple results demonstrating a high degree of fidelity when behaviors were learned from group members and when learned from other groups. At this point, researchers have observed complete cycles from development of behaviors, including social transmission to group members and to other groups, and perseverance of the behavior over generations and across decades. Existence of primate culture is now widely accepted as a given, though not by all.

Humans engage in social diffusion on a constant basis. Children can observe a modeled behavior and pass on the learned task with 100% success. That task can then be transmitted to other children by subsequent learners who never see the original model. Hopper, Flynn, Wood, and Whiten (2010) put this ability to the test, and their participants learned and passed on the original learned task, maintaining fidelity across 20 generations of transmission.

## Overimitation

The puzzling tendency of humans to copy all parts of a process, including irrelevant steps, and even when shortcuts are available, is termed overimitation. Why would this inefficient process be a seemingly natural part of human learning? Indeed, given the preponderance of Western researchers and participants, is it actually a human universal? Nielsen and Tomaselli (2010) set out to investigate the universality of overimitation with a series of experiments comparing children of European descent from Brisbane, Australia with Bushman children from groups historically living as hunter-gatherers in the Kalahari Desert.

In their first experiment, 16 Brisbane and 16 Bushman (African) children were presented with a series of boxes that had a toy inside, along with an irrelevant wooden dowel. Experimenters observed whether they (a) discovered how to open the box and (b) used the object to do so. Half of the children were randomly selected to see an experimenter open the box by first performing an irrelevant action that had no effect, and then using the object to open the box in an inconvenient way. The other half saw no demonstration. Children in the demonstration condition overwhelmingly reproduced the irrelevant and inconvenient actions, while those who saw no demonstration did not. There was no difference between Brisbane and Bushmen children by group. The second study included 62 Bushmen children of a wider age range, to check for age effects. Demonstration was by community members, to be sure the effects were not due to the ethnicity of the experimenter/modeler. Otherwise, objects and procedures were the same, except that the no-demonstration group subsequently saw the demonstration and were given another try. The children again overwhelmingly copied the irrelevant actions, including 10 from the no-demonstration group who had spontaneously figured out how to open the boxes more efficiently by hand, then added the irrelevant actions after observing the modeler.

Added to evidence from Nielsen and Tomaselli (2010), a number of other cross-cultural studies support the presence of overimitation as a human universal. Nielsen, Mushin, Tomaselli, and Whiten (2016) added aborigines to the earlier study. Hewlett, Berl, and Roulette (2016) documented overimitation among the Aka hunter-gatherers of central Africa, Clegg and Legare (2016) documented it in a comparison of US and Vanuatuan participants, and DiYanni, Corriveau, Kurkul, Nasrini, and Nini (2015) in Chinese American children, all part of a growing list of cultures in which overimitation has been observed. Studies of multiple transmissions, child-to-child repeating, show that the unnecessary elements are quickly lost after a few transmissions (Bebbington, MacLeod, Ellison, & Fay, 2017), providing evidence of how cultural practices improve.

### Why Overimitation?

Humans across cultures go to extremes to copy a model they want to be like, replicating much more than just the desired behavior. Humans are especially faithful imitating an admired role model (Bandura, 2009; Sarapin, Christy, Lareau, Krakow, & Jensen 2014), for instance a famous actor or sports figure. The overimitation is probably an unconscious strategy to emulate the success of the model, the learner copying the desired activity (e.g., basketball) and also how the model talks, dresses, and behaves. This leads to successful marketing of shoes that might actually be relevant to athletic success and of clothing or fragrance lines that are arguably irrelevant to the figure's fame; fans will buy both.

Overimitation also leads to concern over criminal and violent behavior by role models and media publicity of such events. The 2009 suicide of German soccer star Robert Enke was followed by a significant increase in suicides in Germany and the rest of Europe (Koburger et al., 2015). The largest copycat effect followed Marilyn Monroe's suicide in 1962, which generated 303 additional suicides. In a meta-analysis of 10 studies from North America, Europe, Asia, and Australia covering 98 celebrity suicides, Niederkrotenthaler and colleagues (2012) found some increase in suicides in all regions, especially after suicide by elite entertainers, with the highest increases in East Asia. Even fictional suicides can inspire copycats, as was first noticed with Goethe's 1774 novel *The Sorrows of Young Man Werther* (Stack, 2003).

Several explanations have been proposed for the tendency to overimitate. One is simply that overimitation enables the learner to succeed even if she does not know how the action leads to the goal. The learner can eventually sort out what actually causes the desired outcome, but she has tools to achieve the desired goal, even if less efficiently (Lyons & Keil, 2013). Another approach instead emphasizes social motivations in over-imitation, tying the phenomenon to children's need to belong (Over & Carpenter, 2013). Overimitation increases the sense of similarity between model and observer and increases the sense of affiliation. Thelen, Miller, Fehrenbach, Frautschi, and Fishbein

(1980) observed that 10-year-olds would imitate the actions of a peer as a Machiavellian strategy when they knew they would need to persuade the peer to do something unpleasant later. Keupp, Behne, and Rakoczy (2013) found evidence that normativity was a motivator for overimitation in children; in other words, overimitation formed an avenue to demonstrate that one fits in, confirming membership and affiliation.

# REALITY CHECK

*What have you learned by copying someone else?*

*Are there certain activities that you and your close friends all do or styles that you all follow? For instance listen to a particular*

*band, watch a show, or dress in a certain style? From where did that style come?*

*Have you ever bought clothing in order to look like an actor or athlete you admire?*

## 2.2 TRADITION AND CULTURAL CREATION

### LO 2.2 Explain how social intelligence facilitates cumulative culture as humans adapt and learn as groups.

#### Tradition vs. Culture

Biologists studying primates have attempted to differentiate processes of imitation, social learning, and culture. A *tradition* has been defined as "a distinctive behavior pattern shared by two or more individuals in a social unit, which persists over time and that new practitioners acquire in part through socially aided learning" (Fragaszy & Perry, 2003, p. xiii). In biology, this definition is accepted by some to describe culture, but others require further qualifications that distinguish tradition from the greater complexity of human culture. Others insist an accumulation of complexity over time is required for an activity of a species to qualify as culture (Whiten & van Schaik, 2007). Whiten (2005) suggests that the presence of *multiple* traditions in different domains is required to meet a minimal definition of culture, such as practices of agriculture and religious ritual.

Humans now possess superb mechanisms of social cognition that facilitate language and cooperation, allowing us to pass multiple types of knowledge to young group members during their protracted developmental period. We now gain skills and abilities outside the realm of survival-based natural selection, such as reading, which appeared only within the past 10,000 years and is not ubiquitous for all humans (Bjorklund & Pelligrini, 2002; Geary & Bjorklund, 2000). Verbal and mathematical literacy requires creation of specific neural connections in the brain—an epigenetic expression—because those neural patterns are stimulated and grown via processes of social transmission rather than genetic inheritance (Ostrosky-Solís, 2004; Polk & Hamilton, 2006). Much of human life now revolves around activities not directly related to survival, using cooperatively acquired skills like math and reading. The genetic survival motive may not adequately explain the entire human story.

Alternatives to gene-preservation theories of evolution have emerged in recent years, including expanded evolutionary theory (Gould, 1980), process evolution (Ho, 1991), group selection (Wilson & Sober, 1994), and evolutionary developmental (evo-devo) psychology (Machluf, Liddle, & Bjorklund, 2014). These theories may better explain factors that drove human evolutionary selection toward our current condition: sometimes characteristics benefitting group survival may contradict or supersede individual survival needs, or even kinship survival motives, and altruistic actions may require explanatory models beyond self-interest (e.g., Baumeister & Leary, 1995; Caporael, 1997; Caporael & Brewer, 1995; Gintis, Bowles, Boyd, & Fehr, 2008).

## Social and Cultural Intelligence

Humans possess cognitive skills not found in even the nearest of primate relatives, especially regarding our ability to manage life in large groups and to collaborate on overcoming major obstacles. Intelligence is often equated to problem-solving ability, which would make social intelligence the ability to resolve problems in social life. In psychological literature, however, *intelligence* can also refer to ability to reason or to innovate, or the speed at which new responses can be associated with stimuli, called *associative learning* (Whiten & van Schaik, 2007). Because *intelligence* is an inordinately broad term, researchers began to narrow the definition to specific phenomena, including social applications of intelligence.

The Machiavellian Intelligence Hypothesis (MIH) attempts to explain ways socially organized primates (or other creatures) maneuver to establish dominance or achieve other interpersonal goals. Byrne and Whiten (1988) distinguished three hypotheses in MIH, increasingly specific in their focus:

(i) Intelligence is manifested in social life.

(ii) Complex society selects for enhanced intelligence.

(iii) Complex society shapes the forms intelligence takes. (p. 604)

The manifestation of intelligence hypothesis (i) refers to problem solving observed in social interactions of animals. The hypothesis of selection for enhanced intelligence (ii) proposes that complexities of social life entail challenges, and that increased general intelligence yields greater evolutionary success. The hypothesis that complex social life shapes intelligence (iii) suggests that it is not general intelligence but specific forms of intelligence that lead to success. Theory of Mind would be one domain, allowing individuals to understand the states of mind of other individuals.

Boyd and Richerson (1996) point out that culture appears in many species, but only humans exhibit cultural activity that no individual can produce alone. This involves transmission, usually by observational means, and diffusion, but also novel innovations improving or enhancing the initial behavior. Tomasello (1999) has termed the collection of modifications to learned processes over time the **ratchet effect**. Rather than starting over, successive learners have a starting point on which to improve, eventually leading from stones to hammers to pneumatic drills. **Cumulative cultural evolution** describes changes accumulated in human populations over time (Caldwell & Millen, 2009). The overimitation of process, including nonessential parts, may be key to ratcheting effects in cultural advancement (Acerbi et al., 2011), allowing emergence of cumulative culture (Shipton & Nielsen, 2015).

Emergence of cumulative culture requires not only the ability to imitate, but also exceptional ability to collaborate and cooperate in groups large enough to facilitate sufficient innovation and to insure survival of the improvement. Herrmann, Call, Hernàndez-Lloreda, Hare, and Tomasello (2007) found that human and chimpanzee children have similar levels of intelligence when dealing with the physical world, but that humans have far greater skills dealing with social interaction. Humans have the ability to create distinct cultural groups with specific artifacts and practices forming multiple traditions. Humans learn these in complex social interactions, including acquisition of language and math skills. The ability to navigate the social world and use social processes to learn a vast array of skills very quickly within a cultural setting differentiates humans from other primates, forming the basis of the **cultural intelligence hypothesis** (Herrmann et al., 2007). This specialized cultural intelligence provides a more comprehensive explanation of humanity's unique achievements than general intelligence.

## Adaptation to New Environments and Situations

Up to this point, the chapter has discussed mechanisms that can be described as **transmitted culture**—culture passed from one individual or group to another. Broadly, cultures are shaped by ecological, social, and biological factors. Ecologically, a culture may be located in a desert or a jungle. There may be plentiful fish or buffalo. Humans respond to these situational factors by creating new behaviors such as fishing, resulting in what Tooby and Cosmides (1992) term **evoked culture**—cultural elements arising in response to external factors. Changes in weather or food availability may evoke new behavioral repertoires for finding sustenance. These may become permanent parts of a culture that are then transmitted between generations (Gangestad, Haselton, & Buss, 2006).

A growing body of research suggests that climates across Africa varied in cycles of 19,000 to 23,000 years between 150,000 and 30,000 years ago. This timespan corresponds to increasing cultural development of early humans and marks the shift from Middle Stone Age to Late Stone Age. As areas received more moisture or dried up, humans had to migrate and adapt. It is possible that this constant need to move and deal with new situations pushed humans to develop more quickly and propelled the genetic and cultural diversification of early humans (Blome, Cohen, Tryon, Brooks, & Russell, 2012; Carto, Weaver, Hetherington, Lam, & Wiebe, 2009; Scholz et al., 2007). A megadrought from 135k to 75k years ago was particularly brutal, and it probably drove the Blombos group mentioned in Chapter 1 to their isolated caves on the South African coast while killing off hominids in other regions (Cohen et al., 2007). The archeological record indicates changes in subsistence patterns, land use, and social behaviors corresponding to these times of environmental change (Blome et al., 2012).

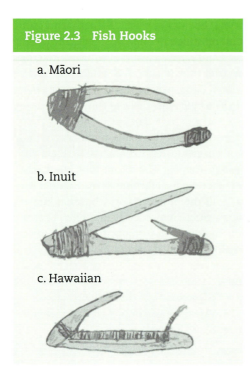

**Figure 2.3   Fish Hooks**

a. Māori

b. Inuit

c. Hawaiian

As migrating groups faced unique challenges, they used existing cultural resources and the physical properties of their new ecologies to create solutions. Similar challenges evoked similar solutions independently, as appears to be the case with the variety of fishing techniques and tools found in widely separated cultures around the world (see Figure 2.3).

Novel situations and different resources yielded solutions unique to a particular group. That early knowledge has been refined and improved over many millennia. Small differences 70k years ago have diverged to yield massive differences today, including cross-cultural variation in material culture and beliefs, emotional regulation, social cognition, and self-concept (Apicella & Barrett, 2016), topics to be discussed in later chapters.

## REALITY CHECK

*What do you think is required for a species to be considered cultural?*

*Can you imagine what it was like to wander from your home into new areas your species had never visited?*

*If you were on another planet, could you create solutions evoked by the new environmental setting?*

## 2.3. CULTURAL LEARNING AND TRANSMISSION

### LO 2.3 Describe the characteristics and processes of cultural dynamic theories.

So far, we have discussed the basic capacities of emulation, imitation, and teaching, and the diffusion within and between groups of simple skills and understandings. These are basic building blocks in the vast mechanisms of human culture. As discussed, increasing complexity required that humans had the ability to acquire skills and knowledge, then to improve on what was acquired rather than starting from a blank slate. Social transmission involves two phases: learning, in which a new individual stores a process in memory, and reproduction, when the learned pattern is replicated by the new individual. Transmission fuels continuity because a new generation carries on the knowledge and changes when the learner innovates (Tamariz & Kirby, 2014).

Because cultural transmission is inherently a social process affecting the thoughts and behaviors of those involved, and because transmission drives both continuity and change, this is where culture, psychology, and evolutionary theory converge. Alex Mesoudi (2009) argues that human culture itself forms an evolutionary system subject to Darwinian principles of variation, competition, and inheritance.

1. Variation: Within and between groups, knowledge and information differ. People hold different values and beliefs, exhibit different behaviors and language use, etc. Some variations are more adaptive or more successfully transmitted than others.

2. Competition: All transmission of knowledge, skills, and so on is not equally successful for two reasons. Because humans do have limits in attention and cognitive resources, errors and alterations emerge. Also, not all information is equally effective or desirable, and more adaptive information may be more likely to be preserved. Ultimately, some cultural information survives and some does not.

3. Inheritance: We learn cultural information from models around us, receiving and transmitting both faithful information and novel variations between models and learners across generations.

Biological and cultural evolution certainly differ in the details of genetics versus social and psychological phenomena, but the processes are comparable, and the comparison may provide insight on an abstract level into the mechanisms of cultural survival and change (Mesoudi, 2009).

Cultural transmission can be described in several ways, depending on the interests and emphases of the researcher. One system uses spatial terms to describe direction of transmission, as though one is looking at a chart of a family tree. Vertical transmission is from parent to offspring. Oblique transmission goes from a parental generation to members of an offspring generation who do not have a familial connection to the source. Horizontal transmission describes transmission between members of the same generation (Mesoudi, Whiten, & Dunbar, 2006; Cavalli-Sforza & Feldman, 1981). Another system describes transmission in terms of the qualities of the model or behavior. Conformist transmission emphasizes copying the most common or popular behavior. In prestige or success bias, the learner copies the cultural trait of the most prestigious model (Boyd & Richerson, 1985). Both strategies can increase chances of acquiring adaptive behaviors, one assuming commonality indicates something works better, the other that models of high status do things best. Neither strategy is likely to be conscious. Conformist transmission also serves as a stabilizing force in culture in the same way that overimitation increases affiliation, by normalizing a behavior and confirming shared membership of those doing it (Henrich & Boyd, 2001).

### Enculturation and Socialization

When you enter college or graduate school, you begin to learn the rules, customs, roles, and behavioral norms of universities in general and of your school or department in particular (Casanave & Li, 2009). This is a process of **enculturation**, when a person acquires or adopts the characteristics appropriate to a culture or group, learning the functions and usage of physical objects and the meaning of symbols, along with the practices enacted in daily life such as greeting a friend, or of greater events such as religious ritual. We are all enculturated in a particular setting as children, and those around us modeled, taught, and admonished us toward becoming a functional member of whatever culture surrounded us.

Russian cultural-historical psychologist Lev Vygotsky viewed children as fully hominidized at birth, in other words, having a fully formed human structure, but not at all humanized (Blanck, 1990). The child becomes humanized in the processes of enculturation. In Russia of the 1930s, Vygotsky believed formal education was the primary engine of enculturation (Jaramillo, 1996), an observation that holds true in other cultures and times when a formal education system exists (Laouira, 1999). Vygotsky did not limit enculturation to schools, however. He believed that children learn primarily through experience, both in and out of school. Parents also enculturate values, behaviors, and general cultural elements, primarily via language (Jaramillo, 1996).

*Pedagogy* is the term for formalized teaching, especially of academic subjects. Whether pedagogy exists outside Western cultures has actually been argued, despite 2500 years of formal education and examination in China, for example. A better question is whether there is active, intentional teaching in small-scale societies (i.e., people living in small groups with low levels of technology, manufacturing, or economic activity). Teaching involves a triangular interaction between a more experienced teacher, a learner, and an object or concept about which information is transferred. Wild meerkats teach their young how to kill scorpions in a process using live, injured, or dead scorpions, depending on the skill level of the youngster, so teaching is not solely Western or even solely human (Thornton & McAuliffe, 2006). The debate privileges Western methods of schools, with roles for teachers and students, above other practices. Csibra and Gergely (2011) prefer the term **natural pedagogy**, to include the many ways children learn and information is transferred by communication outside of schools. Although many cultures do not emphasize verbalization in teaching, natural pedagogy appears to be a human universal (Csibra & Gergely, 2011). Early anthropologist Kaj Burkey-Smith wrote,

> One cannot say that there is a lack of purposeful education among the Caribou Eskimos, as the parents little by little teach their children what they think is right. It might rather be said that there is a want of systematic education, but I am not sure even of that, for the necessary manual accomplishments and moral principles . . . are gradually impressed upon the children. (1929, p. 288, in Sugiyama, 2017, p. 471)

In cultures without formal education systems, cultural activities sometimes provide the setting for enculturation (Schweigman, Soto, Wright, & Unger, 2011). When a young girl in the Solomon Islands learns to weave baskets, for instance, the basket weaving forms a relatively small portion of the activity compared to other interactions. Certainly, the traditions and techniques of weaving baskets are crucial to survival of the traditions, and those are demonstrated and explained. But much of the actual time in a weaving session also includes conversation about family, traditions, and life (Fox, 2010). In numerous cultures, conveyance of the physical techniques involved requires less time than it takes to complete production of the artifact. This leaves time when the people present will alleviate boredom of an otherwise repetitive task by conversing about group history, beliefs, and norms, and about penalties for violations of norms (Greenfield, 1999; Greenfield, Maynard, Boehm, & Schmidtling, 2000). The latter could take the form of gossip, which serves functions of moral regulation and group stabilization (Peters, Jetten, Radova, & Austin, 2017; Fernandes, Kapoor, & Karandikar, 2017).

## Cultural Dynamics

Enculturation, teaching, and pedagogy all primarily deal with transmission across generations, in other words, vertical transfer. The information transferred comes from a culture's body of knowledge, but cultures change over time. Some information fades away, and new information becomes part of a culture. New information must diffuse horizontally in a culture and become accepted if it is to be part of the ongoing culture. Also, new information may pass from younger to older members, as is often the case when a parent or grandparent needs to do something new on a smart phone, but this has undoubtedly happened with new methods and technologies since the invention of stone tools and fire. How does information survive, spread, and/or disappear?

A number of theories have been proposed for how and why ideas spread and survive. In the early 20th century, the idea of cultural diffusionism arose from European anthropology and ethnology, championed by anatomist and Egyptologist Grafton Elliot Smith and others. Smith (1933) proposed that culture originated in one location, the European Mediterranean and Egypt, and spread from there, an idea that itself faded following new evidence. Alfred Kroeber (1940) was more successful with his concept of stimulus diffusion, which will be discussed later. Diffusion does factually happen with cultural knowledge, and the idea resurfaced later in the century, perhaps most notably with Richard Dawkins (1976, 1999). He saw ideas as units of instruction that transmit person to person like viruses you can catch from someone else. He called these units **memes**, from the term *mimesis*, or copying. Pictures of grumpy cats on the internet do transmit in ways explainable by Dawkins's theory, but really the concept is much deeper. Memetics provides a Darwinian model of cultural diffusion dependent on fitness of the idea. The ideas that are most fit, through usefulness or effectiveness, for instance, are the ones that survive and replicate.

Argument continues over the exact psychological mechanisms of transmission. Is the idea from the mind of the source implanted into the mind of the learner, or does the receiver create her own mental representation that may or may not be an exact replica? Dawkins's meme would essentially travel from person to person as a kernel of culture, while others argue that mental representations are not discreet transmittable items (e.g., Atran, 2001). Henrich, Boyd, and Richerson (2008) suggest both camps may hold elements of truth. To transmit, there must be observable behavior generated by the idea that is then recreated in the brain of the observer with more or less accuracy, but not necessarily exactly like a genetic transfer. On the other hand, the transfer of stronger over weaker replicators can be modeled as an evolutionary dynamic between discreet cultural traits. This is not to say, though, that the model is entirely successful: maladaptive traits can spread, such as the myth that vaccines cause autism, and no matter how much you like rock, dubstep, or reggae, there is really no inherent superiority of one musical style over another for survival.

More recently, Yoshihisa Kashima (2008) has proposed that **cultural dynamics**, studying rules of cultural stability and change, may form a more effective path to understanding the formation, maintenance, and transmission of cultural knowledge and behavior. The core concepts of cultural dynamics are as follows:

1. There exists cultural information.

2. Cultural information is instantiated in a material form that can be communicated from a sender to a receiver.

3. The receiver learns (or relearns if the receiver has already learnt it before) cultural information via a communicated form.

4. The distribution of cultural information within a population results in this population's group characteristics. (Kashima, 2008, p. 109)

Information enters cultures by interaction between people. For a discovery or external idea to spread and become part of a culture, people must share the information and reach some agreement on what the information is and on its value. The agreement establishes common ground between the people interacting. This can be described as **grounding** of the information. The information must then be accepted by a larger number of people, eventually becoming commonplace, and it becomes a characteristic of the broader culture.

Kashima (2008) describes two categories of information shared. **Content information** includes concepts about objects, events, practices, and other matters of the world context. **Identity information** regards interpersonal relationships, including memberships in groups and who one is in those groups, and will be discussed in section 2.4 below. As people interact with others, information received may be generalized to other situations and shared further, establishing shared realities and boundaries where the information is no longer relevant. Three rules apply: *sharedness*, that members share some but not all information; *perceived sharedness*, what information is taken for granted as shared; and *perceived endorsement*, the extent to which people value and agree with information. A cultural representation that meets these conditions of sharedness can distinguish members from outgroups if only members hold that knowledge.

Survival of knowledge in human culture requires compressibility, especially regarding processes. In other words, a complex process must be describable in simpler terms, and repeated learning makes a system simpler. Patterns of the activity and explanation become predictable over successive generations of transmission, compressing them into increasingly transmittable form (Tamariz & Kirby, 2014). For example, languages have rules of structural regularity by which new learners begin to understand what is communicated to them and eventually create novel phrases that are comprehensible by using those rules. In language and in other arenas of learning, the novelty added by new learners increases innovations that can also become heritable.

Ideas that conform to the existing concepts of how things should be certainly stick around. Culturally consistent ideas are easier to ground, in smoother interactions with fewer questions or challenges (Kashima, 2008). This sort of information contributes to connectivity and stability in the culture. On the other hand, inconsistent or non-conforming ideas provide more useful information, though they reduce connectivity. Relationship tips the scales: people pass more consistent information when the relationship is less stable, making the relationship more secure by shared understanding. People contribute more novel information when relationships are already stable because novel information has more value and there is no risk of losing connectivity. Stereotype-consistent information is transmitted more easily and accurately than information that runs counter to stereotype (Clark & Kashima, 2007). A football player's workout stereotypically involves weight lifting. And inconsistent activity would be ballet, although the novelty of that incongruence made for an interesting device in *The Game Plan* (2007), with Dwayne Johnson as a quarterback sent to ballet class to develop agility.

## Content Information Biases and Counterintuitive Elements

Content information includes the when, what, where, why, and how of existence, in short, knowledge of everything that is not specific to identity and membership. The information is too diverse to list, but cultural dynamics is concerned with the functions and processes more than specific content. We humans talk, write, sing songs, make symbols, create videos and cat memes, and generally spew forth and receive constant streams of information all day every day. We do not, however, place equal importance on all content. On a meta level, there are observable patterns to what and how we share.

Psychologists have observed a number of biases in informational content. One is bias toward social as opposed to nonsocial information. In other words, we like to talk about people and relationships. Mesoudi et al. (2006) demonstrated that people are more accurate in transmission of gossip, which they defined as pertaining to "intense third party social relationships" (p. 405), than other types of information. That accuracy implies that social information may be more important, or that mechanisms of transmission or reception favor social information. For your next exam, try turning a list into a story in which the items are characters interacting. You will definitely remember more.

Humans also favor certain qualities of the information they share. Bebbington and colleagues (2017) studied bias toward negative information in transmission with 368 Australian university students, using serial reproduction of a fictional girl's flight from the UK to Australia. The story included unambiguously positive and negative events, along with several ambiguous ones, to see whether positive or negative information was preferred and whether resolution of ambiguous details tended toward negative outcomes. Results showed that negative events survived multiple transmissions better and that negative resolutions of story events increased as the story was repeated. This may also be an evolutionary adaptation; in acquiring new information, information about negative events could be more important to survival than positive information. It might be nice to know about a tasty new berry to eat, but knowing whether something is poisonous is crucial.

Much of the information we share is passed in narration of experiences. Humans love to tell stories, to transmit ideas via narrative. The billions of dollars generated by movies, television, and books attest to the continuing power of stories in human life. We now have such a huge volume of information that we may not perceive the process, but in simpler times, we shared only a few stories that we deemed most relevant to pass on. Stories tell us how to live, how to relate to others, and who we are. Traditional stories encapsulate particular information in ways that are entertaining and memorable. The resulting question is, what makes something memorable?

As discussed, stereotype-consistency facilitates easier transmission, but with low informational value. Conversely, violations of norms, or even laws of nature, are exciting elements of narrative. A story must pique our interest to be remembered, and an interesting story, well-remembered, does a better job of cultural transmission. Sitting around a campfire or in a movie theater, does anyone prefer a story describing humdrum daily mundane existence? Instead, you will probably be more apt to like and remember a story with something that defies expectation. A great story mixes normal life, needed so people can relate, with unexpected or strange elements, referred to as **minimally counterintuitive ideas (MCI)** (Boyer, 1994; Chaudière & Mercier, 2017; Norenzayan, Atran, Faulkner, & Schaller, 2006). The MCI will be most effective if it is not outlandishly hard to imagine, adds to the overall cohesion of the story (Gonce, Upal, Slone, & Tweeny, 2006), and contains strong visual imagery (Slone, Gonce, Upal, Edwards, & Tweeny, 2007). If the story spreads and the idea becomes commonplace, such as killer robots eventually manifesting with the invention of drones, the MCI becomes less memorable and culture moves on.

If the MCI can be visualized easily and fits into the narrative context, the story, character, and lesson may survive for centuries. Anthropomorphized animals create memorable images requiring only suspension of disbelief that animals talk and can undertake tasks. Three little pigs and a wolf argue over opening a door, making the message more memorable that we need solid materials for our houses, and by inference, a solid foundation in our lives, if we are to block out disaster. The demigod Maui pulls islands from the sea, much as navigators follow stars and currents until their island destination rises on the horizon, and his tricks and troubles teach us how to live a harmonious life. *Kitsune* of Japanese legend are fox spirits who may appear as beautiful women, young scholars, or old men. The story usually revolves around a weakness of character the *kitsune* uses to teach a lesson or dispatch an offender. In contemporary life, superheroes may be unobtrusive reporters by day but spring into action when a good person must be saved or a miscreant punished (Carney & Carron, 2017).

Why does it matter? Stories have been told by humans everywhere for as long as we have evidence. In fact, other than artifacts, the ancient stories and legends *are* the evidence. The processes engaged in story are interesting from perspectives of a cognitive, social, and developmental psychology. They also contain a body of information about the beliefs and values of a culture. A great deal of intercultural understanding can be gained by listening to stories.

Sugiyama (2017) relates that stories form a widespread method of natural pedagogy. One requirement of teaching is the deliberate participation of the teacher. In stories, intent is often signaled, for instance by the opening phrase "Once upon a time." Native American coyote stories sometimes begin "Coyote was going there" (Sugiyama, 2007, p. 471), to signal the start of the story and to reference Coyote's wandering ways. Some cultures combine song with storytelling, either chanting them, punctuating stories with songs, or using song and vocal alteration as a performance feature. The *pansori* singers of Korea use a ritualized style of singing and speaking described as *seongeum* (Ha, 2015), telling tales from history and folklore but also poking fun at important people of the town. Cultural information is transmitted, and as a bonus, the *pansori* singer provides a voice for the people to speak to power (Park, 2006).

Storytellers transmit generalizable knowledge. Lessons of a story provide cognitive resources that may be applied in ways unlike the story, often about approaches to problem solving or difficult situations. The Skokomish of the Pacific Northwest have a tale of Dashkayah, a huge, horrific witch who eats children (Tafoya, 2003). She had grabbed several children to eat, as was her habit. One clever boy got all the children together to push her into the fire, and as her sparks went up, she was transformed into mosquitos. Working together, a monstrous, frightening problem can be transformed into something manageable, and while mosquitos are annoying, even a child can easily kill one.

Stories also carry identity information, which will be discussed in the next section. Stories provide examples of not only how we should live, but also the underlying ethos of our culture. Dan McAdams (2013) studied the stories of America and Americans and found that stories of redemption resonate most in the American psyche. The heroes of favorite American tales often rise from obscurity to greatness, as in classic underdog stories like *Rocky*. Alternatively, heroes of some stories start out with wealth and advantage, fall from grace, and become notable by climbing back to the top. Barack Obama exemplified the former, as the son of a single mother. George W. Bush followed the latter path, a ne'er-do-well arrested for drunk driving and cocaine possession in his younger days, but finding religion with his future wife and ascending to the presidency. McAdams also sees a darker side because many people live lives of frustration, unable to reach the promised resolution, and those on top often become self-righteous and cruel.

## REALITY CHECK

Have you learned more via vertical or oblique transmission?

Do you remember the stories you were told as a small child? What did they teach you?

In your childhood stories, what counterintuitive elements were presented?

Who is your favorite superhero and what makes the character memorable?

# 2.4 IDENTITY INFORMATION AND CULTURAL PROCESSES

**LO 2.4 Assess ways people share and use cultural information to cooperate as they construct their sense of reality and identity.**

> *The central fact about our psychology is the fact of social mediation. Higher mental functions in the individual have their origins in the social life of the individual.*
>
> *Vygotsky, 1978*

Perhaps our most important information is about identity—who and what we are in social context. All cultural processes occur in interactions by and with groups. We are born into particular groups in which we learn the knowledge and behaviors that enable us to (hopefully) flourish, and embodying that knowledge cements our membership. Humans deeply need to belong, and rejection or social exclusion can be destructive to a person's health and well-being (Baumeister & Twenge, 2003). Knowing we are part of a group helps us feel connected to others, keeping us happier and physically healthier (Cacioppo & Hawkley, 2003; Hale, Hannum, & Espelage, 2005; McLaren & Challis, 2006). This section discusses the role of groups and group membership in cultural processes.

John Turner (1982) emphasized the element of psychological interdependence, "for the satisfaction of needs, attainment of goals, or consensual validation of attitudes and values" (p. 15) of group members. To Turner, social identification involves developing awareness that there *is* a group and that one is a member of that group. We must share in the values and beliefs comprising the perceived reality of the group and develop some sense of membership and role in the group or groups to which we belong. For these understandings to emerge, cultural knowledge is required, which is gained during normal enculturation processes, beginning from birth and continuing as we assume adult roles in our cultures. Psychological interdependence is key in relationships of all sorts, forming a universal element across cultures.

## Layers of Groups

We are most aware of our close relations with immediate family and friends, the dyads, task groups, and demes discussed in Chapter 1. From these immediate levels, we interact with surrounding levels of groups in multiple directions, as described in Uri Bronfenbrenner's (1979) ecological systems model. Though we are all actually interconnected, we experience less immediate awareness of and effect on relationships as they radiate out and away from us. Our family is more familiar to us than people from across town, who are more familiar than unrelated others from another state, and we hold less potential influence over those with less connection to us. Conversely, those surrounding levels all exert inescapable influences that affect us

**Figure 2.4   Bronfenbrenner's Ecological Systems Model**

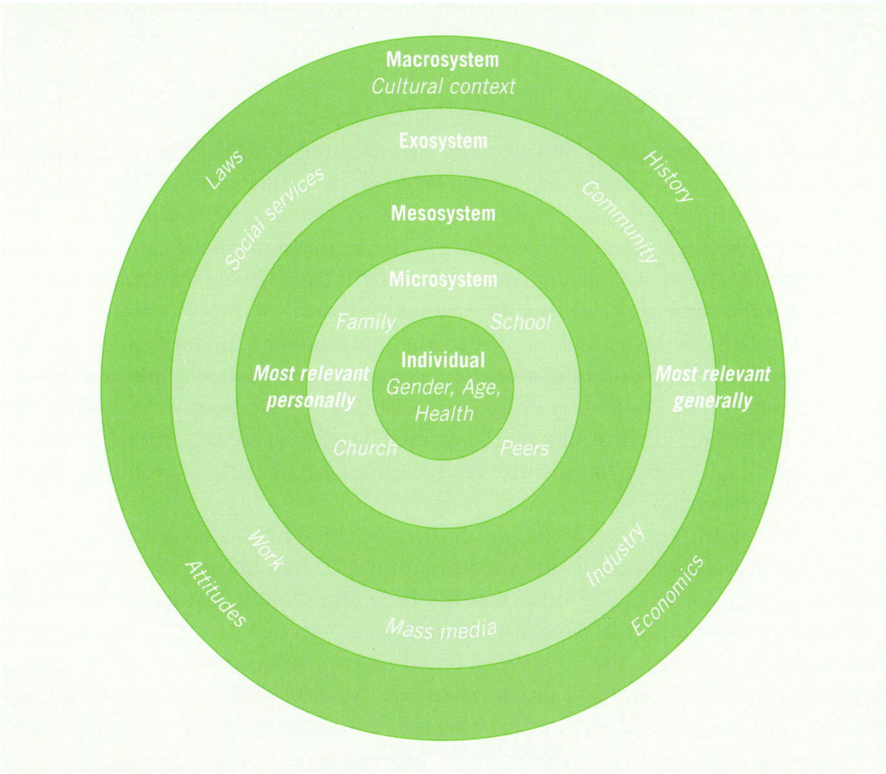

*Source:* Image courtesy of E. J. van Leeuwen.

cradle to grave. The underlying forces that shape our values, behaviors, and beliefs run in the opposite order from our personal perspective, big to small, like Russian nesting dolls with smaller dolls contained within the larger ones. All of these levels happen within the chronosystem of the time in which we live. Bronfenbrenner's (1979) ecological systems model describes how the individual arises as a product of surrounding layers of influence that shape us and, in turn, shape how we relate to others (see Figure 2.4).

On the broadest human level, we share generalized commonalities with every other human, as we relate to our terrestrial environment and to other people, including more than 99% universal genetic similarity. Within that outer layer, we may share a set of more specific characteristics with others in our nation, or who speak our language, or who share our religion. To some degree, residence in the US gives everyone in the country a shared identity, though we are probably more like people of our own state. We have even more specific elements in common with people of our age, gender, ethnicity, and socioeconomic standing from our local area. We share the most in common with our particular immediate family, whether nuclear or extended. These form levels of groups with which one can identify or feel membership.

## Social Identity Theory

Layers of social structure as described by Bronfenbrenner (1979) interact to shape our minds and lives in one very important way; our particular memberships and roles in these layers inform our sense of identity. Henri Tajfel's (1978) concept of **social identity** describes a sense of self based on group membership. Social identity requires some degree of consensual understanding of reality, including who the group members are and the meaning of social situations those individuals occupy. Tajfel and Turner (1979) extended the theory as a way to explain intergroup interactions and, especially, intergroup conflict and discrimination. People may categorize themselves by membership in organizations, by gender or age, and especially by ethnicity or race (Ashforth & Mael, 1989). Our identity may also be defined by who we are *not*, especially in cases of opposition between groups, with race forming a particularly contentious way of assigning membership.

Social identity theory (SIT; Tajfel & Turner, 1986) has been used subsequently as a platform to examine a wide range of culture-related behaviors and mindsets. Hamer (2012), for example, discusses the long and violent history of interracial interaction and conflict in America, including indigenous people killed for their lands and Africans brought for slavery, based on complex constructions of identity by the groups involved. On a much more positive topic, Sammyh Khan and colleagues (2014) examined ways well-being was enhanced by sense of identification within ethnic groups of Northern India. Marilyn Brewer (2007) emphasizes the importance of identification, saying that "as a consequence of our evolutionary history, our sense of personal security and certainty are maximized in the context of shared in-group membership and clear in-group/outgroup distinctions" (p. 735). As humans evolved, we needed to know who would aid or kill us, and we benefit still from connection to in-group. Prejudice and discrimination form unfortunate remnants of the same processes.

## Shared Reality

Our upbringing enculturates a specific sense of reality and a way of thinking. We learn explanations for how the world works, for how we should treat others and be treated, and for everything our culture deems necessary to live a good life. We learn patterns of thought, which may, for instance, be more analytic or holistic (Nisbett, Peng, Choi, & Norenzayan, 2001), to be discussed in Chapter 7. Interpersonally, we are most comfortable with people who think like we do (Na, Choi, & Sul, 2013).

The drive to share understanding of reality arises for both relational and epistemic reasons (Hirst & Echterhoff, 2008). The relational motive simply refers to our drive to feel connected to others, and this connectedness supports our well-being. The epistemic motives arise from our need to find meaning and to develop an effective way of understanding the world and our place in it, the inherent epistemology of our culture. The relational and epistemic drives work together. We connect with others within our cultures knowing that they share our understandings of the world and life, and our connections to others reinforce our beliefs. This combination allows us to function in cooperation with much greater efficiency than if we were negotiating each step of every process: a pack of wolves cooperates based on shared understandings they began to learn as pups. Humans, with many more cultural variables, can cooperate or quickly create chaos, depending on congruence of their conceptualizations of reality. With shared understanding and terminology of medicine, a surgical team can cooperate to save lives. A shared framework of understanding allows people to work together in functional groups (Fiske & Fiske, 2007).

Echterhoff, Higgins, and Levine (2009) refine the concept of sharing further, discussing four possible definitions of *share* and how they apply to social relations. The first involves the act of communicating something to others, for example, to share an idea or a recipe. Humans can share in this way verbally and nonverbally, and they can do so across time and distance via art, text, and digital modalities. The receivers must understand the symbolic signals used by the communicator, whether or not they agree. The second meaning of share is to divide and distribute, as in resource allocation activities. This requires that actors agree on the goal of the behavior, whether or not they agree on the purpose or outcome of the action. Third is the sharing of understanding, the epistemic drive, in which case people hold consensus on beliefs, values, or other opinions. People who do not know each other can share an opinion about who the best rock guitarist or author might be without ever interacting directly. Finally, people can share experientially, whether simultaneously, as when one goes on a roller-coaster with a friend; asynchronously, as when a friend later goes to a restaurant you recommended; or in conditions of a larger context, as when millions of Jews experienced horrors of Nazi rule during WWII. Instances of each of these definitions of sharing occur with frequencies following patterns of Bronfenbrenner's ecological model or Caporael's deme system, being more likely to occur within families or workplaces than between different companies or nations (Hirst & Echterhoff, 2008; Semin, 2011; Yamagishi, 2011; Younes, 2007).

Despite the risk of wars, or on the smaller scale, disagreements about religion and politics at family dinners, humans continue to flourish by virtue of collaboration and cooperation rooted in the relational and epistemic drives that generate shared reality. We have evolved to face challenges by cooperation with each other, capitalizing on shared social identity to unify higher order groups and on shared cognition to coordinate actions in achieving goals (O'Gorman, Sheldon, & Wilson, 2008). Our most comfortable times are spent with those most congruent with us (Na et al., 2013), and those are usually people who share our cultural origin. Our cultural companions are more likely to share our historical, linguistic, and material backgrounds and thus to hold similar values and beliefs, making cooperation and coexistence easier.

## Shared Values and Beliefs

Leon Festinger (1950) described our shared opinions, attitudes, and beliefs as *social reality*, which he said must have a tangible basis for validity. One basis is degree of physical reality. If you believe a hammer can smash a piece of glass, your belief will not be affected much by someone saying they do not believe hammers smash glass. On the other hand, opinions on the outcome of an election are low in physical reality and depend more on perspectives of particular people. Subjective beliefs like this draw validity from the extent to which they are shared by interacting group members and by congruence with perceptions of the reference group. Festinger used the example of the Ku Klux Klan, whose deeply prejudiced views relied on consensus within the group, primarily white males in the southern US at that time. Those views would not be swayed by contradicting views of liberals from the North who said prejudice was wrong. In Festinger's day, interaction between blacks and whites outside of routine tasks was shocking, and merely seeing a Negro drink from a water fountain used by Caucasians caused a racist to shudder with revulsion. Asking a white woman on a date could result in lynching of a black man.

Most values and beliefs are far more subtle and operate without much conscious thought. As Kashima (2008) states, our shared understandings allow us to interact in a coordinated manner, but these understandings are internalized and really only become noticeable when someone acts outside our accustomed consensus social reality. Within cultures, humans usually share values and understandings. Between cultures and religions, intercultural prejudice and misunderstanding underlie a great deal of the hatred and violence in our world. We turn next to ways the variations might be understood and explicated.

## Dimensions of Cultural Variation

As discussed, a great deal of variation has accumulated over time, generating some marked differences between cultures. Researchers have proposed several parameters of psychological variation between cultures that underlie differences in thought and behavior. Typically, we are unaware of these aspects of our cultures or their implications in our daily choices and interactions.

In the post-WWII era, companies rapidly expanded internationally, manufacturing and selling goods in multiple countries. Larger companies suddenly had staff from different cultures, speaking different languages and bringing very different values and norms into the workplace. Managing diversity on that level was a new thing and not entirely comfortable. A new branch of industrial-organizational (I-O) psychology sprang up to deal with these issues.

Geert Hofstede (1980) used his national-level analysis of international employee survey data from IBM to establish a set of **dimensions of cultural variability** that is still considered effective in predicting organizational behavior after three decades. They include individualism-collectivism (I-C), power distance, uncertainty avoidance, and masculinity–femininity. The I-C dimension describes whether a person feels more autonomous or more an inseparable part of a group. Power distance describes whether people relate to authority as approachable or absolute, and whether they feel power is concentrated or more equally shared. Uncertainty avoidance indicates motivations toward risk or stability, how people deal with ambiguity, and, ultimately, whether they are philosophically disposed toward fixed absolutes or more flexible views of reality. Masculinity–femininity does not relate to gender, but rather to whether people are motivated to gain power, status, and material wealth or to nurture and support others. Hofstede found that these dimensions combined predicted much of the variation in behavior, and the resulting problems, faced by international business organizations. They are useful tools in studying and describing cultures from local to national levels.

## Culture-Specific Concepts of Group Interaction

Outside of Western culture the interpersonal terrain changes, and many cultures have concepts of group dynamics very different from the experience and vocabulary of relationship in the West. Numerous concepts are expressed by single words that cannot be translated into English easily or succinctly. Some words reflect, for instance, core values of interpersonal trust and responsibility that were uncommon in Western European cultures but are central to understanding collectivist cultures. These concepts reveal some of the deep structure of these alternative ways of being.

Dong and Liu (2010) identify the concept of *guanxi* as crucial in understanding how business and business management work in China. The term refers to reciprocal relationships and networks developed via common origins, interests, and experience, nurtured by exchange of favors and consideration. Understanding of *guanxi*, and painstaking development of a *guanxi* network, allows Chinese managers to achieve results more quickly because of their networks of interconnections and collection of favors given and owed (Farh, Tsui, Xin, & Cheng, 1998).

A related concept is **xinyong**, or personal trust (Leung, Lai, Chan, & Wong, 2005). *Xinyong* is similar to the Western concept of personal integrity, that a man's word is his bond. Leung and colleagues stress the importance of this concept in doing business in the People's Republic of China (PRC). *Xinyong* is more important than the wording of any legal document: a contract could be broken, but an agreement with someone who has the quality of *xinyong*, with whom one has developed *guanxi*, forms an agreement that will not be violated. If a person were to violate these relational imperatives, the person would lose face, his socially acknowledged integrity and status, and that is a deeply troubling prospect in China (Hu, 1944). The senses of social connection and interpersonal obligation outweigh Western concepts of contract and legal obligation; concrete relations with real people are eminently more important than abstract legal constructs (Lee, Pae, & Wong, 2001; Buttery & Wong, 1999).

Polynesian cultures represent an exceptionally collectivist way of living. Life on isolated islands and travel by voyaging canoe for weeks and months required people to develop skills for cooperation and conflict reduction. They achieved this by evolving a system of values that emphasize interpersonal harmony and relatedness. Although many norms of daily life are unspoken, Polynesians have a relational vocabulary learned during childhood enculturation and used regularly as people interact (See Spotlight: Relational Concepts From Hawai'i and Table 2.1: Hawaiian Collectivist Concepts in Translation).

# SPOTLIGHT

## RELATIONAL CONCEPTS FROM HAWAI'I

*Hawai'i and the Perfect Wave of Collectivism*

The State of Hawai'i is the most collectivist part of the otherwise largely individualistic United States. The cultural history of the islands gives Hawai'i a triple dose of collectivist influences, settled first by the extremely collectivist Hawaiians, now hosting an Asian majority population, and dynamically engendering collectivism by practicality because the islands are the most isolated archipelago in the world. Many people in Hawai'i tend toward collectivism by ethnic origin, and that tendency is enhanced by forced proximity. The year 2014 brought a bumper crop of difficult issues, among them landfall of hurricanes Iselle and Ana and a lava flow from Kilauea volcano that wreaked havoc on the town of Pāhoa. The people of Hawai'i must depend on each other existentially: the nearest help is over a thousand miles across the ocean and several days by barge from arrival. Concepts like *aloha* are more than quaint greetings; they reflect the crucial reality that life in the midst of a vast ocean is, of necessity, interdependent.

Aloha does not mean hello and goodbye, though it can be used as part of those exchanges. Kīʻope Raymond, a doctor of Hawaiian Studies, prefers not to translate the word, though he is a native speaker of Hawaiian and eloquent in English. "You have to live *aloha*; then you understand it," he says (personal communication, March 20, 2014). Indeed, the word is complex, encompassing numerous concepts of fondness and respect between humans (see Table 2.1). Essentially, interactions should be positive and nurturing, especially toward one's in-group, but with an expectation of hospitality toward strangers. The latter forms the source of Hawai'i's stereotype as the Aloha State, with gentle breezes and warm sands and a frosty Mai Tai waiting at the bar. In reality, *aloha* is most important for in-groups, especially children and elders, but generally, life is civil by design.

A person should maintain *lōkahi* (balance) with self, with others, and with the *'āina* (land). Raymond explains, "the *'āina* feeds you, so obviously we need to maintain harmony with the land." The same sense of connection applies in other Polynesian cultures. Māori psychiatrist Mason Durie (2004) states that "good health is seen as a balance between mental (*hinengaro*), physical (*tinana*), family (*whanau*), and spiritual (*wairua*) dimensions" (p. 1141). In the Hawaiian language, a person who maintains this balance would be described as *pono*, a very respectable way to be. That sort of person treats others well and makes responsible, ethical decisions. Someone who is *pono* maintains his *kuleana*, which is literally a plot of garden land, but metaphorically, applies to social and practical obligations. It is *pono* to *kōkua* (help) unasked: "If you see someone laboring, you would not stand there with your arms crossed watching. You would help," Raymond explains, "You would pitch in."

As the Polynesians voyaged across the Earth's largest ocean, interdependence was crucial. Their journeys rivaled modern human journeys to the moon in planning, provisioning, and technological implementation for their time. On a voyaging canoe crossing hundreds or thousands of miles of open ocean, cooperation was a matter of survival, so collectivist values and norms were crucial to continued existence. Had the ancient Polynesians emphasized individual action and independence, the migration may never have occurred.

## Table 2.1  Hawaiian Collectivist Concepts in Translation

| | |
|---|---|
| *Aloha* | Love, affection, compassion, mercy, sympathy, pity, kindness, sentiment, grace, charity; greeting, salutation, regards; sweetheart, lover, loved one; beloved, loving, kind, compassionate, charitable, lovable; to love, be fond of; to show kindness, mercy, pity, charity, affection; to venerate; to remember with affection; to greet, hail. |
| *'Ohana* | Family, relative, kin group; related. |
| *Pono* | Goodness, uprightness, morality, moral qualities, correct or proper procedure, excellence, well-being, prosperity, welfare, benefit, behalf, equity, sake, true condition or nature, duty; moral, fitting, proper, righteous, right, upright, just, virtuous, fair, beneficial, successful, in perfect order, accurate, correct, eased, relieved; should, ought, must, necessary. |
| *Lōkahi* | Unity, agreement, accord, unison, harmony; agreed, in unity. |
| *Kōkua* | Help, aid, assistance, relief, assistant, associate, deputy, helper. |
| *Kuleana* | Right, privilee, concern, responsibility, title, business, property, estate, portion, jurisdiction, authority, liability, interest, claim, ownership, tenure, affair, province; reason, cause, function, justification; small piece of property, as within an *ahupua'a*; blood relative through whom a relationship to less close relatives is traced, as to in-laws. |

*Source:* Pukui & Elbert (2019).

*Note:* Some of these concepts were explained in vivid detail in the TV show *Anthony Bourdain: Parts Unknown*, Episode: Hawaii (6/15/2015).

### Why It Matters

We are usually unaware of the underlying concepts that organize our lives. As one learns more about the interrelationships between culture and the mind, ways culture has taught us to think and live, from relationships to motivations to well-being, become more evident. Looking at the underlying beliefs of another culture can help you to see your own.

Enacting and sharing concepts like these provided a strong sense of belonging and interconnection in traditional culture. Global communication and omnipresent American media have disrupted traditional culture to varying degrees around the world, though not entirely. For example, Neville, Oyama, Odunewu, and Huggins (2014) investigated a concept they term *racial-ethnic-cultural (REC) belonging* among self-identified black indigenous Australians (Aborigines and Torres Strait Islanders). Participants benefitted from five dimensions of REC belonging: history/memory, place, and peoplehood; sense of community; acceptance and pride; shared language and culture; and interconnections. Their well-being was undermined by their very dark-complected phenotype, social identity, and history of colonization. The strength of their connection to a traditional past provided protective factors in the aftermath of brutal colonization by the British.

## 2.5. CULTURAL CHANGE

### LO 2.5 Discuss the reasons and ways cultures change.

Cultures change for a number of reasons. External forces such as ecological conditions evoke adaptive inventions and modifications, as discussed earlier. Cultures change internally, from gradual innovations and even from mistakes, as knowledge transmits imperfectly but sometimes works out well. Moving toward the future involves a certain element of "mental time travel" (Vale et al., 2012), which is perhaps one of the most unique features of human thought. We can imagine past events, whether from personal memory or from description, and learn from them to direct our decisions. We can also imagine futures that have never existed. We can use these imaginings to move toward the imagined situation, as when we build homes or airports. We can move to prevent an undesirable outcome, for instance by adding engineered features to prevent damage from earthquakes or hurricanes (Vale et al., 2012).

Environmental change can cause massive upheaval, as when the Great Dustbowl of the 1930s forced relocation of millions of midwestern farmers in the US. Rising seas are currently forcing relocation of the citizens of the Maldives, Tuvalu, and the Seychelles, and drought has forced relocation of literally millions of people in China, the largest movement of population in history (Doherty, 2012; Farrell, 2009; Sekiguchi, 2006). Deep changes to cultures and their members happen in these processes. Ways of living and being may be completely abandoned, not by choice.

Novel challenges from new conditions combine with previous knowledge and experience to drive cultural diversity. Some challenges are different now; internet hackers and global climate change require responses very different from dealing with angry wooly mammoths or predatory saber-toothed tigers, but the underlying processes are not so different. People have usually faced challenges together in cooperation, using socially acquired knowledge and skills, or ratcheting up from previous knowledge to create a new solution.

Cultures also change in negative ways due to demographic alterations, including generational losses from war, disease, or isolation. Joseph Henrich (2004) discusses the case of Tasmania, which was first settled about 34,000 years ago as part of the Australian continent. At the end of the last ice age, about 16,000 to 18,000 years ago, the land bridge connecting Tasmania disappeared, isolating the inhabitants. At that time, they possessed a fairly complex cultural range of material goods, including nets, bone tools, barbed spear points, and stone tools hafted to wooden handles, numbering hundreds of types. By European contact in the 1600s, the variety of tools had shrunk to 24 item types. Henrich proposes that the loss resulted from imperfect copying exacerbated by an insufficiency of skilled models. If a person will copy the most skilled or prestigious model available and a variety of models are available for comparison, cumulative improvement will probably result. With insufficient experts, transmission errors may instead accumulate, resulting in gradual cultural erosion.

### Effects of Modernization

Eminent cultural psychologist Patricia Greenfield (2009) proposed that socioeconomic and lifestyle shifts can bring deep changes in cultures. Her theory of social change links changes in economics, education, and technological access to increasing individualism and values changes she has observed among the Mayans of Mexico's Yucatan and other groups leading traditional lifestyles. In 1887, German sociologist Ferdinand Tönnies (1887/1957) described two types of social groupings: *Gemeinschaft* (community) and *Gesellschaft* (society). *Gemeinschaft* is typically rural, agrarian, and low tech, with a subsistence economy and no formal education. *Gesellschaft* groupings are urban, large scale, and hi tech, with formal education and a focus on goods and capitalist economy. *Gemeinschaft* groupings are close-knit, self-contained, and interdependent, and relationships of all sorts tend to be lifelong. *Gesellschaft* groupings are fleeting and independent, with little commitment to community and openness to outside contact.

In the Yucatec villages Greenfield studied, babies received constant direct body contact, being carried or strapped to the mother; children learned traditional crafts and agriculture; and caretaking of the old happened at home. During the four decades she has observed them, more and more of the Mayans have gone into commercial activity, entered formal education, and reduced their connection to extended family. As a result, the children follow different developmental pathways and have different characteristics in values and abilities from their parents (Maynard, Greenfield, & Childs, 2015).

Garcia, Rivera, and Greenfield (2015) replicated an experiment called the Madsen Marble Pull Game (Madsen, 1970), comparing results to archival data from four decades of research. The game has a marble held between two pieces of wood connected by magnets that separate easily, sending the marble off the board. Success requires children to cooperate, taking turns allowing one or the other to win. Typically, more collectivistic children, such as those of *Gemeinschaft* cultures, tend to do much better than children of individualistic cultures, and Madsen's (1970) results showed a significantly higher success rate for Mexican than American children. Greenfield's (2009) model (see Figure 2.5) predicts that the Mayan children would score progressively lower on the game over time, as their culture changed. This was the case, supporting the theory that socioeconomic and lifestyle changes would alter underlying values such as sharing (Garcia et al., 2015).

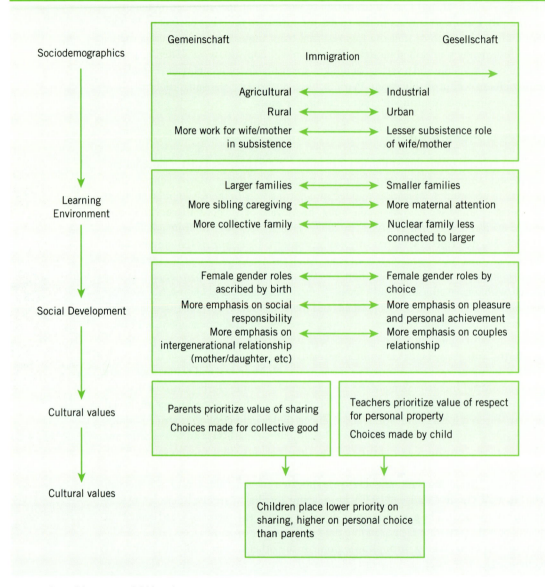

**Figure 2.5    Greenfield's Model of Social Change Regarding Development**

Sociodemographics

Gemeinschaft                                                                Gesellschaft
                                    Immigration

Agricultural ⟷ Industrial
Rural ⟷ Urban
More work for wife/mother in subsistence ⟷ Lesser subsistence role of wife/mother

Learning Environment

Larger families ⟷ Smaller families
More sibling caregiving ⟷ More maternal attention
More collective family ⟷ Nuclear family less connected to larger

Social Development

Female gender roles ascribed by birth ⟷ Female gender roles by choice
More emphasis on social responsibility ⟷ More emphasis on pleasure and personal achievement
More emphasis on intergenerational relationship (mother/daughter, etc) ⟷ More emphasis on couples relationship

Cultural values

Parents prioritize value of sharing

Choices made for collective good

Teachers prioritize value of respect for personal property

Choices made by child

Cultural values

Children place lower priority on sharing, higher on personal choice than parents

*Source:* Adapted from Greenfield (2009).

Though the march from *Gemeinschaft* to *Gesellschaft* seems inevitable, some cultures are revitalizing their traditions as support for well-being and connectedness. Elders in two villages of Yup'ik Inuit in southwest Alaska work with community psychologists at the University of Alaska Fairbanks in a program supporting traditional activities.

They particularly focus on youth, who are at risk of substance abuse, suicide, and numerous other ills as their way of life modernizes. Charlie Moses and James Charlie Sr. write of the program's focus on revitalizing culture and context through kinship:

> It is this model of increasing protection and strengths through the revitalization of traditional practices and ways of life that guides our work with children in our community. We have realized through this work that the proven ways of our ancestors still impact our people today. We need to continue these ways to continue as communities. We need to continue to recognize the natural ways to prevent and/or recover from the modern ills like alcohol abuse, and revive the identity of Native individuals as well as communities, thereby enabling them to "evolve" into the twentieth-century *Yupiit*. (Ayunerak et al., 2014, p. 97)

## Intercultural Transmission

In addition to natural forces pushing cultures to change, another external force comes from interaction with other human groups. When cultures meet, for good or ill, both experience changes. On an individual level, this is called acculturation, defined as the psychological processes of accommodation in prolonged exposure to a culture not your own. It is distinct from enculturation, which refers to the learning of a culture's values, beliefs, norms, etc. during development, and from cultural change, which is changes in a culture at a population level as a result of dynamic events within the culture such as innovation, invention, and discovery (Berry, 1995). Chapter 10 will discuss acculturation in depth. Culture-level changes also happen with intercultural contact, both fleeting and extended, and it is these processes we discuss in this section.

Humans historically met other groups in several ways: migration, trade, war, religious proselytization, or conquest and colonization. On the most benevolent level, one culture can gain needed knowledge or material goods from another. All humans have to have food and shelter, and better methods to produce these are received readily. If someone from the next tribe makes a better bowl, perhaps the item or technique transfers. Everyone may needs such things, or find out they do once they see it, and the new item or process fits right into the point of need. Great ideas, useful goods, and ways to do things better diffuse readily across cultures.

We cannot know what would have happened if all intercultural encounters had been friendly; we can only examine the historical and archaeological record, and it is all but friendly. Armies also traveled the trade routes, spreading destruction along with other elements of culture. Empires from Persia and Rome spread around the Mediterranean, China and the Mongols battled for control of Asia, and the Manding Empire ruled West Africa. Later, Europeans planted their flags on every continent. The colonial era ushered in unprecedented intercultural contact. That contact included trade and migration and the extermination of many indigenous peoples. Areas conquered by Spain and Portugal converted to Catholicism at sword-point, only coming to understand the values and beliefs they professed much later. Soldiers raped and pillaged, forcibly spreading new genes, but thousands did marry local women and join communities. Merchants also spent extended time in new lands, and with them came European ideas, technologies,

# SPOTLIGHT

## THE HAWAIIAN STEEL GUITAR

In 1889, the story goes, a young man named Joseph Kekuku walked along a railroad track in Hawaiʻi. He strummed the guitar he carried as he walked, and then he happened to pick up a railroad spike lying on the ground. Out of curiosity, he held the spike to the neck of the guitar to hear what it would sound like, and the steel guitar was born.

The new sound caught on like a fire in a cane field, and the silky gliding sound became a trademark of Hawaiian music. The century turned, and exotic images of Hawaiʻi caught the world's imagination. Sheet music for tunes like Queen Liliuokalani's *Aloha ʻOe* sold all around the world in the days before phonographs and radio. As the "teens" turned to the Roaring 20s, more and more hula troupes travelled across oceans and continents, bringing the Hawaiian steel guitar with them. WWII brought thousands of GIs through Pearl Harbor on their way to Asia and the South Pacific, and Hawaiian music again topped the charts.

In the US, country and western music has always been happy to borrow from other cultures. Mandolins were brought by Italian stone masons in the 19th century, and banjos descended from instruments made by slaves, modeled after the instruments they knew in Africa. The Hawaiian style of guitar found its way into country and western music in the 1950s, riding the wave of post-WWII tiki bars, exotica music, and hula hoop fads. There, the pedal steel and dobro remain, though few who hear or play them know their island origin.

### Why It Matters

The spread of Hawaiian guitar forms a perfect example of cultural dynamics. Usually, diffusion is easiest when there is a manifest need in the receiving culture, and perhaps steel guitar filled a hole in the sonic landscape of country music. Even if there was no void in the adopting musical styles, the sound provided a unique addition, making a lucrative contribution to several genres.

Cultural exchange generally describes reciprocal transfer of material or ideas between willing participants from two or more cultures (Rogers, 2006). A trader could sell goods from one culture to another or a technique could be taught. In Medieval times, widespread exchange of goods, artistic techniques, technologies, and religion occurred simultaneously around the Mediterranean (Hathaway & Kim, 2012). Cultural exchange requires a symmetrical power structure in which the transfer is not coerced. The spread of religions by missionaries could be described in this way, though greater affluence or political power of the proselytizing culture often suggests that the receiving culture may not be in a position to consent to the transfer.

*Cultural appropriation* is the term for usage of cultural assets, knowledge, or artifacts without authorization, usually done in an asymmetrical structure of dominance. The term has received attention in recent years in incidents like Karlie Kloss donning a Native American headdress at the 2012 Victoria Secret fashion show and Katy Perry wearing *geisha* attire at the 2013 American Music Awards. Perry described her choice as an *homage* to Japanese culture, but Asian Americans disagreed (Nittle, 2017). The year 2017 saw Native American feather headdresses blossom as a widespread but unwelcome hipster phenomenon at music festivals and other events (Wood, 2017). *Transculturation* is a term that describes creation of culture elements from multiple cultural sources, whether by exchange or appropriation.

One of the stranger episodes of transculturation resulted from the encounter between General Douglas MacArthur and the Guna of Panama during WWII (Fortis, 2016). Obviously MacArthur was a man who held great power, and the Guna began to carve wooden effigies of him for use in ritual. The Guna transformed their tradition of carving wooden representations of powerful forces by adding imagery from the US military. In the 21st century, all of these intercultural processes are in constant play, but really they underlie creation of culture in general as cultures have differentiated and recombined across the millennia (e.g., Rogers, 2006).

and economics. Western/European values have been exported to the rest of the world forcibly. Colonization by military conquest eliminated or vastly reduced whole cultures. Those who survived often were so decimated that indigenous knowledge and technologies were lost. But there have also been some benefits to all sides in the process.

Ancient trade routes carried salt inland from the ocean, minerals to places without them, and foods to other regions. The great Silk Road carried silk, of course, but also spices, rugs, manufactured objects, musical instruments, and a host of other goods and ideas. Islam spread from the Middle East as far as China and West Africa. The violin, guitar, and piano's ancestor cymbalom also owe their existence in Europe to the Silk Road, with *erhu*, *pipa*, and *yang chin* as equivalents at the other end. The bagpipe came to Scotland in the form of *gaida* played by Roman soldiers from the Balkans. Cultures can exchange science, technologies, philosophies, and medical knowledge. Algebra and "zero" traveled with the caravans from Persia.

## REALITY CHECK

*Would you say your upbringing happened in a more Gemeinschaft or Gesellschaft setting?*

*Can you think of five items you use or eat that came from another culture?*

## 2.6 ARTS AND CULTURE: CREATING, TRANSMITTING, AND LEADING THE CHANGES

### LO 2.6 Evaluate the utility of arts practices and products as avenues for understanding cultural processes.

*We may regard a work of art as a sort of map of the society in which the artist—and his public—live.*

*Fischer, 1961, p. 89*

Arts weave the fabric of interpersonal connection within and across cultures. We rally around flags that symbolize our nations and the values and events on which they were founded. Icons grace our altars. Anthems start and end sports events. Stories transmit our most treasured legends and the concepts they encapsulate. In old age, patients with Alzheimer's and other forms of dementia still respond to music from their younger days. Arts arguably form the glue keeping us together across every level of analysis in human relations, from the broadest to the most intimate.

## Visual Arts

Overtly, subject matter of visual arts may be drawn from the specific myths, legends, and religious stories of a culture. The content obviously changes from culture to culture, depending on history and other factors, so ancient Greek art will include the pantheon of Zeus and the other gods, ancient Chinese art might have dragons, and Southwest pre-Columbian art may include Kokopelli, the humpback flute player. Whether Krishna, Mother Mary, or a trickster Coyote, iconic images traditional to a culture do not merely convey a visual representation of a character or deity. The images serve as memetic proxies for an entire story and its related concepts. Embedded in the figures on a totem pole or carved into the supports of a Māori *marae* is a body of knowledge. In oral cultures, these served as mnemonic devices to aid recollection. In modern culture, the simple Apple corporate logo carries with it the reputation and history of the company, as well as a carefully shepherded set of perceptions that Apple is cool and the people carrying those millions of identical devices are somehow unique and boldly different.

**Figure 2.6  Shepherd Fairey's Obama "Hope" Poster**

*Source:* MICKE Sebastien/Getty Images

In politics, visual iconography provides shorthand to unify supporters around central messages. The Obama campaign poster by artist Shepard Fairey placed a simplified image of the candidate above the word Hope, intended to galvanize millions of voters who felt demoralized after years of war and hegemony of the rich under the preceding administration.

In 2015, controversy over the Army of Northern Virginia Battle Flag (commonly called the Confederate Flag) erupted when it was found displayed in photos and belongings of Dylan Roof, after his racially motivated massacre of black churchgoers. The flag was incorporated in the State Flag of Georgia in 1956 to protest *Brown v. Board of Education*, the case that banned racially segregated schools. South Carolina and Alabama soon raised the flag at their state capitols, openly displaying the whites' desire to perpetuate the racially discriminatory system of Jim Crow that followed slavery (Forman, 1991). These examples represent overt social functions of visual cultural content, intended to sway opinions and actions of large populations. Visual arts also contain layers of latent content of which even cultural insiders are usually unaware (Peregrine, 2007). In terms of social structure, the Pharaohs of ancient Egypt towered over their subjects in the statues and paintings that survive, illustrating an extremely high power distance and rigid hierarchy.

Manet painted his colleague Monet's family enjoying their summer in a French garden. A woman in light-colored clothing sits on the ground with her child; she enjoys, rather than toils, as her dress shows, which means others of lesser status, like the man behind her, maintain the garden (see Figure 2.7).

In another garden in 1437, Xie Huan painted *Elegant Gathering in the Apricot Garden*, depicting gentlemen discussing the contents of scrolls as they enjoy the day (see Figure 2.8). Behind them, women peer over their shoulders, listening politely to the debates. Depicted at about three-quarter size or less, servants hold the scrolls and perform other tasks. The social hierarchy and the power distance of the culture are obvious, if one follows the visual clues.

Fischer (1961) found a more subtle indication of social hierarchy in ceramic designs from archaeological record, observing that egalitarian cultures emphasized repetition, empty spaces, symmetrical elements, and unenclosed figures, compared to the opposite in hierarchic cultures. Peter Peregrine (2007) confirmed Fischer's (1961) results, and

**Figure 2.7   The Monet Family in Their Garden at Argenteuil**

*Source:* Courtesy The Met Museum, Bequest of Joan Whitney Payson, 1975.

**Figure 2.8   Elegant Gathering in the Apricot Garden**

*Source:* Courtesy The Met Museum, The Dillon Fund Gift, 1989.

suggests that we have a great deal to learn about extinct cultures from visual artifacts. We might also learn much about living cultures, if we are sensitive to what their visual arts convey.

## Musical Arts

*My point is not that a social group has beliefs which it then articulates in music, but that music, an aesthetic practice, articulates in itself an understanding of both group relations and individuality, on the basis of which ethical codes and social ideologies are understood.*

*Frith, 1996, pp. 110–111*

Rock and roll sprang up in the 1950s, following the progression of blues and gospel to jazz, and then onward to the syncopated rhythms and wild performance styles of swing artists like Louis Jordan (Koch, 2014). A synthesis of many cultures over many years built toward the enormous variety of styles available now.

A generation before, music was heard only in the presence of performers, either at home or at theaters, bars, and concert halls. Phonographs were relatively new, allowing music to persist in fixed, portable form, and radio freed music from proximity, allowing songs to ride along in the new automobiles people began to drive. Rock and roll provided a soundtrack for the children of WWII's victors, reveling in their new military successes and moving toward a supposedly bright world of fun and freedom. Music now follows us anywhere we have a device and speakers or headphones, accessed on the internet, downloaded, stored to the cloud, or played from a smart phone, in virtually any genre worldwide. We have generated amazing technologies to experience music, and these technologies now are changing our experience of music, along with the ways music affects our lived experience.

Not everything in music relates to sex, though its ubiquity as a topic is not surprising. After all, sex must happen in all cultures for them to survive. Music forms a crucial component in many sorts of social congress, from lullabies to funerals. Music traditionally happens in social contexts (cf. Hargreave & North, 1999; Turner, 1982; Merriam, 1964). All cultures include activities that can be described as musical (Cross, 2001). Though some strict Muslim regions prohibit music per se (al-Qaradawi, El-Helbawy, Shukry, Siddiqui, & Hammad, 1985; Otterbeck, 2004), *muezzin* call the faithful to prayer with melodic sounds of the *adhān* (Jouili & Moors, 2014). As a transcultural universal, musical activities and social processes should be fertile fields for social and cultural psychology to explore. From long before recorded history, humans danced and sang their way to unity in annual cycles of ritual, developing and enhancing sense of *communitas*, in Victor Turner's (1982) terminology. The form of unifying rituals has changed as humanity has modernized, but music has continued to play a central role.

Alan Merriam (1964) enumerated a comprehensive set of 10 functions of music he felt covered everything observed by ethnomusicologists in his day. Four connect explicitly to our lives as members of groups:

helping to enforce conformity to social norms,

validating social institutions and religious rituals,

increasing the continuity and stability of culture, and

enhancing integration of society. (pp. 219–227)

Religious music and national anthems historically touched the greatest numbers of people of any art prior to modern commercial media, sung by whole religions and entire countries well before recorded media, radio, or Spotify existed. Hymns developed gradually over the history of Christianity (Westermeyer, 1998), and anthems form a key component of national identity (Cerulo, 1993), all reaching billions of lives. The singing enacts ritual connection as we identify cognitively with the lyrical content of these songs that reinforce our ideas of God and/or country. But the act of singing itself may add power to our connectedness.

When people hear music, their heart rate and breathing shifts into synch with the rhythm (Bernardi, Porta, & Sleight, 2006; Clayton, Sager, & Will, 2005). This happens individually, and it happens to entire groups of people, for instance at concerts or dance clubs. Recently, researchers began investigating neurochemical effects of music, including studies of oxytocin, a neurochemical widely associated with bonding, social, and empathetic behaviors (Fukui & Toyoshima, 2014). A number of studies show marked effects of music on oxytocin levels (e.g., Chanda & Leveitin, 2014; Fukui & Toyoshima, 2014; Kreutz, 2014). Kreutz (2014) demonstrated increased oxytocin levels specifically from singing in groups. Music increases the key chemical component in social bonding, providing a possible explanation for the power of music in shared experiences and for the ubiquity of music as a social activity across cultures.

Observed social functions of music also include construction and expression of identity, transmission and support of cultural values, and the fostering of interpersonal relationships (Boer, Fischer, Strack, Bond, Lo, & Lam, 2011; Hargreave & North, 1999). Relationships are fostered by the unifying and bonding effects of musical participation, but also by the sharing of cultural knowledge. Music accomplishes these functions, in part, because it is built of semiotic units of meaning (Nattiez, 1990). A major chord implies bright emotions in Western music, though major and minor sounding scales have different emotional valence in different cultures and may be interpreted only in context. In Pharrell Williams' 2013 global hit song *Happy*, most of the melodic content follows the minor tones of a blues scale, but it is unquestionably upbeat. Music communicates, absolutely, but it is often language and cultural context that enables decoding of the message.

As an activity or experience, music is complex, with multiple psychological, physiological, and social processes happening simultaneously. Perhaps music gains its power from this complexity; whatever the mechanisms, we know the power is there to move hearts, souls, and armies by the sense of bonds it creates. Diana Boer and colleagues (2011) found that shared music preferences increase social attraction between people from several cultures, primarily in that people believe music preference also indicates important shared values. Earlier, Boer (2009) had demonstrated that fans of particular genres, such as heavy metal, were predisposed to like other fans, even if the other fan was imagined to live in a different country. Bollywood music provides a way for the millions of Indians living around the world to bond, even if they are descended from different ethnicities or parts of India. Bollywood clubs and films provide a nexus for these young people to gather, whether in Bombay, New York, London, or Sydney, connecting them to similar others and to their culture of origin.

People bond via music in phenomenal ways. In 1985, drought was ravaging parts of Ethiopia, and popular singers came together to create the song *We Are the World*, bringing global attention to the famine and selling more than 20 million copies worldwide. On an ongoing basis, an even bigger phenomenon has been growing for nearly two centuries. In 1824, Ludwig van Beethoven premiered his *Ninth Symphony*, with its iconic fourth movement, "Ode to Joy." Beethoven used a poem by Fredrich Schiller of the same name for his libretto, in the first use of choir in a symphony. In part, the words translate as follows:

Joy, beautiful spark of divinity,

Daughter from Elysium,

We enter, burning with fervor,

heavenly being, your sanctuary!

Your magic brings together

what fashion has sternly divided.

All men shall become brothers,

wherever your gentle wings hover.

This powerful message of universal brotherhood grows more popular as time passes. Politically, it has underscored Chilean women's protests of the brutal Pinochet dictatorship in the 1970s and the 1989 protests in Tiananmen Square. The film *Following the Ninth: In the Footsteps of Beethoven's Final Symphony* (2014) traces a recent phenomenon of symphonic flash mobs performing the work in shopping malls, plazas, and other unexpected places all over the world. In Japan, the piece has become a symbol of hope, brotherhood, and renewal, played by hundreds of orchestras each December to usher in the New Year. Beethoven's *Ninth* may be most powerful example of international musical bonding, but it does not stand alone. Music always has brought people together, and probably will continue to do so as long as there are humans.

## REFLECTING ON YOUR READING

- Think about yourself as a member of a culture or cultures. From whom have you received your cultural information?

- Is your list short or long?

- If you have or might have children, what cultural information will you pass to them?

- Are there particular activities, like fishing or baking, that are traditional for your family?

- Are there ways your identity has been informed, like a bar mitzvah, confirmation, or quinceañera celebration?

## CHAPTER 2 SUMMARY

Other organisms besides humans exhibit behaviors that could be considered cultural. Only humans have achieved a high degree of complexity in cultural processes and products. This chapter examines the hows and whys of culture.

### 2.1 Social Learning

An important feature of human culture is the ability to transmit information between individuals. Social learning describes acquisition of knowledge from others. Social learning includes three primary processes: *imitation*, where a learner copies a process exactly; *emulation*, where the learner copies only what is needed to achieve the outcome; and *teaching*, where the model intentionally instructs the learner. For a behavior to survive, it must spread to others within the group, and it may spread to other groups in a process called *social diffusion*.

Overimitation is the tendency to copy all actions of the model, even irrelevant ones. Human children tend to do this exclusively, while chimpanzees may emulate at times. Overimitation allows a learner to reproduce the effect of a behavior even before understanding the process. It may happen so the learner is assured of success, but it also stimulates feelings of affiliation and may serve a social purpose.

## 2.2 Tradition and Cultural Creation

A tradition is a shared behavior that continues over time. Culture requires accumulation of multiple traditions, which seems to be a uniquely human ability. Humans now have many traditions not related to survival.

Intelligence refers to problem solving ability. Social intelligence regards navigation the social world. Social and cultural intelligence allows us to evolve as cultures.

In addition to transmitted elements of culture, situations often evoke new cultural elements in response to challenges. Novel responses accumulated over time have led to cultural diversity.

## 2.3 Cultural Learning and Transmission

Ideas and behaviors survive transmission because of certain characteristics, somewhat like genetic survival. Behaviors that are most widespread tend to be copied in conformist transmission. Those done by a prestigious model also tend to be spread.

Humans naturally adopt the behaviors and beliefs of their cultural context in the process of enculturation. This can happen in a formal educational setting, but it happens across cultures in informal social settings, in a process of natural pedagogy. In some cases, skills are learned while other concepts are shared in conversation.

Cultural dynamics is the study of stability and change in cultures. When information spreads until there is widespread agreement on value of the idea, it is grounded in the culture. This applies to content information about objects, events, and practices, and to identity information regarding roles and memberships.

Humans tend to transmit social information more accurately and tend to transmit information as stories. Stories with unexpected or contradictory elements tend to be remembered better. Stories teach lessons of how to deal with situations and about our identity as member of a culture with particular beliefs.

## 2.4 Identity Information and Cultural Processes

We learn and exist as members of an interdependent group. In that context, one type of information is about roles and membership. Understanding our connections helps us to be healthier and happier.

Bronfenbrenner described our memberships as being like concentric circles more related to us in the inner levels, and less so outward, though all levels interact to shape our lives. Tajfel's social identity theory describes how membership affects interactions with others. Our groups teach us a view of what reality is, and we get along best with those who share that view.

Values and beliefs are particular types of shared information. Social reality includes ideas supported by physical reality, like breakability of glass, but also subjective ideas like prejudices.

Hofstede used data from thousands of IBM employees to find ways cultures differ, including include individualism-collectivism (I-C), power distance, uncertainty avoidance, and masculinity–femininity.

These differences can be manifested in culture-specific concepts of how people should live and interact. Chinese business people depend on their social and familial networks and on reputation for trustworthiness. Hawaiian culture emphasizes working together and keeping relations harmonious. Traditional values can protect people from adverse effects of cultural trauma.

## 2.5 Cultural Change

Cultures change with innovations and inventions and also from large-scale environmental disruption.

Challenges can spur positive adaptations. Isolation can cause loss over generations.

Greenfield's theory of social change suggests that people are moving from rural *Gemeinschaft* living to more urban *Gesellschaft* lives with less collective interconnection. This is changing how children grow up and the values they learn, especially around sharing.

Ideas, goods, and technologies have been shared between cultures for millennia. Sometimes cultures come together violently, but changes happen from many types of exchanges. Equal status exchanges can be called reciprocal. Cultural appropriation occurs when members of one culture use elements of another without permission. Transculturation occurs when elements of cultures are combined into something new.

## 2.6 Arts and Culture: Creating, Transmitting, and Leading the Changes

Arts connect deeply with people and can provide a map to cultures. Visual arts contain cultural symbols, providing visual reminders and representations of the ideas and ideals they represent. Some content of visual arts conveys the social structure of cultures, even if the artist is unaware that is being conveyed.

Music conveys a variety of cultural information. Modern American music reflects the deep changes to culture and lifestyle of the past century. Music, including lullabies, anthems, and religious music, connects people. Connection happens on a physiological level in group singing. Music conveys identity content and helps people to connect to others ethnically and even globally.

## GLOSSARY

**Acculturation:** The psychological processes of accommodation in prolonged exposure to a culture not your own.

**Content information:** Information about objects, events, practices, and other matters of the world context—everything that is not specific to identity and membership.

**Cultural change:** Changes in a culture at a population level as a result of dynamic events within the culture, such as innovation, invention, and discovery.

**Cultural dynamics:** The study of cultural stability and change.

**Cultural intelligence hypothesis:** The ability to navigate the social world and use social processes to learn a vast array of skills very quickly within a cultural setting, which differentiates humans from other primates.

**Cumulative cultural evolution:** Changes accumulated in human populations over time.

**Dimensions of cultural variability:** Hofstede's four dimensions along which organizational behavior can be analyzed: individualism-collectivism, power distance, uncertainty avoidance, and masculinity–femininity.

**Emulation:** Actions leading to a consequential result that are reproduced.

**Enculturation:** Acquisition of knowledge or characteristics appropriate to a culture or group, usually during childhood development, that results in learning the functions and usage of physical objects and the meaning of symbols, along with the practices enacted in daily life.

**Evoked culture:** Cultural elements arising in response to external factors.

**Grounding:** The process by which a cultural group reaches agreement on the meaning and/or value of a new idea.

**Identity information:** Information regarding interpersonal relationships, including memberships in groups and who one is in those groups.

**Imitation:** Copying the actions or product of a model.

**Memes:** Units of instruction that transmit person to person, like genes or viruses.

**Mimesis:** Imitation, copying, or reproduction.

**Minimally counterintuitive ideas (MCI):** Concepts, characters, or situations with a small number of characteristics that defy expectations or logic.

**Mirror neurons:** A special class of neurons found in primates, including humans, that fire in sympathy to observed actions.

**Natural pedagogy:** Transmission of information from a more to a less knowledgeable individual done outside of formal teaching settings or statuses.

**Overimitation:** To copy all parts of a process, including irrelevant steps, and even when shortcuts are available.

**Ratchet effect:** The collection of modifications to learned processes over time.

**Social diffusion:** The spread of a behavior to others within a group, and sometimes to other groups—a process necessary for the behavior to survive.

**Social identity:** One's sense of self based on group membership.

**Social learning:** The acquisition of information or skill by new individuals, typically transmitted between related individuals of the same species.

**Social transmission:** Repeated learning by new individuals from generation to generation.

**Teaching:** Occurs when a more experienced actor intentionally conveys knowledge or skill to a less experienced one in an organized manner.

**Transculturation:** The creation of culture elements from multiple cultural sources.

**Transmitted culture:** Culture passed from one individual or group to another.

**Xinyong:** The Chinese concept of personal trust.

# RESEARCH CONSIDERATIONS AND METHODS FOR CULTURAL CONTEXT

## Chapter 3 Outline

## Learning Objectives

LO 3.1 Critique the issues that make culture a problematic topic for psychology.

LO 3.2 Summarize the history of cultural concerns in psychology.

LO 3.3 Differentiate the primary approaches to studying psychology and culture.

LO 3.4 Identify the particular ethical and practical concerns that must be considered regarding participants in cultural research.

LO 3.5 Evaluate the methodological considerations affecting the design and execution of psychological research in a cultural context.

LO 3.6 Discuss the ways culture may illuminate issues of replicability in psychological research.

LO 3.7 Review the ways the arts of a culture may be useful in psychological research.

- If you travel to a country very different from your own, what might you do to understand how to behave there?

- Have you ever experienced a misunderstanding because of differences in language or customs?

*Once upon a time in the early 2000s, a group of researchers in, let's say, Boston were very interested in the effects of shared family meals. The names, cultures, and locations have been fictionalized, but children sharing a meal with parents each day really do tend to be physically and psychologically healthier and have better academic outcomes in Western cultures (e.g., Utter et al., 2017). If this were universal, it would be a wonderful way to help young people be healthier, happier, and more successful. These researchers wanted to check.*

*Robert, the principal investigator, regularly attended conferences about cross-cultural psychology, and he had met Hari from Indonesia several times at those events. Indonesia is a nation of 14,000 islands with dozens of cultures, and Robert knew Hari came from a very traditional culture on one of the smaller islands. He asked Hari if he would be willing to set up a qualitative observation of several shared family meals in his home area. Hari agreed, though Robert thought the e-mail response sounded a little odd. He chalked it up to language differences.*

*Robert's group applied for and received a grant for the research. They scheduled flights and hotels, spent days traveling, and finally arrived at the first house where Hari had arranged an observation. There was no dining table, but Hari said the meal would happen in a living room. The researchers set up cameras to record the interactions for analysis later. The food smelled delicious, and soon the women brought in food and the family sat in a circle and began to eat. Everyone seemed tense and there was little interaction between family members. People seemed unsure how to act.*

*Hari invited Robert to a café afterward. The two men reminisced and discussed their various projects for a while. Then Robert brought up the observation, asking if the meal seemed normal. Hari said of course it did not, but he thought the family held up well, given that in their ethnic group, women and children always ate separately from the men. Robert had asked to observe a situation alien to Hari's culture. The trip was enjoyable, but a complete waste of time and resources.*

# WHY IT MATTERS

*Everyone brings certain attitudes and assumptions to any situation. Psychology itself has a certain set of assumptions and approaches about the whats, hows, and whys of research. This chapter discusses approaches to research, some common issues, and some solutions.*

# 3.1 ISSUES IN THE PSYCHOLOGICAL STUDY OF CULTURE

## LO 3.1: Critique the issues that make culture a problematic topic for psychology.

*Horatio: O day and night, but this is wondrous strange!*

*Hamlet: And therefore as a stranger give it welcome. There are more things in heaven and earth, Horatio, Than are dreamt of in your philosophy.*

*Hamlet, Act 1, Scene 5*

*Cultures are a collective, not an individual phenomenon. They belong to anthropology, not to psychology. Their meaning for psychology is that they set the scene on which psychological processes play. They determine, among other things, what is "normal" and "abnormal" behavior in a particular society.*

*Hofstede, 2000, p. 116*

The relationship between culture and psychology is not without difficulty. This contradiction led anthropologist Clifford Geertz (2001) to opine, "Bringing so large and misshapen a camel as anthropology into psychology's tent is going to do more to toss things around than to arrange them in order" (p. 26). The first area of difficulty pertains to level of analysis and the second to philosophical approach. These issues have interacted to shape the current approaches to culture in psychology. The methodologies to be discussed later include considerations to accommodate some inherent conflicts between Western psychology and cultural perspectives.

The first conflict is that, as Hofstede (2000) points out, culture is a phenomenon of groups, by definition, while psychology focuses on the individual. The simple problem concerns levels of analysis: are you investigating individuals or groups? Methodological issues of levels of analysis will be discussed later, but conceptually, scientific method requires definition of the who, what, and how of an investigation. As discussed in Chapter 2, culture is a product of human interaction in a particular historic context, and enculturation shapes humans of that culture to believe and behave in certain ways. We think using symbols and ideas of that culture, and we act in certain ways that have meaning in that culture, which in turn affects the culture around us. Does culture cause the individual, or do individuals cause culture? Scientific method is rooted in empiricism, the idea that knowledge comes from observable data interpreted using logic. Rules of logic do not easily accommodate circular propositions like culture causes humans who cause culture that causes humans, and so on. In the Western intellectual tradition, definitions must be exclusive (Kashima & Gelfand, 2012).

Philosophically, science seeks universal laws by which phenomena can be reduced to components that operate in predictable ways. Psychological theories, as products of science, should apply to all humans, regardless of where they grew up. "The belief that only one answer is the true answer and the others are false is the ideal toward which, in their Enlightenment spirit, the social sciences have aspired" (Gusfield, 1989b, p. 26). If there are cultural differences in what you study, many psychologists say, you are not digging deeply enough and culture is causing noise that is confounding results. American social psychology seeks to solve this dilemma by eliminating culture from experimental conditions, for instance by creating minimal groups in which the only commonality is being assigned to Group A or Group B (e.g., Brewer, 1979). To psychologists who deal with culture, stripping cultural factors is an impossibility, and in fact, recent research has found cultural variation even in minimal group experimental conditions (Falk, Heine, & Takemura, 2014).

Cultures and cultural differences do exist, however messy they may be, and this text is rooted in the premise that they shape the human psyche. Growing evidence indicates that, beyond simply causing people to believe or behave differently, culture affects human physiology, including neural and limbic development. The chapter begins with an overview of the history of culture and psychology, then discusses schools of thought and their approaches to research, and then looks at methodological considerations in research involving culture.

## REALITY CHECK

*Why would Geertz use the analogy of bringing a camel into a tent when talking about psychology and culture?*

*How is your current cultural and historical context different from what your grandparents experienced? From life on another continent?*

*Can you imagine ways that culture might affect how people change as they grow, for instance? Should psychology consider culture in research?*

## 3.2 HISTORY OF CULTURE AND PSYCHOLOGY

### LO 3.2: Summarize the history of cultural concerns in psychology.

### Before the Science of Psychology

People have been interested in the minds and thoughts of others, especially those different from themselves, for millennia. Hammurabi's Code (1754 BCE) included accommodation for the various ethnic groups living in Babylon. Homer's *Iliad* and *Odyssey* (±800 BCE), along with Virgil's *Aeneid* (±20 BCE), included detailed observations of cultures around the Mediterranean, both civilly compatible and monstrously different. Plato (428–348 BCE) pondered the strange nature of the Locrians and other neighbors of ancient Greece, and Aristotle (384–322 BCE), in his *Physiognomica*, discussed other cultures and the nature of human behavior in general. Ssu-ma Ch'ien, the historian and scribe of China's Han Dynasty, described the odd behavior of what he considered barbarian cultures beyond the Chinese borders (Watson, 1958). From 394 to 414 CE, Fa-Hsien travelled the Buddhist countries around China, describing those he met (Fa-Hsien/Legge, 1886/1995). Novelty entertains us, and there is nothing more titillating than the exoticism of cultures unlike our own. Culture and cultural difference are inherently interesting and have long prompted musings about human nature.

John Locke (1632–1704) laid the foundations for consideration of culture in psychology with his concept of *tabula rasa*: that people are born blank slates and their minds are shaped by learning and experiences (Marsella, 1993). Rousseau (1704–1788) enshrined the notion of the noble savage in Romantic thought with his statement, "Man is by nature good, it is only our institutions that have made him bad" (in Marsella & Yamada, 2010, pp. 103–104), by which he asserted that civilization was the source of humanity's ills, and our salvation might be found amongst savage cultures. Esquirol (1845) reiterated this view in his exhaustive *Treatise on Insanity*, in which he relayed that indigenous cultures of the Americas and the non-European cultures of the Mediterranean and other areas seemed to lack serious mental disorders, except in sharing difficulties following trauma, revolution, and war (see Figure 3.1).

## The Early Years of Psychology

Academic study of culture and the psyche began when psychology was still a branch of philosophy. In 1860, Steinthal and Lazarus began publication of a journal called *Zeitschrift für Völkerpsychologie und Sprachwissenschaft* (Journal of Folk Psychology

### Figure 3.1   Causes of Insanity

## II.  CAUSES OF INSANITY.

The causes of mental alienation are as numerous, as its forms are varied. They are general or special, physical or moral, primitive or secondary, predisposing or exciting.

Not only do climates, seasons, age, sex, temperament, profession and mode of life, have an influence upon the frequency, character, duration, crises, and treatment of insanity; but this malady is still modified by laws, civilization, morals, and the political condition of people.  It is, also, produced by causes, whose influence is more immediate, and easily appreciated.

*Source:* Esquirol (1845).

and Language Science). *Völkerpsychologie* remained an area of interest for several decades, but scientific and medical advances pushed the main body of psychology in a different direction.

Psychology in Europe began as a branch of philosophy and became a separate modern scientific discipline when Wilhelm Wundt established a laboratory for psychological research at Leipzig University in 1879. Wundt was the first to call himself a psychologist. He was a Structuralist, focusing on the physical components that allowed humans to think and feel. He was a strong advocate of scientific method, which was an emerging idea at the time, and he began by measuring a perceptual phenomena by which sensation becomes thought. His use of objective experimentation set him apart from Freud, who often quoted Wundt, but whose subjective introspective methodology Wundt criticized as weak. Wundt (1900–1920) would himself develop an interest in *Völkerpsychologie* later in life and published a 10-volume work called *Völkerpsychologie. Eine Untersuchung der Entwicklungsgesetze von Sprache, Mythos und Sitte* (Cultural Psychology. An investigation into developmental laws of language, myth, and conduct), with chapters on language, myths and religion, society, law, and culture and history.

Wundt's students included James Cattell, who would become the first professor of psychology in the US, and Emil Kraepelin, who was a pioneer in psychopharmacology and clinical diagnosis. By the turn of the century, Kraepelin had developed a system of diagnosis based on years of superb observation. Kraepelin believed strongly in scientific method, and his carefully crafted, scientifically constructed system of diagnosis arguably set the foundation for the diagnostic systems used today. Kraepelin was quite confident he had developed a sound system by which any mental disorder could be diagnosed, and he took his system on a celebratory worldwide tour in 1903 (Steinberg, 2015), to be discussed in Chapter 11, though he encountered some unusual disorders on the trip. He proposed the term *Vergleichende Psychiatrie* (Comparative Psychiatry) and recommended that psychology pursue study of other cultures' illnesses (Marsella & Yamada, 2010).

Despite these early proponents, the issue of culture largely passed from discourse after the first three decades of the 20th century, laid to rest by the popularity of Freudian psychodynamic theory and the contrasting rise of behaviorism (Watson, 1913). Inspired by Pavlov's classical conditioning experiments, behaviorism said that only observable behavior constituted valid evidence, in stark contrast to Freud's theories of unconscious drives, and did not consider culture to be an important factor. Behaviorism continued to gain ground with B. F. Skinner and operant conditioning, extending Pavlovian classical conditioning into the realm of volitional behavior. Though other schools of thought like gestalt and social psychology had proponents, behaviorism and psychodynamics arguably dominated Western psychology past the mid-20th century.

In the Soviet Union, Lev Vygotsky (1896–1934) and his collaborators Alexander Luria (1902–1977) and Alexsei Leontiev (1903–1979) took an entirely different approach. They formed the core of what came to be called the Cultural-Historical School, though they did not use that term. They believed that cultural influences inseparably shaped human interaction and development, as children internalize and replicate the cultural interactions they observe around them.

Every function in the child's cultural development appears twice, on two levels. First, on the social, and later on the psychological level; first, between people as an interpsychological category, and then inside the child, as an intrapsychological category. This applies equally to voluntary attention, to logical memory and to the formation of concepts. The actual relations between human individuals underlie all the higher functions. (Vygotsky, 1978, p. 57)

Vygotsky died in 1938 before he could complete his model of human development. Luria went on to great fame, but left culture behind. The Cultural-Historical School remained virtually unknown outside Soviet circles until Harvard published Vygotsky's *Mind in Society* in 1978.

## The Late 20th Century

The world changed greatly during and after WWII. Soldiers and refugees traveled across continents and oceans, forced into contact with other cultures, even in remote areas. For example, when the Japanese sank John F. Kennedy's PT boat (a light, fast attack vessel), it was two Solomon Islanders, Biuku Gasa and Eroni Kumana, who assisted the crew in contacting the Allies ("John F. Kennedy and PT 109," n.d.). Gasa and Kumana's generation had very little contact with outsiders, and in fact tribes in the Solomons practiced cannibalism into the 1960s (Hoffman, 2014).

The shocking violence of WWII, with tens of millions of casualties, including millions of Jews killed, led psychologists to question how humans could commit such horrific acts. These questions led to a resurgence in social psychology, for instance Muzafer and Carolyn Sherif's 1954 study of Realistic Conflict Theory, using boys randomly assigned to two groups at summer camp. Intergroup violence quickly erupted, but forced cooperation to overcome a water supply problem brought them back together (Sherif, Harvey, White, Hood, & Sherif, 1961). Stanley Milgram's (1963) infamous study of obedience used a fake electrical shock machine to test why people comply. More than half continued to administer shocks past the lethal point in obedience to the experimenter/authority figure. Phillip Zimbardo's (1973) disturbing 1971 Stanford Prison Experiment demonstrated how average college student "guards" could become inhumane in treatment of "prisoner" students with very little prompting, similar to abuses much later in 2003 at Abu Ghraib prison in Iraq. Reaction to WWII also led to increased interest in culture by psychologists (e.g., Segall, Lonner, & Berry, 1998).

After the war, transportation became increasingly convenient, fast, and affordable, and international travel became commonplace. At the same time, the manufacture and sale of goods quickly globalized, with companies like IBM making and selling products all over the world, employing workers from dozens of cultures. Reconstruction of Japan included building of a massive manufacturing infrastructure, and "Made in Japan" appeared on cheap toys and electronics across the West. As Japanese quality increased, manufacturing moved to ever-cheaper locales. This internationalization of business led to organizational management research into culture and cultural difference, such as Hofstede's (1980) analysis of IBM data, which resulted in his seminal work *Culture's Consequences*.

In the last few decades, a small but growing element in psychology has begun to focus on culture as an essential component in understanding how people think and behave, and which cannot be ignored (e.g., Segall et al., 1998). To these researchers, culture cannot be eliminated from understanding of humans, and diversity requires that psychology resist the monolithic ideal of psychology based only in positivistic universals. The idea that general theories will apply equally to all people regardless culture has recently begun to bump against evidence that neural paths and brain activity differ depending on a person's culture of origin. Concepts of absolute objectivity were buffeted by Postmodern and Discourse theories. Entry of non-Europeans into the discipline, as well as intercultural experiences of certain American and European psychologists, has gradually increased attention on culture (Kashima, 2000; Marsella, 1999; Marsella & Pedersen, 2004).

## Psychology Recently

Despite inroads of culture, psychology remains a largely Western science, dedicated to scientific method and rational positivist paths to truth. As such, mainstream psychology uses empirical methods to study fundamental processes, under the assumption that, at some deep level, the same mechanisms exist for all humans. Misra and Gergen (1993) describe this goal as "a culturally decontextualized science of behavior" (p. 227). Theories are expected to predict what will happen in all equivalent situations or populations, or put succinctly, they must be **generalizable** across humanity. If a concept cannot be applied to all humans regardless of culture, as mentioned earlier, perhaps it is not a scientific law. Mainstream psychology says that if culture causes variation in outcomes, perhaps the investigator must dig deeper to find a true law of human existence. Cultural, cross-cultural, and indigenous psychologists have fought an uphill battle to return culture to the discourse of psychology. The American Psychological Association does, however, have a division specific to culture: the Society for the Psychological Study of Culture, Ethnicity, and Race.

Psychology still suffers from a startling lack of diversity. The modern discipline continues to be dominated by researchers from Western Europe and North America. In a 2018 ranking of psychology programs around the world, 29 of the top 50 are in the US, 11 on the European continent, three in the UK, three in Canada, and two in Australia. None are in Africa or South America. The highest ranked Asian program is Peking University's at number 43, and the University of Hong Kong completes the list at number 49 (Times Higher Education, 2018). The US does have more universities than any other country, but the country also dominates journal and textbook publication by sheer volume of research produced. Further, most research is conducted using students overwhelmingly of European origin as participants, meaning psychology is largely white people researching white people. This led Henrich, Heine, and Norenzayan (2010) to say psychology is WEIRD (Western, Educated, Industrialized, Rich, and Democratic).

In keeping with Manifest Destiny and a general ethnocentric belief in the superiority of Western thought, 19th-century psychology largely assumed people of other cultures to be underequipped intellectually and prone to certain weakness of the mind, which is still reflected in disproportionate diagnosis of non-Caucasian people in Western clinical practice (Durie, 1994). From Freud onward, the discipline has focused heavily on treatment of disorders assuming that a fully functional European formed the hallmark of normalcy. With deeply held assumptions of the superiority of the Western mind, cultural differences equaled pathology, and that trend still exists (Roland, 2006). Actually, many of the supposed universals of psychology may be limited to European cultures. Currently, psychology is considered to be part of the replicability crisis in science, meaning many of the old foundational studies have failed to achieve similar results in recent attempts to duplicate results. But the students in studies today, while still largely white, do include other ethnicities whose thought and behavior may differ from those old studies due to their origins. Culture provides a solution, as comparisons are made across cultures, and as diverse voices are heard. We turn now to approaches to including culture in psychology.

## REALITY CHECK

*How has the focus of psychology on behaviorism affected the consideration of cultural elements in psychology?*

*What do you think of the idea of universals in human behavior and thought?*

## 3.3 APPROACHES TO STUDYING PSYCHOLOGY AND CULTURE

### LO 3.3: Differentiate the primary approaches to studying psychology and culture.

In the later 20th century, several trends emerged in cultural research in psychology. Three of the main approaches are cross-cultural psychology, cultural psychology, and indigenous psychology. Each has a history of development, an underlying philosophical stance, and a set of researchers who prefer the approach. Each also has certain relations to the origins of psychology in Europe and America. These three are not a complete listing of alternative approaches in psychology and culture, but they are arguably the most influential at this time.

### Cross-Cultural Psychology

Cross-cultural psychology emerged first, carried on the wave of post-WWII change and buoyed by the Cold War competition to establish footholds in non-Western countries. In 1966, a conference was held in Ibadan, Nigeria to discuss problems in developing countries related to social psychology. Attendees felt they needed a way to collaborate on research, and the *Cross-Cultural Social Psychology Newsletter* resulted (Triandis, 1967). Harry Triandis of the University of Illinois was asked to serve as editor. Wayne Holzman then published a paper titled "Cross-Cultural Studies in Psychology" in 1968, in the *International Journal of Psychology*. By 1970, the *Journal of Cross-Cultural Psychology* began publication. Volume 1 opened with an editor's greeting by Walter Lonner and ultimately included articles by a number of central figures in cross-cultural psychology, including Richard Brislin and John Berry. Articles discussed research in Mexico, Ghana, Hungary, and a host of other cultures. A new discipline was born. At the first meeting of the International Association of Cross-Cultural Psychology in 1972, Patricia Greenfield (2000) described attendees as "an assemblage of expatriates who had lived and worked in countries of the former British Empire" (p. 226).

Triandis (1980) set forth a mission statement for the discipline in the opening of his *Handbook of Cross-Cultural Psychology*, stating, "Cross-cultural psychology is concerned with the study of behavior and experience as it occurs in different cultures, is influenced by culture, or results in changes in existing cultures" (p. 1). At its core, cross-cultural psychology views culture as integral to understanding human development and behavior. In cross-cultural comparison, culture is often treated as an independent variable, the thing that causes different outcomes in dependent variables such as what values are most important to people (e.g., Schwartz, 2001). Culture serves as an independent variable in some studies of self-construal (discussed in Chapter 4), in which cultures may emphasize independence or place more importance on interdependence (e.g., Markus & Kitayama, 2010). Understanding that humans themselves play an active role in creating culture, cross-cultural psychology can also at times examine processes of cultural change. In those cases culture may be more of an outcome variable in the change process (Segall et al., 1998).

From the beginning, cross-cultural psychologists sought to confirm or disprove universal theories, such as the fundamental attribution error, which will be discussed in Chapter 4. Faced with criticism that personality theories had been developed in Western contexts only, cross-cultural researchers began testing personality theories across cultures, attempting to demonstrate universality (e.g., Church & Katigbak, 1989). Cross-cultural psychologists may also seek universal structures or rules of culture, as with Shalom Schwartz's decades-long search for a universal structure of human values (e.g., Schwartz & Bilsky, 1990; Schwartz & Boehnke, 2004), to be discussed in Chapter 9. Schwartz and his colleagues have, over the years, constructed a series of questionnaires about values, translated them into many languages, and compared results for similarities and differences.

Largely, cross-cultural psychology began firmly within the assumptions of Western psychology, using empirical methods focused on variables and dimensions, evaluated with statistical analysis techniques (Misra & Gergen, 2001). Berry, Poortinga, Segall, and Dasen (1992) proposed three potential orientations toward culture in psychology: **absolutism**, **relativism**, and **universalism**. The absolutist view says all human phenomena are the same, so depression in one culture is the same in others, and culture makes no difference. A relativist view holds that no phenomenon can be understood outside of a specific cultural context, making cultural comparisons irrelevant. Most cross-cultural psychologists would fall somewhere between those extremes. A universalist view would hold that there may be shared basic processes, but these would have to be tested across cultures for verification (Berry et al., 1992; Segall et al., 1998).

Crucial to cross-cultural research are distinctions of **etic** and **emic** perspectives. The etic view brings outside perspectives into a culture, while the emic view would come from within a culture or from cultural insiders. An absolutist might use an **imposed etic** in application of an outside concept to another population, as when a researcher tests Western-developed personality theories in another culture. An emic concept could be studied within a culture, as is practiced in indigenous psychology. An indigenous concept could clarify processes in other cultures by creating a **derived etic**. Cheung et al. (1996) first developed the Chinese Personality Assessment Inventory (CPAI) to assess an indigenous Chinese concept of personality structure, but it was translated and administered to people in other cultures, as shall be discussed in other sections.

Cross-cultural psychology is by no means a unified field of study, with a wide variety of topics researched using a range of methodologies in virtually any level of analysis. Brislin and Hofstede came from the world of business, while John Berry is famous for studying adaptation in cultural transitions, the topic of acculturation, to be discussed in Chapter 10. Greenfield's decades spent studying effects of culture on development among the Mayans and others sometimes employed ethnographic techniques associated with anthropology, which is not to say Greenfield practices anthropology. Although Greenfield may use methodologies shared with anthropologists, her focus on psychological processes in social learning distinguish her work from anthropology. Hofstede (2003) wryly commented on the lack of interest from anthropologists in his own work, which he considered national level rather than cultural, pointing out that business studies focus on objectivity and comparison, while anthropology focuses on meaning and subjectivity.

Criticisms of cross-cultural psychology include its origins in European intellectual tradition and its inception mostly by white males. Actually, the discipline quickly diversified, and soon included David Sam from Ghana, Japanese-American David Matsumoto, and Çiğdem Kağıtçıbaşı, who was a Turkish woman. Some of the early founders have passed away, including Kağıtçıbaşı, Gustav Jahoda, and Paul Pedersen, and others have retired. The current practitioners are quite internationalized and multi-ethnic, based in many countries. Another criticism does linger, however, that it relies heavily on imposed ethics investigated using Western methodologies, though this too is changing.

## Cultural Psychology

*Cultural psychology aims to develop a principle of intentionality by which culturally constituted realities and reality-constituting psyches continually and continuously make each other up, perturbing and disturbing each other, interpenetrating each other's identity, reciprocally conditioning each other's existence.*

*Shweder, 1995, p. 71*

Cultural psychology gradually emerged from cross-cultural psychology, led by psychologists who took a more anthropological approach, attempting to understand cultures on their own terms. Shweder and Sullivan's (1990) article "The Semiotic Subject of Cultural Psychology" described the discipline, writing "Cultural psychology is, first of all, a designation for the comparative study of the way culture and psyche make each other up" (Shweder & Sullivan, 1993, p. 498). Semiotics, from the Greek word for *sign*, began as a philosophical theory of linguistics under the name *semiology* (de Saussure, 1916/2011), and was expanded by Charles Pierce to include signs and symbols, within which linguistics is included (Elicker, 1997). Shweder and Sullivan (1990) indicate that it is the meaning of a situation that activates a person's response. People base their interpretation of situations and events on meanings they have learned culturally, in a particular historical context. Cultural psychology would therefore take the very relativistic view that behavior can only be understood contextually.

While the ideal of cross-cultural psychology is to bring theories and procedures from one culture into another for comparison, the ideal of cultural psychology is to derive these from a culture itself. Cultural psychology views the psyche as both product and producer of culture, a process of mutual constitution (Eom & Kim, 2014). Language, interpersonal interactions, teaching and learning methods, or other aspects of lifeway could provide material for theory or procedure. Greenfield (2000) describes an experiment she conducted to assess ways indigenous Mayans develop certain cognitive skills related to their traditional weaving practices. This protocol is not relevant or transportable to another culture, but Greenfield provides a fascinating description and analysis of the Mayans as participants in cultural transmission and change.

Richard Shweder (2000), one of the early proponents of cultural psychology, specifies mentality as the unit of analysis, distinct from mind. Mind, he writes, is the species-wide totality of potential cognitive processes that allow humans use ideas and attain knowledge. The term mentality, by his definition, refers to the cognitive content and manner of a specific person or groups. A Japanese mentality would have particular conceptual content, and specific ways of thinking, feeling, and sensing. Psychology as a whole studies the mind, and cultural psychology studies mentalities, according to Shweder. A cultural psychologist would document and describe the mentalities she encounters, and the processes by which people develop and construct meaning across their lives (Greenfield, 2000). Cultural comparisons may be of little or no interest.

Cultural psychology understands culture as a system of meanings shared by members of the culture. Instead of a postmodern emphasis on validity of subjective views, it acknowledges an objective experiential world and potential for common psychological processes (Miller, 1999). The idea of a self-contained individual person that mainstream psychology considers healthiest, however, with strong personal boundaries and a drive for self-directed attainment, is not universally desirable. The concept of personhood, and identities of people themselves, are constituted by the community and cultural context, and a strongly collectivist person may be describable more in terms of relationships and roles (Gergen, Gulerce, Lock, & Misra, 1996). For cultural psychology, the Western concept of bounded, independent self is a culturally constructed idea of personhood.

Whether or not one subscribes to a culturally determined definition of self, it is a radical charge to view the classical psychological concept of bounded self as essentially a folk psychology. Personality theory goes all the way back to Freud himself, and psychology has long assumed its universality. Cultural psychology takes a stance allowing that Western dimensions of personality may have little relevance to the way Asian or African populations view selfhood, for instance.

Cultural psychology also challenges Piaget's stages of cognitive development. Piaget assumed cognitive development proceeded independent of culture, but the work of Barbara Rogoff (1996) challenges that view. Rogoff comments that the very question of the age at which a child acquires a cognitive skill treats the process as if it were contained in the child. The better questions are about how participation and social supports assist the child in understanding the purpose of reading and then how the supports allow the child to make sense of letters and words. Cognitive development, in this view, could be better understood by including participatory process of social learning.

Cultural psychology primarily emphasizes emic modes of understanding, but not in a vacuum. The leading names in cultural psychology, such as Hazel Markus and Shinobu Kitayama, Patricia Greenfield, Jon Haidt, Arthur Kleinman, and others (Shweder, 1999), began in social or cross-cultural psychology, and studied in programs including training in classical psychological methodologies. The field also draws techniques from psychological anthropology. Whereas Hofstede (1980) analyzed national level samples that certainly included ethnic subgroups, cultural psychology would treat those groups as separate entities with their own systems of meaning. The focus of cultural psychology is on ways of life and how practices and beliefs in a lifeway reinforce and perpetuate the culture. Common denominators certainly exist and should be investigated, but the focus here is on examining a particular culture and understanding how it answers the universal questions we share about life, relationships, and mortality (Shweder, 1999).

## Indigenous Psychology

*While the academy expects that its members will contribute to the scholarly community through rigorous intellectualism, Native Hawaiian communities expect that their members will contribute through vigorous activism.*

*Kaomea, 2004, p. 28*

Indigenous psychology further extends the idea that meanings and personhood are culturally constructed and best understood from an emic perspective. The movement began as more and more non-Europeans entered psychology and found the theories and constructs did not accurately represent their identities or experiences. Çiğdem Kağıtçıbaşı (1984) described the experience of psychologists in non-Western countries, saying, "they have inherited the field ready made from the West rather than having participated actively in its development" (p. 145). A decade later, Bame Nsamenang (1995) of Camaroon commented that "many African psychologists are largely unaware of the Eurocentric nature of the discipline. They inadvertently promote Euro-American values and epistemologies to the neglect of their own. As a result, the psychology that is developing on the continent is Eurocentric in cognitive and value orientation" (p. 729). In non-Western countries around the world, psychology began with the assumption of universality and no validation of existing indigenous concepts.

Indigenous psychology represents a reaction against this imposed system, and a movement to develop psychologies based in the constructs of a particular culture, using the culture's own concepts of personhood and explanations of mental processes. As such, there is no single indigenous psychology; rather, there is a growing number specific to particular countries and cultures. Practitioners are usually members of the culture, though the pioneers were typically trained in North America and Europe, for instance Korean psychologist Uichol Kim, who trained with John Berry in Canada (Greenfield, 2000).

By the 1970s, researchers in Hong Kong, India, and the Philippines began actively developing indigenous psychologies (Enriquez, 1977, Mataragnon, 1979). In her address to the First Regional Conference on Cross-Cultural Psychology, Filipina psychologist Rita Mataragnon quoted Triandis (1972):

> If we are to compare apples and oranges, we can do it only on those dimensions they have in common, such as size, thickness of skin, and acidity, and not on unique dimensions such as "apple flavor." We can formulate "laws" that describe the relation between size and price or thickness and price, that are applicable to all "fruit," but we also need laws that are unique to apples or oranges. (in Mataragnon, 1979, p. 8)

The various indigenous psychologies share several elements, beginning with their origins separated from the Greco-Roman influences that form the foundation of European thought. Most also share the ongoing implications of a colonial past and extending to current effects of globalization. The post-WWII era wrought massive changes in so-called developing countries, as industrialization and resource extraction altered ecologies and economies on an unprecedented scale. Hiroshi Azuma (1984) pointed out that the scale and speed of change went far past anything developed countries had seen because the West experienced a more organic pace of change spread over centuries instead of decades. Traditional ways of living and thinking were destroyed, at times violently, in the wake of those changes. Anthropologist Victor Turner (1986) described ritual in traditional or aboriginal cultures as a primary mechanism for creating sense of unity, equality, and interconnection, which he called *communitas*. Along with the natural environment, cultures all contain histories, bodies of knowledge, and traditional activities forming symbolic resources to support identity and well-being (Markovitzky & Mosek, 2005). Rapid development and Westernization disrupted or destroyed these mechanisms, and Western psychology itself contributed to cultural loss by devaluing indigenous concepts of mind and mentality, at best categorizing them as folk psychologies.

These folk theories form an object of study in cultural psychology. Indigenous psychology takes the folk theories as its raw material to construct the formal theories and models for that culture. The indigenous psychologist then takes these culturally based theories and uses them to design and conduct research (Greenfield, 2000).

## India

In India, psychology began with imitation of the European-American tradition. Great Britain controlled the subcontinent for two centuries, first under the East India Trading Company, then under direct rule of the British Raj. Heavy taxation impoverished the people, and rebellions were put down with deadly force. Convinced of their superiority, Britain subjugated India politically, economically, and in no small way, intellectually. India had 4,000 years of history including ancient writings on health and healing, but British dominion subordinated India's ancient knowledge and traditions to Western ideas and ideals (Gergen et al., 1996). Indigenous psychology in India would not emerge until well after British rule ended following WWII.

Sikh psychiatrist Jaswant Singh Neki (1925–2015) of India observed a disconnect between his patients and the psychoanalytic therapies he had been taught. Psychology pathologized dependency, while cultures of India tend toward collectivism and historically considered feelings of independence to be a problem (Neki, 1976). Neki (1973) proposed that a more effective therapeutic relationship would reflect the indigenous Indian bond between *gurū* and *chēla*, which roughly equates to teacher-student roles but is more complex. The *chēla* devotes herself completely to the *gurū* as a font of wisdom and guidance. The classical *gurū-chēla* relationship is that between Krishna and the warrior Arjuna, described two millennia ago in the Bhagwad Gita. Krishna was the god Vishnu, manifested as Arjuna's charioteer, but Krishna's true role was to teach Arjuna about the nature of consciousness, motivation, cognition, and anger control (Pandey, 2004).

## Japan

Psychology in Japan traveled a different path, partly because it was never colonized. Japan remained closed to Western trade until 1853, when Commodore Matthew Perry of the US Navy brought a small but heavily armed fleet of ships to Edo (Tokyo) harbor. Perry forced Japan to allow trade under threat of attack. The country then undertook an organized effort of modernization. Psychology was embraced enthusiastically as a way to modernize Japanese thinking. When the University of Tokyo opened in 1877, its curriculum already included psychology, only two years after physiologist William James taught the first psychology classes in America. Japanese psychology proceeded to create its own research using Japanese subjects but remained within constructs imported from the West for several decades. Japan continues to host a robust array of psychology programs in its universities, though now with much greater inclusion of Japanese concepts.

Similar to India, indigenization in Japan took a great leap when Takeo Doi (1962) realized that the individualistic concepts of Western psychology were incongruent with centuries of Japanese mentality. Dependency is a key component in healthy interpersonal relationships, with families intertwined for generations in business and friendship. He proposed that understanding of the Japanese personality structure required inclusion of the concept of *amae*. Doi explained that the noun *amae* derives from the verb *amaeru*, "to depend and presume upon another's love." This word has the same root as *amai*, an adjective which corresponds to "sweet." Thus *amaeru* has a distinct feeling of sweetness, and is generally used to express a child's attitude toward an adult, especially his parents. (Doi, 1956, p. 92)

Far from pathological, this sweet sense of dependency permeates Japanese culture, reflected in the phrase "*Okage Sama De:* I am what I am because of you" (Japanese Cultural Center of Hawai'i, 2018).

## Critique

Gustav Jahoda (1920–2016), a founder of cross-cultural psychology, issued a harsh critique of indigenous psychology in 2016, in which he declared the movement in decline from inherent weakness. Jahoda details a number of criticisms, among them positing that as a reaction against colonial influences, the movement was emotionally rather than rationally based. He points out with some justification that several terms are used, somewhat interchangeably, including indigenous psychology and ethnopsychology, and that definitions are at times contradictory.

Indigenous psychologists disagreed vehemently. Hwang (2017) criticizes Jahoda's selection of literature as incomplete and points out decades of literature providing evidence for differing mentalities and their effects on the psyche. Sundararajan (2016) describes indigenous psychology as a global intellectual movement. The lack of consensus Jahoda describes stems from its diversity, and that diversity is its strength. Sundararajan points also to growing impact of indigenous psychology literature, which she says is challenging categories of disorders in in the *Diagnostic and Statistical Manual* (American Psychiatric Association, 2013). Hwang (2017) anticipates steady growth in the movement.

## Other Cultural Trends

A number of other approaches in psychology address issues of culture and ethnicity. Notably, the *Journal of Black Psychology* began publication in 1974. Mexican ethnopsychology dates back to Esquiel Chavez's 1901 *Ensayo sobre los rasgos distinctivos de ia sensibilidad como factor del caracter mexicano*, an essay on the differing characteristics of Mexico's three main ethnic groups (Diaz-Guerrero, 1991). A number of psychologies emerged in Africa over the past few decades (e.g., Bodibe, 1993; Nsamenang, 1995; Nwoye, 2015). These and other ethnic and national psychologies fall on a spectrum between indigenous, cultural, and cross-cultural psychology. Researchers often attempt to address issues of their group, such as Hall and Yee's (2012) observations on the underrepresentation of Asians in American mental health treatment. The Association for Asian Social Psychology includes researchers in indigenous, cultural, and cross-cultural psychology, bonded by their interest in Asians and Asian culture. These organizations and approaches will continue to grow and diversify as psychologists from various ethnicities are trained.

A different approach is taken by multicultural psychology, a term that appeared by 1983 (Ossorio, 1983). The discipline has its origins in the US, acknowledging that the country is inescapably diverse. In their text entitled *Multicultural Psychology* (Mio, Barker, &

Tumambing, 2012), Lori Barker begins, "My whole life is a multicultural experience. I first learned to love and appreciate different cultures from my parents, who immigrated to the United States from the island of Barbados in the West Indies" (p. 2). Hall and Barongan (2016) offer the definition, "Multicultural psychology is the study of the influences of multiple cultures in a single social context on human behavior" (p. 2). The inclusive and multidimensional nature of the approach has been embraced by researchers studying factors of gender identity and feminist theory.

Polycultural psychology goes a step further, taking the view that identities and worldviews are no longer unitary in the midst of increasing diversity (Morris, Chiu, & Liu, 2015). People in multicultural societies may draw ideas and influences from a variety of cultural sources, and they may, in fact, have multiple ethnic ancestries. By census, Hawai'i's population includes 23% mixed ancestry people (Department of Business, Economic Development & Tourism, 2016), but really, categories like "Asian" conflate cultures as diverse as Chinese, Korean, Vietnamese, and Filipino, so the percentage who consider themselves as having multiple ethnic heritages is much higher. Morris et al. (2015) point out that an individual may identify with multiple origins, and further, identity is not fixed. Six percent of Americans reported a different ethnicity on the 2010 census from what they reported in 2000.

With the increasing diversity of the US population, this is a time of change in demographics, policy, and academics. Psychology is also changing. These approaches all represent attempts to break free from an ethnocentric view and explore universals and uniqueness with an open mind. What is researched, by whom, and from what perspective is in flux. The ways of conducting this research is discussed next.

## REALITY CHECK

*Of cross-cultural, cultural, and indigenous psychologies, does one fit better with your way of thinking? How do you think researchers in these disciplines would shape the questions and interpret outcomes of research?*

## 3.4 PARTICIPANT CONSIDERATIONS IN CULTURAL RESEARCH

### LO 3.4: Identify the particular ethical and practical concerns that must be considered regarding participants in cultural research.

A number of considerations must be taken into account when doing research with cultural components. First is the overall approach. As discussed, cross-cultural research inherently involves multiple cultures, each with particular characteristics that may affect research. Etic constructs may or may not cause issues across certain cultural boundaries. Cultural and indigenous psychologies entail sensitivity to emic elements that may inspire theory or indigenous methodologies. Broadly, a researcher must begin with a solid idea of who and what will be researched, the approach to be used, and hopefully, an awareness of cultural assumptions the researcher brings. These sections are not comprehensive; a number of excellent books and chapters are available on the topic of methodology and culture (e.g., Matsumoto & van de Vijver, 2010), but some major issues will briefly be discussed, beginning with issues regarding the people to be researched.

## Levels of Analysis

A first question in cultural research is whom one is studying. Basic approaches include case studies of limited individuals, cultural contextual studies of groups in place, and intercultural studies of multiple cultural groups. Each has benefits, depending on the question being investigated, and varying relevance to the research approaches. As discussed in Chapter 2, we exist simultaneously as members of families, tribes, cultures, and nations. Those layers interact, forming differing characteristics, and revealing different processes depending on which level is being investigated. In social sciences research, the nested layers of interaction comprise **levels of analysis** because people tend to share characteristics or differ relative to these patterns.

On broader levels, such as global or national, researchers would usually collect information from a randomized sample of enough people to represent the bigger population. Typically, scores or ratings are averaged to reveal tendencies of the whole group, which actually may include many different kinds of people. Within the US, California, Mississippi, and Maine differ in ethnic, economic, and environmental characteristics, though they contribute to US aggregate scores. Members of African American, Korean, and Latino communities in Los Angeles have shared residency in the city and in the state of California for decades. They contribute to the average characteristics of the city and state, though when examined on a finer community level, their characteristics are very different. This is why level of analysis and sample demographics are crucial in interpretation and reporting of social science research.

Research on broader levels cannot predict behavior of every individual group member, but such research is valuable in understanding the general forces shaping group values and norms, and therefore illuminating tendencies of a workforce. As our levels of analysis become more specific, understanding of a particular type of person's ways of relating to others may become clearer, but social sciences normally focus on drawing conclusions that are generalizable to as much of humanity as possible. Of course, cultural or indigenous psychologies may not care about generalization. In those approaches, a case study or ecological or cultural context may be the better setting. Small, specific samples may yield rich information on those particular individuals or cultural groups. Each level of analysis has its purposes.

## Sample Representativeness

Once the level of analysis is chosen, the next question may be **representativeness**, or how well the sample represents the people to be studied. In general psychology, random selection forms the highest standard because the diversity of the sample is more likely to match characteristics of the broader population (Boehnke, Lietz, Schreier, & Wilhelm, 2010). Early cross-cultural research tended to compare participants by nation, as with Hofstede's (1980) study of IBM employees. Studies do still make national comparisons, as in Fang, Sauter, and van Kleef's (2018) comparison of emotion perception in Taiwan and Holland.

For cultural research, narrowing selection to members of a specific cultural group may be necessary. In that case, one could randomize from the set of all group members, but this may be impractical for a number of reasons. Members may be unavailable to the researcher due to practical issues such as remote location or work schedule. Less tangible cultural issues may also inhibit access, for instance in the numerous cultures that restrict contact between genders. This may be particularly difficult with groups displaced by war or disaster, where many women experience sexual violence during or after events. If a same-gender researcher and translator are unavailable, their voices may not be heard. Ultimately, it becomes the responsibility of researchers to report who was selected and by what process, along with how limitations may have affected outcomes.

## Issues for Ethnic Communities

*Researchers are like mosquitoes; they suck your blood and leave.*

*Native American saying, in Cochran et al., 2008, p. 22*

Despite its potential importance to health and well-being, ethnic groups often share little enthusiasm for cultural research, especially when researchers are not part of the community. Investigation and observation of non-Western cultures blossomed in the late 1800s, as academics ventured into exotic and newly colonized territory. British anthropologist Edward Burnett Tylor (1832–1917) published his observations of Mexican culture in 1861, titled *Anahuac: or, Mexico and the Mexicans, Ancient and Modern*. John Wesley Powell (1834–1902) documented Native American tribes as he travelled the US frontiers on geological expeditions (e.g., Powell, 1881). German anthropologist Franz Boas (1858–1942) began as a geographer and became fascinated with culture when he encountered the Inuit of Baffin Island. Scientists, whether from anthropology, sociology, medicine, or psychology, plied the globe studying "primitive" peoples (e.g., Boas, 1911), a practice that continues today, though without active use of the term *primitive*.

Indigenous and aboriginal groups grew tired of being studied for a number of reasons. Like the mosquitos in the quote above, researchers took information and artifacts from cultures and gave little in tangible benefits, also taking no responsibility for how the research is used or affects the participants (Deloria, 1991). Māori researcher Linda Tuhiwai Smith explains:

From the vantage point of the colonized, a position from which I write, and choose to privilege, the term "research" is inextricably linked to European imperialism and colonialism. The word itself, "research," is probably one of the dirtiest words in the indigenous world's vocabulary. When mentioned in many indigenous contexts, it stirs up silence, it conjures up bad memories, it raises a smile that is knowing and distrustful. (Smith, 1999, p. 1)

The trend continues, as was revealed when the Havasupai of Arizona discovered that researchers distributed blood samples taken for diabetes research around the country and used them for a number of unauthorized projects (Shafer, 2004). Even huge and ancient cultures are not immune to research excesses. In 1995, researchers at the University of Mississippi received a patent for the use of turmeric in treating wounds, a practice that began in India well over a thousand years ago. The patent was overturned in 1997, after numerous complaints were filed. Ironically, the researchers, Suman Das and Hari Cohly, are Indian-Americans (Chengappa, 1997).

Primary in cultural research is the need to acknowledge rights of self-determination and autonomy of the cultural community (e.g., Smith, 2013). Academics have a reputation for valuing only knowledge generated through positivist rules of objective observation and logical interpretation. Researchers hurt their chances of acceptance and of really understanding their participants if they fail to acknowledge legitimacy of indigenous ways of knowing (Cochran et al. 2008). Smith (1999) advises that designs based in community values and indigenous knowledge will have greater reliability and validity. Collaborative research in which the community determines, or at least advises on, research trajectory is more likely to elicit participation and cooperation and to generate knowledge that reflects the source community (LaFrance, 2004). An outside researcher does well to learn as much as possible about the history, knowledge base, and customs of a group to avoid offense (Cochran et al. 2008; Deloria, 1991). Crucially, participants should have a sense of ownership of the process and results (Cochran et al., 2008).

The terms *decolonization* and *indigenization* are used somewhat interchangeably, and both are used to refer to inclusion of indigenous knowledge and research methodologies. Smith (2013) explains that decolonization of research examines underlying assumptions and values of research, critically examining the imperial and colonial influence of European academics. This involves understanding of history before colonization, the process of colonization, and the time since. A key concept is that colonizers have not left; the process is ongoing. Decolonization asserts the humanity of indigenous people, whose intellectual capacities were denigrated and whose cultures were considered inferior. As explained in the previous section on indigenous psychology, underlying assumptions in indigenized research are drawn from the culture, making the research much more acceptable to ethnic communities.

## Informed Consent Issues

> If you apply this life force feeling to all things—animate and inanimate—and to concepts, and you give each concept a life of its own, you can see how difficult it appears for older people to be willing and available to give out information. They believe it is part of them, part of their own life force, and when they start shedding this they are giving away themselves.
>
> *Rangihau, in King, 1992, pp. 12–13*

Ethical standards in research exist to protect participants. The movement for these protections grew in the latter 20th century following several serious cases in which participants, or subjects, as they were called, experienced physical or mental harm. Most notorious of these was the Tuskegee Syphilis Study, running from 1932 to 1972, in which 399 African American men with syphilis went untreated (Thomas & Quinn, 1991). Ironically, the study began with intent to improve the health of rural African Americans by testing prevalence of syphilis and providing treatment. The Great Depression devastated the resources of the Rosenwald Fund, who provided funding, and the study simply lacked resources to follow through on treatment. Rather than inform participants, researchers decided this provided an excellent opportunity to clear up questions of racial differences in progression of the disease. The men remained intentionally uninformed and untreated until the study was exposed in 1972. Thomas and Quinn (1991) quote former Public Health Service venereal disease director Dr. John Heller's 1976 interview: "The men's status did not warrant ethical debate. They were subjects, not patients; clinical material, not sick people" (p. 1501).

Milgram's (1963) experimental study of obedience and Zimbardo's (1973) Stanford Prison Experiment observing abuse of authority drew widespread media attention to negative effects of research on participants. Milgram's (1963) participants believed they were administering electrical shocks to a subject in a learning experiment, though they themselves were the object of study. Of 40 participants, 26 went to the maximum shock, well beyond indicators of severity and risk of death, and despite strong feelings of distress. Zimbardo selected subjects "judged to be most stable (physically and mentally), most mature, and least involved in anti-social behaviors" (Haney, Banks, & Zimbardo, 1972, p. 5), and assigned them randomly to be prisoners or guards. The "prison" quickly spiraled out of control, partly because Zimbardo played the role of warden and encouraged bad behavior by the guards, which is why only commentaries and not the study itself have been published. In both of these studies, some subjects experienced great distress in the experiments and for years afterward.

These studies and others prompted a widespread movement to establish and enforce ethical standards for research. The academic community as a whole now requires ethical approval for any study involving living creatures, especially humans. General issues such as freedom from coercion apply, though the issue may be clouded when researchers are from a more affluent or dominant culture. In a qualitative study of people in Qatar from Arabic-, Hindi-, English-, and Urdu-speaking origins, Killawi and colleagues (2014) heard concerns about anonymity, privacy, and gender boundaries, and some participants had issues about need to consult family members before consent. These concerns are not entirely unique to cultural research but may involve more rigid barriers in some cultures.

Issues of consent become particularly important for indigenous groups, considering they are often lower in socioeconomic status and political power, and many suffer ongoing effects of harsh colonization (Sobeck, Chapleski, & Fisher, 2003). Fitzpatrick and colleagues (2016) pointed out that ethical guidelines often stress importance of upholding indigenous values in research but fail to provide instructions for achieving this goal. Sherman and colleagues (2012) interviewed people in Shawi and Shibo communities in the Peruvian Amazon to gain perspective on informed consent in remote indigenous communities. Informed consent was an unfamiliar concept, and detailed forms were considered intimidating. Distribution of consent forms engendered nervousness and suspicion, and the detailed information appeared excessive. They did want to know the purpose of the study along with risks and benefits but were not interested in details of how data would be handled. Participants wanted time to consider before granting consent and viewed the process as ongoing, often stopping researchers' questions to ask for reiteration of the study's aim and design. They also emphasized that researchers should consult community leaders often throughout the study.

A unique issue in cultural research is that ethical standards are based on Western concepts of personhood, and of individuals' ability to consent to participation and sharing of information. To indigenous cultures, personhood may be construed more broadly, applying even to animals, plants, and minerals (Grim, 2004). Agency, the ability to choose, varies by culture (see Chapter 4). Kara (2007) observed that people in Turkey consider themselves to be integrally part of a community rather than individuals free to make their own choices, and therefore cannot be expected to consent as autonomous individuals. Lasser and Gottlieb (2017) explain that in Chinese tradition, concepts of personhood are duty oriented, rather than revolving around individual rights. Consent in these cases concerns family and community, leading Korean Americans, for example, to prefer that medical decisions be familial rather than individual.

A final consent issue concerns concepts of ownership. Ownership, control, access, and possession, or OCAP, became an issue in Canada in the 1990s regarding topics including research, statistics, cultural knowledge, and other information gathered from First Nations (indigenous) people (Schnarch, 2004). The issue has a number of facets, including control of resulting data collected and outcomes of analysis. A deeper issue of consent concerns ownership of cultural knowledge because consent is defined as an individual right, but cultural knowledge is more properly a collective possession.

The issue also arises in genetic research because to Māori, for instance, the body is *tapu* (sacred), and to sell or give away anything *tapu* could be a great violation of cultural rules (Gillett & McKergow, 2007). OCAP issues remain unresolved in Canada and elsewhere, though Canadian researchers now appear to be striving to maintain OCAP equity (e.g., Wright, 2017).

## REALITY CHECK

*Does your family have any recipes usually served on special occasions? Are any of those "secret recipes" that are never shared with anyone outside the family?*

*Do you really read the terms and conditions when you buy a cell phone or install software? Do you understand all of those conditions?*

## 3.5 METHODOLOGICAL CONSIDERATIONS

### LO 3.5: Evaluate the methodological considerations affecting the design and execution of psychological research in a cultural context.

Anthropologist Russell Bernard (2017) opens his book on research methods with a description of the origins of various methods. Anthropologists, he says, developed methods to recognize patterns in written text, time use, and decision-making processes. Questionnaire surveys he credits to sociologists and experiments to psychologists. They now belong to everyone. All of them are elements of epistemology, ways of knowing something, and in practice, choice of method is strategic: What is the best tool to investigate [insert your topic here]? Or, on the borders of what is known, will a new tool be required?

Psychologies of culture have bitten off a very big mouthful to chew, as Geertz (2001) cautioned. This chapter discussed earlier that the endeavor began from a strictly European mindset and approach. Expanding around the globe, limitations of those efforts appeared, often pointed out by non-Europeans when the psychology they were taught seemed unlike themselves or their culture. The toolkit of psychology still includes techniques of experiment, interview, inventory, biometrics, and so on. Culture pushed the boundaries, requiring adaptation of old techniques and invention of new ones. The previously discussed approaches to study of psychology and culture lend themselves better to particular methods. Cross-cultural psychology, with its origins most firmly in European tradition, began with preferences for quantitative tools to measure intercultural similarity or difference objectively. Cultural and indigenous psychologies require tools that allow discovery of new constructs, or more properly, that allow existing psychological components of a culture to reveal themselves to researchers. Those may include existing qualitative methods, or the research process may generate or uncover culturally specific methods.

### Quantitative Studies

Quantification in psychology predates the formal discipline, going back to Gustav Fechner's (1801–1887) measurement of sensations, leading to his famous law of "just noticeable difference" in weight, brightness, etc. (Tafreshi, Slaney, & Neufeld, 2016). His work formed a foundation for psychophysics and eventually for Wundt's lab. In Great Britain, Francis Galton (1822–1911) and Karl Pearson (1857–1936) enthusiastically endorsed quantification and numerical representation of psychological phenomena, which could then be averaged and compared using statistical analysis. The mathematical approach supports the assumption of objectivity in psychological science, in which the investigator is separate from the object of research, and a reductionist approach where phenomena are understood by examination of component parts. This objective representation was thought to increase precision and rigor and facilitates statistical analyses. Cross-cultural psychology assumes that quantified behavioral (or survey) responses can provide evidence of cultural effects.

**Quantitative studies** in culture fall into several categories. **Generalizability studies** intend to establish equivalence of concepts or phenomena across cultures (van de Vijver & Leung, 2000). On the other end of the spectrum are **difference studies**, which attempt to demonstrate and explain cross-cultural differences. Their weakness is that a difference may be observed, but interpretation may be problematic. In other words, do groups differ for the reason proposed, or are other factors actually driving the differences?

**Unpackaging studies** are a special type intended to identify underlying causes of cultural differences, to unpack the ingredients contributing to differing cultural outcomes (Matsumoto & Yoo, 2006). Rather than simply tapping a nominal factor of culture, influence of a more specific factor would explain differences (Bond & van de Vijver, 2011). Singelis, Bond, Sharkey, and Lai (1999) found that independent self-construal (discussed in Chapter 4) was the key to unpackaging differences in embarrassability of Americans and Hong Kong Chinese because the independence of Americans made them less susceptible to embarrassment from their own action. The concept of self-construal provided a mechanism to explain the differences.

## Bias and Equivalence

The most important considerations in cross-cultural research are questions of equivalence and bias (Matsumoto & Yoo, 2006; van de Vijver, 2000). When drawing comparisons or stating similarities across cultures, several issues must be addressed. At a most basic level, what units are being used? Length of A in centimeters cannot be compared to length of B in inches without adjustment (Poortinga, 1989). On a deeper level, do concepts hold the same meaning in both cultures? Chen (2008) cautions that we must be careful not to compare forks and chopsticks. Both are eating implements, but they function quite differently, are used in different cuisines, require different skills, and hold different implications for identity of the user.

### Bias

*Bias* is a term for anything that challenges comparability of data (He & van de Vijver, 2012), it may refer to differences in measurement or to differences in response. **Construct bias** occurs when the construct being measured differs across cultures, either because definitions do not align, or because associated behaviors do not match. Method bias may stem from several problems, including **sample bias**, when the set of participants is somehow unrepresentative, or **administration bias**, when there is an issue in data collection, perhaps because of the materials or qualities of the administrator. A mismatch of ethnicity between participants and the researcher administering the study may make participants uncomfortable, affecting responses. **Instrument bias** may occur when an instrument includes unfamiliar content, such as use of a computer in a low-tech context.

Cultural tendencies may lead to bias in response styles. For instance, people who tend to agree rather than disagree exhibit **acquiescence bias**, which is often found in low-SES and collectivist contexts. **Social desirability bias** leads participants to respond in the way they think the researcher wants or in a way they think makes them look best. Participants with a **moderacy bias** may choose items in the middle of a scale, whereas **extremity bias** responders choose the most extreme answers available (Matsumoto & Yoo, 2004; McGrath, Mitchell, Kim, & Hough, 2010).

## Equivalence

This section discusses several issues of equivalence that may cause problems in cultural research. Equivalence, or lack thereof, can yield particular types of bias, including the following:

- *Conceptual equivalence* means the concept can be discussed in all cultures involved and holds the same meaning in each (Hui & Triandis, 1985). If an American says she feels blue, her friends may know what she means, but for someone from a culture that does not characterize emotional states by color, "I feel blue" becomes a bizarre statement.

- *Functional equivalence* refers to the process by which something works. In other words, there must be an identifiable goal, outcomes that can be assessed, and antecedent-consequence relations that are the same (Hui & Triandis, 1985). Berry (1969) stated that "only skills developed in response to a shared problem may be validly compared in two or more cultures" (p. 125). Marriage between two people is functionally different from marriage in cultures where a man can marry multiple women, or where a woman might marry multiple men, both of which are traditional in certain cultures.

- *Measurement equivalence* describes the validity and reliability of instruments in different cultures. In other words, are the same constructs being measured using comparable units of measurement that function predictably when used repeatedly (Matsumoto & Yoo, 2004)?

- *Item equivalence* presupposes equivalence of concept and function, and of construct operationalization. If numeric scores are to be compared, each item must have the same meaning so that outcome scores can be compared (Hui & Triandis, 1985).

- *Linguistic equivalence* A final area of difficulty regards equivalence of words and concepts in different languages. Words, even when precisely the same in denotative meaning may hold different emotional implications. Idioms and colloquial expressions really can never be translated precisely. Usually, translation of an instrument involves a number of stages and processes. These may include back translation, where items are translated to another language and back to the original to see if the meaning remained the same. A bilingual committee may be formed to discuss meanings and best translation.

Poortinga (2016) describes the need to test for structural equivalence, metric invariance, and full score equivalence, all of which relate to patterns of response to an instrument. The idea is that if all elements of a scale are equivalent, then patterns of response and total scores would share similarity. Poortinga says it would be rare for a scale to exhibit exactly the same quantitative and qualitative performance in different cultures because differing interpretation of items as well as differing attitudes may lead to variation in scores, and entire concepts on which a scale is based may hold different meanings. While this lack of precise equivalence has at times formed reason to reject measures, these differences may actually provide evidence of underlying differences.

## Qualitative Studies

**Qualitative studies** examine the contents and meanings of cultural products and processes. A number of qualitative techniques were developed by anthropologists, including ethnography. Ethnographies typically describe the practices and customs of a group, such as a tribe or culture. These can be rich in detail and convey excellent understanding of the people or situations described. When starting into an untested area of research, one way to begin is with a qualitative study to find information about the situations or processes involved. *Talanoa* is a Samoan concept described as "a personal encounter where people story their issues, their realities and aspirations" (Vaioleti, 2006, p. 21). It provides an example of indigenous qualitative methodologies. Topics are discussed until clarity and resolution are reached. The dialogue provides evidence to construct theory and investigate further. Information from qualitative sources may then be used to design subsequent research, for instance quantitative studies such as surveys. At that point the research is considered *mixed methods*.

## Mixed Methods Studies

Mixed methods research mixes two or more different research techniques or strategies (Creswell, 2013). Harkness and colleagues (2006) provide an example of mixed methods in cross-cultural research, in their work with a developmental niche framework to understand early development of children at home and at school. Methods derived from anthropology and psychology worked especially well in combination to understand the multiple factors influencing early development across cultures, in a framework emphasizing interplay between characteristics of the child and of the sociocultural environment. From psychology, the team drew measures of individual characteristics, while anthropology provided methods to understand the meaning of processes and experiences. For the International Study of Parents, Children, and Schools (ISPCS), researchers selected 60 families in each of Australia, Italy, the Netherlands, Poland, Spain, Sweden, and the US, with children ranging from 6 months to 8 years of age. Parents participated in weekly interviews, kept diaries, and completed questionnaires their sources of advice and support and contact with extended family, and on the children's temperament and school success qualities.

The team developed a derived etic by analyzing words parents used to describe children in all of the countries, translating and finding common meanings, and dropping the rare unshared terms. Analysis revealed immediate differences, with American parents using words like "independent" and "intelligent," while Spanish parents emphasized

## DEVELOPMENT OF THE CHINESE
## PERSONALITY ASSESSMENT INVENTORY (CPAI)

Development of the Chinese Personality Assessment Inventory (CPAI) was a marvelous and monumental example of mixed methods research in indigenous psychology. Similar to the Japanese and Indian indigenous researchers mentioned earlier, Cheung et al. (1996) found that Western personality theory did not provide a relevant description of elements important in their culture. They set out to create a personality theory based in Chinese culture, beginning with a qualitative study to determine what traits had been used to describe people in traditional and popular Chinese culture. Possible traits were drawn from a selection of contemporary Chinese novels, books of collected proverbs, 300 statements of self-description by Chinese participants, 433 professionals' descriptions of co-workers in Hong Kong and the People's Republic of China, and analysis of psychological characteristics that have been described already in research.

The researchers categorized these ideas by theme and winnowed them down to 37 personality traits. They then generated about 900 survey items for a trial survey to measure these potential traits. Thirty people examined the list and rated them for relevance, then the scale was tested with hundreds of participants over time, and eventually reduced through factor analysis to 524 items for the final version. Those items measure 22 sets of traits such as family orientation, face, *ren qing*, harmony, *ah-q*, thrift, and graciousness. *Ren qing* has no English translation, but roughly means human sentiment and reciprocity, and *ah-q* mentality is roughly a defensive disposition. These scales were further analyzed in subsequent testing and fall into four broader factors: dependability, Chinese tradition, social potency, and individualism. "Chinese tradition" was renamed "interpersonal relatedness" in subsequent studies.

If this sounds like a great deal of work, it is, and it extended over years. The research trajectory began with qualitative methods, then went through multiple stages of further investigation. Psychology is considered by some to be a soft science, and the relevance of culture is questioned within that discipline. Psychologists who deal with culture respond with increased rigor. The constant questioning of legitimacy of cultural research keeps these disciplines dedicated to high quality, precise methodology.

### Why It Matters

Indigenous psychology inherently seeks to investigate cultures on their own terms. The CPAI provides an example of painstaking work to develop a Chinese model of personality. While the concept of personality may itself have European origins, the dimensions of the CPAI are congruent with a uniquely Chinese sense of self, using concepts that are important in Chinese life.

social competence characteristics such as "good character." Parents also completed the Behavioral Styles Questionnaire (BSQ; McDevitt & Carey, 1978), an established measure of temperament in nine dimensions, including activity level, adaptability, emotional intensity, quality of mood, distractibility, and persistence. Researchers first assessed comparability of these constructs by analyzing fit of items across the cultures. For instance, "watches TV programs (over an hour) without getting up" did not correlate with other items in the Dutch sample because children in the Netherlands are usually restricted to 30 minutes of TV per day. Generally, items were dropped that did not fit in six of the seven national samples, leaving 64 of the original 100 items of the BSQ. Researchers compared BSQ scores to interview data, finding low adaptability and negative mood were considered most difficult across all cultures. "Approachability" was highly valued only in Italy, where parents also preferred descriptors like "lively" and "sensitive."

The data from multiple methods and sources allowed researchers to construct a picture of developmental experiences across cultures. Qualitative interviews allowed feelings and attitudes to emerge uniquely from each culture where they differed, and the quantitative portions provided objective comparisons. All samples valued emotional closeness and endorsed characteristics allowing the child to develop social relationships. Establishment of comparability in meaning and conceptual structure demonstrated validity of cross-cultural comparisons. Although the study was limited to cultures sharing Western European roots, the multiple methodology technique provides a model for cross-cultural investigation of developmental processes in context.

## REALITY CHECK

*What if you were studying how people interact with taller or shorter others? What if your sample was from Holland, where* *the average height is greatest, or among pygmies of the Ituri rainforest in Africa, where the average height is least?*

## 3.6 ISSUES OF REPLICABILITY

### LO 3.6: Discuss the ways culture may illuminate issues of replicability in psychological research.

John Ioannidis rocked the scientific world in 2005 with a provocatively titled article, "Why Most Published Research Findings Are False." The news media went wild, and the article became fodder for anyone with a grudge against science. Pitched battles have waged on for years since then, attempting to support or refute Ioannidis and others who joined the fray (e.g., Goodman & Greenland, 2007). Ioannidis himself has published several more articles on the topic, not backing down on the claim of an overload of false reports or failure to replicate studies but getting more specific in his critique (e.g., Szucs & Ioannidis, 2017).

Several issues are at play, most prominently the idea that it should be possible for another researcher to replicate a valid study, well conducted, with accurate analyses and reporting. Verification by replication forms a cornerstone of science as a credible, self-correcting avenue of inquiry. Also at issue are statistical procedures, primarily based in null-hypothesis testing, in other words, attempting to disprove that the

# SPOTLIGHT

## THE REPLICABILITY CRISIS AND CULTURE

Einstein's general theory of relativity is a theory that explains why things fall toward the earth, and the explanation is not yet perfect. Attempts to revise theories of gravity have proposed concepts like dark matter and dark energy to fill the gaps, but no one theory fully explains gravity at this time (Ezquiaga & Zumalacárregui, 2017; Ishak, 2019). The lack of a sure explanation does not mean one should try jumping off buildings. Theories are explanations created by examining the best evidence available, and then they are refined as new evidence and analyses become available.

When psychologists observe a phenomenon, they may undertake a study to understand it better, like the way people behave when faced with an ethical dilemma. Without unlimited resources, it will probably be a study done at a particular university using students. Will it show how people in another country behave? Maybe not, but it is a start, and then hopefully other researchers undertake replication studies. This book discusses cultural issues in psychology, so replication across cultures is a particular concern when people start talking about universal laws in psychology. As new evidence comes in, scientific method demands a theory be modified to include the new evidence.

Mainstream American social psychology has at times considered culture a confound and has tried to strip cultural elements from controlled experiments, for instance by creating minimal groups based on random assignment to categories (e.g. Brewer & Yuki, 2007). Rather than a confound, culture may be a factor in this replicability crisis in the press. It is true that some highly respected studies are not turning out as expected when someone tries to repeat them. A failure of replication may really be no crisis; it may simply reflect the process of scientific method where new data may appear that requires a new analysis and a revised theory.

The fact is that a vast majority of psychological studies have been done in US universities because the US has historically had the most universities and the most psych departments. The vast majority of participants were of European ancestry, reflecting the historic predominance of whites in college. Most other non-US studies so far have been done in Europe, with similar demographics. But two things have happened: (1) lots of non-Europeans have now become psychologists and universities all over the world have psych departments, and (2) the composition of student bodies has changed even in the US. Cultural diversity gives us new opportunities to look at assumptions of universality.

hypothesis is false and effects happened by chance. The economic and institutional pressure to "publish or perish" may contribute to rushing toward publication, and replication studies are not highly valued, so researchers building reputation may avoid them (Everett & Earp, 2015).

Psychology relies heavily on statistical analysis, given that thought has only recently become measurable via fMRI and other direct observations. The field has long suffered accusations of fluffiness, and early articles on the crisis were by psychologists who observed the problem in their field. This made psychology an easy target in the media, despite findings of failure to replicate across other sciences as well (Achenbach, 2015). Ultimately, there are real issues in how science is done, and challenges as we go forward.

Rather than a crisis, Patricia Greenfield (2017) pointed out a great opportunity for social and cultural psychology in the situation. Over the past century, a massive shift has occurred in where and how people live, moving from rural agrarian life to urban or suburban environments. Demographically, many of the foundational studies of social psychology, including Milgram's and Zimbardo's infamous studies, drew on white Americans as participants, and this was the norm for universities. Those same universities now include student bodies that are ethnically and internationally diverse. Characteristics of the participants in attempts to reproduce studies may differ markedly in their upbringing and ethnicity, but they have also experienced incredible access to communication, travel, and media content, exposing them to a world of ideas unknown when Asch, Milgram, and Zimbardo conducted their studies, and completely alien to the worlds of Freud, Watson, Skinner, or Erikson. Rather than a problem, failure to replicate may provide direct evidence of social and cultural changes in the intervening years since the original study.

## REALITY CHECK

*How might ethnicity or historical context affect studies in psychology or results in science more generally?*

## 3.7 WHAT CAN WE MEASURE IN THE ARTS OF A CULTURE?

### LO 3.7: Review the ways the arts of a culture may be useful in psychological research.

In research, arts have generally provided data or prompts. In many of the studies cited in this text, artistic images might be used to stimulate a particular cultural frame of reference. For instance, Ng, Han, Mao, and Lai (2010) used visual images from Chinese and British/American culture to prime bilingual participants in an fMRI study examining neural responses when asked about self and significant others. One pair of prompts used Bruce Lee and Roger Moore (as James Bond) to stimulate Chinese and English modes of thinking. In Han and Ma's (2014) meta-analysis of 35 cross-cultural brain studies, three used stories as stimuli and nine used pictures.

A very common practice in psychological research is to use music to stimulate an emotion or emotional response. The practice is widespread, and it goes on without consideration of how music should be evaluated or what underlying mechanisms are involved (Eerola & Vuoskoski, 2013; Juslin & Västfjäll, 2008). Eerola and Vuoskoski

(2013) reviewed 251 studies using music as stimuli, finding a very confusing and inconsistent set of concepts about emotions and music, with a small set of familiar Western classical music pieces dominating the research. Cultural origin of participants was not mentioned, but the point is that music appears widely in research as a stimulus.

Another category of use of arts in research is as data for qualitative inquiry. In example, lyrics were used by Dewall, Pond, Campbell, and Twenge (2011) to track psychological and emotional changes in American culture over three decades. A number of examples of this type appear throughout the text, for instance using love songs or poetry as examples of cognitive and emotional processes in relationship. Techniques like this have been used extensively in anthropology and other social sciences, but remain relatively less common in psychology. More common are studies where historic records including news stories and correspondence are used to describe psychological phenomena of the past (e.g., Hatfield & Rapson, 2002, 2005; Liu & Khan, 2014; Rapson, 2007).

## REFLECTING ON YOUR READING

- Think of a cultural phenomenon you find interesting. How would you approach the research?

- What would be your level of analysis?

- Would your project require qualitative or quantitative methods, or both?

- What ethical issues would you need to consider?

- What kind of concepts might require agreement from people other than your participants to be revealed?

## CHAPTER 3 SUMMARY

### 3.1 Issues in the Psychological Study of Culture

Culture and consideration of culture creates a number of difficulties on practical and philosophical levels in psychology. The first is level of analysis, where culture is a collective phenomenon affecting issues that psychology intends to study individually. More generally, psychology seeks universals, and if culture affects psychological states and outcomes, it invalidates universality as a gold standard.

### 3.2 History of Culture and Psychology

Throughout history, writers have mused about differences of people from other cultures they encountered. From its earliest days, psychologists considered that culture might be an important consideration, generating such concepts as *Völkerpsychologie*. With the advent of behaviorism, however, culture faded from research except in the USSR. Culture reemerged in the later 20th century, partly in response to challenges resulting from internationalized business.

### 3.3 Approaches to Studying Psychology and Culture

Predominant stream of research in culture and psychology include cross-cultural psychology, which tends to compare cultures from a Western philosophical and methodological stance; cultural psychology, oriented toward study of cultures using their own concepts and methods wherever possible; and indigenous psychology, which focuses exclusively on a culture's inherent ways of understanding thought and behavior. India, China, and Japan are among countries with histories of indigenous psychology.

## 3.4 Participant Considerations in Cultural Research

In considering participants, the level of analysis is a first concern for clarity of approach and representativeness of samples. The individualist construction of consent forms an emerging ethical issue in light of research in collectivist cultures where rights and ownership may require consultation with other group members, especially elders.

## 3.5 Methodological Considerations

As psychology has spread throughout the world, it brought techniques and tools that may be more or less effective outside Western culture. Among these are surveys, which generate data in affordable and effective ways but may be alien to other cultural contexts. Inherent bias may affect research on conceptual, linguistic, and practical levels. Further, frame of reference and communication style may affect participant responses. Careful consideration is required to assure equivalence throughout research and interpretation of results.

Certain topics may lend themselves to qualitative rather than quantitative methods or some combination of approaches. Indigenous methods may also form valuable tools in cultural research.

## 3.6 Issues of Replicability

Recent headlines claim that science, and particularly psychology, is filled with false claims due to failure to replicate results of previous research. Cultural considerations may provide explanation of these failures. With most foundational research in psychology having been designed and executed by white males using white participants, expansion of the field into other countries and demographic shifts in student populations may account for some changes in results.

## 3.7 What Can We Measure in the Arts of a Culture?

Arts, including visual, textual, and auditory products, have long been used as primes or prompts in psychological research, often without consideration of the cultural implications of the materials. Arts have also served as raw data for research, particularly in quantitative or historical studies.

## GLOSSARY

**Absolutism:** The view that all human phenomena are the same across cultures.

**Acquiescence bias:** The tendency of a responder to agree rather than disagree, often found in low-SES and collectivist contexts.

**Administration bias:** Occurs when there is an issue in data collection, perhaps because of the materials or qualities of the administrator.

**Construct bias:** Occurs when the construct being measured has different meaning or expression across cultures.

**Emic:** The use of only concepts or values found within a culture for research in that culture.

**Etic:** The use of universal or external concepts, imposed on a cultural setting for research purposes.

**Derived etic:** The process of using an emic concept derived from one culture as an etic in another.

**Difference studies:** Studies that attempt to demonstrate and explain cross-cultural differences.

**Extremity bias:** The tendency of a responder to always choose the most extreme answers available.

**Folk psychology:** Informal systems cultures and individuals develop to explain and predict behavior.

**Generalizability studies:** Studies that intend to establish equivalence of concepts or phenomena across cultures.

**Generalizable:** The idea that research in a limited context or sample can or should be applicable to broader contexts or populations.

**Imposed etic:** The application of an outside concept to research in another population.

**Instrument bias:** Occurs when an instrument includes unfamiliar content, such as use of a computer in a low-tech context.

**Levels of analysis:** The scope or focus of research, for instance, individual, local, or national.

**Moderacy bias:** The tendency of a responder to always choose items in the middle of a scale.

**Qualitative studies:** Research in which data are gathered in non-numeric ways, such as interviews, records review, or naturalistic observation.

**Quantitative studies:** Research emphasizing numeric measurement.

**Relativism:** The view that no phenomenon can be understood outside of a specific cultural context.

**Replicability:** The possibility of reproducing results of research.

**Representativeness:** How well a sample represents the group to be studied.

**Sample bias:** Occurs when the set of participants is somehow unrepresentative.

**Social desirability bias:** The tendency of a responder to respond in the way they think the researcher wants or in a way they think makes them look best.

**Universalism:** The view that there may be basic processes shared across cultures, but they would have to be tested across cultures for verification.

**Unpackaging studies:** Studies intended to identify underlying causes of cultural differences by identifying contributing elements.

# THE SELF ACROSS CULTURES

## Learning Objectives

**LO 4.1** Contrast historic theories of self in Western psychology with perceptions of self across cultures.

**LO 4.2** Differentiate universal and contextual factors of self across cultures.

**LO 4.3** Summarize ways self is perceived and enacted differently across cultures, including independent and interdependent self-construal.

**LO 4.4** Discuss constancy and changeability in perception of self and how this may affect behavior and agency.

**LO 4.5** Evaluate evolution of sense of self in terms of gender, ethnicity, and online environments.

**LO 4.6** Illustrate the ways arts reflect our concepts and construals of self across cultures.

# PREPARING TO READ

- How do you define who you are?
- What are your boundaries?
- What are your obligations?
- Who decides what you can and cannot do?
- How do you think your culture might shape your answers to those questions?

*If you have the good fortune to be around when two traditionally aware Māori first meet, they will probably* whakapapa, *which is a formal description of ancestral and geographic origins. If they like you, it might happen in English, just to be polite. The full* whakapapa *process can take a half hour or more for each person, and it would probably be done in te reo Māori, or Māori language. It will start with identifying the person's* iwi, *or tribe, and their home mountain and river. All enculturated Māori know this, even if they grew up in England. If their parents are from different* iwi, *that information is also included. The full recitation could go back to which* waka, *or ocean-voyaging canoe, the person's primary ancestors were on when they arrived in* Aotearoa *(New Zealand) in about 1200 C.E.*

*To a Westerner, this may seem an excessive level of detail. To the Māori people who are meeting, at the conclusion, they know each other's lineage, place in society, innate loyalties, and sense of who they are in the grand tapestry of life. In the Māori understanding of self and the world, a healthy person is made of these connections to nature and family, the* whare tapa wha, *or four-walled house (Durie, 1994; see Table 4.1). As they* whakapapa,

| Table 4.1 | *Whare Tapa Wha*, the Four-Walled House of the Healthy Self | | | |
|---|---|---|---|---|
| Concept | *Taha Wairua* | *Taha Hinengaro* | *Taha Tinana* | *Taha Whanau* |
| Focus | Spiritual | Mental | Physical | Extended family |
| Key aspects | The capacity for faith and wider communication | The capacity to communicate, to think, and to feel | The capacity for physical growth and development | The capacity to belong, to share, and to care |
| Themes | Health is related to unseen and unspoken energies | Mind and body are inseparable | Good physical health is necessary for optimal development | Individuals are part of wider social systems |

*Source:* Durie (1994).

*choice of words and style of speaking are also important because eloquence is highly valued in their traditional culture (Taha Wairua and Hinengaro). If the meeting happened at a marae, or traditional sacred meeting house, how well they sing is also important because you have to sing who you are and what you intend before you are invited in. Before colonization, how well you sang and what you expressed could mean the difference between life and death, if you went to visit another iwi on their home turf.*

## 4.1 PERSONA: THE SELF AS INDIVIDUAL

### LO 4.1 Contrast historic theories of self in Western psychology with perceptions of self across cultures.

*Every man is in certain respects*

*Like all other men*

*Like some other men*

*Like no other man*

*Kluckhohn, Murray, & Schneider, 1950, p. 15*

*All the world's a stage, and all the men and women merely players.*

*Shakespeare (1603), As You Like It, Act 2, Scene 7*

Superficially, identity is simple, being that "set of ideas about who they are and with whom they belong by which humans define themselves" (Grahame, 1998, p. 156). In actuality, understanding differences in the concept of self is perhaps the most difficult aspect of cultural psychology. Our most intimate, familiar knowledge is our sense of self. Every day, we awake to the same self as our only constant faithful companion. We assume everyone feels basically the same underlying sense of individual person-hood. You may not know exactly what you will do after graduation. You may get married or divorced, you may move to another state or country, but you probably assume that you will still be the same person, that same individual you see in the mirror. On the other hand, that strong sense of **individuality** may seem shallow and isolated to someone from a different culture. Trying to convey that there are radically different ways of viewing who one is, that among humans or among classmates your perspective may be different from most, is one of the greatest challenges in teaching the psychology of culture. To understand a completely different sense of self requires stretching beyond your known world. It is also perhaps the most important component of cross-cultural understanding because how we construct ourselves mentally is at the heart of human psychology.

Why does it matter how we think about ourselves? How we think about ourselves influences how we make decisions, how we interact with others and the world around us, and even how we perceive the world. Amid the myriad of ways we live and interact, we are each bound within our particular skin. We all have thoughts, hopes, ideas, and aspirations of our own. These may be narrow or grandly ambitious. Some people's thoughts are limited to survival of self or family. Some are vast: the Dalai Lama wishes for enlightenment of all beings, and astronomer Neil DeGrasse Tyson's goal is to spread understanding of the cosmos. But in very real ways, we are alone inside our thoughts, and our thoughts are what determine how we interact with the world. In distant prehistory, as we developed thought and language, we had to act together for survival, learning roles and specialties, and creating sense of identity within our groups. This section addresses how we are similar and different in sense of self across cultures and what these factors imply for our lives.

*Persona* means "mask" in Latin, and from it, we get the term **personality**. In Roman culture, and many of the ancient cultures, the mask was not worn to hide the actor but, rather, to typify the role being played. In the Renaissance, *comedia dell'arte* had a stock of characters: the doctor, the fool, and the maiden, and so on (see Figure 4.1). The masked actor would behave in certain ways during a hilarious show. These were actually improvised live by Leonardo da Vinci and his friends, among others, using these stock characters built of stereotypic characteristics. Our movies and television shows are still full of heroes and buffoons, acting out challenges, conflicts, and resolutions in much the same archetypal ways we retain from ancient legends (Campbell, 1949/1973). Our own personality could be viewed as a role we play, the mask we present to the world as we play our part each day.

This is the level where Western psychology has long sought to describe the individual, those internal, unique, predictable elements by which we know how our friends and family will behave, and that make us the same person each morning that we were when we went to bed the night before. Personhood, in that system, includes our biological self with its genetic predispositions, unconscious aspects we have learned and internalized as we have grown, ego forces that comprise our self-definition, the ways we interact with others, and the cognitive self that ponders existence and writes or reads psychology books (Allport, 1937; Friedman & Schustak, 2009; Kitayama & Marcus, 1991). Note that this differs greatly from the interconnected *whare tapa wha* of the Māori.

**Figure 4.1 Bonnart (1680–1690), Masked Polichinelle From Comedia Dell'Arte**

*Source:* Courtesy Davison Art Center, Wesleyan University.

## Temperament

Beginning in infancy, children exhibit particular emotional and behavioral tendencies. The term **temperament** commonly concerns differences in reactivity, which refers to level of arousal generated by stimuli we experience, and self-regulation, which is how the person responds to the stimulus (Derryberry & Rothbart, 1988; Krassner, Gartstein, Park, Dragan, Lecannelier, & Putnam et al., 2017). Temperament lies at the core of the ongoing nature–nurture debate, with a century of theorists maintaining that temperament is an innate characteristic, inborn and stable (e.g., Eysenck, 1967; Woodworth, 1921). Indeed, genetic analysis provides evidence of genetic components for some traits, but also of the effects of environment in shaping temperament (Planalp, van Hulle, Lemery-Chalfant, & Goldsmith, 2017). Early temperament characteristics have been linked to adult personality, for instance in a longitudinal study of 1,000 children born in Dunedin, New Zealand in 1972–1973. The Dunedin Multidisciplinary Health and Development Study has provided data for a wide variety of phenomena, including tendency toward risky behavior and likelihood of developing personality disorders (Silva & Stanton, 1996; Stanton & Silva, 1992).

Temperament research provides support for psychological continuity across our lifespans, normally developing into relatively stable adults, though consistency is not emphasized uniformly across cultures and will be discussed later. Cross-cultural studies indicate cultural variation in infant temperament, as exemplified by differing rates of temperament types observed in comparisons of the US, Chile, Italy, South Korea, and Poland (Farkas & Vallotton, 2016; Krassner et al., 2017). Variation was attributed to differences in environment and child-rearing practices, suggesting cultural context shapes our psychological characteristics in important ways.

## Personality Theories

Freud began the modern quest for predictable, psychological laws through introspection, deducing from his own thoughts the laws that he applied to explain the conditions of his patients. His concept of the id, ego, and superego revolutionized psychology, providing the first comprehensive theoretical framework for understanding personality (Freud, 1923/1962; see Figure 4.2). That framework would influence psychology for the next century and continues to serve as the basis of psychoanalytic therapies. Debates raged, and while Freudians and neo-Freudians extended his work, competing streams of thought began proposing alternative theories, often criticizing Freud's methodological lack of objective testing and analysis (Woodworth, 1917).

### Trait Theories of Personality

In response to both Freud and behaviorism, trait theorists pursued an inductive approach, deriving theories from scientific observation. The underlying assumption of trait theories is that we have certain characteristics (traits) that remain stable, can be measured, and can be used to predict behavior. By 1921, brothers Floyd and Gordon Allport had proposed dimensions of intelligence, temperament, self-expression, and sociality. Gordon Allport (1937) and Raymond Cattell (1950) both gathered lists of words for traits describing people and statistically narrowed them to common themes, in what is called a lexical approach (Church, 2016; Saucier, 2009). Using empirical testing and factor analysis of items, Cattell reduced the list to 16 factors of personality.

**Figure 4.2  Diagram of Freud's Conceptualization of the Conscious and Unconscious Elements of Self**

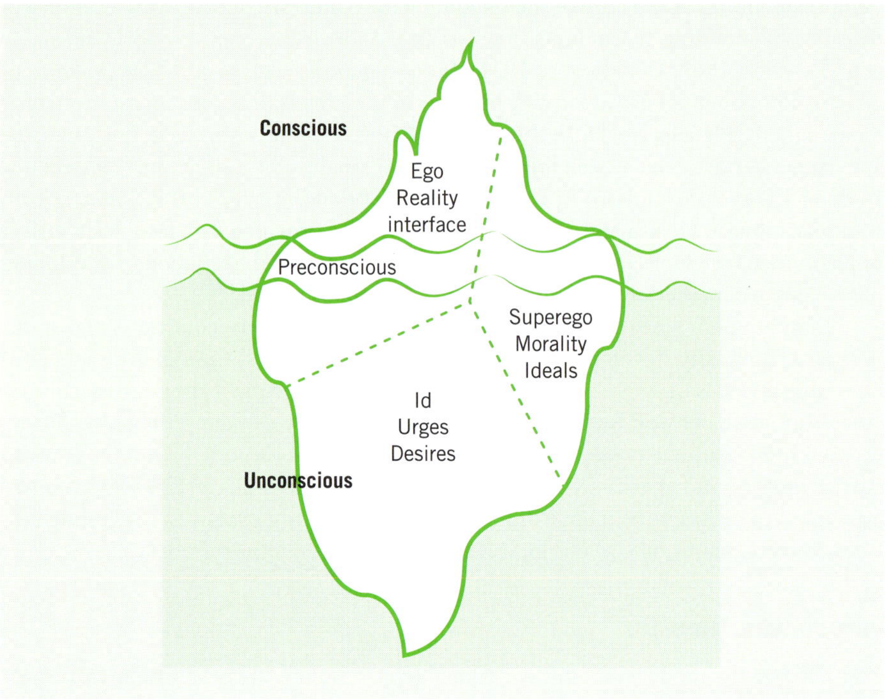

Conscious

Ego
Reality
interface

Preconscious

Superego
Morality
Ideals

Id
Urges
Desires

Unconscious

*Source:* Freud (1923/1962).

By the 1980s, testing and statistical analyses had reduced the trait list to a smaller, stable set of factors, now known as the **Big 5** (McCrae & Costa, 1987; Trapnell & Wiggins, 1990), and the acronym OCEAN (see Table 4.2).

## Trait Theories Beyond Western Shores

In the 1980s, as the Big 5 was being born, cultural activism blossomed, following the Civil Rights movement in the US and postcolonial assertion of indigenous and ethnic rights around the world. More non-Europeans entered academia, and ethnic studies departments sprang up in universities in an increasing number of countries. To be considered a universal, the Big 5 had to be tested across cultures, often in these new bastions of academic research. Largely, traits were reliably observed and measured in an expanding range of cultures, providing support for cross-cultural validity of the Big 5 description of persona (McCrae, 2002; Schmidt et al., 2007). This is an *etic* approach, testing Western constructs in non-Western samples (Church, 2016). One cleverly designed study successfully used ratings from zookeepers to document Big 5 traits in captive chimpanzees (King & Figueredo, 1997).

| Table 4.2 | Big 5 Factors of Personality |
| --- | --- |
| **Factor** | **Description** |
| O  Openness to experience | Includes imagination, wit, and creativity. People who are low on this would be shallow and simple. |
| C  Conscientiousness | Includes dependability and responsibility. People who are low on this trait would be considered disorderly and undependable. |
| E  Extraversion | Includes enthusiasm and sociability. Someone who is low on extraversion would be considered introverted. |
| A  Agreeableness | Includes friendliness and cooperation. People who are low on this trait would be considered cold and caustic. |
| N  Neuroticism | Includes tension and nervousness. People who are low on this would be emotionally stable and contented. |

*Source:* Friedman and Schustak (2009).

As with most psychological research, testing of the Big 5 has predominantly been done among white Americans and Europeans. Cross-cultural testing has happened primarily using university students, all of whom are literate and arguably well-exposed to Western culture and ideals. Sampling bias is certain, and indeed, inconsistencies have emerged regarding nonliterate and less technological cultures such as the Tsimané of Bolivia (Gurven, Rueden, Massenkoff, Kaplan, & Lero Vie, 2013) and the Mooré in Burkina Faso (Rossier, Ouedraogo, Dahourou, Verardi, & de Stadelhofen, 2013). Gurven and colleagues suggest that this is troubling news for the Big 5 and that the structure of personality may vary more across human cultures than currently thought.

Further challenges to the Big 5 came from indigenous psychologists, who question whether the construct of personality is even applicable to other cultures, and if so, whether the traits of the Big 5 are the most relevant in all cases. The constructs and traits may be measurable in diverse cultures, but may not be relevant to life in those cultural world-views (Cheung et al., 1996; Gurven et al., 2013). Western culture lauds independence as an important trait, for example, while Japanese culture holds in high regard the exceptional dependence expressed in the term *amae,* "to depend and presume upon another's benevolence" (Doi, 1988, p. 20). Several studies employed an indigenous lexical approach using terms from their languages, including Cheung et al.'s (1996) CPAI (see Spotlight). More recently, these scales have been compared in meta-analyses, with structures of six or seven factors emerging (Church, 2016; Saucier, 2009). Saucier (2009) found the resulting Big 6 to be relatively stable across cultures, with traits of conscientiousness, honesty, agreeableness, resiliency or emotionality, extraversion, and intellect/openness.

# SPOTLIGHT

## THE CHINESE PERSONALITY ASSESSMENT INVENTORY (CPAI)

In the field of indigenous psychology (see Chapter 3), the belief that individuals may be more accurately described in the terms drawn from their own cultures led Cheung et al. (1996) to develop the Chinese Personality Assessment Inventory (CPAI). At the time of development, people of Chinese ancestry comprised one quarter of the world's population, and the authors felt classification based on Western terms of such a huge portion of humanity constituted a deficiency in scientific understanding.

The CPAI eventually yielded 22 traits such as family orientation, face, and harmony. The Chinese concept of *ren qing* is untranslatable but is described as human sentiment. The traits further reduce to four broader factors of dependability, interpersonal relatedness, social potency, and individualism. In the English translation study by Cheung, Cheung, Leung, Ward, and Leong (2003), the authors tested the CPAI in a non-Chinese sample and compared the structures of the CPAI and the NEO-FFI measure of Big 5 traits. Through factor analysis, they found an interesting pattern when they combined responses to the two instruments: in a six-factor solution, the Big 5 were clearly present, along with a sixth factor that corresponded to interpersonal relatedness. In an American sample, a similar factor structure appeared, though with differing levels. For the interpersonal relatedness constructs of *ren qing*, harmony, modernization,

and flexibility, the American sample predictably scored lower than Chinese samples, but the traits are measurably present. Interestingly, Kwan, Bond, and Singelis (1997) found that for student samples in both the US and Hong Kong, more harmonious relationships predicted higher life satisfaction. Cheung et al. (2003) suggest that the interpersonal relatedness factor may address an important gap in the Big 5.

Testing a non-Western instrument in a Western sample is a valuable way to examine perceptions of self without the inherent ethnocentric biases of what Poortinga and van Hemert (2001) term "indigenous Euro-American" psychology. Many questions arise from this sort of research. Is *ren qing* relevant to Western people? If your *ren qing* score was overly low, should you be concerned? If you are confused about this, it is not surprising, and your reaction is not that different from the confusion a Japanese or Chinese person might feel upon being told, by a gravely concerned psychologist, that they showed signs of being highly dependent, as though it was a bad thing. On the other hand, the appearance of the interpersonal relatedness factor in an American sample may indicate that we can learn more about the self by including perspectives from other cultures, and the Big 5 may not include quite enough traits to describe the human experience.

In subsequent research, Saucier, Thalmeyer, and Bel-Bahar (2014) analyzed descriptive terms from 12 unrelated languages in a further quest for universal traits. Few existed in all 12, and only four of those terms corresponded to Big 5 descriptors: cold, angry, fearful, and jealous. Universals appear to be in short supply. What does this inconsistency mean for personality as a concept? Certainly, we all depend on characteristics that let us know how companions will act in various life situations, a truth in any culture. We know that our mothers, friends, and lovers will usually behave as they always have before, and that people most often meet the expectations of consistency we need to function socially. Particular personality traits may be less important or transferable across cultures than the pioneers of personality imagined, but we all have some relatively stable characteristics, and lexical studies inform personality science of which traits may be important (Church, 2016). We still face hurdles describing the self reliably across cultures, and there may be better ways to understand people and how they behave than reliance on sets of fixed traits. Personality forms one approach to study of the vastly complex human creature, and the following sections explore other approaches to understanding the concept of self.

## REALITY CHECK

What is personality?

Define "trait" and explain why we might want to know people's traits.

What are the primary ways "self" is defined and described in Western psychology?

What are the Big 5?

How is the self described in the CPAI?

## 4.2 PERSPECTIVES ON THE SELF IN CONTEXT

### LO 4.2 Differentiate universal and contextual factors of self across cultures.

We are here to awaken from our illusion of separateness.

*Thich Nhat Hanh*

No man is an island, entire of itself; every man is a piece of the continent, a part of the main. If a clod be washed away by the sea, Europe is the less, as well as if a promontory were, as well as if a manor of thy friend's or of thine own were: any man's death diminishes me, because I am involved in mankind, and therefore never send to know for whom the bells tolls; it tolls for thee.

*Donne, 1624/1994, Meditation XVII*

The idea that a person can be defined by a set of individual personal characteristics, no matter how nuanced, has been challenged when applied outside Euro-American culture. Differences from Euro-American assumptions of self and personhood emerge immediately. Clifford Geertz (1975), the noted anthropologist, summarized the issue as follows:

The Western conception of the person as a bounded, unique, more or less integrated motivational and cognitive universe, a dynamic center of awareness, emotion, judgment, and action organized into a distinctive whole and set contrastively both against other such wholes and against a social and natural background is, however incorrigible it may seem to us, a rather peculiar idea within the context of the world's cultures. (p. 126)

Can any human self really be described without considering connection to others? The Māori *whare tapa wha* describes a person in terms of quality of connection, and definitions of self that extend beyond the boundaries of our skin may be more appropriate in any culture.

Children are born with certain characteristics, but in those first few moments when it is ejected painfully into sudden separate existence, the child almost certainly has no sense of individual self. Self-awareness develops gradually as it interacts with those around it (Welsh, 2006). Langfur (2013) presents evidence that the infant becomes self-aware exclusively by being the object of attention. Of the Big 5 and Saucier's (2009) Big 6, only the dimensions of neuroticism (Big 5) and resiliency and intellect/openness (Big 6) are not contingent upon interpersonal interaction. Although the child may be born with temperament tendencies, temperament and personality appear to be shaped significantly by interaction.

All living creatures adapt to and interact with an ecological niche. Humans exist in a social ecological niche, collaboratively creating existence around us by our actions and interactions with our social convoy (Yamagishi & Hashimoto, 2016). We draw our own contribution from our unique attributes, genes, skills, learning, and inspirations. We balance our personal narrative, the story of *my* life, with the worldview narrated by the *other* lives, *your* life, and *their* lives, within the cultures and institutions around us (Hammack, 2008). The child discovers an identity and role negotiated in relation to people around her, enacting ways of being that are proper for that cultural context. The question of who we are really hinges on who we are to others. The self expands across time collecting memories of past self and imaginings of future, and across social dimensions of relations with others (Kashima, Koval, & Kashima, 2011). In this way, we eventually become our mature selves.

## The Multi-Layered Self

Culture-oriented researchers have explored a range of ideas drawn from a number of disciplines and perspectives to explain how we become who we are and to describe the factors that determine our actions. Several of these consider surrounding layers of contacts and contexts. Outside of the Western viewpoint of bounded self, it is difficult to describe a person *without* considering how we exist within social role and context. To Markus and Kitayama (2010), who are pioneers in this cross-cultural study, the self and the sociocultural environment are inseparable. There is no self without sociocultural context; the self and the environment collaboratively shape each other. That process is the true human universal, so contextual approaches are likely to work best across cultures. The theoretical models of Bronfenbrenner, Triandis, and Sue each explain human contexts in slightly different ways.

Uri Bronfenbrenner (1979, 1994) created his ecological model of development to address the multilayered contexts that shape our lives. This is discussed in more detail in Chapter 5. Briefly, people develop by interacting with environmental systems: individual (gender, age, etc.), microsystem (family, school, other direct interactions), exosystem (neighborhood and other systems not necessarily directly connected to the individual), macrosystem (overarching culture), chronosystem (changes and stability across a lifespan, such as the Great Depression or development of cell phones), and mesosystem (bidirectional linkages within and between systems, such as school and home or individual and chronosystem). The person is the product of these forces interacting all around us, with the person also simultaneously acting upon those levels. Figure 4.3 shows Bronfenbrenner's model compared with the Triandis and Sue models that follow.

## Figure 4.3   Three Contextual Models of Self in Comparison

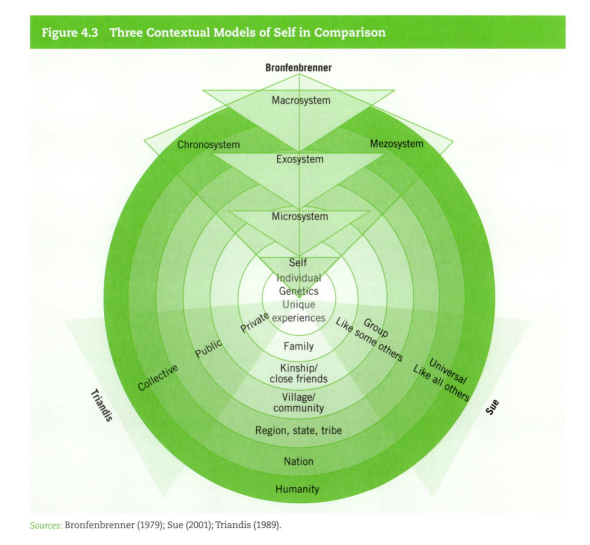

Sources: Bronfenbrenner (1979); Sue (2001); Triandis (1989).

| Table 4.3   Tripartite Model of Self | |
|---|---|
| **All individuals, in many respects, are** | |
| Individual level | like no other individuals |
| Group level | like some other individuals |
| Universal level | like all other individuals |

*Source:* Sue and Sue (2008).

Harry Triandis (1989) discussed what he calls *sampling*, or calling to mind, three major aspects of self: private, public, and collective. The private self is our unique internal qualities, the public self is concerned with how we are perceived by others, and the collective self refers to our connection to the larger group in which we claim membership. For Triandis, we create ourselves mentally by how often we sample each of these and how important they are to us. In Western culture, we sample the private self most, which means that we primarily think of our own views, needs, and abilities. In more collective cultures, the public perception of how we are relating to those around us or the collective elements we share with our in-group are more accessible in our thoughts and more important in our lives. Measurement of these aspects may yield higher or lower scores, depending on our cultural origin, so **individualism** would increase the prevalence of private self-sampling and decrease public and collective sampling (Kashima et al., 2011). How we behave in any situation depends on prevalence of these self-references, influencing how thoughts arise from internal or external perspectives.

In a similar vein, Derald Wing Sue (2001) proposed a slightly different tripartite model of self (see Table 4.3). The inner level, Individual: Uniqueness, includes the person's particular constellation of genetics and experiences. The surrounding level, Group: Similarities and Differences, includes ethnicity, religion, age, location, and other identifying characteristics describing relationship to others. The outer level, Universal level: *Homo sapiens*, includes the characteristics shared by all humanity. Sue is a clinician and has written extensively about the necessity of acknowledging these aspects of self to understand the person one is counseling.

Another pioneer of multicultural counseling, Paul Pedersen, was key in developing the Inclusive Cultural Empathy (ICE) system of therapy. Pedersen, Crethar, and Carlson, (2008) propose that a therapist must understand a collection of factors to connect with a client on a meaningful level. Across his life's work, Pedersen emphasized that each element contributed an important facet to the individual being, and each provided a voice in his client's mind that the therapist should hear, at least peripherally, as he attempted to help the person. These constructs "converge in different ways on the basis of one's experiences, contexts, interactions with the converging identities of others around, and one's resulting beliefs and emotions" (p. 216). The ICE models lists these contributing factors:

- race,

- language,

- religion and spirituality,

- gender,

- familial migration history,

- affectional orientation,

- age and cohort,

- physical and mental capacities,

- socioeconomic situation and history,

- education, and

- history of traumatic experience.

(Pedersen et al., 2008, p. 116)

For Pedersen and his collaborators (2008), each of these aspects, these internal voices, have contributed to what makes up the individual client, and what is shaping the thoughts and disorders of that person.

Each model describes a perspective on the self, including elements that may be more or less important when that person thinks of who she is. A person of any origin (Korean, Irish, etc.) might mention characteristics of self, family, ethnicity, or nationality to describe who they are, but perhaps not all of those at once. Some aspects are more or less important in what that person considers to be crucial to their identity in a particular situation. Bronfenbrenner particularly emphasizes that there is a bidirectional flow between the levels and elements of his model. This means that our family certainly shapes who we are, and our actions subtly change our family. This happens differently depending on the context of region and country where we are born. Two people who consider themselves Samoan will have very different experiences depending on whether they are born and raised in Samoa, Hawai'i, New York, or New Zealand. These unique experiences lead to different ways of thinking and being, which in turn affect what that person contributes to his environment, as well as how she thinks of and relates to the other selves around her. These individuals will, in turn, affect their communities and societies differently. These same processes are present across cultures.

These contexts of self make us who we are, with a particular sense of **self-awareness** and **self-concept**, which shall be addressed shortly. The way we use these attributes as we interact with others is how we gain particular sorts of social acceptance to participate in our culture. Our unique abilities and attributes play out in the roles that our cultural situation allows, but to understand the self, we must also look at how people *perceive themselves* in relation to others around them.

What is consistent about self from culture to culture?

What are the contextual factors that shape self?

Describe the general layers of self from the three main theories discussed.

## 4.3 I AND WE: IDENTIFYING SELF AND OTHERS

### LO 4.3 Summarize ways self is perceived and enacted differently across cultures, including independent and interdependent self-construal.

We began in a Euro-American conceptualization of self, which is internal, stable, and singular. We then examined the idea of self as a product of interaction with the social environment. Another approach examines functional components of the self in daily existence, often categorized as **self-knowledge**, **interpersonal self**, and **agentic self** (Baumeister, 2010). Concepts in this section provide tools to describe self in ways that are less implicitly Euro-American, and to facilitate explanations of the mechanisms underlying differences. The categories are highly interrelated and reminiscent of the tripartite models already discussed.

*Self-knowledge* includes information about one's identity, including self-awareness and self-concept. Self-knowledge also includes evaluative aspects such as self-esteem. As discussed earlier, we gain this knowledge by interacting with those around us. Outside of the Euro-American context, knowledge of self may be deeply intertwined with group membership. *Interpersonal self* describes how a person connects with others and the public persona presented to the world. This is where people attempt to manage impressions, for instance by saving face. The *agentic self* aspect regards a person's ability to make choices, in other words, executive functions, along with complex processes such as juggling multiple goals. Because the concepts overlap so thoroughly, they are presented in an order designed to build progressively toward an overall understanding of self across cultures.

### Self-Construal—Standing Alone or Standing Together

*A single bracelet does not jingle.*

*Congolese proverb*

For Hazel Markus and Shinobu Kitayama (1991), the primary distinguishing factors of self lie in how we construe, or interpret, ourselves as **independent** or **interdependent** in thoughts of ourselves and others. Independent **construal** would mean that we interpret events and make choices based on our own individual perspectives and needs, unlike an interdependent construal, in which we consider the needs, wants, and perspectives of some number of significant others conjoint with our own. The independent self is just me, a self-contained entity, with a firm boundary between self and other (see Figure 4.4a). My unique collection of defining characteristics is mine alone, and people can exist nearby, but I have primary volitional control over sharing and proximity. People vary within cultures, but averaging measurement of many, many people on cultural or national levels of analysis, independent **self-construal** is normative in America. It is not the predominant view around the world.

As an *interdependent* being, I would tend to think of myself primarily as part of a family or group, enmeshed with particular people. Marcus and Kitayama (1991) illustrated this as a dashed, permeable line around the personal self, with certain other people overlapping into our dotted bubble, as in Figure 4.4b. A person's defining characteristics *include* roles and connections to others, with strong ties to in-group members actually comprising some characteristics of self. For example, everyone may respect great-grandfather because he directs the entire family wisely, an accepted role nobody questions. The youngest daughter might be the one who always has to help mother cook, and responsibility for doing this work sets her role in the family and forms part of her identity. The person, in interdependent models, cannot be understood outside of role and context (Markus, 2004).

Interdependence is difficult really to feel if you come from a culture that values individuality and independence, but it is equally difficult for someone from a highly interdependent culture to imagine life without those constant, intimate connections. Absent those links, life may seem very shallow and lonely to an interdependent self, and life in their midst may seem confusingly crowded to an independent person.

Differences in self-construal go beyond psychological or behavioral theories. Recent research demonstrates differences in brain activity between Asian and Western participants related to self-construal (Han & Humphries, 2016). Significant differences have been detected using functional magnetic resonance imaging (fMRI) and event-related brain potentials (ERPs) in a number of cognitive and perceptual processes, and more recently in construal-related processes. For instance, Ma and colleagues (2014) found that Western participants showed increased activity in the medial pre-frontal cortex (mPFC), which is associated with self-relevance of stimuli, compared with East Asian participants. The East Asian sample had greater activity in the temporoparietal junction (TPJ), associated with processing beliefs and perspectives of others. Patterns of activity change when participants are primed with independent or interdependent prompts, showing a causal link between brain activity and cultural frame of reference (Han & Humphries, 2016). In a meta-analysis of 35 fMRI studies, Han and Ma (2014) confirmed differences between East Asian and Western participants in both social and nonsocial thought processes. Availability of advanced technology to measure brain activity is an exciting avenue providing evidence of how culture shapes the physiology of our thought processes.

## Boundaries of Self and Others

*There is no fool who is disowned by his family.*

*African proverb*

*A close friend can become a close enemy.*

*African proverb*

**Figure 4.4a Independent Self-Construal**

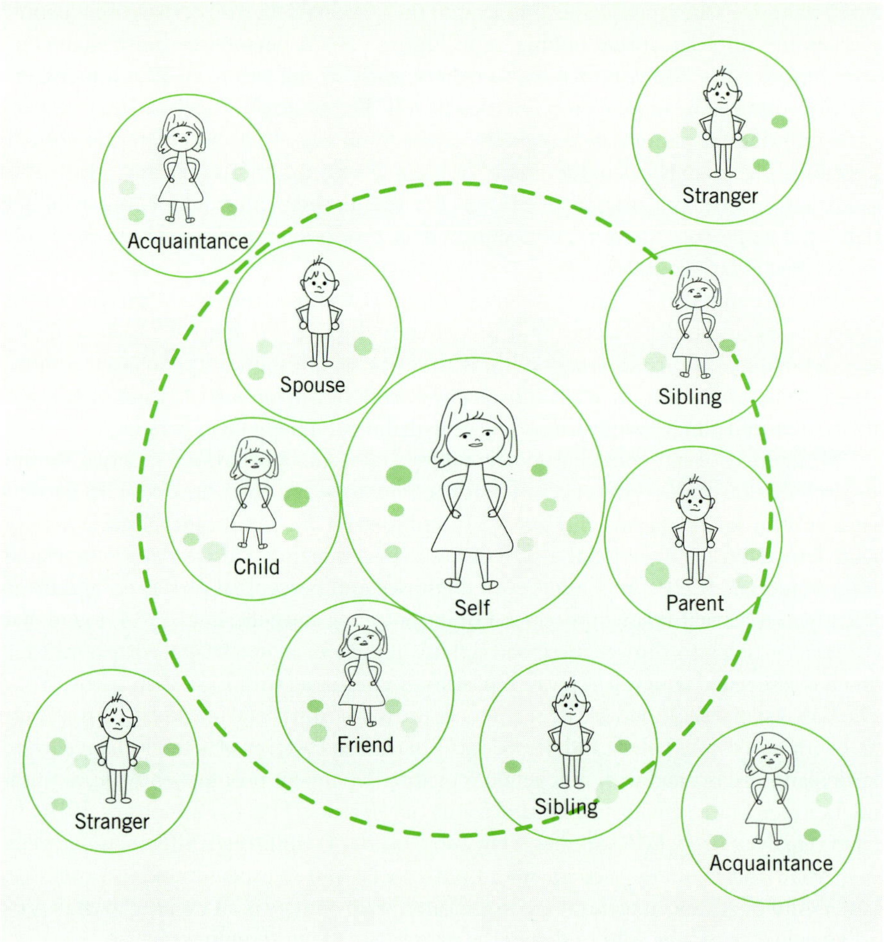

*Source:* Marcus and Kitayama (1991).

# Figure 4.4b  Interdependent Self-Construct

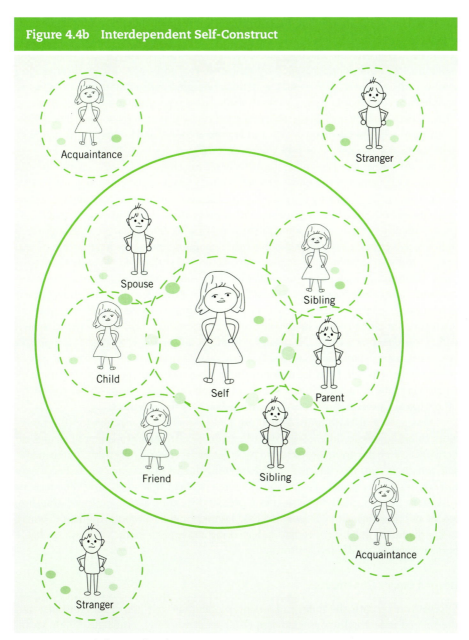

*Source:* Marcus and Kitayama (1991).

Part of understanding myself is knowing where I stop and others start, and who can come in and out of my inner circle. Because our relationships with others can be so important in defining our sense of self, the permeability of those boundaries may be crucial to who we are. The fluidity with which others can come in and out of our lives changes depending on whether our construal is more independent or interdependent. If you are an isolated, independent individual, you may feel happy or sad about people coming and going in your life, but your sense of who *you* are remains largely the same. As in Figure 4.4a, your defining aspects of self are internal and separate from those around you. You are, as Geertz (1974) says, actually a bounded entity, and others exist in the periphery beyond that border. The small shaded dots represent your personal defining characteristics, like being a math whiz or a great rugby player, and are yours alone. Your in-group may be loosely defined, with a wide zone of friends and intimates who may shift in closeness and intimacy over time (Triandis, 1989).

An interdependent person, on the other hand, may have a very specific line between in-group and out-group and much stronger feelings about who comes and goes; when a new person enters the family or circle of close friends, they become part of your collective sense of self. Someone moving out of that inner circle is taking away a part of your group's identity of you, while someone moving in adds entanglements that may need to be considered on a daily basis. If your relationships define who you are and how you behave, and your defining characteristics are somewhat communal, then the stability of these relationships may be very important to you. Additional commitments and more responsibilities make movement inward from an out-group less likely. An independent person can just let the call go to voicemail if an inebriated friend has a flat tire outside town at 1 a.m., and if it keeps happening, the friendship will probably dissolve. In a small village with centuries of interconnection, there is no such liberty, even if the person keeps making constant bad decisions. You may sleep better if you do not have to answer every call for help, but if you are the one calling, those independent friends may not help when you really do need it in the middle of a dark and rainy night. Ability to rely on others has been very important to human survival over the centuries.

Yamagishi and Hashimoto (2016) use a social niche construction (SNC) framework to explain these differences. Interdependent relationships happen in strong-tie networks where the group protects and provides for members collectively. Independent self-construal leads to weak-tie networks in individualist institutions where people are not constrained by threat of exclusion. The independent individual must then present consistent internal traits to be seen as a predictable, safe participant in relationship. Social and material capital is awarded based on internal consistency of the individual, rather than from a stable collective, underscoring and explaining the emphasis on stable personality traits in Western cultures.

## Beyond Binary Constructs

Discussions of both the independent-interdependent self-construal construct and the related individualism–collectivism (I-C) spectrum (e.g., Hofstede, 1980; Mead, 1961) have often treated individuality and sociality as fundamentally opposed tendencies in culture, despite ample literature showing that they coexist in all cultural systems (Vignoles et al., 2016). Levine and colleagues (2003) found in meta-analysis that results of self-construal research do not show consistent differences in independent-interdependent self-construal and that the entire concept may need revision. Markus and Kitayama (2010) later clarified that they should be seen not as distinct dimensions but rather as poles of a single dimension on a cultural level. Individuals would be incentivized by cultural norms to behave in more or less interdependent ways but fulfill the cultural mandates in different ways.

Vignoles and some 71 colleagues (2016) conducted a massive study to deconstruct and clarify self-construal. In a study of 2,921 students in 16 nations, the researchers found seven dimensions of variation in independence-interdependence self-construal: difference vs. similarity, self-containment vs. connection to others, self-direction vs. receptiveness to influence, self-reliance vs. dependence on others, consistency vs. variability, self-expression vs. harmony, and self-interest vs. commitment to others (p. 989). These dimensions allow for a much more nuanced view of self- construal. They then used the survey they developed with 7,279 adults from 55 cultural groups in 33 nations. The researchers found that people in developed and Western nations did endorse some independent construals but not all, and that cultures cannot be labeled as simply independent or interdependent. Rather, it is more useful to examine patterns of how self-construal is defined in a particular culture.

## REALITY CHECK

*How are subjective and objective senses of self different?*

*Why do self-construals lead to different ways of relating to others?*

*What strategies do people use for self-enhancement in different cultures?*

## 4.4 SELF-AWARENESS, PERCEPTION, AND CHOICE

### LO 4.4. Discuss constancy and changeability in perception of self and how this may affect behavior and agency.

The previous section discussed how we perceive ourselves in relation to others, our place in the world and our connections. The following section deals with how we perceive ourselves. Do we evaluate ourselves based on how we feel, or on how others might feel about us? Do differences lead us to take different paths to feel better about ourselves or to manage impressions? How do these factors affect our choices?

### Objective Self-Awareness (OSA) Theory

Humans have the seemingly unique capacity both to consider their own point of view looking outward at the world from within, and also to imagine how they are perceived by the world from without. Duval and Wicklund (1972) described the ability to consider external attention as "objective self-awareness" (OSA), in which self becomes the object of attention, contrasted with subjective self-awareness. With self as object of attention, evaluations were expected to be negative, observed-self comparing to ideal-self in inevitably unflattering ways because nobody is perfect, and someone else may be doing a little better. In subjective states, comparisons happen less because attention is directed to internal feelings (Insko, Worchel, Songer, & Arnold, 1973).

OSA theory has provided explanation for attribution of causation, desire for consistency in behavior, comparisons of self to standards, and other concepts in psychological research (Silvia & Duval, 2001), and cross-cultural differences subsequently have been observed in a number of domains related to OSA (see Figure 4.5). In a classic experiment, Beaman, Klentz, Diener, and Svanum (1979) instructed children to take only one candy from a Halloween bowl and observed fewer transgressions when a mirror placed behind the bowl reflected the child's image, proposing that the mirror heightened OSA. Heine, Takemoto, Moskalenko, Lasaleta, and Henrich (2008) proposed that greater interdependence in non-Western cultures would reveal differences in OSA effects, and indeed found that the presence of a mirror made no difference to Japanese participants, while their North American participants behaved consistent with earlier OSA research.

### Subjective Self-Awareness

**Subjective self-awareness** is the term for that view of self, looking out from within, that is more concerned with the individual as an independent actor. If this is my view, I am most concerned with figuring out the world outside myself as it affects me. My attention is directed outward, away from myself as I look at what is going on around me to understand and affect my world. I am concerned with my own wants and needs as a primary way of navigating through my day, and my thoughts about other people principally regard how they affect achievement of my goals. This is the view of independent or individualist ways of being.

**Figure 4.5  Objective and Subjective Awareness of Interdependent Dog and Independent Cat**

### Objective Self-Awareness

**Objective self-awareness** also describes my viewpoint in my own thoughts, but I am more concerned with how I look to others. I am conscious of how other people are likely to be evaluating me and their perceptions of me more than my own moment-to-moment needs and wants. Certainly I will have needs and wants, preferences and opinions, but I am also highly aware of what my actions say about me. I am conscious of my social context and my first concern is how I am interacting with those others around me. As I prioritize the importance of my wants, needs, and opinions, that objective self-awareness would make me most cognizant of how my actions relate to others in my social sphere, and that awareness will shape my choices and behaviors. Heine and colleagues (2008) suggest that the people of Japan have a metaphorical mirror in their heads, and a constant objective awareness of themselves.

## Self-Esteem, Self-Enhancement, and Self-Improvement

An intimate part of our self-awareness is how we feel about ourselves, which has implications for our choices and how we modify behavior as results of our actions become apparent. Am I a person of value? Am I having positive effects on those who are important to me? Am I going the right direction? Can I or should I do better? The ways we answer these questions and what we do about our answers form another aspect of self that varies across cultures.

**Self-esteem** is the term for how favorably we evaluate our worth or like ourselves (Twenge & Campbell, 2002). The topic has been of interest philosophically for centuries, with Pierre Nicole (1696) discussing moral and interpersonal perspectives on self-love over three centuries ago, both positive and negative. Psychological research generally supports a positive correlation between self-esteem and well-being (Baumeister, Campbell, Krueger, & Vohs, 2003; Branden, 1994). These findings led to an industry of research on promotion of self-esteem in the US, and a steady increase in scores since 1979 (Gentile, Twenge, & Campbell, 2010; Twenge & Campbell, 2001). The US consistently ranks among the highest internationally (Schmitt & Allik, 2005). Cross-cultural research has found a strong correlation between self-esteem and life satisfaction across numerous cultures around the world, though how self-esteem functions in different cultures is a topic of ongoing debate (Sedikides, Gaertner, & Vevea, 2005). Self-esteem is also associated with interpersonal problems, aggression, and destructive behavior (Sanderson, 2010), and excessive pride may be particularly inappropriate in some cultures.

People in all cultures normally want to feel good about themselves. We seek good jobs and relationships, and we strive to achieve in a massive variety of domains, including building homes, herds, and monuments, writing novels and psychology texts, and generally moving toward goals that are only peripherally relevant to our physical survival. **Self-enhancement** refers to ways we seek actively to improve our self-esteem through several cognitive strategies (Trope, 1980). The self-enhancement motive is thought to explain ways we think about ourselves and make **attributions** for success or failure of ourselves and others. Psychologists have described several of these strategies, including self-serving biases and beliefs, a sense of being exceptional, and the **fundamental attribution error** (Davies, 1985; Locke & Pennington, 1982; Sanderson, 2010; see Table 4.4). Primarily, Westerners tend to say our own successes come from our skill and effort, while our failures are blamed on external factors, enhancing our evaluation of self. We do the opposite regarding others, crediting their successes to circumstance and their failures to internal factors. We feel good about our accomplishments and maintain esteem over failures not our fault, reducing risk of unfavorable comparison to others.

## Table 4.4   Self-Enhancement Strategies

| Self-Serving Biases | |
|---|---|
| False uniqueness | A pervasive belief that we are better than others at certain things that are important to us |
| Misremembering | Improving degree of success and reducing magnitude of failure in recall |
| Self-serving attributions | Taking credit for success but denying responsibility for failure |
| False consensus effects | Believing that more people agree with our position than may really be the case |
| **Self-Serving Beliefs** | |
| Unrealistic optimism | Believing that things will come out better than is statistically or practically likely |
| Perceived control | The belief that our thoughts and actions can influence outcomes beyond what is possible |
| Overconfident judgments | Assessing risks as less and success as more likely than the reality of a situation suggests |

*Sources:* Brown and Kobayashi (2003); Boucher (2010); Sanderson (2010).

Self-enhancement strategies do not appear to hold universal importance in cross-cultural studies, particularly in Asian cultures (Brown & Kobayashi, 2002; Diener & Diener, 1995). Heine, Lehman, Markus, and Kitayama (1999) propose that self-enhancement does not fit with the collectivist, interdependent culture of Japan. As a member of a culture that values harmony with the group, there is little benefit in standing out, and humility is a highly regarded virtue. A similar sentiment comes from Polynesian culture. Pacific cultures tell young people that the nail that sticks up gets beaten down, much like the European saying that the tall poppy gets cut off. As an instructor in Hawai'i schools, this does not make it easy to get student participation during a lecture with the over-used technique of whole class questions ("Class, who can tell me . . . ?"). The students normally avoid rather than seek the extra attention. In a ground breaking study in the 1970s at Kamehameha Schools (a system funded by bequest of the last of the Kamehameha line to educate children of Hawaiian descent), Tharp and colleagues (2007) determined that the best way to elicit participation was to have children work in smaller groups with co-participation by the teacher and little singling out of students to speak to the class by themselves.

### The Debate on Self-Esteem

Is it true that that more collective people have less need for feelings of positive self-regard? Heine, Lehman, Markus, and Kitayama (1999) proposed essentially this, that the need for self-esteem and corresponding self-enhancement strategies are artifacts of contemporary North American cultures, stating, "Conventional interpretations of positive self-regard are too narrow to encompass the Japanese experience" (p. 766). For Japanese culture, the most important feeling would be connectedness to an intricate web of relations, both familial and hierarchic. A person would not feel better by differentiating and elevating sense of self above others, but rather would seek greater harmony with those who are significant in one's life. A more formal "thank you" in Japanese is *okage sama de*, which means, metaphorically, that I exist thanks to your generous benevolence. The sentiment is somewhat archaic, but it arises from the culture's deep feeling that our lives are intertwined, and we exist by the grace and support of family, community, and (in the old days) our rulers.

An alternative explanation is that all people seek to enhance their self-image and that it is the mode and expression that change depending on culture (Brown & Kobayashi, 2003; Sedikides et al., 2005). Some evidence shows that self-enhancement may be affected by social context. Takata (2003) observes that Japanese participants are self-deprecating in the absence of competition when around people for whom they have fond regard, but will self-enhance similar to Americans when in competition with others with whom they do not share an emotional connection. Sedikides et al. (2005) argue that Americans self-enhance by amplifying their individual characteristics while Japanese participants self-enhance regarding their collectivistic attributes. Social capital arises in collectivist cultures by consistent mutual action in support of the group. Enhancement by highlighting individual characteristics works against the spirit of mutuality and can actually reduce a person's value as a member of the collective. Rather, in interdependent contexts, a person benefits from highlighting commonalities to strengthen group ties (Hashimoto & Yamagishi, 2016). If this is true, an American wants to feel better by establishing she is better than others, and a Japanese person feels better by being a harmonious and humble member of the collective. In other words, the desire to feel as good as possible about one's self may be universal, but the means used to improve the feelings and the conditions under which the means are employed are different.

In practical terms, these two modes of controlling self-image look very different. The interdependent person presenting great harmonizing skills will not go far in an American company seeking someone who stands out as an independent leader. The stereotypic American setting out to impress an interdependent organization could come off as egotistical and very difficult to work with because of the great pride he takes in his personal work skills. Interpersonal style, mismatched to context, can adversely affect relationships (Jung & Jason, 1998). Happiness and satisfaction for the independent person comes from personal achievement, while the interdependent person's satisfaction, on average, is associated with social harmony (Uchida & Kitayama, 2009). Culture most definitely moderates the connections between self-esteem and the ways we evaluate well-being in our lives (Diener & Diener, 1995; Kim, Schimmack, & Oishi, 2012).

In another perspective, self-enhancement motives may be replaced by a desire for self-improvement in Asian cultures. Choi and Ross (2011) observed that in cards congratulating students on graduation, Chinese families chose messages emphasizing hard work and an ongoing commitment to process of improvement, whereas American cards emphasized fixed traits such as intelligence. The Chinese values conveyed are that a person can achieve value by putting forth effort and that effort brings collective improvement (Gaertner, Sedikides, & Cai, 2012). The positive feelings come from self-improvement to fulfill one's familial role with excellence.

## Constancy and Face

The question of self-improvement returns us to the issue of traits and stability of self-concept. Collective institutions require constant integration into the group, consistently contributing what is required at the time. Without strong ties to automatically maintain relationship, individualists must earn trust by internal consistency and reliability. People in European-origin cultures tend to express thoughts and feelings more to generate trust and perceived behavioral consistency (Hashimoto & Yamagishi, 2016).

The need to exhibit consistency is internalized in a sense of unchanging self, referred to as **entity theory of self**. In this view, one's traits and abilities form a fixed constellation of permanent features, and change is less desirable, even if that change is improving on one's abilities. Conversely, if we form our sense of self based on our in-groups and association, we may logically shift depending on situation. This view is termed an **incremental theory of self**, in which abilities and traits are malleable and can be improved with effort (Chiu, Hong, & Dweck, 1997). View of self as incremental or fixed has particular importance when encountering failure: if you have an incremental theory of self, you will respond by increasing your efforts; those who hold entity theories of self tend to blame innate lack of ability and therefore have little motivation to increase effort.

In an interesting extension of incremental/entitative research, Festinger's (1957) highly regarded **theory of cognitive dissonance** has not turned out to be consistent across cultures. The theory is rooted in the idea that, when people do something that violates their values system, it causes a discomfort that must be resolved either by changing the value or diminishing the violation. The differences arise from expectation of consistency in behavior across situations and time: what one does from moment to moment in more interdependent cultures depends on context and who is present, and variability is acceptable (Kashima, Siegal, Tanaka, & Kashima 1992). As a result, there is little evidence of personal cognitive dissonance in non-Western cultures (Choi & Choi 2002; Markus & Kitayama, 1991). Participants from Western cultures demonstrate a need to justify their personal decisions, but Asians tended more to justify decisions made for a friend, showing they were less concerned with variation in their own behavior but were protective of consistency for friends (Hoshino-Browne et al., 2005).

Na and Kitayama (2011) used measurement of a known brain activity phenomenon of event-related potentials (ERPs) 400 microseconds following a semantic incongruity to test for cultural differences in attribution and trait consistency. Participants were presented with pictures of people, paired with traits and with behaviors that were either consistent or inconsistent with the associated trait. The researchers anticipated that European Americans would exhibit a reaction to incongruity between trait and behavior, whereas Asian Americans focus less on trait stability and would react less. The predictions were confirmed, moderated by the participants' independence or interdependence of self-construal.

Although internal consistency may not be as critical in non-Western cultures, the concept of face forms an area of Asian culture in which one must be absolutely consistent. Hu (1944) described face as, "the respect of the group for a man with a good moral reputation: the man who will fulfill his obligations regardless of the hardships involved, who under all circumstances shows himself a decent human being" (p. 45). Face is how one is evaluated by family and community (Ho, 1976), providing the perfect example of objective self-awareness in interdependent cultures. This objective appraisal from significant others may provide an important motivation for consistent thought and behavior, at least in certain contexts. Rather than presenting one's personal traits in the best light, face requires a person to be consistently reliable and supportive to enhance group function, amplifying the characteristics most essential for one's role. If you are perfectly respectful to your elders and agree with your grandfather's politics while at the family lunar new year dinner, but have entirely different views while with your friends, this may not really be a very big worry in terms of your feelings of consistency. English and Chen (2011) found that East Asian Americans were relatively more accepting of inconsistency across situations, but that they were similar to European Americans in negative feelings about inconsistency within relational context.

The concept of face spotlights differences in how self-concept derives from one's roles, how the self is presented to others, and how and why the impressions of others are managed. Face is conferred upon a person by others (Hu, 1944; Trommsdorf, 2012), and therefore, the interdependent person must maintain a thorough knowledge of social surroundings (Markus & Kitayama, 1991). The interdependent person must have a more elaborate set of memories and representations of the other people filling her social sphere and of their enterprises. The independent person needs only clarity on personal attributes and goals. The independent person needs to maintain internal psychic harmony, at times via self-enhancing and reducing cognitive dissonance, thereby demonstrating consistent competence as a stable self. The interdependent person must maintain external group harmony, and so must perform in the presence of others in ways that do not ruffle feathers, either by poor performance, inconsiderateness, or arrogance.

## Agentic Self: The Self in Action

If we differ in our concerns about staying true to ourselves or to others, this difference also affects how we perceive our ability to make choices and take action. Everyone has particular tasks that must be done each day. We may have parents, children, and/or siblings who depend on us, and we may have jobs, positions of responsibility in community or church, or other obligations that dictate what happens once we awaken each morning. Some of these may be forced on us by circumstance or chosen happily as we make our way through life. Who does the choosing and how we can act is another dimension of cultural difference: the topic of agency (Kashima et al., 1995).

Burke (1989) described what he termed the "dramaturgical pentad" of "the act itself; the scene, or the context in which an act happens; the agents or actors; agency, or the means to action; and the purpose or goals of action" (Farrer, Suo, Tsuchiya, & Sun, 2012, p. 268), to be discussed further in Chapter 9. In modern America and Western Europe, people basically begin in a nuclear family and grow outward toward increasing independence, making choices based on personal inclination. In other cultures, the agentic pathways to action may not be personal, but might rest in the hands of elders or other superior actors.

The sense of agency affects how we feel about why things happen. Imada and Ellsworth (2011) observed that Americans feel proud of successes, a self-agency emotion, whereas Japanese participants reported feeling lucky, a situation-agency emotion. These observations show differences related to the concept of **locus of control** (LOC; Cheng, Cheung, Chio, & Chan, 2013; Rotter, 1966). People may believe to greater or lesser degrees that things happen to them because of their own behavior and characteristics (internal LOC) or because of forces beyond their control like fate or chance (external LOC). The concept initially explained differences in how people responded to rewards (Rotter, 1975), but by 1969, Stephen Abramowitz and other Western researchers began tying LOC to depression: if a person perceived events around them to be beyond their control, they were more likely to be depressed than people who felt they *could* take control of their situations. In a meta-analysis of 152 studies across 18 cultural regions, Cheng et al. (2013) found, however, that people in more collectivist cultures feel more favorably about external LOC, and that the relation between LOC and depression is weaker.

In more **collectivist** cultures, where people think of themselves as part of a group, the idea of decisions made for you by someone else is not a bad thing. In fact, these cultures tend to see life as more interconnected in general, which is termed a holistic view. It may be that someone else will arrange your marriage or job, and this may be just fine with you. These ways of coming to a decision, with or without consulting someone else, reflect differences in what is called *entitativity*, which describes who holds authority to make particular decisions. A high level of individual entitativity indicates ability to make one's own decisions. A person with high entitativity exists, in her own mind, as a person defined by her own characteristics and able to make choices for individual advantage from moment to moment. If entitativity is placed more at the group level, selfishly personal choices make little sense. As shall be discussed later, through most of history and many existing cultures, choosing a mate is normally negotiated by one's family, and surprisingly, some studies show those marriages to be statistically happier and more stable over time

## REALITY CHECK

*Why do our self-construals and self-perception lead to different ways of relating to others?*

*Define "individualism" and "collectivism" and how these affect personal boundaries.*

*What is "face" and does it affect desire for self-esteem?*

*How do incremental and entity views of self differ?*

*What is "cognitive dissonance" and is it the same for everyone?*

*What are "agency" and "locus of control," and how do cultures differ in who chooses what we do?*

## 4.5 EVOLVING DIMENSIONS OF SELF

### LO 4.5 Evaluate evolution of sense of self in terms of gender, ethnicity, and online environments.

In addition to ways of defining self discussed above, other characteristics and categories may affect our self-perception and how others perceive us. These include characteristics we have at birth, such as our sex and ethnic heritage. Gender and ethnicity are now somewhat fluid, with changing attitudes toward both, depending upon where we live and surrounding belief systems. Our lives also reach into digital realms, where self is presented and perceived as disconnected from our physical presence.

### Gender and Self

*Wives, in the same way be submissive to your husbands so that, if any of them do not believe the word, they may be won over without words by the behavior of their wives, when they see the purity and reverence of your lives.*

*1 Peter 3:1–2 New International Version*

*In youth, it was a way I had,*

*To do my best to please.*

*And change, with every passing lad*

*To suit his theories.*

*But now I know the things I know*

*And do the things I do,*

*And if you do not like me so,*

*To hell, my love, with you.*

*Dorothy Parker*

One of the most basic ways we identify ourselves is by sex or gender. We call ourselves a boy or girl, man or woman, lesbian, bisexual, gay, transgender, or other non-binary descriptors. The latter are relatively new in some cultures, though precontact Polynesian culture included non-cisgender identities. *Māhu* hold both male and female aspects of identity, may be transvestites, and may or may not engage in homosexual activity. Identity features distinguish *māhu*, not the sexual behavior (Bolin, 2001). In Western, Christian tradition, until recently, most people were at least publicly heterosexual in their roles and identities. The number of potential identities has increased around the world, though it is still possible to die for having one of the alternative identities in certain cultures, or even for promoting women's rights to education. Assigned sex and gender yield a series of choices in whom we become, negotiated within (or by violating) cultural constraints.

Certain roles such as parenting are associated with gender, with some variability in how those roles function. Cultures normally have tasks and descriptors related to gender. The roles, tasks, and characteristics may be starkly different and discreet, or may be relatively low in division of labor or differences, depending on culture. The contemporary stay-at-home dad would represent the flexible end of the spectrum in terms of gendered roles and tasks.

Biologically, certain differences are unavoidable. Women bear children, men typically have more muscle mass, and hormones bring about predictable emotional differences, regardless of culture. Music plays more of an emotional role in females' lives (Boer, Fischer, Tekman, Abubakar, Njenga, & Zenger 2012). Stereotypes about differences in expected cognitive abilities appear to be consistent across cultures, if completely inaccurate, with women considered more adept at reading and men better at math (Reilley, 2012), but these counterfactual ideas may simply be learned factors. There are certainly differences between genders in physiology and in self and identity, but how expectations relate to and differ by culture is difficult to define. Males in traditional Polynesian culture would sometimes participate in childbirth events, and women could at times become chiefs. Conversely, some fundamentalist Christian and Islamic groups maintain large hierarchic distance between men and women in their rights and responsibilities and in what they are allowed to express.

Cultures differ in basic assumptions about agency and esteem granted by gender, and as a result, people also differ in their sense of self-esteem and self-concept. Korean culture retains significant differences in treatment and roles for women despite transformation to a modern, developed economy (Hovland, McMahan, Lee, Hwang, & Kim, 2005). Traditional Arabic culture includes strong hierarchic distinctions based on both age and gender, with women holding lower status and agency (Ember & Ember, 2003). Interestingly, the Minangkabau of Sumatra maintain matrilineal inheritance of property, and women have a great deal of decision-making power, despite several centuries of Islam as their religion. American culture has increasingly expressed equality by gender, but in reality, women in 2016 were paid 79% of men's wages (Joint Economic Committee, 2016). Women holding CEO positions in the US reached record levels in 2016, which still left women with only 5% of those positions (Long, 2016). The overt emphasis on equality has led American culture to engage in what has been described as benevolent or ambivalent sexism to justify the continued lower status and inferior roles (Lee, Fiske, & Glick, 2010).

We differ greatly across cultures in our ideals and expectations of how men and women should think and behave. For men, concepts of masculinity often relate to being a protector and provider for one's family. These expectations arise from our beliefs about what it means to be a man or woman and our corresponding roles and responsibilities. Our cultures teach us to shape our behavior to conform to perceptions of preferred behavior to match our gender identity. *Machismo*, masculinity, femininity, blended, and alternative gender identities all have related scripts for behavior and are rooted in our culture's values.

Keeping individual variations in mind, *machismo* remains a serious component of a man's life in some Latino cultures. One who is *macho* is expected to be more physical in pursuits and more aggressive. Arciniega, Anderson, Tovar-Blank, and Tracey (2008) differentiated *machismo* from *caballerismo*, a more pro-social male mode associated with higher ethnic identity and sense of affiliation with others, but also with a much more adaptive problem-solving mechanism of coping. Around the world, roles and expectations are changing in an uneasy negotiation between tradition and modernity (Naidoo & Mahabeer, 2006). In New Zealand, young men are stereotypically expected to demonstrate their masculinity by being strong, drinking large quantities of beer, and engaging in reckless behavior (Willot & Lyons, 2012), though these standards are fading. Kiwi women now also may drink in excess publicly, and men may find alternative ways to feel like real men, the latter being particularly true among more educated professionals.

These factors also affect interpersonal behavioral expectations and their consequences. In some cultures, it is a challenge to a man's sense of self if he is not respected and obeyed in the home. Disobedience threatens the man's integrity, position, and authority, and disparities resulting from women's liberation have increased this threat and corresponding reactions from men who have come to feel more insecure. At the same time, abortions of female fetuses have skyrocketed in East and South Asia from preference for male offspring, and may leave tens of millions of young men unable to find women with whom to procreate in the near future. In those cultures, a shift to hyper-masculinized and hyper-feminized ideals is anticipated (Mahalingam & Jackson, 2007), which may lead to a wider cultural distance with Westernized nations.

Certain ideals remain strong despite a global trend toward equity, with cultural constraints still applying to chastity, particularly for women (Buss, 1998; Mahalingam, 2007). Feminism in the US promotes equality between men and women, parallel to civil rights for African Americans and other minorities. Although inequities in pay and job advancement continue, gender-based roles and identities of men and women in the US have changed markedly, particularly for affluent women of European ancestry. Notable feminist Alyse Gregory observed,

> However unwilling one may be to acknowledge it, girls begin to sow their wild oats. . . . Girls, from well-bred, respectable middle-class families [have] broken through those invisible chains of custom and asserted their right to a nonchalant, self-sustaining life of their own with a cigarette after every meal and a lover in the evening to wander about with and lend color to life. (in Calverton, 1928, p. 91)

Conversely, Filipino-Americans express pride in maintaining traditional expectations of chastity. The professed chastity of their young women provides a symbol to assert moral superiority over the otherwise dominant white culture. This places constraints on the autonomy of the women and restrains their range of opportunities for self-expression, but provides a source of self-esteem despite being denied mobility to equal status in American socio-economic achievement (Espiritu, 2001). Chastity also remains a highly valued commodity among certain conservative and more fundamental religious communities.

People also vary by gender in their sense of ethnic identity, which will be discussed shortly. For instance, African American and Asian American women scored higher in their sense of ethnic identity than the men of their cultures (Martinez & Dukes, 1997). With women providing much of the effort in raising and educating children, the future promises to be interesting if unpredictable. Gender roles and options are inexorably changing. Our ways of thinking and being will shift as well.

Knowing these differences in roles and expectation prompts questions of whether gender differences align with other observed dimensions of cultural variation. The concepts of individualism–collectivism, independence–interdependence, and agency–communalism have been used somewhat interchangeably in research on cultural differences in self-construal, with an assumption of West–East dichotomy. Females have been considered to fall on the collective, communal side of the spectrum, aligning with the non-Western way of thinking. Although division of labor could explain evolution of gender differences, Kashima and colleagues (1995) found it unlikely that the same mechanism would explain cultural differences. They undertook a study comparing students in Japan, Korea, the mainland US, Hawai'i, and Australia to discriminate cultural and gender trends in self-construal. They used scales of collectivism, friendship cohesiveness, allocentrism (self-other similarity), and Kanjin-shugi, a Japanese concept of emotional relatedness.

Factor analysis of responses revealed discrete dimensions of individualism, agency, assertiveness, and relatedness. The greatest effects of culture were on the collectivism factor, with Japanese and Korean participants scoring significantly more collectivist than Americans and Australians, and with Hawai'i students falling in between. Groups differed in similar ways on agency and assertiveness, but with a great difference in assertiveness scores between Hawai'i students and the individualist cultures than for other dimensions. The Hawai'i results may reflect inclusion of Euro-American, Asian, and Pacific students in the Hawai'i sample. Gender differences were not significant on these dimensions. Students did differ by gender and culture in relatedness, but the effect was much stronger for gender. On the relational scale, differences emerged for both gender and culture, with a greater effect from gender. In other words, there is little overlap between differences of gender and culture, leading the researchers to opine, "Women are not like Asians" (p. 932).

## The Electronic Self

In the past century, humans increasingly developed the ability to interact in ways that did not involve meeting face to face. Admittedly, petroglyphs and cave paintings conveyed messages beyond the moment of creation, and we have developed increasingly interactive indirect communication via performances, paintings, and speeches. A hundred thousand years ago, your chances of exchanging ideas with someone who had not seen your face were quite small. Now, you get ideas from someone you may never have met every time you listen to the radio, watch TV or read a book, or from anything else in your environment you did not make, including the architecture and furniture design.

With life moving so far beyond immediate contact with family and friends, we do have ways to create a less restrictive sense of self, and to interact without ties to our physical characteristics. We can interact as fictional characters, as demonstrated by the scandal beginning in 2012 between a football player, Manti Malietau Louis Te'o, born in La'ie, Hawai'i, and Ronaiah Tuiasosopo, another male from Hawai'i who masqueraded as a woman online to create a romance with Te'o.

Tuiasosopo claims he was in love with Te'o, and his feelings were genuine. Te'o was a young Mormon man from a conservative community who claimed he was in love with a beautiful female who stole his heart, despite never having met her in person (Gupta, 2013). Our brains are literally hard-wired to process verbal information, and that skill has now transferred to words received over the internet, so a person may believe all of the burning, passionate intimacy poured into an electronic love letter, despite never having met the person face to face. This type of deception became so widespread that it spawned a name, "catfishing," and a popular television show (Zimmer, 2013).

When the internet began to take off outside of academic and military applications, people quickly began interacting in romantic ways, in an increasing array of contexts. One early avenue was called multi-user domains, or MUDs (Turkle, 1997, 1994). The early MUDs were text-based and lacking in frills, but it quickly became obvious that not everyone was who they said they were. Turkle and others celebrated the freedom to explore different identities, including alternative gender identities (e.g., McKenna & Bargh, 1998), and she and others proposed that online identities reflected real, alternative selves that could outlive their creators.

Subsequent research evolved to seeing online and real-life selves as inextricably intertwined (McGerty, 2000), but in numerous domains such as Second Life, people engage in highly complex digital interactions and relationships that they deem important and real (Velleman, 2008). Relationships and infidelities online have very real implications in the real world for the physical person (Craft, 2012), and the online self has effects on the physical health and well-being of the user (Behm-Morawitz, 2013). Online therapy in Second Life provides a number of benefits, including effective treatment for people with social anxiety disorder and other conditions preventing them from going to a therapist's office (Yuen et al., 2013), improving the relational self-concept of adolescents (Knutzen & Kennedy, 2012), and helping returning soldiers to reintegrate into civilian life (Morie, Antonisse, Bouchard, & Chance, 2009). Online communities are sufficiently real to have evolving cultures (Boellstorff, 2009) and material culture that can be "excavated" digitally and examined using techniques from archaeology (Harrison, 2009). The selves populating these worlds may not be separate from their creators, but even if the character's gender does not match the sex assigned at birth to its owner, they are a real part of our world and they are among us to stay.

## Ethnic Identity and the Self

A crucial aspect of self for the psychology of culture is a person's sense of cultural, racial, or ethnic identity (EID). These terms may be treated as conceptually equivalent, but have certain political and social implications, particularly in regard to minority and non-Western groups undergoing intercultural contact or change (e.g., Hill, 2006; Jones, Cross, & deFour, 2007; Saylor & Aries, 1999; Umaña-Taylor, 2004). A number of researchers have addressed this aspect of self and identity. Phinney (1996) defines

EID as "an enduring, fundamental aspect of the self that includes a sense of membership in an ethnic group and the attitudes and feelings associated with that membership" (p. 922). Social identity theory (Tajfel, 1981) concentrates on the person's sense of membership in social groups and the feelings and meaning one holds about the membership(s) in contrast to other groups. Gone (2006) says we intentionally construct "cultural identities," to render life comprehensible in conjunctions of differing political and cultural forces, where the individual must stake some claim of self in situations of disadvantage and disenfranchisement. EID is primarily important in cases of opposition to a dominating group.

Joseph Gone is a clinical psychologist and professor, and he is a Native American. Gone scoffs at the term "post-colonial," considering that the descendants of the colonizers still absolutely control North America. Life at the Fort Belknap reservation exposed Gone to harsh realities of existence on the low end of the power hierarchy, but he also inherited millennia of profound cultural traditions, which he blends into his clinical practice (Gone & Trimble, 2012; Wendt & Gone, 2012). In his own quest for cohesive identity, Gone had to ask what makes him who he is; is it heritage, behavior, ways of thinking, or perhaps what others think? We all must ask, to some degree, what part of our self comes from our ethnic origins.

EID is another concept with evolving definitions. Tajfel's (1981) social identity theory definition provides a starting point: "that part of an individual's self-concept which derives from his knowledge of his membership of a social group (or groups) together with the value and emotional significance attached to that membership" (p. 255). Others have described key aspects of EID, including attitudes and feelings, such as belongingness, commitment, and values; evaluations toward one's group, and/or toward contrasting groups; and practical dimensions including language, behavior, values, and cultural knowledge (Phinney, 1990).

Ward (2001) lists four superordinate categories of identification: belongingness (the degree to which one feels group membership), centrality (the degree to which one bases identity on group membership), evaluation (perceptions of the group), and tradition (participation in and practice of cultural activities, and acceptance of values and norms). In presentation of her Multigroup Ethnic Identity Measure (MEIM), Phinney's (1992) list of components included self-identification and ethnicity, ethnic behaviors and practices, affirmation and commitment, and ethnic identity achievement (a developmental process by which one comes to a secure sense of self as a member of the group).

EID operates on multiple levels. There is the personal sense of self, if that is part of your thoughts. There are group levels, addressed elsewhere, regarding membership and meaning. Wider levels, such as how one relates to other cultures, will be addressed in discussion of acculturation (see Chapter 10). On an individual level, what does EID mean and how can it be measured?

Listed above are issues of membership and evaluation, and of behaviors one might exhibit for various reasons. These are not separate, nor can characteristics be isolated from context. Gone (2006) cautions, "Reality, of course, is more complicated than superficial attributions of the *intrinsic* (what one is) versus the *enacted* (what one does)" (p. 58). If I eat at an Ethiopian restaurant every day, and eating food of one's groups is included on measures of EID, I will not become Ethiopian. Conversely, if I am of Ethiopian origin and assiduously avoid Ethiopian food, this may indicate that I either do not identify with my heritage culture or I outright reject it for some reason.

A growing body of literature positively connects level of EID with better mental health, via a variety of improved outcomes and indices related to positive well-being in a number of studies (e.g., Gray-Little & Hafdahl, 2000; Ryff & Keyes, 1995; Tsai, Ying, & Lee, 2001; Umaña-Taylor, 2004; Umaña-Taylor, Diversi, & Fine, 2002). Higher levels of ethnic identity and higher regard for one's ethnic group are also associated with higher quality of life (QOL), another concept or indicator of well-being (Kiang, Yip, Gonzales-Backen, Witkow, & Fuligni, 2006; Utsey, Chae, Brown, & Kelly, 2002), and increased self-esteem (Rowley, Sellers, Chavous, & Smith, 1998). Noh, Beiser, Kaspar, Hou, and Rummens (1999) found that stronger EID provided their participants with inner psychological resilience to cope with the effects of prejudice.

## REALITY CHECK

*How is technology changing sense of self?*

*Explain how culture interacts with gender identity.*

*What differences might culture make in how people of different genders behave?*

*What is ethnic identity?*

*How does EID relate to well-being?*

## 4.6 ARTS AND THE SELF

### LO 4.6 Illustrate the ways arts reflect our concepts and construals of self across cultures.

As the most human form of expression, arts are loaded with perspectives on self. These have varied over many millennia, reflecting the styles and technologies of their times and environments, but also demonstrating the ways we thought about the self at the time and place of creation. We have told stories for inestimably longer than we have records, and probably longer than we have stories we remember. The sagas of the Polynesians go back far into the Great Pacific Migration, when they left the mythical land of Hawaiki, according to the Māori (Royal, 2008). As mentioned at the start of the chapter, a culturally aware Māori can tell you names of ancestors back to arrival in Aotearoa, eight centuries ago and beyond, and knows the stories and teachings reaching back to the *whare wānanga*, places of learning, in the dim recesses of time (White, 2001). The ancient stories live on in *waiata* (songs) and in the material culture of the Māori, each post of the *marae* (meeting house) ornately carved to convey visual reminders of legendary characters (Walker, 2004; White, 2001). The exact details and aesthetic styles vary by island group, but significant figures and broad stories remain constant, such as the demigod Maui slowing the passage of the sun to make day and night (King, 2001). The cultural learning conveyed across the centuries through retelling of those stories inform identity of the selves of successive generations.

The connection between self and personality has been made manifest in theater for millennia, where the actor intentionally takes on a persona, shaping behavior to fit characteristics of a particular identity. Barba and Savarese (2006) describe the performer as existing on three levels:

1. The performers' personalities, their sensibilities, their artistic intelligence, their social personae: those characteristics which make them unique and once-only.

2. The particularities of the traditions and socio-historical contexts through which the once-only personality of the performer is manifest.

3. The use of physiology according to extra-daily body techniques. (pp. 308–309)

These correspond to Sue and Sue's (2008) Tripartite Model of Self. The first obviously corresponds to "(a) like no other individuals." The similarities to "some other individuals" are particular to the tradition and socio-cultural context. The third level refers to the physical techniques that must be learned: how to move, to project the voice, to emote. Performers all over the world learn physical skills to perform, and are therefore like all others.

The mask removes a certain amount of the individual personality, and transforms the individual into an archetype with a particular, limited set of traits. From ancient times, they shifted the focus from the person performing to the message being conveyed. A performance gathered the community, reaffirming connections and passing on cultural knowledge via inspiring and cautionary tales, in essence telling us what sort of self we need to be.

Music, theater, and dance often happened as part of rituals of transition, as we passed from one phase of life to another. A first birthday *luau* might celebrate that a child survived the risk of infant mortality. At adolescence, ritual song and dance accompanied a person into their new role as adult, as at a girl's *quinceañera*. For marriage, death, or coronation, we are accompanied and instructed through the liminal state between our old self and the new (V. Turner, 1982a, 1982b).

Views of self and other are clearly explicated in song lyrics. Traditional topics included important people and events, for instance the great leaders lauded by the Djeli musicians of West Africa. Hawaiian radio is full of songs about beaches, mountains, and surf, elements of island identity. Topics are becoming more individualistic, however, following the general trend of globalized culture, and topics on a group level are receding. Popular music has also declined in the amount of specific information about cultural identity that is available, becoming more homogenized and international.

The audience also sees itself differently now. Schechner (1988) proposed a model he called the *efficacy/entertainment braid*, in which the *efficacy* participants shared a common set of understandings and goals in a ritualized performance. The *entertainment* strand is a show for the enjoyment of an audience that does not participate directly in the performance and may not share much with the performers in attitudes or beliefs. (also see Schechner, 1985). These differences relate directly to the shift toward independent self-construal in Western culture, with audience and performer sharing less identity and purpose.

Despite the trend toward individualism in media, connections between ethnic identity and sense of self continue to be important factors in theater, music, and visual imagery. National anthems represent very broad levels of self and identity. Genres such as Polish, Irish, or K-Pop Korean music may be important in establishing and maintaining self-concept and identity. Expression of ethnocultural identity is particularly important in group-level interaction and in acculturation, and will be discussed further in those sections.

## REFLECTING ON YOUR READING

- How has this chapter informed or changed how you see yourself?

- Do you know people who seem to have a different view of self?

- What do your group memberships say about you?

- What do you do to create and maintain your self-concept?

- How do your gender and ethnicity relate to who you feel you are and what you can do?

- Are you the same online as you are in person?

- What music do you usually listen to? Are your tastes similar to your friends' taste?

## CHAPTER 4 SUMMARY

### 4.1 Persona: The Self as Individual

Self would seem to be easily defined, but across cultures, people differ in the importance of our sense of individuality and the roles we enact in our lives. Western psychology approaches the self via study of personality, from the Latin for mask. Personality describes a set of lasting core characteristics, including genetic predispositions and ways of being we learn as we develop. Freud established the first laws of personality in Western psychology with his concepts of id, ego, and superego, which were criticized for lack of empirical bases.

Trait theories followed, developing lists of defining characteristics that were refined through statistical analyses to form dimensions by which people can be described in relevant and predictable ways. Presently, the Big 5 factors are considered most accurate: openness, conscientiousness, extraversion, agreeableness, and neuroticism.

The Big 5 can be measured in all cultures, though they vary in strength. They are also viewed with some skepticism by indigenous psychologists and others who feel that they are only really relevant in describing Western people. People are relatively predictable and stable across cultures, and other measures, including the Chinese Personality Assessment Inventory, have been developed to measure factors relevant in other cultures. These systems reflect aspects of self more important to certain cultures, but may be based on an empirical system that is inherently Western.

## 4.2  Perspectives on the Self in Context

Humans do not exist free of social contexts. We have personal characteristics and abilities, but the idea of the isolated self is uniquely Western. Broader definitions may be needed to describe self across all cultures.

Several theorists have proposed contextual models of the self, including Bronfenbrenner's ecological model. Triandis proposes that we "sample," or call to mind private, public, and collective aspects of self, or how we see our internal qualities, how we think we are perceived externally, and how we see our connections to larger groups. Western culture samples the private self most often. Sue's Tripartite Model includes individual, group, and universal levels.

Pedersen's Inclusive Cultural Empathy system of therapy included a list of factors contributing to construction of self, ranging from race to individual traumatic history. These factors interact to form the individual, shaping our self-awareness and self-concept.

## 4.3  I and We: Identifying Self and Other

Baumeister and Bushman describe three functional parts of the self: "self-knowledge (or self-concept), interpersonal self (or public self), and agent self (or executive function)." These influence our behavior and whom we become.

Markus and Kitayama discuss self-construal, how we interpret our meaning and purpose as independent from or interdependent with others. Generally, Western individuals emphasize independent self-construals, while other cultures emphasize interdependence. I may define myself by my own traits and characteristics, as in personality theory, or I may define myself in terms of my relationships.

Our self-construals and sense of independence–interdependence also affect our personal boundaries, affecting who is close to us and how easily they come and go. With an independent self-construal, people can become close parts of one's life, remain outside of the essential self, and can come and go over time without necessarily changing one's sense of self. In an interdependent view, self includes an inner circle of relationships that define the person, and people do not pass easily in and out of relationship.

Close, interdependent relationships come with inherent obligations that are more voluntary in independent cultures.

A closely related concept is individualism–collectivism. While independence–interdependence describes internal sense of self, individualism-collectivism describes more how people's attitudes about behavior in relation to others.

## 4.4  Self-Awareness, Perception, and Choice

People may differ in the perspective from which they think about and describe themselves, depending on their cultural origins. We may value more our internal view looking out as the central actor, or we may be more concerned with how others perceive us, imagining the external view looking in.

Subjective self-awareness is the view from inside the self looking out and concerns how those around are affecting me. I am most concerned with my own goals and how I can achieve them. This is primarily a perspective associated with independent, individualist cultures.

People who emphasize objective self-awareness are more concerned with how they think others perceive them and how they see their actions affecting those around them, particularly their significant others. These viewpoints affect our actions and behaviors.

Our awareness of ourselves includes evaluation of our personal value, our abilities and achievements, and our effects on others. *Self-esteem* is the term for how favorably we evaluate ourselves, and for the past few decades, psychology has held that self-esteem is positively correlated with well-being. This correlation has been observed in numerous cultures. How self-esteem functions to increase well-being is a source of debate because high self-esteem is also associated with interpersonal problems.

People want to feel good about themselves and what they do. *Self-enhancement* refers to ways we seek actively to improve our self-esteem, and we may do this by how we attribute causes for success or failure of ourselves or others.

These strategies are not used equally or in the same ways across cultures. Cross-cultural research may indicate that self-enhancement is not a primary motive in other, non-Western cultures. Conversely, those results may be the result of cultural bias in how the questions are asked—people in other cultures may enhance self-esteem by making their group look better instead of themselves individually, but this may still arise from the same motivation. Happiness comes from helping one's group do better.

Another view is that people of some cultures derive better feelings from self-improvement.

Traits are considered to be stable aspects of self. Across cultures, people endorse two views of stability: entity and incremental theories of self. The entity view is that traits are inherent and fixed, while the incremental view is that people change and improve over time.

In some cultures, people have very different roles at different stages of life.

Festinger's theory of cognitive dissonance proposes that people are highly motivated to maintain consistency in action and attitude. This fits with entity theory of self, but does not seem as important in cultures with incremental views.

The concept of face is very important in Asian cultures, being the status one earns in one's community. Rather than simply presenting a most favorable view, face is earned over time by consistency, achievement, and consideration of relevant others.

People in interdependent cultures must be highly aware of their contexts and those around them, maintaining group harmony, while and independent person is most concerned with personal achievement to create positive reputation.

Interdependence brings additional requirements: the person must be aware of the needs and feelings of others and must behave in nondisruptive ways.

The term *agency* describes the ability and right to choose and act. Different cultures have different views on a person's right to decide depending on cultural roles and statuses. Western culture encourages independence and personal responsibility for choices. People in other cultures sometimes have to obey elders and superiors.

Rotter's theory of locus of control says that people may see life as within or outside their control, and that people who feel they have control are happier. In collectivist cultures, people are happier if they see control as being outside of them. To some degree, authority is respected and seen to lead one to better outcomes.

## 4.5 Evolving Dimensions of Self

Cultures have different acceptable gender roles and identities, ranging from strict heterosexuality to cultures that have defined roles for transgender and homosexual individuals.

Also connected to gender are parenting roles and responsibilities, which also vary across cultures, with men sometimes having more or less involvement with children.

Traditional cultures, including some religious groups in the US and elsewhere, sometimes have very constrained rights and roles for women. Genders also seem to vary in certain cognitive abilities, but this is difficult to separate from early learning. Hierarchic status and esteem are granted differently by gender across cultures.

Kashima et al. identified four factors related to cultural differences in gender formulations: collectivism, agency, assertiveness, and relatedness. Collectivism, higher relational orientation, external LOC, and lower assertiveness are generally associated with females and Asia, and individualism, etc., with masculinity and the West. Research actually shows clearer variation in I-C by culture.

Hofstede's dimensions include masculinity-femininity, with focus on achievement and assertiveness or on nurturance and caring, respectively.

Cultures higher in *machismo* related expectations of men exhibit adaptation and coping problems.

Changing roles and expectations are affecting men's sense of identity as women gain more autonomy. Feminism is changing the expectations and possibilities for women, especially around sexuality.

Modern technology including the internet is changing contact between people at distance, and new types of identities, including fictitious ones, are emerging. Generally, psychology considers that the online self is inescapably intertwined with the actual self. Social media and role-play environments do also provide healthy avenues not available in real life, such as ways to interact socially despite social anxiety or disability. Online communities are evolving and will probably form new cultural contexts.

Our sense of membership in ethnocultural groups forms our cultural identity. For minority groups, this identity can be associated with conflict and oppression.

Key aspects of EID include attitudes and feelings, such as belongingness, commitment, and values; evaluations toward one's group, and/or toward contrasting groups; practical dimensions including language, behavior, values, and cultural knowledge. Ethnic identity is an important component in study of multicultural environments. Higher identification with one's heritage group is associated with better adjustment, especially in relation to self-perceptions of minority youth. Identity is negotiated in a dialog with those around us.

## 4.6 Arts and the Self

Our cultural songs and stories provide the material that informs our sense of self, and the images we replicate reminds us of our origins and beliefs.

Dramas parallel the arc of overcoming adversity and gaining a new sense of self, and the dramatic self has similar components to the Sue Tripartite Model.

Arts accompany our transitions from one state and identity to another, for instance in marriage, and the ritual confirms our new identity.

The traditional artist was an integrated part of the social order, but artists have always had a unique identity including acceptance of eccentricity. In modern times, the artist has increasingly been expected to stand outside of traditions, making a unique contribution. What is expressed as a result lacks the old functions of social cohesion. The audience is now disconnected to some degree from the art and the artist. Arts do continue to provide significant material and avenues for cultural identification.

## GLOSSARY

**Agentic self (or executive function):** The aspect of a person that makes choices and takes action.

**Attributions:** The assignment of agency and causation in outcomes.

**Big 5:** A set of traits currently thought to be most reliable in describing personality in the Western psychological tradition.

**Collectivist:** An internalized doctrine of being in which people exist as inseparable components of a group.

**Construal:** The meaning one gives; what one comprehends something or someone to be.

**Entity theory of self:** A self-perception in which a person remains largely constant and unchanging.

**Face:** A person's status and standing in the community as a person of consistent worth and integrity.

**Fundamental attribution error:** The tendency in Western culture to overemphasize the causative agency of the person in lieu of considering situational factors.

**Incremental theory of self:** A sense of self in which a person can change and/or improve over time and across situations.

**Independent:** In social psychology, the concept and perception of the self as an isolated being without particular obligation to others.

**Individualism:** An internalized doctrine of the self as ultimate authority with sovereignty over one's choices and destiny.

**Individuality:** The concept of the self as independent of others, as an isolated construct.

**Interdependent:** In social psychology, the concept and perception of self and others as interconnected and sharing certain duties and obligations.

**Interpersonal self (or public self):** The person or image one presents to others.

**Locus of control:** Where a person places causation of events in one's life, either within or outside personal control.

**Objective self-awareness:** Thoughts of one's individual being in context and contact with others, including evaluation of how one affects others.

**Personality:** A stable set of traits by which a person can be characterized, unique to an individual, but sharing similar dimensions to others.

**Psychoanalytic:** Referring to the system of therapy developed by Sigmund Freud, including theories of developmental stages and common characteristics.

**Self-awareness:** Our active cognitions about self.

**Self-concept:** Who and what we believe our self to be.

**Self-construal:** How one comprehends, perceives, or interprets one's individual being.

**Self-enhancement:** Strategic improvement of our personal worth via changes in behavior or cognition.

**Self-esteem:** Our evaluation of personal worth and value.

**Self-knowledge (or self-concept):** The set of information believed about one's own person.

**Subjective self-awareness:** Perception of one's individual being as central and primary, focusing on how forces around us affect our lives.

**Temperament:** Emotional and behavioral tendencies, evident from early childhood.

**Theory of cognitive dissonance:** Festinger's theory that discrepancies between one's beliefs and actions cause a discomfort that must be accommodated internally.

**Trait:** A defining characteristic that is generally stable across time.

# LIFESPAN DEVELOPMENT AND SOCIALIZATION

## Learning Objectives

**LO 5.1** Relate the major theories of developmental psychology to the study of culture.

**LO 5.2** Explain the earliest ways cultural elements set trajectories to culturally differing outcomes.

**LO 5.3** Summarize cultural learning and contrast ways knowledge is transmitted in different cultures.

**LO 5.4** Critique constructions of adolescence and achievement of adulthood.

**LO 5.5** Appraise the differing roles older people play in different cultures and potential cognitive approaches to death and how these shape behavior.

**LO 5.6** Evaluate the roles of arts in cultural transmission, life changes, and social processes.

## PREPARING TO READ

- How did you learn to be a good person (or a bad one)?

- Who helped you to learn as a child?

- What ideas were important in your childhood home?

- How will you raise your own children, and why?

- What skills did you learn growing up?

- What makes a person an adult?

- When you get old, how do you think you will be treated?

*Two seventh-grade basketball teams faced off on December 12th, 2013, in Browning, Montana, a normal rite of passage for young males entering puberty and eager to show off their budding athleticism. The De LaSalle Blackfeet School's Native American boys adopted an unusual strategy against their rivals from nearby Conrad when they noticed that Conrad's Aaron Kleinsasser has Down Syndrome. Kleinsasser got the ball and took a shot. He missed. The De LaSalle Blackfeet rebounded the ball and passed it back to Kleinsasser, who shot and missed again. The Blackfeet team rebounded and returned the ball until Kleinsasser finally made the shot. What would trump the testosterone and heat of competition and induce these boys to give away points to the opposing team? Station KRTV's news team reported that the team said they wanted Kleinsasser to play "a game he would always remember." How did these boys come to make this decision? The De Lasalle school's motto is "Touching hearts, touching minds." Are there factors unique to the upbringing these boys experienced that led to this selfless moment? (adapted from KRTV, 2013)*

# 5.1 PERSPECTIVES ON DEVELOPMENT

## LO 5.1: Relate the major theories of developmental psychology to the study of culture.

*We all begin with the natural equipment to live a thousand kinds of life, but end in the end having lived only one.*

*Clifford Geertz*

Birth is the admission ticket to the grand drama of human life, and death is the ultimate price, no matter who you are. Everything that happens between those fixed points depends upon cultural and environmental context. This chapter discusses the ways culture shapes our journey from conception to death. From the beginnings of psychology in the 19th century, debate has raged over the importance of **nature versus nurture**, whether we think and act as we do because of our physical inheritance of genetics or because of the influences and experiences in our lives. We now know that genes affect many aspects of our potential abilities, but we are learning that our environmental influences and experiences also affect everything about us to some degree, down to our developing neural structures. Our experiences arise in cultural context, and variations in formative experiences continue to push us toward increasingly divergent thoughts and actions across the lifespan.

Developmental psychology studies the ways people change over time across biosocial, cognitive, and psychosocial domains (Rogoff, 2003). **Biosocial** changes include the normal alterations of growth inherent in an organism, but also the ways the person is affected by factors such as nutrition that vary by environmental and social setting. **Cognitive** development includes how we learn and think, in turn shaping decisions and adaptations throughout our lives. In the **psychosocial** domain, influences of those around us affect development of our behavior and personality, our social skills and our feelings, and expectations about how we interact with others.

The historical context and location provide a particular set of cultural, technological, scientific, and political conditions. People born around the same time and place form a generational **cohort**. Cohorts usually share culture and ethnicity, with a common language and history. They share what happens around them, whether that might be popularity of leisure suits or an outbreak of Ebola. An American family today may have members whose grew up dancing the jitterbug, disco, the Macarena, twerking, or the nae nae. Cohorts may share **socioeconomic status (SES)**, which is their relative wealth or poverty and social standing, along with the opportunities and resources the status affords or denies them. All of these factors, along with the foods available, disease epidemics, and other natural phenomena shape the humans we become.

Psychologists began studying development from the field's origins in the 19th century, seeking to understand how people end up behaving as they do, and particularly examining what factors at the beginning might cause them to become abnormal or dysfunctional. They proceeded by generating developmental theories, describing principles that form a framework explaining how and why people change in certain ways. The first comprehensive developmental theory in psychology was Sigmund Freud's psychoanalytic theory, developed from his observations of patients in 19th-century Vienna. He proposed that people go through a series of stages centered around pleasure and sexual awakening, a theory that has been criticized for its lack of evidentiary basis, but that remains influential a century later. Erik Erikson expanded on Freud's concepts after moving to the US in the 1930s, switching from psychosexual stages to a series of psychosocial challenges that happen across the entire lifespan instead of simply in childhood. John Watson, teaching at Johns Hopkins University in the early 20th century, took an opposite view from Freud, saying that only observable behavior is important and conditioning rather than sexual urges and frustrations control our outcomes. Watson famously said that given a group of children, he could "take any one at random and train him to become any type of specialist I might select—doctor, lawyer, artist, merchant—chief and yes, even beggar-man and thief, regardless of his talents, penchants, tendencies, abilities, vocations, and race" (Watson, 1924, p. 82). French psychologist Jean Piaget rounds out the major trajectories of early developmental theorists, focusing on cognitive abilities expanding in predictable stages through childhood.

## Stages in Development

Anthropologist Arnold van Gennep (1909/2004) observed that all humans in all cultures go through the same set of life events in the same order, which sounds painfully obvious, but really contains a profound truth. The physiological processes are universals dictated by biology, but anthropology also observes that we celebrate these cardinal junctures in similar rituals and a common conceptual map of the lifespan. Lloyd Warner described the life process as

> the movement of a man through his lifetime, from a fixed placental placement within his mother's womb to his death and ultimate fixed point of his tombstone and final containment in his grave as a dead organism— punctuated by a number of critical moments of transition which all societies ritualize and publicly mark with suitable observances to impress the significance of the individual and the group on living members of the community. These are the important times of birth, puberty, marriage, and death. (in Turner, 1967, p. 94)

We share ideas that life happens as a series of distinct states in a particular order. We all hold certain roles, statuses, and responsibilities that change across life phases, and these are unique to our time and culture. As we make the transitions through life, Warner's critical moments form the limina between stages or phases, the transition points where a person goes from one state to another; during the *bar mitzvah* or the wedding, the person is neither child nor adult, unmarried nor married. We celebrate with different songs and stories, but we mark these transitions because they are times when we must redefine our perceptions of self to accommodate our new positions. We use rituals to prepare psychologically for the new role, and for the new roles to be acknowledged and integrated into the minds and hearts of the community around us.

A century ago, the states in between those transitions appeared stable and predictable to the early researchers. People were born, underwent childhood, and finally became adults, either at puberty or a certain chronological age, and development was complete. They usually remained married until a spouse died. Developmental psychology, as practiced by Freud and Piaget, dealt only with that time between birth and adulthood when a child grows and learns most rapidly (see Table 5.1). These men saw life as a series of discreet stages, though they differed in how they explained what happened in these stages, Freud's explanations dealing with pleasure and Piaget's focused on ability to think logically. Each assumed that events of childhood conclusively set the trajectory of the adult life that would follow.

Erik Erikson took the broader view that people continue to change across the lifespan, facing predictable challenges at each of what he termed *psychosocial stages*. Trained as a psychoanalyst in Freud's Vienna home, Erikson came to the United States during the rise of Nazism and joined the faculty of Harvard in 1936. He soon studied Sioux children in South Dakota who felt torn between their traditional culture and the Western culture forced on them in school, and later children of the Yurok tribe in Northern California. These experiences helped shape his theory, in which the person gains skills in the context of expanding social spheres. He viewed play as an important part of development, in which the child learns social norms and empathy, and where they imitate roles and behaviors of their elders. Successful navigation of the challenges led to a happy, well-adjusted person, and failure would cause issues that could haunt the individual for years or forever (Erikson, 1963).

Each of these theorists described a set of linear steps happening at more or less specific ages, one following another. Real life may actually be messy and unpredictable, and wars or natural disasters may disrupt the course of development. In all lives, our developmental situations are negotiated in an ongoing process, depending on our innate abilities and what we are handed by the circumstances of our existence (Johnson-Hanks, 2002). Subsequent research increasingly shows the stages divide less precisely, and more nuanced gradations fill each stage than were previously acknowledged (Rogoff, 2003).

In contrast to stage theories, Lev Vygotsky and his colleagues focused on the context in which the child was growing. Vygotsky (1896–1934) was a member of a Soviet group termed the Cultural-Historical school, unknown in the West until posthumous translation and publication of his book *The Mind in Society* in 1979. They studied how the child is influenced by people in the immediate environment, including siblings and other children. These close contacts help the child to learn skills and concepts and to develop cognitively, in a process that is more gradual than the steps of a stage theory. Similar to Erikson's views, Vygotsky considered play an important part of development, in which the child learns the norms of society and practices skills for life (Rogoff, 2013; Berk, Mann, & Ogan, 2006). Vygotsky's theories are very important in cultural psychology because they provide a model for how culture is transmitted during normal childhood processes (Rogoff & Morelli, 1989).

Context of development also formed the foundation for Uri Bronfenbrenner's ecological systems theory, called the bioecological model of development.

**Table 5.1   Prominent Developmental Stage Theories by Time of Life**

| Theorist | Stage | Description | 0–1 | 2 | 3 | 6 | 7 | 11 | 18 | 25 | 30 | 40 | 50 | 60+ |
|---|---|---|---|---|---|---|---|---|---|---|---|---|---|---|
| **Freud** | **Psychosexual development** | | | | | | | | | | | | | |
| | Oral | Child receives pleasure primarily via the mouth. Under- or overfeeding may lead to oral fixation later in life. | X | | | | | | | | | | | |
| | Anal | During toilet training, the child experiences pleasure from successful control of bladder and bowel. Harsh or permissive training leads to overcontrol or disorganization in life. | | X | X | | | | | | | | | |
| | Phallic | The child discovers his or her genitalia as a focus of pleasure and competes against same-gender parent for affection from the other. Child begins to identify with same-gender parent. | | | X | X | | | | | | | | |
| | Latency | Child identifies positively with same-gender parent, models that parent's behavior, and seeks same-gender peers for play. | | | | X | X | X | | | | | | |
| | Genital | Beginning at puberty, the person begins to adjust to life as a sexual being. | | | | | | X | X | X | | | | |
| **Erikson** | **Psychosocial Stages** | | | | | | | | | | | | | |
| | Infancy | Conflict: Trust–Mistrust. The child learns it can depend on caregivers for reliable sustenance or fails to learn trust of others. | X | | | | | | | | | | | |
| | Toddler | Conflict: Autonomy–Shame. Successful children learn skills for tasks, developing independence, or fall into failure and doubt. | | X | X | | | | | | | | | |
| | Preschool | Conflict: Initiative–Guilt. The child develops purpose and will to achieve goals or begins to feel guilt over too much or too little accomplishment. | | | | X | | | | | | | | |

*Age in Years*

| Theorist | | | Age in Years | | | | | | | | | | | |
|---|---|---|---|---|---|---|---|---|---|---|---|---|---|---|
| | **Stage** | **Description** | **0–1** | **2** | **3** | **6** | **7** | **11** | **18** | **25** | **30** | **40** | **50** | **60+** |
| | Childhood | Conflict: Industry–Inferiority. The child must develop a sense of confidence in meeting new challenges or face lowering self-esteem from failure. | | | | X | X | X | | | | | | |
| | Adolescence | Conflict: Identity–Role Confusion. The person develops a confident sense of whom she is in the world or has only a weak sense of self with no resolve. | | | | | | X | X | | | | | |
| | Young adulthood | Conflict: Intimacy–Isolation. The person learns to create strong and meaningful relationships or fails and faces a life of loneliness. | | | | | | | | X | X | | | |
| | Middle adulthood | Conflict: Generativity–Stagnation. The person should feel useful and accomplished by nurturing children and projects that will outlive her or face feelings of uselessness. | | | | | | | | | X | X | X | |
| | Maturity | Conflict: Integrity–Despair. The person feels a sense of fulfillment and meaning in her life or faces regret and despair from having lived life poorly. | | | | | | | | | | | X | X |
| **Piaget** | **Cognitive Development** | | | | | | | | | | | | | |
| | Sensorimotor | Children gather knowledge through physical sensation and making things move. | X | X | | | | | | | | | | |
| | Preoperational | Pretending and playing are primary paths for learning. The child has difficulty with logic and assuming others' perspectives. | | X | X | X | | | | | | | | |
| | Concrete operational | The child can think more logically but is limited to observable, actual reality. Abstract thought and hypothetical ideas remain difficult. | | | | | X | X | | | | | | |
| | Formal operational | The person can think more logically and use reasoning processes and can think abstractly. | | | | | | X | X | | | | | |

161

To Bronfenbrenner, development happens in response to influences of surrounding nested layers of social groups, including family, community, and country. The influences are bidirectional, meaning the child is acted upon, but also affects the world around her, and these interactions shape the developing person. The ecology affects the individual who simultaneously affects the environment by her presence and actions. To Bronfenbrenner, development of the individual cannot really be understood without acknowledging these contexts (Rogoff, 2003; Bronfenbrenner & Morris, 2006).

## Lifespan Emphasis in Development

Recent models of development, following Erikson's lead, emphasize a lifespan perspective. People continue to develop and change throughout the situations and experiences of an entire lifespan, first physically growing and developing language skills or secondary sexual characteristics, and later *developing* hair loss or grandparenting skills. We are in a constant state of becoming something slightly different. Certain trends are predictable, like early neural growth and levels of happiness at certain ages. The lifespan approach adds a number of additional phases of life, including prenatal, infancy, early childhood, childhood, adolescence, emerging adulthood, adulthood, middle adulthood, and old age, with old age now including "young old" and "old old" (c.f. Chou & Chi, 2002). Some developments happen normally to everyone, such as losing baby teeth and puberty's hormone levels, while others vary depending on exact conditions. Several changes happen during **sensitive periods,** when developments are *likely* to occur, or **critical periods,** when something *must* happen, and crucial differences arise depending on conditions at those times. Beyond basic genetic coding, all of these stages and periods are affected by our cultural and environmental milieu.

## REALITY CHECK

*What phase or stage of life are you in? Your parents? Your grandparents?*

*Did your family have a celebration or ceremony when you were an adolescent?*

*In what contexts did you grow up? Culture? Country?*

## 5.2 BIRTH AND INFANCY

### LO 5.2: Explain the earliest ways cultural elements set trajectories to culturally differing outcomes.

Each human child is born into a particular cultural context where he or she will learn ways of understanding the world. The child will learn a specific set of understandings about life, including where babies come from and why, with particular understandings about how a child should be raised, and with definite preferences about best outcomes. What constitutes a good life differs markedly across culture and subculture. Each person learns a system of beliefs that, to them, makes sense of the process and that constitutes truth within their world-view.

## Having Children: Parental Roles and Perceived Realities

Biologically, an ovum and sperm from a female and a male must be involved for conception to occur. Beyond that, roles, definitions, and expectations of parents differed across cultures long before technological innovations opened new possibilities for procreation like *in vitro* fertilization. Cultures know the physiology of copulation producing babies, but may vary in beliefs about why a particular child comes to be born into a family, and especially regarding who and what the father is.

Malinowski (1927/2002) described a culture in the Kiriwina Islands of the Solomon Sea where conception was believed to occur when a spirit grows tired of life in the ethereal world and enters the body of a woman of the same clan. The woman lives in the village and home of her husband, who is fondly involved with the children, but he is an outsider to the relationship between mother and this child who has come directly to her alone. Stories like this are also found in Western culture, with certain religious and spiritual groups believing souls choose their families and life situations. In another variation on fatherhood, people in some regions of India practiced polyandry, usually with several brothers marrying one wife and raising the children as one family without knowing precisely who fathered a particular child.

These beliefs about parenthood are part of the **ethnotheory** of a cultural group, comprising the values, practices, and beliefs that explain life and the world for them. Ethnotheories underlie every aspect of how we raise children, and this is true of all cultures, including modern Western culture. Parents provide a child's first models of interaction and care behaviors, and generally form the primary sources of answers about where babies come from. Some explanations are stated overtly, such as "the stork brought you," even if blatantly false. Behavioral guidance may also be overt, such as "spare the rod, spoil the child." Actually, much of what we learn about treatment of children and others is never spelled out explicitly. Non-verbal cues, such as tone of voice when speaking to a spouse or ways we do or do not physically touch family members, shape our interactions across generations, and shape how we eventually treat our own children (Harkness, Zylicz, Super, et al., 2011; Harkness & Super, 1992; Nitz, Lerner, Lerner, & Talwar, 1988).

## Prenatal Development

Cultural influences begin **in utero**. Cultural preferences and ecological situations determine what foods nourish a fetus, the mother's work and social experiences, and a range of additional factors including stress levels and the hormones and neurotransmitters present in the mother. Immediately, toxins in environment, foods, drugs or alcohol will affect prenatal development. A woman's health can be affected by excessively hard work or exposure to toxins in the work environment, sometimes resulting in low birth weight and related developmental issues (Senturia, 1997). Stress has less direct effects that happen over longer time periods as the mother's physiological resources are depleted. Prenatal maternal stress has been observed to affect kidney development, leading to hypertension decades later in life (Armelagos & Maes, 2006). Interestingly, observation of African American and European American women from early pregnancy through 32 weeks gestational age showed that collectivist lifestyles moderated the effects of stressors regardless of maternal SES (Abdou et al., 2010). In other words, a closely cooperative family or village context can reduce the mother's feelings of stress, lower resulting unhealthy endocrine or hormonal levels, and ameliorate subsequent effects on the child.

These factors begin the process of **epigenetic** influences on development. Epigenetic, in this context, refers to the factors beyond the genetic code inherited by the child. Factors such as nutrition, disease, injury, and even social contact may affect normal processes of development, leading to different outcomes in later stages. During gestation, the toxins and pathogens are termed **teratogens**. Genes provide the basic instructions for the growing child, but the eventual expression of those genes may be very different depending upon contextual factors already mentioned, and those depend on cultural and historic context. For example, Kinney, Miller, Crowley, Huang, and Gerber (2008) found a significant increase in autism rates in areas of Louisiana affected by Hurricane Katrina for children born in the months following the storm. Prevalence increased significantly for the cohort in mid or late pregnancy during the event ($p > .001$). The authors attribute the very strong correlation to the stresses experienced in the hurricane.

In addition to issues of nutrition, stress, and resources, the fetus experiences the movements of the mother and the sounds in her environment, and these set the rhythms of life the child will find regular after birth. The sounds around us and the ways our mothers move vary to a surprising degree across cultures, and the effects are far reaching. By 20 weeks, the child's ears are functional. From that point until about six months after birth, the ear and related neural structures adapt to interpret the surrounding sounds of speech, music, and nature (Graven & Browne, 2008). Between 28 and 32 weeks of gestational age, neural responses to linguistic input have been observed, including specific response to gender of speaker and to change of phoneme (Mahmoudzadeh et al., 2013). One of the first critical periods for cognitive development happens with exposure to meaningful sound including speech and music during this time, and without this exposure, the mechanisms of hearing may not develop properly. Surrounding sounds, even prior to birth, begin to shape development of neural structures to optimize attention to the sounds of a particular context.

The way a pregnant woman moves became a focus of attention in decades of research by Patricia Greenfield and her students with the Zinacantec Mayans. Greenfield's research was intended to examine transmission of cultural knowledge, but also provided compelling evidence for important implications of maternal ways of moving. Zinacantec women do not characteristically make big or sudden motions, generally restraining movement within a small space around the body. The restrained movement provides the fetus with a very peaceful uterine environment, and the resulting children move more calmly even in infancy (Maynard, Greenfield, & Childs, 1999).

Their children exhibit uniquely constrained range of motion and high level of visual attention, traits which become important in indigenous weaving practices they learn early in childhood. The ability to be very still becomes a specific asset for the young girls as they learn to weave using unique body looms that require very precise control of balance in their movements as they weave.

## Birth

*Hail, hail, hail, let happiness come:* Yao.

*Are our voices one?* Yao.

*Hail, let happiness come:* Yao.

*The stranger who has come, his back is towards the darkness:* Yao.

*His face is towards the light:* Yao.

*May he work for his father:* Yao.

*May he work for his mother:* Yao.

*May he not steal:* Yao.

*May he not be wicked:* Yao.

*From a Ga chant for the eighth day after a child is born (Field, 1937)*

Childbirth is a time when uncertainty prevails, even in the world of modern medicine. Mothers still die in childbirth, with the US rating 136 of 184 countries ranked, at 21 deaths per 100,000 live births. Estonia is lowest at 2 per 100,000, and South Sudan is worst at 2,000 per 100,000 (CIA, 2013). Complications can also kill or damage an infant. Perhaps because of the uncertainty of birth, cultures normally have a body of practices and lore designed to reduce anxiety and to make the process as safe and comfortable as possible, given their world-view and the sophistication of their knowledge (Sered, 1994). Over many millennia, lore has developed about what the mother should do, who holds authority and knowledge, and who should be present. Human physiology changed when we began to walk upright, bipedal movement requiring differently configured hips and resulting in a different birthing position. Wenda Trevathan (1987) argued that because of the physiological changes from bipedal movement, combined with increased cranial size and altered fetal position, humans need assistance in giving birth. She ties that necessary presence of another at person birth evolution of our social capabilities. In other words, we had to become socially adept to get help with birthing.

Broadly, elder women tended to be trusted to serve as midwives in traditional cultures, and this is still the case in cultures that rely less on the Western medical model (Jordan, 1978; Sargent & Bascope, 1996). Those assisting in traditional Polynesian cultures may include males with transgender statuses (Bolin, 2001). In a number of cultures, the father is present to assist in the birth or simply to witness the mother's pain. The people present and the roles they play form the cast of a child's first social interaction.

A transition to medically directed birth began in the 1800s, when physicians in industrializing nations were first trained in Europe and particularly in England (Scott, 1982). In the context of colonialism and increasing scientific knowledge, authority shifted from the midwives and the mothers to male medical professionals. Cultural practices and expectations of mothers that do not subscribe to modern medical model standards are often openly derided (Barclay & Kent, 1998; DeSousa, 2013; McElhinny, 2005; Sargent & Bascope, 1996). Non-Europeans frequently bear the brunt of prejudicial practices, as DeSousa (2013) observed among Korean women in New Zealand. Korean immigrant women received less quantity and poorer quality of prenatal and perinatal care than European origin women, and medical staff spent less effort explaining conditions and treatment to them.

Many cultures actually do not celebrate birth itself. Ceremonies may occur as much as a year later, when the specter of infant mortality has faded. Conversely, baptisms in Christian cultures tended to be early, specifically so that the baby would die already blessed. Throughout the 19th century, numbers of infants who died in their first year often exceeded 30% (Kyler & Munz, 1993). In 1876, France and England recorded 216 and 170 infant deaths per thousand live births, respectively (Rollet & Bordelais, 1993). A century ago, the infant mortality rate in the US was about 15 per 100 live births in the first year (Wegman, 2001). In 2017, 18 out of 1000 infants died in the first month, with 12 more dying by age 1 (Hug, Sharrow, Zhong, & You, 2017). Deaths of children under 5 years was 5 per 1,000 in Europe, 7 per 1,000 in North America, and 76 per 1,000 in sub-Saharan Africa. The highest infant mortality rate in 2017 was in the Central African Republic, at 87.6 per 1,000 births. The lowest rate was in Iceland, at 1.6 per 1,000. The United States recently ranked 52nd, at 5.7 per thousand (Group for Child Mortality Estimation, 2018). Although the recent rates in developed countries have fallen, throughout history, one in five infants died, and it was psychologically risky to feel emotionally attached to a baby.

## Infancy

At birth, human infants are completely helpless and must be fed, cleaned, and carried for years before becoming self-sufficient. The child does, however, possess a disproportionately large brain connected to an array of sensory equipment that is well-developed at birth. Perceptually and neurologically, the child arrives wired for social interaction, which begins immediately. The ability to recognize generic face shapes at birth appears to be an innate, biological ability (Johnson, Dziurawiec, Ellis, & Morton, 1991; Goren, Sarty, & Wu, 1975). There the shared experience ends. Subsequent interaction is determined by culture, influencing every aspect of development and ensuring perpetuation of the specific culture in which a child develops (Keller & Greenfield, 2000). Is the child held constantly or is she left alone to stimulate independence? Particular parenting practices represent ethnotheories of proper treatment, and shape the child into what parents hope she will become later in life (Keller, Borke, Lamm, Lohaus, & Dzeaye Yovsi, 2011; Sabatier, 2008; Stewart, Bond, Deeds, & Chung, 1999).

### Neural Specialization

The child has billions of neurons at birth and these continue to proliferate for the first few months. Very quickly, however, unnecessary connections begin to be pruned (Nelson, Thomas, & de Haan, 2006). This happens as the infant learns to focus on stimuli in its environment, with neural structures optimizing to discern those specific stimuli most readily. For instance, over the first few months, the infant begins responding less to generic face shapes, instead responding to specific faces of known social contacts (Johnson et al., 1991).

An early cultural adaptation of neurons relates to phonemes, the smallest recognizable sounds of language. Infants begin life with the ability to perceive and differentiate sounds using neural processing strikingly similar to adults (Dehaene-Lambertz, & Gliga, 2004). For the first few months, the infant's well developed sense of hearing can distinguish the phonemes of any language, which include 107 letter sounds, 52 diacritics (modifications of letters indicated by adjacent added marks), and 4 prosodies (specific rhythms, intonations, or stresses in language), comprising 163 phonemes in total (IPA, 2014). Infants can perceive these distinct sounds better than adults (Werker & Desjardins, 1995). By just 6 months of age, the infant is more attuned to the phonemes of its surrounding primary language (Polka & Werker, 1994). At that point, recent advances in measurement by near-infrared spectroscopy (NIRS) show that neural activity is beginning to focus on specific left-brain locations of normal language use, and stabilizes by about 13 months of age (Minagawa-Kawai, Mori, Naoi, & Kojima, 2007). From that juncture onward, the child's brain has adapted to perceive one specific language best, and may not perceive phonemes of another language at all, such as the stereotypic difficulty of native Japanese speakers to discriminate "L" and "R" sounds.

This time of rapid language specialization forms an early sensitive period for language acquisition. Children can acquire additional languages later, but language is most readily acquired beginning in infancy. Debate continues as to whether there are critical periods for language acquisition, especially for learning to speak without accent, but acquisition in early childhood progresses at similar rates across cultures and includes bilingual infants (Conboy & Montanari, 2016). There may be a sensitive period for acquiring a second language without an accent, but some people retain accents despite learning the second language in childhood, and some people do a marvelous job of learning another language in adulthood (e.g., Piske, MacKay, & Flege, 2001).

### Important Milestones

Erikson (1963) would say the infant must develop a sense of trust and secure bonding with caregivers in order to form a foundation for subsequent development and later healthy relationships. In Western psychology, secure attachment is assumed to contribute to the child's sense of well-being and later efficacy (Easterbrooks, Bartlett, Beeghly, & Thompson, 2013), a process that may not be identical across cultures (Keller, 2016).

Infant care takes very different forms across cultures. Americans of European descent favor verbal and distal interaction, in other words interacting primarily by speaking to the child rather than touching, maintaining enough distance to allow mommy

# SPOTLIGHT

## CO-SLEEPING NORMS ACROSS CULTURES

By the time a child is several months old, and certainly when it begins toddling around, cultural patterns affect sleeping arrangements. These reflect ethnotheories of best practice in childcare and reveal underlying values and beliefs of each culture (Welles-Nyström, 2005; Super, 1981). A body of Western literature, primarily from American and British sources, has promoted the belief that the child should be sleeping alone very early in life. Euro-American ethnotheories and expert advice have told American parents that their child must learn to sleep alone to become a functioning, independent person. Pearce and Bidder (1999) tell parents, "Believe it or not, leaving your child alone to cry in bed is a way to show your love and care for him. . . . If you can help your child get himself to sleep, you'll be preparing him for a life of independence" (p. 66). Co-sleeping has been described as a deeply dangerous practice that would lead the child to become dependent on its mother, especially, in ways that could affect mental health for the rest of the person's life. The practice raises concerns about inappropriate sexual contact in the US (see Ball, Hooker, & Kelly, 1999 and Rath & Okum, 1995 for discussions).

These views are definitely not held across cultures. From an evolutionary perspective, co-sleeping formed an excellent way to protect the young, in times when monsters in the night were real, and human predators still roam urban environs today. Co-sleeping is thought to generate security and happiness for the family in Japan. In Sweden, culturally and geographically fairly close to the British Isles, co-sleeping is considered normal and healthy (Welles-Nyström, 2005). Morelli, Rogoff, Oppenheim, and Goldsmith (1992) found that highland Maya of the Yucatan considered sleeping alone to be an unwelcome hardship. I have had students from non-Western cultures who never slept without a sibling or parent in the bed until they left for college. In these cultures, co-sleeping is seen as a way to enhance sense of security in the child, and there are certainly no concerns about sexuality expressed. People from these cultures are as adamant about the rightness of co-sleeping as Western Europeans and their American descendants are about sleeping alone.

Beliefs about infant sleeping, including those of Western cultures, are arguably ethnographic in origin. The cultural values implicit in the beliefs are clear, such as the Euro-American practice of letting the child "cry it out" to make them more self-reliant (e.g., Pearce & Bidder, 1999), even though an infant lacks the cognitive capacity to link those concepts. Sleeping practices are another way parents attempt to shape the child into the type of adult a culture values, even if the attempt is misguided. The Euro-American cultures that frown on co-sleeping value autonomy and independence highly, whereas other cultures value connectedness, reinforced in nocturnal closeness. In those cultures, even when the child no longer sleeps with its mother, it probably shares a bed with other siblings (Luijk et al., 2013; Mileva-Seitz, Bakermans-Kranenburg, Battaini, & Luijk, 2017). Opinions about bed sharing are strong, even among researcher, and consensus does not exist; in a review of 659 published studies, Mileva-Seitz and colleagues (2017) found no clear answers and encourage multidisciplinary research. For now, it seems parents will be making the choice culturally.

to do the dishes and the little child to start feeling independent. Conversely, in many traditional cultures, the interaction tends to include more constant, proximal physical contact (Greenfield, 1972; Hewlett, Lamb, Shannon, Leyendecker, & Schölmerich,

1998; Super & Harkness, 1991). The Efe pygmies of the Ituri rainforest normally care for their children collectively, to such an extent that the child's early nursing is often not at its own mother's breast (Hewlett, 1989). These differences in early interaction styles play out constantly across the life span, creating a person uniquely suited to dynamics of a particular culture.

## REALITY CHECK

*When does culture begin to shape a person?*

*What is similar and what differs in beliefs about birth?*

*Does a baby have language abilities at birth?*

*As a baby, did you sleep alone or with other people in the bed? As a child?*

## 5.3 CHILDHOOD

### LO 5.3 Summarize cultural learning and contrast ways knowledge is transmitted in different cultures.

Early childhood is a time of rapid growth, both physically and mentally. The child is swiftly learning language and learning limits of what she can and cannot do. For a young child in a culture with stoves, not touching a hot one may be important. A Hispanic-American toddler may be learning two languages. A toddler on a tributary of the Amazon may instead be learning caution around open fires and machete, and skills to avoid snakes and crocodiles.

### Toddlers

When a child begins to take its first steps, he or she becomes a "toddler," in English vernacular. Hominids have shared this stage since our *australopithecine* ancestors began to walk consistently upright. As the child becomes more mobile, she begins to move physically further from caregivers and interact with a wider social network. At this point, marked differences begin to emerge in expectations of independence and autonomy, demonstrated to the child in how caregivers relate to each other and to the child herself. Okimoto (2001) compared mothers in the US who were Caucasian American from California and Washington state with immigrant Japanese and Chinese Vietnamese residing in the Seattle area. He found that the Caucasian American mothers encouraged independence via toddler-initiated play and decision making, while the Japanese mothers subtly directed activity and the Chinese Vietnamese mothers overtly directed children to play in certain ways. These modes match cultural norms for adult behavior.

## Attachment

World War II left countless orphans in its wake, prompting the emerging United Nations to commission a study of their needs. Among the problems these children faced was what René Spitz termed *anaclitic depression*, depression from having nobody dependably supplying basic needs or affection (Spitz & Wolf, 1946). British physician John Bowlby took on the study, travelling Europe and the US interviewing caregivers for many thousands of needy orphans. Bowlby determined that the absence of maternal connection may be a driving force in mental health problems more generally. He published his findings in *Maternal care and mental health* (1951) and eventually developed attachment theory (Bowlby, 1969), holding that a person's mental well-being requires a secure sense of connection to the mother or some caregiver in infancy.

Mary Ainsworth expanded the theory, observing children in Uganda and then Boston, describing three types of infant behavior from her results: securely attached, insecurely attached, and non-attached. She proposed that these were the result of the mother's "ability to perceive and interpret accurately the signals and communications in the infant's behavior and, given this understanding, to respond to them appropriately and promptly" (Ainsworth, Bell, & Stayton, 1974, p. 127). Following her return to Boston, Ainsworth failed to replicate her observations and eventually designed her "strange situation" experiments to elicit stronger reactions (Keller, 2013). Infants faced varying types of new and uncomfortable contexts in a laboratory setting, and Ainsworth sorted their reactions into four categories: secure, in which the child is comfortable with the mother, will explore when she is there, and is consolable upon her return; insecure-avoidant, in which the child plays independently without maintaining connection with the parent; insecure-ambivalent, in which the child may refuse to leave the caregiver's lap and may be inconsolable upon return after separation; and disorganized, in which the child may switch affect and go from hitting to kissing the caregiver in unpredictable order.

Attachment became a very popular topic of cross-cultural research, with researchers investigating numerous cultures for similarities and differences compared to Ainsworth's Boston experiments. Generally, researchers identify behavioral patterns that fit Ainsworth's model in proportions that differ from her Boston sample, which still serves as the reference standard. Van Ijzendoorn and Kroonenberg (1988) investigated mother-infant bonds in Japan, the US, and Northern Europe, while Posada and colleagues (1995) looked at relations in China, Colombia, Germany, Israel, Japan, and the United States. Much later, Jin, Jacobovitz, Hazen, and Jung (2012) observed Korean mother–infant dyads, and again identified evidence of attachment behaviors in somewhat different proportions from Ainsworth's reference sample. Cultures share a view of benevolent attachment between mother and child (Arnett & Maynard, 2013), though the ideal form varies. The Japanese concept of *amae* exemplifies a more interdependent bond than Western culture promotes (e.g., Morelli & Rothbaum, 2007). These differing proportions are thought to reflect the underlying cultural systems, values, and ethnotheories, which in turn reflect traditions of childcare and of the ideal end state in adulthood.

Rothbaum, Weisz, Pott, Miyake, and Morelli (2000) suggested that the core elements of attachment theory are rooted in Western culture, with the child's autonomy, individuality, and exploration forming the basis for measurement of attachment style. These qualities are important if one wants to raise a child suited to mainstream Western culture but may be less desirable in other cultural contexts. Behaviors of children in different cultures may observably match behaviors measured in the strange situation, but what parents want and encourage may not fit so easily into Ainsworth's categories, especially regarding her preference for secure attachment behaviors.

The mother–child dyad is most valued in Western and technologically developed areas, and many cultures do not emphasize it at all. That dyad has formed a virtually exclusive focus of psychological theory (Weisner et al., 1977). Barry and Paxson (1971) used coded data from Murdock and White's (1969) standard cross-cultural sample of the 186 best-described cultures to analyze prevalence of child-rearing practices, finding only 2.7% in which the mother provided exclusive care of the infant. In 20.4% of sampled cultures, a majority of time was spent away from the mother. More normatively, older siblings and family members, along with other children and adult neighbors or employees, would provide significant childcare (Weisner et al., 1977). Children in those situations develop sense of trust with a network of others, making security a matter of context or environment rather than dyadic interaction (Keller, 2016). Even in Western culture, relatives and professional childcare providers play important roles in childcare, and examination of contexts and care networks may yield greater understanding of attachment.

The corollary of infant attachment is parental attachment style, which influences how a child is treated and has definite consequences in adjustment of the eventual adult (Vivona, 2000). We get our earliest lessons in childcare from our own caregivers as they raise us, probably determining how people will eventually treat their own children, forming a chain of transmission across generations (Keller, 2013; Main & Goldwyn, 1998). Essentially, the way we were raised seems the natural and proper way because that is our native environment, whether peaceful or hostility filled. Current views of attachment acknowledge that children may benefit equally from feelings of closeness to people besides the mother, such as a grandparent or foster parent, as long as the sense of connection is present (Arnett & Maynard, 2013), the alternative caregiver(s) then providing the behavioral model.

## Terrible Twos

Toddler years also bring the dreaded "Terrible Twos," if one lives in a Western cultures, particularly English-speaking ones (Gallacher, 2005). The toddler may act out in loud, violent tantrums when its will is thwarted. This may be a product of cultural emphasis on independence and autonomy, the very qualities encouraged by sleeping alone and by distal maternal attention. The child is learning a language that emphasizes personal pronouns—I, me, and mine—which the child may learn before she has developed the cognitive skills to regulate behavior. In other cultures, peace and harmony of the group are emphasized in early training of a child, encouraging interdependence rather than independence (Greenfield, 2012, 1972). Linguistically, in Bahasa Indonesia and the closely related Malaysian language, *saya* (I) and *anda* (you) are among words commonly omitted as simply superfluous in daily speech, and the cognitive spotlight is shifted from individuality to mutuality. In keeping with Greenfield's (1972) observations, my African friends laughed when I have asked them about toddler misbehavior. They wonder why anyone would let a child have such a bad effect on the group as they have seen visiting American homes. Far from being a universal, the terrible twos seem to be an effect of Western language and cultural values.

## Early Childhood

In our early years, a great deal of learning takes place in a number of domains. The child gathers skills of language and movement, learning how to do and make things, and learning how to interact with others. By around age 3 or 4, children develop theory of mind (ToM), which means they understand that others have different thoughts from their own, and others may not know what the child thinks. This happens for all children, regardless of culture, as they learn to pretend and play, and the presence of others such as older siblings may help them develop ToM related skills more readily.

The child must also learn self-regulation, including control of bodily functions and emotional expression (Holway, 1949). We share basic functions and common processes of expression, but the ways we express emotion differs, perhaps by temperament, but certainly by cultural rules of acceptable communication. Whether innately outgoing or reserved, your expression style largely reflects the norms your parents and those around you followed when displaying their emotions as you grew. How much we control our expression is a function of our cultural context. For instance, Americans of European ancestry value positive affective expression of enthusiasm and elation, while Asian Americans emphasize serenity and calmness of expression to maintain group harmony (Engelmann & Pogosyan, 2013; Ruby, Falk, Heine, Villa, & Silberstein, 2012).

Psychologists debate whether our temperament is primarily genetic and already set at birth, or is modified by our experiences. Some researchers propose that milieu pushes our temperament toward cultural norms, in other words suggesting that temperament is at least partly a product of culture rather than an innate characteristic (Kohnstamm, 1989). Super and Harkness (1986) conceptualized the "developmental niche" in which "cultural structuring" of development takes place, including "the physical and social settings in which the child lives, the customs of childcare and childrearing, and the psychology of the caretakers" (p. 545). The qualities of the developmental niche mold the child, resulting in the cultural differences observed in Big 5 personality traits and other temperament constructs across cultures (Slobodskaya, Gartstein, Nakagawa, & Putnam, 2013).

## Middle Childhood

Childhood is generally a time of good health, mostly free from new diseases and disorders, once a child survives the first couple of years. Children become increasingly mobile, able to run around, play, and dance. Vocabulary blossoms, enough to express a multitude of needs and feelings. Ability to learn and to focus on completing tasks expands enough that the child can handle more responsibilities and become a functional part of family and community, and demands upon her expand. Erikson would say the growing person is negotiating the challenge of industry versus inferiority, learning skills that let her feel secure in her competence as an actor in her cultural context. Competencies differ radically: ability to excel at video games, Little League baseball, and spelling bees may be of less value in a Tuscan vineyard or the Siberian tundra. Further, depending on what happened during the first couple of years, the child is developing a concept of self that may emphasize uniqueness and individuality, or may instead revolve around a deep feeling of embeddedness in family, tribe, or ethnicity. What happens culturally from this point on continues to shape what we come to believe and how we behave.

## Cultural Learning

Through the childhood years, which are roughly from ages six or seven to adolescence, the child particularly adapts to and learns about the items and activities of a specific culture. Remember that pruning of our neural networks begins very early in life, and that we delete what we do not need, keeping what is encouraged in our environment. Five- to 7-year-old Mayan children continue to demonstrate a greater capacity to pay attention for longer times as they grow (Correa-Chávez & Rogoff, 2009). We quickly become accustomed to a host of culturally specific material goods and behavioral processes. Differences in our material environs are why the Müller-Lyer Illusion is more likely to fool people from cultures with squared walls and less so the Bashi of the Congo (Bonte, 1962) or traditional Navajo (Pedersen & Wheeler, 1983), who historically lived in round dwellings (see Chapter 7).

## The Ways We Learn

Our early learning has similarities, regardless of culture. Vygotsky (1978) would say that our minds develop via the social processes around us and the guidance we receive in our interactions with those at least a little older, wiser, and/or more advanced than we are. Vygotsky proposed that we are helped from our current state of learning to the next accomplishment we can *nearly* do, but not without help. Proximal means "near," and what we can almost do unaided falls in our **zone of proximal development (ZPD)**. Patricia Greenfield and her students spent many years observing the ways weaving is transmitted by siblings and other children, slightly older, who have mastered a technique (Maynard et al., 1999). Rogoff (1995) refers to this as *guided participation*, being mentored in the skills we need to function in our cultural setting, and it happens naturally as we begin to try out those tasks. Broadly, this is just how humans begin learning, though who guides us and what we are learning depends upon culture. The processes of learning the many facets of a culture is called **enculturation** (Lancy, 2012).

Entering the 21st century, the ethnotheory of parenting in Western culture places the parent at the helm of a child's education, enlisting a host of teachers, counselors, and technological tools to help (Lancy, 2010). From the time a child can enter preschool, most people in the developed world consider formal schooling to be the

### LEARNING IN THE *DJELI* TRADITION

Lansana Kouyate grew up in the ancient West-African *djeli* tradition. The *djeli* are musicians and storytellers who enjoy a privileged place in cultures across West Africa, including the former Manding empire. Lansana described how his musical learning process started at about age 2. Young *djeli* children might take a liking to an instrument and, when the adults take a break, creep over to strike a couple of notes (Lansana plays *bala*, which is a marimba relative). Adults pretend not to notice until the child starts to catch on, at which point an uncle or aunt may come over now and then to suggest a technique. Euro-Americans spend years going to a piano teacher's house and later to professors' offices for lessons if they continue to play in adulthood. Lansana became a master player without anything remotely like a formal music lesson. He learned primarily through observation, with an occasional informal suggestion when he needed it, as his family has for centuries.

primary way people learn the important things of life. People really did not learn this way until very recently in human history, though China had already established formal education many centuries ago, including standardized testing for civil service beginning in 606 CE (Suen & Yu 2006).

Direct education by a parent, and formal education in general, have been very rare in human history. More traditional education begins in early childhood with songs and stories, which are linguistic vehicles for transmission of cultural knowledge (Shennan & Steele, 1999). A good storyteller captivates listeners, and this enhances the learning value of the process. By beginning with these lessons early, couched in an easily assimilated form, the child is prepared for the more complex knowledge that will follow as

### TRADITIONAL STORIES IN THE MODERN WORLD

The Tonoho O'odham (Native American tribe) live in southern Arizona and are unusual in simultaneously maintaining their traditional practices and language and participating robustly in Western schooling. On average, they complete 12 years of school and have established the Tonoho O'odham Community College in conjunction with the University of Arizona (www.tocc.edu). Children in traditional families are taught to pay attention to and learn from stories and conversations happening around them, which they call "catching the words as they are thrown" (Tsethlikai & Rogoff, 2013, p. 575). Tsethlikai and Rogoff tested their ability by having African folktales told when children were otherwise engaged, such as in play, and found that the children were very good at retelling the stories. The authors take this as evidence that Western and traditional education can coexist to good benefit.

she develops more complex cognition. Tsethlikai and Rogoff (2013) relate the Tewa (Native American) belief, "We grow them [children] with stories. Our food makes them strong, but our stories make them complete/good (óyyó-'an)" (p. 569).

In addition to the cognitive input of stories, children learn constantly by imitating those around them. Carpenter, Ahktar, and Tomasello (1998) observed that 14- to 18-month-old infants can already differentiate intentional and accidental actions and will more often imitate the intentional ones. Children may model adult behaviors, as with Kouyate's description of musical learning among the Djeli of West Africa, but they also learn by imitating each other, as with Greenfield's descriptions of observational learning and scaffolding among Mayan children. Lancy (2012) lists an impressive range of life skills gathered in early childhood. Some may be considered chores or subsistence activities, but even foraging for edible plants requires considerable knowledge of plant species and stages of readiness, as well as techniques for harvesting.

- Among Kewa horticulturalists, children are competent gardeners by 9.

- Mer Island children are "fairly proficient" reef foragers by 6.

- In Tibet, mixed herds tended by 6–7 year olds.

- 10-year-old Aka pygmies have mastered some 50 foraging skills.

- [Zapotec-Mexico -children's excellent command of ethnobotany is described as] everyday knowledge acquired without apparent effort at an early age by virtually everyone in town.

- [Inuit] children produce a large percentage of their own food supply by gathering shellfish.

- Hadza children not only start foraging at 4, they quickly develop competence in fruit and tuber acquisition and processing.

(Lancy, 2012, p. 8)

### Apprenticeships

Apprenticeships form a long-standing method for transmitting complex information. Some bodies of knowledge and technical expertise require considerable time to impart, such as building canoes or violins, or navigating by stars and ocean currents. These require procedural rather than declarative knowledge and are as difficult to learn from books as riding a bicycle. The apprentice relationship may be informal, as when a child hangs around elders and is eventually given progressively more responsible tasks. Apprenticeship requires the attention of the teachers, which grows less as the student learns, and that the teacher directs the activities of the learner (Maynard & Greenfield, 2005). As with chores and daily activities, other dynamics are happening at the same time as the transmission of knowledge, including the telling of stories, establishment of relationship dynamics, and reinforcement of cultural norms. Apprenticeship, as a way

## INFORMAL APPRENTICESHIP

*Jane (Solomons weaver/musician): That's the tradition way, when you first weave you have to give it to the old people. Everything you learn from the old people. The best friends that I had in Solomons, my favourite friends, are the old people, not young people, but old people.* (Fox, 2010, p. 121)

Jane (not her real name) grew up in the Solomon Islands of the South Pacific, a great-niece of one of the men who rescued John F. Kennedy and the men of PT 109 in WWII. That older generation told tales of hunting parties and cannibalism that were active traditions into the 20th century. After the war, life changed rapidly, and Jane would canoe across the crocodile- and shark-infested lagoon each morning to attend Western-style school. She still spent many hours each week weaving with the older women, an activity that also included singing old songs, telling stories, and generally laughing a lot. The cultural exposure gave her sufficient knowledge to be considered an expert in Solomons culture, with a radio show, media exposure, and gallery showings of her work. She lives in New Zealand now, but she spends time doing these same things with her two mixed-ethnicity daughters, passing on the same stories she heard from her elders as a girl.

to convey a pupil through progressive levels of understanding, constitutes a formalized system of scaffolding (Lancy, 2010, 2012; Maynard & Greenfield, 2006).

In more formal apprenticeships, families may pay a fee, or the youth may be obliged to spend many years in service of the master craftsman. The long duration may not be required for learning of the skills, but instead forms payment for the privilege of acquiring the knowledge (Lancy, 2010). The apprenticeship may create a lifelong bond and obligation, as was traditional in India and Japan (Altekar, 1939/2009; Singleton, 1998). As globalization increases and traditional skills become less essential to survival, many of these skills and learning contexts are disappearing.

### Social Change and Development

In her theory of social change and development, Greenfield (2016) proposes that sociodemographic changes are linked in predictable patterns of shifts in values, learning environment, and development. Cultures are moving from subsistence to commerce, rural to urban life, and extended to nuclear families. Learning is moving from apprenticeship and informal scaffolding to institutional education in formalized Western classrooms. Traditions are being lost and innovation is rising, whatever the cost or gain. In these new settings, individualism becomes more common as collectivism recedes. In her recent field work with a third generation of Mayans, Greenfield (2016) observed that fidelity of traditional weaving patterns was fading, though originality was increasing, following her predicted pattern.

## 5.4 ADOLESCENCE THROUGH ADULTHOOD

### LO 5.4 Critique constructions of adolescence and achievement of adulthood.

### Adolescence

Adolescence marks major physiological changes, as the young human becomes capable of reproduction and a new set of social roles and responsibilities is assumed. This transition is ritualized in many, if not all, cultures, from *bar mitzvah* to Catholic confirmation, to Navajo *Kinaaldá* for women, to the land-diving leaps from towers by young men of Vanuatu (Jolly, 1994). These rituals mark the crossing of the limina between roles of youth and maturity, in other words, the person experiences a brief moment in between being a child and being an adult, and for a few seconds, psychologically identifies as neither one (V. Turner, 1982a, 1967).

Adolescence forms the next set of obvious cultural differences, with some cultures getting married in their early teens, internalizing adult responsibilities, and beginning to have children. In technologically developed countries, teens may be hanging out at malls and playing computer games. A primary goal of puberty years has been achievement of a place in the culture or community, which Erikson would describe as the challenge of finding identity or falling into role confusion. Through much of history, this usually included establishment of vocation and marital alliance. Those choices have traditionally been guided by elders, whereas contemporary media culture promotes individual choice as crucial for living a happy life. In modern, postindustrial culture, adolescents rarely assume adult roles, and the transition from living in mom's basement may take years. In current globalized culture, formal roles may come much later, and in the interim, exploration, irresponsibility, and rebellion are considered somewhat expected if not normative.

The exploratory phase of misbehavior is commonly termed adolescent rebellion. American teens who had grown up protesting the Vietnam War and Civil Rights injustices perpetrated by their elders resoundingly rebelled and changed the shape of parenting, placing themselves on equal footing with their children. Rather than exerting authority based on experience and wisdom, these parents sought a more congenial relationship, which may contribute to loosening mores and bad behavior. Donald Meltzer (2008) observed that American youths had moved from wanting to fall in love as the path to sexual intimacy to the mindset that sex, now a trivial matter, would lead to love. John Savage (2007), on the other hand, traces the Western stereotypes of teenagers and adolescent rebellion back to the 1870s, when Marie Bashkirtseff published a memoir of her teen years and when Jesse Pomeroy went on trial at age 14 for mass murder. By 1955, James Dean had become an icon of teenage angst and died young, which Hassan (1958) views as deeply rooted in the psyche of the American Dream of individual expansion and attainment.

In non-Western cultures, adolescent rebellion is less common. In fact, Nsamenang (2011) contends that the entire construct and study of adolescence is a phenomenon of Western culture. Youths in those age groups around the world are often working to support their families, or simply to survive on the streets, and many grow up with only restricted contact with the opposite gender (Brown & Larson, 2009). Two-thirds of Indian young people willingly accept their parents' choices of an arranged mate, which definitely reduces anxiety about dating (Verma & Saraswati, 2002). These facts contradict the universality of rebellious adolescence as a human norm.

Violence does actually loom over adolescents around the world for a number of reasons. Neurologically, the prefrontal cortex is still developing, making cognition and impulse control more difficult (Gogtay et al., 2004). This is amplified by effects of peer behavior, affecting urban and rural communities across ethnic groups in the US (Blackmon, Robinson, & Rhodes, 2016; Stein, Jaycox, Kataoka, Rhodes, & Vestal, 2003). Violence has different emotional valence depending on culture, such as the normative behavior of Amazonian Yanomamo that seems incredibly violent to Westerners (Chagnon, 1988b). Poverty affects availability of parental supervision and generally corresponds with exposure to violence and substance abuse (Fiaui & Hishinuma, 2009; Rhodes, 2004). Ultimately, teens are among the most vulnerable in war and its aftermath, being conscripted as soldiers when very young, as with the child soldiers of Sierra Leone (Borisova, Bettancourt, & Willett, 2013), or slightly later, as in the US where adolescents can enlist at age 17 with parental consent ("Join the military," 2019).

### Protective Factors and Resilience

Traditional cultures include mechanisms to help youths navigate the transitions of adolescence. Roles were well defined, and rituals accompanied the change from child to adult so that the whole group endorsed and acknowledged new roles. Life has always included the occasional disaster, but close community connection and support provided protection through tough times. Adolescence still brought big changes to a young person's life, but they were predictable and not nearly as psychologically traumatic as the angst-ridden teenage years of our contemporary world. Freedom to step outside of predefined roles has been a benefit of modern culture, but modern freedoms have come with loss of supportive social connectedness and sustenance of cultural resources.

Colonialism wrought rapid devastation of traditional cultures through displacement, forced conversion, and outright slaughter (Hoerder, 2002), causing widespread loss of the cultural and symbolic resources that formerly helped people to cope effectively with change (Markovitzky & Mosek, 2005). Globalization, and especially the global reach of Western media products, continues to erode languages and traditional activities among the cultures that survived (e.g., Garrett et al., 2014; Gone, 2013; Greenfield, 2015). The loss of the traditional mechanisms by which identity was created is particularly hard on indigenous youth, who tend to have very high rates of substance abuse and suicide (Po'A-Kekuawela, Okamoto, Nebre, Helm, & Chin, 2009).

Rather unexpectedly, many minority ethnic groups are rebounding, though actually much concerted effort has gone into the resurgence. A number of cultures have established educational system aimed at cultural revitalization (Widdowson & Howard, 2013). The Māori have established a network of *kohanga reo*, language immersion schools, which provided the model for *punana leo* Hawaiian immersion schools and other language and culture specific educational programs. Youths coming from these systems have now reached adulthood and have children of their own. Results are generally positive in terms of retention and positive life outcomes through teen years (Stiles, 1997; Widdowson & Howard, 2013), but with some concerns about potential for resulting cultural and economic isolation (Rata, 2013).

In another aspect of cultural revitalization, indigenous philosophies and techniques are being used for treatment of mental health and substance abuse problems. These methods emphasize connection to cultural values and indigenous models of holistic health (e.g., Durie, 1995, 1994; Gone, 2013; Po'A-Kekuawela et al., 2009), with favorable outcomes observed among at-risk youth. Traditional interventions have been used to increase resilience in Native American youth (Garrett et al., 2014), and more generally, participation in traditional arts has been demonstrated to increase well-being of New Zealand youth through support of identity, building of social support, and enhancement of self-esteem and resilience (Fox, 2010).

## Adulthood

The point when a person becomes an adult varies across cultures. European tradition recognizes adulthood as a legal concept in which an individual becomes an adult at age 18 or 21 (T. E. James, 1960). As mentioned earlier, Jewish tradition places adulthood as happening at age 13, upon celebrating *bar mitzvah* (males) or *bat mitzvah* (females), and Navajo girls become women at first menstruation, when they celebrate the *Kinaaldá*. The Jewish and Navajo traditions are examples of tying adulthood rights and roles to biology of procreation, while European laws granted full rights upon living more than half of historically shorter lives, the age of majority. Practically, adulthood may be defined by age, role, or responsibilities, depending on country, religion, and ethnicity. These definitions may be simultaneous and conflicting, for instance when a Jewish 14 year old is accountable as an adult within Jewish law and unaccountable as a minor in the Western legal system. Definitions may be even more clouded amid situations of war or crisis, when dire situations necessitate assumption of responsibility by young people.

Erikson proposed that, in early adulthood, a person faced resolution of intimacy versus isolation, which includes finding a life partner in marriage, but should also include meaningful relations with friends and family. As adults, we have a certain amount of agency to choose, within constraints of environmental and cultural factors. A remote fishing village may offer fewer friendship choices than Manhattan, and traditional obligations to tribe, family, or religious group may set other limits. Our romantic relationships may result from individual free choice or be dictated by parents, and the same may be said of our vocations. For an Oriya woman in India, adulthood finds her in an arranged marriage, having children, and doing the hard work of running a house under the stern direction of her mother-in-law (Menon, 2011). In developed countries, the transition to adulthood may increasingly take years to complete. These differences reflect our cognitions and conceptions of adulthood, stemming from what we have observed in our particular elders, and combined with the circumstances of our time in history.

## Emerging Adulthood

*In the life history of every individual who grows to adulthood there comes a time when he must emancipate himself from the thralldom of the home. He must break away from his infantile moorings, go forth into the world of reality and win there a place for himself.*

*White, 1916, p. 147*

In white American culture, this statement has seemed largely self-evident for the past century or so. A person stereotypically becomes an adult at age 18 and bids farewell to mom and dad to either go to work or to college, living alone or with a spouse from then on to achieve independence and success. In reality, even 18th-century British young people might wait and live with parents until their late twenties to marry so they could afford a home. Jobs, property values, and the global economy have altered rapidly following the 2008 financial meltdown, and moving out of the family home is again delayed. Education now takes several expensive years for high value jobs. Many people have trouble settling on a career path or cannot afford schooling for their chosen career, or they simply cannot afford home prices where they live. As a result, more and more Western youths live in their family homes much longer than their parents and grandparents did.

When should a person leave home or should they leave at all? Is staying with parents an undesirable shift toward dependency? When does a person have to assume the mantle of adulthood? Throughout much of the rest of the world, multigenerational households are still common and generally considered desirable, with family members to share expenses, chores, and childcare. People have historically and culturally assumed a wide variety of roles considered adult, at a wide variety of ages. Normative roles and optimal timing are shifting around the world.

Developmental psychologists have adopted the term Emerging Adulthood to describe the new time between adolescence and full adulthood. Neuroscience now tells us that the brain only completes development toward the end of a person's third decade (Gogtay et al., 2004), which explains much of the risk-taking behaviors more common in adolescence and early twenties, such as substance abuse and dangerous sexual practices (Brodbeck, Bachmann, Croudace, & Brown, 2013). Individuals in this stage are in flux, transiting between the rapid physical growth years of childhood and a stable identity and role as an adult. Attitudes toward traditional roles may be abandoned in favor of more progressive attitudes (McDermott & Schwartz, 2013). This is also a time when mental illness may develop, such as schizophrenia, psychoses, or depression (APA, 2013; World Health Organization, 2004). Mental health risks are higher for minorities such as African Americans, perhaps due to additional stresses of prejudice and conflicts of identity in marginalized statuses (e.g., Hurd, Sanchez, Zimmerman, & Caldwell, 2012).

Emerging adulthood is a stage of the modern, technologically oriented world, considering that people were often filling adult roles long before this in traditional and agrarian societies. With rapid globalization, however, these situations and conditions are widespread. People are connected electronically around the world, and young people want upwardly mobile jobs whether they are in America, India, or Zimbabwe. University education is highly desirable, and it takes a longer time to become the type of adult we want to be.

## Middle Adulthood

Chij dyiji'jiyequi *(know how to think [about work and what needs to be done])*

*Tsimané concept of mature years*

Mature years traditionally begin with slowing physiology, around menopause for women and a general lessening of testosterone in most men. At this point, one's children may be entering adulthood and having children themselves. Erikson (1963) describes this stage as negotiating the challenge of generativity versus stagnation, by which he means that the person is either contributing to the growth and prosperity of younger people in the family and community or is sitting around moldering toward old age and death. Generativity describes my motivations for writing this book.

Middle adulthood constitutes another branching in the ways culture affects us. We have learned a series of expected roles to fill that shift as we age, and beginning in the fifth decade or so, one's children have often grown up and some seniority has been achieved. People of this age often begin to assume leadership roles, whether in a village, a tribe, a religion, or Congress, or their relevance begins to fade. When an Oriya woman of Northern India reaches middle age and her oldest son marries, she has it made. The pain and sacrifice of all those years of bowing and scraping in service to her mother-in-law come due and she can demand the same obedience from her new daughter-in-law. She rules the house and none may question her authority, including her own mother-in-law, who may have treated her as a serf but now moves out of power and becomes dependent on her (Menon, 2011).

Across cultures, the quality of relationships, especially marriage, support our sense of well-being, though we differ in how we describe our happiness. Barbara Mitchell (2010) studied relationships among older Canadian residents of European, Chinese, and

Indian origin, and found predictably that the European participants valued personal goals while the Asian participants focused more on family ties.

*Midlife Crisis.* Existential angst and changing quality of life stereotypically send middle-aged Americans into mid-life crises of buying sports cars and having affairs. Outside America, similar concepts exist; Wong, Awang, and Jani (2012) found definite midlife-crisis conditions in Malaysian women, with greater severity for low-income women and better coping by more religious women. For Japanese culture, 42 marks a unlucky *Yakudoshi* year for men, when bad things are thought to happen (Sakashita, 2006). To some degree, our changing physiology and social standing really do erode our sense of well-being, and this is not only true of humans. In a fascinating study, Weiss, King, Inoue-Murayama, Matsuzawa, and Oswald (2012) found signs of mid-life crisis in great apes at zoos, as rated by their caretakers.

Margie Lachman (2004) acknowledged commonality of the midlife crisis, but marveled at the variety of lived experiences. We vary in our midlife expression by factors including "gender, cohort, socioeconomic status (SES), race, ethnicity, culture, region of the country, personality, marital status, parental status, employment status, and health status" (p. 306). Ultimately, while midlife crisis may be common, these many variables affect the experience across cultures. The Tsimané of the Bolivian Andes simply shift roles, the men moving from hunting to more agrarian pursuits. The elder Tsimané are respected for the wisdom they have acquired. Younger people begin to refer to them as *jayej* (grandmother) or *via'* (grandfather) and seek them out for their knowledge of ethics, herbs, and history (Schniter, 2010). Continuing to matter and stay connected as they age, many traditional cultures have no negative concept of midlife crisis. Ironically, even within the US, the midlife crisis is not as common in Western culture as stereotypes lead us to believe, with only 26% of Americans reporting actual crisis symptoms (Wethington, Kessler, & Pixley, 2004).

## Aging and Later Life

*You do not teach the paths of the forest to an old gorilla.*

*African proverb, possibly from the Congo*

A century ago, humans lived 47 years on average. In the US, only 4% made it past age 65. Incredibly, we now can expect to live 72 years if you are male and 79 years if you are female, and those over 65 are now 12% of the population (Gonyea, 2013). If you are Okinawan, you are likely to live even longer, with three times the chances of living more than 100 years (Bendjilali et al., 2014). That frighteningly short 47-year average span was driven in part by high infant mortality, but undoubtedly, there are many, many more old people among us, and we are living longer all the time.

Older years hold very different meanings and experiences across cultures, with variation in how elders are perceived and treated, what duties they must perform, and what roles and positions they fill in a culture. American culture is notoriously youth-oriented, in no small part due to a rapacious media industry focused on novelty and profit potential of the next big thing, which is usually younger and fresher than the last big thing. In the counter-culture movement of the 1960s, a common slogan was "Don't trust anyone over 30." Old people especially embodied a system that was sacrificing its young in the futile Vietnam war. The culture was already rooted in children's stories where the old witches and grandmothers ate little children and poisoned princesses, and respect for elders declined rapidly as the war dragged on. The US is an extreme case, and elders are treated differently in other cultures, as demonstrated in the wisdom section below.

Elders themselves share some similar concerns across cultures. Waugh and McKenzie (2011) interviewed older Aborigines in Sydney, Australia to determine what they felt constituted a life well lived. The researchers identified four themes of concern: identity, family, community, and perceptions of health and aging. Identity referred to sense of purpose and pride as an aboriginal elder. Social connectedness forms the core of the family and community themes. The perceptions theme relates to failing health and abilities and how this affects what they can do for themselves and those around them. Erikson (1963) termed his final stage "integrity versus despair," where the person either feels a sense of accomplishment and connection or faces bitterness and regret. Among the Oriya of Northern India, this is the time when a woman reaches her third stage, having first served her mother-in-law, then ruling the household during middle age, and finally battling irrelevance as a younger woman takes her place and authority (Menon, 2011, 2012). Old age can be a terrible time.

## Caring for Elders

*Among hundreds of virtues, filial piety is the most important one (*bai shan

xiao wei xian*).*

*Traditional Chinese proverb*

At the core of ancient Chinese culture lay the concept of filial piety, reverence and obedience toward one's father and lifelong obligation to care for parents and progenitors. The relevance for cultural psychology rests in the underlying structure of values and beliefs that drive the related motivations and behaviors. In fact, filial piety formed a central avenue of persuasion, as parents pressured offspring toward behaviors and choices they felt were most likely to result in financial stability and care in old age (Wang, Laidlaw, Power, & Shen, 2010). China had an exceptionally institutionalized set of norms for care of elders, but the concept may be widespread across cultures, if not universal: John James (1829) described elders' expectation for love, respect, and caring in the early-American culture of his day. In Arab culture, a similar concept historically exists, but is now stronger in those with traditional values and weaker in urbanized and increasingly individualistic young people (Khalaila & Litwin, 2012).

Expectations for elder care have changed markedly in the West since James's 19th-century observation. Poverty for elders reached highs in the early 20th century but has actually steadily declined (Engelhardt & Gruber, 2004). The peaks followed the industrial revolution, when masses of people moved into cities. That demographic shift broke traditions of extended families under one roof and the norms of caring for elders in the home. Declines in poverty were the result of society-level programs such as Social Security and Medicare.

China, the bastion of enculturated filial piety, faces a struggle between tradition, modernity, and practicality. Young people are leaving rural areas to join industrial workforces and modern culture. Leaving their parents behind is a natural consequence with repercussions as those parents age, and fewer people hold the values and beliefs pressuring them to care for their elders. Beginning in one rural region and gradually spreading to urban areas, a type of contract is now promoted by the government called a Family Support Agreement. What was traditionally taught in childhood has become a matter of legal obligation with substantial penalty if proper care of parents is not provided (Chou, 2011).

## Wisdom

Wisdom represents the culmination of skills and experiences gained through a lifetime, well considered and judiciously shared. Yang (2001) found four factors in descriptions of wisdom by Taiwanese participants: competencies and knowledge, benevolence and compassion, openness and profundity, and modesty and unobtrusiveness. Wisdom stands enshrined in the center of most cultures, from the sages of ancient China to Athena, goddess of wisdom in ancient Greece. Like love, the more wisdom you have, the better, and its absence is universally considered unfortunate (Baltes & Smith, 2008). Wisdom happens suddenly in revelation, as in Christianity and Islam, or through contemplation, as in Buddhism or Hinduism (Walsh, 2011). Wisdom may also be transmitted and nurtured, achieved later in life (Garrett et al., 2014; Kaomea, 2004). Appreciation of wisdom varies with attitudes toward the elderly, who are seen as wellsprings of life by the !Kung (Biesele & Howell, 1981), and as evil, loathsome creatures to be feared in later European folk tales (Grimm, 1883).

Indigenous and First Nations people of the Americas revere elders as keepers of wisdom, the caretakers who nurture and protect the spirit of their tribes and pass on the sacred ways of living in harmony and balance to future generations (Garrett et al., 2014). In Hawaiian culture, elders are called *kupuna*, "the wise ones who have paved the way before us" (Kaomea, 2004, p. 37). *Kupuna* are considered to epitomize Hawaiian values such as *aloha*, *pono*, and *kōkua*. Those words are easy to say, especially *aloha*, which is familiar to anyone who has heard about Hawai'i. The *kupuna* pass these understandings by their example and counsel.

Rather than valuing age and wisdom, American culture lauds youth and stereotypes the elderly as incompetent and cognitively impaired (Hehman & Bugental, 2012). Women particularly suffer from negative views as their bodies change, which fuels momentum to avoid appearance of ageing (Jenkins & Marti, 2012). This is unfortunate, if one considers the benefits advanced age can bring. Wisdom provides perspective to understand and interpret events such that elders are often happier and more cognitively resilient (Etezadi & Pushkar, 2013). Elders are adept at conflict resolution, wisdom providing the skills to strike balance between competing interests and opposing views (Grossman, Karasawa et al., 2012; Yang, 2001). Grossman, Karasawa, and colleagues (2012) observed benefits for young people from a culture that values wisdom, with Japanese youth more capable of using wise-reasoning in conflict resolution than American youth. The youth focus may drive some highly profitable business models, but at the cost of sagacity and the benefits of judicious thought in decision making.

## REALITY CHECK

At what age do you (or did you) expect to assume full adult responsibilities?

How do you feel about the capabilities of old people? Is your evaluation fair?

What happened in your parents' lives when they reached middle age?

Do you expect to become an old person some day? How do you feel about that idea?

## 5.5 DEATH AND DYING

### LO 5.5: Appraise the differing roles older people play in different cultures and potential cognitive approaches to death and how these shape behavior.

*Live fast, die young, have a beautiful corpse.*

Knock on Any Door, *Willard Motley (1947)*

At some point, we all exit our lives, whether gently in our sleep or brutally by inexplicable violence or disaster. Death became our constant companion long before we became modern humans. Archeological evidence suggests that 400,000 years ago our *Homo heidelbergensis* ancestors were laying their loved ones to rest in special ways (Carbonell & Mosquera, 2006) and mortuary practices were certainly present among *Neanderthal* 100,000 years ago (d'Errico et al., 2003). These practices show two things had happened in our brains: we became consciousness of our inevitable mortality and we gained capacity for symbolic thought. Archeology tells us that we actively honored the meaning and memory of the lives and deaths of our loved ones, which highlights ancient awareness of mortality. We memorialized them through symbolic actions of ritual, placing them in particular positions and decorating their resting place with flowers and personal effects, items we imbue with meaning. Our big brains had given us survival skills of cooperation and of making things, with the nasty side-effect of **mortality salience**, which is the psychological term for awareness that we will die.

For all this new awareness, or because of it, we actually spend our lives assiduously *not* thinking about our impending deaths. A hundred-thousand years ago, a lot of large carnivores were eager to kill you, and if you thought too much about them, you might never leave the proverbial cave to get food for the kids, and that is bad parenting in any era. From an evolutionary perspective, we had a problem: the same enlarged brain that was allowing us to flourish by cooperation and communication also informed us that we are doomed. Once we developed the capacity to conceptualize the certainty of death, getting up in the morning became overwhelming, so we had to develop mechanisms to deal with our ongoing existential crisis (Becker, 1971; Greenberg, Pyszczynski, & Solomon, 1986; Rosenblatt, Greenberg, Solomon, Pyszczynski, & Lyon, 1989).

## Mortality and Terror Management Theory

*The idea of death, the fear of it, haunts the human animal like nothing else; it is a mainspring of human activity—designed largely to avoid the fatality of death, to overcome it by denying in some way that it is the final destiny of man.*

*Becker, 1973*

Ernest Becker (1971) attempted to generate a theory that covered all human activity, based in our need to sustain self-esteem and acknowledging our existential struggle with death. We used our mental capacity, in Becker's view, to create formalized belief systems explaining life and what happens after. We have invented myriad daily tasks big and small to make us feel our lives have meaning and importance. We surround ourselves with symbols of our ethnic groups, religions, and football teams to assure us that we are part of a greater family, tribe, or society that will continue after we are gone. These cultural connections link us to a sort of collective immortality. Becker would say that every human activity, everything we think and do as members of a culture, forms a shield built to avoid facing our individual ultimate demise.

Becker may not conclusively have solved the human dilemma, but he succeeded in providing ideas that led to Terror Management Theory (TMT). TMT proposed that, if Becker was correct, we should show the strongest connection to the values and beliefs of our culture when we are most aware of our mortality: we defend against thinking about our death by connecting to our culture. Our ties to a group that will outlive us provide a real sort of immortality via genetics and identity (Routledge, Juhl, Vess, Cathey, & Liao, 2013). Customs and beliefs thereby form our shield against the eternal night. TMT provides a highly cogent model for the ways and reasons culture shapes our thinking.

TMT has now been tested frequently, including work of Greenberg et al. (1986) and extending into the present (c.f. Gailliot, Stillman, Schmeichel, Maner, & Plant, 2008; Yen, 2013). People consistently endorse and protect their culture of origin when prompted with mortality cues, and results are consistent across cultures, ranging from Americans to Tibetan Buddhists (Holbrook & Sousa, 2013). Du and colleagues (2013) found that independent and interdependent ideas of self became stronger in alignment with how participants' cultures think of identity. Cai, Sedikides, and Jiang (2013)

## WHAT IS A GOOD DEATH?

Elderly Mexican American participants said,

- no suffering,

- living life with faith,

- having time for closure with family,

- dying at home, and

- a natural death.

*Source:* Ko et al. (2013)

found that Chinese participants affirmed their familial sense of self when faced with mortality salience. Greenberg and colleagues (2001) found increased acceptance of White Supremacist racism in otherwise-normal white participants reminded of death. Whatever our culture, we cling to it more strongly when reminded of death, providing strong evidence supporting the TMT premise. Culture gives us ways to live better by following what our ancestors have passed down to us, whatever that may be, and connection to culture reduces our anxiety about dying. Whether or not mortality drove creation of culture, the two are inextricably intertwined, providing conscious and unconscious help in dealing with death.

### Thinking About Death

In addition to cultural norms of behavior, we learn ways of thinking that affect our responses to mortality salience and death, and these ways of thinking correspond to the philosophical underpinnings of our cultures. Western culture draws upon Aristotelian logic, which assumes that there is a linear path from question to solution, that life and events move in strict progression, and that reality falls into bimodal categories of yes or no, light or dark, good or bad, etc. Death is absence of life and should be resisted at all costs, and hence was personified into combatable human form, such as Hades among the ancient Greeks or Anubis among the Egyptians (Bryant & Peck, 2009). Modern medical doctors carefully dissociate from death, beginning with their first exposure to a training cadaver (B. Robbins, 2012). Death is firmly excluded from Western thinking, if at all possible, and if it creeps in, Dylan Thomas instructs us to deny that finality: "Do not go gentle into that good night. Rage, rage against the dying of the light."

Asian thought is based in the concept of yin and yang, in which nothing exists without also containing the seeds of its opposite, the white dot in the black half, the black dot in the white, death in life and life in death. What goes down will come up, and even the darkest badness contains some good. All things are connected, and we live better lives by understanding our place in the ebb and flow of events around us. These are characteristic principles of holistic thought. Over the past four millennia of continuous culture, the Chinese have embraced Taoism, Confucianism, and Buddhism, overlapping and continuing together as philosophies underlying their worldview. Part of this way of thinking is the knowing that death and life are connected aspects of a continuous cycle (Hsu, O'Connor, & Lee, 2013). On his deathbed in 1837, 88-year-old Zen monk Sengai Gibon expressed an approach to death very different from Thomas's:

> He who comes knows only his coming.
>
> He who goes knows only his end.
>
> To be saved from the chasm
>
> Why cling to the cliff?
>
> Clouds floating low
>
> Never know where the breeze will blow them.
>
> Sengai Gibon (1749–1837; in Hoffmann, 1986, p. 114)

Christine Ma-Kellams and Jim Blascovich (2012) studied differences between European Americans and East Asians living in California in what came to mind once mortality salience (MS) was triggered. The East Asians' ancestry was either Korean, Chinese, or Japanese, all related cultures with connection to Taoist, Confucian, and Buddhist traditions. In five experiments, the researchers provided an MS prompt, measuring whether participants thoughts related to life or to death, and finally, whether stimulating holistic or analytic thinking altered participants' ways of thinking about life and death. Results clearly showed that, when reminded of their mortality, the Euro-Americans dwelt on death while the East Asians affirmed enjoyment of life activities. When pushed to think analytically or holistically, the way of thinking overrode ancestry, suggesting that thinking style is the important factor and that East Asians naturally exhibited the life affirming, holistic approach to death unless stimulated to think analytically.

TMT studies like those of Ma-Kellams and Blascovich (2012) tell us that we universally react to mortality salience by retreating toward our culture. The resulting thoughts and the effects of those thoughts on our lives are not universal. While both groups defended against thinking of mortality, as TMT predicts, they used different methods. The Euro-Americans shift to rigid cultural adherence, even softening their feelings toward White Supremacists. The holistic way of thinking still moved toward cultural norms, but it endorsed a more positive, life-affirming adaptation style. Studies of holistic thinking styles frequently refer to Asian cultures, but could include other non-Western cultures such as the Māori, who place high value on sense of connectedness to the land, family, tribe, and spirit (Durie, 1995, 1994), and probably choose healthier thoughts relating to death. Culturally embedded concepts such as mindfulness, practiced in meditation, have developed over several millennia to support positive adaptation to mortality. Buddhism arose, their scriptures say, from Siddhartha Gautama's sudden exposure to suffering and death, from which he had been shielded since birth.

Sitting under the bodhi tree, he found unity with everything, and by his connection to the eternal, he moved beyond fears of a finite individual existence. Greater access to life-affirming thoughts may allow us to live more peacefully and with less turmoil about our impending deaths.

## Grieving: Those Who Still Live

*She said she usually cried at least once each day not because she was sad, but because the world was so beautiful & life was so short.*

*Brian Andreas*

What happens to us after we die is the topic of philosophy and religion, but what happens with those left behind is fair game for psychology. We have to cope with loss and adjust in ways that allow us to go on living, paying bills, and feeding the children. We grieve for those we have lost, and it reminds us that we too shall pass (see Figure 5.1). This is true, perhaps minus the bills, no matter what your culture might be.

### The Circle of Life: Connecting Ancestors and Descendants

Mexican culture celebrates *Día de los Muertos*, the day of the dead, connected to the Christian set of All Hallows Eve, All Saints Day, and All Souls Day, beginning with what America calls Halloween. Halloween coincides with the ancient pre-Christian festival of Samhain, which celebrated harvest and, by extension, our human harvest by the grim reaper. Halloween/All Souls draws on rhythms of season and harvest from ancient tradition to normalize death for children and adults much as Easter drew on the life-renewal of festivals in Assyria and Babylon celebrating the fertility goddess Ishtar in Spring. In short, we like to create ways to remember and celebrate our connection to those who have gone before, and tying us to the ongoing continuities of human existence.

Chinese culture has venerated ancestors for more than 4,000 years, based on archeological evidence from the ancient Shang dynasty (Li, 2000).

**Figure 5.1   Weeping Angel in Cemetery**

**Figure 5.2  Temple and Lanterns at Obon Festival**

In rituals each year, the ancestors are invited back to eat, drink, and dance with the living. The ancestors watch over the living, and if we treat them well, they assure our success in this world. In Japan, and especially in Okinawan culture, the ancestors are revered in the summer *Obon* festival, based on an event where the Buddha assisted in liberating a disciple's departed mother trapped in the purgatorial Bardo realm. The format of *Obon* largely follows the ancestral rituals that preceded it, with the departed invited to return from the spirit realm to commune with the living, then sent back with fond thanks to their realm again (see Figure 5.2).

These celebrations have different significance in their respective religions, but they share a common function for the living. If we view these rituals from a perspective of TMT, by connecting to our ancestors and communing with them for a few hours, we also connect ourselves to our descendants (whom we expect to continue the ritual) and therefore to immortality. In truth, we are *literally* connected to both ancestors and descendants, being the active expression of our genetic and cultural line at this moment, from those who provided our genes and toward those we will help create. The psychological mechanisms of TMT are based in reality. We are the living hopes and dreams of those who came before us, and our children carry our own wishes and aspirations into the future (see Figure 5.3).

**Figure 5.3   Memorial Lanterns at Obon Festival**

## SPOTLIGHT

### GIBRAN, THE PROPHET, ON DEATH

*And behold I have found that which is greater than wisdom.*

*It is a flame spirit in you ever gathering more of itself,*

*While you, heedless of its expansion, bewail the withering of your days.*

*It is life in quest of life in bodies that fear the grave.*

*There are no graves here.*

*These mountains and plains are a cradle and a stepping-stone.*

*Whenever you pass by the field where you have laid your ancestors look well thereupon, and you shall see yourselves and your children dancing hand in hand.*

—Khalil Gibran (1923), *The Prophet*

Why would culture help us fear death less?

Have you known anyone who died? How did their death affect you?

## 5.6 ARTS AND DEVELOPMENT ACROSS CULTURES

### LO 5.6: Evaluate the roles of arts in cultural transmission, life changes, and social processes.

Arts weave through our lives in very obvious ways, beginning with lullabies and nursery rhymes, and we remember tunes from our youth even after dementia has claimed the rest of our minds. Finally, we exit life to laments and dirges sung or played to honor our passing, though the music may really be there for benefit of those left behind. Arts convey our systems of meaning and the symbols representing the concepts we use to explain life, packaged so it can be transmitted and remembered as easily as your ABC's, which you probably also learned as a song (Frith, 1996; Hargreave & North, 1999; Kashima, 2000, 2008; Turino, 1999).

Our mothers sing to us, and we learn that music makes us feel good, but the content of our lullabies also begins our early enculturation: we learn language, values, and beliefs from the start (Trehub, 2009). Perhaps because of its close association with language, we enter the world familiar with the scales and sounds of our native music, and cognitions about the things we hear and see begin to optimize our ability to perceive and interpret our world efficiently. Very soon, we know melodies for church or games. Those songs help us to bond with our villages, tribes, or ethnic groups as we grow, the social-psychological functions of music being shared even if it sounds very different.

> Timo (Samoan dance/music): *They [youth] all get stuck into it [Samoan music and dance]—lose themselves in it, but also they learn the skills of dancing in a line, being together, moving together, singing in rhythm . . . you're trying to get them to stand still to show discipline, to show everybody's ready as a team, as one when you move.* (Fox, 2010, pp. 118–119)

Houses are arguably among our most important artistic creations, being the sculptures we inhabit. As mentioned earlier, the presence of square corners in our buildings shape our perceptual skills, including susceptibility to the Müller-Lyer Illusion (see Chapter 7), while those who grow up in a teepee are not affected. We represent the

# SPOTLIGHT

## BEETHOVEN'S YOUTHFUL ANGST

Beethoven's Second Symphony is a crass monster, a hideously writhing wounded dragon, that refuses to expire, and though bleeding in the Finale, furiously beats about with its tail erect.

(Zeitung fur die Elegente Welt, Vienna, May 1804)

concepts of our cultures in visual imagery, and our children use them as cognitive maps of those concepts. We know a cross on a building means church, or the painted carvings of a Māori *marae* tell the stories of ancestors. Across the arts, we remember our origins and systems of knowledge, and from these we create identity.

> Mina (Philippine dance): *Dance would remind us where we come from, where we are now, and where we are heading tomorrow. It's always there.* (Fox, 2010, p. 107)

Learning an art gives people skills beyond the art itself. As with any cultural learning process, whether formal master-apprentice or informal, the relationship between transmitter and receiver of the information and skills will reflect hierarchic structures of the culture. Further, if one learns to paint, the visual content will be drawn from the system of knowledge for that culture, as will the words of a song or the message of a story. In learning an art, the person learns the culture.

We sing out our adolescent angst and bond over new musical styles in our teens, and this is not new. Beethoven's early compositions brought howls of protest that he would bring the fall of civilization with his horrid music, now considered sublime, even into his 30s. We are forging our lasting friendships by adolescence, and music is an important medium for bonding. Rap and hip-hop music form a complex set of issues for adolescents and young adults. In the US, they are associated with gangs, gun violence and misogyny, and years of research supports validity of this connection (Anderson, Carnagey, & Eubanks, 2003; Bryant, 2008). Kopano (2002) conversely finds rap a crucial, healthy outlet for expression of rebellion against continued discrimination. Hadley and Yancy (2012) advocate rap as an effective tool of music therapy, much as Farr (1997) utilized hip-hop dance therapy for at risk youths. Travis (2013) recently examined effects of rap on empowerment and identity, which he judged to be favorable. The genre has now spread widely into Korea, Japan, Germany, the Philippines, and elsewhere. Diana Boer and colleagues found that musical taste formed a basis of favorable feelings toward those who shared a love of heavy metal or rap that spanned across countries and ethnicities (Boer, 2009; Boer et al., 2011).

As adults, the roles of innovation reverse and we are the ones singing the traditional songs and telling the old stories. Outside of Western pop-culture and its focus on youth, music and dance can bring intergenerational bonding.

> Mina *(Filipina dancer): When we get together, we sing and dance, and so perhaps I would see—and I admired my elders who were able to dance, and despite their age, they were able to move their hands and turn and twirl. So perhaps I have also inherited it from them, and I'm glad that the environment encouraged me to develop that liking.* (Fox, 2010, p. 121)

Music provides the background for our rites of passage, including *bar mitzvahs*, weddings, coronations, and funerals. The familiarity of the music of those occasions provides a cognitive bridge to renew our connection to those sharing celebration of the passage with us (V. Turner, 1982a). The Kaluli of Papua New Guinea use music as a medium of communication with the dead after they have left, a process shared across cultures celebrating connection to ancestors (Cross, 2001; Feld, 1982).

Throughout our lives, visual and musical arts provide interactive staging and soundtrack for our existence. Simultaneously, arts help us to be healthier and happier, as a growing body of evidence demonstrates. Musical training nurtures neural development, including a more robust corpus callosum connecting our brains' hemispheres (Schlaug, 2009; Steele, Bailey, Zatorre, & Penhune, 2013). Musical children do better in math, and theater students do better in language tasks, among a growing list of ways arts affect skills in other areas (Lamont, 2009; Rauscher, 2009). Arts programs have documented positive effects on self-esteem, conflict resolution skills, and relationship skills (Rapp-Paglicci et al., 2006).

The strangest thing about research into effects of arts and arts programs on development is that we are researching something that is now unusual, something added to some lives and absent in others. In a hundred thousand years of humanity, arts have never before been separate from our lives. We sang and danced together, we crafted the items we needed, we inscribed our symbols into cliffs and painted them on our cave walls (e.g., Cross, 2009; Gaunt, 2006; V. Turner, 1982b). Our children learned our cultures while they learned our arts and passed them to their children, and they had fun doing it. In our headlong rush toward technology and specialization, we may have lost something crucial for developing into healthy, happy people.

## REFLECTING ON YOUR READING

- From where did your parents say babies come?

- Did you and/or your siblings sleep alone, together, or with your parents?

- Did you learn any special skills from your parents?

- How certain do you feel about your identity at this point in your life?

- Does death frighten you?

# CHAPTER 5 SUMMARY

## 5.1 Perspectives on Development

We humans all face a journey from conception to death that follows a similar process. This chapter discusses how culture shapes us along the way, forming the "nurture" side of the nature-nurture debate in psychology. People change across biosocial, cognitive, and psychosocial domains, and we do this as members of cohorts, born around the same time and place, and often sharing socioeconomic statuses.

To explain these processes, psychologists have proposed developmental theories, ranging from Freud's psychodynamic theories about sexuality and pleasure to Watson's behavioral models, to Piaget's cognitive processes.

Humans generally conceive of life as happening in stages that are more or less the same, even if some details differ. We pass through those stages at social junctures such as maturity and marriage. Some psychologists, however, have described the stages based on achieving capacities or milestones, or as a fluid, without clear points of change.

Early theorists saw development as being complete by adulthood. More recent theories include changes that happen from birth to death.

## 5.2 Birth and Infancy

Cultural differences begin before birth. Differences include concepts of where babies come from and roles of parents. These are part of systems of ethnotheories specific to cultures.

Early differences include epigenetic factors that result in differences in outcome not predicted by our genes, including foods a mother may eat and diseases or toxins (teratogens) she may encounter that affect the fetus.

Childbirth remains a time of uncertainty, and people have developed ethnotheories and practices to make the process as safe and secure as possible, within the constraints of cultural knowledge.

Humans are born with large brains and helpless bodies. The child's experiences and interactions begin to make immediate differences in development.

The child's massive set of neurons continue to proliferate for several months as the child is adapting to a certain language and environment.

Language acquisition happens more easily during infancy, which is an early sensitive period. Infancy is a crucial time for forming bonds with caregivers, setting patterns of relationship that continue through life. Parents immediately begin to treat infants in very different ways endorsed by their cultures, including their sleeping arrangements.

## 5.3 Childhood

Early childhood is a time of rapid growth and learning. Toddlers begin walking, which makes them more mobile and begins a series of cultural differences in upbringing.

Attachment Theory holds that children need to bond with caregivers to grow up secure and healthy. Cross-cultural differences have been observed in the manner of bonding preferred in cultural groups, suggesting the theory may be the product of Western culture. The behavior of parents toward their children reflects what they learned in childhood.

The Terrible Twos are a time when children in Western culture develop behavioral problems as they attempt to assert independence and autonomy. The stage is not necessarily shared as a universal across cultures, and may have roots in characteristics of language.

In early childhood, we rapidly learn language and develop theory of mind, whatever our culture. Those around teach us to regulate our bodies and our emotional expression. Psychology debates whether temperament is genetically determined or molded by interaction styles.

Childhood is generally a time of good health. Erikson posits the child negotiates the challenge of industry versus inferiority, learning to be competent at skills of a specific culture and a particular sense of self in their cultural context. As we learn in a cultural context, our physiology is adapting to our physical environment.

Vygotsky proposed the concept of scaffolding, in which we are helped from nearly having an ability, the zone of proximal development, to mastering it. Our mentors and the content we are learning varies, the process of enculturation.

In Western cultures, parents and schools direct learning. Other systems of learning are also highly effective for the content they convey. In all cultures, learning begins with songs and stories and becomes more complex as the child's cognitive capacities develop.

For cultures to live on, cultural learning must occur, with ways of knowing and being passed to subsequent generations. The child learns her origins, customs, behavioral expectations, and identity during this process.

Apprenticeships be formal or informal, with the goal of transmitting a specific set of complex skills. Simultaneously, the apprentice is learning other aspects of living and being from the mentor. Relationship between apprentice and master also differs in terms of obligations and commitments.

## 5.4 Adolescence Through Adulthood

Adolescence marks the transition when a person gains the capacity to reproduce. The juncture is ritualized in cultures in order to mark changing roles and responsibilities, both internally and socially. The person accepts new roles or identity. Within Western culture, it is a time of rebellion against familial and cultural constraints. In other cultures, choices are more constrained. Adolescence is a time of great risk if the cultural context includes violence or war.

Traditional culture included mechanisms for changing roles and creating identity. Cultural changes of globalization and technology have eroded these mechanisms, causing harm particularly to indigenous youth. Some ethnic groups are rebounding via revitalization of cultural mechanisms and processes.

People continue to change across the lifespan, with specific roles and expectations changing within those contexts. Adults create relationships and families, raise children and contribute to social groups.

Emerging adulthood is a new concept, with technological and societal changes demanding longer learning periods for certain roles. Emerging adulthood draws to a close as neural development maximizes in the late 20s. It is a time when mental illnesses may develop, and this is more common for ethnic minorities. Becoming an adult may take longer now and include more psychological risks.

In mature years, people pass into sustaining and directing roles. The quality of relationships influence well-being. Mid-life crisis is primarily a construct of Western culture, but the changes of ageing bodies and altered social standing causes stress in many cultures. A person may move into a respected position at this time of life.

We live much longer now, so many more people are entering old age. All face questions of failing health and altered social roles. Cultures vary in the esteem imbued or withheld from older people causing worry about sense of meaning and purpose as physical abilities decline. Familial care of elders has become increasingly less common as cultures advance technologically. Concepts of filial piety have been replaced with contractual obligations in China.

*Wisdom* is the term for cognitive and interpersonal skills gained primarily through age and experience. Age and wisdom are valued differently, primarily in greater valuing of youth in modern American culture. Wisdom brings benefits of ways of thinking associated with happiness and well-being, and with effective conflict resolution.

## 5.5 Death and Dying

We all die. We are aware of mortality, termed mortality salience. Becker proposed that we use our mental abilities in part to avoid thinking about death, which is a reason we developed cultures. His ideas contributed to terror management theory, which examined mechanisms used to ignore mortality. Fear of death leads us to adhere to values and beliefs of our cultures more strongly.

Western culture sees life in linear terms, while other cultures have an encompassing, holistic view of life as a cycle. This leads different cognitions when reminded of death, with holistic thinkers tending toward life-affirming thoughts. We all grieve for loved ones who have passed. People maintain cognitive connection across generations by annual rituals in which ancestors are remembered. In TMT terms, this reduces our anxiety about death by highlighting the continuity of our culture and family.

## 5.6 Arts and Development Across Cultures

Arts have been an intrinsic part of human development until recent years. They form a conduit of cultural transmission and maintenance and increase our well-being by connecting us to others.

## GLOSSARY

**Biosocial:** In development, an approach that acknowledges both biological and social influences.

**Cognitive:** Related to thinking processes.

**Cohort:** A group of individuals who share a common locale and timeframe. In developmental psychology, those who are born in the same time and place.

**Critical periods:** Points in the lifespan when something must happen if it is to be.

**Developmental theories:** In psychology, constructs attempting to predict how human growth shapes the cognitions, beliefs, and behaviors of individuals as general laws.

**Enculturation:** The process of natural indoctrination, especially during childhood, wherein a person learns the behaviors and beliefs required of members of a culture.

**Epigenetic:** In development, factors outside genetics that affect how a person grows and develops.

**Ethnotheory:** Implicit beliefs about how things should be that underlie the values and practices of a culture.

**In utero:** The time of life before birth, while the child lives in the womb.

**Limina:** Thresholds, usually of perception of a sensation. Also, a threshold between life stages. (singular = limin)

**Mortality salience:** Conscious awareness of the inevitability of one's own death.

**Nature versus nurture:** Name for the long running debate of whether people are born with innate traits that shape who they become or are shaped by environmental influences.

**Psychosocial:** Concepts related to both psychological and social factors.

**Sensitive periods:** Times in the lifespan when something may happen more easily.

**Socioeconomic status (SES):** The social standing and economic resources that determine available options and conditions in a person's life.

**Teratogens:** Harmful agents that can affect a fetus in utero, such as diseases and toxic substances.

**Zone of proximal development (ZPD):** The developmental concept of skills and abilities a person is nearly achieving and can do with slight assistance.

# CLOSE RELATIONSHIPS

# PREPARING TO READ

- Who should have more friends, a collectivist in Africa or an individualist in North America?

- Does an elder grandfather or grandmother need to be consulted before you make a life decision such as choosing your college major?

- Are marriages chosen for love clearly more or less happy than arranged marriages?

*Once, a very long time ago, even before the Han kingdoms went to war, a young herder took his flock into the hills around the headwaters of the Yangtse to nibble the lush grasses of late spring. His elder brother's wife had driven him out of the family home, and he found relief wandering the valleys day by day, enjoying the solitude and the cool breezes as his animals grazed. One day, Niulang (literally, "cowherd") spotted a fine silk robe on the bank by a peaceful pond. He picked it up and, seeing nobody nearby, began to wander on carrying it.*

*The robe belonged to the youngest of seven daughters of the king and queen of the heavenly celestial realm. Zhinü (literally, "weaver girl") had slipped away from the tedium of weaving clouds, which was her chore, to swim in the soothing waters of that particularly refreshing Chinese stream. Seeing her robe being taken, she gasped, and the herder turned to behold her in her lovely nakedness. The two therefore had to marry because when a virtuous woman is seen disrobed, only marriage to the one who beheld her can restore her honor. They lived for several earthly years in a loving marriage that produced much joy and two beautiful children.*

*Eventually, the queen of the heavens noticed her youngest daughter was missing and ordered her located and brought back to the skies. The two lovers despaired, for they were of different worlds, she a celestial being and he a mere mortal. The daughter was returned to the heavens. The herder happened, as is the case in mythic stories, to have an ox that was a magical creature that then gave its life and hide to transport the herder and the children to heaven. The queen was so angry that the mortal dared violate the heavens that she cast them out and slashed a river of stars across the sky to divide the lovers. We now call that dividing river the Milky Way.*

*The shepherd and the cloud weaver felt bereft, but they were also both beloved of the sky beings and the creatures of the earth. The queen eventually relented, allowing them to reunite for one day each year, and on the seventh day of the seventh month, the birds of earth joyfully fly up to make a bridge across the river of stars so the lovers can meet again.*

—Ancient Chinese tale

The tale of the bridge of birds has been told and retold for many centuries at the time of the *Qixi* festival in China. The details change, but the story always includes romance between the lovers from heaven and earth, represented by the stars Vega and Altair, and forbidden to be together by their social roles and responsibilities. In its basic form, the story mirrors *Romeo and Juliet*, and the earlier Cathar tale of *Abelarde and Heloise* on which Shakespeare based his tragedy. The stories speak of our memberships in groups that existed before we were born, ones perhaps in conflict with other groups, and of fondness that may arise between two people regardless of those larger affiliations.

## 6.1 ROLES AND INTERPERSONAL RELATIONSHIPS

### LO 6.1 Describe how roles form the structure of human relationships.

He aha te mea nui o te ao?

He tangata! He tangata! He tangata!

*What is the most important thing in the world?*

*It is people! It is people! It is people!*

*Māori proverb*

The previous sections discussed general constructs of culture and how culture shapes our lives; we now turn to more intimate contexts of relationship. Over the vast span of human existence, we have established frameworks of organization for our social groups in which individuals hold statuses or perform functions that are predictable and that endure as part of our cultures (Moffett, 2013). We describe our relationships with others by the part we play, what we generally call our role, a terminology taken directly from theater (Gusfield, 1989b). As with theatrical roles, social relationship titles are anonymous in that the role continues to exist independent of a particular person who may hold that status for a limited time. In English, we may be a father, mother, child, brother, sister, or friend, and we may be several of these at once. Fiske and Fiske (2007) describe 15 roles (see Table 6.1) they say are salient across cultures that are "culturally elaborated, socially institutionalized, cognitively schematized, and emotionally motivated" (p. 283). We are motivated, they write, to relate in order to establish belonging,

## Table 6.1 The 15 Categories of Formalized Relationships

| Relationship | Description |
| --- | --- |
| Marriage | Life commitment to one or more spouses |
| In-lawship | Relations with the family of one's spouse |
| Joking and funerary relationships | Parties joke and tease in normative ways and may have obligations to attend funerals or execute estates |
| Compadrazgo | Relationship with the parents of one's godchild, common in Catholic countries |
| Agemates | Typically males of similar age who aid each other in warfare and raiding and who share resources in fellowship and feasting |
| Kinship | An organizing system based on shared social identity, usually transmitted paternally or maternally, involving cooperation and sharing |
| Milk-kinship | Most important in Islamic societies, the bond between a woman and a child not her own whom she nursed |
| Ritual covenant | A bond of aid, trust, and altruism established by ritual sharing of blood |
| Reciprocal exchange of prestige goods | Participants give each other ritual gifts in processes in which the gift may be of little value but the process constitutes a formal bond |
| Rotating credit association | A group that meets regularly in which participants contribute equally to a pool which one person draws at each meeting |
| Sodalities and secret societies | Voluntary groups formed to perform political, moral, ritual, or religious activities |
| Castes | Social categories established by birth that affect social contact, hierarchy, and marriage |
| Slavery | One person owns another and holds rights to the time, activities, and products of that person |
| Prostitution and concubinage | A person is supported or paid in exchange for performance of sexual activities |
| Totemic | A group or individual identified with an animal, plant, or natural phenomenon, often marrying exogamously (outside the group) |

Source: Fiske and Fiske (2007).

understanding, self-enhancement, and trust, goals that all require the presence of others. We achieve those goals by our participation in the relational structures available in our culture. Not all of these roles happen in every culture; a role like president requires a very large political institution. A priest-penitent relationship requires a particular church. We will focus on several more common one-to-one relationships in subsequent pages.

## Friendships

Perhaps the least complex of relationship roles is that of friendship: people simply drawn together by shared interests and enjoyment of each other's company. In the Western ideal, friendships are open-ended and unconstrained, voluntary association, free of monitoring in exchange (Silver, 1989). Involvement with friends provides a healthy, secure base as people move from life with family into adulthood (Fraley, Roisman, Booth-LaForce, Owen, & Holland, 2013), and extended social networks provide support for coping with major and minor stressors (Taylor, Chatters, Woodward, & Brown, 2013). The urge for friendship is shared by our primate relatives and was demonstrated in a recent study involving the chimp-like bonobo (Demuru & Palagi, 2012). Three bonobo were placed in separate cages for each trial, with doors that provided opportunity to share with either a known bonobo or one it had never met. Most often, the bonobo with food shared with the unknown one to make friends, then the new friends together tripped a gate to invite the third to eat with them. The bonobo used the food and the opportunity to forge new friendship bonds. The need for companionship extends across species as diverse as donkeys, birds, and rodents (Murray, Byrne, & D'Eath, 2013), and forms a universal among creatures related to us.

Beyond the basics, the dynamics of friendship start to look different across cultures. The English word *friendship* may relate to several of Fiske and Fiske's (2007) categories, such as joking and funerary relationships, *compadrazgo*, and agemates. In many cultures, relationships may include more formalized obligations or responsibilities that fit poorly into the nebulous Western category of friendship. Non-Western people surely enjoy time spent relaxing and having fun with those around them, if presented with the opportunity, and rely on those people when in need. In most ways, friendship is a common theme but with differences that emerge on closer examination.

In the 1980s, Harry Triandis and colleagues began to explore how concepts like the individualism-collectivism dimension would affect relationships. Triandis, Bontempo, Villareal, Asai, and Lucca (1988) proposed that in collectivist cultures, vertical relationships like parent-child and boss-employee would be most important, whereas in individualist cultures, horizontal relations like friend to friend and spouse to spouse would be paramount. Individualists, they explained, may move fluidly through many friendships, whereas collectivists would have deeper connections with others, but surprisingly, would have fewer friendships. The deeply rooted cultural mechanisms that underlie the differences bear some explanation.

In Western cultures, they saw the self treated as individual and discreet from the people, things, and creatures around us. This would be an implicit view, built into our ways of thinking and perceiving, operating without conscious awareness. In more traditional cultures like those of Ghana, where relational-interdependent constructions of reality are the norm, people do not feel separate; they are connected to each other, and to the land and living things around them (Adams & Plaut, 2003). This is true of other more traditional and collectivist cultures, such as Polynesian cultures like the Māori, and indigenous cultures of North America (c.f. Durie, 1994, and Gone, 2008b, respectively). Adams and Plaut (2003) propose that these are more than simply beliefs, but rather, form the patterns of thought and meaning that we replicate in our relationships and institutions, from friendship to business to marriage.

More friends, for an individualist or a collectivist, mean more support, which is good. More friends also mean more people to whom one must *give* support, and with a deep sense of connectedness, one cannot simply walk away when obligations become too much. Collectivist friendships may span generations, and obligations are not easily shirked. Where an American can simply un-friend that person mentioned in Chapter 4 who becomes overly demanding or who phones drunk late at night one time too many, the collectivist perhaps cannot. Adams and Plaut's (2003) research in Ghana demonstrated expected differences between the two cultures. While Americans may have more friends, they feel more loneliness because the feelings of connection may be shallow and fleeting. Ghanaians expect their friends to provide material and emotional support, and to provide companionship and emotional disclosure. Their friendships are lasting, close, and rewarding, but yield more obligations, and are best considered carefully before making that commitment. For Americans, it is a sad thing to lack friends but not necessarily a sign of character defect, while to Ghanaians, a person without friends is strange and disturbing, and probably is too selfish to keep friends.

Efficacy of the individualism-collectivism relational platform established by Triandis et al. (1988) has been demonstrated many times in cross-cultural research, and research into underlying factors continues. Wheeler, Reis, and Bond (1989) contrasted social versus individual orientation in Chinese and American students, finding that Americans had more interactions, but Chinese interactions with friends lasted longer. More recently, Schug, Yuki, and Maddux (2010) investigated the concept of *relational mobility* as a driving force in variation in dynamics of friendship. Interestingly, high relational mobility, where people can more easily leave friendships, causes people to work harder to maintain friendships, disclosing more information to increase intimacy. Friendships reflect the thoughts and values that shape all of our relationships, whether professional, familial, or intimate.

## Family

*We naturally develop a liking to those, who have long been the objects of our beneficence, especially when we consider them as dependent on us: and it is further natural, for persons who have lived long together, to be unwilling to part.*

*Beattie, 1783*

Family forms a most basic human social unit. The concept of family seems straightforward, but only when viewed within one's own culture. Definitions and descriptions of families differ incredibly between cultures, and families are shifting into new forms and expanded definitions as globalization and commercial media set off massive seismic shifts in traditional social landscapes (Bengtson, 2001; Georgas, 2003; Otters & Hollander, 2015).

Anthropologist George Murdock (1949) provided the quintessential working definition of family: "The family is a social group characterized by common residence, economic cooperation, and reproduction. It includes adults of both sexes, at least two of whom maintain a socially approved sexual relationship, and one or more children, own or adopted, of the sexually cohabiting adults" (p. 1). This definition is severely outdated, given growing trends toward alternative lifestyles in the West, including recent legalization of same-sex marriage in the US, New Zealand, Ireland, Taiwan, and numerous other countries. What does remain across cultures and eras are the common dimensions of structure and function, within which variations occur. Structure includes the number and types of people involved and their defined roles, while function includes raising of children; provision of food, shelter, and clothing; working for economic resources; and satisfaction of emotional and psychological needs (Georgas, 2011).

### Family Structure

The structure of family in Western culture stereotypically revolves around a nuclear family of father, mother, and children. Convention holds that multiple generations lived together in agricultural settings prior to the 19th and 20th centuries, when nuclear families became the desired norm (Georgas, 2011; Ruggles, 2012). People moved increasingly to cities to work in factories, shops, and banks, leaving extended families and farm life behind. Outside of Western origin cultures, this shift was not as prevalent.

In non-Western cultures, families may normatively be larger and more complex, as is typical of agricultural societies (Georgas, 2003). Multigenerational families may share a house or a compound, including multiple parenting couples, elders, and cousins, or the extended family may not live together but may be very actively involved in day-to-day life functions (Georgas et al., 2001). Relations with extended family may be more formalized than in Western culture. Malaysian culture has specific named roles for collateral kinship relationships with cousins, aunts, uncles, and other extended family, so there is a title by which one addresses a parent's eldest brother (*pak long*) or eldest sister (*mak long*). Cousins who are older are called *kakak*, if female, and *abang*, if male, which are the same terms for older siblings. Younger relatives are not always given honorific titles. Further, family obligations may be much more binding, so if your father's cousin's third son comes to town to attend college, you may be expected to host him for several years.

Marriage may take a number of forms in terms of male or female partners, greatly influencing roles and hierarchies, along with distribution of authority. If your father had four wives, you may have a number of siblings and several mothers telling you to do your chores. In a few cultures like the Nyinba of Nepal, women have multiple husbands, so their family structure might include several elder males to respect and obey, though only the oldest one may officially be considered the father (Levine, 1980; Levine & Silk, 1997).

In the 21st century, families are changing, but in complex patterns. An apparent shift toward nuclear families is ongoing in countries and cultures that traditionally live in extended settings, but recent research shows they maintain very close functional relations with their kin (Georgas, 2003; Georgas et al., 2001). Families are still highly intertwined; even if they now live in separate homes or towns, they continue to come together for meals, holidays, religious activities, and so on. Functional interactions among extended family members were more important than family structure, and viewed from the functional level of analysis, the psychological implications of modern roles and family structures become easier to understand. Livelihood and childcare may still be shared in families much as they have been historically, perhaps with small children all going to a grandmother's house when parents work.

Interestingly, multigenerational households are becoming more common again in Western cultures due to increased longevity, shared family functions, and new relational definitions (Bengtson, 2001). Economic and practical realities now push together larger family groups as children may take years to achieve economic independence or boomerang back after leaving, and elderly parents may receive better care for less expense at home (Bianchi, 2014; Duxbury & Dole, 2015; Otters & Hollander, 2015). These issues are compounded for many immigrant families, such as Mexican families in the US, for whom living in multigenerational extended households may be culturally normative (Richter & Pflegerl, 2001), and where families may be forced to live together because parents may lack legal status or economic means (Leach, 2014). Further, as societies become more tolerant of homosexuality, divorce, out-of-wedlock sex, and other non-traditional life choices, single parent and same-sex or nonbinary households are increasingly common (Vespa, Lewis, & Kreider, 2013).

Differences in norms arise from histories diverging across hundreds or thousands or years. The recent family changes due to increased tolerance, migration, and globalization simply reflect our current status in the march of humanity through time, a manifestation shaped by sociocultural and historical context.

## Parenting

From a garden snail to a president, we all have parents who contributed our genetic material. With the snail, parenting ends when eggs are deposited, and the little snails are left to fend for themselves. For warm-blooded creatures, parenting extends beyond birth for some amount of time, fulfilling the biological and social requirements of a species, until the offspring can make its own way. Elephants live in matriarchal herds, while canines live in packs with an alpha-male leader, and emperor penguins live in nuclear families amidst huge nesting colonies. Mother mammals have obvious roles in birth and lactation, and are the primary caregivers for most species. For about 40% of primates, though, the father plays some role in parenting the offspring (Smuts & Gubernick, 1992).

Operating for its first century from a Euro-American viewpoint, some of what psychology assumed should constitute normative and healthy parenting practices may simply be culture-specific norms and ideas, and really may simply be Western *ethnotheories*. When wider cultural variation is considered, some Western practices are considered undesirable elsewhere, such as having babies sleep alone and cry themselves to sleep. Parenting practices derive from the lore passed down across generation, and the resulting families reflect the social structures of each culture. Is the family more individualist or more collectivist? Is there a high power distance with an authoritarian head of household or a more egalitarian structure where all family members have voice and make independent choices? Exposure to our peculiar family lives train us in the values and behaviors we take with us into adulthood, shaping our thoughts and decisions along the way, and making us into whatever types of parents we become. In short, our parents teach us by example how to parent (for better or worse).

## Fathers

> *There is government, when the prince is prince, and the minister is minister; when the father is father, and the son is son.*
>
> *Confucius, Analects XII, 11, trans. Legge, 1861/2014*

Mothers unquestionably hold the paramount position in terms of child rearing, even in highly patriarchal China. They give birth and lactate, and those bonds cannot be surpassed by any male activities in usual situations. Maternal involvement is a cross-cultural universal, though exact details of how mothers and children interact do change, as discussed in the Development chapter. Everywhere, mothers are the ones who most directly transmit culture to their children, from earliest lullabies onward (c.f. Bornstein et al., 2012; Shand & Kosawa, 1985), but fathers also have important roles in many human cultures. Chinese culture is traditionally organized around the concept of filial piety, devotion and obedience to the father as head of the household, a structure that is reflected up to the national level where the emperor or Communist Party chairman is given this absolute respect as father of the country (Jankowiak, 1992).

Paternal roles vary widely, despite the crucially ubiquitous initial biological role. After conception, though the requisite job is done, paternal care is associated with species like humans that have longer gestation and juvenile times, and may play a role in human ability to bond emotionally (Fraley, Brumbaugh, & Marks, 2005). Culture determines the shape of that involvement, guiding variation in practical responsibilities and normative activities that follow birth. Paternal behavior and roles provide some interesting examples of guiding principles that shape a culture, and what changes and stays the same with this common role across cultures.

Social sciences generally place paternal activities into two categories termed investment and involvement (Hewlett, 1992). The concept of paternal investment comes from biosocial and evolutionary psychology, and relates to activities undertaken to insure survival of his genetic material. In other words, the father invests time and resources to protect and propagate his genetic material on into the future. Involvement, as it is used here, can be viewed as a type of investment describing ways the father may be expected to interact with the child.

Fathers can invest in two broad modes, described as direct and indirect activities (Hewlett, 1992). Direct activities are things the father does proximally to assist the child, such as holding her, working closely with the child teaching a skill, and so on. These will differ by gender and will reflect usual activities, such as daily tasks a boy might need to do and ways families might spend leisure time. Proximal investment also may change depending on the age of the child. A boy may be cuddled as a toddler, but perhaps not as a teen, and a father may maintain physical distance from a girl after puberty. As a boy grows, whether playing baseball, hunting, or building houses, interactions shift as the boy can more closely approximate adult skills.

Indirect activities may benefit the child, but apply to the larger context, for instance when the father engages in hunting that feeds the tribe or in standing guard for the village. The activities benefit the entire group, with the father's own offspring enjoying the protection or nutrition as part of that unit. Military service protecting a city or country could be considered an indirect paternal investment in the family lineage. These investment activities are universally geared toward genetic continuity via survival of the child, or at least survival of the genetic line; a young or childless male protecting the group could die in the effort without passing on his own genes, but he would be helping to assure survival of his family. The shape and specifics of this type of involvement depend on environment, resources, and sociocultural factors.

Involvement similarly has two types or styles: active and passive. Active involvement would be feeding the child, talking or playing with her, and other activities where the father acts directly with the child. Passive involvement includes co-sleeping or simply being near the child, or in other words, proximity without conscious, intentional interaction. Perhaps the family watches television together in the evening, but the father does not particularly speak to or otherwise interact with the child. Involvement activities vary more widely across cultures, being tied less to physical survival and more to socialization. The roles and interactions of the father contribute to the microenvironment, or developmental niche (Super & Harkness, 1986), in which the child learns and grows.

Susan Harkness and Charles Super (1992) summarize how fathers' roles are culturally constructed across a range of possibilities, from the harsh and feared disciplinarian to the fun-loving playmate. In some polygynous cultures, fathers may have several wives in different locations, with their children experiencing only occasional contact. Men in East Africa now may work in cities while their families stay on a rural farm, with the father returning only for holidays or important occasions. The post-industrial polar opposite is the stay-at-home dad, becoming more common in Western cultures. Super and Harkness compared paternal involvement in western Kenya (Kokwet ethnic group) and Boston (primarily affluent, European origin), looking at time spent, settings, and activities. Kokwet fathers were passive and distal in involvement for the first two years, when play and chore involvement began to increase. Boston fathers were more proximally and actively involved from the start, a difference which is explained by cultural perceptions of roles.

Abundance and scarcity shape these paternal roles, based on how these conditions may affect the child. Kokwet fathers believe their primary purposes in a child's life are economic provision and moral discipline, while Boston fathers focused on developing close emotional bonds with their children. Subsistence life, as with farmers in Kenya, involves real struggle for survival; children still die without food or medicine, and they must grow up able to cooperate with family and community to bring subsequent generations to adulthood. Children of the affluent Boston fathers in Super and Harkness's study rarely would die. They would face a long, slow educational process that would potentially lead the child to a job far away, as a member of a law firm, a medical practice, or teaching at a university somewhere else in the world. The Kokwet have lifetimes of togetherness in their agrarian lifestyle, if children survive, so togetherness may normatively be abundant and it is survival that must be protected rigidly. Boston families enjoy physical safety, but only have a few years to build sense of intimacy before children may move away.

## REALITY CHECK

*Are there friends from earlier in life that you no longer see?*

*Who lives in your house? Are bills shared or paid by one or two people?*

*What are interactions like with your father? How did you interact when you were small?*

## 6.2 DYADIC RELATIONSHIPS: ATTRACTION

### LO 6.2 Identify the principle components in interpersonal attraction.

Whether collectivist or individualist, in a city or a jungle, much of human life involves dyads, two people interacting over a significant amount of time. We begin nursing at our mother's breast, a formative intimate dyad discussed in development literature. Special friendships may blossom between two children, and these friendships may last a lifetime. Eventually the child grows up and becomes interested in sexual activity, and procreation usually happens in a dyadic act, though human sexuality has covered a far wider range of behaviors. Clinical sounding descriptions drastically understate the importance of intimate relationships in our hearts and minds, and more broadly in our cultures; love fills our imaginations and overflows into our songs and legends, onto our televisions, and into virtually every aspect of our lives.

Relationships begin with attraction, with something that draws people together. That something may be a shared interest, some aspect of appearance, or common ethnicity. All relationships, from friendship to love, require common elements. Despite the adage that opposites attract, we are really more likely to relate to people similar to ourselves in socioeconomic and ethnic origins, and those relationships will be more stable over time (Glomb & Welsh, 2005; Hamm, 2000). Generally, though, when one speaks of attraction in context of love, we mean that special smile, that flip of the hair, some physical characteristic that arrests our attention and leads us to want that particular person more than any other. Fortunately, romantic attraction is an appealing topic, so a great deal of research exists on the subject, both within and across cultures. A great deal of research focuses on physical attractiveness or appearance combined with traits such as the ability to provide resources or nurture children.

## Physical Attraction

Genetics give people who are considered to be attractive remarkable advantages in life, from wider choices of mates to better jobs. Darwin (1871) observed that appearance was the primary factor motivating men of his day in their choice of a wife. A century later, Cunningham (1986) found that men were more willing to make sacrifices and perform altruistic acts for women they rated as more attractive. The legendary face of Helen launched the thousand ships that sailed to fight the Trojan War (Homer, 800 BCE), costing the Trojans their empire. People also assume that attractive people possess desirable qualities such as intelligence, charm, and happiness, at least in Western culture, but across cultures, attractive people are ascribed whatever qualities are considered the most desirable for that group (Anderson, Adams, & Plaut, 2008; Cunningham, 1986).

**Figure 6.1  Artistic Rendering of Prehistoric Venus Stone Figure, ca. 30,000 BCE**

*Source:* Courtesy The Met Museum, Bequest of Walter C. Baker, 1971.

To some degree, standards of beauty and attractiveness shift with changing tides of history, location, and situation. For tens of thousands of years, the ideal of feminine beauty was rotund, corpulent, and maternal, the prototypic great mother with the hips and breasts to bear generations into the future (see Figure 6.1; Coleman, 1998; Huyge, 1991; Józsa, 2011). Among the Awazagh Arabs of the Sahara, girls are fed the richest, most fattening foods so that by adolescence, they are developing the folds of fat on their stomachs and buttocks that are considered most beautiful and sexually attractive (Popenoe, 2012). Some researchers hold that our aesthetic appreciation of body size is an evolutionary adaptation; a plumper woman with some fat reserves was more likely to sustain an infant through its first few years if food is scarce. In times of greater nutritional opulence, thinness becomes more exotic and therefore desirable (Brown & Konner, 1987; Sobal & Hanson, 2011; Sobal & Stunkard, 1989). If indeed preferences for fatness or thinness form a predictable response to food security, the variety of weight preferences do not demonstrate cultural difference, but rather illustrate a common response to situational prompts. Food supply should, then, predict ideal body preferences in evidence across cultures and historical eras.

The theory that beauty norms reflect response to the presence or absence of adequate nutrition is supported by images from American history. In the dawn of the US, two centuries ago, untapped resources provided immediate great wealth to the new country, fertile soils produced bountiful crops, and willowy women were most desirable. After the devastation of the Civil War, when the fertile fields of the South had been burned again and again, a more buxom form came into vogue. Following Reconstruction and recovery, ideal type slimmed down to the waifish flappers of the 1920s, and then the Great Depression and the corresponding Dustbowl in agriculture coincided with Mae West's buxom popularity. After WWII, Marilyn Monroe was curvaceous but slimmer than Mae West, as preferred BMI decreased toward skin-and-bones Twiggy, a top model in the financially booming 1960s. In the modern US, food has actually been sufficient to feed everyone, with only economic inequality keeping the poorest citizens hungry. Predictably, the most successful recent fashion models are extremely slender, verging on anorexia (Banner, 1983; Levenstein, 2003; Stearns, 2002; Wolf, 2013). In other words, our perception of beauty is arguably hardwired into our drive to survive.

Singh (1993) proposed a related cross-cultural commonality, that waist to hip ratio (WHR) is the most important factor for female body attractiveness, building on the view that markers of fecundity (ability to bear children) would be most desirable from an evolutionary standpoint. A WHR of .7 seems to be most desirable, the waist being 70% of the hip dimension. Furnham, McClelland, and Omer (2003) found this to be true of both English and Kenyan participants, though notably all participants were university students, and therefore were well accustomed to Western norms. Evidence does support consistency in WHR across cultures, independent of body mass index (BMI). In a study of participants from Bakossiland, Cameroon, Africa; Komodo Island, Indonesia; Samoa; and New Zealand, a low WHR consistently was rated as more attractive (Singh, Dixson, Jessop, Morgan, & Dixson, 2010). The overall body size and amount of fat varies greatly, while the proportions of the body shape remain more consistent, so the very heavy women of the Awazagh Arabs probably have a similar WHR to the much slimmer average New Zealand girl. Breast size preferences do differ slightly, with some evidence that men from subsistence cultures prefer larger breasts, and that generally, darker areole, indicating sexual maturity, are preferable (Dixson et al., 2010).

## Cross-Cultural Consistencies in Facial Aesthetics

Some additional aspects of attractiveness do not change across cultures, and actually apply across gender. Several of these are explainable for their evolutionary benefits. Clear skin, free of sores and lesions, is always a plus. Good skin indicates the person is free of diseases, an obvious advantage. A second commonality is anatomical symmetry, especially of the face, which is interpreted to indicate an absence of genetic abnormalities. A lopsided face or short limbs may be judged harshly, perhaps from an instinctive understanding that offspring could be unhealthy because lopsidedness may indicate susceptibility to parasitic infection (Grammer, Fink, Møller, & Thornhill, 2003; Thornhill & Gangestad, 1993) or genetic abnormalities (Scheib, Gangestad, & Thornhill, 1999).

Cultures agree on ratings of facial attractiveness to a surprisingly high degree (e.g., Cunningham, Roberts, Barbee, Druen, & Wu, 1995). Laurentini and Bottino (2014) provide a list of studies showing very consistent ratings of facial attractiveness across a global range of cultures, with high agreement between males and females in those studies. Sorokowski, Kościński, and Sorokowska (2013), however, express concern that samples in attractiveness research tend, as usual, to be Western or from cultures with histories of Western influence. They chose a novel approach to counter the trend, using participants in Poland and in the Indonesian region of New Guinea, the latter having very little Western contact. Four photos were used, with one considered highly attractive in Poland, one very unattractive, and two in a moderate range. Interestingly, New Guinea participants did not agree with the Polish choice for most attractive, but both cultures agreed on which was least attractive. The researchers propose that, while standards of beauty may vary, perceived ugliness may be the real universal.

The widespread consensus on attractiveness suggests that deeply rooted universal processes may be in play. Indeed, several studies of brain activity patterns using MRI, near-infrared spectroscopy (NIRS) and event-related brain potentials (ERP) show differential responses to attractive and unattractive faces (Laurentini & Bottino, 2014), indicating possibility of a hard-wired neurological response to facial characteristics. Trujillo, Jankowitsch, and Langlois (2014) used electroencephalographic analysis to monitor ERPs in the brain, and found that fewer neural resources came into play when participants were shown faces approximating population averages. In other words, it was literally easier to look at attractive faces, illuminating another factor in differential treatment of people who are considered attractive.

## Average Is Exceptional

Symmetry, youth, and fecundity form logical explanations for perceptions of beauty, but they do not adequately tell the whole story of human attraction. As Trujillo et al. (2014) explain, "Many perfectly symmetrical faces are not attractive, many youthful faces are not attractive, many faces with big lips are not attractive, and many highly masculine faces are not attractive" (p. 1062). The authors suggest that if these indicators of reproductive viability provided sufficient explanatory power, these exceptions would not exist. Another factor must be in play.

Darwin's (1851) theory of evolution by selection suggests that species stabilize partly by innate preference for a population norm, and those characteristics are biologically reinforced as they become the ever-more desirable choice for mating (Dobzhansky, 1970; Langlois & Roggman, 1990). This trend appears to be true for humans, and ironically, while we think of highly attractive people as exceptional, the faces we think are most attractive are faces that are closest to population averages.

Langlois and Roggman used early digital technology to superimpose photographs of faces and create artificially averaged faces. Perceived attractiveness increased as more and more faces were included in the average, supporting the theory that the population norm is considered most desirable.

Gillian Rhodes and colleagues (2001) hypothesized that if there were a biological basis for this averaging effect, it should be observable in other cultures, and indeed, the effect held true for Chinese and Japanese participants. Rhodes and colleagues then took this research a step further, using faces of Australians of either European or Chinese origin to create averaged faces from each ethnicity, but then to average the two ethnicities into a single set of faces (see Figure 6.2). As with Langlois and Roggman's (1990) experiment, averaged faces within an ethnicity were rated more attractive than the source photos, but averages of both ethnicities blended together were judged most attractive of all.

Trujillo et al.'s (2014) study supported a neurocognitive explanation for the attractiveness of averaged faces. Event related potentials (ERPs) in EKG brain scans of participants were measured while they performed a task discriminating photos of human and chimpanzee faces. The human faces included attractive, unattractive, and averaged faces. Processing time was fastest for the highly attractive and averaged faces, and those faces elicited reduced ERPs, showing that fewer neural resources are used in processing the attractive human faces. From several research approaches, facial attractiveness appears to be a biologically based universal across cultures.

## Figure 6.2  Digitally Averaged Faces: Chinese, Caucasian, and Mixed

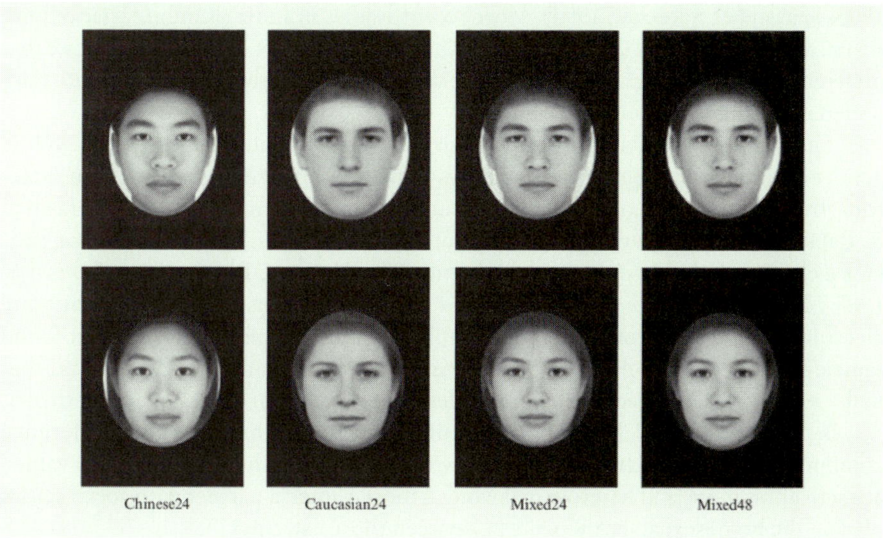

Chinese24        Caucasian24        Mixed24        Mixed48

*Source:* Rhodes et al. (2001, p. 615).

What we seek and value in relationships may differ, as shall be discussed, but our evaluation of facial attractiveness largely follows predictable shared patterns, tending toward population means. Preferences for level of body fat appear to reflect nutritional availability, while WHR may be a cross-cultural constant. Exceptional faces become exceptional by fitting norms for a population most perfectly, so people like Mila Kunis, Angelina Jolie, Zac Efron, and Brad Pitt are actually the least exceptional among us. A facial tattoo is startling when encountered for the first time by someone from a culture lacking the practice, but likewise, a face without tattoo could seem bereft in a traditional culture where that is the norm. Indeed, as the Māori of Aotearoa (Nikora, Rua, & Te Awekotuku, 2004) and the Maisin of Papua (Barker & Tietjen, 1990) have become smaller parts of multicultural societies, the practice had nearly vanished, and is now making a resurgence as a statement of identity.

## Gender and Attraction

From the evolutionary perspective of parental investment theory, males and females could reasonably be assumed to differ in what they find attractive. Both genders would benefit from the indicators of health and fecundity already discussed. With differing biological roles, men and women should differ in what attracts them to a mate. David Buss and colleagues indeed found consistent patterns of gender difference across cultures. In Buss's (1989) study of 37 cultures, he found that men valued appearance more than women and preferred women two to three years younger, both of which he interpreted as signaling reproductive capacity. Women emphasized what he termed resource capacity, preferring men who were three to four years older, who possessed status, and who were industrious and ambitious. Cultures differed in emphasis on female chastity. Results have been replicated in a number of subsequent studies (e.g., Buss & Schmitt, 1993; Hatfield & Sprecher, 1995). More recent studies in India (Kamble, Shackelford, Pham, & Buss, 2014) and China (Chang, Wang, Shackelford, & Buss, 2011) indicate that preferences are changing around topics like virginity and creativity, but the evolutionary preferences remain constant.

The evolutionary perspective has been criticized for a number of reasons. While gender accounts for important differences in mating preferences, sociocultural factors strongly influence people's feelings and behaviors in mate selection (Hatfield & Rapson, 2006; Wallen, 1989). Also notable, evolutionary theories do not provide a clear explanation of homosexual attraction (Howard, Blumstein, & Schwartz, 1987). Howard Russock (2011) examined personal advertisements from print and electronic sources and found the predictable patterns in heterosexual ads, but found female-seeking-female more closely resembled male-seeking-female ads, and that male-seeking-male ads contained no evidence of traits from sexual selection theory. Ha, Berg, Engels, and Lichtwarck-Aschoff (2012) found that all sexual preference combinations desired attractive partners with social status, heterosexual men valued attractiveness most, and heterosexual women most wanted a partner with social status, placing the homosexual participants in between those extremes.

Understanding of human mate choices requires more research in patterns among alternative gender and sexual orientation groups, and particularly requires that researchers not fall prey to stereotypes or limitations of conventionality (Felmlee, Orzechowicz, & Fortes, 2010; West, Popp, & Kenny, 2008). Around the globe, norms and expectations seem to be shifting toward broad acceptance of alternative lifestyles. Actually, cultures have never exclusively favored strict heterosexual definitions of legitimacy in relationship, and many only adopted narrow heterosexual standards after the spread of European colonialism and widespread adoption of sexually conservative Victorian-era European values (e.g., Ajibade, 2013; Roughton, 2014; Ruiz-Alfaro, 2012). A number of other attraction possibilities will probably emerge as cultural research increases around nonbinary and other gender and sexual orientation identities. Further, some individuals are uncomfortable categorizing themselves in any sexual orientation or gender identity (Scheffey, Ogden, & Dichter, 2019). Keeping in mind limitations of current research, we turn now to examination of cultural literature on dyadic relationships.

## REALITY CHECK

*How much are you similar to your friends in terms of ethnicity, geographic origin, and interests?*

*What do you consider attractive in terms of appearance?*

*What qualities would you like your romantic partner to have? Your life mate?*

## 6.3 COUPLES: ROMANCE AND REALITY

### LO 6.3 Compare and contrast research and theories about love and intimacy.

*Out of this bond arises feelings of eroticism, passion, and companionship which somehow merge together to form a unified conceptual whole.*

*Jankowiak & Gerth, 2012*

"Marry me," Mikita wrote to Anna on a piece of birch-bark, "I want you, and you me." The sentiment is not unusual. The fact that Mikita sent the proposal to his love between 1280 and 1300 in Novgorod, before Russia even existed, underscores that some truths remain, and people in all places and eras fall in love (Herszenhornoct, 2014). Survival of a species depends on procreation, to state the obvious. From penguins to primates, creatures mate in particular patterns, sometimes with particular rituals. Male penguins search for a particularly attractive stone to give to their prospective mates before they settle down to raise a single egg in monogamous bliss. Clever marketing of diamonds over the last century has convinced human males in Western culture that they too must find the right stone to induce mating behaviors from a female, in this case set as an engagement ring. The bonobo is very similar to chimpanzees in appearance but much less violent. On the other end of the spectrum from the penguin, bonobo engage promiscuously in hetero- and homosexual liaisons, a practice that keeps their social relations much more peaceful than their chimp cousins. Human relations run the gamut of possible liaisons, but one thing is certain: we are fascinated by love, as demonstrated by the reams of poetry and love songs churned out over the centuries, and perhaps this makes us different from other animals. Our use of language and abstract thought certainly places us in a unique position to examine the myriad ways we have expressed love across history and cultures.

## What Is Love?

*The minute I heard my first love story,*

*I started looking for you, not knowing*

*how blind that was.*

*Lovers don't finally meet somewhere.*

*They're in each other all along.*

*Rumi*

From poets to philosophers, humans have struggled to understand love for as long as we have records. To a Sufi mystic like Rumi, all love is love for the one divine creator, manifest in our many human forms. For most of us, love is for the people in our lives. We have maternal love, filial love, and especially, love for a romantic partner. It is the latter, that special someone, to which we turn now.

The Oxford Dictionaries (online) define love as "An intense feeling of deep affection," or "a deep romantic or sexual attachment to someone." Love has been a troubling topic for psychology from the start, being a hypothetical concept more suited to poetry than science (Carter, 1998). Psychological explanations range from libido expression and ego gratification to strict descriptions of physiological and evolutionary functions. In Irving Singer's (1987) estimation, Freud painted a confusing picture of the topic, variously describing love as sexuality fused with tenderness, libido directed toward a love object, *Eros* (the life force), and *Eros* combined with the death force (*Thanatos*), all of which are impossible to quantify and measure. The other end of the spectrum places love in the increasingly measurable realm of neurobiology, drawing strikingly accurate parallels between human love and mating behaviors of prairie voles, for instance (Carter, 1998), with liberal secretion of the bonding hormone oxytocin in both species when they come together. Neither libido nor prairie vole bears much resemblance to the experience of love in daily life.

Cultures do provide more practical and comprehensible answers about the human experience of romantic love. Intense emotions in pair bonding, what we call "love" in English, is a human universal existing across cultures (Buss, 1988;

Jankowiak & Fischer, 1992; Wlodarski & Dunbar, 2014). The commonalities and differences of how we describe and enact love reveal a great deal about the topic and about our cultures (Hatfield & Rapson, 1996). Cultural parameters determine whom we may love, what our responsibilities are in relationship, and how we may and may not behave with our objects of affection. Serious research into love across cultures was rare until recently, due to an unbelievably ethnocentric view that romantic love existed only in European cultures (Jankowiak & Fischer, 1992).

Increased research over the past few decades, notably led by Elaine Hatfield and her husband Richard Rapson, reveals a set of parameters shared across cultures that are definable and measurable while still reflecting the inner, subjective experience of love. Hatfield and Rapson (1996) generally differentiate between two types or aspects of love that appear consistently across cultures: passionate love and companionate love. It is with these concepts that we will begin.

### Passionate Love

> *I love thee to the depth and breadth and height my soul can reach.*
>
> *Elizabeth Barrett Browning*

In passionate love, a person feels great desire, sexual and emotional, for the other person and longs for union. If that union is fulfilled, love is reciprocated and life is wonderful. If not, if it is unrequited, the person may feel empty and anxious (Hatfield & Rapson, 2010; 1993; Hatfield, Rapson, & Martel, 2007). Jankowiak and Fischer (1992) defined romantic love as "any intense attraction that involves the idealization of the other, within an erotic context, with the expectation of enduring for some time into the future" (p. 150). This is the love of Romeo and Juliet, of Tristan and Isolde, and of the herder and weaver in the bridge of birds tale, all of which speak of love so intense that the characters violate rules of their societies to be together (Jankowiak & Fischer, 1992). Across cultures, stories appear describing emotions that overwhelm the characters, driving them beyond the normal ken. The tales usually end unfortunately for the characters, but they make our hearts beat with passion and our imaginations soar.

Love's excitement and euphoria have physiological correlates including an amphetamine relative, phenethylamine (PEA; Jankowiak & Fischer, 1992). Other researchers focus on the neuropeptide oxytocin, which is also present immediately after childbirth as the mother and infant bond, and vasopressin, which is associated with male mating behavior. Levels of these are very high early in romantic relationships, indicating they play an important role in the biology of romantic bonding (Campbell, 2008; Schneiderman, Zagoory-Sharon, Leckman, & Feldman, 2012). Emanuele and colleagues (2006) measured a number of neurotrophic chemicals (ones that induce nerve growth and maturation) and found a distinct correlation between nerve growth factor (NGF) and intensity of romantic feelings. These chemical components of romance provide evidence that romantic love is a universal, built into human physical being, which explains why love is such a powerful presence in our lives and fills the art and music of cultures around the world.

Cacioppo, Bianchi-Demicheli, Hatfield, and Rapson (2012) summarized the burgeoning field of brain research about love, in which fMRI studies show clear patterns of brain activity for passionate love. Passionate love activates both subcortical and cortical areas, including reward centers rich in dopamine, and some patterns that bear similarity to brain activity after consuming drugs like cocaine. Activity is more intense than for love of parents, siblings, or friends, which in turn are more intense than unknown people or celebrities, when pictures are shown during protocols. In the brain, passionate love is a deeply rewarding, highly pleasurable, and possibly addictive experience.

Despite its intense effects and the popularity of passionate love in media, it has been actively discouraged more often than not throughout history (Hatfield & Rapson, 2002), with Christianity taking a particularly repressive stance for the past 1500 years. Tamils of South Indian compare it to *makkyam*, a state of "dizziness, confusion, intoxication, and delusion" (Hatfield, Mo, & Rapson, 2015). Indeed, Wlodarski and Dunbar (2014) discuss the effects of intense love on mental abilities, citing a number of studies showing impairment when participants are prompted to think of the love object. Paradoxically, the same type of prompt is associated with increased accuracy in perceiving emotion. This means passionate love makes us measurably less effective or rational yet more emotionally sensitive. Passion is inherently unstable: the adolescent infatuation portrayed in *Romeo and Juliet* results in six deaths and provides a poor model for maintaining social order. Passions also diminish over time, as partners wrinkle, reveal annoying habits, and generally become commonplace after the blush of new love has faded. Emanuel et al. (2005) found that the high levels of NGF receded after 18 to 24 months to a point where they are indistinguishable from the control group who were not in love. Passion moves our hearts and souls to create great works of art and perform heroic feats, but eventually it fades. Something else must come into play for our relationships to last.

### Companionate Love

Complementary to passionate love, and sometimes considered its opposite on the love spectrum, is companionate love. After the flood of neurotransmitters has passed, a longer, less tumultuous phase may follow, "characterized by the growth of a more peaceful, comfortable, and fulfilling relationship; it is a strong and enduring affection built upon long term association" (Jankowiak & Fischer, 1992, p. 150). Melvin M. Knight (1924) used the term to distinguish marriage expressly for companionship from the institution of family, which he described as existing expressly for procreation. By 1978, the second edition of Berscheid and Hatfield's *Interpersonal Attraction* included a chapter on romantic love and one on companionate love, which they described as an intense liking for "someone with whom one's life was 'deeply intertwined'" (Berscheid, 2010, p. 3). Companionate love focuses on feelings of intimacy and commitment rather than emotional fire and physical desire (Hatfield et al., 2015).

Companionate love is not separate from passionate love. Practically, long term relationships include both passionate and companionate feelings. People age and become accustomed to each other, and this is a natural part of life. Focus on passion also varies by culture, with companionate feelings forming a more normative part of arranged marriages, for instance. A shift to a more companionate phase does not preclude additional times of passion: the two may both be active aspects of a healthy relationship. The two types of love also provide explanatory power to describe relationships in a wider variety of cultural and lifespan contexts. American media emphasizes high passion with lower concern for companionate aspects, and preferences of other cultures may be compared on level of each dimension.

### The Triangular Theory of Love

In 1986, Robert Sternberg debuted his triangular theory of love. Instead of the two components, Sternberg had parsed love to three factors: intimacy, passion, and decision/commitment. Intimacy describes feelings of closeness and bonding, passion refers to the romantic and sexual aspects, and decision/commitment refers to the cognitive dedication to preservation of the relationship. Noting that love "can be partitioned in a number of ways" (p. 119), Sternberg (1986) proposes that this partitioning "is particularly useful for understanding elements of love, and how they function in close relationships" (p. 120).

Sternberg's theory indeed illuminates some cultural variation. Cheng and Christopher (2010) investigated relationship satisfaction in China, predicting that commitment would moderate the effects of passion and intimacy. In analysis of responses from 263 participants, they found that levels of intimacy and commitment significantly affected satisfaction, but that passion did not. These findings are in keeping with Chinese traditions for relationship, and differ from the Western emphasis on passion as the basis for successful marriage.

### Sex

> Societies take what are essentially straightforward, biologically grounded dispositions, for example puberty, or pregnancy, or menstruation, and weave around them the most intricate webs of custom, attitude, and belief.
>
> Broude, 1975, p. 381

Biological imperatives form an absolute substructure of human life; we all must eat, drink, and find shelter, and at least some members of a culture must procreate for the group to survive. What we eat and wear varies, along with the shapes and materials of our shelters, reflecting our environment, our cultural origins, and the thought patterns we have learned in our journeys across the globe. Sexuality, perhaps more than any other of these absolute imperatives, reveals deep differences in belief systems and ways of thinking, leading to very different answers to questions, who can have sex and with whom? Can we speak of sex? Is it taboo or is conversation normally filled with sexual innuendo? Does sex require a legitimized relationship, is it considered pleasant or unpleasant, and what happens if rules are violated?

### Premarital Sex

Rules and norms about premarital sex form a bewildering tapestry of contradictions, ranging from absolute prohibition to hearty endorsement. Pre-contact Polynesia, including Hawaiʻi, had no equivalent concept of marriage, and hence had no notable proscriptions against genital contact, except between low ranking males and female royalty (Diamond, 2004). Broude (1975) provides an extensive list of cultural attitudes when marriage is a component, including the Chewa of central and southern Africa who believe young women need premarital sex to become fertile, and the Goajiro of Colombia and Venezuela who forbid it as an act against the will of the gods. Christians in the US generally forbid premarital sex, and early missionaries to Pacific islands professed shock at the liberal sexuality of Polynesians, but actual behavior often does not match expectations and prohibitions. The Centers for Disease Control (Kann et al., 2014) estimates 34% of US high school students are sexually active and the Department of Health and Human Services recorded a pregnancy rate of 29.4 per 1,000 teen girls in 2013 (National Center for Health Statistics, 2015).

These values and proscription arise from underlying belief systems. Within the US, some cultural and religious groups speak of children as blessings from God and prohibit both birth control and sex for reasons other than procreation, while the other end of the spectrum maintains strictly biological perspectives and may be more liberal about birth control and sexual mores. Higher educational attainment is associated with higher incidence of premarital sex, possibly because women delay marriage to finish degrees and start careers (Addai, 1999). Higher levels of education and affluence also correlate with secularity (Gallup International Association, 2015), which may reduce importance of religious proscriptions. Addai (1999) tested several hypotheses about prevalence of premarital sex in Ghana. The territory that is now Ghana includes multiple ethnic groups with a range of sexual norms and traditions, but several trends are clear. Premarital sex is increasing over time, likely because parental control and adherence to old norms are decreasing as youth are exposed to new elements of modern culture brought by globalized products and media.

Among cultures that prohibit premarital sex, Broude (1975) provided several examples of what she termed "native explanations for restrictiveness" (p. 382). These range from very practical motivation to prevent unwanted pregnancy among the Fon of West Africa (Herskovits, 1938), to the Kazak requirement of virginity at marriage described by Hudson (1938), to the judgment of the Wogeo of New Guinea that premarital sex was an indicator of later marital infidelity (Hogbin, 1945).

Inheritance practices provide another explanation of mores about premarital sex. In patrilineal cultures, inheritance passes father to son, while in matrilineal societies, mothers control ownership, passing land and wealth to daughters. Matrilineal societies have fewer prohibitions about premarital sex because the child has membership in the line of inheritance regardless of who the father is. Patrilineal cultures remain more invested in female chastity because premarital sex may happen with someone other than the eventual husband, and thus, the activity interferes with inheritance by the male's genetic offspring (Addai, 1999).

Whatever traditions govern premarital sex, modernization and media are unquestionably changing traditional practices. Hawaiʻi traditionally endorsed liberal sexuality before Western contact (Diamond, 2004), but now enjoys a relatively low rate of unwed births (Shattuck & Kreider, 2013), perhaps because sex education has been available in schools and became mandatory in public schools as of 2016. Unwed mothers in America face a number of economic and social consequences (Shattuck & Kreider, 2013), whatever their cultural origins. Promiscuity also brings with it increased transmission of HIV, causing concern in global health efforts. With greater choice come greater risks.

## REALITY CHECK

*Is dating allowed in your culture? How did you meet your romantic partner or those you have dated?*

*If you are in a relationship, can you identify the levels of passionate, companionate, and committed love?*

*How does your family feel about premarital sex?*

## 6.4 MARRIAGE AND INTIMACY

### LO 6.4: Explain how culture shapes the dynamics of our intimate relationships.

Dyadic intimate relationships exist in all times and cultures, fulfilling needs for sex, emotional bonding, and intimacy. Humans have embraced an incredible variety of romantic and marital relationships across history and across cultures (see Table 6.2). In addition to the numbers and types of partners involved, cultures also vary in how relationships come about, who can engage in sexual contact, who makes decisions once the relationship is established, and other factors of day-to-day existence.

| Table 6.2 | Types of Mating/Marital Arrangements |
|---|---|
| Monogamy | Men and women are permitted to have only one regular sexual partner or marry only one person at a time |
| Polygamy | Men or women are allowed to have more than one regular sexual partner or mate at a time |
| Polygyny | Men are allowed more than one regular sexual partner or wife at a time |
| Polyandry | Women are allowed more than one regular sexual partner or husband at a time |
| Polygynandry | Both men and women can have as many sexual and/or marital partners as they desire |

*Source:* Hatfield and Rapson (1996, p. 5).

## The Mating Game

*Burke considers courtship as a form by which social distinctions, such as classes, are transcended.*

*Gusfield, 1989, pp. 37–38*

Discussion of intimate relationships begins with how people can or cannot meet, who determines and/or legitimizes relationships, and what partners may do once they decide to couple. Propinquity has formed a principal avenue of American research, with Bossard (1932) observing that one third of marriages licensed in Philadelphia in 1931 were between people who had lived within five blocks of each other. Abrams (1943) found the same pattern a decade later, and Korson (1968) found evidence of propinquity in mate selection in the very different cultural milieu of 1960s Karachi, Pakistan. The Karachi case raises a very different issue, however, because all of the marriages Korson observed were arranged by parents or others. Newcomb (1956) observed that "what we are concerned with is something that is made possible, or more likely, with decreasing distance" (pp. 575–576), a fact that is true also in friendship (Nahemow & Lawton, 1976). The choices of mate in Philadelphia, influenced by nearness but made individually, are very different from those arranged marriages in Karachi.

In the realm of who marries whom, personal choice has not historically been the path to liaison; entitativity becomes the paramount consideration, the group or individual level at which decisions can be made (Kashima, 2005). Can a person just decide her marriage partner, or must any marriage be arranged or approved? Attraction and the formalized liaison of marriage have often been two different processes. Throughout recorded history and across cultures, mates are commonly chosen by elders or respected matchmakers rather than by individual choice. At minimum, lovers sought parental blessings on the match, and pairings outside family approval were the stuff of Romeo and Juliet type dramas. Broude and Greene (1983) surveyed an extensive list of cultures to determine common patterns of mate selection, shown in Table 6.3.

In Broude and Greene's (1983) cross-cultural comparison of marriage practices, they found that when men choose whom they marry, women do also. In cultures where marriages are arranged, this may happen in a number of ways. Parents may consult a trusted friend or a religious leader, or a professional matchmaker. Questions to address may include religion, family background, and dowry size. In India, caste (whether noble or some level of commoner) along with religious affiliation are extremely important questions (despite official elimination of caste at founding of modern India). The advantage gained by alliance of the families involved may be of paramount importance (Dion & Dion, 1993). In my (Fox, 2010) study of artists in New Zealand, a thoroughly modern Indian woman in her late 20s expressed that she could see herself entering an arranged marriage, especially since she was getting a bit older without having established a marriage on her own.

Generally, marriage quality is a universal predictor of health and well-being (e.g., Umberson, Williams, Powers, Liu, & Needham, 2006; Williams, 2003). Research into outcomes of marriage based on who initiates the match is difficult for a number of

| Table 6.3 | Options for Marriage Choice | |
| --- | --- |
| **Locus of Choice** | **Individual Entitativity** |
| Parents choose | Person cannot choose |
| Parents choose, person can object | Individual can choose |
| Arranged and individual choice acceptable | Person and/or others choose |
| Individuals, kin, and others all must agree | Person has limited choice |
| Approval of kin and/or community highly desirable | Person has limited choice |
| Individual solely selects partner | Individual solely chooses |

*Sources:* Broude and Greene (1983); Hatfield and Rapson (1996).

reasons, including differing marital roles, behavioral norms, and communication styles, and cultural constraints on divorce. Some cultures flatly reject love as a criterion of mate selection in favor of arranged marriages, while others endorse love as the criterion or prefer some combination of love and arrangement (de Munck, 1996). Folk wisdom says that love marriages begin hot and grow cooler, while arranged marriages begin cold and grow hotter (Xu & Whyte, 1990). Research into marital choice shows a mixed picture, with some studies showing no significant differences in satisfaction (Myers, Madathil, & Tingle, 2005; Regan, Lakhanpal, & Anguiano, 2012; Schwartz, 2007). Xu and Whyte (1990) observed better satisfaction in Chinese in couple-initiated love marriages. Two studies separated by decades of time showed very high marriage satisfaction for couples in arranged marriages in Jaipur, India (Bowman & Dollahite, 2013; Gupta & Singh, 1982), which the authors credit more to relational dynamics than to how the marriage began.

Interestingly, Madathil and Benshoff (2008) compared Euro- and Indian Americans and Indians in India, finding that the happiest couples were Indians living in the US in arranged marriages, compared to those in marriages of choice, whether Indians in India or Americans. Happiness, well-being, and satisfaction depend on the stability and conflict in our relationships, as Daniel Shek (2001) found with his Chinese participants in Hong Kong, and as did Quek and Fitzpatrick (2013) in Singapore. Cultural factors in relationship further influence these outcomes because cultures have different norms and expectations for marital behavior, and offer different resources for conflict resolution.

## Engagement and Changes in Relationship Stability

Between the high individualism of Western culture and the breakdown of traditional restraints on marriage (see Spotlight: Shifting Sands), modern love relationships are certainly characterized by high relational mobility. As Schug et al. (2010) observed, individualists are motivated to make greater investment in relationship to counteract this

# SPOTLIGHT

## SHIFTING SANDS: LOVE IN THE 21ST CENTURY

World War II unquestionably involved more humans in war than ever before in history. Death and destruction raged across the globe, and men and boys left hearth and home to fight. As war spread and men departed from farms and factories, women entered the workforce, and particularly manufacturing, in unprecedented numbers. Women built the machines and vehicles of war, represented by the archetypal image of a woman in a work shirt often referred to as "Rosie the Riveter" (see Figure 6.3). Some 6 million American women entered the workforce, most of whom had never held a paying job before. Following the war, many GIs and women from the factories and hospitals never went back to agrarian or domestic lives, and the women now had unprecedented earning ability.

Figure. 6.3    We Can Do It! by Miller (1942)

Source: oberart/istockphoto.com

The economic independence of women, along with voting suffrage, socially acceptable divorce, and greater civil equality, radically altered the hierarchies and power structures of gender relations in Western culture. Women could tell an abusive spouse to "hit the road, Jack" without certainty of becoming a starving outcast, as was historically a real risk for women who left marriages. Realistically, many still remain in abusive relationships because the shift to gender equality is far from complete. Wages still favor males, and males far outnumber females in political and corporate positions of power. Though room for improvement remains, the conditions of women have unquestionably improved on average.

The stability and longevity of relationships, on the other hand, plummeted. A popular misconception is that half of American marriages end in divorce, but trends are complex. The marriage rate in 2011 was 6.8 per thousand people, while the divorce rate was 3.6 (Copen, Daniels, Vespa, & Mosher, 2012). The half that divorce include many second or third marriages, and do not reflect the growing number of stable cohabitations. In 1995, 34% of women cohabited as a first union, increasing to 48% in 2006–2010 data, with 23% of births occurring in cohabitation (Copen, Daniels, & Mosher, 2013). What is certain is that traditional marriage is less popular and less stable, and that alternative choices are better tolerated.

In addition to the changes above, modern entertainment, including the seemingly harmless Disney films, promotes an ideal of lasting, passionate love that is not supported by cultural precedent or empirical research. The motherless princess of most Disney movies falls in instant love at first sight, an impractical condition lampooned in *Frozen*.

The older films portray the woman as lacking in personal power, dependent on the handsome prince for her rescue. More recent films such as *Brave*, *Frozen*, and *Moana* from the Disney brand show increasing independence of the princesses, but those heroines still promote an individualist path to success.

Disney forms the mildest end of the media relationship spectrum. American media has produced brilliant films, music, and other media, but there is a dark side. Media endorsing promiscuity and oozing sexuality is aggressively marketed around the world, spreading cultural instability in its wake.

With loss of proscriptions against divorce, increased economic power of women, and the general drift toward individualistic ways of being, the old reasons marriages lasted are gone. New reasons to stay together have not fully emerged, in one of the fastest cultural shifts of human history. But research consistently shows that people who do not divorce are happier and live longer. Only time will tell how we solve this dilemma.

type of mobility. It is interesting to note that the diamond engagement ring, a literal financial investment, only began to appear outside royal circles in the later 1800s. The expensive ring increased in popularity after elimination of a legal concept called "breach of promise to marry" (Brinig, 1990), in which failure to marry could result in lawsuit. Engagement rings became common after 1945, amid the massive relocation of soldiers and families following WWII (see Spotlight: Shifting Sands). As relational mobility has increased, the popularity of a specific large cash investment in a tangible symbol of relationship (the ring) has become normative. Similarly, the double ring ceremony, in which the man also receives and wears a wedding band, only became a "tradition" in the later 20th century (Howard, 2003). The rings form an alternative way to induce compliance in sexual and relational fidelity as religious and social pressures have waned.

## Problems in Relationships

All bleeding eventually stops, and all relationships end, at least in our finite physical world. People naturally face conflict as they attempt to negotiate existence together. Partners change, mature, and disagree over time in all cultures, necessitating redefinition of relationship (Hatfield & Rapson, 1996). Lisa Dillon and colleagues (2015) surveyed 2,600 married couples from the United States, Britain, China, Russia, and Turkey, finding fairly consistent sources of conflict across cultures. Primary issues were sexual activity, financial issues, labor division, and parenting. Kindness, including positive communication, was the primary factor reducing conflict.

Infidelity is considered to be a source of problems across many cultures, despite scarcity of systematic review of evidence on the topic (Jankowiak, Nell, & Buckmaster, 2002). From an evolutionary standpoint, infidelity should be endorsed more by males, in a double standard where males enjoy more opportunities to procreate. Indeed, this gender difference has been supported in research (e.g., Brase, Adair, & Monk, 2014), with notable exceptions. Cultures do differ in acceptance and perceived effect of sexual infidelity (Jackman, 2015). Harris and Christenfeld (1996) found that the seriousness of infidelity depends on whether the culture links sexual infidelity to feelings of

**Table 6.4** Percentage of Cultures Allowing Divorce, Rated by Conditions and Gender

| Standards for Divorce | Males | Females |
|---|---|---|
| No grounds required for divorce | 59% | 42% |
| Grounds are not necessary, but grounds ease financial, legal, or social consequences | 19% | 33% |
| Divorce is only possible with grounds | 7% | 9% |
| Divorce is not allowed | 3% | 4% |

*Source:* Broude and Greene (1983).

love. Zandbergen and Brown (2015) found that culture predicted jealousy about sexual infidelity, but that gender predicted jealousy over emotional infidelity. Women do appear to be more strongly affected by emotional infidelity across cultures, in keeping with predictions of evolutionary psychology (Brase et al., 2014) because emotional infidelity affects a partner's willingness to remain in relationship until children mature.

Relationships reach an early end for variety of reasons, many of them shared around the world. The Austin Institute for the Study of Family and Culture (2014) cites 17 reasons for divorce in America, including emotional abuse, poor partner match, infidelity, financial differences, and spouse's immaturity. These reasons parallel Dillon et al.'s (2015) cross-cultural comparison, and the literature of relationships across cultures in general. Abandonment also constitutes grounds for divorce in many cultures, including within Sharia practice (Mashhour, 2005), and may form grounds for annulment in Catholicism, which does not actually allow divorce (Vannoy, 2000). Divorce as a legal and ethical issue largely affects ability to remarry (Rheinstein, 1953). Broude and Greene (1983) included a compilation of conditions required for divorce across cultures, rated for frequency of acceptability by gender (see Table 6.4). Their findings definitely show more flexibility for males, but while divorce may technically be allowed, implications may be severe and lasting, with divorce creating a lasting stigma, especially for women. Romantic love is a common experience, but so is loss, and misfortunes in love fill the songs and poetry of many cultures.

## REALITY CHECK

*Who did or will decide whom you may marry?*

*Do you think emotional infidelity is a serious infraction?*

*Are your parents still married? What proportion of people you know are from homes where someone divorced?*

## 6.5. ART AND RELATIONSHIPS

### LO 6.5 Explain the roles of the arts in defining and sustaining relationships.

No topic is more powerful in arts across cultures than close relationships. Your desk and walls likely contain photos of friends and family. Before photography, artists painted tiny cameos worn close to the heart, and large portraits to grace grander walls. Shah Jahan commissioned the exquisite Taj Mahal in memory of his most beloved wife, Mumtaz Mahal, and it has stood for four centuries in silent testament to his affection.

Songs and poems describe our expectations and experiences in relationship. Heroes in myths and movies frequently have a side-kick and love interest. In the Hindu epic the *Mahabarata*, the deity Krishna is the charioteer of the hero warrior Arjuna, who offers wisdom in the *Guru Gita* to prepare Arjuna for the battle to come. Friends in tales from many cultures teach how to be a good and faithful friend, and how to be alert for treachery. Songs sing praises of ancestors, and especially mothers. And of course, love songs fill our hopes and dreams as we move into sexual relationships. The world's songs and literature are filled to the brim with relationships too numerous to discuss, though the topic is fascinating. A few examples regarding romantic love will illustrate some of the commonalities and variations on the theme.

The words of songs and poems convey the deepest thoughts of lovers across time.

All your young beauty is to me

Like a place where the new grass sways

After the blessing of the rain,

When the sun unveils its light.

—Somali Poem (Andrzejewski, 1969)

The sentiment of this Somali poem may be unfamiliar: Somalia is a dry land where rain means life. Bright sun on new grasses compare the lover's presence to nourishment to sustain the writer's heart and soul. *The flower song* is from ancient Egypt's New Kingdom 3,000 years ago. It contains the same theme of sustenance from the lover's presence:

*The Flower Song* (Excerpt)

To hear your voice is pomegranate wine to me:

I draw life from hearing it.

Could I see you with every glance,

It would be better for me

Than to eat or to drink.

—Egypt, c. 1000 BCE, trans. by M.V. Fox)

Less familiar imagery also appears in ancient Egyptian love poems: *I'll go down to the water with you/and come out to you carrying a red fish*. The fish may represent the lover's heart laid bare. Pollen becomes the metaphor for evidence of infidelity in this Indian poem calling out an unfaithful lover from about the 9th century:

> Did you sleep in the garden, dear,
>
> On a bed of magnolia flowers?
>
> I suppose you know that your breast
>
> Is smeared with the pollen dust?
>
> —India, ca. 800 CE, in Wright (2011)

The conditions and emotions would appear to be similar across time and culture, with the allusions and metaphors changing with the environment, but people may also think differently about love.

In Japan, love poetry is shaded by *mono no aware*, a sentiment of simultaneous sorrow and joy at the fleeting nature of life and love, made all the more precious in its impermanence. Moto-Yoshi Shinnō (died 943 CE) was a son of the Emperor Yōzei, famous for his many love affairs. Of a woman who rejected his advances, he wrote:

> *Wabi nureba*
>
> *Ima hata onaji*
>
> *Naniwa naru*
>
> *Mi wo tsukushite mo*
>
> *Awamu to zo omou.*
>
> We met but for a moment, and
>
> I'm wretched as before;
>
> The tide shall measure out my life,
>
> Unless I see once more
>
> The maid, whom I adore.
>
> —Shinnō, Japan, ca. 10th century

His melancholy seems a lasting condition central to his self-concept, "wretched as before." *A Tale of Genji* was written by Lady Murasaki Shikibu about another roguish charmer, and published in 1008 CE as a pillow book read by wealthy ladies. Illegitimate son of the ruler, Genji pursued many women, never quite finding happiness even in achieving his goal. Genji also had male friends, notably his confidant Koremitsu. The friends shared pleasures and adventures, but Koremitsu was obliged to help Genji when situations ran afoul, as when a fragile woman died in Genji's bed. Something of a scoundrel, Genji's fictional friendships were not easy on his friends, who, in that hierarchic collectivist setting, had to help him no matter what.

*Mono no aware* fits well with remorse and nostalgia, and particularly with grief. The sentiment actually was influenced by Chinese poetry. Mei Yao Ch'en wrote a poem mourning his first wife in the 11th century, translated as "In Broad Daylight I Dream":

A Dream at Night

In broad daylight I dream I

Am with her. At night I dream

She is still at my side. She

Carries her kit of colored

Threads. I see her image bent

Over her bag of silks. She

Mends and alters my clothes and

Worries for fear I might look

Worn and ragged. Dead, she watches

Over my life. Her constant

Memory draws me towards death.

—Mei Yao-ch'en (1002–1060), in Chaves (1976)

## Music and Love

*If music be the food of love, play on.*

Twelfth Night, *Act 1, Scene 1*

One of the oldest surviving songs from Europe is Greensleeves, with 16th-century lyrics set to a melody probably older still. Like many songs and poems about relationship across culture, Greensleeves is a song of sorrow and loss:

Your vows you've broken, like my heart,

Oh, why did you so enrapture me?

Now I remain in a world apart

But my heart remains in captivity.

Greensleeves was all my joy

Greensleeves was my delight,

Greensleeves was my heart of gold,

And who but my lady Greensleeves.

At the dawn of rock and roll, traditional life had thoroughly been disrupted by WWII, and in the void, teens with the new mobility of widespread automobile ownership sought new excitement. Arts always reflect and interpret social change, particularly in music (Walters & Spitzer, 2003), and predictably, the greater mobility and independence of women flavored popular music as the Civil Rights movement and feminism expanded. Sexuality definitely played a huge role in rock and roll.

Hobbs and Gallup (2011) examined a large number of songs for reproductive messages, first beginning with Top Ten songs from 2009 (174 songs), then the annual Top Ten for one year from each of the past six decades (60 songs). The authors comment, "A content analysis of the lyrics revealed 18 reproductive themes that read like an outline for a course in evolutionary psychology" (p. 402). Reproductive messages did not start in this modern era, however. Hobbs and Gallup eventually examined classical and operatic repertoire dating back to 1597 (327 songs) and found the same patterns. Mozart was only one of the many respected composers who wrote a set of overtly sexualized madrigals to be enjoyed at parties.

The situations of love vary incredibly, from monogamous heterosexuality to multiple wives or husbands, to the somewhat relaxed liaisons of old Hawai'i. What does not change is the need to bond closely with at least one or more individuals. How we describe those relationships may change depending on our culture and epoch, but the existential need for affiliation remains.

## REFLECTING ON YOUR READING

- Looking at the relationships in your life, how might you describe them using the theories presented in this chapter?

- Would you describe your upbringing as more collectivist or individualist? What evidence could you present to support your claim?

- How might your relationships be different if you grew up in another culture?

## CHAPTER 6 SUMMARY

### 6.1 Roles and Interpersonal Relationships

*Role* is a theatrical term describing particular relationships, statuses, and responsibilities people may hold. These roles form enduring components of cultures.

Friendships form a generally less formal set of roles. Relational mobility, how easily a person can move in or out of friendships, affects how friends behave toward each other.

Family generally includes genetic relatives and shared residence, though this varies across cultures. Structure also varies in terms of who holds authority or controls resources. Parental roles and responsibilities also vary, particularly for fathers, who may invest energy, time, and resources in proximal (close and direct) or distal (more general to the group) ways.

## 6.2 Dyadic Relationships: Attraction

Much of human relating is enacted in dyads, whether friends of sexual partners.

Attraction is what pulls people together in relationship. Physical attractiveness may include a range of body types, often reflecting food scarcity. Facial attractiveness across cultures includes symmetry and freedom from blemishes, and an averaging of population norms in specific feature configuration. Males slightly prefer women with higher fertility characteristics, while women tend to prefer evidence of social standing and better resources, both of which reflect evolutionary selection to maximize survival.

## 6.3 Couples: Romance and Reality

Although love appears to be a universal, cultures differ in descriptions. Generally, love includes elements of affection and attachment. Research describes elements of love, which Hatfield and colleagues suggest may be passionate and erotic, or companionate and comfortable. Sternberg describes three components: intimacy, passion, and commitment. These components are useful in understanding different manifestations of love relationships across cultures.

Though sex is a biological universal, rules and norms about sexuality vary widely across cultures. Acceptance of premarital sexual activity appears to correlate with inheritance practices, with patrilineal cultures assuring genetic connection of father to children through chastity.

## 6.4 Marriage and Intimacy

Marriage has included numerous configurations across history. A primary difference arises in who can choose, whether people marrying, parents, or matchmakers.

Problems happen in relationships in all cultures, and the causes are strikingly similar. The ways we deal with those problems and the solutions available differ.

## 6.5 Art and Relationships

Arts contain detailed information about relationships, especially in music. Visual arts convey information about attractiveness and family structure. Love songs and poetry describe relationship dynamics, desires, and expectations for a given era and culture.

CHAPTER SEVEN

# COGNITION AND PERCEPTION

## Chapter 7 Outline

## Learning Objectives

**LO 7.1** Differentiate holistic and analytic cognitive styles.

**LO 7.2** Describe ways culture may shape perception.

**LO 7.3** Explain non-Western concepts of intelligence and limitations of intelligence theory.

**LO 7.4** Discuss regular and altered states of consciousness.

**LO 7.5** Elaborate the ways the arts can serve as useful tools in the study of cognition and perception.

# PREPARING TO READ

- Can you imagine that other people have thought processes entirely unlike yours?

- Can you be fooled by visual illusions that do not affect people in other cultures?

- Would what you are learning in school prepare you to solve problems in a jungle? On the Arctic tundra?

*If I say "I hear a church bell," it would seem a simple enough statement, but a great many steps happened between a precipitating event and those words passing from my lips. First, something struck a concave metal object such that vibrations emanated into the surrounding air. I must have been close enough for a certain amount of those vibrational waves to reflect from the pinnae of my ears into the ear canal and strike my tympanic membrane. That disturbed the tiniest of bones, my malleus, incus, and stapes, then arousing microscopic hairs within the cochlea, the snail-shaped sensory apparatus resting just inside my ear. Those hairs, given enough stimulus, cause an electrical charge to pass through nerves to my brain. Those events only regard sensation, and not my conclusions about "bell" or "church" as origin of a sound.*

*Up to this point, my experience is the same as any other human who can hear. In the next step, culture works its magic. In processes of perception, I interpret the neural signals to begin figuring out what I heard. Out of the many sound waves in my environment, those particular vibrations caught my attention. Then cognition kicks in, and I think about the sound. I had to realize the vibrations had a particular source, one of human origin. Before my statement can occur, I must already know what a bell is, and I must have a concept of church somewhere in my mind. Perhaps the process goes further, and I know it is Sunday morning so those must be church bells. If they ring in the wee hours of the night, I may understand that there is an emergency, and I am called to action. My culture shaped everything after the sound wave was transduced into neural signals, and without my cultural background, the statement is impossible.*

This chapter discusses perception, which is the interpretation of sensations, and cognition, the working of the mind and of thought. Humans face a dizzying array of stimuli and issues in each moment. You may find that statement odd because you probably do not feel overwhelmed at the moment. Thank your brain's efficiency for that. You are simultaneously maintaining balance and bodily processes, your ears and eyes pour in constant stimuli that are filtered down only to the most relevant items, and you are translating symbols in this text into meaningful concepts. You may also have passing thoughts about what to have for dinner, your romantic partner, or other events of your day all at the same time. Somehow, you make sense of it all enough to function.

We do this by selectively perceiving and ignoring certain things, taking heuristic shortcuts in thought, and generally responding habitually as much as we can.

The path of neural events goes from sensation to perception to cognition. Beyond very minor genetic variation, people share the same sensory capabilities. If culture affects perception, the differences probably begin as we learn to think about the world, shaping habitual paths by which sensations become perceptions and thoughts. Distinctions between culture, thought, perception, and language may exist only in academic parlance: the topics actually blur and overlap, but for clarity, we first discuss some basics of cultural effects on cognition. Reasons for intercultural differences may be clearer if we begin with research on underlying thought patterns associated with cultures and then turn to discussion of perception, and finally to some mysteries of consciousness.

## 7.1. THINKING ABOUT THE WORLD: CULTURE AND COGNITION

### LO 7.1: Differentiate holistic and analytic cognitive styles.

Cognition refers to mental processes, beginning with how we evaluate physical sensations and growing increasingly complex as thoughts become more abstract and less rooted in the physical world. We engage in social cognition as we think about relationships between ourselves and others. Scientific consensus holds that what differentiates human cognition from other creatures' is theory of mind, discussed in Chapter 1. More recent research suggests that uniquely human cognition depends on understanding of others first as intentional agents, then as mental agents. A 1-year-old child begins to understand that others do not share the child's intention, for instance, to receive food. Understanding intentionality, how others are initiating activity, allows new forms of interaction and learning. Later, at around 4 years old, the child begins to understand that others' thoughts may differ from their own (and even from reality), seeing others as mental agents (Tomasello & Rakoczy, 2003). Cognitive skills develop in interaction with others, our languages, survival and technical skills, and worldview learned from our families and community. Intentionality provides the basis for human learning and social interaction, "with understanding of persons as mental agents representing a kind of 'icing on the cake'" (Tomasello & Rakoczy, 2003).

We engage in practical cognitive processes deciding where to live or what movie to see, in short, on a constant basis making every choice every moment of our lives. Our beliefs, values, aesthetic preferences, and judgments are all cognitive products. You may notice by now that the list resembles the components of culture we have discussed throughout the previous chapters. In fact, a number of researchers have suggested that culture *is* cognition (e.g., Bax, van Heusden, & Wildgen, 2004). Some models of cognition assume a mechanism analogous to a computer's central processor, inspiring Hofstede's (1980) suggestion that culture provides shared programming of our minds.

A school of thought called associationism underlies traditional psychology, a view that the mind is composed of linked ideas and sensations learned and connected through experience (e.g., James, 1890; Mill, 1829/1878; Brown, 1827). Aristotle listed four laws of association, laws of contiguity, frequency, similarity, and contrast, by which humans understand the world. Associations of color, taste, smell, and texture inform us whether a fruit is an apple (Warren, 1921). John Locke (1632–1704) later applied association to ideas and to the process by which a human goes from blank slate (*tabula rasa*) to possession of knowledge (Locke, 1693/2007, 1690/1836). James Mill (1773–1836) described how experience of the physical sun lingers in the mind as an idea:

> After I have seen the sun, and by shutting my eyes see him no longer, I can still think of him. I have still a feeling, the consequence of the sensation, which, though I can distinguish it from the sensation, and treat it as not the sensation, but something different from the sensation, is yet more like the sensation, than anything else can be; so like, that I call it a copy, an image, of the sensation; sometimes, a representation, or trace, of the sensation. (Mill, 1829/1878, p. 52)

To Mill, the sensations of sun and sunlight, seen and felt, become linked thoughts that remain in his mind. Associated thoughts become part of the stream of consciousness (e.g., James, 1890), the concept of sun perhaps linking to star, planet, and solar system for an astronaut. We can talk with others about these concepts and link them to other thoughts. If you are a Polynesian navigator, stars become part of a different flow of thought helping you map your journey across otherwise trackless oceans.

Associationism has branched into several different philosophical stances (Warren, 1921), forming a foundation of very different fields like behaviorism and *gestalt*. For the purposes of this chapter, associationism provides a starting point explaining how humans collect experiences and ideas, associating them as we go, and adding up to very different minds and mindsets in diverse cultural and ecological contexts. Children growing up in an urban center must navigate subways and densely packed sidewalks, eventually feeding their families as bankers, engineers, or shop clerks. Those skills may be useless in a desert, jungle, or marine environment, and a brilliant tax accountant may be utterly clueless about survival on the banks of the Amazon. Our social environment likewise provides a particular ecology of ideas.

Concept is a term for basic units of thought. John Stuart Mill (1806–1873), son of James Mill, termed them "general notions," formed as sensations associated with ideas, enabling logical thought (Mill, 1884). Concepts form the building blocks of knowledge. Interpersonally, they may be transmitted, as is the case with memes, discussed in Chapter 2 (Dawkins, 1976). *Semiotics*, from the Greek for "sign" (Oxford English Dictionary, 2003), began as an explanation of ways meanings are ascribed and transmitted symbolically with language (de Saussure, 1916, in Elicker, 1997). Whether delineated as concepts, semiotes, or memes, when added together, these units of cognition add up to ways of thinking. When they are transmitted within groups of people over time, they comprise stable sets of beliefs, worldviews, symbols, and artifacts, the building blocks of cultures (Atran, 2001; Blackmore, 2006; Kashima, 2008).

Our collections of concepts and the ways we organize them form our epistemological orientations (ojalehto & Medin, 2015), in other words, what we know and our ways of knowing. A collection of concepts about raising children would form a folk theory of parenting, as discussed in Chapter 5. Scientific method comprises a collection of concepts about best ways to conduct unbiased research, developed in Europe over several centuries, drawing on Cartesian principles of observation and experimentation. Cartesian epistemology is by no means the only way of thinking, and in fact stands on one end of a continuum of cultural differences in cognition ranging from analytic to holistic.

## Holistic and Analytic Thought

We are surrounded by far too many objects, situations, and choices to ponder each one separately, so we take shortcuts. One shortcut depends on a capacity to organize knowledge so we can access it quickly when we need to react to a situation. All humans observe and catalog the world around them using an evolved capacity to organize knowledge, but we organize in different ways. Few people are aware of their organizational system, but it affects virtually every aspect of our lives. We have discussed how individuals may think of themselves in terms of their own individuality or by their memberships and how relationships differ depending on how the culture values interdependence. Underlying these differences are enculturated patterns of thought, influencing choices including relationships, resource distribution, and cognitive organization.

Among the most documented ways cognition differs across cultures regards the attention people pay to focal or contextual information. Focal information is the main character of a story, the figure at the center of a painting, or the head of the company. Contextual information tells us where the person is, who they are with, or what is going on around them, also termed the ground in a visual image. In nature, the focus or figure is a tree, while the context or ground is the forest. This emphasis causes surprising shifts in other aspects of thought and behavior. In thought, focus on context versus actor affects how we evaluate people and situations, as discussed earlier regarding fundamental attribution theory. Perceptually, a number of effects emerge that will be discussed later.

If my focus is the individual actor, for instance, I may assume that the way a person behaves arises only from the person's characteristics because I value influences of the context less. If someone slips and falls in the cafeteria, do I think, "what a klutz" or consider the floor may have been wet? This describes the fundamental attribution error (FAE) discussed in Chapter 4, formerly thought to be a universal, but now known to demonstrate a cultural difference in cognition about context and behavior (Miyamoto, 2013). Dispositional attribution shows emphasis on focal information in which the actor is assumed to determine her own behavior independent of context. Paying more attention to context will lead me to situational attribution. FAE is a phenomenon of Western culture not found in Asia, where people focus more on context and less on internal attributes (e.g., Norenzayan & Nisbett, 2000). In other words, Asian thought processes are more likely to consider the relationship between the person and the context when making attribution of cause for behavior, while Western culture assumes that the actor acts independently from the context. The Western thought process underlies susceptibility to the error.

This difference in thought is part of a constellation of cognitive characteristics that cultural researchers describe as holistic and analytic modes of thought. **Analytic thought** relies on logic, focusing on the central actor, the individual delineated from context. **Holistic thought** emphasizes the interdependence of actors or objects in relation to each other and to context (Miyamoto, 2013). To an analytic thinker, situations and things are best understood by reducing them down into their component parts for analysis. Time is a linear experience from past to future in a direct line. Analytic views of human development gave us stage theories such as Piaget's cognitive progression from sensory-motor on toward formal operations. Descartes and scientific method sprang from analytic modes of thought. Analytic thought appears more commonly in Western culture, urban environments, and fields of science and technology. The modern university stands as the bastion and defender of analytic approaches. Individual accomplishments are most valued, and not the cultural environment or infrastructure that made them possible.

Asian and other non-Western cultures are more likely to employ a holistic style of thought. A holistic thinker understands via connections and context. To know a frog, one would observe where it lives, what it does, what it eats, and who eats the frog. Dissection might show how its organs look, but a dead frog reveals little about what a frog is in relation to the creatures of its ecosystem. A Cartesian might disassemble a clock to understand its workings, but that clock tells no time. To holistic thinkers, time goes in cycles, what is old will be new, and what goes up will come down. A practitioner of Chinese medicine looks for blocks in a patient's flow of energy to understand illness, not to specific symptoms. Whereas urban, industrialized people tend to use analytic thinking, holistic thinking appears more among rural, agrarian, and collectivist cultures.

### Social Orientation

One explanation for analytic-holistic variation is social orientation; research shows more reliance on analytic thinking among independent cultures, while holistic thinking coincides with interdependent orientation (Varnum, Grossmann, Kitayama, & Nisbett, 2010). Social organization and practices affect how people pay attention to the world, their beliefs about causality, their understanding of knowing and knowledge, and ultimately, the way they learn to think (Nisbett et al., 2001). Ancient Greece and China provide the historical roots of these differences for European and Asian cultures respectively. The Greeks emphasized individual freedom, valuing debate, and proposing rules to model how the world and its categories of things work. In contrast, the ancient Chinese saw people as inextricably linked in relationships, with a moral code based on obligations between ruler and subject, husband and wife, parent and child, etc. Harmony within the group formed a highest value still paramount in Asia today, thousands of years later. Rather than relying on categorization and abstract logic, Chinese culture has relied on experiential knowledge and acceptance of contradiction and change symbolized by yin and yang. Nature was never considered something separate from the human world. These differences have huge implications in aspects of thought and behavior.

In situations and interactions, analytic thinkers tend to focus on a prominent central figure, politically represented by the boss, king, or president who stands isolated as final authority. "The buck stops here" was Teddy Roosevelt's famous statement of ultimate responsibility. Holistic thinking, with its emphasis on connections and contexts, is associated with collective views of self and others. A ruler in Confucian culture maintains a harmonious kingdom through strong connections from his ancestors to the present and future. In idealized form, the country is a harmonious family working together.

Extensive research supports the connection between analytic-holistic thinking styles and social orientation. Markus and Kitayama (1991) explain, "If one perceives oneself as embedded within a larger context of which one is an interdependent part, it is likely that other objects or events will be perceived in a similar way" (p. 246). In a collectivist culture, how one relates to other people and how actions affect the group form the crucial elements of interaction. An individualist can simply focus on the task at hand to achieve personal wants or needs without consideration of effects on others. These approaches each require attention to particular environmental and social elements, making for very different resulting thought processes (Nisbett et al., 2001).

## Categories

Universally, humans keep track of the incredible diversity of creatures, things, and ideas in our worlds by associating them into some set of groupings. People do this organizing according to the culturally influenced cognitive styles already discussed. People with analytic thinking styles tend to use attributes of a creature or thing to create rules-based and taxonomic categories, differentiating one thing from others. Scientific classification of warm-blooded vertebrates as mammals exemplifies this process. Holistic thinkers tend to group things into thematic categories by relationships and similarities, associating rather than differentiating (Nisbett et al., 2001).

In an early cross-cultural study, Lian-Hwang Chiu (1972) compared effects of cognitive style on categorization in China and America. He presented 25 Chinese and 13 American children with pictures of humans, animals, vehicles, furniture, tools, or food in sets of three, instructing them to pick the two that go together and explain their choices. A total score was then calculated for number of responses in four possible categories:

- descriptive-analytic, referring to observable parts of an item, such as fur or scales
- descriptive-whole, including total representations such as size
- relational-contextual, choosing similarity based on function or theme
- inferential categorical, including function (e.g., cutting), class membership (e.g., fruit), attribute (e.g., motors of boats and cars) or location (e.g., farm)

As Chiu expected, American children based significantly more choices on descriptive-analytic and inferential-categorical reasons, while Chinese children used significantly more relational-contextual and descriptive-whole reasons. In Chiu's and a number of later studies, dog, rabbit, and carrot formed one of the prompts for association (see Figure 7.1). Typically, analytic thinkers group the dog and rabbit together taxonomically, both being warm-blooded mammals with fur. Holistic thinkers tend to associate the rabbit and the carrot because rabbits stereotypically eat carrots (Brown, McDonald, & Roman, 2014).

Figure 7.1   Images From Categorization Research

*Source:* Brown, McDonald, and Roman (2014).

Presented with a man, woman, and child, an analytic thinker most often pairs the adults, while a holistic thinker would choose the woman and child because of maternal interaction (Price & Briley, 1999).

As with much of cross-cultural psychology, analytic/holistic comparisons are most frequently made between Asian and European/American samples, corresponding to independent/interdependent concepts of self (Marcus & Kitayama, 1991) and Hofstede's (1980) dimensions of individualism and collectivism. As research continues, though, other factors are emerging that may influence patterns of thought. Miyamoto and Ji (2011) found that SES (socioeconomic status) and sense of agency (power to choose actions) differentiated American students, for whom higher SES and personal agency correlated with taxonomic categorization.

Leaving the Asia-Euro-American world, still more possibilities emerge. In the first study to use Chiu's (1972) categorization task in the Caribbean, Brown and colleagues (2014) found a third rationale: usefulness. Brown had taught psychology in the Dominican Republic for several semesters and had her cross-cultural psychology students go out and test Chiu's stimuli with Dominican participants. The expectation was that as a country identified as collectivist on Hofstede's (1980) dimensions, Dominicans would favor a holistic approach, but responses often were neither holistic nor taxonomic. Eventually, a pattern emerged, exemplified by the statement, "The dog and the carrot are both useful to me," meaning people could imagine a function for the thing in their own lives (Brown et al., 2014, p. 64).

To test whether this proposed cognitive style would hold up to scrutiny, Brown and colleagues (2014) arranged a study. Dominican lifestyles range from affluent and urbane to rural and poor, and to evaluate SES influences, they recruited 76 participants, 32 from the city, and 44 in rural/poor areas. Each was shown five choice triads. The researchers predicted that scarcity in the lives of the rural poor would lead them toward functional categorization. Results showed overwhelmingly holistic choices from the urban sample, in keeping with the collectivism of the culture. The rural sample primarily chose the functional grouping (see Table 7.1).

| Table 7.1   Dominican Categorization Styles | | | |
|---|---|---|---|
| | Number of Responses | | |
| Sample SES | Functional | Holistic | Taxonomical |
| Urban/Abundance | 9 | 139 | 7 |
| Rural/Scarcity | 150 | 51 | 19 |

*Source:* Brown et al. (2014).

All over the world, biology forms a core domain of cognition and categorization (Medin & Atran, 2004). Humans have forever had to use the plants and animals around them for survival, though availability of species has changed as humans migrated from our common African origins. Moving further away from Western culture, cognition about organization operates very differently. To the Yupno of the remote New Guinea highlands, all things, from plants to people to states of health, traditionally fall into categories of *tepm* ("hot"), *yawut* ("lukewarm," "fresh," "cool"), or *mbak* ("cold") (Wassmann & Dasen, 1994). The extremes of hot and cold present danger, so Yupno prefer the safer *yawut* choices. Things that are colored black or red are typically *tepm*, while white is *mbak*. Certain bananas are cold, while insects are hot. We all organize in some way, though schema from a culture not our own may be difficult to understand. Interestingly, as the Yupno adapt to outside cultures, those who are educated in schools tend to categorize by color, an attributional choice.

## Time

The Yupno also have a very unique way of conceptualizing time: past is downhill and future is uphill (Núñez, Cooperrider, Doan, & Wassmann, 2012). Everyone experiences time, events passing with no way to actually re-experience them. Time is an inherently abstract concept, being something we experience but cannot see or hold. Linguists describe two types of time concepts: **deictic time**, with "now" as the reference point between past and future, and **sequence time**, which is unanchored, as in saying summer comes before autumn. Cultures all tend to describe time metaphorically, in spatialized terms like front/back or up/down. Western culture conceives of time as a line from past to future, hence the term *timeline*. The past is behind me and the future is in front, a seemingly egocentric description. The Aymara, an indigenous culture of the Andes, provide a rare example in which the past falls metaphorically in front and the future in back because you know and see the past. What is behind you is unknown and unseen, like the future (Núñez & Sweetser, 2006).

The Yupno uphill–downhill description is environmental, not connected to the self. If a Yupno is facing uphill while describing a past event, he will gesture behind him to indicate past, but to the front if facing downhill. This defies linear conceptualization of time as a line from past to future and disconnects time from the person. The future may

# SPOTLIGHT

## PHYSIOLOGIC IMPLICATIONS OF CULTURE: NEURONS AND CULTURAL BRAINS

Definitions of culture in psychology tend to emphasize cognition. Our definition of "constellations of thought and behavior" certainly follows a trend so common that some have suggested that culture is cognition. van Willigen, Chada, and McDonald (1999) caution that psychology is guilty of locating all explanatory models between the ears in the brain, but that anthropology and other social sciences would take issue with the culture = cognition equation. A better question might be to ask how deeply culture affects our neurology, and fortunately, recent technological advances in imaging (e.g., fMRI) allow unprecedented access to the physiology of mental processes. A growing body of evidence, appearing throughout the text, shows marked differences in areas activated when people are prompted to think in particular cultural modes.

Kitayama and Park (2010) called for a new field of cultural neuroscience to expand knowledge in this area. As evidence of the importance of culture in brain morphology, they offer a variety of cases where differences have been documented. One example involves the areas of the brain activated during mathematical computation. Children in East Asia are taught to use the abacus, moving beads that represent numbers to perform calculations, and master users are incredibly fast. Non-users show activation in linguistic centers (e.g., Broca's area), while young users add activation in motor cortices. More advanced users show activation in parietal centers involved in visual and spatial processing, with bilateral activation in advanced users.

London taxi drivers must navigate an exceptionally complex tangle of streets, finding destinations using creative ways around heavy traffic. Maguire and colleagues (e.g., Maguire, Woollet, & Spiers, 2006) investigated differences in the hippocampus of the drivers, a brain structure involved in memory and navigation. Indeed, differences were found between taxi drivers and bus drivers, who follow only consistent routes. Further, to check for effects of expert-level expertise, they compared the taxi drivers to medical doctors, who also must use training and experience to find novel solutions, finding no effect on the grey matter of the doctors (Woollet, Glensman, & Maguire, 2008). These changes can only be explained by effects of training and repetition of practices specific to a cultural activity and context. Culture is unquestionably sculpting our brains, optimizing us for our cultural milieu.

### Why It Matters

For culture to be a valid area of inquiry in psychology, evidence must exist that culture explains phenomena beyond foundational universals of human thought and behavior. If culture results in significant differences in brain structure and activity in addition to variation in behaviors and beliefs, perhaps this is sufficient evidence that culture should be a central topic in the study of human psychology.

be uphill because the Yupno believe their ancestors traveled from an offshore island up to their current highland home, but this is conjecture (Núñez et al., 2012). Mandarin speakers use back/front spatialized terms for past and future like English, but they also use vertical metaphors *shàng* (up) and *xià* (down) to refer to order of events (Boroditsky,

Furhman, & McCormick, 2011). Rather than a topographic representation like the Yupno, the Mandarin conception is an abstract verticality without a slope, with the past below and the future above.

In each case, these directional concepts are built into the language. Boroditsky (2001) demonstrated that bilingual Mandarin/English speakers maintained a bias toward vertical spatialization even when speaking English, despite the dual horizontal and vertical options in Mandarin. She provided either horizontal or vertical spatial primes (statements including ahead/behind or above/below with a horizontally or vertically oriented graphic) before asking a series of true/false questions about statements such as "March comes before April" or "March comes earlier than April." Her hypothesis was that horizontal primes would speed up responses for native English speakers and vertical prompts would slow them, with native Mandarin speakers exhibiting the opposite effect. Her hypothesis has been supported across multiple inquiries (Boroditsky, 2001; Boroditsky et al., 2011). A number of cognitive differences are connected to language acquisition processes of childhood and will be discussed in a later chapter.

Another cultural effect on reasoning about time appears in prediction of what the future will bring. Western culture and the analytic style of thought views trends as consistent, so rising house prices will be expected to continue to rise. Asian holistic perspective brings expectations that trends will change, as represented by the yin-yang symbol. Rising prices will someday drop and life is a mix of good and bad, but even unfortunate events yield to good eventually.

## Reasoning and Contradiction

The differing views of time reflect a deeper pattern of cognition that affects how people deal with decisions, contrasts, and contradictions. This has been examined in a literature that again relies heavily on Western Europe, the US, and East Asia. As with categorization and social orientation, holistic thinking considers ideas, objects, and other people in terms of context and relationships. By its nature, reality is seen to be in flux and everything exists as part of a complex whole. Inherent in this view is contradiction, which Asian culture deals with by seeking the compromise of a "middle way" (Peng & Nisbett, 1999, p. 742). The ancient Chinese systematized the shifting nature of reality in the *I Ching*, or *Book of Changes*, as a systematized tool of divination. Yin gives way to yang and yang to yin in complex patterns of six lines, creating 64 hexagrams. Each represents a set of conditions, named and described more than two millennia ago. Centuries of subsequent commentary provide advice on questions being asked, given the energy fluctuations in that moment when the oracle is cast.

Western thought, conversely, sees the world as stable, with thoughts and things remaining consistent and true to definable and constant traits. Everything can be considered on its own merit, independent of context. Contradictions violate the rules of logic, as advocated by Aristotle (384–322 BCE) a few centuries after the *I Ching* reached its basic form. If two propositions contradict each other, those rules of logic are used to discern which is true and which is false. In that system, all questions, properly examined and debated, come down to a single, unchanging answer.

Peng and Nisbett (1999) describe the Asian mode as dialectical, willing to consider opposing views and find a compromise between them. The Eastern view looks outward into the environment with its complexities and contradictions amid the world of creatures, ideas, and things, all of which must be accommodated and accepted. Holistic thought, with its dialectical negotiation of process and change, explains the more malleable views of self and others in contrast to Western essentialism (Ma-Kellams & Blascovich, 2012).

Westerners, they say, are much less willing to compromise and consider the attributes of things and situations to be fixed. It is perhaps the focus on field and context that allowed the Chinese to understand acoustic resonance, magnetism, and tides some 1,500 years before Europeans. Peng and Nisbett acknowledge, however, that neither system is without flaws, and that the analytic style of Western thought allowed for the development of modern physics. This is not to say that Western people never consider context or that cultures are homogenous in thinking style, but Eastern and Western cultures arose based in distinct tendencies in patterns of thought dating back millennia, and these affect what we think and perceive today.

## REALITY CHECK

Do your own thoughts tend to be more holistic or analytic?

Dog, rabbit, or carrot—which is the odd one out? Why?

Can you think of a few hours in the future as being behind you? The past in front?

## 7.2 CULTURE AND PERCEPTION

### LO 7.2: Describe ways culture may shape perception.

Perception is the process of converting sensation into thought, something everyone does all the time. Several of the topics already discussed influence how we perform those processes, including the analytic/holistic styles of thinking and independent vs. interdependent self-construal. In one of the most interesting aspects of cultural difference, culture shapes how we literally see the world.

The idea that culture influences perception is an old one, but empirical demonstration took time (Segall, Campbell, & Herskovits, 1966). The underlying hypothesis was that environmental conditions would lead to different processing of sensory data. A classic difference in perception arises from growing up in rectangular buildings, leading to susceptibility to the Müller-Lyer illusion (see Figure 7.2). The illusion was designed by Franz Müller-Lyer in 1889, and by 1905, William Rivers reported differences in susceptibility among the Todas of Southern India and indigenous people of Australia's

Figure 7.2   Müller-Lyer Illusion

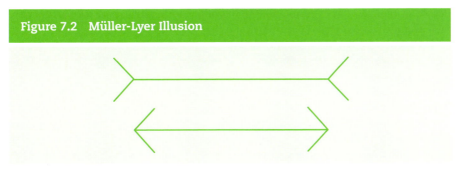

*Source:* Müller-Lyer (1889).

Torres Straits. The illusion depends on adaptation of visual perception to judge distance and size, in this case specific adaptation to life in squared buildings. The lines in Figure 7.2 are the same length, but to most people reading this book, the top line, with lines radiating outward at each end, will appear to be longer because it looks as though it is an inside corner farther away.

People who grow up in igloos, hogans, or other round structures are not fooled by the illusion. To show that susceptibility comes from the developmental environment, Pedersen and Wheeler (1983) measured the effect with two groups of Navajo students at Brigham Young University in Utah. They identified 10 students who spent at least their first six years living in a hogan, a traditional round or octagonal dwelling made of wood and clay. They were matched with a second group of 10 who grew up in rectangular houses. The researchers used a device that allowed participants to slide the end of one set of lines, attempting to match the size of the corresponding set (see Figure 7.3).

Figure 7.3   Müller-Lyer Illusion Measurement Device, Lafayette
             Instrument Company

*Source:* Lafayette Instrument Company.

People susceptible to the illusion tend to misjudge line length. The size of errors were then averaged across trials, and they found that the students from the curved hogan environment were significantly more accurate in their matches.

## Attention

A more subtle effect of culture is found in where our attention goes as we look around, and therefore what we perceive and retain more readily. Holistic versus analytic thought is associated with differences in visual perception that manifest in several ways, one of which is how people look at a picture. The earliest evidence for differences in attention came from Abel and Hsu's 1949 study of responses to Rorschach tests. Chinese Americans tended to respond based on the entire inkblot shape, whereas European Americans tended to give responses referring to a restricted part of the inkblot (Ishii, 2013). Research on this phenomenon has continued and branched into several streams.

Masuda and Nisbett (2001) asked American and Japanese participants to describe the scene in animated videos showing focal fish set against a natural looking background. The Japanese participants included much more information on the background of the scene than Americans, who gave more details about the fish. In the second phase they were asked whether they recognized objects that were new or already seen and recognition accuracy followed the same pattern. This attention pattern can be observed by computerized tracking of eye movement. Chua, Boland, and Nisbett (2005), for instance, showed participants pictures of objects set against realistic backgrounds. North American participants focused on the central object faster and longer, and Chinese participants spent more time attending to the background. Masuda and Nisbett (2006) tested sensitivity to change in Japanese and North American participants, alternating photos with a change in either the foreground object or background until the change was noticed. North Americans were more adept at noticing foreground than background changes. Japanese participants were equally good at both conditions but were faster than Americans at noticing background changes.

Sharon Goto and colleagues (2013) documented physiological evidence of cultural effects on perception, testing sensitivity to emotional incongruity between facial emotion and elements of a background scene by measuring the N400 ERP. Magnitude of the N400 brain response has been found to increase when mismatches of meaning occur. They showed pictures with happy or sad faces against happy or sad background pictures to 23 Asian American and 23 European American students, asking them to identify the facial emotion in 50 congruent and 50 incongruent pairings. As expected, significantly larger N400s were measured for Asian American students when the background did not match the facial emotion, and interdependent self-construal was also positively related to the larger N400s. No differences were observed for the European Americans. These results are consistent with earlier findings of differences between analytic and holistic thought on a neural level: mismatch between foreground and context interferes with perceptual processes of holistic but not analytic thinkers.

Miyamoto, Nisbett, and Masuda (2006) questioned whether something in the physical environment influenced attention. They selected scenes at random from small, medium, and large cities in Japan and the US and asked participants to rate elements in the pictures, for instance, "'How many different objects do there seem to be?' (1 relatively few; 5 enormous number)," and "'To what degree is the scene either chaotic or organized?' (1 organized; 5 chaotic)" (p. 115). Japanese scenes were rated as more complex and ambiguous with more items. The researchers then used the scenes as primes for detection of contextual changes and found that Japanese participants detected more contextual changes than Americans, but that both groups detected more contextual changes after priming with Japanese scenes. Ueda and Komiya (2012) presented 32 Japanese students at Kyoto University with American and Japanese scenes, finding that participants moved their eyes more broadly when viewing Japanese scenes than for American ones, and continued to exhibit broader movement when viewing a neutral scene after priming with Japanese scenes than American ones. Whether Japanese society constructs more complex environments intentionally is unclear, but it would appear that their environments are conducive to more holistic visual perception.

### Field Dependence/Independence

In the late 1940s, Herman Witkin encountered an odd phenomenon he called the field-dependence/field-independence dimension. Witkin and Asch (1948) designed a test of how people identify which way is up and what is vertical, processes we normally do with a combination of bodily sensation and visual cues. The test uses a frame and a rod, both of which can be rotated independently, with an assistant moving the rod until the participant says it is perpendicular. They were surprised to find that, while some people could place the rod in a true vertical position regardless of the frame's position (field-independent), others would align the rod with the frame, even if it was 30 degrees off-kilter (field-dependent). The same applied when people were asked to position themselves upright in a tilted room. They were dependent on the visual field to determine position.

This perceptual test eventually led Witkin to understand that people responded to a number of situations in the same way, including tests of functional fixedness, with field-independent people more easily finding the novel solution. Field-dependent thinkers made fewer distinctions and bigger categories in grouping tasks and paid more attention to social information in defining feelings. Witkin found a range of consistent differences in what he came to call cognitive styles. These affected how people learned and taught, did therapy, and related interpersonally in pervasive patterns, with field-dependent people retaining information with social content more easily, for instance (e.g., Witkin, Moore, Goodenough, & Cox, 1977).

Field-dependence–independence forms a facet of interconnected concepts in perception and cognition. Subsequent cultural research finds that field-dependence is associated with sedentary agricultural settings and tight social organization, while field-independence ties to sociocultural looseness in nomadic hunting ecologies (Witkin & Berry, 1975). Ji, Peng, and Nisbett (2000) found that Chinese, Japanese, and Korean participants were more affected by frame position in the rod and frame test than were their American participants. Masuda and Nisbett (2001) connected field-dependence–independence to context sensitivity and more broadly to the analytic-holistic cognitive styles discussed earlier, which in turn connect to independent–interdependent self-construals, modernization versus traditional contexts, and other dimensions of cultural variation.

## Language and Perception

The emergence of language marked an evolutionary revolution without which human history would not exist. Language identifies the things and creatures of the world in verbal symbols that can be pondered and transmitted to others, allowing us to develop science, technology, philosophy, and cuisine, for example. Words inherently categorize, so we can pair "cuisine" with "French nouvelle" and not with "oil well." As cultures differ in cognitive style, they also differ in how words map onto concepts. In English, eating is discrete from drinking or smoking, but the Turkish word *içmek* can refer to all three (Lupyan, 2016). Lupyan gives language a central place in cognition, words providing cues pointing to meaning. Words can convey knowledge, like where to find food, or internal states like hunger that are not externally visible. Words can also convey abstractions like education or honor, and the terminology will prioritize and link concepts. The Hawaiian word *pono* is similar in definition to "honor," but it emphasizes interpersonal responsibility and reliability, as expected in a collectivistic culture, whereas honor is more of an internal, individual state.

Language unquestionably influences how we organize our thinking about the world. Indonesian language uses signifiers when counting like *ekor*, or tail, when talking about animals. One would say "*dua ekor kucing,*" "two tails cat," rather than "two cats." Houses are *rumah*, using the indicator *buah*, or fruit, interestingly, so "three houses" would be "*tiga buah rumah.*" Paper is more obvious, using the signifier "*daun,*" for leaf. How crucial language is to cognition is a subject of debate, but to some researchers, language *is* cognition. I personally think primarily in words, which seems normative, though the famous autistic animal researcher Temple Grandin says she understands animals so well because she thinks visually as they do, in pictures rather than words (e.g., Grandin, 2013). Language and cognition are certainly connected, but how, and at what level of universality or effect?

In the Eurocentric 19th-century view of evolution, anthropology considered unwritten languages and their associated cultures inferior. This prompted Franz Boas and his students to embark on a mission to demonstrate that languages of non-Europeans are as complex and richly descriptive as those of Europe, whether written or not. To his student Edward Sapir (1929), what we perceive is a world "to a large extent built up on the language habits of the group" (p. 209). Sapir's student Benjamin Whorf took the idea further, describing the world as "a kaleidoscopic flux of impressions which has to be organized by our minds—and this means largely by the linguistic systems in our minds" (Whorf, 1956, p. 213). Whorf's ideas form the radical extreme of linguistic relativity, proposing that differences in linguistic systems parallel differences in cognition, and that native language determines perceptual experience (Kay & Kempton, 1984). My perceptual experience might be completely different from yours, if we speak a different language.

The theory became known as the Sapir-Whorf hypothesis. It since vacillated between acceptance and outright rejection. Early research largely focused on color, with the idea that language would lead to differing color perception, following Whorf's own idea that Eskimos would surely have multiple and exclusive terms for snow, making them more sensitive to differences. The ultimate test is to demonstrate that language does (or does not) affect perception.

## The Language of Color

Color is continuous, spread across the vibrational frequencies our retinas can capture. We perceive them as discrete, however, as in the bands of color we think we see in a rainbow. Color perception forms an important area of cross-cultural research. A number of disciplines including biology, physiology, psychology, and anthropology have studied and defined the processes of sight (Jameson, 2005). While theories of color perception remain unresolved, there is no question that we all have the same rods and cones stimulated by photons to fire messages into optic nerves and visual cortices. Vision and color perception seem universal, excepting color blindness, but variations have been observed in individual capabilities. Because of its ubiquity, vision provides a superb testing ground for cultural differences in cognition and perception. The question is whether culture leads us to see color differently, much as carpentered corners lead us to fall for the Müller-Lyer illusion (Figure 7.2).

The ways we name and categorize colors, if Whorf was correct, may provide a window into perceptual and cognitive processes (Bornstein, 1975). A universalist would propose that all people follow the same rules of categorization and will group and remember colors in ways generalizable across languages. A relativist would expect variation in categories, and for the categories to affect color perception. The debate still rages, but with decades of research only now reaching some interesting conclusions.

Berlin and Kay (1969) undertook a major effort to catalogue color lexicons (verbal categories or terminologies) from different cultures. They, along with a number of other studies, have relied on the Munsell (1912) color system, which charted colors in a three-dimensional space based on hue, lightness, and color purity. Generally, researchers would ask participants to identify colors by pointing them out on a chart of 320 Munsell chips of 40 hues plus nine black to white chips. While paint companies have hundreds of names for their products (Exuberant Pink and Adrift were two top colors for one paint company in 2018), English splits color into 11 basic terms: black, white, red, green, yellow, blue, orange, purple, pink, brown, and gray (Davies & Corbett, 1995). The Aguaruna Jivaro of Peru have only four color terms, translating to black, white, red, and grue (green blue) (Berlin & Berlin, 1975). Rosch Heider and colleagues (e.g., Rosch Heider, 1972; Rosch Heider & Olivier, 1972) performed studies with the Dugum Dani of Irian Jaya, the Indonesian portion of New Guinea, whom she reported had only two color terms, *mola* (dark and cold colors) and *mili* (light and warm). Rosch Heider claimed that despite the linguistic differences, the Dani exhibited similar cognition and memory of colors to English speakers and could learn to identify what she termed focal colors with equal facility, supporting the universalist stance. Roberson, Davies, and Davidoff (2000) attempted to replicate Rosch-Heider's results, comparing

Berinmo (with five colors) and Americans, but concluded there were relativistic effects of language on color perception. The controversy grew.

The World Color Survey collected data from speakers of 110 unwritten languages and compared groupings (Cook, Kay, & Regier, 2005). Linguistic categories of color do indeed vary widely in number and characteristic, but they tend to cluster in patterns that are more similar than chance would allow, suggesting a universal perceptual similarity. On the other hand, a number of studies have shown that people differ in memory, learning, and discrimination of colors, with greatest difficulty at the borders between linguistically created categories (e.g., Kay & Regier, 2006; Pilling & Davies, 2004; Roberson, 2005). This would indicate a Whorfian effect on the tasks. More recent research using fMRI technology shows that there is an effect of language on brain activity, but surprisingly, only in the right visual field, leading Regier and Kay (2009) to declare with some sarcasm that Whorf was half right. Further neuroimaging research shows that these effects persist even in non-linguistic tasks, suggesting that language may be so deeply integrated into cognitive processes that lexical categories are still accessed in non-lexical tasks (Imai, Kanero, & Masuda, 2016).

The universal-relative debate on language and color continues, and probably both sides are correct to some degree. Gibson and colleagues (2017) studied recognition of colors by name with participants who were Bolivian Spanish speakers, Tsimané hunter-gatherers of the Bolivian Amazon, or English speaking students in Boston. Despite linguistic differences in color categories, communication was more effective for warm colors (yellows/reds) than for cool colors (greens/blues) in all three groups. The authors also examined colors of human created objects in all three environments, finding much more use of warm colors. Chattopadhyay, Gorn, and Darke (2010) found that Chinese and American participants favored similar colors and only differed in their expressed color preferences when asked about colors associated with a holiday. These results indicate a potential universal bias toward particular colors despite differences in categorization.

## REALITY CHECK

*Looking at the Müller-Lyer diagram (Figure 7.2), do the lines look the same length? Even if you know they are?*

*Do you speak a second language? Are the color names slightly different? Do you agree with your friends and family when coming up with color names?*

## 7.3 CULTURE AND INTELLIGENCE

### LO 7.3: Explain non-Western concepts of intelligence and limitations of intelligence theory.

Taking concepts of awareness, perception, and thought to the next stage, intelligence generally deals with how well or poorly people can add knowledge and, using knowledge gained, learn to respond to the stimuli they perceive. Few topics in social sciences so inflame passionate debate as those related to race and intelligence. Underlying these topics are the great dilemmas of universalism versus relativism, scientific ethnocentrism, and white male academic privilege. Usual definitions of intelligence include ability to learn and solve problems, though definition of intelligence is itself an ongoing debate. Historic definitions included Wechsler's (1944) opening to his book on measurement of intelligence, "the aggregate or global capacity of the individual to act purposefully, to think rationally, and to deal effectively with his environment" (p. 3). Piaget (2005) wrote, "intelligence constitutes the state of equilibrium towards which tend all the successive adaptations of a sensori-motor and cognitive nature, as well as all assimilatory and accommodatory interactions between the organism and the environment" (p. 10). Adaptation to what the individual encounters environmentally forms a commonality between the two statements, but other definitions have been proposed and the debate is certainly not over.

Need to quantify and measure the concept grew a century ago as educators and psychologists sought to identify what was described as feeble-mindedness, retardation, or idiocy (Terman, 1921). At the end of the 19th century, France mandated compulsory education for all children, but not all children could succeed in the classroom environment of the time. Within a few years, psychologist Alfred Binet was engaged to create a test to assess mental deficiency. The Binet-Simon test first appeared in 1908, and soon after, Lewis Terman began publishing the revisions eventually called the Stanford-Binet Intelligence Scales (Terman & Childs, 1912). Terman himself only considered the test a rough diagnostic tool, saying "that no intelligence scale gives an entirely accurate measure even of intelligence" (Terman, 1921, p. 403). Though Terman became associated with the eugenics movement, he strongly opposed the idea of racial superiority, stating, "any proposal to apply in practice the doctrine of the biological inequality of human beings, whether in politics or education, infringes upon some of our deepest-lying prejudices, and challenges our fundamental philosophies of life" (Terman, 1921, p. 362). He saw intelligence as a product of heredity and environment together, and intended his test as a tool to channel youth toward their best chance of success.

One of the most resilient theories is Spearman's (1904) *g* factor of general intelligence, which he developed after observing similarities of scores in different scales. People who score high on one test or scale tend to do so on others, leading Spearman to propose people have some degree of general intelligence underlying all mental capacities. The theory remains influential among universalist researchers. Psychologists who work across cultures, however, often will say that cultural differences in experience and thinking style lead to differences in scores that do not reflect actual differences in cognitive ability. A relativist would say you cannot measure intelligence without considering culture and context.

WWII created a great need to assess abilities of recruits rapidly and accurately, but the variety of ages and life experiences people brought to the war effort meant many were unprepared for a paper test, and language presented barriers for others (Cattell, 1943). In 1940, Raymond Cattell proposed a culture-free intelligence test intended to minimize effects of cultural mismatches on outcome. His work led him eventually to break intelligence down into crystalized intelligence (Gc), which would include vocabulary and other formal ideas that can be recalled and recited, and fluid intelligence (Gf), describing abstract reasoning and problem solving ability (Brown, 2016; Cattell, 1943; Sternberg, 2004). His tests began an effort toward greater cross-cultural accuracy.

Two notable theories further depart from the orthodoxy of a single universal intelligence: Gardner's theory of multiple intelligences and Sternberg's triarchic theory of intelligence. In their research, both saw examples that did not fit the prominent theories. Gardner observed highly talented youth with intellectual impairments and adults with stroke-induced impairments. Sternberg did extensive international research in non-Western cultures. Both developed theories intended to expand the field beyond conventional Western understandings of intelligence.

Sternberg (2004) developed a concept he called *successful intelligence*, in other words, the cognitive abilities needed to do well in a particular cultural setting. He had collaborated on research in numerous cultures, studying the Dholuo of Kenya, the Yu'pik of Alaska, and other groups in Russia, Zambia, Jamaica, and elsewhere. He and his colleagues found that children in many of these contexts did not do well on Western style tests geared toward academic achievement, but they had intricate knowledge of their immediate culture and environment. They could find and prepare foods, utilize medicinal herbs, or navigate across snow-covered tundra, finding solutions to complex problems posed in situations that could be lethal to an American student. His triarchic theory of intelligence includes domains of componential (analytic), experiential (creative), and practical (contextual) intelligences, with which he hoped to explain the wider variety of cognitive expertise he encountered.

Gardner (1995) pushed further, questioning the need to focus on analytic conceptualizations of intelligence that rely on design and analysis of testing instruments. He posits that humans recognized intelligence and ability long before Binet's tests, and that we could continue to do so even if every measurement instrument disappeared tomorrow. Further, he found the idea appealing that perhaps intelligence included an array of independent faculties, present to greater or lesser degrees in everyone.

Gardner (1995) based his ideas on observations of some people with very unique abilities. They included older stroke victims who retained significant abilities despite losing others. Perhaps more important were young people with profound talents, some of whom were then called idiot savants. They had, for instance, exceptional ability to solve math problems or to remember and play musical pieces, despite having severely limited communicative or intellectual abilities. He took the isolated appearance of these abilities as indications that they may represent independent aspects of intelligence. He proposed seven domains of intelligence:

Linguistic intelligence (verbal abilities)

Logical-mathematical intelligence (numeric/math ability)

Spatial intelligence (ability with visual and physical space)

Bodily-Kinesthetic intelligence (athletes, dancers, people with fine and great motor skills)

Musical intelligence (musical ability)

Interpersonal intelligence (ability to understand and/or communicate with others)

Intrapersonal intelligence (understanding of one's own feelings and thoughts)

To this list, Gardner eventually added naturalist intelligence—an understanding of the natural world and its components. Much later, he also added creative and existential dimensions.

Gardner's (1998) theory of multiple intelligences (MI) has received criticism for what some see as inherent contradictions. Distinguished scholar Hans Eysenck (1995) critiqued both Gardner's and Sternberg's theories in a scathing review. Still, their ideas resonate among cultural and cross-cultural researchers, particularly in education (e.g., Kim & Cha, 2008; Suprapto, Lu, & Ku, 2017; Wu & Alrabah, 2009). Each provides a rich explanatory framework for interpersonal differences in ability, but also as underpinnings for broader intercultural differences. Ultimately, the evidence presented here supports that people engage in different types and modes of thinking, and that these modes reflect differences on a broader cultural level.

## Beyond Euro-American Conceptualizations of Intelligence

So far, we have discussed Western concepts of intelligence and forays into broader ideas by Western researchers. These are all etic conceptualizations of intelligence exported from Europe and the post-colonial nations like the US, Canada, and Australia. As Gardner (1998) suggests, however, people recognized ability and intelligence long before attempts at scientific definition. One must also wonder about emic conceptualization of intelligence and intellectual ability within cultures. What follows is a brief look at concepts of intelligence in a few other cultures.

In Confucian traditions of East Asia, intelligence is cultivated over a lifetime through self-discipline. An intelligent person has acquired knowledge and maintains social relationships through politeness and respect, knowing what to do in the right moment. This forms an incremental view of intelligence, as opposed to the fixed trait view more typical of Euro-Americans where a person is either smart or is not. Buddhism and Hinduism consider knowledge to be gathered through the senses and experience, much as associationists might, but value a further stage of transcendence, when the individual mind merges with the greater universal mind (e.g., Chen, 1972; Cocodia, 2014). Hinduism refers to that transcendence as *pratibha*, and the related concept *Buddhi* adds determination and affective elements to aspects of understanding and knowledge (Das, 1994; Singh, 2012).

Nevo and bin Khader (1995) undertook a study designed to tease out cultural conceptions of intelligence. Their participants were Indian, Chinese, and Malay mothers in Singapore, providing a cross-cultural comparison. They began with a pilot study in which 63 mothers were asked to describe characteristics of intelligent and unintelligent behaviors. The resulting set of 55 items was used to create a survey completed by 708 mothers. Four factors emerged in analysis: cognitive/academic ability (learns quickly, good in counting and using numbers), appropriate behavior (disciplined, shows patience), socially interactive behavior (playful, makes friends easily), and unintelligent behavior (is not active, reads with mistakes). The mothers were in agreement overall on their ratings of importance of items, which is not surprising given their residence in the small but diverse nation of Singapore. One overall difference was that Malaysian mothers rated the first two factors higher than the Chinese mothers. There were also item differences, with the greatest difference on "has high score on intelligence test" which Chinese mothers rated much more important, though this contradicts the lower valuing of Factor 1 by the Chinese mothers. Unfortunately, the study has not been replicated to clarify results.

Klein, Freeman, Spring, Nerlove, and Yarbrough (1976) undertook an early exploration of concepts of intelligence in rural towns of Guatemala. The Spanish term *listura* translates as "intelligence" in English, with associated qualities of alertness, verbal acuity, and physical activity. The children were part of an ongoing study on effects of malnutrition and had taken a battery of IQ type tests repeatedly. A number of adults from their communities rated the children on *listura*. Agreement between judges was very high (correlations around .70). Correlations between the composite cognitive scores from the Western tests and the *listura* ratings were also significant at <.05. The researchers hesitated, however, to conclude that the study provided evidence of equivalence between the concepts.

West Africa consists of 17 countries on the southern half of Africa's western bulge, covering about 8 million square kilometers. By comparison, the area of the entire US, including Alaska and Hawai'i, is 9 million square kilometers. Borders of the countries cut through ancient kingdoms, tribal territories, and language groups. Though there were dozens of languages in the past, most people currently speak eight languages, with Hausa most common at 25 million, followed by Yoruba at 19 million (Linguistic Data Consortium, 2018).

Swiss psychologist Pierre Dasen began traveling to Côte d'Ivoire (Ivory Coast) in the 1970s to study development using Piaget's cognitive stage theories. He spent time with the Baoulé of Côte d'Ivoire and was surprised to find little difference in development of concrete operations skills in their children despite poverty and consumption of half the calories of a European child (Dasen, 1984; Dasen et al., 1985; Dasen, Lavallée, Retschitzki, 1979). He became curious about other cultural constructs of intelligence, expecting that languages would have an equivalent term. The Baoulé did indeed have such a term: *n'glouélè*. He was told that *n'glouélè* has several social components, including *ô ti kpa*, with meanings including responsibility, obedience, and honesty. Of the eight components he lists, others include *i gni ti klè*, referring to observation, intelligence, and memory, *angyhiè*, meaning politeness and respect, and *angundan*, meaning wisdom in adults and maturity in children (Dasen, 1984).

Further concepts emerged with creation of indigenous African psychologies, plural because hundreds of cultures call the continent home and the psychologists engaged are diverse. Born in Nigeria in West Africa, Michael Durojaiye earned his PhD in psychology in England, returning to teach in Nigeria in 1968. Durojaiye was Yoruba. He explained the Yoruba view of intelligence:

There are different words used to indicate the components of the Yoruba concept of intelligence. For instance, there are different words for wisdom (*ogbon*), understanding (*oye*), planfullness (*eto*), knowledge (*imoran*), attentiveness (*ifokansi*), brains (*opolo*), and thoughtfulness (*ironu*); there are other words for ingenuity, creativity, originality, and discretion. Finally, there is a distinction made between constructive intelligence (*ogbon ewe*) and destructive intelligence, or skill in deception or cunning. The former is admired, the latter despised. (Durojaiye, 1993, p. 215)

This is a sophisticated delineation of the forms, functions, and effects of what, in English, is simply intelligence.

Cameroon lies just south of West Africa, home to 250 languages. It was home to Bame Nsamenang, who taught at Yaoundé University's Advanced School of Education. He pointed to development of social thought as a primary aspect of intelligence in the cultures around him. Healthy development requires "the acquisition and growth of the physical, cognitive, social, and emotional competencies required to engage fully in family and society" (Nsamenang, 2006). Children learn social responsibility through participatory learning through tasks such as neighborhood errands in which they must interact with others, learning values and skills as they go about this "work." Elders can evaluate the child's level of social cognition, for instance the concept of *tumikila* in Zambia, meaning intelligence about social responsibility. Serpell, Mumba, and Chansa-Kabali (2011) explain that for the Chewa, the term *nzelu* may be closer conceptually to intelligence, including wisdom, cleverness, and skill. *Chenjela* indicates cleverness or advanced cognitive skills, but to be *nzelu*, one must also display *tumikila*. Otherwise, with cleverness and no sense of responsibility, one poses a threat to the social group.

How do we understand these similarities and differences in conceptualization of intelligence? We can look at established dimensions of cultural difference (e.g., Hofstede, 1980), and we will see some expected variation. Euro-American cultures place great value on literate individuals who can think logically, mathematically, and rationally, and this is reflected in much of psychology's literature on intelligence. The West African cultures are more collectivist, valuing people with nuanced interpersonal intelligence who add to the smooth functioning of the family and community. We can look to Gardner's multiple intelligences to see if predictable patterns of scores on the dimensions emerge. On a deeper level, though, are questions of whether intelligence is fixed and measurable, or if the Confucian view of gradual development holds more merit, and of the legitimacy or practicality of a universal construct of intelligence across cultures and contexts.

## 7.4 CULTURE AND CONSCIOUSNESS

### LO 7.4: Discuss regular and altered states of consciousness.

"Cogito ergo sum," declared Descartes, providing the Western academic tradition with its definition of consciousness, "I think therefore I am." For Descartes, consciousness and the physical being were separate, intermingling at the pineal gland. Scientists in in Descartes' 17th-century milieu saw the natural world as mechanical, like processes built by an ultimate craftsman. This view, with their knowledge of physiology and physics, could not explain human processes like language and imagination, which they ascribed to a nonphysical substance of thought (Chomsky, 1995). More recent definitions, though less poetic, attempt to explain neurological mechanisms of consciousness, revolving around awareness of surroundings, as in when one awakens from sleep. Still stoking our curiosity are dreams and other unusual states of consciousness, imagination, and creativity.

Numerous mysteries remain in the biology of consciousness. Why is consciousness controlled in the cerebral cortex, the outer layer of the brain, when many times as many neurons fill the cerebral medulla? Further, the cerebral medulla remains active during sleep; we cease conscious thought and yet we still exist, despite Descartes' prescription. A number of theories connect the experience of events and cognitions to neural substrates during wakefulness. Dreaming poses another quandary, falling outside our conscious control and often forgotten when we wake. Freud, of course, held that dreams were a key to the unconscious mind, with our frustrated urges burbling up into the content of dreams. His theories have largely fallen from favor, failing to hold up in empirical research, but remain a part of popular culture. More recent theories include the activation-information model, which suggests that we interpret random neural firings during sleep using experiences from our waking time. Indigenous and folk theories vary in their explanations.

For the aborigines of Australia, two concepts are often confused by outside observers. Human dreaming happens normally during sleep, though a dream might carry psychological or spiritual significance. The Dreaming or Dreamtime exists beyond this world, beginning when the world was created by the great eternal beings of legend and continuing with no known end (Petchovsky & Cawte, 1986). The many cultures and languages of the continent have different words for Dreaming or Dreamtime, sometimes translated as the eternal times, ancestral times, or creation (Price-Williams & Gaines, 1994), leading Berndt and Berndt (1984) to describe the term as an unfortunate choice of translations. Some of these beings paused at particular locations, creating or becoming features of the landscape with heightened spiritual energy where ceremonies may take place. Called Ayers Rock by the British, the region and landmark named Uluru by the Yankunytjatjara who traditionally own the land has several sacred sites. A place becomes sacred because a Dreamtime being performed some action there, and considering they exist beyond time, are still doing the action.

Petchovsky (1986) collected a number of dreams from Yolngu people in northern Arnhem Land, Australia, who still had relatively little outside contact at that time. He found most (78%) had dreams containing imagery from traditional spiritual practices or Christianity. The latter arrived with Methodist missionaries in 1942, four decades before Petrovsky's project. He noted that, having heard hundreds of dreams from his psychoanalytic patients, aborigines living in the city seldom related dreams with religious content (6%). In nighttime dreams, the Yolngu say a person's *mali* (shadow) travels to the spirit world. They awake a sleeper gently to allow the *mali* to return. In these forays to the spirit world, the dreamer may to some degree interact with beings from the greater Dreamtime, for instance if a human dreams about a geographic site or metaphysical being of The Dreamtime (Bell, 2002). These are not Dreams; the terms only overlap due to lack of clear English equivalent. Bringing back knowledge from contact with spirit, though, these dreams may help a person adapt to a life transition or find other answers (den Boer, 2012). In case of powerful dreams, they might be shared with others or may give insight to the dreamer.

## Altered States

Moving across cultures, entirely different descriptions and experiences of consciousness emerge including trance, visions, and meditative states. The term **altered state of consciousness (ASC)** refers to experiences outside what is considered normative daily waking consciousness. These could be intentionally induced through drugs or specific activities or could happen spontaneously for a variety of reasons, but most are considered pathological in psychology and psychiatry. Visions, voices, trance, and possession are considered to indicate schizophrenia, psychosis, or a dissociative disorder, despite their presence for eons across cultures and religions the world over. For brevity, we will discuss trance and possession, though other states are certainly important within cultures.

The American Psychiatric Association published the *Diagnostic and Statistical Manual of Mental Disorders*, the DSM-5, to be discussed in Chapter 11. It describes diagnostic criteria and treatment for mental illnesses and disorders. Dissociative disorders are described as "a disruption or discontinuity in the normal integration of consciousness, memory, identity, emotion, perception, body representation, motor control, and behavior" (APA, 2013, p. 291). This can describe any altered state, though meditative states would probably not result in diagnosis. Trance and possession, along with hallucinations, are often considered diagnosable. A growing set of studies use imaging technology to examine physiological evidence of trance (e.g., Carhart-Harris et al., 2012), finding a number of effects, though small samples of different ASCs thus far yield a confusing picture of results. Flor-Henry, Shapiro, and Sombrun (2017) used EEG mapping and electromagnetic tomography to map the brain of a single subject trained in Mongolian trance. Brain activity in trance shifted from right hemispheric dominance to left, and from anterior prefrontal to posterior somatosensory activity.

Most cultures worldwide recognize existence of trance and possession phenomena (van Duijl, 2014), though trance states occur on a spectrum of experiences from distressing to joyful, and from controlled onset to involuntary (Venkataramaiah, Mallikarjunaiah, Chandrasekhar, Rao, & Reddy, 1981). A person in a trance ASC experiences loss of volition or subordination of identity to an outside force. The person loses internal agency, relinquishing control to what they perceive as another entity or energy. The DSM-5 differentiates dissociative disorders from culturally accepted states, describing the pathology as involuntary, uncontrolled, and persistent, involving conflict with family, social contacts, or the workplace. Prominent theories of trance connect dissociation to previous trauma or to excessive stress or internal conflicts. Trance and dissociative disorders communicate distress to loved ones in cultures with reduced channels of expression, according to the psychiatric view (Bhavsar, Ventriglio, & Bhugra, 2016). Studying trance sufferers in Uganda, van Duijl, Kleijn, & de Jong (2013) found that symptoms matched those of the DSM-5 list for dissociative trance disorder (DTD), including tremors, altered consciousness, and voice change. These people would be sufferers of involuntary trance.

In a great many cultures, trance and possession are normative behaviors, and psychology has begun to acknowledge that these cannot be understood without examination of the cultural context in which it occurs (Bhavsar et al., 2016). Even in Euro-American cultures, these states may be more than acceptable; they may be revered. Healers and sages often reach their status via visions or other mystical experience. In fundamentalist churches across America, parishioners speak in tongues. Millions seek counsel from psychics and mediums. In many cultures, people who have such experiences are considered blessed by their encounters with supernatural or divine realms.

The term shaman refers to a person who uses culturally legitimized altered states to heal or otherwise reshape reality. Their trances, voices, and visions were long assumed to be pathological, though this judgment holds little sway outside Western medical and psychological circles (Stephen & Suryani, 2000). Shamanic trance is considered to be a voluntary experience, though descriptions of how people become shamans or trance participants may include difficult involuntary processes such as illness or possession. Shamans and others who enter culturally accepted altered states often receive high social status. Trance appears in cultures from Siberia to Bali to West Africa, to Native America.

Possession forms a specific type of trance in which an external entity is thought to take over or inhabit an individual. Ward (1980) described two broad types of trance, the distinction being useful in psychological study: central or ritual trance, functioning to reinforce officially recognized morality and power in socially legitimate contexts, and peripheral trance, which happens outside social institutions and morality. Ritual possession happens in particular processes, usually in a religious or spiritual setting, and effected by known deities or other entities. It enhances status, providing psychological benefits including emotional catharsis, improved esteem, elevated social standing, and better adjustment. Peripheral possession is unsanctioned, primarily involving low status, low-SES individuals with little power. It happens often in regions with high male-female power differential, especially when domestic abuse is a factor.

In Muslim tradition, shamanic trance or possession may involve *djinn*, Anglicized as genie. The process may begin with a distressing mental and physical illness as described from Uganda (van Duijl et al., 2013), with ritual trance forming a cure. Berger (2012) describes the initiates experience in the *jinè* cults of Mali, writing

> the jinni was thought to settle within the novice . . . , enter into her, and take control of her mouth . . . , eyes, ears and entire body . . . the jinni descends upon and is inside you ("He is in your body, it is his mouth that speaks. It is wrong to say that it is your mouth that speaks"). (p. 169)

Metaphorically, the human in trance becomes a horse for the *jinè* to ride. The trances eventually heal the initiate of their trance sickness symptoms, moving from peripheral trance at the onset to ritual trance after initiation.

Trance states are reality to the people involved. Without passing judgment or pathologizing these experiences, cultural approaches to psychology seek models of ways altered states function in the lives and cultures of participants. Through various methods, a number of effects and benefits have been documented, including "(1) escape from unpleasant situations, (2) diminution of responsibility and guilt, and (3) group support in a clearly defined subculture" (Ward & Beaubrun, 1980, p. 207). Cultural research continues to support psychosocial benefits of ASCs (e.g., Reddish, Fischer, & Bulbulia, 2013; Nielsen, Fischer, & Kashima, 2018). Many of the cultures maintaining ASC practices experienced suppression and death under colonial rule, for instance cultures practicing voodoo rituals descended from Yoruba slaves brought from West Africa. ASC rituals helped people of these cultures deal with slavery, and later, with socioeconomic suppression. Whatever their realities or pathologies, ASCs serve to benefit many of the participants in trance across cultures.

As with fraternity hazing, pain and stress during initiation increases sense of social bonds for the participants (Bulbulia et al., 2013). Bulbulia's team observed photographs from an annual fire-walking ceremony in Spain, in which the people being initiated carry family members or friends as they walk across three meters of burning coals (see Figure 7.4). The researchers recorded a temperature of 677° C at the surface of the oak coals before the ritual. The predicted outcome was that the passengers would show empathy for the suffering of the initiate, the initiate would exhibit increasing suffering, and all, participants and audience, would feel more cohesion afterward. Empathy did not appear as expected, which the team compared to examiners' enjoyment of student apprehension at dissertation defenses. The increased suffering of the initiate and subsequent cohesion of all did appear, the authors referring to the likelihood of student and examiner celebrating after defense. The divergent effects on participants by role was surprising, and it points to a complex set of factors in ASC rituals. Aesthetic aspects of trance and trance induction will be discussed in the next section.

### Figure 7.4 Spanish Fire-Walking Ceremony

*Source:* Courtesy of Dimitris Xygalatas.

# REALITY CHECK

*What do you think about your dreams? Are they random neural firings or something more?*

*Have you ever seen a person go into trance?*

## 7.5 ARTS, PERCEPTION, AND COGNITION

### LO 7.5: Elaborate the ways the arts can serve as useful tools in the study of cognition and perception.

As examples of cognition and perception, arts provide superb examples. Inherently intended to be perceived, creators of all arts incorporate the thinking styles and symbols of their cultures into every aspect of their creations. The artist, thinking in the modes of her culture, draws from the stories, images, and sounds that shaped the artist she has become. Artists, whether they work in music, dance, story, or visual media, generally achieve a high degree of sensitivity to sensory and cognitive input. Respected artists, whether musicians, painters, or authors, display the greatest skill at expressing the mindset of their culture or historic milieu.

Ways of thinking are most obviously conveyed in arts that include representations drawn from a culture's stories and myths. Jung's (1936) concept of archetype posits that humans share basic characters and roles such as the hero, crone, or maiden. In stories, these epitomize the highest and best of a culture or the worst, depending on the character and the story. Campbell (1949/1973) found the same basic story structure in myths from around the world, his concept of the hero's journey. These cultural patterns shape our sensitivities and preferences, our thoughts, hopes, and dreams, and along with them, provide the story outline of myths, sagas, and movie franchises.

### Visual Arts

Visual arts show us the ocular perceptions of the artist and the thoughts and feelings associated with the subject matter, filtered through context, era, and milieu. Viewing the cave painting of Lascaux, we know the painters saw the creatures around them much as we do, rendering the images with considerable skill. We know something of their thoughts from the choices they made of which animals to paint and techniques of stylization. We know of the importance of women in those days from the rotund Venus figures celebrating their fertility. Moving closer to our own times, we also know the stories from some cultures, so we know the reverence for wisdom in Greece from the majesty of the Parthenon. Vitruvius designed it with the perfect math of the Golden Ratio, tilting and curving its columns and floors carefully to correct perceptual distortions when viewed from a distance. The Elgin marbles from its walls are currently still held by the British Museum.

Subtler cultural elements can also be conveyed visually. Kim and Markus (1999) compared magazine ads from East Asia and the US, finding a marked slant toward collectivist values in the Asian advertisements compared to very individualistic choices in US advertising. These can be conveyed by who appears in ads, for instance individuals or groups, and whether they are depicted interacting or not, with American ads favoring models engaging in solitary pursuits.

Keiko Ishii and colleagues (2014) investigated ways cultural values like harmony and uniqueness could influence artistic expression in physical media. Their project compared Asian and Western participants asked to color geometric patterns using their own choice of colors. As expected, the Asian sample tended toward using colors that were harmonious and more predictable, in keeping with collectivists' valuing of conformity to maintain group cohesion. Western participants made color choices that were bolder and more intense, in keeping with individualists' desire to be distinctive.

Takahiko Masuda and Richard Nisbett have been involved in a number of studies investigating differences in aesthetic preferences and their relation to holistic versus analytic thinking. A distinction between Asian and Western art illustrates differing emphasis on field and ground, with Asian artists filling more of the image with contextual elements. The horizon is characteristically much higher than in European pictures and focal figures will be smaller compared to background (Masuda, Gonzalez, Kwan, & Nisbett, 2008; Nand, Masuda, Senzaki, & Ishii, 2014). These choices provide evidence of culturally based cognitive styles affecting aesthetic expression.

## Music

Music provides a rich trove of cognitive and perceptual information specific to a culture, weaving sonic information with very specific characteristics through time in particular patterns. In addition to lyrical content discussed earlier, the aesthetic and temporal elements of music reflect its unique origins. Time forms a fascinating element of culture reflected in music, with very linear compositional norms in Western classical music moving from beginning to end, left to right on the page. The music of India, conversely, evolves over repeating rhythmic patterns called *tala*, drummers and soloists interacting to create unique performances guided by shared understanding of *tala* and *raga* (the melodic structure), expressed within cultural norms of improvisation.

### Effects of Music in Brief

A number of effects have been ascribed to music's ability to change states of consciousness, ranging from scientifically verifiable to subjective and mystical. We know, for instance, that choral singing seems to increase oxytocin levels, inducing feelings of love and bonding (e.g., Keeler et al., 2015). Also established is that there are effects of music on brain wave patterns and that learning to play music is associated with more robust neural networks.

European and East Asian cultures use scales based on what is called the overtone series. A bugle uses the series to make music without keys or slides, using only the natural physics of vibration. Those related pitches create the familiar scales of Western and East

Asian music. Similarity of those frequencies make them sound good together, coherent waveforms resulting from their combination in harmony. Strike two adjacent keys on the piano at once, and the resultant dissonant frequencies conflict creating interference patterns. In an evolutionary sense, interference patterns correspond to squawking birds and screaming monkeys when a predator attacks or the crashes and mayhem of natural or human-induced disasters.

All gamelan throughout Indonesia uses scales absolutely unlike those of the West and East Asia. Craftspeople tune each orchestra differently, with a unique scale and slightly different frequencies. All diverge from the consonance of the overtone series, creating interference patterns that are simultaneously very pretty and somewhat disturbing neurologically. The music taps the ancient reptilian brain structures that stimulate adrenalin releases, but while simultaneously providing emotionally and cognitively positive input.

Javanese gamelan is described by Indonesians as elegant, a shimmering soundscape of gongs, flutes, and zithers. The music moves mostly at a gentle pace. The metallophones emit hypersonic frequencies that interact to create complex interference patterns; these create measurable alterations to brain waves patterns (Oohashi, Nishina, Kawai, Fuwamoto, & Imai, 1991). The music is simultaneously soothing and stimulating, generating a wash of neurotransmitters and novel brain waves.

Balinese gamelan underwent a change in the early 1900s, the older style replaced by *gong kebyar*, often translated as "exploding gong," describing its volume and furious pace. Paired instruments tuned to slightly different frequencies exchange notes alternating back and forth, each covering half of 20 notes per second or more. All gamelan requires extreme cooperation, certainly for the *kotekan* of alternating notes in Balinese music, but also in gentler gamelan Java. Hardja Susila, esteemed leader of the gamelan at University of Hawai'i school of music for more than three decades, said of all gamelan that one only really plays gamelan when aware of all of the instruments, hearing moment by moment instructions via the drummer/conductor, and meeting the concluding note of each cycle. What one is playing personally becomes a selfless part of a much greater sonic whole.

## Altered States in Performance

The term *shaman* describes traditional healers and visionaries in many cultures. Each culture has names and terminologies but they share the basic concept of an individual who can access metaphysical energies and enter altered states of consciousness. They serve as healers, to be discussed in Chapter 11, and are thought to provide a sense of control when people otherwise feel disempowered. Shamanic ritual may include musical components such as fast drumming to induce the trance state (e.g., Fachner & Rittner, 2011; Krippner, 2009).

The people of the island of Bali in the Indonesian archipelago teach children to dance from a young age. Accompanied by the shimmering sounds of gamelan, an orchestra of gongs, flutes, xylophones, and cymbals, most dances recount stories from Hindu classics like the Ramayana and Mahābhārata. The gods and other spirits take possession of the children as they dance, trance forming part of the tradition for as long as people can remember. *Topèng*, a masked dance form, appears in Javanese texts from the 13th and 14th centuries (Hobart, 2007). In *Lègong*, girls entering puberty become nymphs of Hindu legend. Far from a frightening experience, possession is considered a great blessing, and children hold a special place in Balinese society in part because it is easier for them to enter trance.

A different selflessness emerges in *qawwali* songs of India, Pakistan and the Middle East. *Qawwali* grew from the Sufi religion, as did the dances of the whirling Dervish. *Qawwali* provides a vehicle of transcendence, moving the practitioner beyond the bounds of individuality into a state of unity with the universal divine consciousness (Bailey, 1986; Becker, 1994).

Redfield and Thouin-Savard (2017) studied electronic dance music (EDM) events, hedonic scenes usually including light shows and very loud music produced by DJs, some of whom are highly paid and enjoy international followings. EDM has a ritual quality, taking attendees through hours of nonstop dancing, eventually yielding a transpersonal ecstatic state. The authors propose that EDM forms an important support for well-being equivalent to shamanic and religious rituals of the past.

## REFLECTING ON YOUR READING

- Looking back over this chapter, have you discovered anything about your own thought processes?

- Can you see ways culture has shaped how you perceive the world around you?

## CHAPTER 7 SUMMARY

### 7.1 Thinking About the World: Culture and Cognition

Humans receive and interpret sensations to navigate the physical and social environment. A number of theories explain our cognitive processes, the ways we think, some of which compare our mentality to computer processors and culture to the software. A very old concept, associationism, says we link concepts by laws of contiguity, frequency, similarity, and contrast.

Cognition may be more analytic, focused on discreet categories, focal figures, and individual actors, or holistic, emphasizing contextual information and situation. These appear more in independent and interdependent cultures, respectively. Analytic thinkers categorize by descriptive individual characteristics, while holistic thinkers attend to relational and contextual factors. Analytic thinkers also tend to want one exclusive answer while holistic thinkers have more tolerance for contradictory concepts.

Humans all conceive of time in spatial terms, but may prefer deictic time, anchored in the now, or sequence time, without a fixed point of reference.

### 7.2 Culture and Perception

Perception happens when sensation is converted to thought. A primary piece of evidence for influence of culture on perception is the Müller-Lyer illusion, which only affects people who grow up in square-cornered buildings. Cognitive styles affect how people attend to foreground and background, as well as contextual information. Background can interfere with recognition of incongruent facial expressions.

Field dependence–independence concerns how people can recognize direction, depending on bodily sensation and visual cues. It relates also to how people respond to a number of other types of input.

For more than a century, theorists have pursued the idea that language shapes perception. Some evidence comes from color perception, where categories affect speed of recognition in intermediate areas between colors.

### 7.3  Culture and Intelligence

The concept of intelligence is controversial. It is a Western concept, measured with Western tools, but it has implications for how people are perceived and treated. Ideas of racial superiority continue to be believed by some people. Intelligence, if the concept has merit, can really only be measured with consideration of culture and context. Gardner's theory of multiple intelligences and Spearman's tripartite model provide concepts more sensitive to cultural considerations.

Beyond Euro-American conceptualizations of intelligence, a study of mothers across cultures revealed four factors all considered indicative of intelligence: cognitive/academic ability, appropriate behavior,

socially interactive behavior, and unintelligent behavior. Terms for intelligence in other languages reflect cultural values.

### 7.4  Culture and Consciousness

Consciousness is that mysterious quality of awareness, primarily experienced during waking hours. Dreams form a different kind of consciousness. Cultures value these states in particular ways. The Aborigines of Australia come from many tribes but share ideas consciousness beyond limits of time and space.

Altered states describe consciousness outside normal parameters. These may include trance or sense of possession by outside entities. Psychology is skeptical of these states, but they may serve necessary psychological functions.

### 7.5  Arts, Perception, and Cognition

Arts are inherently creations of thought and perception. The arts of a culture contain numerous clues about ways of thinking and about how culture shapes perception. Cognitive components include the stories and characters of a culture's myths and legends. Music also includes concepts of time. The sound waves of certain music can change brain waves. Music can aid in inducing trance states.

## GLOSSARY

**Altered state of consciousness (ASC):** Experiences outside what is considered normative daily waking consciousness.

**Analytic thought:** Thought that relies on logic and focuses on the central actor.

**Concept:** A term for basic units of thought.

**Deictic time:** Concept of time with "now" as the reference point between past and future.

**Holistic thought:** Thought that emphasizes the interdependence of actors or objects in relation to each other and to context.

**Sequence time:** Concept of time that is unanchored (e.g., "Summer comes before autumn").

**Shaman:** A traditional healer or visionary.

CHAPTER EIGHT

# COMMUNICATION AND EMOTION

## Chapter 8 Outline

## Learning Objectives

# PREPARING TO READ

- When you're talking with a friend, how much must be spelled out and what can be left unsaid because you "just know" already?
- Can you tell how people feel without them putting it in words?
- Have you had difficulty communicating with someone from another culture?

*Bill fell in love with Akiko at first sight in their Chem 100 class, where she was one of several international students. He was delighted that she agreed to go out with him at all, given their different cultural origins. Three months later, Bill was showing his affection for her openly around friends and family. By six months, he really wanted to formalize the relationship, at least becoming boyfriend-girlfriend, but while Akiko continues to go out with him and treats him well, she does not kiss him in public or expressing her emotions toward him in the ways he would like. Bill wonders if she feels the same as he does.*

*Arthur is a Polynesian faculty member invited to attend a prestigious conference in Mumbai, India. He enjoys going into the everyday world of any country he visits and begins to walk the streets near his hotel. When he passes someone on the street, he raises his eyebrows slightly, in the way Hawaiians, Māori, and other Polynesians casually greet people around them. The people he passes seem upset, especially the men, who seem like they expect aggression from him.*

*Bill and Arthur both expect people to understand their expression and to respond as they would. Bill is an American guy who shouts at the TV when watching football and gives his buddies bear-hugs at parties. He has no frame of reference to understand that a Japanese national is rarely loud or public in their emotional displays. Arthur will find that raised eyebrows, a respectful acknowledgement of the humanity of people around him, signals intent to fight in parts of India.*

# WHY IT MATTERS

*Intercultural communication presents challenges of language barriers, but also more subtle differences in how people create and express meaning. Emotions present particular challenges because they can be deeply personal and cultures differ greatly in norms of what can and should be expressed, and the forms the expression takes.*

Humans spend considerable time communicating with one another, which is not unusual; most creatures interact with others of their species to some degree. All creatures must eat and mate to survive, of course. Mating requires interaction, while feeding may not. Beyond that, species vary enormously in type and level of interaction, with humans communicating complex information frequently.

Human life now involves an incredible amount of nonsurvival information, including complex negotiations of hierarchies, cooperative arrangements, food production and preparation processes, mating and child rearing, defense, emotion, and shelter (Matsumoto, 2006). We do this with complicated communication systems involving verbal and nonverbal cues. We eventually developed writing, telephones, and social media, to name a few recent communication options. Emotions form a particular set of cognitive and neurological states internally, which we communicate externally via gesture, tone, facial expression, and other means. As a special case of communication, emotional information is crucial to bonding and close cooperation, but also to persuasion, control, and intimidation. We begin the chapter with communication in general and move on to language and emotion, discussing how each shapes and is shaped by culture.

## 8.1 EVOLUTION OF HUMAN COMMUNICATION

### LO 8.1: Describe the evolutionary steps leading to current human communication universals and differences.

Among the broad range of capacities humans have evolved, communication is perhaps most important, allowing us to send and receive knowledge with others around us. We tell people how we feel and what makes us happy, sad, or angry. We pass along knowledge of how to live well, including interpersonal skills, often in the form of folklore encoded in stories and songs. We transmit practical skills for doing and making things. These have been improved upon and passed generation to generation in a continuous chain of communication.

Ability to communicate is not unique to humans or even to the animal kingdom. Plants emit chemicals to attract or repel microbes in the soil around their roots to maintain a beneficial environment (e.g., Estabrook & Yoder, 1998). They send airborne chemicals to warn nearby plants when they are under attack, for instance by caterpillars, allowing their neighbors to begin production of chemicals to resist infestation (e.g., Ali, Sugimoto, Ramadan, & Arimura, 2013). Creatures developed ever more sophisticated methods of communication as they became more complex. Birds and whales chirp and sing elaborate messages to each other. They even develop their linguistic abilities in processes similar to humans; young birds produce imprecise calls imitating their parents just as baby humans babble until they learn to speak proper words (Hauser, Chomsky, & Fitch, 2002).

As mentioned in Chapter 1, dogs and humans utilize similar brain regions in communication, a homologous remnant of our evolutionary split long ago. Similarities include primary regions in communication and also nonprimary auditory regions involved in emotional perception (Andics et al., 2014; Andics & Miklósi, 2018).

## Figure 8.1 a, b, and c   fMRI Scans of Canine and Human Brains During Language Stimulus

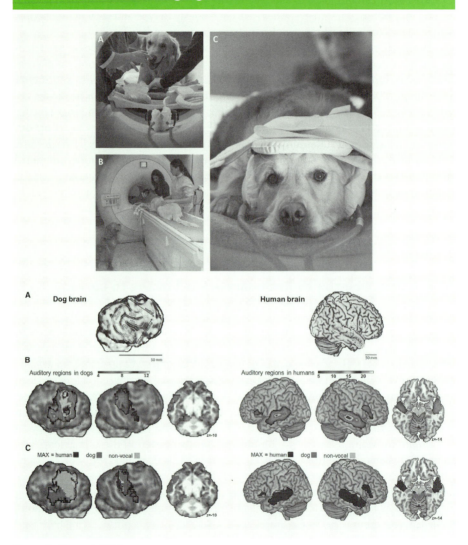

*Source:* Andics et al. (2014).

Although the dog's brain and the area of activation are smaller, our shared mechanisms for communication of both language and emotion go surprisingly far back on the evolutionary tree (see Figure 8.1). Perhaps this explains the ancient and durable friendship between our species.

Humans branched from apes much more recently, sharing 99% of our DNA with chimpanzees and bonobos, our closest surviving relatives (Staes, Bradley,

Hopkins, & Sherwood, 2018). Because language leaves no fossil traces, those primate cousins present our best window into the evolution of communication skills. Grooming provides a primary mechanism of social bonding among primates, but vocalization allows social interaction with a larger cohort at greater distance, facilitating coordination of life in a complex social group (Roberts & Roberts, 2018). Synchronized pant-hoot choruses provide opportunities for social bonding with several individuals at once, not unlike the effects of human choral activities. Gorillas, chimps, and bonobos also employ a wide range of gestures, some including contact (e.g., hugs) and using sound.

No other species (as far as we know) has the capacity for the rich descriptive detail of human communication, allowing for infinite variation across situations and topics (Hauser et al., 2002). We may never understand exactly how or why language developed, but we do know that the abilities emerged as group size increased, probably paralleling advances in social cognition. The social brain hypothesis, discussed earlier, posits that our relatively larger brains evolved to enable life in larger, more complex social groups (Staes et al., 2018). The 1% of genetic difference between us and other primates has played out in neural and physiological structures that facilitate a range of cognitive and communication abilities, including language and abstraction (Staes et al., 2018). Without these, humans would never have developed culture, computers, or Reality TV, whether or not those are all adaptive outcomes.

## Tools and Language

Recent research in language and communication suggests simultaneous evolution of language and tool-making ability. We discussed earlier that certain creatures use simple tools, such as otters using rocks to crack mollusks or chimps using twigs to fish termites from a mound. Hominins took tool use to another level when they began crafting materials to suit their needs, an evolutionary process that coincided with changes in social structures, brain configuration, and memory capacity (Ambrose, 2010). Our ancestors began chipping stone into tools about 2.5 mya in processes that were undoubtedly transmitted from one individual to another. The oldest, found at Gona in Ethiopia, were made by *Homo habilis* and took considerable practice and skill to create. They did not improve, however, until Acheulean tools appeared about 1.5 mya, leading some to propose that language had only then developed sufficiently to facilitate complex cultural transmission (Morgan et al., 2015). A number of studies support the parallel between tool improvement and appearance of more complex neural structures (Stout, Toth, Schick, & Chaminade, 2008). Coevolution of cognitive and cultural traits has been observed in other domains (Lotem, Halpern, Edelman, & Kolodny, 2017), and it is likely that tool-making, cognitive advancement, and language ability all evolved together.

Morgan and colleagues (2015) undertook a study to demonstrate the likelihood that early tool makers began to use language increasingly as tool processes were refined. They proposed that reliance on low-fidelity transmission processes of imitation/emulation led to the 700,000-year stasis of tool design, and that more effective proto-language enabled the later phases of advancement. A total of 184 participants produced 6,000 flint tools, passing the skill one person to another in multiple chains using one of five transmission methods: reverse engineering, imitation/emulation, basic teaching, gestural teaching, and verbal teaching. Only gestural or verbal teaching elicited clear improvement in flake quality, with verbal teaching doubling the performance of reverse engineering learners. Language use improved fidelity of transmission, a crucial component in ratcheting-up of knowledge.

## Language as a Universal?

Linguist Noam Chomsky (1995) maintains that, given the consistency of language acquisition across languages and cultures, language facility and the resulting languages qualify as naturally evolved objects. Language would be as natural as opposable thumbs. Nature, Chomsky suggests, shaped humans into perfect language acquisition devices, born with exactly the right physiology to imprint with and reproduce language. He has argued that the architecture of the human brain facilitates capacity for language and that common brain structures shape our languages. He maintains that while languages differ somewhat in sound and structure, they share common computational processes by which meaning is constructed and understood, leading to similarities in the underlying structure of all languages. "A rational Martian scientist would probably find the variation rather superficial," Chomsky imagines, "concluding that there is one human language with minor variants" (p. 13). The concept of universal grammar (UG) proposes that input during early childhood is insufficient to allow a learner to understand and produce the complexities of adult language without the presence of innate mechanisms (White, 1985). Languages then blossomed into incredible variation in less than a hundred millennia, many incomprehensible to each other.

## Linguistic Communication

Words represent objects or concepts symbolically, transformed into agreed-upon sounds understood within a group. Humans combine phonemes, particles of sound like "ah," to build words. We have also developed visual representations like the letters on this page. These particular symbols, like "tree," exist as patterns of ink or pixels on a screen, but if you speak English, the word tree points to knowledge of large plants with dense branching structures above and below ground. Words become language when combined in patterns of meaning grouped by syntax, an ordering of words by type, used to build phrases, sentences, and paragraphs.

Language would seem to be a completely human modality, but really the ability began evolving long ago and numerous species have related abilities. Dogs bark warnings and excitement and whine their pain, sympathy, and affection. Those constitute communication, but are they language? Western science sets a high bar for language, including syntax structure, and has long considered humans to be the sole possessors of these abilities. A tiny bird, the *shijukara*, or Japanese tit bird in English (*parus minor*), rattled the scientific world when researchers identified syntactic composition in the bird's calls. The birds use at least 11 distinct calls in 170 combinations, for instance to sound an alert and specify danger from a predator (Griesser, Wheatcroft, & Suzuki, 2018). Suzuki (2014) documented different sounds by which the *shijukara* indicate type of predator, for example, snakes or aggressive bird types. When recorded calls were played in correct syntax, the birds responded, but they ignored alarms played out of order.

Humans use complex syntax in flexible ways, providing tools to communicate a virtually unlimited range of nuanced thoughts. Miyagawa, Berwick, and Okanoya (2013) propose that syntax emerged as a combination of two simultaneously evolving systems. The first, Type E (expression), is the expressive function by which basic information is expressed, such as territory, mating, or alarm, for instance the *shijukara* calls indicating predators. Type L (lexical) connects a predicate to an explanation, such as the compass heading indicated in a bee's dance of direction to food or the *shijukara*'s direction for the flock to repel a predator. The two systems interact in human language, allowing its unbounded possibilities of expression. These are the universals of language: phonemes, words, structure, and syntax, along with processes such as turn taking.

## Turn Taking

One procedural component of communication is turn taking, in which speakers alternate who speaks (or tweets) and responds. Shared across many species, human cultures and languages contain implicit social rules for turns (Levinson, 2016). Turns may be ordered by hierarchy, such as oldest to youngest speakers, and despite a huge range of possible situations of conversation, transitions between speakers usually happen with minimal interruptions, gaps, or overlap (Sacks, Schegloff, & Jefferson, 1974). Within our own language, we recognize blocks of words or phrases, termed **turn constructional units (TCUs)**, including intonations, words, or phrases signaling completion of a turn. Though turn taking forms a universal of communication, languages and cultures vary considerably in how turns are taken. English, despite a number of complexities in grammar and spelling, signals turns with straightforward grammatical conclusion of a sentence or phrase, normally in subject-verb-object order (SVO): I (subject) want (verb) cupcakes (object).

Japanese language follows a subject-object-verb order (SOV): I (subject) cupcakes (object) want (verb). Appearance of the verb may not signal change of turn, however (Tanaka, 2000). Japanese language speakers often employ an interrogative element as a TCU such as *neh*, which works something like "isn't it?" or "you know?" in English. The speaker asks for agreement, thereby preventing appearing too assertive, and indicates the turn. These Japanese TCUs are especially prevalent for females, acknowledging traditionally lower social status in the culture.

In Korean language, also SOV in ordering, Park (2016) proposes turns occur at a transition-relevance place (TRP). A native speaker of Korean, he recorded hours of conversation in Korean language, which was then transcribed and analyzed for content and patterns. He observes that speakers often entirely omit the end of a sentence, following a rule of transition at completion of action. The listener will know from context what the remaining content should be (see the high and low context discussion in section 8.3). Gestures, intonation, or other cues replace what might have been a grammatical conclusion in English, and the conversation flows on unabated. Koreans, rated as collectivistic in Hofstede's (1980, 1991) research and subsequent studies, tend to share understanding of contextual information not made explicit in communication.

# REALITY CHECK

How are humans different from other creatures in terms of communication?

Why is communication important for humans?

Why does Chomsky call humans "language acquisition devices"?

How does syntax affect communication of messages?

## 8.2 LANGUAGE ACQUISITION

### LO 8.2: Explain how humans acquire language and communication skills.

We learn our primary language and communication rules through a natural process of enculturation. Children usually produce initial words after their first birthday and begin producing word pairs around age 2, though age at these milestones varies. Language skills develop simultaneously and interdependently with motor skills, object recognition, and social skills (Floccia et al., 2018). The learning of a language is a monumental achievement, even if it is happening naturally in every culture every day. The child must gain a working understanding of syntax, add hundreds of words, eventually thousands, while connecting words to objects and ideas, and learn rules of expression, learning both when to speak and when to stay quiet, all without any formal training. It is this amazing process that led Chomsky (1995) to refer to humans as "language acquisition devices."

Beyond the universal developmental processes, a number of conditions may affect outcomes. These could include norms of interaction between children and their caregivers and peers and of expectations for what a child's duties should be. Evidence discussed earlier says that language shapes our thinking (and perhaps perceptions), so language acquisition involves learning ways of thinking, and the simultaneous development of our brains and language abilities lead to differences in cognition later. Another set of conditions arise from environmental and social conditions. These could include availability of food and shelter, options for education, and the level of safety from harm and criminality. In extreme cases of war or widespread famine, the effort needed for simple survival may overwhelm ability to develop language skills normally.

In less extreme conditions, life circumstances still affect developmental outcomes. The Family Investment Model proposes that higher SES leads to greater parental investment in a child's development, which in turn yields more favorable outcomes including earlier language learning (Lohndorf, Vermeer, Cárcamo, & Mesman, 2018). In Western samples, family income has been linked positively to both parental education and child vocabulary. Wealthier parents have more material and social resources, allowing more time for playing and interacting with children. Higher-SES families also have greater variety of age-appropriate learning materials. Lohndorf and colleagues compared outcomes of Chilean preschoolers of majority Spanish-speaking ethnicity and indigenous Mapuche. The Mapuche primarily live in the Araucanía region, with the highest poverty rate in the country. The comparison supported the correlation between SES and language learning, but it also revealed an expected moderating effect of home environment, probably due to the reduced attention available to the children.

The Mapuche children face a double challenge: they must fight their uphill learning battle while simultaneously speaking a second language in school. Laws passed in the 1920s made speaking the Mapuche's Mapudungun language illegal, similar to the historical trauma of Native North Americans, Hawaiians, Māori, and other indigenous groups. Education still happens in Spanish, while Mapuche families may speak Mapudungun at home. Learning of second languages (or more) has received a great deal of attention in psychology and in educational research, though the hostile conditions faced by the Mapuche amplify their challenges.

## Second Language Acquisition

Even more impressive than learning of one language are children who learn two or more languages in early childhood. Typically, the mother's language of primary familial communication would be considered the first, with additional languages acquired termed second languages. Second language acquisition (SLA) in any situation touches on topics of cognition and learning, human development, and acculturation, among others. It has drawn academic attention for a number of reasons including differences in success of acquisition. In terms of acculturation, second language skills are particularly important for businesses when people move for jobs, an area with considerable funding for research, and in education for immigrant and minority children. A number of factors have been investigated for effects on outcome, including age of learning (AOL), length of residence (LOR), length and quality of language instruction, motivation, and aptitude (Piske et al., 2001). Oddly, time spent in language classes has correlated negatively with accuracy of pronunciation in some studies, perhaps because not all classes emphasize correct pronunciation, and some instructors may be second language speakers themselves. Other factors would include language of friends, family, and coworkers, presence of co-ethnic communities, and other factors of social environment.

Age at time of SLA has been shown to influence outcomes in a number of ways, though results are inconsistent. Broadly, the younger learning begins, the better the learner's ability will be and the less accent the person will have in adulthood. A number of developmental factors may affect when SLA must begin for the person to be accent free in the second language. As discussed in the development chapter, perception of phonemes becomes restricted by age two. Beyond that early neural pruning, researchers suggest reduction of neuroplasticity makes learning progressively more difficult. Several ages for the end of the critical period have been proposed, including 6 years (Long, 1990), 12 years (Scovel, 1988), and 15 years (Patkowski, 1990). A famous example in US politics is Henry Kissinger, Secretary of State to Richard Nixon, who fled the Nazis before WWII and reached America at age 15. Kissinger's thick German accent is legendary, but his brother, who was three years younger, has virtually no German accent (Dahl, 2004).

Globally, a majority of children grow up speaking two or more languages (Floccia et al., 2018). In standard assessment practices, bilingual children tend to underperform when tested in only one language, leading some researchers to conclude that early learning of second languages interferes with language development. Research through the 1970s assumed that words and phrases from the primary language would interfere with the second language in a process called negative transfer (Dulay & Burt, 1974). More recent research includes use of neural imaging technologies to be discussed shortly.

In other research, language distance predicts fluency in the second language. In other words, the greater linguistic similarity between French and English or Spanish and English leads to better language competence than Chinese-English bilinguals, who face low similarity in those languages (Floccia et al., 2018). Floccia and colleagues (2018) measured vocabulary for 372 toddlers learning British English and one other language using the Communicative Development Inventories. The first languages included Bengali, Cantonese, Dutch, French, German, Greek, Hindi-Urdu, Italian, Mandarin, Polish, Portuguese, Spanish, and Welsh. Linguistic distance predicted vocabulary outcomes and may also indicate differences in cognitive processes, given the effects of language on thought. Overall, studies like this show that second languages are not inherently a problem, but rather that difficulties arise due to other factors such as age of acquisition and language distance.

## Linguistic Relativity

In Chapter 7, we discussed the Whorfian hypothesis, that the language we learn shapes our thoughts and possibly our perceptions. Conversely, patterns and words of the languages we speak may provide insight into thought patterns of our cultures, a way to reverse engineer the influences that shaped a language. One such pattern involves the use (or omission) of personal pronouns. Languages vary in the personal pronouns they include, for instance I, me, mine, you, yours, and so on in English. Other languages include fewer, some only one. Further, quite a few languages allow the omission of pronouns in certain circumstances. Indonesian language is one of these, with *saya* (I) and *anda* (you) often left out of sentences. In conversation, overuse of *saya* can seem especially immodest, calling too much attention to one's self. To say "I have to go to the market," an exact translation would be "*saya harus pergi ke pasar*," but more commonly, one would simply say "*harus pergi ke pasar*," omitting the personal pronoun.

Emiko and Yoshihisa Kashima (1998) undertook a comparison of languages by culture, using Hofstede's dimensions of national cultural variation and data collected by Hofstede (1980, 1991) and others. Their hypothesis was that personal pronouns would be used more often in individualist cultures and omitted more commonly in collectivist cultures. They examined pronoun use in 39 languages across 71 cultures, finding support for their hypothesis; the less individualistic cultures were more likely to drop pronouns. Much as with the linguistic influences on conception of time discussed in Chapter 7 (e.g., Fuhrman et al. 2011; Boroditsky, 2010), language, culture, and thought have interacted, each shaping the other across eons of human generations, transmitting verbal symbols in particular configurations that support and perpetuate our cultural ways of living.

## The Bilingual Brain

The development of PET scan and fMRI technology provides particularly rich information regarding brain activity in bilingualism. In previous chapters, several examples of differences in brain activity have been discussed. Language understanding and production in a single language are based in specific known brain regions. Bilingualism provides potential to explore how one brain can produce two or more languages and shed light on neural processes of language in general (Spivey & Marian, 1999).

The difficulty for bilinguals lies in reducing interference from the nontarget alternate language on language production in the target language needed at the moment. This allows you to say *dog* (English) instead of *chien* (French) at the right moment and not to confuse *kepala* (head) with *kelapa* (coconut) when speaking Indonesian. The language suppression hypothesis assumed an input switch of sorts that would activate one language and turn off the other as needed. Spivey and Marian (1999) tested this theory by tracking eye movements of Russians who learned English in adulthood when asked to name pictured items with sonic overlaps between the languages. Eye movements showed the participants would look first to the incorrect language choice, showing that both languages were active. More recent theories propose that two slightly different neural systems operate depending on which language is spoken (Hernandez, 2009). Imaging and ERP studies provide evidence of this interference, for instance when German-Spanish bilinguals are asked to choose names of items with similarities between the languages (Rodriguez-Fornells, de Diego Balaguer, & Münte, 2006). In fMRI studies of young bilingual speakers of English and Spanish, differences were observed in activation of areas associated with language, providing direct evidence of parallel systems. More interestingly, there were also differences in areas associated with emotion, memory, and somatosensory processing (Hernandez, 2009). Within bilingual brains, one finds physiological evidence of variation in language processing, but also in associated thought patterns.

## Dialects and Language Variants

When my mama went to the store with my auntie I stayed over to my Big Mama house with my cousin and my baby brother. We was watchin' t.v. and eatin' cookies. We was playin' with our toys and ridin' bikes too. My mama came home and she said "this a really fun day." I laughed. 'Cause I was thinkin' the same thing. (Story told by a 5-year-old African American girl, Washington & Thomas-Tate, 2009, p. 147)

The paragraph above reflects normal usage of African American English (AAE), a dialect widespread in African American families and communities of the US. The term *diglossia* refers to a community's use of two or more languages, with one language considered superior, in this case Standard American English (SAE) holding dominance over AAE (Washington & Thomas-Tate, 2009). The two differ in accent but also in syntax, word usage, and concepts emphasized, as well as communication norms. In notable ways, though they are spoken on the same land mass by citizens of only one country, they are different languages, with implications for the speakers of each. The high status language tends to be used exclusively in education and in formal legal and public functions. Low status language(s) mark the speakers' social status and may bring denigration by the dominant group.

Scholars continue to debate two topics regarding AAE: its origins and its legitimacy. The Creolist view assume that AAE developed from the African languages brought by slaves into Creole combinations with English. The Anglicist view holds that slaves quickly adopted English from the English-speaking people enslaving them and retain a form of the linguistic structure and accents of those sources. In fact, examination of historic recordings of European descendants and former slaves born before the Civil War showed no significant differences in vowel duration, meaning the two groups spoke Southern US English and AAE with the same timing, indicating shared origins (Thomas & Carter, 2006). Though creolization may partly explain AAE, stronger evidence points to AAE reflecting the language slaves learned from their settler masters, who spoke dialects from Scotland and other areas of the British Isles (Howe & Walker, 2000). Similarly, Chota Valley Spanish, an African-Spanish vernacular found in Ecuador previously thought to have origins in a Portuguese-African creole, instead appears to simply be a second-language adaptation of Spanish learned by slaves from Spanish masters (Sessarego, 2013).

The legitimacy issue can be summed up as a question of difference versus deficit. Historically predominant, the deficit view says that AAE is a corrupt version of English and implies that its speakers are cognitively flawed. The difference view holds that AAE evolved into an altered version of English due to a number of sociohistorical factors and comprises a legitimate version of the language. AAE operates by a vocabulary and system of rules that vary slightly from SAE but are as regular, complex, and robust, shared by African American communities across the US. This led to use of Ebonics as a name for AAE. The Oakland Unified School District resolved that it could legitimately be used in educational settings in 1998, though the move remains controversial (Wassink & Curzan, 2004).

Children arrive at school enculturated in the language or dialect spoken at home, in this case AAE, and face issues similar to the language difficulties faced by minorities and immigrants in many regions. A negative bias against AAE speakers has been observed even among African Americans themselves, including African American teachers (Billings, 2005). This places AAE speakers at a disadvantage as they face challenges in producing standard American English, and unfortunately, bring assumptions of lesser intelligence from the start of their education. Further, for children who may have language learning disabilities, elements of AAE are sometimes diagnosed as pathology (Seymour, Bland-Stewart, & Green, 1998). This places children in an unfair position of having to overcome bias in addition to any other issues they face.

## 8.3 CULTURAL PATTERNS IN COMMUNICATION

### LO 8.3: Identify modalities of human communication and differences in those domains.

### Nonverbal Communication

Chances are you can tell how your friends and family feel without a word being spoken. Nonverbal communication includes facial expression, posture, and gesture, plus a variety of behavioral signals (Matsumoto, 2006). Drooped shoulders may mean someone is sad or tired. Dilated pupils may indicate romantic attraction or it might indicate substance abuse. Humans also use a wide variety of intentional gestures, movements made to express feelings and other communicated messages. Winks, smiles, nods, pointing, or frowns can at times express more than words. We also communicate unintentionally when we blush or grimace with pain (Thomas, 1991).

Humans begin to use gestures in infancy, parents communicating with babies by sign months before verbal skills appear (Wang & Vallotton, 2016). Beyond basic physiological cues, messages become more difficult to understand without context. Cultures especially differ in use and meaning of gestures, and even facial expressions of emotion form a complex topic to be discussed later. Gestures can convey specific meaning, such as the American thumbs-up sign or the circling of thumb and forefinger to signal things are good or working well. Those specific signs can also express sex-related profanity in other cultures.

Franz Boas and his students (e.g., Boas & Efron, 1936; Efron, 1941) undertook a number of studies to understand similarities and differences in gestural expression across cultures. They observed Polish and Lithuanian Jews along with immigrants from southern Italy in New York in the 1920s and 1930s. What they found were marked differences in meaning and effect of gestural communication. More recent research identifies several areas of cultural variation in gesture. Gestures vary in meaning associations within cultural systems such as the "ok" sign already mentioned. Cultures also vary in spatial gestures, in how people describe size and shape in gesture. Another variation stems from different conceptualizations of time and space discussed in Chapter 7, with the past behind or in front, for instance. Finally, cultures vary in pragmatic rules of gesture, including syntax and politeness, for example when and why a person should nod in agreement (Kita, 2009).

Italian culture is particularly rich in gestures, a stereotype with a basis in reality. Speakers frequently use elaborate gestures, often in place of speech, and meanings are easily understood within the culture. Jana Iverson and her colleagues (2008) compared Italian children from monolingual families in Rome to monolingual English-speaking children in the US. All were 10 to 24 months in age. They found that both groups used gestures, with the Italian children using more. Both groups also began using word-gesture combinations several months before they used two-word combination, indicating that gesture forms an important part of language acquisition.

## High and Low Context

A framework for understanding cultural difference in communication stems from the degree of contextual information stated overtly. Edward Hall (1976) proposed that cultures tend to be either high or low in the portion of unspoken contextual information needed to understand a communication. Context consists of the information surrounding an event or situation, including environment, social settings, and meanings needed for understanding (Nishimura, Nevgi, & Tella, 2008). Northern Europeans, such as Germans, Scandinavians, and Swiss, tend to communicate via explicit verbal and textual statements that include explanation of context, for instance clear listing of all steps and documents needed to register for college. They are low-context cultures because little additional context information is needed beyond what is overtly stated. In high-context cultures, members are preprogrammed with knowledge of how things work, and a speaker will omit the contextual information. The listener understands unspoken messages implied by shared understanding of the situation (Wurtz, 2006).

As with so many topics already discussed, context dependence relates to the individualism-collectivism dimension. Hall (1976) viewed low-context cultures as individualized and fragmented, with people relatively uninvolved in others' lives. In high-context cultures, relationships tend to be more stable, often extending across generations (Kakabadse, Kouzmin, Korac-Kakabadse, & Savery, 2001). This is typical of collectivist cultures including East Asians and Polynesians and of places with limited population and few degrees of separation between people such as small towns or villages. In Japan, some businesses operate under agreements struck between parties centuries earlier.

Conversation in a high-context culture may flow very differently. The collectivist aspect shifts emphasis from efficient transmission of complete information to efficient maintenance of trust and connectedness. Further, topics are often addressed obliquely, talking around the point, which of course the listener will ascertain from knowledge of the context. Servaes (1989) described a continuum from direct, explicit communication, exemplified by Euro-Americans, to indirect, implicit communication, typified in Asian culture. The differences can be infuriating for a brusque American business person with an attitude of "time is money" who wants to waste no time "beating around the bush." Of course, that person may lose the business opportunity from failure to build a strong enough relationship sufficiently to obtain an agreement, as numerous anecdotes in international business classes will tell.

# SPOTLIGHT

## PIDGIN IN HAWAI'I: EH! YOU LIKE DA KINE, YEAH?

The past two centuries brought radical changes to the shores of Hawai'i. European and American traders hauled away primeval forests a ship load at a time, then began acquiring lands from the *ali'i* (ruling class) for sugar cane and pineapple plantations. All the while, the indigenous Hawaiians suffered huge losses from diseases new to their immune systems. For labor, expanding plantations shipped in recruits from China, then Japan, the Philippines, Portugal, Korea, and Puerto Rico. Each group arrived indentured, required to pay for their passage and purchase food and supplies from expensive company stores. As each worked their way up out of debt, a new group arrived to take their place at the bottom rung.

Gradually, a unique language emerged, an amalgam drawing from all of the languages present so these disparate groups could communicate. In Hawaiian Pidgin (actually a creole), the end of work is *pau hana*, from Hawaiian language. Food is *kau kau*, from Chinese. Appetizers are *pupu*, also from Hawaiian. Some letters are dropped, like the "d" in *kind*, so something little is *small kine*. The term *da kine* is a unique Pidgin creation that can refer to almost anything, as long as the two parties share enough mutual history to infer the correct referent (Drager & Grama, 2014). Hawaiian Pidgin, and especially the term *da kine*, inspired efforts and publications of a number of researchers (e.g., Marlow & Giles, 2008).

*Da kine* is the ultimate high-context word. *Da kine* can refer to a person, place, thing, or condition. If someone says your car is *da kine*, it can mean anything from excellent to dirty or broken, depending on inflection and situational knowledge. If someone asks if you saw *da kine* at the mall, they could mean your friend Bob or a new store, and the amazing thing is that people communicate successfully every day using da kine to replace a huge array of words.

*Da kine* is "a Pidgin term that serves as a referent to a previously established or contextually known lexeme" (Drager & Grama, 2014, p. 39). In other words, *da kine* can replace any word or phrase as long as speaker and receiver both can access shared referential information.

*Da kine* only works for cultural insiders and those familiarized enough to be sensitive to the contextual cues. As such, Pidgin also serves a social identity function, marking who is within and who is outside the group. Pidgin differentiates between locals and people from elsewhere. Through its many permutations, even in a small and isolated state such as Hawai'i, particular words and phrases can mark one's island and area of origin (Drager & Grama, 2014; Ohama, Gotay, Pagano, Boles, & Craven, 2000). As such, pidgin marks a sensitive gradient of in- and out-group, from foreigner, to US mainland, to Hawai'i born, to immediate in-group.

### Why It Matters

Hawai'i presents an interesting example of how pidgins and creoles come about, facilitating communication between a very diverse set of people from different cultures and languages. Further, the concept of high versus low context is not easy to grasp, and da kine provides a unique example on the extreme end of high-context communication.

High- versus low-context communication styles also leads to differences in conflict resolution (Croucher et al., 2012). High-context cultures discourage direct public disagreement because such displays disturb the collective. Communications are often indirect and affective, leading toward compromise solutions. Low-context cultures want direct, logical communication in open confrontation. Croucher and colleagues (2012) measured conflict style of participants in India, Thailand, Ireland, and the US. They used Oetzel's (1998) measure to compare propensity for dominating, integrating, avoiding, obliging, and compromising styles. An integrating style shows highest concern for interests of both parties, whereas a dominating style puts interests of one party ahead of others. All four most endorsed an Avoiding style, hoping conflicts will fade on their own. Americans (low context) rated the dominating style higher than other groups, while Thai (high context) rated it lowest. Conflict resolution may be particularly difficult when one party with a high-context communication style disagrees with people from a low-context culture. These variations in communication style have caused many issues in cross-cultural interaction, but understanding of the parameters presents solutions.

## REALITY CHECK

*What examples of nonverbal communication have you seen today?*

*Do you think your culture is more high or low context in communication?*

*Can you think of an example of low-context communication in your school life?*

*Does communication style affect how disputes are processed in your home?*

## 8.4 EMOTIONS

### LO 8.4: Discuss theories of emotion and how those theories interact with cultural factors.

Emotions characterize our human condition, filling our interactions and experiences and flavoring our arts, literature, and music. Psychologists have been fascinated with emotion from the field's beginnings, though emotions present psychology with a few headaches, including definition. To begin with, the terms *affect*, *emotion*, and *mood* tend to be used somewhat interchangeably. Affect is the more general term for evaluative responses to events that may include intense or brief emotions and longer-term moods, along with how those states are expressed or displayed externally. Affect arises from internal states but can also transmit from one person to another, such as when a friend smiles, you smile back, and you both feel happier. Anger also transmits easily and on a large scale can lead to riots or brawls. The transmission of affect in social contact is called **affect diffusion** (Peters & Kashima, 2015).

Emotions might be slightly easier to define, happening in response to events, changes, or thoughts people experience. They are familiar, named in our languages, and experienced constantly. Within a huge body of emotion research in psychology, a substantial literature looks at emotion in cultural and cross-cultural context. The cultural literature exists, at least partly, because of the difficulty of measuring or describing them objectively. We know that emotions play out in cascades of neurotransmitters and complex neural connections, and that many of these structures and chemicals appear in other creatures (Ledoux, 2012). The biology and neurochemistry, however, fail to capture the deeply personal and subjective experiences.

Shweder (2004) states, "The idea of an emotion is a complex synthetic notion, composed of wants, beliefs, feelings and values" (p. 81). We *feel* emotions *intra*personally, and although we may share words like "love" and "happiness," my experience of these may differ substantially from yours. Emotions involve both process, such as a precipitating stimulus followed by physiological changes, and content, including my thoughts about the emotion. They also involve a rather messy set of overlapping affective, linguistic, and sensory experiences (Barrett, Mesquita, Ochsner, & Gross, 2007). I may "see red" if I am very angry or "feel butterflies in my stomach" if I am nervous. Fear or hesitation may give me "cold feet." A breakup may cause me to feel "heartache," or if I speak Malaysian or Indonesian, I might ask, "*kenapa ada sakit hati*?" Although the literal translation is "Why have you got an ill liver?" the meaning is really the same as heartsickness, though it is conceptualized in a different organ.

Psychologists have proposed a number of theories to explain emotion, beginning with the James-Lange theory, proposed independently by psychologist William James (1884) and physiologist Carl Lange (1887). In this model, you notice that something happens, your body reacts, you interpret the situation, and then you decide you are experiencing an emotion. James (1884) explained his theory that "the bodily changes follow directly the PERCEPTION of the exciting fact, and that our feeling of the same changes as they occur IS the emotion" (pp. 189–190). For example, you are walking in the woods, you see a bear, your heart starts to race, and you thereby decide you must be afraid. Though the theory seems counterintuitive, it has received empirical support in the intervening decades from studies showing that people can be tricked into believing they are feeling a particular emotion when given a stimulant or placed in a situation of excitement.

In the 1920s, Walter Cannon and Phillip Bard pointed out that the same physiological reactions, increased heart rate, vasoconstriction, and pupil dilation, accompany a variety of emotions (Cannon, 1927). Based only on those physiological signals, humans could never distinguish fright from anger. The Cannon-Bard Theory proposed that the sensations and emotion happen simultaneously. One more major theory remained prominent in the 20th century: the Schachter-Singer two-factor model in which the physiological sensation and the cognitive evaluation of the stimulus together create the perceived emotion.

These theoretical models form the foundation of emotion research in psychology, though they were developed almost entirely by Westerners observing Westerners. Major questions remain about whether emotions are truly universal or if they vary from culture to culture. In fact, researchers generally agree that animals feel certain emotions, described as basic emotions (Demoulin et al., 2004). Psychology seeks universals, so if theories regarding emotion are valid, they should apply across cultures. Particularly, the cognitive components become relevant when considering how humans understand and describe emotions.

## Emotions Across Cultures

Cross-cultural research in emotion begins with the question of universality, whether there are differences in emotions and what differences can be ascribed to cultural factors. Cross-cultural psychology emphasizes comparisons to illuminate universals or differences empirically, often split between research on expression or recognition (van Hemert, Poortinga, & van de Vijver, 2007). The recognition research stems from Darwin's view that emotions are universal and innate, and that basic emotions should be recognizable everywhere. Ideas of difference underlie expression research. An additional line of research looks at dimensionality of emotions, such as positive and negative valence (van Hemert et al., 2007).

### Basic Emotions

**Basic emotions** are emotions based in biology or found so commonly that they are ubiquitous, though the term has also been used to describe simplest elements that combine to form complex emotions (Ekman, 1992). Oddly, the concept of basic emotions was not popular in early psychology. In 1938, Klineberg published what would now be called a qualitative study of emotions and facial expressions as portrayed in Chinese literature. He found the norms and descriptions so unlike his own experiences that he determined universal emotions unlikely. The topic remains a battleground in the nature-nurture debate. The universalist side would say emotions are natural, arising from our physical characteristics, while the nurture side would say that we learn our emotions and their expression. Over the subsequent decades, research has supported a set of six universal emotions: happiness, sadness, anger, fear, surprise, and disgust; this is the same list included in the emotions nonhumans probably experience (Demoulin et al., 2014). Research also supports that cultures differ in what and how people are allowed or supposed to express, which Ekman and Friesen (1969) termed **display rules**.

A number of differences in emotional experience and expression have been linked to ecocultural variables such as political democracy, wealth, religiosity, temperature, mode of subsistence, and Hofstede's dimensions. It was proposed that people in warmer places tend to be more emotionally expressive and tend to show more negative emotion. Evidence of negativity would include more frequent armed attacks and riots, though the premise is questionable. In a major meta-analysis of 190 cross-cultural emotion studies published between 1967 and 2000, a different picture emerged (van Hemert et al., 2007). Temperature and wealth were not predictive of cultural differences. Democracy and human rights correlated with greater emotional expression, as did Hofstede's Individualism dimension. Political stability was associated with more positive emotions like optimism.

While the meta-analysis showed fewer areas of cross-cultural difference than one might expect, some areas of difference did appear. Mode of subsistence, ranging from agrarian to service economies, was correlated with a number of differences. Mode of subsistence affects level and type of cooperation required. Agricultural societies instill compliance in their children, increasing cohesion and conformity and restricting emotional expressions that could cause interpersonal strife (van Hemert et al., 2007).

Modern postindustrial cities and towns employ far more people in services jobs, including financial, retail, restaurant, cleaning, and educational services in which companies and individuals compete for jobs and clientele. Individualism was strongly related to emotional expressiveness, part of the complex of individualism-collectivism (IC) effects appearing so often in cultural research.

David Matsumoto worked with dozens of colleagues around the world on the first large-scale international study of emotional display (Matsumoto, Yoo, & Fontaine, 2008). As with van Hemert et al. (2007), more similarities than differences were observed. In all cultures, participants endorsed about the same level of expressiveness, suggesting great similarity in emotional regulation (discussed below). All groups express more emotions to in-groups than to out-groups. Contempt and disgust were least favored for expression to both in- and out-groups, which is not surprising given their potential for disruption of social relationships. Endorsement of sadness and fear expression was also low, but sadness had the greatest difference between in- and out-group endorsement. The authors attribute the difference to the vulnerability sadness reveals. In-groups provide a safer space to express vulnerability and ask for help.

Predictably, individualism correlated positivity with norms for higher expressiveness. This may be explained by country-level differences in personality traits, particularly extraversion. Extraverts tend to be more expressive, and their greater presence in individualistic countries could make expressiveness more normative. Also unsurprising was the negative correlation between individualism and expression of negative emotions to out-groups, while expression of happiness and surprise were endorsed. Individualists have a greater need to put their best foot forward to maintain connections that are not at risk in collectivist life.

Cross-cultural research in emotion continues to reveal differences in other areas, including their connection to values. People from cultures valuing benevolence want to feel empathy, those valuing self-direction emphasize excitement, and so on, in a topic to be discussed in the next chapter. Some cultural differences appear incredibly early in development. Camras, Bakeman, Chen, Norris, and Cain (2006) studied emotional responses of 3-year-old girls of different origins: nonadopted European American girls, Chinese girls adopted into European-American families, nonadopted Chinese American girls, and nonadopted Chinese girls living in Mainland China. The girls were shown photos that were amusing, such as a rabbit with Groucho Marx glasses, or mildly disturbing images that mothers had rated as acceptable. They were also presented with vinegar to smell as a disgust stimulus. European American girls smiled more than Mainland Chinese and Chinese American girls. European American girls were more expressive overall. For disgust, Chinese American and adopted Chinese girls expressed more than Mainland Chinese. The authors say this indicates rapid influences of culture and socialization on emotional expressiveness in early development.

## Facial Expression

Everyone's face expresses a constant stream of emotions. We smile, frown, and widen our eyes in surprise. These expressions provide the most objectively observable evidence of our internal emotional states, and their recognition is crucial to interpersonal

Figure 8.2 Duchenne Using
Electrodes to Simulate
Emotional Expression

Source: Duchenne (n.d.).

communication (Kosonogov & Titova, 2018). Duchenne attempted to document standard expressions in 19th-century France (see Figure 8.2). As potential universals, facial expressions also provide an avenue to investigate similarities and differences in expressing and recognizing emotions across cultures. Studies testing emotional recognition across cultures began in earnest in the 1960s, showing photos of faces to people of different cultures who were asked to judge the emotion (c.f. Ekman & Friesen, 1971). Although high agreement was found between college students in Europe, Brazil, the US, Argentina, and Japan, this could be attributed to similar cultural origins or contact with Western media.

To control for cultural familiarity, Ekman and Friesen (1971) studied the Fore of the New Guinea Highlands, who had remained completely isolated until 12 years prior. Further, they selected participants who had only minimal contact with outsiders. The project was beset with methodological issues; while Western participants could simply choose an emotion word from a list, the Fore did not read, and having the list repeated verbally for each photo was confusing. Ultimately, they were told a story with an emotional outcome and asked to pick the corresponding picture of facial expression (see Table 8.1). Of the six accepted basic emotions, the Fore reliably recognized happiness, sadness, anger, and disgust. They had difficulty, however, distinguishing fear from surprise in the photos.

The idea of universal recognition of basic emotions has continued to receive partial support in the intervening years, but issues with the research have emerged. The strategy of showing participants a limited set of pictures to match with a list of emotions or set of stories increases the chances of response bias (Jack, 2013). Research characteristically used an alternate forced choice design, with a prescribed set of expressions and labels. Accuracy is calculated by whether scores exceed chance. Emotion matches could exceed chance for other reasons, including misunderstanding of categories. Also, limiting choices to approximate translations of the basic emotions may force participants into choices that fit neither the "universal" emotions nor the emic emotions of the target culture. Free labeling, in which participants themselves offer the label, should avoid the issue, but results have been mixed. Further, there are really no objective criteria for judging conceptual similarity, with the researcher typically coding responses into preselected categories that may misrepresent cultural or linguistic concepts of emotion.

Inconsistency in cross-cultural recognition of basic emotions has led some researchers to pursue new directions. Marsh, Elfenbein, and Ambady (2003) propose the concept

**Table 8.1   Stories From the Study of Fore Facial Emotional Recognition**

- Happiness: His (her) friends have come, and he (she) is happy.

- Sadness: His (her) child (mother) has died, and he (she) feels very sad.

- Anger: He (she) is angry, or he (she) is angry, about to fight.

- Surprise: He (she) is just now looking at something new and unexpected.

- Disgust: He (she) is looking at something he (she) dislikes, or he (she) is looking at something that smells bad.

- Fear: He (she) is sitting in his (her) house all alone, and there is no one else in the village. There is no knife, axe, or bow and arrow in the house. A wild pig is standing in the door of the house, and the man (woman) is looking at the pig and is very afraid of it. The pig has been standing in the doorway for a few minutes, and the person is looking at it very afraid, and the pig won't move away from the door, and he (she) is afraid the pig will bite him (her).

*Source:* Ekman and Friesen (1971).

of nonverbal accents, the idea that expressions differ subtly across cultures and nations. Their participants saw pictures of either Japanese nationals or Japanese Canadians, correctly identifying national origin at an incredibly significant rate of $p < .000001$, or a less than one in ten million chance. Other research demonstrates that participants recognize expressions modeled by people of their own culture with greater accuracy, particularly the often-confused expressions of fear and disgust (Yan, Young, & Andrews, 2017). The same-group advantage may be due to cultural differences in the way expressions are produced or their intensity or in display rules governing what and how expression should occur (Beaupré & Hess, 2005).

Real emotional expression involves muscular movements that happen in series rather than isolation. Some, called microexpressions, are very brief, lasting only 1/25 to 1/5 of a second (Shen, Wu, & Fu, 2012). They include involuntary movements, for instance a "tell" that indicates lying. Microexpressions are surprisingly important in communicating and perceiving emotion. One approach to explaining inconsistencies in cross-cultural emotion research expression looks at **dynamic expression**, examining recognition as the face moves, because static photos do not represent human expression in real life (Chen & Jack, 2017; Delis et al., 2016). Delis and colleagues (2016) identified temporal sequences in facial expression and found that confusion of fear/surprise and disgust/anger are the result of similarity of units in the process of expressing those emotions. Use of temporal sequences allows researchers to observe eye movements as receivers watch an expression. Asian and Western participants differed in the part of the face they watched most, with Asians attending to the eyes and Westerns watching across the face, including eyes and mouth. The emotional accents discussed earlier may be perceived via these microexpressions, providing a direction for future research.

## Emotional Regulation

Part of human development involves learning when and how to express emotions appropriately, to manage the outward display of our internal affective state to fit our situation, and to maintain functionality in difficult situations (Gross, 2014). The process is universal, but culture shapes how we self-regulate our emotions by reinforcing or discouraging certain modes of expression (Butler, Lee, & Gross, 2007). The term **emotional regulation (ER)** refers to intentional management and modification of emotional reactions to facilitate goal-directed outcomes (Matsumoto et al., 2008). Research has shown effects of gender, age, and ethnicity on ER, and differences in strategies used in regulation. A number of factors may explain cross-cultural variation including which emotions are considered desirable and to what extent they may be displayed openly, influenced by cultural norms and values, national heterogeneity, collectivism, religiosity, and social hierarchy.

Gross (2014) discusses a process model of ER over time (see Figure 8.3). It begins with a situation that elicits an affective change. The person pays some degree and type of attention to a stimulus, makes an appraisal, and responds in some way, then the cycle begins again with attention to the now-modified situation. Is the situation important? What do I notice? What do I make of it? How should I respond? Our emotional reactions change the dynamics, modifying the initial stimulus and causing new cycles. We may regulate our expression due to the reaction of others or to our own changing feelings at any stage of a cycle.

Emotions can be regulated by changing the situation, changing one's perceptions, or altering the response. At each step, cultural scripts influence what happens next. If my daughter gives me a sarcastic response to a question, do I think she is cute and funny, decide I am happy, and laugh? Or am I intensely aware that she has overstepped her place in the family and am deeply offended by her disrespect, which enrages me. Of course, there are situations in which a normally cute and funny child pushes buttons at the wrong time, making a parent angry. Hopefully, one can tamp down the anger and diffuse the tension using coping and regulation skills appropriate to the culture. For this discussion, we will acknowledge that factors like environmental conditions, statuses, and norms will limit choices for changing situations or attention, so we will move on to appraisal and response.

In terms of response, both positive and negative emotions can be increased or decreased. Calming down describes decreases of anger or other negative emotions. Getting fired up for a sporting event such as football or wrestling increases emotions

---

**Figure 8.3   Gross's (2014) Process Model of Emotional Regulation**

Situation ⇨ Attention ⇨ Appraisal ⇨ Response ⇨ Situation ⇨ etc.

*Source:* Gross (2014).

some might consider extremely negative. Feeding friends or family a great meal could increase positive emotions. Adolescent girls giggling past bedtime at a slumber party might need help reducing their positivity (e.g., Gross, 2014). How do we change our responses? Two tools of emotional regulation that vary by cultural characteristics are reappraisal and suppression (Matsumoto et al., 2008).

**Reappraisal** means deciding to look at a situation differently, construing the situation in a different way to change its emotional impact. To feel less sad, one might say, "It's OK that Uncle Pete died because he's in a better place now." In cognitive psychology, this is called **cognitive reframing**. Uncle Pete still died, but "better place" is a Euro-American trope that sounds less sad, based in a Judeo-Christian beliefs of a paradisiacal afterlife. To a Hindu, it would make sense only if Pete's *karma* was particularly positive, in other words, if he had primarily good and few bad effects on the world around him during life. In fact, crediting *karma* or God for misfortune also reframes a negative event into an acceptable causal structure that is very specific to culture. The Arabic phrase *Insha'allah* can reduce worry during stressful times; what will happen is God's will.

In **suppression**, a person actively controls or neutralizes their emotional display. This process begins when a mother shushes her baby's crying. Suppression happens every time a soldier faces hostile fire and has to overcome fear. When an airline pilot tells passengers to keep calm and stay in their seats, she is asking them to suppress their panic. One might want to downplay disappointment or grief to save face if you lose a game, don't get a job you wanted, or get jilted by a significant other. In East Asia, appearing too happy could seem inappropriate; given the Asian awareness of impermanence, happiness will yield to sadness eventually, so overt displays may tempt fate and make your friends and coworkers uncomfortable (Ma, Tamir, & Miyamoto, 2018). Sims and colleagues (2018) compared responses of Asian Americans, European Americans, and Hong Kong Chinese to excitement-focused or calm-focused physicians. The Asian participants responded less favorably to the excitement condition, and further, their memory of information from the excited physician was worse. The authors say the emotional mismatch may explain why Asian Americans routinely report worse healthcare encounters. Cultural norms and mores may require some suppression of positive emotions, though certainly negative emotions like anger hold the most potential for turmoil.

*Anger Regulation.* Anger is a universal emotion, and strong cultural norms regulate its expression or suppression. Research on the topic predictably covers Western and East Asian cultures in more detail, but differences emerge already in that limited sample. A primary difference in expression of anger arises from the need to maintain group harmony in collectivist cultures. Broadly, East Asians will be more circumspect in expression of anger, employing more ER. Those of European origin will express anger more externally and aggressively. In North African and Middle Eastern cultures, all collectivistic cultures, the Arabic word *aql* describes the sensible, responsive behavior expected of people, even in anger (Novin, Baanerjee, & Rieffe, 2012).

Moroccan immigrants form a large bicultural group in Holland, currently including many young people born there. Novin and colleagues (2012) studied differences between European-Dutch, Moroccan-Dutch, and Moroccan youths in how they managed anger, expecting the Moroccan-Dutch youths to maintain an *aql* style of restraint in anger response. Interestingly, European-Dutch and Moroccan-Dutch youths responded similarly, both differing from their peers in Morocco. This would indicate that Moroccan youths have shifted toward Dutch norms as they adapt to life in that culture.

*Emotional Regulation in Organizations and Workplace.* Organizational settings and work environments place people in situations that require communication and cooperation, though people largely consider conflict inevitable (Runde & Amon, 2016). Conflict can spur excitement and innovation or cause catastrophic failure, meaning conflict management is key. Whether the setting is a PTA meeting or a multinational corporation, differing goals and understandings can cause friction and, if emotions are unchecked, erupt in conflict with potential for lasting effects. Strategies to regulate emotion are among the most important in mediation and negotiation because people must be aroused enough to move toward solution but not so emotional as to damage the process (Folger, Poole, & Stutman, 2016). Organizations now frequently include members from multiple ethnicities, adding cultural differences in emotional expression and conflict style to already challenging situations, and leading researchers to investigate the interaction of ER and culture in organizational settings.

Kim, Bhave, and Glomb (2013) studied 2,072 employees in 274 workgroups, looking at factors that influenced ER. They did not find effects for "racial" diversity on regulation, probably because it was moderated by social interaction; the more interaction, the more regulation. Age diversity also correlated positively with use of ER. In multicultural groups, low ethnic diversity correlated to higher ER for members of outgroups (with fewer members and/or status), while high diversity was associated with more ER for ingroup members. The study was done in universities, and younger workers are fewer and hold less power, effectively making them an underprivileged outgroup. It may be that lower status led the younger workers to take more care not to cause trouble, or perhaps the elders inspired better behavior. Certainly, older workers know how to regulate already and young workers are more likely to regulate in age diverse groups, whether because of their status or the presence of experienced role models.

## REALITY CHECK

*Have you seen differences in how people express emotions?*

*Have you seen emotions spread from one person to another? Through a group?*

*What do you think of the evidence for basic emotions and facial expressions?*

*Can you think of a time when you needed to regulate your emotions this week?*

# 8.5 CULTURAL DIFFERENCES IN EMOTIONAL EXPERIENCE AND EXPRESSION

## LO 8.5: Discuss how cultural factors interact with and affect emotional experience and expression.

Although psychology as a whole is oriented toward universals, cultural psychology seeks underlying influences that shape processes and meanings to illuminate psychological diversity (Shweder, Haidt, Horton, & Joseph, 2008). Rather than pursue basic or intrinsic emotion, Shweder and colleagues suggest that emotions are "content-laden processes, which are contingent on the implicit meanings, conceptual schemes, and ideas that give them life" (p. 410). Emotions would be dynamic, not snapshots of a facial position, arising from a culture's way of thinking, perceiving, and knowing, and reflecting their social structures and interpersonal norms. Further, people gravitate toward emotions that are congruent with their values system (to be discussed in Chapter 9), for instance influencing whether and how people savor positive emotions (Ma et al., 2018).

In real life, emotions are rarely simple. A person may be both happy and sad at graduation, happy for the success and new opportunities, but sad to leave that phase of life and set of friends behind. A breakup can make one sad for the loss but happy to get out of a dysfunctional relationship. **Emotional complexity (EC)** refers to the experience of simultaneous and potentially contradictory emotions. Similar to the relative ease with which Asians can holistically embrace opposing ideas (Peng & Nisbett, 1999), one could expect a dialectic approach to conflicting emotions. Grossmann, Hyunh, and Ellsworth (2016) undertook a series of studies to clarify differences in EC across cultures. They found robust cultural differences in EC along with a tendency for older people toward greater complexity in their emotional reflections. Surprisingly, they found that dialecticism did not explain differences in EC, but Individualism did. The more Individualist United Kingdom and United States showed the least EC, and the more Collectivist Malaysia, Philippines, Japan, and India were most complex, with Germany, Russia, and South Africa falling between.

Evidence exists for differences on national levels in emotion-related factors. Is this indicative of differences in the experience and processing of emotion on national or cultural levels? Russian culture has been characterized as oriented toward brooding and melancholy, leading Grossman, Ellsworth and Hong (2012) to investigate differences in attention to negative stimuli. In the first study, their participants were Russian students in Moscow and European American students in Michigan. Students were presented with a series of positive or negative images from the International Affective Picture System (Lang & Greenwald, 1988), a set of pictures chosen to elicit particular emotions. Participants controlled when they switched from one image to another, and the time spent looking at each image was used for analysis. Americans spent similar time looking at positive and negative valence images, while Russians spent significantly more time on negative images. In the second study, participants were primed with either Russian or Latvian images and presented with words describing positive or negative traits or with random letters. The Russian prime resulted in faster recognition of negative trait words, with the strongest effect observed in those who identify more as Russian.

## Folk Emotional Concepts

Over the past century, the pendulum has swung between a universalist view of emotion and cultural constructionist views. The idea of culture-specific emotions arose from those lacking linguistic and conceptual equivalents, words that cannot be translated, and feelings that may be incomprehensible outside of a culture (see Shiota & Keltner, 2005; Harkins & Wierzbicka, 1997 for contrasting views). If there are universal emotions, perhaps there are also ones not shared, stemming from cultural differences in other arenas. Developmental conditions shape our very neural structures, and we know that scanning technologies reveal differences in neural activities in domains including cognition and perception. What if some of those differences lead to emotions unique to particular cultures? We are born into and enter different types of relationships; for instance, although mothers are generally loved, East Asians have a unique sense of filial piety, a sentiment specific to fathers. A number of cultures have emotional terms with no English translation and potentially no parallel in any other culture. Psychology generally describes these as "folk emotions," which are criticized for their very specificity, being inherently difficult to define and categorize and impossible to generalize (Scarantino, 2012).

A growing body of literature does take folk or culture-specific emotions seriously, describing them and looking for their roots in parameters of their cultures. In cultural psychology, for instance, some researchers describe all emotions as culturally constructed scripts (e.g., Dzokoto & Okazaki, 2006; Markus & Kitayama, 1994; Menon, Morris, Chiu, & Hong, 1999), and some emotional concepts contain elements traceable to cultural dimensions already discussed. The feeling of *amae*, mentioned earlier, describes the Japanese sense of deep emotional and cognitive connection with family and social convoy (Doi, 1989). *Amae* clearly reflects the collectivism of traditional Japanese culture and the sense of connection underlying their social and business relations. Among the meanings of *aloha* is a warm interpersonal affection and regard that can be deeply and viscerally emotional. *Toska* translates from Russian as "sadness," perhaps a deep, yearning sadness of the soul (Fitzpatrick, 2004), but without the sociohistorical experience of suffering through harsh winters and brutal governance for centuries on end, one would be hard pressed to really grasp the feeling existentially. Nor would one make the cognitive link to *schast'e*, translated from Russian as "happiness," and the tragic irony of its use in propaganda under Stalin. In the 20th century, English became the *lingua Franca* of science, and Wierzbicka (2009) cautions that unless we can move beyond an Anglocentric emphasis on reduction to English terms, we will not understand emotion.

Other languages have marvelously descriptive terms that, even if untranslatable, export across languages because the meaning is just so relevant to life experience. Feeling an existential boredom so deep that nothing seems fresh or exciting? The French word *ennui* describes the feeling. Only in the mid-1800s did the concept *bore* enter English, and Charles Dickens coined the word *boredom* in his 1850s novel Bleak House (Lombardo, 2017). *Ennui* provided more depth and color and the borrowed emotional concept entered English.

If someone who has done me (or others) wrong now faces adversity, I might feel *schadenfreude*. **Schadenfreude** is the German word for taking pleasure at another's misfortune. Someone arrogant gets cut down to size. Someone wins a falsified lawsuit then loses a justified suit that costs more than was won. A particularly arrogant football team loses in the finals. I probably would not feel sad. I might not be happy, given that people already suffered, but I may feel a certain righteous satisfaction that makes me smile wickedly for a moment. *Schadenfreude* feels better if the misfortune befalls a person or group outside our own, adding a social identity aspect to its processes. In fact, *schadenfreude* has added to theoretical literature on social identity and intergroup processes (e.g., Leach, Spears, Branscombe, & Doosje, 2003).

## Cultural Understandings of Emotion

Arguably, cultures include cognitive models of emotion, including beliefs about mechanisms, causes, or purposes of emotions, evaluations of occurrences, and appropriateness of reactions (Russell, 1991). Going beyond particular folk or culture-specific emotions and the controversy surrounding their legitimacy, some cultures have sophisticated conceptual systems for understanding emotion, affect, mood, and feeling, and these may be quite unlike Western European models. The ancient Greeks, considered foundational to Western culture, had a very different conceptualization of emotions, considering them not a mental phenomenon but rather agitations of and in the body (Belfiore, 1985; Dzokoto & Okazaki, 2006). India and China are home to highly elaborate and refined systems, each going back thousands of years. Generally, Western researchers classify all other approaches as folk systems, regardless of their antiquity, and differentiate modern scientific study from those other systems as a group (c.f. Sundararajan, 2009).

Japanese and American understandings of emotions present an immediately apparent difference concerning agency and the constructs of self versus other (Uchida, Townsend, Markus, & Bergsieker, 2009). Americans and Western psychology in general consider emotions to be intrapersonal phenomena, happening within a person. In Japanese culture, emotions happen *between* people, interpersonal phenomena. Recall that self-construal in Japan is interdependent, with the self constructed and described in terms of relationships, while the Western model of self is bounded and separate. In Japanese culture, emotions arise conjointly, the product of relationship and interaction, occurring in the overlaps between self and surrounding others. Uchida et al.'s (2009) team based four studies on Japanese and American Olympic athletes interviewed on television after their competition, anticipating that the emotions expressed would reflect group or individual focus respectively. Analyses supported a relationship focus for expressions by Japanese athletes and self-focused emotions for the Americans.

A number of languages include body references, including English, where loss of love results in heartache or hesitation comes from cold feet (Barrett, 2017), as mentioned earlier. Dzokoto and Okazaki (2006) caution against confusing idioms of the English type, where they are understood as metaphorical, with understanding of emotions in cultures and languages where there is no demarcation between affective and bodily states. This confusion could necessitate a reevaluation of African American psychology from beyond a Eurocentric lens. Examining Dagbani and Fante, two West African languages found in Ghana, the researchers found widespread somatic references placing emotions in the body rather than the mind. In Fante, the word for anxiety translates to "stomach burn," and "heart grow" describes anger. *Ninimooi*, literally "eye red," is worry in Dagbani. Dzokoto and Okazaki (2006) suggest that rather than an abstract linkage between body and emotion, the linguistic emphasis on these somatic descriptions arises from a cognitive system in which body and emotion cannot be separated. The concept of embodiment would therefore be crucial to future theoretical models of emotion among non-Western cultures and minorities.

The Chinese term *qing* appears as an equivalent translation for emotion but it actually expresses a much broader construct. *Qing* includes moods and sentiments, but also the "ever so subtle emotional nuances that color everything we see through the affective lens" (Sundarajan, 2016, p. xii). Similar to the Japanese conceptualization of emotions as interpersonal phenomena, Chinese emotions cannot be understood from a perspective of subject-object polarity. Sundararajan (2009) explains by discussing the term *ganlei*, from *lei*, responsiveness, and *gan*, categorical similarity. *Ganlei* expresses the commonality between self and other that allows us to understand and respond when experiencing emotion, similar to the mechanism of mirror neurons. We attune to the emotions of those most like us, making mind to mind connections rather than self-other perceptions. Emotion happens embedded in, not separate from, a responsive surrounding environment.

The culture of ancient India created the oldest treatise on emotional and affective states, the *Nātyaśāstra*, actually a treatise on aesthetics, particularly dramatic arts. *Nātya* translates to "drama" and *śāstra* means "treatise." Traditionally credited to the mystic sage Bharata Muni, it is probably the work of a number of scholars, written and revised around 300 BCE to 200 CE. It was written as a guide to aesthetics and artistic expression, primarily addressing dramatic production, but advising on poetry and arts in general. The sixth chapter, *Rasādhyāya*, is most specific to communication of emotion. It discusses how emotions are represented dramatically to create aesthetic experiences and revelations through the narrative structure of a performance.

The term *rasa* literally translates as "essence" or "relish" (Paranjpe, 2009), but also describes flavor in foods (Kumari & Nishteshwar, 2013) and moods created by music. *Rasa*, as it relates to the *Nātyaśāstra* and this chapter, applies to emotions, mental states, or feelings (Shweder et al., 2008). There are eight *rasa* described as *sthāyī bhāva* in Sanskrit, which could be translated as basic, universal, or principal: erotic feeling (*rati*), mirth or amusement (*hāsa*), sorrow (*śoka*), anger (*krodha*), dynamic energy or heroism (*utsāha*), fear or terror (*bhaya*), disgust or disillusionment (*jugupsā*), and astonishment or amazement (*vismaya*; Pandit, 2011; Shweder et al., 2008). Created two millennia earlier, the list is similar but not identical to Eckman's list of basic emotions, especially varying with the inclusion of the erotic and heroic domains of experience. Further, the descriptions and associated expressions differ, with *vismaya* falling closer to the English word "wonder" than to "surprise" or "shock." Rather than an open mouth, *vismaya* is conveyed with a closed mouth and a slight bemused smile. Their purpose and use in the arts will be discussed later.

### Intercultural Competence in Expression

As should be apparent by this point, cultures and their ways of thinking can lead to very different norms of communication. We grow up learning who can speak to whom, in what way, and under what circumstances. We learn to be loud or soft to fit the situation, who to hug or not, and what it looks like to be happy, sad, angry, or any of the many more complex emotions. Our communications reflect our values, a topic for the next chapter (Awang, Maros, & Ibrahim, 2012). We also learn to feel uncomfortable when our expectations are violated.

Around the world, communication norms are shifting as media products diffuse norms from dominant cultures across the globe. Local norms are changing as people encounter ideas and products from external influences, whether brought home by friends or family who travel or by people moving into our area (Durant & Shepherd, 2009). This can lead to conflict in our homes and family, or can simply expand our expressive repertoire. At times, these differences exacerbate otherwise manageable conflict.

Awareness of norms of communication and emotional expression are especially important when people communicate across cultures for business or political reasons, or when conflicts occur between cultural groups. A miscommunication can then have major implications, depending on the scale involved. Points to consider go well beyond issues of language and translation. Well-meaning professionals can stumble into conflict if they do not consider limits of hierarchies of age and status or gender restrictions in communication. High- or low-context mismatch can mean too much or two little information is provided. Norms of emotional expression and specific meanings of non-verbal signals are crucial. Sensitivity to these largely unwritten codes, conversely, can yield effective and rewarding interactions.

## REALITY CHECK

*Have you felt multiple emotions about something lately, perhaps happiness and sadness?*

*Do you think there is a preferred emotion in your culture?*

*Have you used a term like* ennui *or* schadenfreude *to describe how you feel?*

*What do you think about the idea that emotions might be interpersonal instead of internal?*

# 8.6 COMMUNICATION AND EMOTION IN THE ARTS

## LO 8.6: Explain ways that the arts and arts production can illuminate cultural nuances of emotion and communication.

Each chapter discusses communicative aspects of the arts as examples of cultural topics in psychology. All arts are inherently communicative, whether overtly containing linguistic messages or simply conveying images or designs stemming from a cultural aesthetic set. For this chapter, a focus on the emotional content may be most interesting. Three examples of cultural connections between emotion, arts, and culture will be discussed: *rasa* in India as a philosophical system of emotions and their purpose in arts, *saudade* in Portuguese-speaking countries as a culture-specific emotion, and *mono no aware* in Japan as an emotion with widespread influence on aesthetics.

To the Indian culture of Bharata's time, drama provided an opportunity for secondary experience of emotions acted out on a stage. Freed from the personal implications of negative experiences, audiences could witness anger, fear, or sorrow vicariously, transforming these awful experiences into enjoyment (Paranjpe, 2009). Ownership of emotion in drama cannot be ascribed to any one party, being shared collectively by playwright, actor, audience, and the imaginary characters. Those ancient thinkers proposed a theory of generalized emotion (*sādhāranīkarana*) shared across a trans-individual domain. Productions of the *Bhagavad Gita* and *Mahabarata* proliferated through history in India and other regions that experienced Hindu rule including Indonesia. So powerful were the stories and the emotions they convey that they continued to be performed after Indonesia became a predominantly Muslim region. Arjuna and Krsna remain common characters in *wayang tarian* dance performances and the iconic *wayang kulit* shadow puppet plays characteristic of Indonesian traditional arts.

In the stories of incarnated deities like Krsna or Rāma, the love of humans around them, spouses, parents, lovers, friends, and children, is transformed from mortal love to intense devotion, *bhakti rasa*. The audience participates in experiencing this transcendent love by witnessing the drama. The actors provide examples of what this divine love looks like, but they also are considered blessed because they physically embody emotions beyond mortal experience. The Sanskrit term for actor, *patra*, also means pot; the actor is a vessel to transport *rasa* to the audience and to elevate the *rasa* from mundane to divine (Sharma, 2016).

For Portuguese speakers there is a feeling they know well, celebrated in art and song. *Saudade* has no direct translation in English, but is related to melancholy, a longing for something lost or a hope that faded, a love gone away or that never bloomed. *Saudade* is about what makes life wonderful, tragic, and amazing, why we want to keep living in this strange, awful, and terrific world (Bowring, 2008; Holton, 2006). Holton (2006) illustrates the concept with a 1941 poem by José Régio, painting an image of the archetypal sailor at sea, the loneliest of creatures, longing for home, proclaiming an existential truth so resounding that *saudade* came to be.

| | |
|---|---|
| O fado nasceu um dia | Fado was born one day |
| Quando o vento mal bulia | When the wind barely stirred |
| E o céu o mar prolongava | And the sky extended the sea |
| Na amurada dum veleiro | On the gunwale of a boat |
| Num peito dum marineiro | In the chest of a sailor |
| Que estando triste cantava | Who, full of sorrow, sang |
| Que estando triste cantava . . . | Who, full of sorrow, sang |
| Ai, que lindeza tamanha | Oh, what monumental beauty |
| Meu monte, meu chão, meu vale | My mountain, my earth, my valley |
| De folhas, flores, frutos de oiro, | Of leaves, flowers and golden fruit |
| Vê se vês terras de Espanha, | See if you see Spanish lands |
| areias de Portugal | Portuguese sands |
| Olhar ceginho de choro | A look blinded by weeping |

—trans. in Holton (2006, p. 2)

*Saudade* fills the streets and clubs of Lisbon, Portugal's capital and polestar of a musical style called *fado* (Gray, 2007). *Fado* is mostly sung by women called *fadistas*. Ethnomusicologist Tom Pryor (2004) described his experience in a Lisbon bar, hearing a *fadista* sing:

> Her song is like nothing you've ever heard: mournful, melancholy, world-weary . . . and yet luxurious, alluring, seductive. It captivates the room like a spell; rolls over the audience like a wave, threatening to pull everyone into its undertow. (p. 27)

*Fado* survives today in traditional form, but also in indie rock and electronica. *Fado* and Spain's flamenco have provided emotional and identity elements for these newer styles as Iberians seek to retain their cultural and historic voice amidst the onslaught of global culture (Arnold, 2013). Popular across Portugal and a deep part of Portuguese culture, *fado* traveled also to Brazil with Portuguese settlers.

Japanese culture prizes a similarly existential aesthetic, *mono no aware*, translated as "the moving power of things" (Ramirez-Christiansen, 1994, p. 15). *Mono no aware* describes the infinite sadness of finite life, the fleeting beauty of a flower, the fragility of a butterfly's wing, the impending doom that faces every man, woman, and child eventually. Whatever we achieve, however much power we amass, we cannot avoid that inevitability. *Mono no aware* reaches its pinnacle in Japanese poetry such as "Plum Blossoms by the Eaves," by Buddhist bishop Shinkei (1406–1475):

Plum Blossoms by the Eaves

When I am gone,

plum blossoms by those eaves

deep with moss fern:

the sadness of a fragrance

drifting alone in the dew.

—in Ramirez-Christiansen (1994, p. 17)

While *mono no aware* may seem like terribly depressing way of feeling, really, it describes a deep, contemplative appreciation of beauty; in the pathos of impermanence, each moment takes on a transcendent beauty (Lomas, 2016). Similarly, in the *ukiyo-e* style, translated as "the art of the floating world," the figures are literally detached from any surface, expressing the sensation of life untethered in this fleeting world. These emotions and aesthetics characterize the drama, music, visual arts, and architecture of Japan well into the 20th century and beyond. Arguably, manga cartoons and comics continue the tradition, with brooding heroes and figures sometimes disconnected from an illustrated ground. Scholars point to manga's historic origins in art going back as far as the Gaki-Zoshi, the 12th-century scrolls depicting the doomed hungry ghosts of Buddhist lore (Papp, 2010). These arts provide an avenue for making this particularly Japanese emotional landscape accessible to outsiders.

## REALITY CHECK

*Do you listen to music specific to your ethnocultural group?*

*What emotions are expressed in the music you listen to?*

*Have you experienced the arts of another culture? Did you feel anything new or different?*

## REFLECTING ON YOUR READING

- Do you speak more than one language? Do you think differently when switching?

- Do you or any of your friends speak a dialect or creole?

- Have you seen someone make a facial expression you did not understand?

- Does your family express emotion loudly or quietly?

# CHAPTER 8 SUMMARY

## 8.1 Evolution of Human Communication

While humans use neuro-physical structures shared with other creatures, only humans seem to use language for complex and abstract communication. This has facilitated development of culture. Tool making may have spurred evolution of complex communication.

A number of creatures use combinations of sounds in communication, arranged according to rules of syntax.

Chomsky proposes that we are language-learning devices optimized to acquire language, and that our languages are more alike than different. The flexibility of syntax allows virtually limitless expression of ideas. We organize our conversations using turn constructional units (TCUs) so we know when one party is ready for the other to speak.

## 8.2 Language Acquisition

We acquire language as children in ways shared across languages and cultures. More parental involvement can facilitate faster learning. Because our brains develop at the same time we learn language, our cognitive processes may differ later in life.

Second languages impose additional effects on development. While earlier thought proposed interference between additional languages, it appears people adapt readily, depending on age of acquisition and similarity of the languages.

Language usage can reveal some cultural differences such as the lower use of personal pronouns in collectivist cultures.

Research suggests that multiple languages can be active simultaneously for bilingual people, unlike the suppression of the alternate language previously assumed.

Diglossia is use of more than one dialect in a community, especially when one is dominant and the other indicates lower status.

## 8.3 Cultural Patterns in Communication

People begin communicating with gestures before they can speak, and nonverbal cues remain important. These differ by culture.

Cultures may tend toward high- or low-context communication, where high-context cultures spell out information that may be shared and assumed in low-context cultures. The context dimension relates also to individualism–collectivism (I-C) and to conflict interaction style.

## 8.4 Emotions

The terms *affect*, *emotion*, and *mood* are all used to describe subjective and mostly internal states. Emotions can spread interpersonally in the process of affect diffusion. Early explanatory models of emotion included James-Lange, where emotion perception follows the stimulus, and Cannon-Bard, where stimulus and emotional perception happen simultaneously.

Darwin proposed that emotions would be universal across humanity. Basic emotions would be ones shared by all cultures. Differences would then be due to display rules governing expression, not actual differences in emotion. Some differences in expression appear related to domains discussed elsewhere like I-C.

Similarities exist in facial expression even among remote cultural groups, but evidence for universal basic emotions remains controversial. Some researchers propose existence of display accents affecting recognition.

In some situations, people must control their feelings and expression for particular purposes, a process called *emotional regulation* (ER). Emotions can be regulated by changing the situation, changing one's perceptions, or altering the response. The process of regulation may change the situation, potentially shaping ER in a dynamic sequence. One method of

ER is cognitive reframing, in which people change how they think about the situation. It may be particularly important to regulate anger and its expression.

## 8.5 Cultural Differences in Emotional Experience and Expression

Cultural psychology prefers to look for explanation of emotion in terms of a particular culture. Emotions are dynamic and shaped by cultural factors. Often more than one emotion happens in the same moment, the concept of emotional complexity. Complexity is greater in older people and collectivist cultures. Cultures also differ in preferred emotions, such as melancholy in Eastern Europe.

Folk concepts of emotion include emotions specific to a culture and cultural ways of explaining emotion. A number of emotion terms cannot be translated and may represent unique emotional states.

While Euro-American cultures tend to see emotions as internal states, Japanese culture considers emotions to be interpersonal. Some cultures consider emotions to be physical states of the body. Cultures including Chinese and Indian have broader concepts in which emotion is a part. The primary Indian treatise related to emotion is more than 2000 years old.

## 8.6 Communication and Emotion in the Arts

Arts provide a major way to express and experience emotion. In India, emotions in arts were used to educate and elevate both performers and audience.

Arts may be filled with culture-specific emotions like *saudade*. Artistic expression of these emotions provides opportunities to share and construct cultural identity.

The Japanese emotional aesthetic of *mono no aware* expresses a deep philosophical approach to understanding life and the world. Experience of Japanese arts provides a glimpse into that way of feeling for outsiders.

## GLOSSARY

**Affect diffusion:** Transmission of affect in social contact.

**Basic emotions:** Emotions based in biology or found so commonly that they are ubiquitous.

**Cognitive reframing:** Changing the way you view events to find more positive alternatives.

**Diglossia:** A community's use of two or more languages, with one language considered superior.

**Display rules:** What and how people are allowed or supposed to express.

**Dynamic expression:** Expression as the face moves.

**Emotional complexity (EC):** The experience of simultaneous and potentially contradictory emotions.

**Emotional regulation (ER):** The intentional management and modification of emotional reactions to facilitate goal-directed outcomes.

*Mono no aware*: Japanese term for the infinite sadness of finite life.

**Reappraisal:** The way in which individuals construe an emotion-eliciting situation to change its impact on emotional experience.

*Saudade*: Portuguese for a bittersweet longing.

*Schadenfreude*: German word for taking pleasure in another's misfortune.

**Suppression:** The inhibition of emotional expressive behavior.

**Turn constructional units (TCUs):** Intonations, words, or phrases signaling completion of a turn.

# MOTIVATION AND MORALITY

## Learning Objectives

**LO 9.1** Discuss how motivations are influenced by culture.

**LO 9.2** Explain the ways morals reflect their cultural context and origin.

**LO 9.3** Evaluate the theoretical models of values across cultures.

**LO 9.4** Describe the role of the arts in transmitting and supporting morality and values.

# PREPARING TO READ

- Did you ever feel guilty or ashamed about a choice you made? Why?

- Have you ever wondered why people make the choices they do?

- Do some choices make less sense than others?

- Is there perhaps a relation between how similar people are to you in origin and how well you can relate to their choices?

*Prophecies foretold Kamehameha's birth and rise to power, a great leader destined to unite the Hawaiian islands, the most isolated archipelago on the planet. When Kamehameha was born in 1758, even the Great Polynesian Migration had ignored the islands for centuries. Haley's Comet lighting the night skies was seen as a potent augur for the infant being born, an ali'i, the ruling class in traditional Hawaiian culture. Monumental changes indeed approached. Twenty years later, in 1778, Captain James Cook would arrive, altering island life forever.*

*Kamehameha grew tall among his people, well over six feet, strong of body and of mind (see Figure 9.1). Fierce in battle, he trod the opposition to dust, gathering lands and allies as he went. He eventually became first to rule the entire island chain, his last few battles fought with artillery provided by British captain George Vancouver.*

**Figure 9.1    Statue of Kamehameha, Honolulu**

*He'iau were the temples, the churches or cathedrals of the island paradise in the form of carefully crafted stone platforms and thatched buildings. In those days, the ali'i of the islands drew authority from ceremonies at he'iau that included human sacrifice on certain occasions. One he'iau remained to be consecrated by sacrifice in Kamehameha's ancestral home area. During a military expedition in the Puna area, the young ali'i and his party spotted a group of commoners from an opposing group and gave chase. Kamehameha outran his party and had nearly caught two of* the commoners when his foot got stuck in a lava crevice. One commoner hit him over the head with a canoe paddle, which splintered on impact, incapacitating the aliʻi. The man did not kill Kamehameha, though he had the ability and motivation, and history pivoted in a new direction.

Kamehameha spared the man, who certainly should have been put to death under the old Hawaiian laws that required a commoner to be killed for simply stepping on the shadow of an aliʻi. Kamehameha awoke from the blow with a profound realization of compassion and shared humanity. Later, when he became ruler of the island chain, he enacted Kānāwai Māmalahoe (the Law of the Splintered Paddle), which became a fundamental law of the entire archipelago. The 1797 law established the right of all people to live free from fear of danger or harm regardless of social standing. Kānāwai Māmalahoe stands as a hallmark of humanitarian law and is often cited as such, especially regarding noncombatants in warfare (MacKenzie, 2010; Andrade, 2010).

Kānāwai Māmalahoe

E nā kānaka,

E mālama ʻoukou i ke akua

A e mālama hoʻi ke kanaka nui a me kanaka iki;

E hele ka ʻelemakule, ka luahine, a me ke kama

A moe i ke ala

ʻAʻohe mea nāna e hoʻopilikia.

Hewa nō, make.

Law of the Splintered Paddle

Oh people,

Honor thy god;

respect alike [the rights of] people both great and humble;

May everyone, from the old men and women to the children

Be free to go forth and lie in the road (i.e., by the roadside or pathway)

Without fear of harm.

Break this law, and die.

—Kamehameha I, 1797

# WHY IT MATTERS

*All cultures have rules and ideals for how to live, some stated implicitly, some unspoken. Kānāwai Māmalahoe overtly states a moral standard unusual for its time in history. The law reflects a humanitarianism inherent in Hawaiian culture.*

An overarching goal of psychology is prediction of behavior, particularly human behavior. Freud saw human choices arising from the unconscious, in a battle between primal urges and restraints learned in early childhood. Watson viewed behavior as the result of conditioning that could be engineered to yield virtually any behavioral outcome. Seeking a more nuanced process, Skinner proposed operant conditioning to explain volitional behaviors. Humanists argued that humanity goes beyond such mechanistic predictability, striving instead for self-actualization, yearning to reach its greatest potential of expression. Psychologies of culture, along with sociology, anthropology, and other disciplines, instead examine the impact of cultural processes and social constructions on norms and behaviors to explain the myriad of choices billions of people make each day.

Physical survival is, of course, as universal a drive for humans as for any organism. Are there human activities that can be distinguished from instincts for survival or are humans acting out seemingly complex tasks simply to achieve those same basic goals beneath their guise of sophistication? What, if anything, distinguishes an instinctual drive or need from something more lofty? What leads people to live the lives they do, and are the laws governing our choices universal or culturally determined? In basic terms, this chapter discusses goal directed behavior, and the apparently increasing importance of culture as humans engage in a myriad of activities less directly related to survival.

This chapter discusses motivations, values, and morals, an overlapping set of parameters that guide human behavior. To get started, definitions are in order. **Motivation** is a person's reason for doing something. Value is the importance or cost placed on something, while **values** describe the principles or standards for judging importance in how we live. **Morals** are standards for judging right from wrong and good from bad. Morals allow us to discern and administer justice. All three represent aspects of how humans, unlike other creatures, thoughtfully choose what they do and do not do. Perceived differences in these areas form a primary source of intercultural hostility and violence. Each has been a topic of extensive research in psychology and each has a body of cultural research to be discussed in the following pages.

## 9.1 MOTIVATION: WHY WE CHOOSE WHAT WE DO

### LO 9.1: Discuss how motivations are influenced by culture.

The most basic motivation, physical survival, is a drive that explains a vast majority of behaviors across species and includes obtaining food, water, and needed shelter.

The next level of drive would be procreation, the instinctual drive to pass on genetic material to subsequent generations. The motivation for genetic survival spans all life forms. Although intent to achieve these goals can be called motivation, they are all instinctual biological imperatives, unlike human activities that are apparently volitional. Quite a few creatures choose to play, sometimes frolicking like lambs in the springtime or practicing hunting behavior like young wolves or kittens. Human motivation involves intentionality, conscious decisions to direct effort toward a goal (McClelland, 1987). No creatures but humans seem to make decisions in such a vast array of domains, many apparently unrelated to survival at all.

Plants and animals all draw on their environments for survival, but plants lack mobility. Animals move around to obtain resources but make few choices beyond survival needs. Human motivation has evolved in new directions unknown to other animals as cognitive and affective components of human ability appeared, supporting and reinforcing motivations and their outcomes. We eat, but the experience is made richer through our refined aesthetics, motivating us to create cuisine. We hold concepts of family as a source of fulfillment and meaning in our lives, enhancing what is otherwise simply biological reproduction. Humans are unique in the level of support we provide for our offspring and spouses, beyond even other primates, something Baumeister (2016) posits is one of humanity's most noble characteristics.

Approaches to the study of human motivation have tended to focus on particular motivations such as achievement, power, or intimacy (Baumeister & Leary, 1995). Baumeister (2016) suggests that this limited approach has hindered progress, and a more general theory of motivation is needed. That theory should explain both state (impulse) and trait (drive) motivations. Although both move people to change themselves and/or their environment, they can be differentiated by duration and relation to survival, drives being more permanent and crucial to physical existence. He further says that a general theory of motivation should operate at such a deep level that other processes, such as cognitions and emotions, can be attributed to the underlying motivational structure. A general theory of motivation should also remain valid across cultures.

In earlier research, Baumeister and Leary (1995) discussed fundamental motivations, those being motivations so basic that they would underlie all other human activity. They laid out a set of criteria for a motivation to be fundamental:

(a) produce effects readily under all but adverse conditions,

(b) have affective consequences,

(c) direct cognitive processing,

(d) lead to ill effects (such as on health or adjustment) when thwarted,

(e) elicit goal-oriented behavior designed to satisfy it (subject to motivational patterns such as object substitutability and satiation),

(f) be universal in the sense of applying to all people,

(g) not be derivative of other motives,

(h) affect a broad variety of behaviors, and

(i) have implications that go beyond immediate psychological functioning. (p. 498)

A fundamental motivation must exist regardless of situation, including cultural context. It must affect thought and feeling, and failure to achieve satisfaction should lead to medical, psychological, or behavioral pathology. Consequences from lack of fulfillment differentiate a fundamental need from a want. A flashy new car would be nice, but if a bus or your mother's old car gets you where you need to go, you will survive. If a motivation is universal, this implies evolutionary or physiological origin, or it might not be present across cultures. Fundamental motives should not be possible to reduce or eliminate via cultural conditions. Finally, a fundamental motivation should account for multiple behaviors and outcomes beyond basic functions.

One school of thought, including Baumeister and Leary (1995), maintains that belongingness is a fundamental human motivation. Humans everywhere need some level of positive interpersonal relationships, and these relationships must endure over time to be satisfying. Humans without connection tend toward physical and psychological illness, and people with good social relations tend to be happier. Need to belong may explain why people want that flashy car, listen to particular music, or color their hair pink; those actions solidify membership in a specific group. Belongingness or connectedness thus satisfy criteria for fundamental motivation, and appears just above physical needs (food, water, shelter) and safety in Abraham Maslow's hierarchy of higher and lower priority needs.

Maslow (1943) considered these topics at length as he developed his theory of human motivation, which included his famous hierarchy of needs. Humans are creatures that perpetually want, he said, often with aspirations predicated on achieving layers of goals: a job to pay bills and to buy a house to start a family. Maslow was a humanist, and he wanted to understand human achievement far beyond somatic drives like hunger; he wanted to explain why Beethoven wrote symphonies, Vermeer painted, and Einstein found laws of physics. Maslow wanted to explain the highest achievements of humanity. He envisioned that getting there requires a series of steps, each predicated on the one before, first physical needs, then safety, then belonging, then esteem being fulfilled before seeking that final step. Maslow (1943) described that lofty stage:

> Even if all these needs are satisfied, we may still often (if not always) expect that a new discontent and restlessness will soon develop, unless the individual is doing what he is fitted for. A musician must make music, an artist must paint, a poet must write, if he is to be ultimately happy. What a man can be, he must be. This need we may call self-actualization. (p. 382)

Maslow's hierarchy will be discussed as it pertains to well-being in Chapter 11, including some issues in its applicability across cultures.

## Agency and Goals

White men, with white students as their participants, created the overwhelming bulk of motivation research, as is true of most psychological work (Usher, 2018). This fact calls into question the fundamental assumptions of the field and their universality. Some concepts are self-evident and likely to hold true across cultures, for instance, the primary motivation for humans to create and maintain lasting bonds with other people, to create a sense of belongingness (Baumeister & Leary, 1995). People are certainly motivated to maintain positive relations with some number of others, though variation in how that is approached and accomplished highlights the effects of culture on people and their behavior. Other motivations, such as those for pro-environmental behavior (Barbarossa, De Pelsmacker, & Moons, 2017), are not necessarily shared, despite the potential to assist human survival.

A number of researchers have proposed generalizable constructs for describing motivation across cultures. Broadly, these usually include motivations for survival, achievement, belonging, pleasure, growth, and spirituality (e.g., Schwartz, 1992; Grouzet, 2013), though different theorists have proposed a variety of categories and sub-categories. Motivations may be more or less emphasized in cultures, and some motives conflict with others. As is the case with so much cultural research, a primary driver of difference depends on the emphasis on individual or collective self-construal, with influences in play from Hofstede's dimensions like uncertainty avoidance and long-term orientation, from cognitive styles, and other topics to be discussed in the following pages.

## Achievement Motivation

The term achievement motivation first appeared in the 1950s, notably in the work of David McClelland, who defined it as intent for "success in competition with some standard of excellence" (McClelland, Atkinson, Clark, & Lowell, 1958, p. 181). The concept quickly gained traction as a means of understanding productivity in the workplace and likelihood of success in education or other endeavors requiring perseverance and skill. The US military hired McClelland and his colleagues to research achievement motivation and its measurement, which they stated had "proven useful in predicting widely different kinds of behavior—e.g., performance., learning, memory, perception, etc." (de Charms, Morrison, Reitman, & McClelland, 1954, p. 1). It remains a popular topic in education research (e.g., Azman, 2005).

Researchers in achievement motivation almost immediately began looking for differences due to social class (e.g., Douvan, 1956) or culture (e.g., Kerckhoff, 1958). Typically, these early studies predicted lower achievement motivation in minority or low SES group. In comparing white and Chippewa children, Kerckhoff (1958) found higher achievement motivation among the white children, but qualified his results by pointing out that Chippewa who identified more with whites scored higher than those with mixed or Chippewa identity. Mingione (1968) measured need for achievement (N-Ach) in fifth and seventh graders in a low-SES northeastern school, finding whites scored highest, with "Negroes" [sic] scoring lower and Puerto Ricans scoring lowest.

These were not insensitive researchers, despite their use of prejudicial terminology, but rather people trying to find solutions to social inequities. Mingione (1968) comments that in the white dominated culture of the time, "The culture offers Negroes and Puerto Ricans less encouragement than whites to be concerned with personal achievement; in consequence, they are less likely to become productive and achieve at a level commensurate with their abilities" (p. 94). Although this situation has brightened somewhat in the past 50 years, inequities do still abound.

McClelland's research has been criticized for its ethnocentricity on a number of levels (c.f. Zusho & Clayton, 2011). His methodology employed the Thematic Apperception Test (TAT), which requires participants to tell stories about pictures or drawings, a task most suited to people with Western schooling. He also approached achievement from a view that success equals making money, much in the tradition of Weber's Protestant ethic. Further, though concepts of individualism-collectivism had been discussed for decades, his theories were based on individual achievement.

Fortunately, subsequent research has provided much more nuanced views. King, McInerny, and Nasser (2017) based their research on the idea that culture would tend to promote patterns of motivation, much as cultures include patterns of emotional display or parenting style. They used the four types of goals set forth in personal investment theory, mastery, performance, social, and extrinsic, to compare patterns of goal orientation across nine cultural groups. Mastery orientation focuses on learning to meet self-set standards and personal interest. They sampled participants in Hong Kong, Singapore, Vietnam, Qatar, and Lebanon, along with Anglo-Australian, Aboriginal Australian, and Navajo samples. Mastery was the strongest predictor of engagement for all groups except Qatar, but with considerable variation; in the Qatar sample, it predicted 22% of engagement, while for the Anglo-Australians, it predicted 80%. The other samples ranged from 34% (Hong Kong) to 61% (Vietnam) with the Navajo sample at 40%.

## Self-Enhancement and Self-Improvement

Among the basic assumptions of psychology is the connection between self-esteem and well-being, and a great deal of research has sprung from the idea that people seek ways to feel good about themselves. Positive self-esteem makes people healthier, happier, and more productive, the logic goes. Diener and Diener (1995) found self-esteem to be the strongest predictor of life satisfaction across 31 countries and 13,118 participants, supporting the view. Educational and business settings want productive employees and high-achieving students, leading to a continuing body of work on the topic and various theories about how to optimize self-perceptions. In North American schools, self-efficacy and optimism have been linked to enhanced achievement, and an industry of self-esteem programs blossomed over the past four decades.

Western researchers predictably emphasize the need to feel good about one's self *individually.* Their cultures reward people motivated to seek praise for personal accomplishments and to diminish failings, termed self-enhancement bias. In the fundamental attribution error (FAE), discussed in Chapter 4, individuals attribute personal successes to internal factors and blame external influences for failure. The reverse is true when considering attributions for others. When researchers began trying self-enhancement questionnaires on non-Western participants, curious results appeared, and as with FAE, cross-cultural research weakened the case for universality of self-enhancement motivations. Cultural researchers now generally accept Asians will tend toward modesty, downplaying their successes and eschewing praise. Instead, they hold an incremental view of self and abilities, increasing positive regard through self-improvement rather than self-enhancement (Tsai et al., 2015).

Two explanations have been offered for differences in self-enhancement and self-improvement biases. Perhaps the self-enhancement motive is a Western phenomenon and not universal at all. Collectivists would tend modestly to emphasize group harmony over praise and seek self-improvement to increase group success instead. Conversely, perhaps self-enhancement is universal but differing display rules lead to behavioral variation (Brown & Kobayashi, 2003). Both possibilities could be tied to differences in self-construal, those holding independent self-concepts seeking distinction while interdependent self-construal emphasizes collective good (Kurman, 2001). A common axiom in New Zealand and Australia says the tall poppies get cut down, meaning the collective will punish rather than praise overly conspicuous success (Harrington & Liu, 2002). A number of studies have attempted to clarify the complex picture of research variously confirming and contradicting conventional assumptions about self-enhancement bias.

Heine and colleagues (2001) undertook a series of studies that supported the self-enhancement and self-improvement differences between American and East Asian cultures, using samples in Japan, Canada, and the US. In the first three studies of the series, persistence was measured by observation through a hidden camera to prevent attempts by participants to create socially desirable appearances. For Japanese participants, failure served as a motivating force, leading to greater persistence in the tasks. They used negative information to facilitate self-improvement. The North Americans followed a diametrically opposed path, persisting less in the face of failure than when they succeeded. Successes affirm self-esteem while failures threaten self-image. Both groups want to appear as successful as possible, the Japanese by efforts at improvement, and the North Americans by persisting in tasks where they are already successful. The authors propose that fundamental differences in how cultures view the nature of ability and the effect of effort underlie these differences, as discussed in previous chapters. The persistence of Japanese participants indicates an incremental or growth mind-set view of self and abilities, culturally supported by emphasis on effort and self-improvement. North American culture, conversely, views ability as fixed, minimizing effectiveness of efforts at self-improvement.

A growing number of researchers are seeking alternatives to individualism-collectivism in explaining cultural differences, especially given inconsistent data regarding self-esteem bias. One alternative paradigm distinguishes cultures of face versus cultures of dignity (Lee, Leung, & Kim, 2014). In face cultures, esteem depends on externally granted hierarchic status and recognition. Dignity cultures assume that people have an intrinsic value from birth, theoretically equal to other people. To claim recognition beyond what one has earned is highly inappropriate in face cultures, leading to a humility bias. Face is easily lost and difficult to gain, leading to a prevention focus in what one presents to others and moderating external expression of self-enhancement (Lee et al., 2014). When privacy is assured, East Asians express similar levels of self-enhancement as displayed by Westerners.

To face and dignity, Leung and Cohen (2011) add cultures of honor. Honor has both internal and external elements: an internal, personal evaluation and an external evaluation by others of the culture. An honorable person can be trusted to fulfill promises or pay debts. Cultures of honor appear in cultures with herding as opposed to horticultural lifestyles (Henry, 2009). Nisbett and Cohen (2018) found that murder rate in the Southern US varied between flatter, moist areas suited for plants compared with steeper, arid areas, with higher rates in herding counties. Honor cultures appear in lawless areas and may be associated with low socioeconomic status (Henry, 2009).

Honor can be gained or taken away in contest with others and may be jealously guarded. Challenges to one's honor may induce violent response, and domestic violence is more frequent in honor cultures. Reciprocity forms a key characteristic, with both good and bad actions being repaid in kind, leading people to defend their honor vigorously when wronged. The focus on honor in the Southern US may explain the much higher levels of interpersonal violence there compared to the North (Ayers, 1984). In a meta-analysis of 92 countries, Henry (2009) found a significant relation between murder rate and herding, but he found the effect was mediated by economic status disparity.

Modernization provides an additional factor affecting self-enhancement bias research, with norms changing as people leave traditional lifestyles behind. Bai and Chow (2013) led a study that expected no self-enhancement bias, in which 445 Chinese aged 60 or older were asked about their perceptions of themselves and others. Contrary to predictions, more than 75% rated themselves more positively than their peers, despite being of an age where traditional values would be expected. The researchers proposed that the surprising results can be explained by gradually diminishing respect for older people following years of exposure to Western media and ideas. This idea was supported by more positive evaluation of peers by those in rural areas than in the city.

## Agency and Control

Europeans and Euro-Americans are more strongly motivated when they can choose what to do (Uchida & Kitayama, 2009). If they achieve successes, their happiness is a personal, internal experience so important that it is codified in the US Constitution. Individual agency facilitates achievement of individual goals, regardless of others' wants or needs, and with emphasis on a person's own hard work. Personal self-esteem generated by those achievements correlates highly with happiness (e.g., Diener & Diener, 1995; Mesquita & Markus, 2003), and relational harmony has little effect on goal choices. In failure, individualists tend to externalize agency, blaming others or external factors, and thereby fulfilling the goal of protecting individual self-esteem (Imada & Ellsworth, 2011).

In an interdependent view of self, individuals exist embedded in a web of relationships, their agency conjoined with the goals and desires of others around them (Uchida & Kitayama, 2009). As such, Asians feel stronger motivation when others make choices for them and may feel anxiety over disapproval of their own choices or subsequent need to request help. The need to maintain relational harmony leads to restraint in expression such that one does not seem boastful or ungrateful. This is not to say that hierarchies do not exist or that people are not proud of individual accomplishments, but norms encourage humility, at least on the outside.

These independent versus interdependent models of motivation underscore questions of agency and expectations of how social obligations affect life satisfaction (Eisen, Ishii, Miyamoto, Ma, & Hitokoto, 2016; Miller, 2003). European culture's stance, and Euro-America by extension, is that any infringement on personal choice impinges on free will and individual agency, while Confucian cultures emphasize collective agency (Buchtel et al., 2018). The assumption of mainstream psychology has been that full exercise of independent agency leads to healthy, fully functional adulthood, inspiring self-determination theory (SDT; Ryan & Deci, 2000). SDT associates intrinsic motivation and self-regulation with the greatest chances for well-being.

Miller, Das, and Chakravarthy (2011) undertook a series of studies comparing perceptions of students in New York City and Mysore, India regarding helping, obligation, and satisfaction with some interesting results. Results demonstrated that Indian participants internalized the role expectations of family and friends, leading to strong correlations between duty/responsibility and both choice and satisfaction. Ambiguity of interpersonal obligation and reduction of personal choice for helping led Americans to feel less satisfaction from helping others in high expectation conditions, but Indian participants felt equal satisfaction from helping regardless of strength of expectation.

Eisen and colleagues (2016) undertook a study comparing choice preferences of Japanese, German, and North American workers. They found a number of country-level differences in workplace control preferences for participants. The Japanese participants were much more likely to prefer workplaces with compensation schemes that maintained social order instead of rewarding individual achievement, indicating an interdependent sense of agency. American and German participants demonstrated preference for independent agency, wanting much more control over their work environment.

These differences found their ultimate expression in Amy Chua's (2011) book *Battle Hymn of the Tiger Mother*. Chua, a Yale law professor and self-described tiger mother, made the bold claim that the deep involvement of Asian American mothers in their children's lives leads to greater excellence compared to children of more lenient Euro-American mothers. Controversy ensued. Citing prior research showing that people in interdependent cultures do not perceive parental influence and pressure as constraining, Fu and Markus (2014) undertook studies of European American and Asian American high school students in California to examine perceptions of maternal support and pressure. They found that Asian American students felt more interdependent connection with their mothers than did European American students. Maternal pressure helped the Asian American students to persist in difficult tasks and was unrelated to sense of support. European American students, conversely, felt independent from their mothers and experienced a negative relation between support and pressure. Pressure reduced feelings of support for the European American group and reduced motivation.

What motivates you to get out of bed in the morning?

How important to you are success and recognition for the things you do?

Will your goals be of more benefit to you or to your family if they are achieved?

## 9.2 MORALITY: DECIDING WHAT IS RIGHT

### LO 9.2: Explain the ways morals reflect their cultural context and origin.

We judge actions based on moral codes, culturally based bodies of prescriptive norms including ideas about fairness, justice, and rights in interactions with those around us (Killen & Dahl, 2018). The origins of morality will remain forever shrouded in primeval mystery, but these processes are shared universally. We benefit by pooling our resources and efforts into social institutions, whether families, tribes, villages, states, or nations, and for those to exist, we need a common set of rules to coordinate our coexistence and reduce conflict. In nature, conflicts are resolved with aggression and physical dominance; morality provides more peaceful and adaptive mechanisms for order and compromise (Baumeister & Vonasch, 2012). For the most part, humans get along, notwithstanding occasional wars when moral codes differ. Morality informs how we judge ourselves and others and influences our personal choices of what we do and do not do. The latter describes the concept of self-regulation, when we do not pursue urges, however tempting they may be. Morality also provides reasons to set aside self-interest and undertake dangerous or damaging actions when needs of the group conflict with our own.

The human brain lacks structural components for morality; neural activity observed while a person engages in moral judgment is the same as other processes such as risk-reward evaluation (Greene, 2018). Instead, the natural social orientation of children combines with developing cognitive capacity to enable inferences of whether acts are right or wrong (Killen & Dahl, 2018). Very early actions, including the social smile at four to six weeks of age, set foundations for later acquisition of moral norms. As a child's social sphere expands, more experiences with others, including antagonistic encounters, add complexity to moral considerations. Dilemmas and conflicts can at times lead to non-moral considerations or outright violations of moral codes, and children eventually internalize which codes can be violated under what condition. For instance, one question commonly used in research asks whether it is acceptable to steal to obtain life-saving medicine that you cannot afford.

In European origin philosophy, Kant's ethical theory defines moral decisions as those made by an individual without coercion, rationally chosen with free will

(Buchtel et al., 2018). This view contrasts with some religious moralities, where individuals are required to behave in particular ways to align with supernatural or spiritual forces for some ultimate outcome. In the Hindu tradition, moral action wins freedom from suffering and rebirth. The scriptures of Christians and Muslims exhort them to behave morally as prerequisite for a paradisiacal afterlife. More a social philosophy than a religion, Confucian culture revolves around roles, hierarchies, and inherent obligations, the fulfillment of which maintains balance of nature and human order. Ancestors exist on a spiritual plane, nourished by descendants to whom they dispense benevolence. Of course, moral systems can be quite complex, with lists of what one must and must not do, but these can be viewed as products of the cognitive and social structures of their cultures. All presuppose free will because a moral decision must be a choice; compelled activity cannot really be moral if the actor lacks agency to choose otherwise (Baumeister & Vonasch, 2012).

## Sex and Sexuality

Despite it being a universal imperative crucial to survival of species and culture, humans have spent enormous time and energy making rules about sex: who can have it, with whom, with what preconditions, and with what future implications? Chinese culture traditionally places high value on female chastity, but sex is not taboo. Rather, sex and discussion of sex remained behind closed doors (Chu, 2017). A notable sex scandal erupted in Hong Kong in 2008, when prominent Chinese actor Edison Chen took his computer in for repairs and photos of him with female celebrities were stolen and published. The press painted Chen in such a negative light that he issued two apologies, while the females, all of whom had consented to private photos, were cast as victims (Chu, 2017). In light of the #MeToo movement, their consent may no longer be considered valid, given Chen's high-powered star status (Zarkov & Davis, 2018).

Few aspects of culture generate as much controversy as questions regarding sexuality of young people. Euro-American mainstream assumptions about youth sexuality are by no means homogenous, but research tends to normalize Euro-American adolescent experiences and stigmatize other groups (Stephens & Few, 2007). In the US, the idea of teens having sex, especially before marriage, violates religious mores and cultural expectations, despite decades of data showing no generation has been remotely abstinent. Using public health records and survey data from the National Family Growth Survey (NFGS) for 1982, 1988, 1995, and 2002, Finer (2007) demonstrated that almost all American have premarital sex. For those turning 15 between 1954 to 1963, 82% had premarital sex by age 30 and 88% by age 44. For those turning 15 between 1964 to 1993, 91% had premarital sex by age 30. In the 2002 survey, 85% of all women indicated they had sex before marriage. Even in the 1600s, an estimated 30% of Puritan colonial brides were pregnant before marriage (d'Emilio & Freedman, 1997), though a minister in the Massachusetts colony reputedly complained the number was likely half (Bryson, 2010). If the US has a moral stance on youth and premarital sex, it is to condemn it in public, though statistics say Americans tend to have covert sex anyway.

Morals around sex and sexuality can become particularly problematic crossing cultures, and despite some claims that panic over sexualization of youth are overblown, images in music videos are shocking to people in cultures where female bodies are always covered. Again, not everyone is following the rules; after the US, which watches by far the most internet pornography, and Great Britain in second, third place goes to India (Ray, 2017). Conflicts over sex and sexuality also arise within national cultures when factors of multiculturalism or modernization place differing moral systems in conjunction.

## Morality and Gossip

People love to gossip. Gossip relays personal information about an absent party. Originally *godsib*, the word described conversation between godparents, people who were close and held shared interests in the moral enrichment of a child (Dunbar, 2004). It now implies speaking ill of someone or sabotaging social relations. Gossip is inherently judgmental, containing evaluations in addition to factual information. Keenly attuned to and entertained by gossip, it is estimated to fill two-thirds of our conversational time (Dunbar, 2004).

Mesoudi, Whiten, and Dunbar (2010) used gossip in an experiment testing accuracy of transmission in a transmission chain (like the telephone game). They found social information of a relationship gossip type was recalled and transmitted with much greater accuracy than individual or nonsocial information. The researchers interpreted the results to support the social brain hypothesis, that human intelligence evolved to facilitate social interaction. In that paradigm, language increases our communication network, allowing us to communicate with and transmit information about more people. Gossip forms one important medium for social information (Dunbar, 2004).

Gossip's reputation as an act of idleness, or a waste of time, may be undeserved; consider that gossip also serves several social and moral functions. First, gossip is a time-honored tool of instruction. People learn from gossip what is acceptable and what will cause a backlash. By extension, gossip provides a means of social control, reinforcing norms and punishing infractions, and this process continues evolving across generations into the future. Gossip appears to be one of the few ways to regulate behavior in online interaction, where normally polite people engage in brutal flame wars and horrific criticism. In nongaming virtual realities like Second Life, Gabriels and colleagues (Gabriels & De Backer, 2016; Gabriels, Bauwens, & Verstrynge, 2012) found that fear of gossip provided a rare means of restraining trolling and other bad online behaviors.

## Cross-Cultural Theories of Morality

### Kohlberg and Moral Development

Lawrence Kohlberg's 1958 dissertation marked his first step toward creating a universal theory of moral development. The dissertation focused on thought and choice in adolescence, leading to adult morality. He sought to define the stages through which an infant with no knowledge of self-regulation eventually grows into an adult, normally with some moral compass. Kohlberg (1971) felt confident he had found the universal elements and process:

All individuals in all cultures use the same thirty basic moral categories, concepts, or principles, and all individuals in all cultures go through the same order or sequence of gross stage development though they vary in rate and terminal point of development. (p. 175)

Kohlberg (1971) saw his stages as discrete and whole systems of thought, each level acting as a cohesive way of thinking and being (see Table 9.1). Development moves in only one direction toward higher levels, never skipping steps and never going back except under effects of extreme trauma. Each level includes knowledge and understanding of the previous levels (Kohlberg & Hersch, 1977).

Babies are born without any moral system, but they quickly learn about punishment and achievement of pleasure through behavior. The conventional level is reached when the child understands that there are rules and begins to internalize them. The post-conventional stage is reached when a person understands that rules are made by humans for the sake of social functionality and serve as means rather than ends in themselves. An advanced person ultimately moves beyond need for authority and makes choices for the good of humanity. The aim of formal education, according to Kohlberg, should be to assist the developing person in moving toward higher stages. The sixth and final stage remains hypothetical, with no clear testing criteria in Kohlberg's research to differentiate Stages 5 and 6 (Snarey, 1985).

### Table 9.1 Kohlberg's Theory of Moral Development

| Level | Description | Stages |
|---|---|---|
| **Preconventional level** | No internalized morality, code is based on consequences of following or breaking rules. | **Stage 1:** Punishment-and-obedience orientation. Physical consequences determine right or wrong; punishment is to be avoided. |
| | | **Stage 2:** Instrumental-relativist orientation. Right action provides satisfaction of needs. Fairness, equality, and reciprocity are present but interpreted pragmatically. |
| **Conventional level** | Conforming to expectations and following rules are intrinsically valuable, system is supported and defended. | **Stage 3:** Good boy/nice girl orientation. Conforming to stereotypic behavior. Rules are internalized. Being good is a reward in itself. |
| | | **Stage 4:** Law and order orientation. Respect for authority and adherence to social order are paramount. |
| **Post-conventional level** | Principles have value apart from and beyond group or individual authority. | **Stage 5:** Social contract orientation. Rights and standards are seen as mutually constructed by society. Laws are good but can be renegotiated. |
| | | **Stage 6:** Universal-ethical orientation. Guided by abstract principles of universal justice, fairness, human rights, the dignity of human individuality. |

*Source:* Kohlberg and Hersch (1977).

## Cultural Critique of Kohlberg

Kohlberg's theory undoubtedly forms a milestone in psychological research, but science moves on, and critiques have arisen, particularly regarding the claim of universality. Methodologically, Kohlberg based his initial theory on observations of young white males in a private school, and a number of his later studies were with young males, such as a 20-year longitudinal study in Chicago and a five-year study in Turkey (Kohlberg, 1975). The claim of universality across cultures followed testing only in the US, Taiwan, Turkey, Mexican cities, and a village in the Yucatan, though Kohlberg continued to add further locales. By 1985, consensus found his interview reasonably fair across cultures and evidence of Stages 1 to 4 credible. Stage 5 was quite rare, however, and Stage 6 remains unverified (Snarey, 1985).

The scant evidence for postconventional reasoning outside Western samples calls into question Kohlberg's underlying assumptions about what constitutes morality and moral behavior. Testing depends on responses to a series of scenarios, and although Kohlberg claimed they were universal topics (rights, property, trust, etc.), critics point out that regardless of care taken in translation, they are still scenarios generated from a Western perspective. Dien (1982) maintained that Kohlberg's theory missed fundamental aspects of Chinese culture, with his emphasis on individual rather than collective moral principles and personal choice. Particularly, concepts like *guanxi*, emphasizing obligation and reciprocity in relationship, brings a mix of socioemotional and instrumental concerns even to business dealings. Chang and Chen (2017) found that people would make seemingly immoral business choices due to *guanxi* obligation, clouding interpretation of responses and skewing results.

As research expands to other cultures around the world, the moral landscape has become complex and a universal moral theory seems less likely. Tietjen and Walker (1985) found evidence of development only to Stage 3 among indigenous men on the Maisin coast of Papua New Guinea. They suggested this was because Kohlberg's methodology does not address the complex interpersonal norms of the highly egalitarian and collective culture. In the Maisin example, standing higher than others violates egalitarian norms, so one would never stand on a raised porch or platform with others nearby. From India, Mulla and Krishnan (2014) propose Karma-Yoga as a model for moral development in India. Explained in the ancient Bhagavad Gita, Karma-Yoga bases morality on duty orientation, indifference to rewards, and equanimity. The authors see teaching of Karma-Yoga in business schools as an antidote to the greed and selfishness inherent in amoral pursuit of profit idealized in corporate culture.

One last issue to address in Kohlberg's ideas stems from his linkage of moral development to cultural evolution:

> Not only are the moral stages culturally universal, but they also correspond to a progression in cultural history. Principled moral thinking appeared first in human history in the period 600–400 B.C., when universal human ideas and rational criticism of customary morality developed in Greece, Palestine, India, and China. (Kohlberg, 1981, p. 128)

## RETIRING FROM ROBBING BANKS

I have a friend, we'll call him Rip (not quite his real name). I know Rip from a music scene in which I participated for several years. He is a great singer and songwriter, but his origins left him with some issues. A member of a low-SES minority, his father was leader of a very bad gang, engaged in drugs, robberies, prostitution, and extortion at a minimum. During the years I knew him, Rip would disappear for a few months now and then, while enjoying the hospitality of a federal prison for his past crimes.

I know so much about Rip (who people sometimes called "Rip You," as in "Rip you off," behind his back) because he was trying to make some positive changes in his life. He had taken a liking to me and knew about my research. He wanted me to know who he really was and why it was important for him to change, so he told me.

"I used to rob banks," he said, "I've done some bad things. But I'm making a change now."

It was an uncomfortable conversation, but I was hopeful this was a breakthrough for him. It sounded like he was heading for the Conventional levels, at least. He continued, "You know the problem with banks these days? Everything is electronic. You get what, maybe $200,000? And you have to split it four or five ways with your crew. It's just not worth it."

That Rip was making strides toward developing a moral code at all is amazing, given his origins. Perhaps he has gone further in the years since I moved away, but at that moment, Rip had only reached Level 2. Rather than deciding that robbing banks is something to avoid because it is bad or illegal, he relied, in part, on a cost-benefit analysis in which the potential benefit of a relatively small amount of money was outweighed by the likely punishment. This instrumental analysis placed Rip squarely in Level 2.

### Why It Matters

Kohlberg came up with a brilliant theory, and he never said development was uniform across cultures and contexts. Rip provides an example of someone from a tragic environment who exemplifies contextual factors delaying or preventing moral development. He is also an inspiring example of someone moving toward a higher level against all odds.

Kohlberg carefully explained that he was not an evolutionist and did not intend to say Western culture was better than others. Conversely, his rankings placed the US at the top of moral development and non-technological cultures at the bottom. Whether intentional or not, he privileged literate cultures and complex social organization (Snarey, 1985). Perhaps ironically, Western economic interests contribute to some of the gravest threats to global survival as carbon emissions hit record levels and rainforests fall. These should be top priorities for those achieving Level 6 moral reasoning.

### Other Views of Moral Development

Kohlberg continues to hold a respected place of influence in morality research, but other approaches are gaining ground in the literature. As with the different theories of human development, some are not stage theories and give greater emphasis to the social and cultural context of development. Mark Tappan (1997) suggests a Vygotskian approach in which moral development follows acquisition and internalization of language in a specific cultural context. As with Vygotsky's (1978) other thoughts about development, a child's status at any given moment is the product of a particular set of influences, enhanced by the coaching of others through the zone of proximal development (ZPD). In this view, moral development would have no discernable stages. The child learns language, practiced and perfected as inner speech, and develops a vocabulary including concepts of good and bad. Development of the moral system is verbally mediated as the child internalizes concepts, with significant others assisting in ZPD transitions. The process is social, not individual, and the outcomes, if something continuously evolving over a lifetime can have outcomes, are specific to the temporal, historical, and cultural milieu where the person exists.

## Shweder's Systems of Ethics

A different view of morality across cultures was developed by Richard Shweder, making him one of the most cited authors on the subject, largely due to the "Big 3" ethics of autonomy, community, and divinity (see Table 9.2). Cultures contain ideas of how to evaluate human behavior in part because we need to explain suffering and unfortunate events. Up until very recently in human history, few cultures based explanations on logic and physics. Most cultures considered illness, misfortune, or death to be results of metaphysical influences such as evil spirits or divine vengeance, often due to misdeeds that offended gods or violated spiritual laws. The construction of systems of norms and violations contain clues about the thought processes of the culture. In South Asia, moral ideas of sacredness, ethics, and justice include karma, describing how good and bad actions return to the doer. Bad actions are seen as a cause of suffering, perhaps lifetimes later. Rather than disregarding these ideas a superstition, they can provide evidence for understanding psychologies of cultures and the moral and ethical systems they generate.

The Big 3 developed from Shweder, Much, Mahapatra, and Park's (1997) analysis of interviews conducted with 47 people in Bhubaneswar, Orissa, India, regarding situations where morals may have been violated. The people were Oriya and situations had been generated using ethnographic knowledge of the area, with 39 items like the following:

- A woman is playing cards at home with her friends. Her husband is cooking rice for them (p. 131).

- A beggar was begging from house to house with his wife and sick child. A home owner drove him away without giving anything (p. 131).

- A brother and sister decide to get married and have children (p. 134).

The interviews were transcribed and combined by situation. Statements were then coded using categories such as social order, duty, and hierarchy. Qualitative and statistical techniques were used to reduce statements to thematic categories, eventually

## Table 9.2  Ethics of Autonomy, Community, and Divinity

*Autonomy*

The ethic of autonomy emphasizes individual freedom and rights. The individual is of primary concern, with agency to choose and to exercise liberty. Morality or rightness in this ethic is determined by considering fairness, rights, justice, freedom, and harm. You violate the ethic of autonomy if you hurt another person or impinge on his or her rights. Violations generate anger. That person who cuts you off in traffic or constantly interrupts you makes you mad. A burglar who breaks in and steals your TV makes you very mad.

*Community*

The ethic of community emphasizes the good of the collective, whether family, community, or religious or ethnic group. Agency in this ethic rests at a group level, requiring individuals to consider or consult others in their decisions. Morality or rightness in this ethic depends on loyalty, interdependence, and group honor. You violate the ethic of community if you fail to fulfill your role obligations, disrespect hierarchy or authority, or somehow harm the collective. Examples would include causing discord or disrupting the normal functions of the group. Selfishness or personal choices are discouraged. Shweder (1995) associated contempt with the ethic of community. It is possible that many Asian dentists gave up dreams of an arts career to meet family expectations.

*Divinity*

The ethic of divinity emphasizes sacredness, the spiritual, natural order, and purity. The individual is of primary concern with agency to choose and to exercise liberty responsibly within moral bounds. People are moral or righteous in this ethic if they practice the traditions and follow the prohibitions codified in their culture or religion. If you step outside the sacred or natural order or otherwise break the moral rules, you violate this ethic. Violations of the ethic of divinity bring emotions of disgust. Eating of pork is repulsive to Jews and Muslims because the animals are considered unclean. Sitting on a table where food will be served or stepping over another person causes noticeable distress for Māori because the posterior is *kapu* due to elimination functions.

*Source:* Shweder et al. (1997).

clustering in patterns they named ethics of autonomy, community, and divinity. Each situation was then rated by frequency of statements related to each ethic. For example, the wife playing cards failed to fulfill her role of cooking (community) and the family hierarchy where she serves the husband (divinity/natural order). The homeowner committed an injustice driving the beggar away (autonomy/justice), and he had better hope it was not a god in disguise. The brother and sister violated norms against incest (divinity), which is a common concept of natural order across cultures.

Each situation we face can activate more than one ethic, and this is normal in the complexity of human life. Cultures may emphasize one ethic over another, for instance the emphasis on the ethic of autonomy in individualistic American culture, or the ethic of community in Polynesian life. There are situations, however, where a collectivistic Polynesian may be more mindful of autonomy in achieving a personal goal, or an individualistic American may be highly collectivistic in dealing with her family or her workplace.

## REALITY CHECK

*Of the moral ethics of autonomy, community, and divinity, which most resembles your own?*

*What is your own stage of moral development? How about children in your family?*

*Have you engaged in any gossip lately? What did you learn the last time you gossiped?*

## 9.3 CULTURE AND VALUES

### LO 9.3: Evaluate the theoretical models of values across cultures.

#### Theoretical Values Models

The term *values* describes the set of motivational criteria by which people prioritize and select actions, evaluate self and others, and decide what is important. In the words of Milton Rokeach (1973),

> [A] value is an enduring belief that a specific mode of conduct or end-state of existence is personally or socially preferable to an opposite or converse mode of conduct or end-state of existence. A value system is an enduring organization of beliefs concerning preferable modes of conduct or end-states of existing along a continuum of relative importance. (p. 5)

Viewed as the primary mechanism influencing voluntary behaviors, Rokeach advised a central role for values in research across the social sciences (Schwartz, 1992). If behaviors and beliefs differ across cultures, values are likely at the core of those differences.

#### Kluckhohn's Values Orientation Model

Anthropologist Clyde Kluckhohn (1951) describes three assertions about how a culture's values come about: "divine revelation or command, tradition and custom, and human intelligence" (p. 2). No culture relies on only one source, and usually cultures describe a combination of sources for their values. Each culture would see its own values as natural, right, and good and would see conflicting values in other cultures as abnormal, strange, and inferior. Kluckhohn, his wife Florence, and their colleagues undertook the Harvard Values Project, an unusual endeavor in anthropology for its time. More like a psychological study, they developed a theory-driven survey measure, gathered data from randomized samples, and analyzed their results using what were, in those days, innovative statistical techniques (F. Kluckhohn & Strodtbeck, 1961).

From Clyde's concepts and the subsequent research, the value orientation theory developed (F. Kluckhohn & Strodtbeck, 1961), proposing that all cultures face certain universal problems for which values provide answers:

(1) What is the character of innate human nature? (human nature orientation),

(2) What is the relation of man to nature (and supernature)? (man–nature orientation),

(3) What is the temporal focus of human life? (time orientation),

(4) What is the modality of human activity? (activity orientation),

(5) What is the modality of man's relationship to other men? (relational orientation). (pp. 10–11)

All cultures share the dilemmas, but would differ in their values orientation combination, in other words, how they answer the question (See Table 9.3). For instance, human nature could be seen as immutably good, with man and nature harmonizing, oriented toward the future and doing, emphasizing collateral relations. Note that positioning in the diagram does not imply any hierarchic ordering.

Like the Kluckhohns, Rokeach (1974, 1973) also believed it possible to describe a set of universal human values. Where the Kluckhohns proposed a broad theory based on a few overarching values constructs, Rokeach proposed a comprehensive set of values

**Table 9.3  The Five Value Orientations**

| Orientation | Postulated Range of Variables | | | | | |
|---|---|---|---|---|---|---|
| Human nature | Evil | | Neutral | Mix of good and evil | Good | |
| | Mutable | Immutable | Mutable | Immutable | Mutable | Immutable |
| Man-nature | Subjugation to nature | | Harmony with nature | | Mastery over nature | |
| Time | Past | | Present | | Future | |
| Activity | Being | | Being-in-becoming | | Doing | |
| Relational | Lineality | | Collaterality | | Individualism | |

*Source:* Kluckhohn and Strodtbeck (1961).

shared across cultures; these could be rated using his Rokeach Values Survey (RVS) to examine patterns of priorities that might differ by culture. He constructed a list of 18 terminal values, which are end states such as a comfortable life, world peace, and equality, and 18 instrumental values representing modes of behavior, including ambitious, loving, obedient, and polite. This list of values and the RVS itself have been widely used in subsequent research.

### Schwartz's Theory of Basic Values

Shalom Schwartz (1992) has used the RVS in his projects developing a universal theory of values. He has identified types of values, their content and the equivalence of content across cultures, and examined consistent conflicts and compatibilities in how those values work together. He took three questions as his starting point: How do social experiences shape values? How do values shape choices and behaviors? How might values be the same or different across cultures and what factors drive those differences?

Schwartz began by reviewing the many definitions and descriptions of values already filling the literature, finding five features common to all the lists. Values are "(a) concepts or beliefs, (b) about desirable end states or behaviors, (c) that transcend specific situations, (d) guide selection or evaluation of behavior and events, and (e) are ordered by relative importance" (Schwartz & Bilsky, 1987, p. 551). Over multiple studies of samples in dozens of countries, Schwartz and colleagues initially derived eight types of values: prosocial, restrictive conformity, enjoyment, achievement, maturity, self-direction, security, and power (e.g., Schwartz & Bilsky, 1987). In subsequent publications, Schwartz has proposed 6 to 19 values domains (Schwartz, 2014), which prompted one critique that his theory lacks precision and parsimony (Gouveia, Milfont, & Guerra, 2014). Schwartz (2014) explained that values form a continuum of motivations, and rather than discrete categories, values across cultures more resemble the continuous changes across the color spectrum. Groupings of value types are somewhat arbitrary, with divisions reflecting the interests and perspectives of the researcher. Ultimately, Schwartz says, all values could be reduced to as few as two motives: growth versus self-protection.

Schwartz began mapping the structure of values with the idea that values could be clustered in domains by similarity, for instance by goal type, interests served, and motivational domain. Some values would be closely related and some are different to a point of incompatibility. A model would be useful to demonstrate the relations between values and to illuminate what values are emphasized in a culture. Over several years, Schwartz and a number of colleagues gathered data for cross-cultural comparison, for instance German and Israeli samples (Schwartz & Bilsky, 1987), then samples from Australia, Finland, Hong Kong, Spain, and the United States (Schwartz & Bilsky, 1990). They initially used values from the Rokeach list that participants rated for importance in their lives and for similarity to other values pair by pair. The research expanded to dozens of countries over subsequent decades in their own data collection (e.g., Schwartz & Bardi, 2001) and in reanalysis of data collected by many others (e.g., Schwartz & Boehnke, 2004).

Schwartz (2008, 2014) has returned a number of times to a set of three bipolar dimensions with seven value domains: harmony versus mastery, hierarchy versus egalitarianism, and embeddedness versus autonomy, with subdomains of affective and intellectual autonomy (see Figure 9.2). These pairs represent how cultures answer three basic questions. The dimension of hierarchy versus egalitarianism addresses maintenance of the fabric of society, such that people remain productive and adhere to behavioral norms. Hierarchic cultures accept unequal distribution of power and resources, while egalitarians prefer the opposite. To answer questions about relating to the world, harmony orientation values fitting into and appreciating the flow of society and nature, whereas mastery urges people to take control, make changes, and dominate. Intellectual autonomy encourages free thinking, curiosity, and creativity, while affective autonomy emphasizes positive experiences full of pleasure and excitement. Conversely, the value of embeddedness promotes identification with the collective, working toward shared goals, and maintaining group harmony. The research illuminates cultural patterns of importance, such as American cultural emphasis on mastery and affective autonomy, while embeddedness and hierarchy are emphasized in Southeast Asia (Schwartz, 2008).

Schwartz (1992) described his approach to study of values as working on a culture level, though most of his analyses either rely on national level averages or contrast individual and national data (Fischer, Vauclair, Fontaine, & Schwartz, 2010; Schwartz, 1994, 2006). This may cause some clouding of results on a cultural level, given the ethnic diversity of many nations. Another problem in research concerning values and culture is

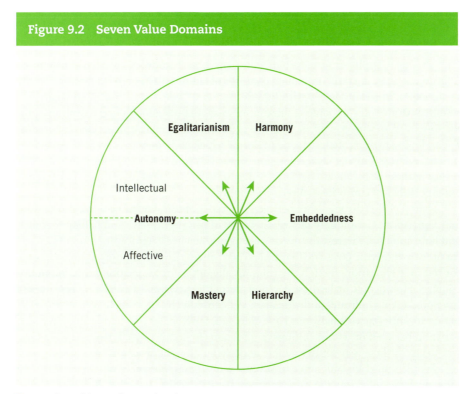

Figure 9.2    Seven Value Domains

*Source:* Adapted from Schwartz (2006).

the difficulty of parsing motivation for valuing; is something seen as important because the person has internalized a cultural value or because it holds value on a personal level? Vauclair and colleagues (2015) point out that wealth may be rated highly important for personal reasons and not because of its broader social desirability.

Vauclair, Hanke, Fischer, and Fontaine (2011) performed a meta-analysis using RVS data from 37 cultural groups in 344 samples from 173 studies with a total of 44,047 participants, a massive amount of data. They followed Schwartz's method of using multidimensional scaling of all 37 Rokeach values to map overall structure, their analyses confirming Schwartz's findings. The analyses also revealed a set of value items correlated in a pattern indicating a previously unidentified value. They called the value *self-fulfilled connectedness (SFC)*, which includes an intriguing blend of individualistic and interpersonal values. The values of SFC include both profound attachment to others and of self-fulfillment. These also correlated highly with country indices for subjective well-being and post-materialism in regions where basic needs are met and individualism is valued. Although lasting relationships and mutual caring are assured in norms and relational structures of embeddedness cultures, SFC may indicate ways people find meaning and satisfaction through voluntary relationships in cultures without such guarantees. Connectedness is crucial to human well-being, but it seems rare in individualist cultures. SFC may represent a mechanism for maintenance of connectedness in cultures lacking the assurance of fixed social networks.

## Resource Distribution

One practical application of values concerns how resources are shared (or not). *Distributive justice* is a term describing concepts of fair distribution of resources (Enright et al., 1984). In a finite world with limited resources, who gets what? A company has resources to give only a couple of substantive raises but not enough to give a meaningful increase to all, so who gets the increase? In extremes like famine, who gets food? Families in developing nations often struggle to decide which child goes to school. Allocation of resources always happens in some organized way (Dalton, 1962), and though we may not realize it, these decisions are made according to values systems we learn long before we enter positions of authority to direct distribution.

Dalton (1962) distinguishes between two types of social organizations, community and association. Community describes groups of people who live and belong together and hold common interest for major aspects of their lives. Associations are organized for pursuit of specific goals and may be less permanent than community. Both form sites for resource allocation, though the rules usually differ for association and community contexts. How people make these decisions certainly varies, and a number of researchers have predictably indicated individualism-collectivism (IC) as a likely source of explanation for differences. Questions have emerged, however, as to whether there is more variation between or within cultures (e.g., Leung & Bond, 1984; Triandis, 1989). One way to clarify these issues is to examine underlying thought processes.

People approach outcomes in several ways, being cooperative, competitive, or individualistic, reflecting the values activated as they make allocation decisions (Carlo, Roesch, Knight, & Koller, 2001). An individualistic approach, of course, values maximum personal benefit. A competitive approach is geared to generate personal benefit at an opponent's expense, either out of rivalry, superiority, or need. In a cooperative approach, a person could altruistically seek to maximize the other's outcome, minimize differences between outcomes to enhance equality, or seek benefit for the entire group. If IC makes a difference, only collectivists would favor cooperative approaches, for instance. Given the complexities of human behavior, it is also possible that other forces exert influences, for instance contextual factors and lifespan development.

Carlo and colleagues (2001) compared resource allocation by Brazilian and Euro-American children aged two to twelve, rating allocation choices as individualist, cooperative, or competitive. They expected that all children would follow individualistic patterns of allocation while very young, when they are developmentally unable to see beyond their own egocentric needs. Differences due to culture and gender would emerge more as they aged. Culturally, the Brazilian children would be expected to become more cooperative, in keeping with the more collectivist culture of Brazil, and the Euro-American children would become more competitive. The study supported these predictions and also revealed gender differences that increased with age. Girls made fewer competitive choices and more cooperative choices, and boys made more competitive choices. The authors caution, however, that the standard view of girls as more prosocial may be overrated because the girls as a group increased to similar levels in both cooperative and competitive allocations. The boys did engage in far more competitive behaviors, and the Brazilian sample differed significantly by gender, but the Euro-American sample showed little gender difference.

Values differences help to explain the results of Marble Pull Game studies discussed in Chapter 2, for example the competitive US children and the more cooperative children in Mexico (e.g., Garcia et al., 2015), though those differences have lessened recently. The various clusters of values in different contexts and eras help to explain why those results are not precisely reflected in all cross-cultural studies. Zeidler, Hermann, Haun, and Tomasello (2016) used a similar game in research with 168 pairs of children from Germany and from two African societies, the Samburu and Kikuyu of Kenya. In this study, children fished containers with a bead inside from a tube, first in a learning trial, then in a condition where they watched videos of children playing the game together and either taking turns to split winnings, or with one child taking all the turns. Children all watched both videos, but in randomized order, and were then asked which children played the game correctly. German children all said the taking of turns was correct, while 75% of the Kenyan children said not taking turns was right. When they actually played, it was the German children who immediately began taking turns allowing each other to win. In the Kenyan trials, one of the children would usually dominate a round of play, but sometimes the next round would be given to the other child.

## Forgiveness

People do bad things. They cheat, rob, and steal intentionally, but often cause unintentional harm through accidents, anger, or ignorance. Adaptation to such experiences often requires that we forgive the transgressor. Forgiveness appears to be a universal value that varies greatly in how and why one seeks and grants it across cultures (Ho & Worthington, 2018). Rokeach's (1973) RVS forgiveness item describes it as "willingness to pardon others." Hanke and Vauclaire (2016) discuss forgiveness as "a symbolic process involving apology and its acceptance or as an intrapersonal release from holding onto grievance" (p. 216). The process generically involves a transgression followed by a series of interactions, cognitions, and emotions. Interactions include recognition of the infraction or injustice, a need to receive and/or give forgiveness, the offering of apology or restitution, acceptance of that offer, and the renouncing of the right to harbor resentment.

Forgiveness involves two or more parties, including offender(s) and someone(s) wronged, whether individuals or groups. Forgiving may happen as a response to apology or it may be an internal experience of the one(s) offended, independent of offenders' actions. Apologies and pardons are external process between parties, the release of grievance is internal. Forgiveness may be an individual matter, as in forgiving oneself for mistakes or misdeeds; it may be interpersonal, as when wrongs are committed in friendship or business; or groups may be involved. In sustainable interpersonal forgiveness processes, the offender must admit blame and express remorse (Hanke & Vauclaire, 2016; Shafa, Harinck, & Ellemers, 2017). For people to be forgiven, the victim(s) must trust and believe the apology and abandon the aggrieved thoughts, feelings, and behaviors. Forgiveness on all levels is contextual, the need to forgive attached to specific events at a particular point in history (Hanke & Fischer, 2013).

Forgiveness happens in cultural context by culture-specific rules that shape the shared parameters discussed above. Ho and Worthington (2018) compared Chinese and American idioms and writings about forgiveness looking for similarities and differences in cognitions about the topic. The basic parameters of transgression and debt cancellation were shared. English idioms had more emotional content, such as anger and revenge. Chinese idioms included concepts like benevolence and harmony, intended to preserve relationship.

Individually, most research links forgiveness to better well-being, happiness, psychological pain cessation, and reconciliation. Forgiveness brings healing and allows people to move beyond conflict to repair damages (Hanke & Fischer, 2013). Effects are debated, however. In contrast to conventional wisdom that forgiveness is good, some authors have argued that forgiveness allows transgressors to evade consequences and continue their bad acts (c.f. Rata, Liu, & Hanke, 2008). From these broad descriptions, cultures diverge in expectations and norms. Further, research regarding forgiveness on group, cultural, and national levels has only begun relatively recently (e.g., Hanke et al., 2013) and will be discussed further in Chapter 12.

One point of divergence in forgiveness relates to the cultures of honor/dignity paradigm. Shafa and colleagues (2017) found that honor culture participants were less willing to forgive than dignity culture members, perceiving apologies as less sincere. Cultures of honor tend to recognize certain violations, for instance of ethics of divinity such as proscriptions of chastity, that are unforgivable. Though the value of forgiveness is endorsed in Confucian philosophy, Stankov (2010) found that people from modern Confucian countries are less likely to forgive. In short, a number of factors may affect how and what people forgive.

### Modeling Forgiveness

Ho and Fung (2011) proposed a process model that they claim helps to explain cross-cultural differences in forgiveness. They based the model on Gross's (1998) model of emotion as a product where evaluation of emotional cues leads to a set of affective, physiological, and behavioral responses. Emotions are thus person-situation interactions. Similarly, forgiveness has multiple influences, including "perceptions of transgression, dialectical thinking, causal attribution, approach- versus avoidance-focused motivation, and socially engaged versus socially disengaged emotion" (Ho & Fung, 2011, p. 279).

Perception of transgressions is affected by the I-C continuum, with individualists more concerned about justice and identity preservation while collectivists are more concerned with maintenance of positive relationship. This provides motivation to assess and reassess situations in certain ways to achieve those goals. Causal attribution places blame for the transgression, and as discussed earlier, responsibility may be attributed to the person or situation, with cultural biases as to which. The Western tendency toward the fundamental attribution error means they are more likely to blame the transgressor, while other cultures will consider contextual causes more readily. Dialectical thinking, associated with non-Western cultures, involves greater consideration of the context rather than the focal person or event and greater tolerance of contradiction. These perceptions, filtered through culturally influenced cognitions and emotions, will determine the likelihood and conditions of forgiveness.

The approach/avoidance dimension determines behavioral components of reaction to grievance. An approach-focused motivation could lead one to direct interaction in response to offenses, seeking to generate positive outcomes to heal a transgression. Asian culture tends toward avoidance-focused motivation, tending to avoid overt argument and negativity to preserve the relationship. Although this is more peaceful in the immediate sense, it can mean positive and conclusive solutions remain undiscovered.

Finally, socially engaged emotions include friendliness, guilt, and respect, while socially disengaged emotions include anger and pride. Socially engaged emotions are preferred by interdependent cultures, oriented toward relationship preservation and harmony. Socially disengaged emotions are more common in cultures oriented toward independent self-construal. The independent self has less at stake in loss of relationship and more to lose when personal self-esteem is damaged. Cultural patterns of forgiveness diverge with each of these possibilities.

## REALITY CHECK

*What are most important among your personal values?*

*Do your values reflect those of your parents? Your culture of origin?*

*How important is it to forgive people? Is it easy or hard for you?*

## 9.4 MORALS, VALUES, AND MOTIVATIONS EXPRESSED IN THE ARTS

### LO 9.4: Describe the role of the arts in transmitting and supporting morality and values.

Arts have appeared in psychological literature in two domains related to motivation, morals, and values, one regarding the content and its place in transmission across generations, the other regarding motivations to create arts and excel in execution thereof. To reveal the cultural orientations in a society, we could look at the themes of children's stories, at the systems of law, at the ways economic exchange is organized, or at socialization practices (e.g., Schwartz, 2008). Arts, of course, draw their themes from the legends, myths, and stories of a culture. This is why the literature of cultures has been used so often in development of criteria in personality and values research. We begin with the motivational aspect.

### Arts and Motivation

Curiosity about the motivations of artists arises for two primary reasons: biographical interest in prominent artists and musicians, and pedagogical interest in how best to nurture developing artists. As a journalist, I heard a surprisingly famous female singer, answering why she makes music, say the completely predictable, "Why does a bird sing?" A more interesting answer came from African American saxophonist Bobby Watson, who said, "It's like a beautiful painting or a sculpture. They can convey something that can't be put into words. That's what music does, it can take the ineffable and make it real" (Fox, 2001). The motive here is self-expression on a transcendental level by an already skilled professional artist.

A more frequent topic of study regards education and development of young artists as they learn. Music educators have studied motivation in Western context attempting to assess methods to encourage habits like practicing, with the ultimate goal of producing excellent performers. Most of this research involves classical music played by people of European origin (Mok, 2014). Predictably, Euro-American classical music provides the most intense individualistic achievement motivation. The structure and subculture of orchestra inherently drive competition; beneath the absolute authority of the conductor comes the concertmaster (first violin), followed by the first seat of each instrument section. For those positions, the best performance wins, and with the win comes prestige, higher pay, and more solo opportunities.

Chinese culture presents some quandaries when it comes to music. Although the culture generically emphasizes collective action (Buchtel et al., 2018), the Confucian ideal for music is a wise male scholar playing a *guzheng* (plucked zither) alone. The music calms the emotions, and accolades are superfluous to his intrinsic motivation. Asian cultures also do value modesty.

In practice, current Chinese culture is quite competitive, with achievement motivation common in school settings. Mok (2014) found achievement motivation was a prominent motivation among Hong Kong musicians that she interviewed who played popular genres (e.g., rock, heavy metal). Several reported that they love music, use music as an avenue of emotional expression, or cannot imagine life without music. Her sample did, however, relish being on stage, hearing applause, and perceiving signs of enjoyment from their fans. As is the case in many cultural settings, opportunities for performance are limited and highly competitive.

This brief discussion in no way covers the research into music, motivation, and education. It is intended only to provide a glimpse into the diverse reasons people learn to create music. These reasons may reflect some of the motives of artists across cultures and media, but psychological research in arts motivations across cultures is relatively recent and has room for development.

## Arts, Morals, and Values

Arts serve as repositories and mechanisms of transmission for morals and values. As with other elements of culture already discussed, they are represented in words, characters, and symbols, depending on the medium and culture. The melodies and motifs embed this information in the cultural context memorably, reinforced as they are experienced again and again. Whether described as memes or semiotes or simply as motifs and melodic hooks, repetition hammers these messages into our minds, like the chorus of a song on the radio.

From its beginnings in the ancient world, theater has served as teacher, conscience, and example, supporting the moral values of cultures. Gods and heroes of Greek tragedy showed the right ways to live and the consequences for transgressions. Greek tragedy was ritual, enacted to edify, educate, and liberate the community. Watching the drama freed the audience from need to experience the missteps and misdeeds portrayed. The ethics, morals, and motivations of those ancient characters remain relevant, as does the ritual process. Joseph Campbell's archetypal journey takes the hero through challenge, difficulty, discovery, and return, bringing back new knowledge to his or her people, the edification of that lesson transmitted again and again as the story is read or acted.

Kenneth Burke (1897–1993), writer and critic of theater and literature, said that people attribute motives based on five elements he termed the *dramatistic pentad*: the act (what was done); the scene (when and where it was done); agent (by whom); agency (using what method or instruments?); and purpose (the why). Burke later added the element of attitude, which described how to prepare for the act (see Figure 9.3). Although Burke was superficially referring to drama and fiction, he viewed the pentad as a way to understand human action in regular life. To Burke, language is symbolic action; action is understood, explained, and expressed in language, whether lived or fictionalized. Burke saw in his pentad a way to understand and explain the inextricable link between motivation and behavior, whether actual, literary, or historical, "for every judgement, exhortation, or admonition, every view of natural or supernatural reality, every intention or expectation involves assumptions about motive or cause" (Burke, 1969, p. xxii).

**Figure 9.3   Burke's Dramatistic Pentad**

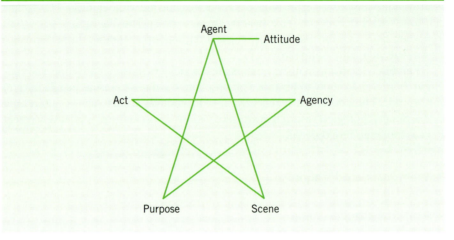

*Source:* Burke (1969).

Songs, of course, convey copious information about what people want and how they should behave. As mentioned in Chapter 5, an itsy-bitsy spider admonishes children to persist even when facing setbacks, instilling the value of perseverance. A host of moral and motivational messages fill the songs we hear:

- To Aretha Franklin, "R.E.S.P.E.C.T." meant she valued being treated with dignity as an African American female human being.

- "Onward Christian Soldiers" demands the values of dedication and sacrifice from parishioners.

- Katy Perry's song "Firework" promotes a blazing level of individualism, telling us to value our uniqueness and explode with success.

Many songs, if not most, support the status quo and majority values system, but times and values do change. Keyboardist Billy Preston played with The Beatles and numerous other acts beginning in the 1960s and was sometimes called the fifth Beatle because he appeared on so many of their recordings. The music scene was smaller and very tightly interwoven, and most popular artists knew each other. Evidently, Preston once advised folk-rock legend Steven Stills, who was in the midst of a frustrating romantic issue. The sexual revolution was in full swing, and from Preston's comment, Stills wrote "Love the One You're With." In a context where old norms of chastity were being cast aside, the idea that you might as well be having sex with somebody, even if it's not your first choice, resonated widely. The song remains a mega-hit, mostly relegated to oldies stations, but the message continues reverberating across generations.

In Prince's "1999," he also took the bold step of endorsing hedonistic values. He encourages us to embrace celebratory excess as a means of coping with an erroneously predicted apocalyptic end of days as the year 2000 would arrive. When Prince sang it in 1982, 1999 was so far in the future that the adolescents and young adults in his target demographic lacked the full development of their prefrontal cortices necessary to plan for events in a distant future. Hedonism, in those cocaine-fueled days of the early 1980s, helped Prince craft a wildly popular hit, though nobody on the dance floor was stopping to consider the implied values structure. Music can sell a value and values can sell music. Ironically, Prince was initially raised Seventh Day Adventist and converted to become a Jehovah's Witness, both conservative branches of Christianity. Privately, Prince was reportedly shy and meekly polite in person, which is not unusual for performers. How he resolved the differences between the values of his faith and those he espoused on stage was known only to Prince and his confidants. Publicly, he provided endorsement for shifting values in the extremely selfish pursuit of profit and pleasure in 1980s America.

## Semiotics of Moral Values

Visual arts provide semiotic links, often via images from stories, myths, and legends that typify moral concepts. Jesus on a cross, blood dripping from his wounds, reminds believers of his sacrifice, that through his pain we are redeemed. This exemplifies forgiveness and a path to righteous living. The faithful also see someone suffering a worse fate than theirs, providing a reason to persevere.

Gautama Buddha, sitting serenely, reminds Buddhists that the world is illusion. Attachment to the people, situations, and things of that illusion brings pain. In letting go, consciousness eventually expands to embrace all of existence, and consciousness moves beyond suffering. The bodhisattva Kuan Yin, a feminine embodiment of Buddhic compassion, represents a spirit so pure that she has committed to be reborn over and over, to suffer, until all creation reaches enlightenment. Found in temples, on home altars, and in Buddhist-owned businesses wherever they might be found, these images inspire people to follow particular values and ways of being, renouncing materialism and working for the good of all life.

In Hinduism, the universal energy manifests as Brahma, the creator, Vishnu, the preserver, and Shiva, the destroyer. In some images of Shiva, he dances blissfully on a pile of skulls and bones. We humans die and decay, Shiva's image tells us, our bones ground to dust beneath the deity's happy feet. The message is stark but not sad. Gautama was a Hindu, a believer in gradual rebirth evolving toward release. Galaxies, stars, and planets, along with the myriad creatures inhabiting them, burble into and out of existence. When we finally shuffle off these mortal coils for the last time, Shiva says, when the illusion of physical separateness fades away completely, only then do we reach sweet release.

Tricksters appear in cultures around the globe. The hump-backed flute player Kokopelli wandered the Southwest deserts, possibly derived from actual merchants who roamed those lands for centuries before Europeans arrived. He appears in countless drawings and stories throughout the region. An archetypal figure, probably amalgamated from many people across centuries, he told stories as he travelled and played tricks on those who needed a moral lesson. In the Great Plains, Coyote hoodwinked those who strayed from the right path to get them back on track. In parts of Africa, the spider Anansi served the same purpose. For Japan, it was *kitsune*, fox spirits, who manifest as maidens, scholars, or old men to teach lessons and make examples of people who violate norms. Perhaps a greedy person gets fed to bursting point, or a young man making unwanted advances finds out the lovely maiden is actually deadly. The *kitsune* stories can be scary, stories told to children to entertain and frighten. Coyote stories can be very funny and sometimes quite lewd, a bawdy example of how *not* to behave.

Arts have intertwined with our ethics, values, and morals since long before we distinguished between art and daily materials or between audience and performer. To know a culture, the clues are there waiting. Even better, in the diversity of these systems, the ease with which they are conveyed in creative production provides a great way to learn the ways other cultures answer the fundamental questions of coexistence.

## REFLECTING ON YOUR READING

- How are the terms *motivation*, *moral*, and *value* the same or different?

- Can you describe ways your own culture has shaped your thinking in this domain?

- Do you think the choices that brought you to where you are at this moment might have been different if you had grown up in another culture?

## CHAPTER 9 SUMMARY

Psychology has always included prediction of behavior as a primary goal. Three descriptions for human reasoning about choice are *motivation*, a person's reason for doing something; *values*, the principles or standards for judging importance in how we live; and *morals*, the standards for judging right from wrong and good from bad.

### 9.1 Motivation: Why We Choose What We Do

Human motivation includes cognitive components beyond what has been observed in other species. Fundamental motivations are ones underlying all other motives and thought about motive. Maslow theorized a series of conditions fulfilling fundamental motives and eventually allowing humans to reach their highest potential.

Achievement motivation is the drive to succeed in our endeavors. Often, earlier research in achievement motivation assumed Western goals to be best and other cultures to be under-motivated. Self-enhancement motivation describes the urge to improve individual self-esteem. Self-improvement seeks to build skills rather than seek praise, and is seen more in collectivist cultures. Japanese participants persevered more than Western ones in the face of failure. Agency describes ability to choose action. Research shows an individual orientation in Western culture's sense of agency, and a collective orientation for decisions and actions in Asia.

### 9.2 Morality: Deciding What Is Right

Evolutionary evidence indicates that morality serves as a tool to facilitate coexistence, instilled during development. Sex has a particularly rigid set of moral standards in some cultures. Gossip may serve as a means of instructing morality and punishing transgressions through social pressure.

Kohlberg developed a theory of moral development with three main stages: preconventional, conventional, and post-conventional, where convention represents social rules. The child goes from seeking pleasure and avoiding pain to internalizing rules, and eventually realizes that rules and ethics are there to help humans achieve universals like justice and human dignity. Shweder proposed the "Big 3" ethics of autonomy, community, and divinity as primary categories in answering moral dilemmas.

### 9.3 Culture and Values

The Kluckhohns proposed that values are ways cultures answer universal problems of relations of humans to nature, other humans, and temporal life. Several researchers have attempted to describe systems of universal values, including Rokeach and Schwartz. A list of values that translate across cultures has been developed, and although they are shared, different cultures emphasize some more or less in predictable patterns.

Values affect resource distribution, cultures generally tending to be cooperative, competitive, or individualistic. Individualists may tend to maximize personal gain while collectivists may share more.

Forgiveness is important in a world where wrongs and injustices happen interpersonally and interculturally. Forgiveness is given or not depending on rules and parameters about context, severity of infraction, causal attribution, and sincerity of the transgressor.

### 9.4 Morals, Values, and Motivations Expressed in the Arts

Research in the arts, morals, motivation, and values includes what is transmitted by art but also why people choose to engage in artistic production. Theater forms an ancient vehicle for transmission and reinforcement of cultural values. All arts contain symbols and stories meant to remind us of values. Values and changes in a culture's values are especially evident in popular music. Tricksters are found in stories of many cultures, teaching lessons to characters who stray from righteousness.

### GLOSSARY

**Morals:** Standards for judging right from wrong and good from bad and discerning and administering justice.

**Motivation:** A person's reason for doing something.

**Value:** The importance or cost placed on something, describing the principles or standards for judging importance in how we live.

# ADAPTATION AND ACCULTURATION IN A CHANGING WORLD

## Chapter 10 Outline

## Learning Objectives

**LO 10.1** Identify global issues affecting modern intercultural contact.

**LO 10.2** Define and differentiate adaptation and acculturation, describing the processes involved.

**LO 10.3** Explain and critique the theories and research contributing to an understanding of acculturation.

**LO 10.4** Appraise the effects of context on acculturation experiences and outcomes.

**LO 10.5** Evaluate the current understanding of acculturation conditions and outcomes for individuals and communities.

**LO 10.6** Explain the psychological and practical purposes the arts serve in acculturation.

## PREPARING TO READ

- Have you been outside of your usual culture?
- Can you imagine what it would be like to move suddenly to a different culture?
- What do you think you would have to do to live day to day?
- Have you known anyone who immigrated to your country or area?
- What did they experience in the process?

In 2011, 15-year-old Jakadrien Lorece Turner was already a troubled young girl when she ran away from her Houston home. Arrested for shoplifting, she claimed, for some reason, to be a woman named Tika Lanay Cortez. Cortez, it turned out, was a Colombian who was in the US illegally and had a criminal history. In a conservative state and a political environment demanding tough action on illegals, Jakadrien suddenly found herself deported to Colombia. She was trapped for months in a living nightmare, unable to return to her native country, though she was born and raised in the US (Crimesider Staff, 1/6/2012). The situation recalls Cheech Marin's movie Born in East LA (1987), a comedy in which the main character was deported to Mexico though he was an American-born citizen and spoke little Spanish. Jakadrien certainly was not laughing; she was a teen thrown into a foreign country with no social or economic resources and little grasp of the language or customs.

Hopefully, Jakadrien's story is unique, but the issues she faced were not. She lost normal social and economic supports and found herself in an alien environment without the ability to navigate or communicate in regular social interactions. Certainly there were psychological effects from the experience. How can we understand acculturation experiences, even in more normal circumstances? This chapter discusses the processes of adapting in intercultural contact and clues from research for adapting well.

# 10.1 MULTICULTURALISM AND MIGRATION

## LO 10.1: Identify global issues affecting modern intercultural contact.

Human cultures grew apart over vast spans of time, as **migration** across the globe brought different ecologies and challenges. The result is an incredible array of remarkably distinct cultures so different that we no longer share languages or lifestyles. Things and situations that are commonplace in our lives would be difficult for our own ancestors to understand. If our great-great-great grandparents suddenly materialized at a Starbucks in an airport terminal, nothing there would make sense to them. They may have had coffee in their day, but the terms "airport" and "Starbucks" would be meaningless to them, and the setting with its noise and hubbub could be quite frightening, especially with the take-off and landing of flying machines.

In the **diversity** of cultures, worldviews, and social systems now existing, we often fail to understand each other, despite our common origins. People in China or Chad or Chile may equally love their children or music or good food, but they may differ greatly in how they view their lives and the world around them. As we humans have expanded around the world, our cultural groups have interacted peacefully and/or violently over ever-greater distance and difference. Changes happen on personal, social, and psychological levels when cultures come together, and this has become a more common experience as humans have diversified and interacted throughout human history. With airports and internet, we meet and communicate across those divides more and more often, and we must adjust to accommodate these forgotten relatives we encounter.

Intercultural differences unquestionably affect how people think, relate, and behave. The term **multiculturalism** describes a diversity of cultural and ethnic groups within a sociopolitical entity such as a community, state, or nation (see Figure 10.1). **Indigenous** cultures may be part of the ethnic landscape, and they may not welcome new groups into ancestral lands already overrun by a newer dominant culture. Politically, multiculturalism often describes policies embracing immigration and inclusion, especially in nations around the world where ethnic and **immigrant** cultures form growing segments of the population (Kivisto, 2011). These policies appear more in developed countries that have a high need for immigration to cover skill and labor shortages, often because of declining birthrates and longer lifespans in majority groups that alter demographic patterns of age and ethnicity (Espenshade, Guzman, & Westoff, 2003). These demographic

**Figure 10.1    Multilingual Bank Sign**

shifts have also led to nativist and xenophobic backlash against immigrants, appearing dramatically in the 2016 US presidential election and England's Brexit vote to leave the European Union.

Increasingly frequent migration and interaction brings people together in complex cultural landscapes. How does intercultural contact affect us psychologically, and how can we achieve best outcomes in the process? To understand these conditions and their implications, this chapter discusses the psychological processes and outcomes described in acculturation literature of the social sciences. A number of examples are provided to give some perspective on this complex subject.

## The Birth of Nations and Beginnings of Modern Migration

After tens of thousands of years of migration and change, even the remotest areas of the world host larger and larger populations. We interact and compete interculturally on national levels, and have for centuries. Egypt, China, and Rome were winning teams in some early encounters, expanding their domains across multiple ethnocultural regions. The nation-state (the modern concept of country) is a relatively recent phenomenon, arising as winners of feudal and regional conflicts created larger political entities with bigger armies and firmer borders. Countries with the biggest armies and navies set off across oceans and continents to form colonies and outposts from which to send the best resources back home. Colonialism flourished, with Spain, England, France, Holland, and eventually the US controlling vast expanses across continents, dominating local cultures and sometimes establishing an immigrant majority. The system gradually eroded, beginning with the Revolutionary War and birth of the US, and followed by a stream of countries rebelling against colonial powers, though even successful rebellion rarely brought equity or reparation for indigenous inhabitants. In the aftermath of World Wars of the 20th century, treaties and negotiations between winning parties led to modern definitions of national boundaries, carved without regard to traditional ethnic regions. Internal strife results, as different groups fight for autonomy or control of resources (Hoerder, 2002). This is the case in Iraq, with Shiites, Sunni, Kurds, and Armenians all forced into one uneasy national entity.

Added to the internal issues of ethnic variety within nation-states are issues of mobility and migration *across* national boundaries. Countries with greater economic resources have become a destination for people seeking a better life for themselves and their families. At the same time, women with better education tend to work more and spend less time in pregnancy and childrearing, leading to lower than replacement birth rates for dominant groups in the most developed nations (Espenshade et al., 2003; Matthews & Ventura, 1994). Improved medical care helps us have longer lives, but proportionately fewer young people are available to care for the expanding elderly population. These factors motivate people to move to more affluent countries to fill labor and professional positions, especially as medical workers caring for the elderly.

In addition to these factors pushing cultures together directly, technological advances allow people to travel long distances more affordably and to communicate and experience entertainment media on a global level. Donne's axiom "No [person]

is an island" has never been more factually true; physical, digital, and metaphorical bridges abound between cultures and countries that Donne could not have imagined (see Figure 10.2). On this planetary island spinning through the universe, our lives are all inextricably intertwined.

## REALITY CHECK

*What is diversity in human society?*

*How do multiculturalist policies affect cultural experiences?*

*How has the rise and fall of colonialism affected intercultural contact?*

*How does the concept of nation-state differ from country or culture?*

*Why has migration between countries increased?*

## 10.2 ACCULTURATION AND ADAPTATION

### LO 10.2: Define and differentiate adaptation and acculturation, describing the processes involved.

**Acculturation** is the term for processes that happen when individuals or groups of two or more cultures meet for extended periods of time, one of the most important topics currently researched in Cultural and Cross-Cultural psychology. As Hofstede (1980) points out, a fish does not understand water until it is on dry land, and rapid development of technologies for communication and travel now constantly push us out of our natural environs. The topic of adaptation, in terms of intercultural contact, deals with how we adjust to new cultural interactions. We learn our own cultures as we develop (enculturation), transmitting and preserving the behaviors, values, and beliefs across generations. Changes to those enculturated elements due to intercultural processes are addressed in the study of acculturation.

Amidst the flurry of exploration and migration, intercultural contact has reached a point where no cultures, not even the remotest tribes of the Amazon or Kalimantan, remain in isolation (Chagnon, 1988a; Enzlin-Dixon, 2004; Hoerder, 2002; see Spotlight: Media, Marketing, and Acculturation). Each new contact, however it happens, exposes societies and their members to differing ideas and ways of being. The more benign encounters have given us knowledge and resources to live longer, healthier lives in more material comfort and safety. Conversely, contact via colonization and invasion have decimated cultures and their resources, as with the many indigenous cultures devastated by European colonization, eliminating traditional social structures, community supports, and symbolic resources. For good or ill, intercultural contact brings changes on both societal and individual levels, and these changes lead to a range of potential psychological effects and outcomes, depending on conditions of contact and the resources and responses of those involved (Ward, 2001).

## Acculturation as a Concept

Adaptation is a process of achieving some degree of stability in relationship with one's environment (Brody, Stoneman, Flor, & McCrary, 1994). Humans have historically lived in relatively stable situations until recently, with only the rare adventurer traveling more than 30 miles from their birthplace before the 20th century. Changes happened incrementally over hundreds or thousands of years, and were probably accommodated with little notice. With the exceptions of war or natural disaster, you would have had to live for millennia to see much difference. Colonization, transportation, and communication technology, along with other factors of increased migration, have disrupted this pace of adaptation, and more frequent (if not constant) intercultural contact has disrupted the stability of our cultures and their institutions in sudden and shocking ways. As a result, we have to adapt to increasingly diverse cultural situations on individual and group levels.

Acculturation is not a new experience. Plato commented on processes of change in intercultural contact as the Greeks expanded around the Mediterranean and toward Asia in trade and military conflict (Fine, 2008). These processes happen in more or less predictable patterns, differentiated by the strength of groups and of cultural elements involved. Usually, the weaker group is forced to change the most, though dominant cultures may also change from the contact, as shall be discussed later.

The term *acculturation* was coined by John Wesley Powell (1880), who explored what would become the Western US (see Figure 10.3). He was a pioneer in the developing field of anthropology, studying indigenous North American cultures and languages during their brutal suppression in the late 19th century. A brilliant visionary for his times, he accurately predicted that farming and depletion of water resources would lead to the Dustbowl that eventually happened in the 1930s. He also firmly believed that Anglo-American culture was the epitome of human evolution, destined to righteous dominance. "Judged by these criteria," he said in comparing indigenous North American, European, and English languages, "the English stands alone in the highest rank" (Powell, 1881, p. 16), an incredibly chauvinistic conclusion. The concept of Manifest Destiny held that divine providence granted European colonists and their descendants dominion over North America (O'Sullivan, 1845). It was widely assumed in the late 19th and

**Figure 10.3   Etching of John Wesley Powell**

MAJOR POWELL.

early 20th centuries that "primitive" cultures rightly should fade into the past as their surviving members willingly embraced the "superior" European-origin cultures.

During this same time period, immigration to the US increased rapidly, leading researchers to shift focus from declining indigenous groups to study of expanding immigrant communities in the burgeoning cities (see Figure 10.4). By the 1930s, the fields of anthropology and sociology were actively engaged in immigration research, predicting an inevitably difficult process in which minorities would be marginalized or, in the best outcomes, assimilated into the mainstream (e.g., Park, 1928; Redfield, Linton, & Herskovits, 1936). The concept of the **melting pot** entered common usage by that time, and a play with that name was first performed in Washington, D. C. in 1905 (Zangwill, 1908). The concept had been considered for more than a century before, dating back at least to St. John de Crevecoeur (1782/1905) who observed of the new US, "Here individuals of all nations are melted into a new race of men" (p. 55).

Intercultural contact and immigration continue to be a hot topic of discussion and debate. During development of this book, millions of refugees have fled war in Iraq, Syria, and Afghanistan and have been blocked from entry into some European countries ("Migrant Crisis", 2016), despite tragic circumstances and international accords on acceptance of refugees. Certain candidates in the 2016 US presidential race called for a total ban on immigration by Muslims (Berman, 2015), and laws have been passed subjecting Hispanic Americans to unusual detention by police if they are only suspected of being from outside the US (Cooper, 2010). In early 2017, Donald Trump began attempts to ban people from several Muslim countries by presidential order. Politicians

Figure 10.4   Graph of US Migration by Decade and Origin

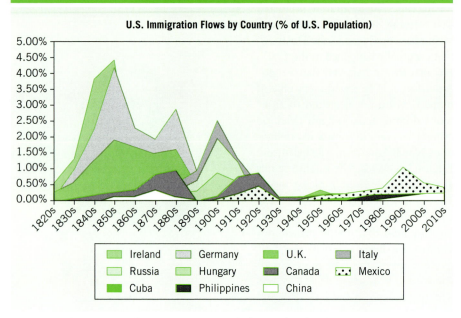

**U.S. Immigration Flows by Country (% of U.S. Population)**

Legend:
Ireland | Germany | U.K. | Italy
Russia | Hungary | Canada | Mexico
Cuba | Philippines | China

*Source:* Image by Metrocosm, http://metrocosm.com/animated-immigration-map/

around the world have fanned xenophobic fears and prejudice to gain political power in a process causing increases in interethnic violence and tensions that may last for years.

Inter-ethnic tensions are unfortunately frequent in developed nations including the US, New Zealand, Canada, France, England, Sweden, and Australia, among others (Canadian Council for Refugees, 2000; Human Rights Watch, 2012; le Mesurier, 2012). In less developed nations, deadly violence erupts between ethnic, immigrant, and indigenous groups, especially in cases where a government has encouraged internal migration for political or economic goals (Human Rights Watch, 2001). Intergroup relations on social and political levels shape the psychological outcomes for the individuals involved, and the language of sociopolitical discourse on migration frames debates that determine well-being for millions around the world.

## Processes of Acculturation

Processes of acculturation happen on both group and individual levels. Theorists have suggested that acculturation at the group level and **psychological acculturation** at the individual level are distinctly different processes that should be studied separately (Graves, 1967). Further, there are semantic differences between "acculturation" at the individual-level of changes and **psychological adaptation**, which describes outcomes of the process (Ward, 2001). Historically, the processes of acculturation have often happened on larger scale as groups move en masse, as with the Irish Potato Famine or the Jewish Diaspora of WWII. But even huge groups are composed of individuals who may have very different adaptation experiences depending on the specifics of their situation, as well as the material and psychological resources they bring. We begin with group-level dynamics, and then focus in greater depth on the psychological processes of individual acculturation and adaptive outcome.

## Group-Level Processes of Acculturation

People move in large numbers for a number of reasons. Sometimes people face dire conditions such as war or famine forcing them to move. In the Irish Potato Famine, between 1845 and 1854, nearly two million people left Ireland due to hunger and poverty, most moving to North America or to British colonies including New Zealand and Australia. This was a massive number of people in a time when far fewer people lived. They began a process of adapting wherever they went, facing different customs and **prejudice** that pushed them to band together as ostracized communities. The general process has been repeated with variations in the Jewish Diaspora following the Holocaust, Vietnamese refugees escaping the fall of Saigon, Ethiopians fleeing civil war and famine in the 1980s, and victims of ethnic cleansing leaving the Balkans in the 1990s.

The groups above are described as **refugees** or **asylum seekers**, defined in international law as people who are forced by circumstances beyond their control to cross international boundaries for safety and survival. In acculturation terminology, they experience "involuntary" acculturation (Berry & Sam, 1997; Ward, 2001). Other people who experience involuntary acculturation include indigenous people who encountered cultures as the result of colonization, such as Native American cultures and the Māori of New Zealand. A further set of people who may face involuntary acculturation are described as **internally displaced persons** (IDPs), who are forced by warfare or environmental factors to flee their traditional homes but do not cross international borders, and may or may not cross regional cultural boundaries. **Civil war** and drought in Somalia and the Sudan have forced millions to flee, though many have not crossed a border. People migrate and acculturate for numerous different reasons, but may share psychological experiences along the way.

## Motivations to Migrate

Voluntary acculturation describes the experience of ethnocultural groups who *choose* to interact with a different, dominant society. These groups might include the Amish who have lived in the United States for generations and maintain a distinct lifestyle. Permanent immigrants and temporary sojourners who move by choice for economic or educational purposes form the greatest number of contemporary migrants. Large communities of people from the Indian subcontinent can be found in the US, England, New Zealand, Australia, and many other countries. From every part of the globe, millions have chosen to seek their fortunes or education in other countries, some moving permanently, and others returning when their goals are achieved. **Sojourner** is the term for those moving temporarily to work or study in another country, but who may return after a few months or years to their native lands (Berry & Sam, 1997; Kuo & Roysircar, 2009; Ward & Rana-Deuba, 1999).

# SPOTLIGHT

## MEDIA, MARKETING, AND ACCULTURATION

Visiting the Malaysian Sabah portion of the island of Borneo in 2008, I did not expect to encounter multiculturalism: only a few decades ago, it was jungle full of orangutan and rhinos and barely contacted tribes. Actually, I stayed at a hostel owned by Chinese-Malaysians who told me they were saving to send their son (then 3 years old) to school in New Zealand for high school. In the common area at the base of the building was a café that featured

**Figure 10.5    KFC Sabah, Malaysia**

music each night by bands playing old pop music from the US and England. Adjacent was a Pizza Hut. A block away were a Kentucky Fried Chicken franchise (chicken can be *halal* if prepared by religious rules and can be eaten by the Muslim majority) and a multi-story mall with T-shirts, handbags, and CDs of dubious copyright or trademark (see Figure 10.5).

Movies and music are distributed globally, especially in context of the internet. It would be difficult to classify media factors in terms of acculturation research: if the children of a traditional family enjoy Euro-American songs and movies, the family may be disrupted by a very different set of cultural values. American media often portrays children mocking their parents, which may not be so strange in the US, but may be disturbing to a family expecting respect for elders. A young girl in a strictly hierarchic, patriarchal family may be in big trouble if she copies behaviors even from Disney shows. If she researches further, she may find video of Miley Cyrus twerking. In marketing, research does not discuss the effects of scantily clad women on the minds of those who see an ad, but those images may fly in the face of traditional or conservative cultures, violating ethics of divinity (Shweder et al. (1997). Elements of other cultures enter our homes and lives constantly, through aggressive marketing of American media, and the sustained encounter is essentially an acculturative process. In a world of constant intercultural contact, is acculturation the new cultural constant?

The distinctions between categories may be overly fine. A family that makes its way to the United States illegally from Central America because they lack opportunity and resources, a student of Chinese ethnicity born in Malaysia who cannot find a place at a national university because of preferential quota laws, or a manager who is offered a choice between unemployment or international relocation are technically voluntary migrants, but they may have had few real choices in the matter. Some who relocate may intend to return home but stay permanently, or conversely, intended permanent residency may not turn out well and the person may return home. Whatever the reason for migration, all acculturating groups or individuals share the experience of dealing with a different set of cultural rules and activities in the new setting for some amount of time (e.g., Nayar, 2009).

Groups experiencing acculturation may be categorized as voluntary or involuntary, reflecting the differing intentions described above. They can also be described as *pushed* by circumstance, such as poverty, or *pulled* by need or desire for some outcome, such as higher education. Other important factors include what resources they bring into the new situation, whether they are welcome or not, whether there is a community of people from their heritage culture, and whether or not opportunities are available to create a good life for themselves and their loved ones. Over generations, these factors may set trajectories for entire families adapting to their new homes (Liebkind, 1996; Miller & Rasco, 2004; Nguyen, Messe, & Stollack, 1999).

## Hurdles in Acculturative Adaptation

Difficulties may be encountered by acculturating groups in any of the categories described above. All must find new means of livelihood and must somehow understand ways of living and being that are not necessarily in harmony with their heritage cultures. The new situations involve changes in "identity, values, behaviours, cognition, attitudes and affect" (Bemak, Chung, & Pederson, 2003, p. 31). New skills may be required simply to shop for food (Nayar, 2009) or to behave in ways that fit in with norms of those around them (Nguyen, Messe, & Stollack, 1999). All may face pressures to adapt to life amid dominant or majority group societies and may face greatest pressure to do so when economic and social power structures are stacked against them (Berns-McGown, 2007; Hoerder, 2002; Marsella & Ring, 2003).

Much of the psychological literature of acculturation focuses on immigrant groups whose actual experiences may vary depending on their reasons for migration. The worst of these experiences are faced by refugees and forced migrants (Bemak et al., 2003), but all migrants face some risks. Jablensky, Marsella, Ekblad, Jannsonn, Levi, and Bornemann (1994) state, "There is compelling evidence that specific configurations of migration and displacement have a major impact on both short-term and long-term mental health and well-being" (p. 329). The risk factors shared by groups before and during migration include the following:

- Marginalization and minority status
- Socioeconomic disadvantage
- Poor physical health
- Starvation and malnutrition
- Collapse of social supports
- Mental trauma
- Adaptation to host culture

# SPOTLIGHT

## THE VIETNAMESE REFUGEE EXPERIENCE

The regions comprising modern Vietnam have been in almost continual armed conflict for more than a thousand years as different groups have tried to unite, dominate, or divide the region. Mountain ranges and a pinched waistband in the middle of the country have isolated the North and South to some degree and made them difficult to hold together as a unified political entity. The Chinese have dominated the region at various times over the centuries. During the Colonial era, the French controlled the country and established lucrative plantations and other ways to exploit the area's resources. France completely lost control of the region during WWII and gave up attempts to regain domination in 1954 (Yu, 1985). At that point, the US stepped in, and Vietnam became a pawn in the Cold War between the US and the USSR.

The Vietnamese had never passively accepted outside domination. The Chinese, Japanese, and French all expended huge resources and suffered great losses in the attempts at domination, and the US fared no better. The North, with Communist backing from the USSR and China, waged highly effective guerrilla warfare, and eventually the US had to withdraw in 1975, evacuating tens of thousands of those loyal to the US-backed government of the South, and leaving behind hundreds of thousands more to suffer brutal retribution under the new regime. Many of those left behind escaped in subsequent migration waves under terrifying conditions, and eventually, a third large wave began with normalization of political relations in the 1990s.

A total of 130,000 Indochinese refugees came to the US in the first wave (Nguyen et al., 1999; Thai, 2002). They included political elites, wealthy merchants, medical doctors, military officers, and others who were fortunate enough to escape immediately. Unlike the mayhem of millions relocating during and following WWII, the first wave was a finite group, and all passed through the Philippine First Asylum Camp. The US made efforts to plan and control relocation, beginning with screenings at the camp. These were people who had known years of war, and many suffered PTSD or other psychological conditions on arrival. An alarming 41% of youths exceeded the clinical diagnosis threshold on the General Health Questionnaire (GHQ), and 15% of young adults showed clinical-level scores on the HSCL-A measure of anxiety disorder (Felsman, Leong, Johnson, & Felsman, 1990).

This highly organized migration, while certainly tragic, led to some very good research opportunities, and to a number of theories about the acculturation process and adaptation outcomes. High rates of diagnosable mental illness have continued into the present in those populations, partly because of the vast *cultural distance*, or differences they face between their origin and destination cultures. The great differences in culture influenced outcomes in ways that will be discussed in the following Social Learning and the Stress and Coping paradigm sections of this chapter.

Sue le Mesurier, then Senior Policy Officer Migration of the International Federation of Red Cross and Red Crescent Societies, said at the 21st Session of the UN's Commission on Crime Prevention and Criminal Justice,

> Violence against migrants can take many forms. Physical, moral and psychological abuses against migrants are a growing phenomenon which is exacerbated by the current dialogue on migration and immigration

policies. The migrant population, especially those in irregular situations, are particularly vulnerable to labour exploitation.

Other horrendous crimes such as human trafficking and smuggling are also highly affecting migrants. These are issues that the International Community needs to address to ensure that the human rights of all, including migrants, are respected and upheld. (le Mesurier, 2012)

Although the negative aspects of migration are most immediate and pronounced among refugees, the shared hurdles can be exceedingly difficult for anyone acculturating. This is especially true in cases of pushed migration due to military, environmental, or economic hardship, when few physical or social resources are likely to be brought along on the journey. Many migrants were minorities or held low socioeconomic status in their land of origin. Both in their place of origin and in their new homes, their life situation may include such factors as very low socio-economic status, dangerous living conditions, language issues, prejudice, and political persecution or exclusion (Arroyo & Zigler, 1995; Green, 2009; UNDESAPD, 2011; Wilton, 2005). Indigenous groups often face these same issues, sometimes for generations, though they never leave traditional homelands (Hoerder, 2002; Murray, 2004). Sojourners also face stresses and difficulty in their host cultures in a number of socio-cultural domains (Kuo & Roysircar, 2009; Ward & Rana-Deuba, 1999). In other words, basically anyone who is not born a member of the dominant ethnic or national group where they live potentially faces some of these risks as they are pressured to adapt.

Acculturation is a two-way street because all cultures involved are placed in contact with ideas, products, and behaviors different from their origins (e.g., Berry, 2006). Some degree of cultural and psychological change may be experienced by any or all of the groups and individuals involved. European Americans have adopted the peanut as a common food and enjoy jazz music that includes numerous elements of African source culture (see Figure 10.6; DiMaggio & Ostrower, 1990; Neto, Barros, & Schmitz, 2005). In evaluating the individualism and collectivism scores of students of different ethnic groups in New Zealand, results followed interesting patterns. The New Zealand Māori were less collective than Polynesian immigrant participants, which is predictable given the long contact between Māori and Europeans. More surprising was that the New Zealand European students were less individualistic than other Western groups, suggesting that

**Figure 10.6  Peanuts, Brought to America to Feed Slaves**

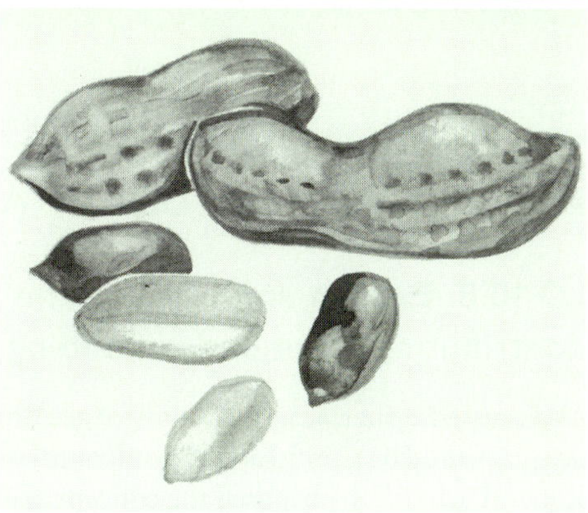

*Source:* nats77/istockphoto.com

they had accommodated somewhat to the more collectivist mode of the Māori with whom they share the country (Podsiadlowski & Fox, 2011). The minority group may be most pressured to adapt, given the range of social, political, and economic pressures they face (Berry, 2006), but all groups may face some measurable changes when in intercultural contact.

Immigrant or minority groups have little choice but to learn the dominant language and customs if they want to earn a livelihood and eventually be included in society. The dominant culture may hold all the cards and has relatively little pressure to accommodate the less powerful others. Minorities sometimes also form a convenient target for politicians who use divisive issues to garner support. Frequently, economic woes are blamed on the minority in a *scapegoating* process (Baumeister & Bushman, 2010), such as Jews in Nazi Germany, or illegal immigrants in the 21st-century US. Simply having a different skin color or accent can cause someone to be targeted. This happened to University of Pennsylvania economics professor Guido Menzo in May 2016, as he sat on an airplane working a mathematical equation while awaiting take-off. The Caucasian American woman sitting next to him reported him for suspicious behavior, assuming this dark-skinned man was a terrorist. Despite being Italian, not Middle Eastern, and despite his respected position, he was removed from the plane (Rampell, 2016). Racial profiling is an ongoing issue for minorities around the world and especially in the US.

## REALITY CHECK

What types of groups experience acculturation?

What is the difference between immigrants, refugees, and sojourners?

Historically, what were the expected outcomes of acculturation?

What life changes might an acculturating person have to make?

What are the potential problems faced in acculturation?

What may happen to a person's status and employment after migration?

## 10.3 APPROACHES TO THE PSYCHOLOGICAL STUDY OF ACCULTURATION

### LO 10.3: Explain and critique the theories and research contributing to an understanding of acculturation.

As discussed earlier, academic study of acculturation began with the assumption that the process would be painful and the outcomes were all negative. In this context, sociologist Robert Park (1928) proposed the concept of The Marginal Man, which assumed that the acculturating individual would be caught in the margins between two cultures, accepted by neither the culture he had left nor the one in which he arrived. Park believed this situation would lead to **marginalization** and that dark psychosocial outcomes would be inescapable. In the best-case scenario, the person would successfully assimilate, giving up his culture of origin entirely, and acquire the self-image of an unhyphenated American (Sam, 2006). This view is no longer endorsed in psychological research, but assimilation remains part of political debate.

Decades after the study of acculturation began, Kalervo Oberg (1960) coined the term **culture shock**, still assuming that the acculturative process included primarily negative emotional experiences and outcomes, and indeed, there is evidence that international students and others crossing cultures do sometimes experience negative health and well-being effects (Furnham, 2010). The concept became a part of popular culture and remains a commonly used term. It was not until Berry (1970) proposed the concept of *acculturative stress* that alternative views became part of serious research. Berry drew upon psychological models of stress and coping (c.f. Lazarus & Folkman, 1984) to describe a range of ways an individual might respond to stresses in intercultural contact. Berry proposed a more balanced model assuming that acculturation included stressors, but also including coping strategies and other factors affecting outcomes. Most important, Berry had found a way to draw on volumes of previous research about resources or skills people could use to promote more positive psychological outcomes when dealing with acculturative stressors.

## The Strands of Acculturation Research

Each individual experience of acculturation is unique, potentially bringing a variety of resources into the process, or bringing only needs. Understandably, given the wide variation in circumstances and options of humans in intercultural contact, research has focused on many different aspects and a number of theoretical streams have resulted. Colleen Ward (2001) summarized acculturation research overall as falling into three theoretical approaches: stress and coping, social identity, and cultural learning. The stress and coping framework focuses on the stresses faced in intercultural contact and the ways individuals deal with the stressors. The social identity approach revolves around ways people construct identity on a cultural basis and how different groups interact. The cultural learning approach discusses knowledge required to function successfully in a new or different cultural milieu.

### Stress and Coping Research

The stress and coping framework of research deals primarily with aspects of contact that cause stressful feelings for the individual and how the person deals with the stressors. Stress and coping as an avenue to understand acculturation originated with Berry's (1970) proposal that the acculturating individual encounters stressors in the process of dealing with new environments and worldviews, and that the ways the individual copes with them shapes psychological outcomes in the process. Inclusion of coping concepts allows a framework for understanding healthier and more successful ways acculturation might proceed (e.g., Berry, 1997; Ward, Bochner, & Furnham, 2001).

Factors affecting individual adaptation outcomes in the stress and coping paradigm include the **demographics** of the new environment, the availability of social support, the cultural differences between the culture of origin and the new environment, whether there is discrimination from dominant and other ethnic groups, and knowledge and skills the person brings or gains (see cultural learning paradigm below). Personal characteristics are also important in this paradigm, depending on whether the person can normally deal with stresses in a resilient and adaptive way (Berry, 1997; UNDESAPD, 2011; Ward, 2001).

The milieu of acculturation may be a major factor in stressors and adaptation: Is the individual accepted by the dominant or host community? Is diversity tolerated, or do attitudes of prejudice and exclusion prevail (Green, 2009; Marsella, 1994; van Oudenhoven, Ward, & Masgoret, 2006; van Tubergen, 2006)? If the dominant ethnic group is strongly prejudiced against the acculturating group, it may affect the acculturating group's ability to earn a fair livelihood, and thus yield lower socioeconomic status. This may lead to **ghettoization** and/or economic disenfranchisement of entire groups (Green, 2009; Ward & Masgoret, 2006, 2007). Differences between the heritage and host cultures, whether they are more or less similar, may affect the amount of accommodation or learning required of immigrants or indigenous groups and resulting stress (Markus & Kitayama, 1991; Tadmor, Tetlock, & Peng, 2009). A number of others of the same ethnicity in the community may provide social support, mitigating stressful problems and ensuing psychological disturbances (van Tubergen, 2006). Honolulu's Chinatown hosted successive waves of immigrants, beginning with the Chinese, and more recently, Vietnamese (see Figure 10.7). **Co-ethnics** may simply make life easier by providing employment opportunities within the community (Brody, 1994; Liebkind, 1996; van Tubergen, 2006). Conversely, other research suggests that strong co-ethnic presence inhibits the process of acculturation because less interaction with the host culture, language, and customs is required (Brody, 1994; Liebkind, 1996).

**Figure 10.7 Vietnamese Language Business Sign in Chinatown, Honolulu**

Berry's (1970) foray into the stress and coping framework marked a shift from the previous views that acculturation was a difficult and painful process leading only to negative outcomes of marginalization or cultural surrender in assimilation. Stress and coping research outside of acculturation had already discussed ways people could deal successfully with difficulties and trauma. The framework included mechanisms that could be identified and measured on interpersonal levels, such as social support, and intrapersonal levels, such as cognitive reframing and resilience skills. The potential for positive outcomes led to investigation of more possibilities in adaptation outcomes.

### Social Identity Research

The second theoretical approach, social identity, drew its inspiration from the social psychological literature of social cognition (how we think about group membership). It includes research streams focused on individual or group processes, either investigating individual sense of cultural identity or dynamics of interaction between groups involved. On the individual level, this approach studies how people identify with their culture of origin or an alternate (i.e., dominant) culture. Social identity research studies how people vary in their sense of belonging to these groups, the importance of membership, and their evaluations and appraisals of the groups involved (Ward et al., 2001). Individuals may identify as part of their culture of origin, as part of the dominant culture, or as some combination of both. In multicultural settings, a person may have heritage from a number of cultures, with parents, grandparents, and great-grandparents all having one or more different heritages. A person may have more or less knowledge of any of these cultures, may practice different traditions to greater or lesser extents, and may identify themselves as members of one, two, or more cultural groups. Each group may be held in higher or lower esteem.

On the group level, social identity research focuses on perceptions of groups and relations between groups. Individuals may have different perceptions of in- and out-groups regarding similarity of their group to others, the status and power held by each group, and boundary permeability, which refers to whether a person can move between and interact with different groups (Crocker & Major, 2003; Turner, 1999; Ward et al., 2001).

In the social identity paradigms, much of the acculturation research revolves around either Berry's (1990, 1997) acculturation strategies (discussed below) or Phinney's (1990, 1992) developmental approach to how people achieve sense of identity. Both approaches discuss ways people arrive at the sense of identity and what happens because of their choices. Strengths of these approaches are that they can be applied in complex cultural landscapes that may include indigenous groups, long-term minorities in decades or centuries of intercultural contact, and to groups in recent migration. These paradigms can also be applied to children and subsequent generations of these groups. Both paradigms assume the presence of a different, more dominant group and that there may be psychological repercussions from choices people make as they create their sense of identity. Phinney's concepts concern the ways a person makes decisions about identity during development, while Berry's concepts focus more on psychological ramifications of strategic identity choices in acculturation.

The ways we perceive and identify with heritage and other groups have been shown to affect psychological states and outcomes. In acculturation research, the general conclusion is that the marginalization strategy leads to the worst psychological outcomes and the integrations strategy is healthiest. In other words, we need a positive sense of group affiliation to be healthy, and multiple affiliations seem best. The ways one's own and other groups are compared may also play a role, with favorable feelings about the group(s) with which one identifies being most likely to lead to better outcomes adjustment (Berry, 1997; Ward et al., 2001).

## The Cultural Learning Paradigm

The cultural learning paradigm forms a third stream of psychological research in acculturation. The underlying idea is that the acculturating individual experiences difficulties because she lacks knowledge and skills needed in the new cultural context. To adapt successfully to a new culture, a person needs to be fluent in the language, to understand the rules and norms of communication and interaction, and to have skills necessary to make a living. Skills may be as seemingly simple as learning how to shop in a supermarket or whether or not to tip the staff at a restaurant. Without the needed knowledge and skills, the person faces great difficulties and may experience negative psychological effects from the resulting troubles (Ward, 2001). Does the waiter you tipped think you are a nice person or feel insulted? Can you buy food for your children, or are you intimidated and frightened by rows of cereal boxes in an unfamiliar language, illustrated with bizarre pictures of rabbits, tigers, and leprechauns? The beauty of this paradigm is that it describes a particular set of hurdles and remedies that can be measured and monitored. You can learn the word *granola* or read a map to find an Asian grocery, and data have been gathered to establish how assistance can lead to better outcomes.

Research in cultural learning has shown that effects and outcomes follow a predictable learning curve that corresponds to time spent in contact with the alternate culture. The person needs to learn a language and how people normally interact, how to do profitable work, and how to complete daily tasks of shopping, banking, having a home, and so on. This just takes time. As the person spends more time in contact with the different culture, simultaneous learning occurs in terms of knowledge of the new culture and skills needed to adapt. This experiential learning yields improved adaptation outcomes. The simple set of skills and information needed and the demonstrably improved outcomes when those are gained have made this paradigm very attractive for international business and education, when people are moving in scheduled ways. Research in this paradigm has understandably focused on these sojourner groups (Cushner & Brislin, 1996; Ward & Kennedy, 1994).

The cultural learning paradigm is a highly effective avenue of research in practical terms. It provides a clear way to describe and measure aspects of acculturation and the potential to influence beneficially the outcomes. It does not address issues of how people reshape their identities or how effects of combined stressors may come into play, and does not address effects of prejudice or violence from the host culture. It is highly effective, however, at what it is intended to do: increase understanding of the new culture and thereby improve practical outcomes. Cultural learning provides an approach that, for instance, shows why it would be valuable for sojourner students and workers to learn about their destination culture before they even depart, thereby preventing some bad experiences altogether.

## Acculturation Strategies

John Berry's studies of acculturation have included Canadian First Nations (Berry, 1974), immigrants and refugees (Berry, 1986), and numerous other groups in Canada and around the world, illuminating the processes and outcomes of their experiences. Berry's (1990, 1997) acculturation strategies originally described the degree to which individuals identified with their heritage culture or the host/dominant culture, assuming that high identification with one indicated low identification with the other. The theory evolved to recognize that individuals may maintain the heritage culture identification and, orthogonally, participate in the dominant culture (Berry, Kim, Power, Young, & Bujaki 1989; Ward et al., 2001). **Orthogonal** is the term for variables that interact independently. The individual may identify with and participate in the heritage culture(s) and/or in the host or dominant culture to different degrees at the same time. Each aspect may be higher or lower, depending on the individual and the circumstances of that person's life. The degree of identification and involvement with each culture can be measured, and those scores link a person to an acculturation strategy.

Berry (1990) has described four acculturation strategies: assimilation, separation, marginalization, and integration (or bicultural strategy), based on the level of identification with the new/dominant culture and origin culture (see Table 10.1). In Berry's model, **assimilation** occurs when the individual gives up identification with the culture of origin, choosing instead to identify as a member of the dominant culture. That person identifies highly with the dominant culture, and identification with the culture of origin is low. In **separation**, the individual chooses only to identify highly as a member of the heritage culture of origin and on a low level with the host culture. In the marginalization outcome, the person does not identify as a member of either culture, and so she is low on identification with any culture. In other words, the person does not feel or value membership in any culture and probably maintains few traditions of any sort. The final strategy was initially described as **bicultural**, in which the person feels membership in both the heritage and dominant cultures. Identification with both cultures is high. The term **integration** better fits strategies observed in multicultural settings where a person integrates multiple identities, and it is now the preferred term (Ward, 2001).

| Table 10.1   John Berry's Acculturation Strategies | | | |
|---|---|---|---|
| | | **Identification With the New Culture** | |
| | | High | Low |
| **Identification With the Culture of Origin** | High | Integration (Biculturality) | Separation |
| | Low | Assimilation | Marginalization |

Source: Berry (1990, 1997).

## THE MERRIE MONARCH FESTIVAL

Each year since 1964, *hula* dancers, teachers, chanters, musicians, and fans have gathered in Hilo, Hawai'i, for the Merrie Monarch Festival (Merrie Monarch Festival, 2012). The festival honors King David Kalākaua (1836 to 1891), who was the last king of Hawai'i from 1874 to 1891. Kalākaua loved *hula* and other aspects of Hawaiian culture that had been suppressed under the influence of missionaries, following the adoption of Christianity by the Hawaiian ruling class in the early 1800s. Under Kalākaua, *hula* had a brief blossoming, prior to his death and the subsequent overthrow of his successor, Queen Liliuokalani, by a cabal of American businessmen supported by US Marines (Coffman, 1998).

Hawaiian culture went through cycles of popularity, neglect, and outright suppression. Surprisingly, *hula* traveled worldwide throughout much of the 20th century, with hula troupes traveling to England, Australia, India, and elsewhere (Brozman, 2009). Back in Hawai'i, *hula* was not assured of survival as anything more than a quaint photo opportunity for tourists. Hawaiian culture was in peril of being overwhelmed and assimilated (Ariyoshi, 1998; Rayson, 2004). By the 1940s, Maiki Aiu Lake was one of the few *kumu hula* (*hula* master teachers) still practicing in the traditional way, with deep knowledge of the language and underlying cultural system (Ariyoshi, 1998). She and her students poured their hearts and lives into bringing the culture back to life. The Hawaiian Renaissance of the 1970s and 80s saw a resurgence of cultural practices and language, in tandem with Civil Rights and cultural heritage movements on the mainland US and around the world. Assimilation or extinction, as predicted by Powell (1879), did happen to many cultures around the world, but in a surprising turn of events, many traditional cultures are reasserting their value and right to survive (e.g., Mussell, 2008). The Merrie Monarch Festival serves as an Olympian competition of excellence in Hawaiian culture and arts and is a living testament to cultural sustainability (see Figure 10.8).

### Figure 10.8 Kahiko (Ancient Style) Hula

Research has focused on how to measure and describe experiences of people as they naturally utilize one strategy or the other, and how to encourage the best choices of strategy. Published research has primarily supported that the best adaptive outcomes are gained in the integration strategy (Berry, Phinney, Sam, & Vedder, 2006a), though some strongly disagree (e.g., Rudmin, 2006). The acceptance of this research has supported efforts to help immigrants learn more about the ways and beliefs of the dominant or host culture so as to fit in better. Largely, international research such as the International Comparative Study of Ethnocultural Youth (ICSEY) in 13 receiving countries (Berry, Phinney, Sam, & Vedder, 2006b) have provided strong support for the theory. Less investigated is how people can learn and maintain their cultures of origin when it is not encouraged in the new context, and in fact may have been abandoned by the elder generation (Fox, 2010). This has been the experience, for instance, of urban Māori in New Zealand, whose parents and grandparent may have been assimilated or marginalized, and who may not have much cultural knowledge to offer (Durie, 1995; King, 2001). Many young Māori and Pasifika youth join

cultural groups to learn their language and culture (see Figure 10.9). Additional research may be needed to understand both how people adapt to a new culture and how they enculturate their heritage culture—and how these patterns interact.

One way people deal with multicultural life is called **frame-switching**, where people may be fluent in more than one language and competent in multiple sets of cultural norms (Hong, Morris, Chiu, & Benet-Martinez, 2000). They may behave differently, depending on where they are and who else is present, and the cultural connections with others present. This is not surprising. Everyone may behave differently in the presence of Grandma from how they act around friends their own age. For a person who speaks one language at home and another at work or school, this shift happens several times daily. Going to a family gathering or religious event, one may speak and dress very differently from other situations. Further, people may actually experience a different set of ideas and feelings about themselves and others, depending on context.

Recent fMRI and ERP studies demonstrate that the change of cultural frame may cause alteration in brain patterns (Han & Humphries, 2016; Ng et al., 2010), as discussed earlier regarding self-construal. Frame-switching may involve more than an ability to speak two languages or to follow different behavioral rules as expected in different situations. These studies indicate that truly multicultural people may actually switch the physiological patterns of their thoughts from one context to another. Rather than simply switching from one skill set to another like changing a costume, the change happens internally and a slightly different person emerges on a neurological level.

Hong and colleagues (2016) reviewed recent research in multicultural identities and outcomes. Consistent with Berry's research, multiple strong cultural identifications correlate favorably with better psychological and sociocultural adjustment. Contrary to Berry's predictions, however, some individuals who identify at very low levels with heritage and dominant/host cultures actually function very well, exhibit high degrees of creativity, and excel in international business leadership (Arasaratnam, 2013; Fitzsimmons, Lee, & Brannen, 2013; Hong et al., 2016).

Arasaratnam (2013) proposed an alternative operational definition of multicultural identity that may account for these varied outcomes: "the condition of persons who have formed an identity that is not affiliated with one particular culture but instead a blend of multiple cultures and contexts" (p. 682). Rogoff (2016) suggests that examining participation in cultural practices may form a more effective platform for understanding people's relationships with their cultures than attempting to assign a "static social address" (p. 182) based on demographic information and survey responses.

Bicultural identity integration (BII) conceptualizes the degree to which an individual feels her cultural identities are compatible (Cheng & Lee, 2013; Cheng, Lee, & Benet-Martinez, 2006). The two domains comprising BII are distance, which is how different the cultures are, and conflict, representing perception of tension or integration between cultural identities (Hong et al., 2016; Mok & Morris, 2013). Low BII distance is associated with lower anxiety and better performance in mixed cultural settings. Interestingly, high BII conflict can lead one to examine cultural assumptions more carefully. The internal conflict between identities makes the person more aware of interactional dynamics and less prone to pitfalls like groupthink in teamwork.

## Weaving Together the Strands of Research

The three paradigms discussed all have practical merit and well-developed bodies of supporting research. Ward (2001) synthesized the three theoretical approaches into what she termed the "ABC's of crossing cultures" (p. 415). "A" is for Affect, "B" is for Behavior, and "C" is for Cognition. The terms have been used as a triad in social psychology in general (Baumeister & Bushman, 2012) and are applied more specifically when discussing acculturation. In this case, the affective component corresponds to the stress and coping paradigm and relates to stressful states encountered in the processes of coping with cultural change. The behavioral aspect corresponds to the cultural learning paradigm, including the ways of speaking, interacting, and working one must learn in a new culture. The cognitive component corresponds to theories of social identity, relating to the ways one perceives and thinks about social and cultural groups involved and evaluates membership in those groups. The ABC's of acculturation provided a shorthand for the major theoretical themes in acculturation research, but each of these domains is complex, with a multitude of possible variations in individual lives.

Acculturation research shows that each individual experience and outcome may be as unique as a snowflake, with different psychological and material resources, preceding experiences, and social contexts involved. Stuart and Ward (2015) point out that previous research focuses primarily on the acculturating individual, highlighting intrapersonal processes when acculturation inherently involves interaction between individuals and groups. These interactions happen in a particular place and time, including families, communities, and surrounding institutions. Stuart and Ward recommend an ecological approach, drawing on Bronfenbrenner's (1979) ecocultural theory, to encompass the complexity of these multi-layered experiences.

Acculturation involves ongoing changes and interactions that are affected by a variety of contextual factors, leading Ward and Geeraert (2016) to suggest that a process approach can better account for these multiple influences and their effects over time. Focusing on immigrants and sojourners, they propose a model of processes and factors leading to individual well-being and social functioning outcomes. The model includes context of global culture, the heritage and host cultures and differences between them, the ecocultural layers in which intercultural contact happens, stress processes, and the blending of heritage and host cultural elements that affect individual outcomes. Indigenous experiences of acculturation may require a slightly different model, as would long-term ethnic minorities *in situ*, highly multicultural settings like Hawai'i, or acculturation experiences of dominant groups. The following section addresses effects of social contexts of gender, family, community, and nation, as well as intergroup processes of prejudice and oppression.

## REALITY CHECK

Who is the Marginal Man? Why might marginalization lead to bad outcomes?

What happens when a person switches frames?

How might co-ethnics affect the process of acculturation?

What are the ABCs of crossing culture?

What is culture shock?

## 10.4 SOCIOCULTURAL CONTEXTS IN ACCULTURATION

### LO 10.4: Appraise the effects of context on acculturation experiences and outcomes.

Recent acculturation research acknowledges that level of analysis may be a crucial consideration in studying acculturation (Chirkov, 2009). Recall that Vygotsky (1934/1986) and the Russian Cultural-Historical School developed a theoretical model emphasizing context of development, and Urie Bronfenbrenner (1979) proposed that all human development happens in ecological contexts expanding from family to community and outward toward the broader nation and culture. Current approaches in acculturation research now acknowledge that acculturation happens in ways that may not fit a uniform set of steps and outcomes; contexts shape both process and results (Ward, Fox, Wilson,

Stewart, & Kus, 2010). We craft our identities and roles from a complex set of elements: ethnic and religious affiliation, economic and employment status, social memberships and hierarchies, gender and gender roles, and marital and family structures among them. Our roles and experiences in those contexts shape acculturation processes.

## General Sociocultural Factors

A primary factor in the process of acculturation is **cultural distance**, or the degree of difference between the culture of origin and the culture to which a person must adapt (Berry, 1997; Ward, 2001). If the cultures are similar, there is less to learn to adapt successfully, and the process may be relatively stress free. If they are very different, there may be more to learn in terms how people are expected to behave and interact. Similarly, a shared language makes the process easier, even if terminologies differ, such as boot versus trunk or bonnet versus hood on a car. Dialects of English use similar terms to describe shared physical constructs. A totally different language can make simple communication and life tasks difficult. Seemingly simple processes such as shopping for food can be daunting if a person is accustomed to shopping in a village market and must learn to navigate a large supermarket (Nayar, 2009). Imagine walking for the first time into a huge building where doors slide open without being touched, revealing row upon row of boxed items with labels you cannot read, if you grew up in a village where you knew every person and raised most of your own food.

Cultural identity is enacted in social contexts where "social performers meet social perceivers" (Hong et al., 2016, p. 51). In other words, we stake our claim to identity by our actions, assuming that our actions will be perceived as congruent with our intended identity. In any context, a person may be misperceived. A strongly identified Asian-American may be perceived as only Asian by a white majority perceiver, or a person with integrated Asian and American identities may be perceived as assimilated into American culture and lacking Asian identity. As with cultural distance and awareness, negotiation of identity occurs in all of the contexts to follow.

## National-Level Factors

Laws and policies on a national level can have a great effect on the acculturation process. Governmental policies can address or ignore issues of social inclusion and barriers, social capital, and social well-being (Peace, Spoonley, Butcher, & O'Neill, 2005). Is an immigrant welcomed and protected by laws against discrimination or do laws or policies unfairly favor a dominant culture.

The term *multiculturalism* was first used in Quebec in the 1970s to describe policies designed to value and preserve the multiple ethnic communities there, including large French- and English-speaking segments (Hong et al., 2016; Morris et al., 2015). Multicultural policies facilitate cultural maintenance and integration strategies in acculturation, but have been observed to reduce national unity (Reitz, Breton, Dion, & Dion, 2009). These policies are observed to enhance self-esteem only for highly identified individuals. Support for visible displays such as cultural festivals may either reduce or inadvertently reinforce stereotypes (Hong et al., 2016; O'Hagin & Harnish, 2006; Sousa, Neto, & Mullet, 2005). Whether exclusionist or embracing, national policies affect those who immigrate or seek refuge across national borders.

Malaysia has what are called *bumiputera* laws that favor those of Malaysian ethnicity (Shamsui, 2001), setting quotas for admission to schools and universities, and inhibiting access to higher education even for groups such as Indians or Chinese who have lived there for generations. Within the US, as described above, laws and policies increasingly subject particular groups to identity checks, searches, and potential incarceration or deportation (Cooper, 2010). Unofficial policies can lead to exclusionary practices in hiring or to additional requirements for professional licensure, even when these policies and practices violate legal guidelines (Diego-Mendoza, 2010). Policies and laws affect people in immediate ways, and may affect their psychological condition through stress and demoralization.

In Malaysia, the US, or any other country, the policies, laws, and practices of a nation may affect indigenous or long-term minorities as well as immigrants. Rates of incarceration and institutionalization are much higher for indigenous people in New Zealand and Australia and for Native and African Americans in the US (c.f. Durie, 1995; Western & Petit, 2010). Discriminatory conditions increase stressors and require greater coping effort, and they may result in greater psychopathology for large groups of people. Ethnic Russians who moved to Estonia during the Soviet era enjoyed many advantages during that time, but they now experience resentment and prejudice from the majority Estonian population who regained political power after Glasnost. Contrary to expectation, the Russian participants who adopted an integrated acculturation strategy exhibited lower life satisfaction, underscoring potential complications from historical and contextual factors on national levels (Kus-Harbord & Ward, 2015).

Even well-intentioned national policies may have negative effects. The first wave of Vietnamese refugees from the Indochinese War was dispersed across the United States, often into areas that were previously entirely Euro-American, in an attempt to avoid ghettoization. While the intent was to avoid clumping refugees together in bad neighborhoods, what actually happened was that families and individuals were left with drastically reduced social networks and resources, and few or no people who spoke their language. They had a markedly higher level of psychological disorders and usage of public health systems than other groups, probably partly due to isolation. This was especially true for the Hmong, a fiercely independent minority in Vietnam and Cambodia (Fadiman, 1998), some of whom were relocated to rural "white" areas of North Carolina and Minnesota (Westermeyer, Vang, & Neider, 1984). Already suffering higher levels of PTSD, depression, and anxiety, the Hmong also faced prejudice and discrimination, adding stressors that exacerbate pathology (c.f. Fadiman, 1998).

It is important to keep in mind that, despite some serious issues and inequities around the world, there are many favorable national-level factors in immigration and acculturation. Numerous nations continue accepting numbers of refugees each year, per post-WWII accords, allowing greater life opportunities and/or escape from intolerable life-threatening conditions. In general, most legislation internationally tends to increase protections against prejudice and exclusion. Daily experiences in communities,

# SPOTLIGHT

## MULTICULTURALISM IN NEW ZEALAND

Aotearoa, the land of the long white cloud, is currently known as New Zealand, though the other name has been around far longer. The indigenous Māori are estimated to have arrived in about 1200 CE. Abel Tasman, a navigator for the Dutch East India Company, happened across the archipelago in 1642 but did not land, besieged by hostile Māori in *waka* (canoes; Keightley, 2005; Slot, 1992). Englishman James Cook arrived in 1769 (Beaglehole, 1961). Limited settlement by Europeans began with camps of whalers and sealers in 1792, and missionaries arrived in 1814. Permanent settlement gradually increased, and by 1839, about 2,000 Europeans were present, comprising two percent of the population at most, compared to a minimum of 85,000 Māori (Davidson, 1983; Liu, Wilson, McClure, & Higgins, 1999; Phillips, 2008).

In 1840, British consul William Hobson, proposed a treaty with the Māori, who were assured the document granted them perpetual control over their physical and cultural assets, as well as full rights as citizens of the British Empire. The English and *te reo Māori* (Māori language) versions differ significantly (probably intentionally), principally in use of the Māori words *tino rangatiratanga* (sovereignty, self-management, self-determination) and *kawanatanga* (Māori adaptation of the term *governor*). In the Māori version, the Crown was granted *kawanatanga*, with Māori retaining *tino rangatiratanga*. The English version ceded political dominion over the land and people to the Crown (Barclay, 2005; Liu et al., 1999; Walker, 2004; White, 2001). British immigrants violated even the English version within 72 hours, but the document currently serves as the basis for litigation to gain compensation for two centuries of land theft and domination by military force (Barclay, 2005; Walker, 2004; White, 2001).

In the modern *bicultural* system, the Māori and British descendants are supposed to share governance, but the system has never worked equitably. Added to the situation are new migrants, about whom the Māori were not consulted. Seeking to supplement skill shortages amidst high outward migration and an aging population, the government eased immigration policies in 1988, and in twenty years, the percentage of non-European immigrants swelled from under 2% to more than 20% (Ministry of Social Development, 2008). It is a unique and dynamic setting for rapid acculturation.

Kiwis, as white New Zealanders call themselves casually, perceive theirs to be an enlightened, open, embracing culture. In actuality, they have all of the intercultural problems found in other developed countries, including overt and covert discrimination in public and workplace arenas and great inequality in political power distribution. Governmentally, minorities and immigrants are theoretically supported and protected by Ministry of Māori Affairs, the Ministry of Pacific Island Affairs, and the Office of Ethnic Affairs. Privately, individuals and communities have created organizations for mutual support and collective clout, eventually coalescing into the New Zealand Federation of Multicultural Councils (NZFMC), which has regional councils in many cities around the country.

The New Zealand government, the NZFMC, and numerous communities host festivals each year to celebrate diversity. The Indian community celebrates Diwali, the Festival of Lights, in Auckland and Wellington, with more than 150,000 people attending in 2016 (Asia New Zealand Foundation, 2018). That is 5% of the New Zealand total population. Common thought is that the festivals provide a non-threatening, positive setting for inter-cultural interaction and thereby promote more positive relations. This parallels research following Allport's Contact Theory (Pettigrew & Tropp, 2006), in which constant contact of living in close proximity with other ethnic groups in post-WWII housing projects was seen to reduce prejudice. In the New Zealand case, the contact is less direct, but tolerance of diversity seems to be increasing (Fox, 2010).

Over time, New Zealand is becoming more inclusive of its minorities. The indigenous Māori have made some strides with *te reo Māori* now an official language, and a number of financial settlements for illegal seizures of land have been reached. They do, however, continue to experience lower educational achievement and much higher rates of incarceration (Durie, 1995; Statistics NZ, 2012). The concept of multiculturalism seems a cruel joke to some, with equity as a bicultural Māori-British nation never having been achieved. New Zealand is not a perfect case in outcomes, but it is a perfect example of the factors and processes of acculturation.

work, schools, and other settings tend to reduce prejudice and increase acceptance, as was suggested by Gordon Allport's contact theory (Allport, 1952, 1953; Pettigrew & Tropp, 2006). While exclusion and violence gets media attention, immigration is often positive for both immigrants and receiving communities. Comparing New Zealand and Great Britain, Stuart, Ward, and Robinson (2016) observed better adaptive outcomes for Muslim emerging adults in New Zealand, which is normally more accepting of immigrants, though if they felt acculturative stress they suffered lower life-satisfaction and increased behavioral issues in both countries.

## Community

Culture normally happens in communities. We learn our culture in communities; popular sayings like "it takes a village to raise a child" reflect this truth. Our parents are normally part of a community, and the values, beliefs, and behaviors of culture are passed on in these ecological contexts. We also normally encounter other cultures in context of community, when we encounter other ethnicities in our area (Prilleltensky, 2008; Sabatier, 2008). Exactly how this happens depends on many factors, but there are few ways intercultural contact can happen independent of community.

### Composition, Distance, and Cohesion in Communities

Community factors have been viewed in both positive and negative ways in acculturation research, mostly related to ethnic composition of the community, degree of difference between groups (especially majority and minority), and community cohesion. In terms of composition, differences depend on whether the larger community is diverse or primarily one dominant ethnicity. A homogenous mainstream may be less accepting of other ethnicities, while a multicultural community may be more tolerant (Maira, 1999). Having few people of one's group in a community may lead to a sense of isolation. Presence of a larger group of co-ethnics may enhance sense of inclusion and support, or may facilitate a Separation strategy in which a whole community insulates itself from the host culture (Liebkind, 1996; van Tubergen, 2006). Pockets of an ethnic group or minority are termed **ethnic enclaves**, which includes the Chinatowns of many major cities or the Polish community of Chicago. In short, the makeup of the community sets the stage for the acculturation experience that will follow.

The effects of cultural distance are felt most acutely in community settings. In situations of low distance (high similarity), the immigrant or minority person may pass almost unnoticed. If the distance is high, one may stick out like a sore thumb. Muslim women wearing *hijab* (headscarves) or *burkah* (full body and head covering) have been the target of prejudice and even legislation against wearing their garb in parts of the US and other countries, and Western women are advised to wear these items in certain Muslim countries. Remember that all groups must adapt to each other to some degree, and the less the differences, the easier this will be (Markus & Kitayama, 1991; Tadmor et al., 2009).

A third broad topic is how people connect and interact in communities. Are people supportive of each other within their ethnic group and of members of other groups? Or is there an atmosphere of mistrust, selfishness, and exclusion? A sense of connection to others has been shown to be extremely important to healthy psychological functioning (Barber & Schluterman, 2008; Baumeister & Leary, 1995), and connectedness may be low or missing during acculturation. The presence or absence of social support in community can have a huge impact on well-being.

Ideally, the immigrant or refugee arrives in a hospitable environment. As the Syrian refugee crisis expanded in 2015, a number of countries closed their borders to asylum seekers, flagrantly defying the 1951 Geneva accords on refugees. Justin Trudeau, Canada's newly elected prime minister, responded to the Syrian refugee crisis by stating that Canada would welcome 25,000, greeting the first arrivals personally, and making clear Canada's commitment to providing safe haven (Austin, 2015; "Trudeau Welcomes Syrian Refugees," 2015). Co-ethnics already in the community may also provide support. Co-ethnics share traditions and behavioral norms, can help to nurture children and connect people with jobs, and tend to make familiar foods and other necessities available.

Conversely, community factors may impede healthy adaptation. Immigrants may face exclusionist policies or attitudes, and members of the dominant culture may exhibit great prejudice, leaving the minority persons more aware of their isolation. Close communities that embrace Separation strategies may prevent members from exploring other options for connection and learning outside the ethnic enclave. The social environment may affect immigrants on an individual or family level, or may impact entire communities.

## Family

When people relocate, they often move as a family unit. In families, we have a number of our most intimate relationships and our earliest formative experiences. Acculturation is experienced by all family members together, bringing both benefits and complexities (Ward et al., 2010). Families provide social support and teach us our cultures, and generally give us our best chances for psychological well-being

(Oppedal, 2006; Phinney & Ong, 2002). Surprisingly, family has only recently become a topic in psychological acculturation research, perhaps due to psychology's inherent focus on the individual (Kağıtçıbaşı, 2007), but as with community, one usually finds individuals within families.

Families face a number of challenges in acculturation. Complicated and time-consuming processes of immigration and entry can be costly, potentially draining family resources. Adults who come into contact with another culture may have a very different experience from their children, with some uncomfortable changes in statuses, roles, and behaviors (Chung, 2001). Children may be young enough to learn a new language without accent and to learn normative behaviors more easily, given their greater neuroplasticity. In many cases, children serve as translators in official dealings. This may lead to situations in which parents, who would normally be directing their children's development, become dependent on the children for navigation of the new culture. A child's better adaptation to the alternate culture may give her an unusual amount of power, being the primary member assisting the family with authorities or finding livelihood.

Immigrant children usually grow up attending schools and making friends in the new culture on a daily basis. This exposure makes them likely to adopt different values and beliefs that are not acceptable in their heritage cultures. Conflicts may then result across generations, causing additional stresses in lives of all involved (Phinney, Kim-Jo, Osorio, & Vilhjalmsdottir, 2005; Ward et al., 2010). The migration experience may offer greater freedoms and opportunities, but can place the younger family members at odds with elders rooted in tradition.

Despite some inherent risks and pitfalls, families also provide potential resources for enhanced outcomes. While family cohesion may be threatened in acculturation, strong family bonds provide children with social support and sources of resilience. Families can help to create a strong sense of identity through maintenance of values and traditions, giving children a more cohesive view of who they are (Stuart, Ward, Jose, & Narayanan, 2010). Family-level outcomes are improved by "(1) fostering openness and mutual respect among family members in response to generational conflicts that arise during the acculturation process; (2) enhancing family cohesiveness; and (3) utilizing the social support provided by the family unit" (Ward et al., 2010, p. 29). In these ways, families can actually improve outcomes, providing different trajectories from the expected downward spiral of marginalization.

## Gender Issues

Sex and gender identity determine roles, statuses, rewards, and treatment in any situation, but particularly in migration. In civil unrest and war, women and children experience exceptional hardship that may lead them to relocate; for instance, women may experience rape or widowhood, and children may be orphaned, raped, or conscripted into paramilitary activity (e.g., Bemak et al., 2003). Normal intergender interaction in one culture may be illegal in another, such as using physical violence in disciplining a spouse or child. Life in a different culture often brings about changes in family structure and interaction, such as necessity for women to work or simply to go out of the house. These activities may have been prohibited in their heritage culture. Women may then gain greater independence and autonomy, and men may lose traditional authority.

Attitudes and values always change in the acculturation process, and changes around gender and sexuality may cause particular problems between generations within families, perhaps simply because a teen from a family where marriages are arranged wants to go on a date. Interaction between unrelated males and females is prohibited in many cultures. These changes may cause insecurity, anxiety, and conflict for the whole family, and loss of control has caused some men to react with anger and violence (Denmark, Eisenberg, Heitner, & Holder, 2003; Eckblad et al., 1994).

Challenges for LGBTQ individuals before, during, and after change of cultural context may be exceptionally dramatic (Luu & Bartsch, 2011). Gender or sexual preference issues may have been reasons for immigration or relocation, often under mortal peril in countries where homosexuality is criminalized. Cultural differences in acceptance of alternative gender or sexual identities may press a person to seek a new cultural context, perhaps simply by moving from a rural to a more urban location with more accepting norms, or by fleeing to another country. Oppression may be left behind, or may exist in the new culture. Attitudes toward homosexuality change with acculturation to more liberal cultures, and may bring relief to some. Traditionalists may be extremely uncomfortable with these changes (Luu & Bartsch, 2011; Rosenthal, Levy, & Moss, 2012). Any of these factors can affect the experience of acculturation for better or worse.

## REALITY CHECK

*What is cultural distance and how does it affect people?*

*Why does it matter who lives in your community?*

*What do families often experience during acculturation?*

*How can gender or gender orientation affect acculturation outcomes?*

## 10.5 OUTCOMES OF ACCULTURATION

### LO 10.5: Evaluate the current understanding of acculturation conditions and outcomes for individuals and communities.

Acculturation happens in context of major changes in a person's life situation. In the Holmes-Rahe Life Stress Inventory, stressors have been rated as to severity, with a threshold of 300 marking the point of likely illness. A person will almost certainly face change in financial state (38 points), changes in line of work (36), change in living condition (25), revision of personal habits (24), changes in residence (20), social activity (18), family gatherings (15), and eating habits (15), for 191 points. This does not count a host of other conditions in the new setting or extreme events before departure, like potential deaths of family (63 points). Changes to social roles and deeply held beliefs may also adversely affect the psychological health of people in the process. These factors influenced early assumptions about negative outcomes in acculturation, but other factors are in play as well.

Prior experiences may include horrible traumas that result in post-traumatic stress disorder (Jablensky et al., 1994). Terrible experiences in a new culture may be equally traumatic (le Mesurier, 2011). Throughout those experiences, a person's thoughts and feelings about these conditions may have far-reaching effects on eventual outcomes, including whether a person seeks or accepts treatment resources.

Mental health interacts with physical health, particularly in cases of stress, which causes release of hormones and neurotransmitters related to fight-or-flight reactions. Prolonged stress may cause **adrenocorticotropic hormone syndrome**, where overtaxing of resources may lead to physical and mental illnesses (Dunn & Berridge, 1990; Gallo & Mathews, 2003). This concept ties into the Stress and Coping paradigm of research in terms of how acculturation may increase stresses and how a person's reactions to those stresses may lead to better or worse health outcomes.

Access to and use of healthcare may solve numerous problems. Timely treatment for physical or mental issues may alleviate them quickly and effectively. Cultural learning may be important in health outcomes because access to healthcare requires language skills and understanding of bureaucracies that may be quite alien. If they do make their way to healthcare, migrants' expression or understanding of disorder may differ greatly from that of healthcare professionals. Sometimes, negative mental states are expressed as *somatization*, which is physical perception and/or expression of psychological illness (Marsella & Yamada, 2000; Southard, 1912; Walsh, 1912). Issues of health and treatment are discussed in Chapter 11.

Emphasis on real risks and difficult situations in immigration may misrepresent the actual acculturation experience. Much research up to present has followed the deficit model of the 19th century, assuming that outcomes would be negative. Researchers may be guilty of some confirmation bias in focusing on negative issues. Immigration may actually bring safer, healthier conditions and greater access to better healthcare. While the situations described above are largely negative, it is important to remember that acculturation experiences can also bring healthy, happy outcomes.

The experience of acculturation includes what *actually happens* to the person before, during, and after intercultural contact, and the person's *interpretations* of what goes on during these stages (Marsella, 1999, 2009; Marsella & Ring, 2003). These form experiential and interpretive domains, respectively, and together they shape realities and outcomes of the process. People bring a variety of experiences to the table and can conceptualize and understand what has happened very differently, for good or ill. Acculturation can be an exciting experience of learning a new and wonderful culture, if conditions are right both in the external milieu and in the immigrant's mindset. Positive experiences may lessen effects of previous trauma and positive interactions in the new setting may help make the acculturation process a pleasant one (e.g., Coppens, Page, & Thou, 2005; Son & Kim, 2006). It can be, however, that previous experiences or adverse conditions on arrival may set the stage for mental health issues.

## The Melting Pot and the Salad Bowl

This chapter provides a very broad look at the enormously complex topics of acculturation processes and research. What happens on an individual level depends on an enormous range of possibilities before and during acculturation. These processes extend back centuries in the US, and the conjunctions of indigenous peoples and immigrants have shaped the resulting nation. For the European arrivals, the usually benevolent situation led a French immigrant to remark,

> Whence came all these people? They are a mixture of English, Scotch, Irish, French, Dutch, Germans, and Swedes. . . . What, then, is the American, this new man? He is neither a European nor the descendant of a European; hence that strange mixture of blood, which you will find in no other country. I could point out to you a family whose grandfather was an Englishman, whose wife was Dutch, whose son married a French woman, and whose present four sons have now four wives of different nations. He is an American, who, leaving behind him all his ancient prejudices and manners, receives new ones from the new mode of life he has embraced, the new government he obeys, and the new rank he holds. . . . The Americans were once scattered all over Europe; here they are incorporated into one of the finest systems of population which has ever appeared.

> —J. Hector St. John de Crevecoeur,
> *Letters from an American Farmer* (1782)

In the 19th century, the focus was on ways inferior cultures would be assimilated into dominant culture. At the beginnings of the 20th century, *The Melting Pot* (Zangwill, 1908) described ways multiple cultures would become one, probably dominated by the majority culture, and it was assumed that the burgeoning immigrant communities of the great American cities would blend into a superordinate single culture. The melding never really happened, and civil rights movements around the world made clear the demand that all cultures be valued (Schuck, 1993; Soysal, 1994).

Multiculturalism came to the forefront in the US with a speech in Pittsburgh on 27, October, 1976, when presidential candidate Jimmy Carter said, "We become not a melting pot, but a beautiful mosaic. Different people, different beliefs, different hopes, different dreams." A growing body of social research demonstrates the value of cultural diversity for the health and vitality of communities. Indigenous groups are demanding cultural survival in civil life and in court. Increasingly, it is acknowledged that true social cohesion requires respect for and nurturance of a varied cultural tapestry rather than homogenization (Abele, 2004; Beauvais & Jenson, 2002; Peace et al., 2005).

Emphasis on diversity has led to the metaphor of the salad bowl, in which each culture retains its unique colors and flavors in complement to others (Huddle, 1987). These metaphors and corresponding assumptions in research parallel changes in public policy and effects on acculturative outcomes. The processes are not linear; recent political rhetoric has not always become more accepting, even though social science research supports the ultimate value of diversity. Peace et al. (2005) suggest that governments must balance the need to welcome immigrants inclusively with the need for immigrants to respond to the institutions of the new country. Elements of social inclusion and well-being must be addressed to maintain cohesive societies.

The processes and outcomes of acculturation are relatively recent topics of investigation, and results of inquiry are vigorously debated (e.g., Rudmin, 2010). The acculturation process and its outcomes provide a marvelous area for future research. Many factors in acculturation have already been identified which may interact in numerous ways, and the burgeoning human population leads to dramatically increasing interactions between cultures. Resulting questions include the value of sustaining diversity versus exclusion, balancing potential for intercultural misunderstanding and conflict with benefits of wider ranges of individuals contributing to knowledge and productivity. These dynamics will likely shape progression of research (including funding issues), publication (as it aligns with accepted theories), and public understanding (as theories enter—or do not enter—popular knowledge) for decades to come.

## REALITY CHECK

How can acculturation processes affect mental and physical health?

How does historical context affect acculturation and its outcomes?

Why would issues from before immigration affect outcomes?

How do the concepts of melting pot and salad bowl relate to understanding acculturation?

## 10.6 ACCULTURATION AND THE ARTS IN INTERCULTURAL CONTACT

### LO 10.6: Explain the psychological and practical purposes the arts serve in acculturation.

Arts have formed a core pillar of culture, in the music of our rituals and celebrations, in the clothes and tools we use, and in the images that decorate our lives. When we have migrated through the ages, we have brought our arts with us. The functions of community cohesion and cultural transmission continue as long as a group has its arts, and in fact they may be more important when the group has left their familiar surroundings. The group may lose its sacred ground, but still have their songs and symbols contributing to their sense of identity and cohesion (e.g., Farr, 1997; Gaunt, 2006; de Silva Jayasuriya, 2006).

In migration, traditional musical and artistic practices frequently continue to be preserved and transmitted, sometimes over eons and great distance, as with the Great

Pacific Migration. Much as words follow migration and remain in the deep structure of languages across vast regions, so also do the sounds, images, and stories (Gaunt, 2006; Obeng, 1997; Waseda, 2005). Arts also change to reflect the migration experience, adding elements as cultures meet, and adding stories as the body of experience grows (de Silva Jayasuriya, 2006; Valdez & Halley, 1996).

Despite the obviously large quantity of cultural information within music and other arts, very little psychological research has been conducted regarding the role of arts in acculturation. Study of arts processes has been the academic domain of anthropology, ethnomusicology, and cultural studies (Hargreave & North, 1999). Arts are only just beginning to be examined and explored psychologically in their roles in culture (Stern, 2004; Sussman, 2010). In psychological inquiry that *has* transpired, traditional or ethnic music and dance, particularly, have been shown to strengthen or maintain ethnic identity (Waseda, 2005), alleviate anxiety and homesickness (Son & Kim, 2006), increase social bonds, and facilitate transmission of cultural values (Hargreave & North, 1999). This list is remarkably congruent with the risks and pitfalls of acculturation. In acculturation, arts can be seen to play four general roles: transmitting and maintaining culture across generations and regions, interpreting and expressing the experiences encountered, coping with stressors and maintaining social resources, and connecting to the other groups met along the way.

## Transmitting and Maintaining Culture in Acculturation

Someone leaving home to attend college brings practical items like clothing, but also some mementos of home, their music collection, and some art for the walls. Families in migration, given the time and opportunity, bring their most treasured items, which might include photos or painting of ancestors, traditional clothing, or musical instruments. These might be passed down through generations along with stories of their meaning and origin, providing connection to familial origin and culture. The images and songs carry layers of information. We learn our culture through arts, and cultures carry these encoded lessons as they travel. The legend of the white stag explains how the Huns and Magyars journeyed to settle Hungary in 896 CE, and continues to form a key element in national identity (Makkai, 2000; Selnick, 2012; West, 2000). *The Aeneid of Virgil* (Virgil, 2004) commemorates the founding of Rome by the fleeing Trojans, following their defeat, and justifies their conquest of the Italian peninsula.

Arts travelled the slave-trade routes, as the music, the dances, and their social functions travelled from Africa with the slaves brought to other countries, serving the same psychosocial functions in new lands. Kyra Gaunt's (2006) study of jumping rope and hand-clap games among African American girls shows how these seemingly simple games transmit cultural values and belief systems, traveling in the lyrics and rhythms, and in the cooperative motions. She credits these as key in the development of rap and hip-hop, establishing links from those styles back to pre-slavery roots in Africa. The games are fun and comforting, and while those participating would rarely be aware of the importance or antiquity of what they are doing, it places young children squarely in a centuries-old chain of cultural continuity. The transport of cultural knowledge extends not only to Europe and the Americas, but also across the Indian Ocean.

Notably, Sri Lanka retains a surviving African subculture, established during slavery under the Portuguese (1505–1658), Dutch (1658–1796), and British (1796–1948) colonial eras (de Silva Jayasuriya, 2006; Farr, 1997).

A resurgence of cultural identities began in the Civil Rights movement and other movements around the world, and artistic elements became hallmarks of these efforts. Soul food, soul and funk music, and dashiki type garments became symbols of African American pride. Master *taiko* drummer Kenny Endo was a jazz drummer from Los Angeles during that time. He sought his Japanese identity in the rigorous discipline of *taiko*, spending years studying in Japan, and subsequently passing his knowledge to those who attend his concerts and to thousands of students in Hawai'i.

Indigenous cultures suffered massive losses of population and cultural knowledge over the past few centuries. Hawaiian children were beaten for speaking their language at school and their parents were told speaking anything but English would make them stupid. Native American, Australian Aborigine, and Māori children were taken from their families and placed in boarding schools or foster families. What survives was largely passed down in songs, chants, dances, and tactile arts, now used to enculturate new generations. Native American powwows provide annual opportunities to reassert and transmit identity. Māori maintain a growing number of *marae* ceremonial houses, where *haka* and other traditions live on. Learning the *Kumulipo* creation chant taps hula students into thousands of years of continuous culture. In 2013, a *hula halau* at the Merrie Monarch festival danced in *kapa* fabric beaten from bark for the first time in well over a century, reviving a traditional art that had completely died out when traders brought more convenient fabrics to the islands (see Figure 10.10).

**Figure 10.10   Sabra Kauka Making Kapa**

## Interpreting and Expressing Acculturation Experiences

Intercultural contact brings about a variety of experiences, both good and bad, which must be incorporated into a person's psyche. Migration means a home is left behind, perhaps loved ones, and certainly, one's familiar life. According to Farr (1997), arts "provided a mechanism for communal coping- an expressive outlet with restorative benefits to ensure healthy adaptive functioning, particularly under difficult circumstances" (p. 184). Koreans migrated to Hawai'i in 1903 to work the sugar cane fields and were trapped, unable to return, when the Japanese took political control of the country by military force. The traditional song *Arirang*, with its lyrics about love and loss, came to symbolize the Koreans' loneliness and homesickness, as they spread to the mainland US and ever further from their homeland (Coffman, 2002).

> Arirang
>
> Look on me! Look on me! Look on me!
>
> In midwinter, when you see a flower, please think of me!
>
> Ari-arirang! Ssuri-Ssurirang! Arariga nanne!
>
> O'er Arirang Pass I long to cross today.
>
> —Traditional song, Sejong Cultural Society (2016)

In intercultural contact, music has played an important role of expression and communication in post-colonial processes (Graburn, 2004; James, 1999; de Silva Jayasuriya, 2006; Kramer, 2004). The Berbers of Algeria, both in their native regions and in France, have embraced music and poetry as a nonviolent way to move toward political acknowledgement and autonomy (Goodman, 2005). Across the vastness of Africa, music and dance have always been particularly salient factors in maintaining social cohesion and negotiating transitions, and these functions continued through colonization and slavery. In the United States, rap music (demonstrably an extension of African musical tradition) provides a means of emotional and social expression amidst continued prejudice and suppression (Kopano, 2002). The music has been filtered through church music, blues, jazz, soul, and funk along the way, but continues to serve functions similar to those served before Africans were enslaved and exported. It is for this reason, Farr (1997) explains, that hip-hop dance therapy is effective in treatment of at-risk African American adolescents.

## Coping With Stressors and Maintaining Social Resources via the Arts

Arts practices provide a way to connect members of communities and families in acculturation. Traditional arts provide excellent ways for young people to learn cultural traditions and to connect in positive ways with elders who might otherwise seem distant and strange (Coppens et al., 2005; Miller & Rasco, 2004; Nguyen et al., 1999). Dole and Csordas (2003) observed development of connectedness through participation in traditional ceremonies for Navajo youth. Coppens et al. (2005) observed and evaluated a Cambodian dance program for young Cambodians living in the northeastern US set up to "increase awareness and pride in Cambodian culture, promote healthy behaviors, and create linkages within the community" (p. 321). Music provides an avenue for increasing social cohesion among Latinos in Toledo, Ohio, helping to unify a population that is actually diverse in countries and cultures of origin (O'Hagin & Harnish, 2006). In Hamilton, New Zealand, Guerin, Fatuma, and Guerin (2006) observed Somali refugee women's groups. The women's participation in parties and celebrations involving music and dance "was easily seen as contributing positively to their mental health and well-being, and their feelings of belonging in their new country, as they changed with the better position of the community over time" (p. 4). Loss of social support and resources has been observed to be sources of stress in acculturation (Markovitzky & Mosek, 2005), and arts provide a way to cope with these losses.

Sharing of popular arts also can provide ways to increase connectedness and reduce stresses. Chinese immigrants in Japan hold "dance parties," using certain favorite musical content, in which the shared contact affirms identity and sense of belonging while also providing opportunities to garner social capital and support (Farrer, 2004). Similarly, the tango subculture in New York City provides a means of accessing social networks and resources in the city's Argentinean community (Viladrich, 2005). By far the most widespread use of a popular genre to provide resources of connectedness in acculturation is found in the worldwide dispersion of Bollywood movies, music, and dance in Indian communities across the world (Punathamberkar, 2005). Bollywood brings together people who identify as Indian and can connect to the genre despite generational differences and origins in entirely different ethnic subcultures back in India. In New Zealand, tens of thousands of Indian immigrants gather for annual Diwali festivals with sold-out Bollywood dance competitions (Asia New Zealand Foundation, 2009). These activities, in cultural contexts far removed from the origins of ethnic groups involved, provide ways to increase social support and reduce stressors common in migration (e.g., Jablensky et al., 1994; Marsella & Ring, 2003), and thereby may bring about better adaptation (see Figure 10.11).

## Intergroup Relations and the Arts

Finally, arts provide an avenue for intercultural understanding and beneficial contact, as well as a platform for negotiation of acculturation issues. Obviously, adoption of jazz by the American mainstream demonstrates the acceptance of transplanted African cultural elements by mainstream white culture. Latin music events in Toledo (O'Hagin & Harnish, 2006) provide a means of connecting the Latin community to other ethnic groups (including the dominant group). The researchers were told that experience of Latino musical festivities was perceived by their respondents to help overcome the "Taco Bell" image of Latinos. Inclusion of Latin music elements in school curriculum was seen to help to increase intercultural understanding. Similarly, inclusion of Cape Verde music in Portuguese curriculum reduced skin-color based prejudice among children less than 10 years of age (Sousa, Neto, & Mullet, 2005).

Figure 10.11    Hare Krishna Festival at Avenida Paulista, Sao Paulo, Brazil

*Source:* AllisonGinadaio/istockphoto.com

Exposure to arts of different ethnic groups may help to reduce intergroup conflict in ways that parallel Gordon Allport's contact theory, in which sustained, positive interaction between residents of integrated housing projects in the 1950s was seen to reduce prejudice (Pettigrew & Tropp, 2006). Arts do not provide the direct contact Allport observed but do provide exposure to the beliefs, values, and behaviors of other groups in non-threatening contexts. The oldest people alive in the US grew up with early jazz and gradual integration of big bands (e.g., Mintz, 2012). Those now in their sixties grew up with Motown, soul and funk, and younger generations have listened to reggae, rap, and hip-hop (Gann, 1997). These musical developments occurred alongside the Civil Rights movement and cultural Renaissance movement among Native Americans, Hawaiians, Asian Americans, and others. As our cultural landscape has become more diverse, so have our tastes and the arts we enjoy.

Arts draw their inspiration from daily life and reflect both our increasing diversity and the cultures we have brought on the journey. My own journey into the study of culture began with experiences of music and other arts from various cultures that were initially exotic and fascinating to me. Through playing music with people of numerous cultures, I came to greater understandings of those people and their cultures of origin—and of the ideas and histories they expressed in their music. Arts form avenues of expression, adaptation, and understanding in intercultural contact. Arts participation does not cure all ills, and use of cultural arts may sometimes constitute theft of cultural property (Cameron, 2005). On the brighter side, communication by artistic media and acceptance of arts from different cultures demonstrate hopeful signs that we are becoming more enlightened in our understanding of other cultures and more tolerant of cultural difference.

## REFLECTING ON YOUR READING

- How did the birth of nations affect the current adaptation of immigrants?

- Can you differentiate between the strands of acculturation research? Does one seem to have more merit?

- What factors influence outcomes in acculturation?

- How do the arts assist adaptation in acculturation?

## CHAPTER 10 SUMMARY

### 10.1 Multiculturalism and Migration

Cultures have differentiated over time to such a degree that mutual understanding is difficult. People from different cultures live in ever closer proximity as migration and globalization break down barriers and people leave their traditional regions.

Current social groups attempt to find solutions to issues of diversity. Diversity in groups can be a great asset because different viewpoints tend to lead to better solutions, or conversely to disagreement and misunderstanding. In some countries, immigrants and minorities are vilified and blamed for social ills, while in others, diversity is celebrated. Situations of inter-cultural contact affect us psychologically as we are forced to adapt to new cultural contexts.

Colonial conquests led to violent cultural encounters on a global level. Differing educational opportunities and resource availability have led to new reasons for migration. Simultaneously, demographics are shifting in more affluent countries, stimulating need for labor and certain skilled workers, especially in healthcare. We have become an inescapably multicultural world.

### 10.2 Acculturation and Adaptation

Acculturation describes the processes of adaptation when two or more cultures meet for extended periods of time. It differs from enculturation, which is the normal learning during development within a culture. Sustained contact affects those involved with a range of outcomes from beneficial to disastrous. Acculturation was assumed to be a painful process leading to marginalization or assimilation, negative outcomes viewed as natural during the post-colonial era. Inter-ethnic tensions continue in many developed countries hosting immigrant populations.

Some theorists carefully differentiate between group processes and individual psychological acculturation, and use the term psychological adaptation to describe the outcome. Often large groups of people have migrated together, at times facing prejudice from host cultures. Extreme circumstances sometimes lead people to become refugees or asylum seekers, forced to flee. Internally displaced people are also forced to migrate, but do not cross national borders. These are termed involuntary migrants.

Some people migrate voluntarily for reasons including economic and educational opportunity. Those who do so temporarily are called sojourners. Migrants can also be differentiated as being pushed by circumstance or pulled by desire for an outcome. All of these factors affect the immigrant and may affect future generations.

People crossing cultures encounter a number of predictable difficulties. They must learn new skills, languages, and behaviors in unfamiliar settings, potentially causing considerable stress. They may have had terrible experiences before migration that continue to affect them. These conditions are most intense for involuntary migrants, but are faced to some degree by all migrants. Acculturation effects are also experienced by host cultures, though they face less pressure to adapt.

## 10.3 Approaches to the Psychological Study of Acculturation

Early acculturation research assumed the process would always be painful and outcomes would be dismal. Oberg (1960) coined the term culture shock to describe the process. In 1970, Berry proposed the concept of acculturative stress, which still assumed a negative process, but one that could be assisted through coping techniques.

Acculturation research overall falls into three theoretical approaches: stress and coping, social identity, and cultural learning. Stress and coping research seeks to identify sources of stress and mechanisms to minimize negative consequences. Social identity research deals with how people identify with heritage and host cultures and how this affects them psychologically. The cultural learning paradigm focuses on how people gather the skills necessary for effective functioning in the new culture.

Berry's acculturation strategies are widely accepted in the social identity stream. People may identify with their heritage or host culture independently, leading to outcomes termed *assimilation* (low heritage ID, high host), *separation* (low host ID, high heritage), *marginalization* (low host

ID, low heritage), and *integration* (high host ID, high heritage), with integration assumed to be most beneficial. Frame-switching happens when a person strategically shifts behaviors and attitudes to match host or heritage contexts.

In Ward's (2001) "A.B.C.'s of crossing cultures" (p. 415), "A" is for Affect, from the stress and coping paradigm, "B" is for Behavior, corresponding with cultural learning and "C" is for Cognition, relating to theories of social identity. All have merit, but philosophical and methodological differences make them difficult to connect.

## 10.4 Sociocultural Contexts in Acculturation

Recent research suggests that different levels of analysis and contexts must be considered in acculturation research. Context shapes the processes and outcomes. Cultural distance, how different host and heritage cultures are, forms a primary general-level factor, affecting how easily the person can navigate the new context.

The laws and policies of the host country have serious effects on the process, making life better or more miserable depending on the conditions. Community forms the usual level where other cultures are encountered. The composition of a community determines its effects on minorities and immigrants, including presence of coethnics and acceptance by the mainstream. Cultural distance becomes most important at this level. This is also the level where support can be strongest. Families face particular challenges, with children learning languages and cultures more easily, and parental authority facing numerous challenges. Family cohesion can be threatened in the process, but family can also provide support in the process.

Cultures are structured in ways that specify roles, statuses, and rewards based on gender. Often, these do not align with the new host culture's set of specifications. Familial structures may change, with women gaining and men losing status. These changes are often sources of serious stress. In addition, gender identities may differ in the new culture, particularly in regard to transvestite, homosexual, and transgender identities.

## 10.5 Outcomes of Acculturation

Two sets of factors affect what happens to the physical and mental health of those who acculturate: what happened before acculturation and the conditions in which acculturation happens. Traumas beforehand may have long-term repercussions. Attitudes toward public resources may limit their use by acculturating people. Conversely, beneficial environments may make rapid and lasting improvements in people's lives.

Views of immigration and acculturation are changing. Multiculturalism is replacing preferences for assimilation. Metaphors of a homogenized melting pot are giving way to the collection of identities of a salad bowl. Even assumptions drawn from acculturation research are being replaced at a rapid rate.

## 10.6 Acculturation and the Arts in Intercultural Contact

Arts have always travelled with people throughout our existence. As a part of culture that can travel with us, arts provide a means of maintaining and transmitting culture in the process. Numerous examples support this view. Arts provide a means by which acculturating people can express their experience and reach greater understanding through dialogic processes. Arts also provide ways to maintain and increase social supports in acculturation, and to engage in therapeutic processes of expression. In acculturation, arts are likely to pass interculturally both directions, regardless of dominance. They provide a relatively non-threatening avenue to experience other cultures, and in that context, they convey rich information that can increase understanding. Arts may serve as a mechanism to increase contact and subsequent understanding.

## GLOSSARY

**Acculturation:** The processes of accommodation that occur when individuals or groups from two or more cultures come into sustained, direct contact.

**Adaptation:** The processes of accommodating new, changing, or different environmental circumstances.

**Adrenocorticotropic hormone syndrome:** The process that occurs when adrenalin and related chemicals are present in the body for a sustained period of time, leading to depletion of physiological resources and susceptibility to illness.

**Affect:** Emotional feelings and expression.

**Assimilation:** The condition in acculturation wherein the individual abandons the culture of origin, instead adopting and embracing the dominant or host culture.

**Asylum seekers:** Individuals seeking shelter and protection from the government of another nation because of repression or persecution in their own country.

**Bicultural:** Having origins in or associations with two cultural or ethnic groups.

**Bicultural identity integration:** A term conceptualizing the degree to which an individual feels two or more cultural identities are compatible.

**Civil war:** Formalized armed conflict between two or more factions within a nation or country.

**Co-ethnics:** People of the same ethnic origin living within a community.

**Collectivist:** A way of being in which one focuses attention more on group affiliation than on individual autonomy.

**Colonialism:** A geopolitical movement primarily occurring in the 15th to 20th centuries, during which European nation states sought political and economic domination of other countries and regions.

**Cultural distance:** The discrepancy between the elements of two cultures, including language, customs, behavioral norms, world view, etc.

**Culture shock:** Oberg's concept of the effects of sudden cultural displacement on the individual psyche.

**Demographics:** Characteristics of a population, such as age, ethnicity, income, social status, etc.

**Diversity:** In politics and social sciences, a term for population characteristics including multiple ethnicities, religious persuasions, gender orientations, and/or other socioeconomic characteristics.

**Enculturation:** The process of learning the ways of being, thinking, and acting as a member of a cultural group, occurring naturally during lifespan development.

**Ethnic enclaves:** Geographic locations with a high concentration of an ethnic group or minority.

**Frame-switching:** Changes in behavior and thought experienced by individuals using an integrated strategy of adaptation in multicultural living situations when they go from one cultural context to another.

**Ghettoization:** Localization of an immigrant or minority ethnic group in a particular area characterized by low income, lack of access to public process and services, isolation from other ethnicities, and/or prejudicial treatment by dominant groups.

**Immigrant:** A person who has left his or her nation of origin to live long term in another country.

**Indigenous:** In social sciences, an ethnic group with a long history of living in a particular region, usually considered to have begun prior to colonization, occupation, or domination by another country or ethnic group.

**Integration:** In political and educational settings, the inclusion of diverse groups as members, clients, or participants. Individually, the acculturation strategy in which a person embraces cognitive and behavioral elements of two or more cultures.

**Internally displaced persons:** People who have been forced to leave their native region due to armed conflict, natural disaster, or other circumstances but who have not crossed a national border.

**Marginalization:** In acculturation, the status in which an individual feels no membership or affiliation with either her culture of origin or the host/dominant culture(s).

**Melting pot:** A term from the late 19th century describing the mixing of ethnic immigrant groups in the cities of the United States. The concept assumed that all of the distinct cultural elements would be subsumed into a superordinate amalgamated culture.

**Migration:** Movement from one region to another.

**Multiculturalism:** The existence or embracing of ethnocultural diversity within a sociopolitical entity such as a community or state.

**Nation-state:** The modern geopolitical entity equivalent to a country, usually with internationally recognized borders and governance systems, often dividing or comingling ethnocultural groups against their wishes.

**Orthogonal:** In statistical analyses, domains that move independently, in other words, ones which can be higher or lower without correlation.

**Prejudice:** An ingrained or systematic attitude applied categorically to a set or subset of people, for instance against a particular ethnocultural group.

**Psychological acculturation:** The behavioral, affective, and cognitive changes that occur when an individual comes into sustained, direct contact with an unfamiliar culture.

**Psychological adaptation:** The processes of accommodating behavioral, affective, and cognitive differences encountered when an individual comes into sustained, direct contact with an unfamiliar culture.

**Refugees:** People who have been forced to leave their country of origin due to armed conflict, natural disaster, or other circumstances and have crossed a national border in the process. Certain international treaties require that nations provide certain levels of accommodation to refugees if they attempt to enter the country.

**Salad bowl:** A recent term for the interaction of different ethnicities in communities that is now preferred to the term *melting pot*. In the salad bowl, each culture can maintain some level of uniqueness, as opposed to the homogenization expected in the past.

**Separation:** The condition in acculturation wherein the individual embraces only his or her culture of origin and does not adopt elements, beliefs, or practices of the dominant or host culture.

**Sojourner:** Individuals who live for a limited amount of time in a different culture or country for purposes such as education or employment.

# HEALTH AND WELL-BEING

## Chapter 11 Outline

## Learning Objectives

**LO 11.1** Describe ways health may be conceptualized and how this may differ around the world.

**LO 11.2** Compare physical health conditions around the world and the relationship of these patterns to mental health.

**LO 11.3** Discuss perspectives on well-being as conceptualized across cultures and ways the concept can be operationalized for measurement.

**LO 11.4** Identify components of mental health across cultures and how differences affect diagnosis and epidemiology.

**LO 11.5** Summarize approaches to maintenance and restoration of mental health and how these relate to underlying belief systems.

**LO 11.6** Identify ways cultural arts affect health and well-being.

# PREPARING TO READ

- What would you say is most necessary for your own sense of well-being?

- Can you define health? Can you define well-being? How can these be measured in a meaningful way?

- Does well-being depend on happiness, or are other concepts, such as meaningful work or freedom, crucial to its achievement?

*Pania spends time by the sea every morning and evening listening to voices in the wind and waves. When she faces life decisions, her father may tell her what to do, and her maternal grandmother, grandfather, and great-grandfather speak to her often. She hears their advice about questions and issues she faces in life, and she always follows their counsel as best she can. Her father died eight years ago, the grandparents died before she was 10, and the great-grandfather before she was born. Pania hears their voices and others in the rustling of leaves in the wind, in the gurgling of the river and crashing of the waves, and in signs conveyed by the birds and animals she encounters. Pania has been this way since her late teens. Were she living in an American city, these characteristics could well be interpreted as symptoms of schizophrenia. If she lives on a remote Pacific island, however, or in a host of other traditionally oriented locales, it may be that everyone consults their ancestors and feels intimately connected to the wisdom of nature. Any other way of being would seem sad and strange, and her people would worry about her isolated condition. Their concern might be well founded.*

## 11.1 HEALTH AND WELLNESS

### LO 11.1: Describe ways health may be conceptualized and how this may differ around the world.

Discussion of health and well-being in any situation involves a number of considerations. Are we talking about physical health, mental health, or both? Are the two separable? What causes people to become ill, either physically or mentally, and how can they be cured, if a cure is needed? Ultimately, we want to understand why people die, and how death can be prevented or delayed. Given that no culture has found an escape from the grim reaper's scythe, we invest massive time and resources into fixing what ails our bodies and to discovering or inventing ways to make our time wandering the mortal realm as pleasant and meaningful as possible, or in other words, toward creating the greatest amount of **well-being** for ourselves and our loved ones while we are here.

As we shall see, cultures normally include understandings of well-being and paths to its achievement, but we do not agree on the paths or even on the exact destination. Science helps greatly with physical health, but is less effective at reliably producing happiness. It would be a rare scientist who has skills for approaching the entire topic: physical and mental health along with social and environmental conditions, equitable use of resources, and a host of other issues that affect the quality of our lives. Then one faces difficulties of quantification for empirical research. Is well-being objectively measurable, or is a person's own perception of their well-being the only relevant indicator? If a person feels healthy and satisfied, is that not sufficient? Are there absolute thresholds of health or well-being, or must we compare groups to establish relative levels? When crossing national or cultural boundaries, these questions may become even cloudier, with differing perceptions of what is sufficient for a good life: A refugee fleeing war may be deeply thankful just to be free of bombings and armed insurgents, while a business executive in Manhattan may feel deeply distressed that she only took home six figures last year. More questions emerge around causes and treatment of disease, and especially of what constitutes a normal or disordered mind.

Pania's story is fictional, but drawn from very real examples: in a great many indigenous and traditional cultures around the globe, connection to ancestors and nature is considered crucial to normal functioning. The Blackfeet of what is now Montana listen to their ancestors, surrounding spirits, and physical environment in this way, finding answers from the sacred spaces and the spirits who walked those lands before (Carbaugh, 1999), and this is true of many traditional cultures around the world. Consulting spiritual sources is surprisingly common in post-industrial cultures as well. Ronald Reagan scheduled his 1967 inauguration as California governor at 12:10 AM for best astrological effect, and celebrity astrologer Joan Quigly visited the White House often during his presidency (Regan, 1988; Roberts, 1988). The question of mental health may hinge more on an individual's functionality and the norms of the surrounding milieu than the objective existence of signs, psychics, and spirits. While reliance on astrology by the leader of a major global power is a bizarre state of affairs, his consultations were widely known, and he remains a respected historic figure. Clearly such behavior and belief is part of the fabric of American life, whether for good or ill, and relatively few people are disturbed by the practice.

Health and well-being span a range of concerns. Physical health seems straightforward, but ways people believe they can maintain or restore health has changed across time and locale. Ancient systems such as Chinese and Ayurvedic Indian medicine have long histories of success and are still widely used, though they differ greatly from modern biomedical constructs. Health includes physical and mental components that interact; physical illness impacts mental states, and mental illnesses such as depression or PTSD can affect physical health. Well-being is a concept used to describe a person's physical and mental states, along with emotional and material stability and satisfaction, a complex calculation even after decades of research. Further, cultures differ in what they value in achieving well-being. Mental health is even more complex, as fictitious Pania and actual Reagan demonstrate, because what is normal thinking for one person or culture may seem delusional to another. The relentless pursuit of power and material wealth may be far more bizarre to some non-Western people than listening to the wind for answers is to a modern American. The chapter concludes, as usual, with arts, which have always been tools for creating cohesive, healthy lives, and which are now a topic of growing interest in supporting psychological health, managing pain, and creating well-being, among other topics.

# SPOTLIGHT

## THE GIFT OF DISEASE

Across cultures and throughout time, humans have battled pestilence and disease as best they can, drawing on the experiences and awareness handed down to them from their predecessors. Every so often, disease has been said to bring great gifts, with lore of diseased or deformed people rewarded with exceptional powers. When the gods gathered at Teotihuacan to create the Fifth Sun that lights our present world, the Nauatl people of central Mexico say only the sickly and tumorous god Nanahuatzin had the courage to sacrifice himself in the sacred fire to bring light to humanity (Florescano & Bork, 2014; see Figure 11.1). The concept of the wounded healer appears as a cross-cultural

### Figure 11.1    Mayan God Nanahuatzin

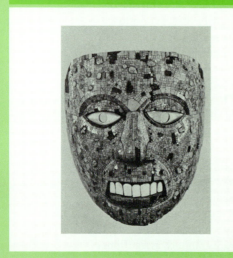

*Source:* Ullstein Bild Dtl./Getty Images

archetype, a person who through tragedy or illness has received the ability to heal or do great things. Carl Jung discusses Chiron, who was one such mythological character, wisest of the half-horse half-human centaurs. He was poisoned by the blood of Hydra, but as an immortal, he could never die. He wandered the Earth healing others despite his own great pain, until he gave up his immortality to save Prometheus. He watches over us today as the constellation Sagittarius. To Jung, the therapist's understanding of his own inner wounds is what allows him to bring healing to the patient (Groesbeck, 1975; Kirmayer, 2003).

The wounded healer archetype reverberates across cultures and epochs, with shaman, sage, and healer learning their art via their own suffering. Black Elk (1932/1991), a revered healer and visionary of the Lakota, had his great vision when he fell unconscious as a child. Sun Dancers of the Lakota and other Plains nations attach themselves to the central Sun Dance pole by piercing their flesh and dance for days without food or sleep in order to bring healing and prosperity to the tribe. Benziman, Kannai, and Ahmad (2012) detail experience of pain or induced illness during initiation of healers in Arthurian and Norse legends, cultures of Africa, India, and China, and in Islamic and Jewish traditions. Across the globe, illness brings suffering, but it also brings opportunity for transformation (Koss-Chioino, 2006). More frequently, however, diseased mortals were reviled not only for the illness they carried, but also for whatever misstep others assumed they had made to bring misfortune on themselves and their compatriots.

## Health vs. Disease

Knowledge of what causes disease has blossomed over the past few centuries, as technology and scientific method have become commonplace. Modern Western epistemology splits health and disease into a mutually exclusive binary, constituted in the physical world. From influenza to Dengue fever to schizophrenia, the Western biomedical paradigm considers pathology, disorder, and disease to exist as objective states described and diagnosed by specific sets of symptoms. These are assumed to arise from particular physical or situational causes such as bacterial or viral contagions, environmental toxins, or bad parenting. The diseased state exists as a hard fact, independent of social constructs or perceptions (Hatala, 2014). For a great many disorders, the biomedical model is fantastically successful; the discovery of microbial pathogens provided explanation for a huge number of illnesses, and provided avenues to fight them. The Western biomedical model is a recent innovation, but after only a couple of centuries of research, medical technologies including genetic analysis, advanced imaging, organ and joint replacement, and many others correct conditions that previously brought untold suffering. It is not perfect, however, and does not prevent or cure all illness, mental or physical.

The dichotomy of health and illness and even the reliance on the Cartesian logic of scientific method arise from particular ways of thinking, the analytical pattern discussed in Chapter 7. The West only progressed from conceptualizations of illness arising from witchcraft and the evil eye in recent centuries. In other cultures and eras, including Chinese and Ayurvedic systems, diseases may be seen to arise from energetic or spiritual origins, leading to more holistic understandings of treatment and health maintenance. Despite its many successes, numerous questions remain unanswered in the Western model, regarding certain conditions, reasons one person thrives while another gets sick, and other mysteries of mortal life. Disease and disorder are understood and experienced differently across cultures, with different prognosis for recovery in some cases, and using other treatment methodologies including acupuncture, herbs, and chanting. By examining other ways of understanding health and disorder, we can learn about the underlying epistemologies that lead to those beliefs, and we may find valuable clues to the unanswered questions of our own systems.

## REALITY CHECK

What has caused you to get sick in the past?

Have you prayed for someone to be healed?

Do you know someone wise? Did that person suffer on the way to wisdom?

Are there things you do to maintain your health?

# 11.2 PHYSICAL HEALTH AROUND THE WORLD

## LO 11.2: Compare physical health conditions around the world and the relationship of these patterns to mental health.

UN Declaration of Human Rights (1948), Article 25(1) stipulates:

Everyone has the right to a standard of living adequate for the health and well-being of himself and of his family, including food, clothing, housing and medical care and necessary social services, and the right to security in the event of unemployment, sickness, disability, widowhood, old age or other lack of livelihood in circumstances beyond his control. (Haworth & Hart, 2007 p. 1)

Health and well-being would seem to be straightforward concepts shared across humanity. After WWII, nations came together to establish certain basic parameters to which all humans should be entitled, enumerated in Article 25 above. Obviously, humanity has not reached these goals, even decades later. While some countries make great efforts to support the welfare of all citizens, others do not, either because they lack resources, because those in control do not distribute resources in such a way as to prevent poverty, or because leaders hold an ideology counter to governmental provision of social supports. In cases of war or of natural disasters such as drought, entire regions may experience hellish conditions for years on end. Intentionally or by happenstance, people experience conditions that differ by country, region, ethnic group, socioeconomics, and many other factors, all of which affect health and well-being, including factors that are cultural in their origin.

Life expectancy data provide a widely accepted gauge for overall health (National Center for Health Statistics [NCHS], 2015). As of 2013, people of Sierra Leone had the lowest life expectancy, at an average of 45.5 years. Highest was Hong Kong at 83.8, followed by Japan at 83.3 and Iceland at 83.1. In that year, the US ranked 47th of the 235 countries monitored, at 78.8 years (World Bank Group, 2015). In the United States, the NCHS provides data for average life expectancy delineated by demographics. The 2013 average life expectancy at birth for the US was 77.4 for males and 81.2 for females, meaning the average child born in 2013 would be expected to live for that long (NCHS, 2015). Of great interest, differences emerge when lifespan is estimated by ethnic group: white American males are expected to live 76.5 years, significantly longer than black males at 71.8 years, but Hispanic males live longest at 79.1 years. The pattern holds true for females also, with projected lifespans of 78.1 for black females, 81.2 for white, and 83.8 for Hispanic women. Explanations for these differences may include diet and other lifestyle choices, as well as different sorts of stresses faced in daily life, which will be discussed in the following sections.

Lengths of these average lifespans are unprecedented in human history. At the end of the 19th century, life expectancy was about 45 years, and in a few short decades, rose to 75 years in the developed world. In developing regions, increases have been slower, but increased by 20 years between 1960 and 2000 (Soares, 2007). By 1822, René Louis

# Figure 11.2  Health vs. Wealth by Country

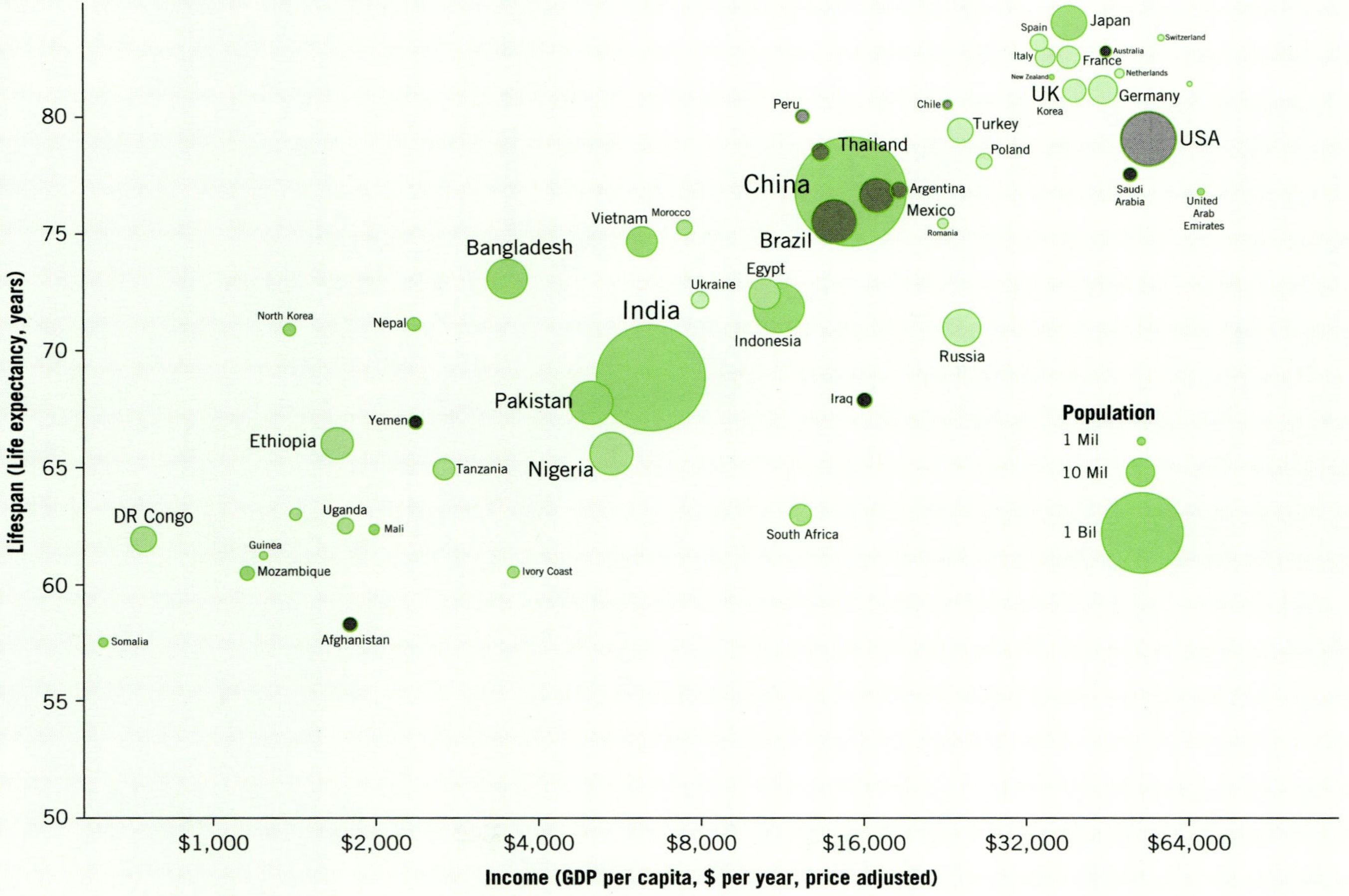

**Population**
- 1 Mil
- 10 Mil
- 1 Bil

Lifespan (Life expectancy, years)

Income (GDP per capita, $ per year, price adjusted)

*Source:* Courtesy of Gapminder.

Villermé observed and documented the relation between poverty and crude mortality rate, and he confirmed the link in the massive cholera epidemic that swept Europe and North America in 1832 (Julia & Valleron, 2011). Poverty remains the confederate of higher mortality today, harbinger of suffering around the world (see Figure 11.2).

The rise in life expectancy in recent centuries has coincided with an increase in per capita income, and conventional wisdom has held that increased income is the driver of increased longevity. A number of factors have caused Soares (2007) and others to question this causal link, including continuing longevity increases in Bolivia and other countries despite economic reversals, and a continuing longevity rise despite stagnation of wages in the US since the early 1990s. Robert Fogel (1986, 2004) instead ties lifespan increases primarily to the rising efficiency of agricultural production and resulting better nutrition.

Fogel and his colleague Dora Costa (1997) use the term **technophysio evolution** to describe changes in human physiology and health that have resulted from technology and our growing knowledge base. The rise of mechanized agriculture has fueled a meteoric rise in human population over the past three centuries. In addition to the greater variety and quantity of food generally available due to improved agriculture, contaminants in water and food supply are drastically reduced, and more robust bodies are more resistant to disease. Clean water alone accounts for an estimated 43% reduction in general mortality between 1900 and 1936, and for a 74% reduction in infant mortality (Cutler & Miller, 2005; Soares, 2007). Effects of improved health and nutrition reverberate across the lifespan, beginning with the health of mothers before and during pregnancy, and continuing throughout the lifespan of her children.

## Mothers and Children

*One third of all that were ever quick, die under five years old.*

*John Graunt (1661, p. 16)*

The average lifespan globally and in most regions drastically exceeds what it was through the end of the 19th century, but it is a common misconception that there were no old people. A huge factor in the increase is the drop in infant mortality. If roughly a third of all children born alive die as infants, the average lifespan drops considerably, no matter how long the survivors of childhood may live. Out of any 300 people before 1700 AD, the deaths of 1/3 in infancy or early childhood were a fact of life around the world. If the other 200 lived to age 50, the average life expectancy would be 33 years. If the other 200 live to 60, the average lifespan is 40 years, which was indeed the norm toward the end of the 19th century; even before modern medicine and agriculture, a goodly number of people lived to a respectable old age. Life for infants and young children was, however, fraught with disease and death, and their loss contributed to the brevity of average lifespan.

The same conditions that allow us to survive infancy and live longer improve our health and well-being from conception onward. Nervous systems and organs require good nutrition for formation, and the result drastically affects people's health and abilities across the lifespan (Fogel, 2004). Poverty, malnutrition, and neglect in utero, in infancy, and in childhood will have lifelong effects on physical growth and health, but also on **mental development**, which is a term used to describe "growth in cognitive, language, social, and emotional capabilities" (Aboud & Yousafzai, 2015, p. 434). A child deprived during these early years will become a person less capable of communication, learning, and critical thinking forever after.

The negative effects of early deprivation are strongest in the poorest nations (see Table 11.1a and b), but poverty affects some portion of children everywhere. In 2012, UNICEF (the United Nations Children's Fund) published a report card measuring child poverty in the 35 most economically advanced countries in the world, including Great Britain and other European Union countries, the United States and Canada, New Zealand and Australia, and Japan (UNICEF Innocenti Research Centre, 2012). Iceland had the fewest children in poverty, with 4.7% living in households earning below 50% of the median income. The United States ranked 34th of 35, with 23.1% below the poverty threshold. Governments differ widely in what they provide their citizens, even when resources are available. Of affluent nations, the US is furthest from providing conditions for its children that meet the 1948 minimum parameters.

A healthy child needs a healthy mother who had good nutrition during pregnancy and enough food to lactate sufficiently during infancy. Women face mortal risks in pregnancy and childbirth, and while modern medicine has improved their chances, women die from pregnancy and birth complications in every country. The clergy of Sweden began collecting maternal death data in 1751, providing the oldest comprehensive data on the topic. At that time, Sweden's maternal mortality rate was 1,046 per 100,000 live births. The rate dropped below 400 for the first time in 1856, and below 1, at .86 per 100,000 in 1993 (Hanson, 2010). The current maternal mortality rate calculation includes the number of women dying during pregnancy or within 42 days of giving birth, and Finland, Greece, Iceland, and Poland have the lowest at 3 per 100,000 live births. Sierra Leone is worst of 216 countries reporting, at 1,360 (World Bank Group, 2015), which is worse than Sweden's rate before the advent of modern medicine.

In very real ways, maternal health determines the health of families, communities, and nations. Of 179 countries ranked on overall maternal health by the Save the Children organization in 2015, the United States ranked 33rd. Norway rated the best and Somalia, unsurprisingly, had the worst maternal health. Due to the major health risks of pregnancy, birth control contributes greatly to improved health of women. Particularly, due to the threat of HIV/AIDS in Africa, condoms save millions of women's lives each year.

Another major contributor to the health of both women and children is education. Gakidou, Cowling, Lozano, and Murray (2010) examined census data from 175 countries spanning the years 1970 to 2009 for evidence of effects of women's educational attainment on child mortality. Globally, the mean number of years of education for all adults over 25 years of age increased from 4.7 to 8.3 years for men, and from 3.5 to 7.1 years for women. In developing countries, education for women of child-bearing age (15–44 years) increased from 2.2 to 7.2 years. The researchers compiled child mortality rates for those years, which included mortality increases due to the AIDS epidemic. Controlling for increase in a country's gross domestic product (GDP) and other factors that could be affecting child mortality, they estimated that 8.2 million fewer children died than predicted by 1970 rates, of which 4.2 million could be attributed to the substantial increase in maternal educational attainment.

Malala Yousafzai comes from a Pakistani family that runs a number of schools. At age 11, she began to blog under an assumed name about her life in the Swat Valley, where the Taliban had forbidden education of young girls. She quickly rose to fame for her advocacy of education for girls, and a 2010 documentary about her brought international recognition and a nomination by Archbishop Desmond Tutu for the International Children's Peace Prize. It also brought the attention of the Taliban. In 2012, a Taliban gunman boarded her school bus and shot her in the head. She survived and was awarded the 2014 Nobel Peace Prize, among a host of international honors (Yousafzai, 2013). When Malala speaks of the rights of girls and women to receive an education, she addresses a wide range of conditions beyond simply learning to read. An educated woman is likely to be healthier and to have healthier children, and she has a better chance of higher income. All of these factors will improve conditions for her descendants over successive generations.

## Education and Health

As is the case with mothers, education brings better health for everyone, and this holds true across nations and cultures. Mary Silles (2009) used historical data from the United Kingdom to ascertain whether the relationship between education and health is causal. Changing laws about compulsory education provided evidence across five decades beginning in 1935 showing that better education clearly improved health. A number of mechanisms may contribute to the education–health link. More education leads to higher income, which is another correlate of better health, but Cutler and Lleras-Muney (2006) demonstrated that income ceases to explain improvement once it is sufficient to provide access to healthcare. Certainly, income is a contributing factor, but so are the more informed lifestyle choices, better knowledge of medical issues and treatments, and higher social status that education brings (Currie, 2008; Gakidou et al., 2010; Silles, 2009). Education related health disparities may actually be more extreme than generally reported in published research, because better educated people report their health behaviors and conditions more accurately, with health problems underreported by the less educated (Cawley & Choi, 2015). Surprisingly, the accuracy gap holds true even for socially undesirable behaviors like smoking, to which more educated people confess more readily. Ultimately, education is a clear path to better physical and mental health.

## Stress and Health

Stress impacts health on both psychological and physical levels. In 1956, endocrinologist Hans Seyle published *The Stress of Life*, describing the consequences of stress exposure for laboratory animals. As exposure to extreme temperatures, electric shocks or other harsh environmental stimuli continued, the animals experienced first alarm, then resistance, and finally, exhaustion, ultimately destroying the creature's health.

The alarm/resistance/exhaustion model was also later confirmed in human subjects, and thus began decades of research into topics of stress and health, and terms such as *stressed out* entered the language.

Thomas Holmes and Richard Rahe (1967) noted that Navy medical records indicated a trend where major changes in patients' lives preceded need for medical care, leading them to apply Seyle's paradigm to stressful events in human lives. They found 43 types of events reported widely by veterans with major health issues, and asked a number of individuals to rate the difficulty of readjustment for each. Death of a spouse was considered worst, and they rated it as 100, worst on their resulting Social Readjustment Scale (Holmes & Rahe, 1967). Divorce scores 73, and death of a close relative and incarceration both rate 63. A positive experience like marriage also requires significant readjustment, with marriage rating 50 on the scale. A change in eating habits rates 15. Scores are added together, and a total of 150 or less is considered good. At scores of more than 300, the model predicts an 80% chance that the person will become sick in the near future.

Numerous studies have used the scale since publication. At first, researchers focused on acute changes in people's lives, but more recent research has highlighted the effects of ongoing chronic stressors, such as insufficient income to pay bills or caring for a disabled child or parent (Thoits, 2010). As with Seyle's animals, damage to the person increases as intensity and duration of stressors goes up. R. Jay Turner and colleagues have spent years cataloging and assessing the effects of negative events, traumas, and chronic stressors, and how cumulative stressors affect mental health (e.g., Barrett & Turner, 2005; Turner & Avison, 2003). They find that chronic strains affect mental health more strongly than acute stresses, when examined over time.

Cumulative life stressors disproportionately affect minorities, immigrants, refugees, and war survivors (Thoits, 2010). Immigrants and refugees often experienced traumas and/or years of highly stressful life conditions prior to their relocation, and face obstacles and difficulties in their new homes. In addition, all of these groups bear burdens of prejudice and discrimination, increasing their daily load of stress through the direct experience of discriminatory acts, but also due to lower income, lower quality housing or homelessness, and a stream of daily hassles. Cumulative advantage/disadvantage theory (Dannefer, 2003) helps to explain how outcomes diverge for dominant and minority ethnic groups and people of higher or lower SES. In short, the small stresses of daily life (or their absence) expand over time to result in very different experiences of mental and physical health, especially in old age. These effects also proliferate across successive generations, widening inequality in health and well-being, but Thoits (2010) points out that high levels of mastery, self-esteem, and/or social support can reduce impacts of stressors on health and well-being. Growing evidence also shows that simply maintaining a happy outlook forms a path to better health (Sabatini, 2014). Protective factors are built into some traditional cultures, as with the social support of *taha whanau* in the Māori's *Whare tapa wha* of healthy self (see Chapter 4). Currently, low SES and cultural oppression work against these cultural resources, often yielding lower health and well-being for ethnic minorities around the world, but they provide a culturally congruent path to health if cultural resources are supported.

## Inequality in Health

In all developed nations, ethnic minorities experience significant disadvantages in health and wellness due to a number of factors. Minority youth statistically experience poorer nutrition, poorer educational opportunities, and physical violence, which lead to poorer health, lower income, and more frequent incarceration as they enter adulthood and begin having children who experience the cycle again. In the US, the Centers for Disease Control and Prevention (CDC) conduct biennial studies of risk behaviors of high school youths, with data from 2013 to 2017 to follow. Only part of these data is parsed by ethnicity, and then only for white, black, and Hispanic categories, with slightly different analysis each time. Some differences by ethnicity defy stereotype. Interestingly, a number of risk behaviors in 2013 were more common among white American youth than either black or Hispanic youth, including cigarette smoking, with whites at 18.6%, blacks at 8.2%, and Hispanics at 14%. Two years later, this had dropped to 12.4% for whites, 9.2% for Hispanics, and 6.5% for blacks (Kann et al., 2016). In 2017, rates dropped to 11.1% for whites, 7% for Hispanics, and 4.4% for blacks (Kann et al., 2018).

Texting or e-mailing while driving follows similar patterns, as does having carried a weapon during the preceding month (Kann et al., 2014). Experience of sexual dating violence was highest in 2013 among Hispanic females (16%), followed by white females (14.6%), and black females (8.8%). Rates in 2017 dropped to 11.4% for Hispanic females, followed by white females (11.1%), and black females (6.8%) Among males, sexual dating violence was experienced by 2.7% of black males, 2.5% of Hispanic males, and 2.6% of white males.

The study also monitors prevalence of mental health concerns, and these show a different pattern. As an indicator of depression, youths were asked if they had felt sad or hopeless during the 12 months before the survey. In 2015, prevalence was highest among Hispanic females (46.7%), followed by white females (37.9%) and black females (33.9%). For males, prevalence was again highest for Hispanics (24.3%), followed by whites (19.2%) and blacks (17.6%). Measured by need for treatment by a medical professional, suicide was attempted most often by Hispanic females (5.4%), followed by black females (3.2%) and white females (2.8%; Kann et al., 2014). Obviously, our ethnic origins affect our health outcomes, for a variety of contextual, social, and cultural reasons. Physical and mental health combine with stress and these other factors ultimately to produce what researchers came to call well-being, described more fully in the next section.

## REALITY CHECK

How has life expectancy changed over time?

Why is it important for women to be educated?

What are the effects of stress on well-being?

Do the data on health by ethnicity surprise you?

# 11.3 UNDERSTANDING WELL-BEING

## LO 11.3: Discuss perspectives on well-being as conceptualized across cultures and ways the concept can be operationalized for measurement.

The UN Declaration of Human Rights Article 25(1) establishes a set of criteria for physical and practical conditions people need to live decently. Absent from the list are less tangible concepts like happiness, honor, satisfaction, or love, but for many people, these are crucial components of well-being. The World Health Organization (WHO, 2006) describes health as "a state of complete physical, mental and social well-being and not merely the absence of disease or infirmity" (p. 1). In their review of well-being literature, Haworth and Hart (2007) found a range of definitions including "happiness, satisfaction, enjoyment, contentment, and engagement and fulfillment, or a combination of these and other hedonic and eudaimonic factors" (p. 1). These are highly subjective factors that may change often, and depend heavily on conditions in surrounding milieu of family, community, region, and nation (Greve, 2008), and these intangible elements are not easily quantified.

### Defining and Measuring Well-Being

Researchers have debated a global definition of well-being over the past several decades, developing scales along the way to measure the components they ascribe to the concept. McKennell (1974) determined that scales at that time included a mix of affective indicators, measuring how people felt, and cognitive indicators, measuring how people thought about their lives. In 1986, Kammann and Flett described two slightly different categories for measurement of well-being: "(a) a complete and lasting satisfaction with life as a whole," which could include elements of McKennell's cognitive component; and "(b) a preponderance of good or pleasurable feelings and a scarcity of unpleasant feelings" (p. 3), which includes affective aspects. Notably, these concepts are still subjective in nature, in other words, measuring the participant's internal perspective, as opposed to more objective, externally observable factors, leading some researchers to prefer the term **subjective well-being** (e.g., Diener, 1984).

In 1985, the World Health Organization published an extensive review of research on well-being by Rup Nagpal and Helmut Sell, who attempted to distill the many concepts and indices available at that time into a cohesive set, in order to establish a concise, measurable list that could be used across cultures. In a process they termed *stepwise ethnographic exploration*, Nagpal and Sell brainstormed with colleagues and conducted extensive interviews and focus groups to identify eight areas of importance for well-being in any culture:

- Subjective well-being—positive affect

- Subjective well-being—negative affect

- Mental mastery over self

- Rootedness, belongingness

- Structural and cohesive aspects of family life

- Density of social network

- Security in crisis (socioeconomic and related to health)

- Expectation-achievement harmony (p. 13)

With the exception of negative affect, which describes bad feelings and is ideally low, these items describe what is good in a person's life. Diener (1984) had recently commented on the irony that, while the great philosophers of history have focused on happiness as the ultimate human goal, psychology has focused on an extensive exploration of human unhappiness. Nagpal and Sell (1985) were among those who intend to change the paradigm. Well-being research is a growing area of interest reaching across national and cultural boundaries.

## Well-Being Around the World

The Gallup survey and research corporation recently undertook the largest global study of well-being in history, completing data collection in 2013. Over a six-year period, the organization interviewed more than a million individuals in the United States, along with more than 133,000 interviews across 135 other countries. The researchers identified five categories of elements crucial to well-being and asked participants to rate two items assessing their subjective views on their status in each (see Table 11.1a). Countries

| Table 11.1a | Global Well-Being Index Categories, Descriptions, and Survey Questions | |
|---|---|---|
| **Category** | **Description** | **Statements** |
| **Purpose** | Liking what you do each day and being motivated to achieve your goals | You like what you do every day. You learn or do something interesting every day. |
| **Social** | Having supportive relationships and love in your life | Someone in your life always encourages you to be healthy. Your friends and family give you positive energy every day. |
| **Financial** | Managing your economic life to reduce stress and increase security | You have enough money to do everything you want to do. In the last seven days, you have worried about money. |

| Category | Description | Statements |
|----------|-------------|------------|
| **Community** | Liking where you live, feeling safe, and having pride in your community | The city or area where you live is a perfect place for you. |
| | | In the last 12 months, you have received recognition for helping to improve the city or area where you live. |
| **Physical** | Having good health and enough energy to get things done daily | In the last seven days, you have felt active and productive every day. |
| | | Your physical health is near-perfect. |

*Source:* Gallup Healthways (2014).

were rated as thriving, struggling or suffering in each domain, and ranked by percentage of the population thriving in each, yielding both predictable and unexpected results (see Table 11.1b).

The results shown for the top 10 countries in the table may be surprising. Notably, the United States does not appear in the top 10 of any category. Sweden's score in financial well-being outstrips other scores, with 72% of citizens feeling secure. The number of Central and South American countries defies stereotypes, with Panama ruling the ratings at the top of four out of five categories.

The set of lowest scores contains few surprises. Those countries with least well-being have experienced years of war, drought, economic failure, or political instability. Greece was among the hardest hit in the recent Great Recession, which may explain the faltering sense of purpose reflected here. Several also provide a steady stream of refugees and migrants. The UN High Commissioner for Refugees (2018) reported 19.9 million people had fled their own country, including a half million Rohingya from Myanmar who fled genocidal purges by their government. By the end of 2017, another 40 million people worldwide were displaced within their own countries due to conflict, persecution, violence, or human rights violations, becoming internally displaced persons (IDP). The numbers have grown since.

Obviously, factors of war, poverty, and disaster drastically reduce well-being. Researchers in topics of well-being face a struggle between extremes; massive numbers of people experience horrid conditions and extremely low well-being, but a small number experience very high well-being, and the vast majority of humanity falls somewhere in between.

The body of SWB research around the world is growing, though still relatively few studies have included assessment of the values or beliefs by which cultures *themselves*

## Table 11.1b  Gallup Healthways Global Well-Being Index (2014) Country Rankings

### All Elements of Well-Being: Top 10 Countries Ranked by % Thriving

| Purpose | % | Social | % | Financial | % | Community | % | Physical | % |
|---|---|---|---|---|---|---|---|---|---|
| Panama | 66 | Panama | 68 | Sweden | 72 | Panama | 58 | Panama | 63 |
| Costa Rica | 50 | Costa Rica | 58 | Austria | 64 | Netherlands | 53 | Costa Rica | 45 |
| El Salvador | 49 | Uruguay | 54 | Denmark | 59 | Austria | 52 | Brazil | 44 |
| Brazil | 45 | Brazil | 52 | Netherlands | 56 | Denmark | 51 | Uruguay | 43 |
| Denmark | 45 | El Salvador | 51 | Germany | 55 | Sri Lanka | 50 | Guatemala | 41 |
| Venezuela | 43 | Argentina | 49 | Iceland | 54 | UAE | 49 | Mexico | 41 |
| Guatemala | 42 | Guatemala | 48 | Belgium | 52 | Costa Rica | 45 | El Salvador | 40 |
| Argentina | 41 | Malta | 47 | Canada | 52 | Sweden | 45 | Trinidad & Tobago | 39 |
| Colombia | 39 | Chile | 47 | Australia | 48 | Canada | 43 | Saudi Arabia | 39 |
| Paraguay | 39 | Colombia | 46 | Bahrain | 48 | Saudi Arabia | 43 | Colombia | 38 |

### All Elements of Well-Being: Lowest 10 Countries Ranked by % Thriving

| Purpose | % | Social | % | Financial | % | Community | % | Physical | % |
|---|---|---|---|---|---|---|---|---|---|
| Afghanistan | 1 | Afghanistan | 0 | Afghanistan | 2 | Armenia | 8 | Ukraine | 8 |
| Syria | 3 | Syria | 2 | Guinea | 3 | Italy | 8 | Syria | 8 |
| Madagascar | 7 | Haiti | 7 | Mali | 4 | Bosnia & Herzegovina | 10 | Croatia | 9 |
| Albania | 7 | Madagascar | 9 | Uganda | 5 | Croatia | 10 | Haiti | 9 |
| Greece | 7 | Uganda | 10 | Niger | 6 | Democratic Republic of the Congo | 10 | South Africa | 11 |
| Croatia | 8 | Democratic Republic of the Congo | 10 | Angola | 6 | Azerbaijan | 10 | Belarus | 11 |
| Armenia | 8 | Chad | 11 | Benin | 6 | Montenegro | 11 | Afghanistan | 12 |
| Tunisia | 8 | South Africa | 11 | Sierra Leone | 6 | Haiti | 11 | Lithuania | 12 |
| Georgia | 8 | Rwanda | 11 | Chad | 6 | Zimbabwe | 11 | Uganda | 13 |
| Burkina Faso | 8 | Lithuania | 12 | Senegal | 7 | Serbia | 12 | Turkey | 13 |

*Source:* Gallup Healthways (2014).

define and support well-being (Moore, Leslie, & Lavis, 2005). There is, however, recognition that cultures will differ in what they believe constitutes well-being, and researchers do try to avoid imposing cultural biases. Nagpal and Sell (Nagpal & Sell, 1985; Sell & Nagpal, 1992) took care to assure that their Subjective Well-Being Inventory (SUBI) scale was flexible enough to allow differing cultural constructions of well-being to emerge. They had attempted to identify necessities that should be universal even if they are emphasized more or less from one culture to the next, so they were measuring common building blocks of well-being rather than components of a particular cultural idea of wellness. Analysis revealed 11 factors, clusters of important building blocks in the final 40-item version of the scale, which differed from the original eight categories (see Table 11.2). Sell and Nagpal (1992) tested the scale in several major ethnic groups of India, and it has been used subsequently in a number of cultures, primarily in Asian, South Asian, and Western settings.

Moore et al. (2005) noted that Pacific Islanders are underrepresented in well-being research, and undertook use of the SUBI with participants from the Ha'apai

## Table 11.2  Factor Structure of SUBI Well-Being Scale

| 1 | General well-being—positive affect | Perceiving life as smooth and joyful |
| 2 | Expectation-achievement congruence | Success in achieving expected goals |
| 3 | Confidence in coping | Adapts to change without breaking down |
| 4 | Transcendence | SWB from values of a spiritual quality |
| 5 | Family group support | Positive items related to wider family group |
| 6 | Social support | Security and density of social network |
| 7 | Primary group concern | Positive & negative items about security and group well-being |
| 8 | Inadequate mental mastery | Inability to deal with life aspects that disturb mental equilibrium |
| 9 | Perceived ill-health | Concerns about real or imagined physical or mental disfunction |
| 10 | Deficiency in social contacts | Feelings of being disliked or of missing friends |
| 11 | General well-being—negative affect | A generally depressed outlook on life |

*Source:* Sell and Nagpal (1992, pp. 11–14).

region of the Kingdom of Tonga, intending to compare the responses with those from other cultures. Polynesians settled Tonga at least 3,000 years ago as they began expansion across the Pacific. Though it experienced colonial and missionary influences similar to other areas of the Pacific over the past two centuries, the islands maintain a very tradition-oriented culture. Uniquely, Tonga has always had indigenous governance.

The researchers compared their Tongan data to life satisfaction data collected in 1990 and 1995 in the World Values Survey (Inglehart et al., 2000). Compared to 17 other nations of the WVS, Tongans were quite satisfied with their lives, less than one point lower than Canada (top score) on a scale of 1 to 10, despite having a drastically lower GDP per capita of $2,200, compared to Canada's $29,400 and $37,600 for the US. The factor structure, however, was drastically different, with only two emergent categories. The strongest factor related to collectivistic and interdependent aspects of life, with the strongest measured elements involving maintenance of smooth family relations. The second factor included items related to income, health, and anxiety. The results differed from previous uses of the SUBI, and the instrument successfully reflected the values of Tongan culture. The concept *mo'ui lelei* indicates health in the Tongan language, and is used as such by medical professionals, but it actually refers more to how one lives as a member of the society (Young-Leslie, 2002). Health and well-being equate with successful fulfillment of social roles and obligations (Moore et al., 2005).

## Positively Well

*What would happen if we studied what is* right *with people?*

*Former Gallup CEO Donald Clifton*
*(Lopez, Pedrotti, & Snyder, 2018, p. 53)*

Well-being research focuses on what makes people happy and healthy. Freud was a medical practitioner dealing with psychological malfunctions, and as Martin Seligman and Mihaly Csikszentmihalyi (2000) point out, the field has historically focused on repair of damage. Especially following the aftermath of WWII, the focus is understandable, but little time has been spent studying healthy people or finding ways to nurture and preserve life satisfaction, fulfillment, or joy. Humanistic psychologists Abraham Maslow and Carl Rogers were among those who bucked the trend, and Maslow's (1948, 1943) hierarchy of needs stands as social sciences' foundational theoretical map toward highest human experience (see Figure 11.3).

Maslow's model begins with physiological needs, and progresses through safety, love, and esteem to self-actualization, and then (in later writings) to transcendence. The subjects of his study were indeed amongst the most accomplished figures of history through the mid-20th century, including physicist Albert Einstein and philosopher/physician Albert Schweitzer, as well as historical figures like Jefferson and Lincoln. They were all from Western culture, however, and the theory has been criticized for the ethnocentricity of its concepts (Hofstede, 1984). Some transcendent individuals contradict the model, such as Nelson Mandela, who spent his years from 1962 to 1990 in prison under cruelly inhumane conditions, yet rose to prominence as a leader of his country

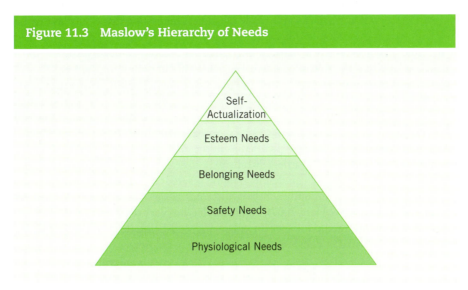

**Figure 11.3   Maslow's Hierarchy of Needs**

Self-Actualization

Esteem Needs

Belonging Needs

Safety Needs

Physiological Needs

*Source:* Maslow (1948; 1943).

and a beacon of freedom for the world (Nelson Mandela Foundation, 2015). His journey violates Maslow's progression, demonstrating the highest qualities of humanity long before he had remotely secured physical safety, but his case is exceptional.

Positive psychology continues to build a case that true health encompasses a constellation of positive traits and evaluations, rather than merely being an absence of disease (Seligman & Csikszentmihalyi, 2000). From this perspective, researchers investigate ways that well-being can be protected and fostered, and positive attributes can be supported and nurtured (Haworth & Lewis, 2005; Vaillant, 2000).

## Context, Connectedness, and Well-Being

Well-being has often been operationalized in subjective terms, and individual factors are certainly relevant to psychological health. It is also true, however, that our health and safety, the opportunities and experiences we encounter, and many other factors including available nutrition depend heavily on connections to our social, cultural, and environmental contexts. These demographic and environmental factors influence the conditions and status of our communities, organizations, and families, which in turn form the contexts where individual well-being blossoms or fails (Haworth & Hart, 2007; Kagan & Kilroy, 2007; Prilleltensky & Prilleltensky, 2007). The term **connectedness** describes the sense of interdependence, belonging, inclusion, caring, or emotional closeness that can be found in positive association with others (Flanagan, Cumsille, Gill, & Gallay, 2007; Hardaway & Fulghini, 2006; Hynie, Lalonde, & Lee, 2006). Active involvement with other people and groups reduces stress, provides coping resources, and promotes well-being (Townsend & McWirter, 2005).

In 1961, psychologist Jack Little made the radical suggestion that clinicians may be more effective if they adopt a role he describes as "social architect." A debate emerged in the American Psychological Association, criticizing the focus only on disturbed individuals, recognizing the role of contextual social factors in both illness and health, and suggesting pursuit of alternative approaches to achieve mental health. Rather than modeling psychological practice in the mold of physician treating diseases after they develop, the psychologist might find more success by engineering healthier communities and social interactions, "assisting people to lead more satisfying lives through their spontaneous associations with other people, that is, in the context of their natural groupings in ordinary community life" (Little, 1961, p. 603). Research in this direction continues in the belief that well-being can deliberately be created, enhanced, and sustained by improving factors like community cohesion and connection to the natural environment (Haley, 2007; Haworth & Hart, 2007). While this has not yet been a widespread focus of Western psychology, methodologies for enhancing well-being through connectedness are surprisingly normal in non-Western and indigenous cultures.

## Indigenous Views of Well-Being

*Well-being is also viewed as a process, something we do together, and as sense-making, rather than just a state of being.*

*Haworth & Hart, 2007 p. 1*

*I never thought it likely they could be so fine a race of people as I now found them [the Māori]. They generally rose above the middle stature, some were even six feet and upwards, and all their limbs were remarkable for perfect symmetry and great muscular strength.*

*John Liddiard Nicholas, 1817, p. 96*

The Western biomedical model defines health and wellness as absence of disease (Adelson, 1998; Kleinman, 1977). Traditional and indigenous worldviews often take a more nuanced approach. Conceptualization of well-being may include a combination of components on physical, emotional, social, and spiritual levels. Those components may be part of sophisticated systems of support whereby well-being is promoted and maintained on individual and community levels. The following section presents brief overviews of several cultural formulations of well-being from very different perspectives.

When Europeans arrived on the shores of Aotearoa, the Māori were fantastically healthy, as Nicholas (1817) attests. Māori traditionally maintained health through holistic systems that balanced things that were *tapu*, translated as sacred, forbidden, restricted, or set apart, and *noa*, which indicates unrestricted and ordinary things (Moorfield, 2019). A corpse would be *tapu*, but a person also becomes *tapu*, or restricted, when entering the sacred space of the *marae* ceremonial house. The person becomes *noa* after exiting the *marae* event by sharing food and socializing, thereby returning to the normal world. *Tapu* and *noa* also serve as a system of public health, from preventing contact with waste and pathogens for physical health, to prescribing ways people should and should not interact to facilitate mental and spiritual health. The system worked marvelously until the arrival of Europeans, who brought new diseases, alcohol and tobacco, and general demolition of the cultural and environmental ecology.

By 1837, the tides had turned to such a degree that James Busby, who held the office of Resident representing the British Crown, felt compelled to describe the deplorable conditions of Māori health to his superiors. On June 16, only 20 years after Nicholas, he wrote,

> It must not be lost sight of that the mortality has not been confined to those who have been the victims of violence, or who have been exposed to the effects of vices or diseases of foreign origin. Disease and death prevail even amongst those native who, by their adherence to the missionaries, have received only benefits from English connexions [sic]; and even the very children who are reared under the care of the missionaries are swept off in a ration which promises, at no distant period, to leave the country destitute of a single aboriginal inhabitant. (Busby, 1837, p. 8)

The Māori did survive, though their numbers decreased by two-thirds by the end of the 19th century (Kingi, 2006). Colonization brought tragic loss of life and devastating disruption to their culture and well-being. Dominated politically and economically by the growing British and European population, the 19th and 20th centuries were not kind to Māori.

Like many indigenous groups including Native Americans, the 1970s saw Māori begin to reassert their traditional ways of being. The New Zealand government suppressed Māori health-ways for over a century, in favor of a British system of medicine that treated disease in isolation from the whole person, going against the holistic Māori worldview. In 1982, Māori psychiatrist Mason Durie presented a model of the Māori health system, developed in consultation with other cultural and medical experts, termed *whare tapa wha*, the four-walled house (see Chapter 4, Table 4.1). Spiritual, mental, physical, and familial elements are balanced to maintain well-being (Durie, 1994). Of these, *taha wairua* is most crucial, because it connects people to spiritual vitality, without which they will certainly be unhealthy, and also to the natural environment. A healthy Māori feels connectedness to a mountain and a river, and to ancestral lands, and these connections help to maintain the person's identity and well-being. The Hawaiian systems of *kapu* (restriction) and *lā'au lapa'au* (healing traditions) follow a similarly holistic approach to well-being, reflected throughout Polynesia. In Tongan tradition, *mo'ui lelei*, translated as "living well" (Young-Leslie, 2002, p. 3), emphasizes maintenance of good social relations.

The Ojibway of Ontario, Canada, along with other Algonquin tribes, describe themselves as *Anishinabek*, or First Peoples. To achieve the state of *mno bmaadis*, "living the good life" (Wilson, 2003, p. 87), a person needs to feel connected to the Creator and to the land, rocks, water, animals, and plants, all of which exist as part of the physical and spirit worlds simultaneously. Health requires balance of physical, emotional, mental, and spiritual elements, represented by the four cardinal directions of the Medicine

Wheel, and living in harmony with nature and the spirit world while maintaining a deep connection to the earth (Gone, 2008a; Wilson, 2003).

Australian Aboriginal and Torres Strait Islander indigenous groups derive well-being from connection to their traditional spiritual beliefs and practices, contained in stories of The Dreaming. The Dreaming speaks of connection to the land, which was formed by the Spirit Beings, and to other groups and people in a continuous reality stretching from The Dreamtime to present and future. The spiritual and physical realms are not separate, and an aware human is linked to the surrounding plants, rocks, and creatures. Through ritual and ceremony, they contact Spirit Beings and connect with the entire cosmos. Two centuries of oppression under British colonial and postcolonial rule have taken a huge toll on the indigenous population, but their spirituality provides a great resource for well-being amidst ongoing socioeconomic adversity (Love, Moore, & Warburton, 2016; Poroch et al., 2009).

Western culture includes a distant history that was much more like what we now call indigenous culture, but the concept of well-being is based in post-Enlightenment Western ideas of self as bounded individual (Christopher, 1999). Framed as a preponderance of intrapersonal good feelings and absence of illness, well-being has been conceptualized and measured in largely individual terms, omitting factors that are paramount in some cultures. Consistently across the indigenous cultures discussed above, well-being revolves around connection, usually to in-group, often to nature, to religious or spiritual constructs or supernatural beings, to nature or earth, or to some combination of extra-personal factors (Angell et al., 2016; Adelson, 1998; Christopher, 1999; Love et al., 2016). Western psychology has recently begun investigating the concept of connectedness, generally defined as feelings of closeness, belonging, inclusion, caring, or interdependence (Barber & Schluterman, 2008; Baumeister & Leary, 1995; Townsend & McWirter, 2005). In modern urban and suburban life, social supports and connections to community, culture, and nature are vastly diminished, leading a small but growing number of researchers recognize the importance of connectedness in promoting and maintaining well-being. Despite the ethnocentric view that modern medicine is the penultimate path to health and well-being, an antidote to the isolation and anomie of info-age modernity may be available in these ancient ways of being.

## REALITY CHECK

*How might you go about defining and measuring well-being?*

*Do the rankings of well-being by country surprise you? Why?*

*What are the prominent features in indigenous ideas of well-being?*

*How does connectedness function in maintain well-being?*

# 11.4 PSYCHOPATHOLOGY AND CULTURE

## LO 11.4: Identify components of mental health across cultures and how differences affect diagnosis and epidemiology.

The opposite of well-being logically must be ill-being, which could include physical, mental, or social conditions. For psychology, the usual concern is mental illness. Founders of the science of psychology were primarily medical doctors and neurologists like Freud, Wundt, Griesinger, and Kraepelin, who began to describe and treat mental illness in Europe during the 19th century. A very brief examination of that history begins this section to acknowledge the importance of European culture in current health practice. The Euro-American biomedical model remains the predominant forces in academic study of mental health globally.

### Modern Definition of Mental Illness

*A mental disorder is a syndrome characterized by clinically significant disturbance in an individual's cognition, emotion regulation, or behavior that reflects a dysfunction in the psychological, biological, or developmental processes underlying mental functioning. Mental disorders are usually associated with significant distress and disability in social, occupational, or other important activities.*

*APA, 2013, p. 20*

The quote above represents current thinking in the Western system of psychological diagnostic categorization. All such systems fall under the term **nosology**, describing the science of disease classification. Classification of mental disorders began in 19th-century Europe, in the time of Darwin and the ascendance of scientific method. German neuro-anatomist Wilhelm Griesinger (1817–1868) had developed an early nosology based in the belief that all mental illness was caused by brain disease. A few years later in 1879, Wilhelm Wundt (1832–1920) established the first lab for psychological experimentation, which attracted a young Emil Kraepelin (1856–1926). Kraepelin was unimpressed by the neuro-anatomists, whom he felt produced too few practical results for treatment and ignored the internal life of the mind (Engstrom & Kendler, 2015). He admired Wundt's carefully crafted scientific experiments designed to reveal the inner workings of perception and thought. His eventual diagnostic system was based in Wundt's style of clinical observation, unlike Freud's introspective methods. Kraepelin's contributions included differentiation of dementia praecox (now schizophrenia) as a permanent neurologic disorder, from the more transitory illnesses of affect he classed as manic-depression. His system of describing illnesses by symptomatology and allowing for differentiation by pathogenesis, or origin of the disorder, still serves as the foundation of the American Psychiatric Association's Diagnostic and Statistical Manual, currently in its fifth edition (DSM-5).

Kraepelin formed the hypothesis that domesticating processes of civilization were driving the frequent pathologies observed in European cultures, an idea echoed a few decades later in Freud's *Civilization and Its Discontents* (1930/2015). More generally, Kraepelin maintained that exterior factors of social context appeared to influence prevalence and outcomes of disorders, including syphilitic conditions. He departed in 1903 for a world tour to promote his nosology and test it among "primitive" people (Steinberg, 2015, p. 531). Despite encounters with *latah* and other culture-specific disorders during his time studying dementia praecox on Java, Indonesia, Kraepelin concluded that all disorders could be explained within his taxonomy, and that only prevalence and expression of illnesses varied by culture (Engstrom & Kendler, 2015). Despite proposing a specialty of *Vergliechende Psychiatrie*, or comparative psychology (Marsella & Yamada, 2000), he remained convinced of the superiority of the white race and was profoundly anti-Semitic throughout his life (Strous, Opler, & Opler, 2016). Wundt also formed an interest in effects of culture on the mind and mental health, publishing his multi-volume *Elemente der Völkerpsychologie* (Elements of Folk Psychology) beginning in 1913.

These were serious attempts to understand other cultures and how contexts affected illness, though the work relied on a very Eurocentric perspective (Goldenweiser, 1914). They formed the foundation of what would become transcultural psychiatry, but in the decades following Kraepelin and Wundt, culture largely receded from the mainstream of psychology. Primary influences were psychodynamic, following Freud, and behaviorist, following Watson and Skinner in strong contrast to Freud. Gestalt and humanistic psychology also found audiences, but an increasingly biomedical approach fit with the growing power of modern biomedicine. By the 1960s, biochemical research into antidepressants and other psychoactive drugs provided dramatic results from medication. Described as neo-Kraepelinians, proponents of the biomedical model place pathogenesis and treatment in neurochemistry and the brain, now the predominant paradigm in psychiatry. Oddly, Kraepelin is held as inspirational both to transcultural and biomedical theorists, despite their great differences in approach and philosophy.

Two documents currently govern diagnosis of mental illness and psychological disorders in Western medicine and psychology: the DSM-5 and the *International Statistical Classification of Diseases and Related Health Problems*, 10th edition (ICD-10). Organization of a comprehensive system for consistent classification of disorders began in Europe during the 18th and 19th centuries, largely to facilitate statistical tracking of disease. Following WWII, the World Health Organization assumed maintenance of the ICD, publishing the ICD-6 in 1946 (WHO, 2006). Inclusion of mental illnesses has increased gradually, but as an internationally developed catalogue of thousands of illnesses, much time passes between editions, and psychological disorders are a relatively small portion. It is used around the world, however, while the DSM system is the product of the American Psychiatric Association and is used primarily in the US.

The first edition of the DSM was published in 1952 by the American Psychiatric Association, who still controls development and publication of the manual. ICD codings are included for each DSM diagnosis, but the DSM is considered important in its level of detail, which goes beyond descriptions in the ICD (American Psychological Association, 2009). Use of these diagnostic manuals across nations and cultures allows international tracking of disorder prevalence and opportunities to compare ways progression and outcomes of disorders might be shaped by cultural context.

## International Prevalence of Disorders

Assessing prevalence of mental disorders internationally is difficult for a number of reasons. Baxter, Patton, Scott, Degenhardt, Land Whiteford (2013) examined 77,000 data sources from around the world and found less than 1% were usable in calculating national averages. Regional coverage varied widely, and methodological issues plagued many of the studies. Steel and colleagues (2014) identified 174 surveys from 63 countries with sufficient detail for meta-analysis, finding 17% of participants had experienced a common mental disorder in that past year, and 29% at some point in their lifetimes. North and Southeast Asia had lowest prevalence, with sub-Saharan Africa also showing low rates. English speaking countries had the highest lifetime prevalence of mental disorders. An examination of 41 studies of children and adolescents in 27 countries (Polanczyk, Salum, Sugaya, Caye, & Rohde, 2015) found an overall prevalence of 13.4% in that age group (anxiety 6.5%, depressive disorders 2.6%, ADHD 3.4%, disruptive disorder 5.7%).

A more complete epidemiological picture is unlikely in the near future, with 30% of countries having no national health system (Mihai, Jordanova, Volpe, & Sartorius, 2016). Concepts of disorder differ widely across cultures, as do access to healthcare professionals, attitudes toward mental illness, and crucially, where people turn for treatment. Use of traditional healers is dropping, but in India, nearly 20% will turn to them first (Oyebode, Kandala, Chilton, & Lilford, 2016). Among Egyptian patients with bipolar disorder, 40% sought help from traditional healers either before or after engaging psychiatric services (Assad et al., 2015). In many cultures, admitting to having a mental illness is a great disgrace, so treatment is unlikely and potential patients will not appear in statistics. Despite difficulties, international research expands gradually, led by organizations like the WHO, often relating to prevalence and course of particular illnesses.

Schizophrenia has received over a century of extraordinary international attention, from Kraepelin's identification of dementia praecox onward. Diagnosis currently requires presence of two or more of the following symptoms during one month:

1. Delusions

2. Hallucinations

3. Disorganized speech (e.g., frequent derailment or incoherence)

4. Grossly disorganized or catatonic behavior

5. Negative symptoms (i.e., diminished emotional expression or avolition)

(DSM-5, p. 99)

Schizophrenia has been described as an egalitarian disorder, affecting rich and poor around the world at similar rates of 1 to 4 per 1,000 people, though some studies have observed up to 18 per 1,000. Onset usually occurs during early adulthood. Schizophrenia tends to run in families, and it affects males more than females (Barbato, 1998; Gejman, Sander, & Duan, 2010; Jablensky, 2000, 1997; McGrath, 2006). The DSM-5 cites a prevalence of .3% to .7%, noting considerable variation by country, region, ethnicity, and geographic origin. The section on culture-related diagnostic issues cautions that experiences that seem delusional in one culture, such as witchcraft, may be accepted in another. Religious experiences that include hearing voices or hallucinations with religious content may not indicate illness, and as discussed at the start of the chapter, some cultures absolutely endorse hearing or seeing spirits or ancestors as part of good health and adjustment.

Schizophrenia's range of symptoms, multiple possible causes, and differing outcomes have led some researchers to question legitimacy of the illness's universality. High incidence has been reported in certain areas of northern and central Europe, in Afro-Caribbean communities in the UK, and among ethnic minorities in a number of countries. Urban areas have more cases than rural, and developing nations have lower rates than developed (Barbato, 1998; Jablensky, 2000; McGrath, 2006). Availability of treatment may explain some of the variation in rates, as could cultural reluctance to admit to mental issues, though most studies attempt to adjust for these factors. More puzzling are variations in outcome, which classical psychiatry described as an inevitable downward spiral without hope. In the landmark WHO 10-year study, rates of remission after a single episode ranged from 3% in the US to 33% in Japan and 54% in India (Barbato, 1998; Jablensky et al., 1992).

## Limitations and Solutions in Epidemiology

The Western system is rooted in a particular world-view and set of assumptions that could be influencing research through methodological choices and confirmation biases (Kleinman, 1987). In fact, the DSM-5 "acknowledges that all forms of distress are locally shaped, including the DSM disorders" (APA, 2013, p. 768). Kirmayer and Ryder (2016) stress that each individual must be understood in cultural context, and each cultural context may influence the prevalence, progression, and outcome of a disorder. Researchers increasingly look for reasons behind the underlying differences in epidemiology and presentation of mental illness. Americans provide a poignant example in their susceptibility to depression and bipolar disorder, in a country founded on the pursuit of happiness (Ford, Dmitrieva, et al., 2015; Kirmayer & Ryder, 2016). Higher valuing of happiness is associated with better well-being in East-Asia and Russia, but with higher incidence of mood disorders in the US, leading Ford, Mauss, and Gruber (2015) to propose that it is the *way* Americans value happiness that causes problems. American pursuit of happiness is more extreme, and in keeping with the country's individualism, tends also to emphasize personal achievement and acquisition, whereas other cultures may associate happiness with social connectedness.

If Western nosology is rooted in culture-based assumptions of normalcy and largely shaped by European experiences and understandings of illness, what differentiates the system from ethnotheory? One difference is understanding of neurochemicals and neurological structure, with a growing push to identify common organic components to explain mental illnesses (Goodkind et al., 2015). Western nosology also enjoys a history of careful observation and research that is not to be discounted. Variations in concepts of mental illness discussed in the following section, however, will show that not every disorder in the DSM-5 is a human universal.

Since the 1970s, interdisciplinary cooperation has been quietly growing between fields of cultural psychiatry and psychology, neuroanthropology, cultural neuroscience, and medical anthropology. The DSM-IV editions included a section on culture-bound disorders, now omitted in the DSM-5 in favor of a Cultural Formulation Interview (CFI) schedule and listing of cultural expressions of distress, along with descriptions of cultural considerations in some disorders. These and other issues are discussed next.

## Cultural Considerations in Diagnosis

Several issues arise when attempting to diagnose psychological disorders across cultures: What constitutes an abnormal or distressed state? How are symptoms expressed or communicated? And at what point is a person sufficiently dysfunctional to require diagnosis? Patients from cultures without terminology to explain mental illness with Western concepts like depression may present explanations from their own cultures.

Implicit in concepts of mental illness are assumptions of abnormality, in other words, deviance from norms. Note that both the ICD and DSM systems include the term *statistical* in their titles, referring to quantification and normalcy of conditions. In the case of mental disorders, the behavior, dysfunction, or impairment must fall outside of population norms. Narcissistic personality disorder was nearly eliminated from the DSM-5 for a number of reasons, but in the age of selfies and the Kardashians, scores on measures of narcissism are soaring (Gray, 2014). In fact, narcissism scores and social media behavior are significantly correlated (Barry, Doucette, Loflin, Rivera-Hudson, & Herrington, 2015). If behaviors associated with narcissism become widespread to a point of normalcy, the diagnosis may indeed disappear in future DSM editions. Basing diagnostic criteria in normalcy, which varies widely across cultures, risks cultural bias in diagnosis. Though the DSM-5 includes a significant acknowledgment of cultural considerations, is it ethical to impose Western diagnoses on non-Western people?

The concept of dependent personality disorder (DPD) provides an excellent case in point. The syndrome is characterized by what are described as "submissive and clinging behaviors" (APA, 2013, p. 675). Diagnosis requires presence of at least five of eight specific features, several of which are controversial in terms of cultural norms. As discussed in Chapter 4, the concept of *amae* is a desirable quality of close, loyal, interdependent affiliation in Japanese culture (Doi, 1988). Chen, Nettles, and Chen (2009) point out that characteristics valued in collectivist cultures and specifically encouraged in Confucian ideals throughout East Asia are pathologized in DPD diagnostic criteria. Criteria include (1) need for advice from others, (2) surrender of personal responsibility, (3) reluctance to express disagreement, (4) reluctance to initiate activities, (5) excessive support seeking, including willingness to do unpleasant tasks, (6) discomfort when alone (see Table 11.3). Rather than indicating dysfunction, these describe normative characteristics of collectivists in a vertically hierarchic culture where agency is externalized by those lower in status. An early indication of problems in cross-cultural research appeared when Western personality tests were administered to Japanese participants, with results suggesting pathological levels of dependence for well-adapted individuals (Doi, 1988).

## Table 11.3    Dependent Personality Disorder

### Diagnostic Criteria: DSM-5 301.6 (F60.7)

A pervasive and excessive need to be taken care of that leads to submissive and clinging behavior and fears of separation, beginning by early adulthood and present in a variety of contexts as indicated by five (or more) of the following:

1.  Has difficulty making everyday decisions without an excessive amount of advice and reassurance from others.

2.  Needs others to assume responsibility for most major areas of his or her life.

3.  Has difficulty expressing disagreement with others because of fear of loss of support or approval.

4.  Has difficulty initiating projects or doing things on his or her own (because of a lack of self-confidence in judgment or abilities rather than a lack of motivation or energy).

5.  Goes to excessive lengths to obtain nurturance and support from others, to the point of volunteering to do things that are unpleasant.

6.  Feels uncomfortable or helpless when alone because of exaggerated fears of being unable to care for himself or herself.

7.  Urgently seeks another relationship as a source of care and support when a close relationship ends.

8.  Is unrealistically preoccupied with fears of being left to take care of himself or herself.

*Source:* APA (2013, p. 675).

Other cultures do have norms of behavior and thought that can be exceeded, and many cultures have indigenous understanding of mental and emotional ailments and their treatment. Chinese and Indian cultures have highly organized systems whose development began in eras when Europe had only Neolithic cultures. Examination of other perspectives on mental disorders is warranted for understanding how distress is expressed and conceptualized in other cultures, but also to stimulate inclusion of diverse ideas in the evolution of mental health practices in a multicultural world.

In a more confusing pattern affecting diagnosis, people from non-Western cultures may describe their psychological symptoms in terms of pains or other sensations, which is called **somatization** (Kleinman, 1977; Rohlof, Knipscheer, & Kleber, 2014; Zhou et al., 2015). Particularly in East Asian cultures, depression tends to be presented as a bodily sensation. Ryder and Chentsova-Dutton (2012) suggest that cultural scripts shape the experience and language of depression among East Asians. Zhou and colleagues (2015) found that a model connecting somatization and depression among Chinese patients could be replicated in South Korea, a culture with similar cultural values. Non-Western refugees especially exhibit a high number of unexplained somatic complaints, perhaps due to traumatization or stigmatization of mental illness, and these are often highly correlated with presence of depression and anxiety (Rohlof et al., 2014). Fenta, Hyman, Rourke, Moon, & Noh (2010) found a significant association between

## DIZZINESS?

South Maui Medical was owned by Eddy Samad (not his real name), who had moved to the US from Brunei on the island of Borneo in about 1970. He grew up on Borneo and completed medical school in Canada under a scholarship that required him to practice in Borneo for a few years. He met and married a lovely nurse and they moved to the US after his mandated service was complete, and they raised their five children in Hawai'i as assimilated Americans. Papi Samad's medical clinic was open every day of the year, a precursor to urgent care clinics.

One day, a Filipino man named Domingo Ruiz (not his real name) walked into the clinic complaining of dizziness. He had been a regular patient, coming in every year or two for his check up and for emergencies and bringing his children

in for occasional ailments. On the day of his visit, a newly arrived mainland doctor was on duty. Mr. Ruiz said he felt dizzy, and the doctor prescribed a standard anti-dizziness medication. A week later, Ruiz returned, telling the same Euro-American doctor that he still felt dizzy, and he was given an increased dosage. The third time Ruiz came in, fortunately Samad's oldest son had joined the practice as a newly minted MD. Though assimilated into American culture, he knew the idioms of Southeast Asian somatization, and he asked Ruiz to describe his dizziness. The sensations of fuzziness and spinning he described were a physical metaphor for depression, but his language had no word for it. Rather than increasing dizziness meds to a dangerous level, he prescribed an antidepressant, and Mr. Ruiz's "dizziness" disappeared.

somatic symptom levels and major depression and PTSD among Ethiopian immigrants in Toronto. These results and many others suggest something different from the DSM-5 somatization disorder where medically unexplained symptoms are present and cause an undue level of concern in the patient. These patients consistently convey their experience of psychological distress in somatic terms, and recognition of this can lead to more accurate and effective treatment (see Spotlight: Dizziness?).

## Cultural Perspectives on Disorders

Moving beyond the borders of mainstream Euro-American nosology, several categories of cultural systems emerge: folkways from many cultures, highly developed systems like Indian Ayurveda and Chinese medicine, and very old oral traditions like Hawaiian *lā'au lapa'au*, Native American medicine ways, and so on. All of these include understanding of unusual or dysfunctional mental states, along with causes and outcomes for people with those conditions. These are widely divergent systems, arising from vastly different world-views in varied historical contexts, making categorization or comparison without ethnocentric biases difficult. The DSM-5 includes perspectives from other cultures by considering three factors that clinicians may encounter, affecting expression, understanding, or experience of illness:

*Cultural syndrome*: A cluster of co-occurring symptoms found within an ethnic community or group. It may or may not be recognized as a disorder within the group, but is recognizable to outside observers (see Table 11.4).

*Cultural idioms of distress*: A way of talking about distress within an ethnocultural group. These may or may not rise to pathological levels, and often use bodily metaphors. Heartbroken would be an example.

*Cultural explanation or perceived cause*: A culture's explanation for how an illness or condition comes about. The evil eye and hexing are examples.

It is expected that consideration of these factors will help to guide clinicians as they complete and evaluate the Cultural Formulation Interview (CFI). The DSM-5 further includes a brief list of cultural concepts of distress encountered with enough frequency to warrant description (see Table 11.4). These include cultural syndromes, such as *dhat* syndrome, idioms of distress, such as *nervios*, and perceived causes of disorders like *kunfungisisa*, where thinking too much is the cause of illness.

## Table 11.4 Cultural Concepts of Distress

| Name | Region/group | Explanation |
|---|---|---|
| **Ataque de nervios** | Latin America, Latinos | Literally "attack of nerves." Characterized by intense emotional disturbance such as anxiety or anger, may include screaming or shouting, crying, trembling. Often follows stressful event in the family. |
| **Dhat syndrome** | South Asia | Among young male patients, a cultural explanation of symptoms such as anxiety, weakness, weight loss, or impotence attributed to semen loss. |
| **Khyâl cap** | Cambodia, Cambodians in the US | Literally "wind attacks." Symptoms are like panic attacks, with dizziness, palpitations, autonomic arousal such as tinnitus. Cognitively, fear that *khyâl* will rise in the body to lungs or head. May occur without warning or after worrisome thoughts, situational triggers. |
| **Kufungisisa** | Shona of Zimbabwe | Literally "thinking too much." Idiom of psychosocial distress. Interpersonal difficulties bring rumination and worry, with symptoms such as depression, irritability, panic attacks. Often used to describe a range of general psychological disorders. |
| **Maladi moun** | Haiti, Haitian communities | Literally "human caused illness." Envy or malice causes a person to send illness or misfortune, such as psychosis, depression, or academic failure. Onset is signaled by an abrupt change in behavior. Good looking and highly successful people are the most vulnerable targets. |
| **Nervios** | Latin America, Latinos in US | A broad idiom of distress describing vulnerability to life stresses, causing emotional distress and difficulty functioning. May include irritability, nervousness, tingling sensations, headaches, etc. Ranges from mild cases to extreme pathologies including anxiety, depression, or psychotic disorders. |

| Name | Region/group | Explanation |
|------|--------------|-------------|
| *Shenjing shuairuo* | China, Chinese immigrants | From Chinese medicine. Meaning— weakness of nervous system. May include weakness or fatigue, disturbed emotions, overexcitement, nervous pain, sleep disturbance. Causes include family stresses, loss of face, failure. |
| *Susto* | Mexico, Central and South America, Latinos in US | A frightening event causes one's soul to leave the body, resulting in persistent illness, misfortune, and psychic disturbance. |
| *Taijin kyofusho* | Japan, Japanese immigrants | Extreme anxiety about interpersonal situations from fear that one's appearance, actions, or odors will offend others. |

*Source:* APA (2013, pp. 833–837).

Culture-bound disorders were subsumed into categories such as anxiety disorders in the interest of creating a cohesive, comprehensive diagnostic system, following in the footsteps of Kraepelin. While practical for diagnosis and treatment within the paradigm, their elimination devalues those concepts and the world-views from which they stemmed. Inherently, millennia of literature from India and China, as well as thousands of oral traditions, are diminished in relevance. Those traditions may be highly relevant to provision of culturally appropriate mental healthcare to people from those cultures. Diagnoses arising exclusively from the Euro-American psychiatric tradition of nosology may make little sense to people from other cultures, and may lead to treatments that bewilder the patient. A broader view may be crucial to developing an encompassing psychology of the human race and effective treatment of mental illness.

## Ecocultural Construction of Distress

As the DSM-5 acknowledges, all psychological disorders are shaped by the cultural milieu. The oldest psychological diagnosis for women was hysteria, which the Egyptians blamed on displacement of the uterus some 4,000 years ago. Madness or aberrant behavior of women has since been ascribed to imbalance of the humors by Galen in Ancient Rome, to demons and the inferiority of women in the Middle Ages, and eventually to frustration of sexuality by Freud, at the end of the very repressed Victorian era (Tasca, Rapetti, Carta, & Fadda, 2012). Primarily affluent Jewish women in Vienna, many of Freud's patients suffered from hysteria, attacks of which included convulsions, anorexia, hallucinations, and other phenomena (Freud, 1909; Putnam, 1906). The diagnosis was omitted from the DSM-III, after several decades of declining diagnosis and issues of definitional clarity, replaced by diagnoses of conversion and dissociation disorders. Whether hysteria has vanished because of changes in the social conditions of women or increased nosological knowledge, the epidemic has passed (Akagi & House, 2002).

As the epidemic of eating disorders spread among young women of America and Europe, a number of researchers noted the culture-bounded aspects of anorexia and bulimia, which are associated with the great pressure from popular media for women to be exceedingly thin (e.g., McElroy & Townshend, 2004; Prince, 1985; Swartz, 1985). Eating disorders are growing more frequent in Asia and other parts of the world, and the global reach of Western media is blamed (Lee, 1995). Eating disorders may be syndromes of modernity rather than a specific culture, but they serve as an excellent example of process, given their origin in culture-provided stressors and their normalization by widespread news coverage. Road rage, male genital flashing, and certain fetishes have also been proposed as culture-bound disorders unique to the US (McElroy & Townshend, 2004).

In addition to the DSM-5 cultural concepts list, a number of the former culture-bound syndromes have been observed and documented over decades and centuries and were included in the DSM-IV's cultural appendix. Unique to Indonesia, *latah* is characterized by exaggerated startle reactions, often including mimicking of a startle stimulus or other atypical responses. *Latah* generally strikes women around menopause. The ailment is not considered terribly unusual, but the *latah* women suffer teasing and harassment, often from children, but sometimes from other adults (see Spotlight: *Latah*). *Latah* was removed from the DSM-5, subsumed as an individual difference in expression of hypersensitivity. Among other syndromes now omitted are ghost sickness, a Native American preoccupation with death and the dead; *hwa-byung*, the "anger syndrome" of Korean culture; *mal de ojo*, effects of the evil eye, found in Mediterranean cultures; and *pilobtoq*, a dissociative episode experienced by Eskimo and Inuit, in which an inexplicable brief period of extreme excitement is followed by a coma lasting several hours. Perhaps most notably absent is the Malaysian term *amok*, from which came the phrase "running amok." *Amok* is a sudden homicidal rampage, historically by a man wielding a sword, sometimes following several days of brooding. The attack goes on until the person is exhausted or has been killed, and if he survives, no memory of the event remains (Flaskerud, 2012; Gaw & Bernstein, 1992; Hatta, 1996; Kua, 1991). Hagan, Podlogar, and Joiner (2015) draw parallels between *amok* and modern mass shootings, with both types of events often following an insult, grievance, or social exclusion that cannot be resolved by the attacker in socially accepted ways (Browne, 2001).

Several of these idioms of distress serve social functions, because in many cultures, mental illness carries significant stigma and bring shame to the person and family, while the cultural idiom carries no negative charge (McElroy & Townshend, 2004). *Latah* provides a culturally acceptable label for Indonesian women who may have anxiety or adjustment related conditions. They often experienced a trauma or loss, and *latah* provides an expressive outlet without stigma of mental illness. The *latah* woman in the Spotlight certainly witnessed deaths of friends and family during WWII, if not personal rape or other violations that could make anyone crazy. But *latah* is not *crazy*. *Latah* is simply *latah*. Of course, the woman experienced some personal discomfort when teased, but she avoided the long-term collective trauma of being an insane family member, as opposed to the silly, funny, *latah* aunt everyone loves.

Anthropologists explain some culture-bound syndromes using the *role conflict* model, where feelings of inadequacy or frustration interfere with a person's ability to fulfill expected responsibilities. The resulting dissonance either causes or exacerbates the condition. One example is *susto*, or fright, which is found throughout Latin America. Sufferers become withdrawn, apathetic, or listless, losing their appetite and becoming

## LATAH

By the time she was 90, Trudy Ezekiel seemed to be a typical mild-mannered grandmother with pure white hair and a Dutch accent, living on the leeward side of Kauai. She would have looked at home in Little Red Riding Hood, except for the intensity of her blue-eyed gaze that could have incinerated an unsuspecting wolf. The piercing blue eyes belied her Indonesian ancestry, but Trudy was also a descendant of Dutch colonialists who had intermingled with the many cultures of Indonesia following the Dutch East India Company's arrival in 1603. Like many Dutch-Indonesians in WWII, the Japanese put her in a concentration camp where the younger of her two small children died from the harsh conditions. For several years after the war's end, Trudy owned and operated a small doll factory, primarily employing Javanese ladies to sew and assemble the dolls. One of the workers was *latah*.

"Every so often, someone would roll a doll's head across the floor and shout '*kepala bergulir!*' (rolling head)," Trudy explained with a wicked gleam in her eye. "The poor thing would jump straight in the air and shout '*kepala bergulir!*' and we would all laugh. I suppose we were terribly mean to the poor thing, but that was just what we did in those days."

depressed, and they may die if the condition persists (McElroy & Townshend, 2004; Rubel, O'Nell, & Collado, 1985). Onset of *susto* can follow a number of experiences, including extreme public embarrassment and fights over infidelity, and suicide in a village once induced an epidemic. In Latin American culture, the person consists of two elements, one physical and one spiritual, and those two may become detached when a person experiences fright. The spirit of the frightened person may wander away or, among indigenous groups, may be captured by spirits, such as the lords of air, mountains, or rivers. The afflicted spirit must be found, possibly ransomed, and led back to the body, which is done by folk practitioners (Rubel et al., 1985). Culture-bound syndromes and idioms of distress may be explainable in terms of face-saving or other self-preservation strategies, but ultimately, it is a person's own culturally constructed understanding of health and illness that will determine course of treatment and outcome. For *susto*, medical professionals are not perceived to know how to treat spirits.

## REALITY CHECK

*Why is it difficult to establish prevalence of mental illnesses across cultures?*

*What issues arise in diagnosis of dependent personality disorder outside Western culture?*

*How does somatization affect diagnosis of mental illness?*

*What are culture-bound disorders?*

# 11.5 CARE AND TREATMENT OF ILLNESS

## LO 11.5: Summarize approaches to maintenance and restoration of mental health and how these relate to underlying belief systems.

Humans and their relatives have nurtured and cared for the unwell for tens of thousands of years. At least 45,000 years ago, injury severely crippled Shanidar 1, a Neanderthal man from northern Iraq, yet he lived to be 35 to 40. A deformed and dwarfed male who lived in Italy about 10,000 years ago and a boy with spina bifida who lived in Florida 7,500 years ago both survived beyond childhood only with assistance from others (Trinkaus, 1982; Dettwyler, 1991). Dettwyler (1991) cautions against assuming that these cases serve as evidence of compassion, which implies the person had no other value to caretakers, but factually, these people survived only because others were willing to provide material and practical assistance.

Care includes three elements: people, knowledge, and behaviors (McElroy & Townshend, 2004). In terms of people, care can come from many sources. Comfort from parents enhances emotional well-being, and mothers routinely stand at the front lines of treatment for their families. Doctors and folk healers appear in many forms. Care may occur at a community level, and may be preventative, as well as curative. Elements of connectedness provide health resources correlated with better health, supported or promoted in celebratory and healing rituals in folk and religious practices. Settings for healing can include the home, a medical office, or a shaman's hut. The knowledge and behaviors encountered in the varied settings depend on the traditions and norms of the healer and patient.

The Western biomedical model of treatment predominates in the developed world, and in the universities that train medical professionals. Drake (2015) posits that overreliance on the biomedical model has degraded mental health care by not providing the type of psychological supports people may need. Minorities suffer gross inequities from insufficient funding and from implicit or explicit prejudice and discrimination affecting the quality of care provided in multicultural settings. Years of research document that people of lower socioeconomic or ethnic minority status receive poorer quality healthcare from biomedical practice in developed nations (DeSouza, 2011; Fiscella, Franks, Gold, & Clancy, 2000).

Though prejudice may be implicit, the result is institutionalized racism, especially in mental healthcare. Māori of New Zealand are underserved in psychological treatment, yet are institutionalized at disproportionally high rates (Baxter, Kani Kingi, Tapsell, Durie, & McGee, 2006; Gibbs, Dawson, Forsyth, & Mullen, 2004). Native Americans also depend on grossly underfunded services, with only 7% of Indian Health Services funding going to mental health (Gone, 2004). Need for treatment is high in indigenous, minority, and refugee groups whose communities have few cultural resources or economic opportunities and high levels of depression and substance abuse (Fiscella et al., 2000; Jones, 2002). Treatment provided may be inappropriate or ineffective, if not offensive, and at minimum providing a poor fit to the understandings and needs of non-Western patients. Joseph Gone is a Native America psychologist with an extensive body of research into Native American mental health and attitudes toward treatment. In 1999, he interviewed Traveling Thunder, a traditionalist from the Gros Ventre tribe in Montana, who said of Western psychology, "Well, go ahead and rid me of my history, my past, and, you know, brainwash me forever so I can be like a Whiteman" (Gone, 2008b, p. 382). A new and improved approach is definitely needed.

Healthcare options outside the biomedical model are often preferred by non-Western people, but also by people in developed nations who seek non-medical treatment. Literature from academic research and popular publications regarding alternative health practices generally follow two strands: traditional medicine, normally drawn from the historic practices of particular ethnocultural groups originating in low and middle income areas, and complementary/alternative medicine practiced in wealthier countries (see Table 11.5).

Beginning in the 1970s, the World Health Organization (WHO) began acknowledging the role and importance of traditional medicine. As described in a 2002 WHO policy paper, "Traditional medicine includes diverse health practices, approaches, knowledge and beliefs incorporating plant, animal and/or mineral based medicines, spiritual therapies, manual techniques and exercises, applied singularly or in combination to maintain well-being, as well as to treat, diagnose or prevent illness" (p. 2). In effect, the term *traditional medicine* describes everything that is not Euro-American biomedicine. Acupuncture, Ayurveda, and other long-standing traditions actually predate modern medicine by millennia, but the WHO shift is the first acknowledgment in decades of traditional practice as legitimate. In low-income and less developed regions,

### Table 11.5 Use of Traditional and Alternative Medicine

| Country (Developing) | Percentage using traditional medicine as primary care |
| --- | --- |
| Ethiopia | 90 |
| Benin | 70 |
| India | 70 |
| Rwanda | 70 |
| Tanzania | 60 |
| Uganda | 60 |

| Country (Developed) | Percentage using complementary/ alternative medicine |
| --- | --- |
| Canada | 70 |
| Australia | 48 |
| France | 49 |
| USA | 42 |
| Belgium | 31 |

*Source:* WHO (2003).

non-Western methodologies are sometimes the only ones available, and they are popular even when modern medicine is accessible (see Table 11.5). Acknowledgment also provides a platform for collaboration between traditional healers and modern practitioners, allowing patients to feel more comfortable with treatment and potentially to draw on the best of both worlds.

## Practitioners and Treatment

Estimating the number of practitioners of traditional, non-Western, holistic, folk, or complementary/alternative systems of healing is impossible. They may be credentialed through family heritage or formal education, and these may overlap, as in the ancient systems of China and India. Traditional practitioners may be the best and brightest to utilize traditional methods in a remote culture where other options do not exist, or they may simply be the most compassionate and empathetic of their locality. A person may be perceived as having been imbued with healing power through illness, a mystical experience, or some other sort of divine intervention. In the many millennia of human progress, myriad attempts have been devised to repair physical and mental damage.

Much remains in "modern" biomedicine from these systems, including aspirin derived from tree bark to alleviate pain, and ipecac to induce the vomiting out of poisons. Mescaline and *ayahuasca* are psychoactive plant-based substances from Central- and South-America considered to yield mental or spiritual healing. Ndetei, Mbwayo, Mutiso, Khasakhala, and Chege (2013) point out that traditional healers are sought out by pharmaceutical companies seeking to develop new drugs from traditional medicine, and often there is little or no compensation to the traditional practitioner. Underlying the substances or techniques used for treatment and practice in any culture are beliefs about the causes and meanings of illness and injury. Those understandings interact with options available to form technologies of health and wellness for a culture, including modern Western culture (Gureje et al., 2015; McElroy & Townshend, 2004).

## Indigenous, Traditional, and Alternative Treatment

Broadly, traditional healers work to repair disharmonies or imbalances. The source of the problem may be internal, as in some improper way of thinking. A problem could come from an external source, most obviously from physical injury, abnormality, or poison, or metaphysically from a curse, spell, evil spirit, or some other non-corporeal force. Each culture includes some belief system cataloging sources of disease and disharmony, and from that set of explanations, solutions are derived.

In Hawaiian culture, healing was done by *kahuna*, traditional priests, healers, and ministers. Healing of illness is the domain of the *kahuna lāʻau lapaʻau*, and practitioners still exist today (Gutmanis, 1976). By the 1840s, Western medical doctors and dentists were also termed *kahuna* (Pukui & Elbert, 2019). The practitioner considers the whole person, their relationships, and their social and natural context, along with the person's sense of connectedness to these surrounding elements. In addition to reducing infirmities, the *kahuna lā'au lapa'au* would also help the person build strength and resilience. Through advice, herbs, massage, and other physical treatments, and perhaps including traditional processes like *ho'oponopono*, the person is brought back into harmony with nature, family, and spirit (Chun, 2016; Gutmanis, 2004).

The Western biomedical model places sources of disharmony primarily in the physical realm, so its practitioners use surgeries and prescription medications to correct problems. Herbalists derive medicines from plants in many cultures, and use herbal medicine for a variety of cultural purpose, including good luck, prosperity, and love, in addition to physical health functions (Cocks & Møller, 2002). The Naua of Mexico use herbs to control balance of hot and cold, much as in the Ancient Greek system of humors (Smith-Oka, 2008). Chinese medicine uses a vast pharmacopeia of herbs, minerals, and animal products developed over thousands of years. Incense and fragrant smoke are used in Asia and Native America to cleanse the atmosphere and the individual of negative influences and to bring in good vibrations (e.g., Ryback & Decker-Fitts, 2009).

Other physical approaches include activities like martial arts and yoga, to maintain harmony or increase capabilities, and massage or other manipulations to correct ailments. In the Native American sweat lodge ceremony, rocks are heated in a fire then placed in a dome covered with hides or, more recently, with canvas or other material. Water is splashed on the rocks, creating steam, somewhat like the cleansing sauna of Scandinavia. More important for the cleansing ritual are the chants and prayers led by an elder, and the entire holistic experience of heat, spirituality, fellowship, and serious intent (Bucko, 1998; Colmant & Merta, 1999; Schiff & Moore, 2006). As with many traditional practices, Western academic researchers are not particularly welcome, given that the logical positivist approach includes a basic denial of unmeasurable spiritual experience. In one of the few attempts to quantify and measure effects of the sweat lodge on well-being, Schiff and Moore (2006) observed improvement in spiritual and emotional well-being of participants, but due to excellent health of their sample, no change in physical well-being.

Acupuncture straddles a line between physiological and energetic, using needles inserted at particular places in the body to correct the flow of *chi*, the universal energy flowing through all things. Ayurvedic health depends on the balance of the three *dosha* energies, *vata dosha* controlling motion of blood breath and heart, *pitta dosha* controlling digestion, nutrition, and temperature, and *kapha dosha* controlling growth and immunity. Each person has a predominant *dosha*, requiring a particular diet, lifestyle, and emotional regulation. In these systems, imbalance leads to illness, including mental issues.

Shamanic healers work in realms of spirits and mystical forces. They go by different titles; for instance, among the Sora of India, a *kuran* is male and a *kuramboi* is female (Beggiora, 2011). Tools of the shaman include feathers and fur, cleansing smoke, and songs and chants. Reaching the spirit world may require the shaman to enter a trance state. Getting there may require a ritual, often including drumming, singing or chanting, and/or dancing. A Sora healer will begin talking with someone seeking a cure, and the process almost inevitably leads to a trance in which departed ancestors will speak through the *kuran* or *kuramboi*.

## SORA SHAMAN

On the eastern side of India, in Odisha state, live the Sora people. At under a half million, they comprise a tiny minority in Indian terms, and they continue to practice many of their traditions regarding communication of the dead with the living via a shaman (Vitebsky, 2016). Some Sora teens and young adults suffer an affliction where they laugh or cry inappropriately, pass out, and experience memory loss due to interest of a spirit in marriage to the youth, though observers suggest the youth may actually be anxious about transition to adult roles and responsibilities. Rather than being treated for the symptoms, the youth marries the spirit, and the symptoms disappear. The person becomes a *kuran* or *kuramboi*, and enters adulthood in a respected position doing the crucial work of negotiating solutions with the departed ancestors of the village (Beggiora, 2011; Vitebsky, 2016).

### Traditional/Alternative Mental Health Practice

Consultation with traditional healers is sometimes normative in cases of mental illness outside of Western context, depending on how mental illness and its causes are defined in a culture. With the Sora teens above, symptoms were not explained as illness, and the shaman who speaks with and for the dead performs a crucial service. In many cultures, those who have visions and hear voices may be revered as saints, as is the case in Christianity, and hence they may be the healers instead of patients. It is notable that trance is classed as a dissociative mental illness in the Western model, despite being present in cultures around the world (Suprakash, Kumar, Kumar, & Kiran, 2013). Whatever the objective validity of trance healing, the practices are essential to numerous indigenous systems of health, and are eminently valid to practitioners and their patients.

Western psychotherapy is clearly not a comfortable option in traditional Chinese cultural context. Strong emotions are frowned upon, and any mental impairment is shielded from exposure to anyone outside the immediate family (Lin, 1983), leaving only traditional medicine. Emotions reside in organs, happiness in the heart, anger in the liver, worry in the lungs, fear in the kidneys, and interestingly, desire in the spleen. Imbalances are treated with the usual pharmacopeia, and illness prevented with Tai Chi or other martial arts practices. Somatization of mental symptoms may be a result of this cultural tendency.

Treatment in Chinese practice is entirely individualized to the flows and turbulence of chi in a particular patient in the particular moment, making controlled experimentation quite impractical. Further, practitioners of a system based in a holistic worldview are unlikely to feel comfortable embracing analytical scientific methods, something I personally experienced when I was hired to teach Western research methods at a highly respected school of Chinese medicine in Hawai'i. Objective studies are therefore rare. In a meta-analysis of what research was available, Butler and Pilkington (2013) found no clear evidence for effectiveness of Chinese herbal medicine in treatment of depression, though it is difficult to say whether this is because of problems with treatment or with the clash between analytical methodologies and holistic practices. Conversely, Yeung and colleagues (2014) analyzed controlled studies of Chinese herbal medicine (CHM) treatment of depression, finding that CHM was as effective as Western antidepressant drugs and had fewer associated adverse events (e.g., side effects). Acupuncture has been shown to increase levels of certain neurotransmitters including serotonin, and is considered to have a positive effect on anxiety and depression, though the mechanism by which this works is unknown (Samuels, Gropp, Singer, & Oberbaum, 2008).

An issue may be trying to measure effects of other systems on disorders as delineated in Western biomedical terms. Looking more broadly and allowing for a diverse range of viewpoints, there is no question that traditional and alternative medicines improve psychological and subjective well-being for millions of people around the world on a constant basis (e.g., Drake, 2015; Schiff & Moore, 2006), often for those with least access to biomedical options. They help, and given rates of usage, alternative treatments and healers are not going anywhere. An expert on Yoruba healers of Nigeria and a psychological counselor herself, Mary Olufunmilayo Adekson recommends synergies of traditional and biomedical models, stating "the end result for all healers (traditional or Western trained) is to help clients solve their problems, which could be physical, physiological, psychological, emotional, mental, marital, family related, gynecological, spiritual, or parenting issues" (Adekson, 2003, p. 109). On a global scale, our best way forward must include mutual respect, embracing diversity in illness and in health.

## REALITY CHECK

*How do people become traditional practitioners?*

*Why might traditional healing be a better option in some cases?*

*Are non-Western treatments effective?*

## 11.6 ARTS AND WELL-BEING

### LO 11.6: Identify ways cultural arts affect health and well-being.

In previous chapters, arts have been discussed in terms of cultural transmission, identity formation and maintenance, communication, emotional expression, and so on. In short, arts permeate cultural and psychological dimensions of human existence. Arts have held a particularly prominent place in health and well-being throughout human existence. Arts provide mechanisms to promote connectedness and for the formation and maintenance of identity, and music, dance, and symbology form crucial components of ritual healing, as discussed earlier.

Effective dissemination of health information forms an innovative use of cultural arts. Indigenous groups and ethnic minorities may not speak the language of the dominant culture, or may simply be more receptive to messages expressed using the symbols and idioms of their own cultures. In a public health initiative in Western Australia, Davis et al. (2004) engaged local tribal artists to create health messages for Mowanjum aboriginal peoples in Western Australia, finding that use of culturally appropriate imagery provided an excellent platform for transmission of health information. The result was increased discussion and unprecedented community involvement in healthy lifestyle choices.

## Communitas

A consistent primary function of arts participation is joining people together. People with strong social bonds are healthy people, leading to growing study of connectedness as a psychosocial support for well-being. Essentially, traditional arts and ritual formed systems of community mental health as humanity evolved.

All of those millennia of social brain evolution still reside within us. That is why we respond to national anthems and hymns, not only with our thoughts, but also with the oxytocin coursing through our veins. Turner (1986) used the term *communitas* to describe the process, meaning a sense of unity, equality, and interconnection, derived from the Latin for community. The modern Pan-American powwow provides a setting for Native Americans to establish collective identity and to connect across tribal boundaries (Browner, 2004; Scales, 2007).

To the great scholar Joseph Campbell (1949/1973), ritual enacts a mythic journey that takes the community collectively out of the everyday world and into transpersonal realms of spirit. The group emerges back into the regular world renewed, with rifts healed and ties strengthened. Campbell observed this process in cultures he termed primitive, such as tribes of the Americas or Africa. Late in his life, he observed a parallel at a Grateful Dead concert, having been invited by the admiring band members who had drawn the name Grateful Dead from Campbell's writings. To him, the concert was a Dionysian ritual, songs evolving toward a section of primal, powerful drumming and frenetic dancing, followed by reunification in uplifting song (Campbell, 1986). Traditional arts help to maintain connectedness and cultural continuity, contributing to individual and community well-being (cf. Fortes, 1936; Geertz, 1993). This process continues in traditional cultures, though many are imperiled by modernization. In popular settings, some functions remain. Diana Boer and colleagues (2011) found that fans experience some degree of connection to other fans of their favorite genre even if they are from different countries; simply being a fan of rap or heavy metal increases liking of similar fans.

## Traditional Arts and Well-Being

Participation in traditional arts such as *hula*, Māori *kapa haka*, Native American dance, or Japanese *taiko* drumming acts in several ways simultaneously to increase well-being for members of ethnic groups in immigration or minority status (Fox, 2010). This is well known to seasoned practitioners, but was tested in cultural psychology in a mixed methods series of studies. Qualitative interviews with 30 New Zealand artists from traditional, Western, and modern arts revealed that traditional arts act uniquely on identity and connection to others, and these effects were supported by data from Māori and Pasifika participants in the longitudinal New Zealand Youth Connectedness Project.

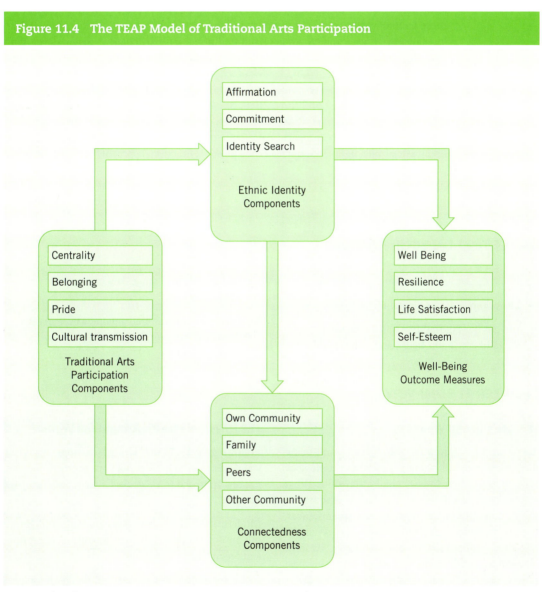

**Figure 11.4   The TEAP Model of Traditional Arts Participation**

Affirmation

Commitment

Identity Search

Ethnic Identity
Components

Centrality

Belonging

Pride

Cultural transmission

Traditional Arts
Participation
Components

Well Being

Resilience

Life Satisfaction

Self-Esteem

Well-Being
Outcome Measures

Own Community

Family

Peers

Other Community

Connectedness
Components

Source: Fox (2010).

Drawing further from the qualitative data, an instrument was designed to measure level of involvement in the art and several ways traditional arts could be influencing well-being. From those data, the following emerged: Learning the art increases knowledge of the heritage culture, providing a richer, more informed sense of identity and cultural pride. Becoming part of the group, embedded in the cultural context, stimulates connectedness with the performing group, family, and community, as well as providing opportunities to connect with other cultures via performances such as cultural festivals (see Chapter 12 for the latter). Figure 11.4 illustrates an interconnected model of how these factors work together to support and enhance well-being. Practicing any art can increase self-efficacy and self-esteem, but traditional arts particularly assist in developing resilience, which helps to maintain well-being when bad things happen, such as prejudice and discrimination. One young leader of a Māori *kapa haka* group explained, "you can build yourself up to be so grounded and so confident that when those things come flying at you they just bounce off" (Fox, 2010, p. 147). Traditional arts form a complex web of interconnected positive influences that can continue to maintain well-being in modern contexts. For this reason, arts are worthy of governmental and community support, because healthier, happier people become positive, functional parts of their communities.

## REFLECTING ON YOUR READING

- What do you think constitutes well-being?

- How do you define mental illness?

- In your heritage culture(s), how did your ancestors maintain well-being? This could be a martial art, sauna, dancing, singing, or something else.

- Have you encountered anyone with a malady described in cultural terms like *susto*, *windigo*, or *shenjing shuairuo*?

## CHAPTER 11 SUMMARY

### 11.1 Health and Wellness

Topics under the heading of health and well-being include mental and physical health as people seek ways to make their lives as good as possible. What constitutes a good life may differ, depending on social, cultural, and environmental circumstances. Norms of thought and behavior also vary. Wellness and disease form a dichotomous binary in Western biomedicine, primarily concerned with physical causes of illness. Other systems exist, with centuries-old methods of diagnosis and treatment.

### 11.2 Physical Health Around the World

Following WWII, the United Nations set forth standards to which all people are entitled, but few nations approach those goals. Current and historical lifespans

Modern and historical lifespans are compared, showing improvement with better agriculture, sanitation, and technology.

Infant mortality has decreased markedly in the past century, but mothers and children still face risks from poverty and malnutrition, and effects of these continue throughout adulthood. Maternal health is better through pregnancy and childbirth, with highest rating for Norway and lowest for Sierra Leone, and with the US at 33rd of 179. Education is a major predictor of mental and physical health. Education leads to better health information and lifestyle choices. Stress erodes mental and physical health. Stressors range from mundane daily stresses to extreme and horrific experiences. SES factors may exacerbate effects of stress, and cultural resources may increase resilience to counteract these effects.

Inequality in health: Socioeconomic and ethnic factors affect health throughout the lifespan. In some cases, minorities have better health outcomes in terms of risk factors and unhealthy behaviors, but mental health issues are often more common with minorities.

## 11.3 Understanding Well-Being

Well-being can be defined in a number of ways, including presence or absence of symptoms, and of good or bad feelings. Ideally, any measurement should be objective, but well-being has often been defined in subjective terms, leading some researchers to prefer the term subjective well-being.

Several surveys of subjective well-being are discussed, along with comparison of ratings around the world. Pacific Islanders are underrepresented, but a study using the SUBI showed that Tongans actually rate quite well, despite low income and a relatively low tech existence.

By the latter 20th century, Maslow had proposed his hierarchy of needs, mapping a path to what he considered highest and best expression of human existence. Contextual factors can support or destroy well-being. Because people are social creatures, community settings can provide resources for well-being, and offer opportunities for promotion of health.

While Western culture defines well-being as an absence of disease, other cultures such as Māori take a holistic view of health. The Māori suffered greatly with diseases brought by Europeans and loss of cultural and material resources, but they and other indigenous groups are regaining well-being by reconnection to traditional ways.

## 11.4 Psychopathology and Culture

Psychopathology has been a primary concern of psychology, and the discipline has dealt with culture and mental illness occasionally in its history.

Major figures in Western nosology include Griesinger, Wundt, and Kraepelin, who began the system of diagnosis still in use. Their early investigations into culture also led to transcultural psychology. Current diagnosis is drawn from the DSM-5 and ICD-10 catalogs of diagnoses.

Comparable epidemiological studies that account for cultural and regional factors are rare. Many cultures use non-Western systems of diagnosis and treatment, partly because mental illness may bring disgrace. Schizophrenia is one illness where outcomes may be better outside Western culture.

The DSM-5 "acknowledges that all forms of distress are locally shaped, including the DSM disorders," but diagnoses still rely on Western norms of behavior and its underlying belief systems. Dysfunction in Western nosology may include biased assumptions. Dependent personality disorder forms a case in point, pathologizing what are normal aspects of being in Japan. Other cultures have ancient systems of diagnosis that far predate European psychology, and other cultures have different ways of experiencing and explaining disordered conditions. Culture-bound disorders, while no longer included in the DSM, are excellent ways to understand other perspectives on illness. Western disorders may make little sense in other cultures, being based on different understanding of how humans and the mind work. The DSM now recommends consideration of cultural syndromes, idioms of distress, and perceived causes of disorder. Hysteria is a very old construction of mental illness in women that formed one of the main disorders encountered by Freud. Researchers have considered the possibility that some Western illnesses may be culture-based disorders. Eating disorders are spreading along with Western media. Several culture-specific disorders are discussed.

## 11.5 Care and Treatment of Illness

Humans have treated disorders for millennia. Care includes three elements: people, knowledge, and behaviors. Māori and other indigenous groups tend to be underserved but overrepresented in institutionalization. Non-Western treatments may be preferred. Practitioners are credentialed in many ways around the world. Western medicine retains numerous naturally derived medicines, though the source culture often was not acknowledged or compensated.

Traditional systems often seek to restore balance. Western system uses surgeries and prescriptions. Other systems use herbs and other medicines, usually to restore wholeness rather than to kill an illness. Chinese and Native American systems have vast pharmacopoeia, but also acknowledge spiritual or non-physical elements. Some traditional practitioners would qualify for diagnosis in Western system. Current research is beginning to recommend acknowledgment of traditional healers and their incorporation into comprehensive treatment programs for minority patients.

## 11.6 Arts and Well-Being

Arts have long held a prominent place in health and healing. Arts provide means of connectedness, an area of growing interest in positive psychology. Arts provide means of connectedness, an area of growing interest in positive psychology. Traditional arts operate on multiple levels to establish and maintain health. These include mechanisms to establish healthy identity and cultural connection, and ways to learn resilience.

## GLOSSARY

**Connectedness:** The sense of interdependence, belonging, inclusion, caring, or emotional closeness that can be found in positive association with others.

**Mental development:** Growth in cognitive, language, social, and emotional capabilities.

**Nosology:** The science of classification of disease.

**Somatization:** Description of psychological symptoms in terms of pains or other sensations.

**Subjective well-being:** A person's own judgment of qualities of his or her life, potentially including physical and mental wellness, life situations, affluence or lack, and other components that make life satisfying.

**Technophysio evolution:** Changes in human physiology and health that have resulted from improved technology, public health, and medicine.

**Well-being:** The sum of positive and negative aspects of a person's life, consisting of health, satisfaction, and/or other subjective or objective measures of quality of life.

# LIVING IN A MULTICULTURAL WORLD

## Learning Objectives

LO 12.1 Describe the ways multicultural interactions are increasing.

LO 12.2 Identify issues that culturally informed psychologists address in the real world.

LO 12.3 Explain how culture shapes conflict and resolution.

LO 12.4 Discuss ways the arts are a positive factor in this increasingly multicultural world.

## PREPARING TO READ

- How many ethnicities are represented in your class? Your college or university?

- How many ethnic groups live in your community?

- The last time you went to a doctor, did you think the staff members were from your area?

*On a Wednesday in early 2018, a judge issued a bench warrant for the arrest of assistant professor Kaleikoa Kaʻeo for failure to appear in court. Kaʻeo had arrived on time for the hearing and at the moment the warrant was issued, he was standing in the courtroom within feet of the judge. He was still in the courtroom when he was handcuffed. To understand this event requires more than a century of context.*

*In 1893, Hawaiʻi was ruled by a constitutional monarchy, in the reign of Queen Liliʻuokalani. The population had the highest literacy rate in the world, at about 80%, and generally enjoyed just and equitable governance under the constitutional monarchy. A group of American businessmen living in the Kingdom of Hawaiʻi, however, wanted more land for plantations and less restriction on what they could do to build their businesses, such as Sanford Dole's growing pineapple empire. A ship full of US Marines lay at anchor in Honolulu harbor, and the businessmen persuaded their commander to provide support in deposing the Queen.*

*Queen Liliʻuokalani was no fool. She knew the US had spent the previous century systematically exterminating or subjugating Native Americans. Hawaiians would not fare well resisting a vastly larger military. She expected other countries that already recognized the kingdom to come to their aid, but the situation remains unresolved to this day. Hawaiians say the US Congress never ratified the articles of annexation, which is true, nullifying the American claim to the territory and subsequent statehood. The monarchy's lands were seized and remain in state or federal control.*

*Kaʻeo was in court over his protests against the building of another observatory on Mauna Kea, an ecologically fragile environment and place of sacred cultural significance.*

*What he had actually refused to do was to speak English, asserting his right to defend himself in his native language. Hawaiian is one of two official languages of the state. Public outcry was massive and swift, and Ka'eo was released on bail. State courts immediately adopted procedures for translation, but the event made clear the ongoing institutional oppression of Hawaiian people and their political voice in a diverse and otherwise seemingly tolerant state.*

# 12.1: MULTICULTURALISM, GLOBALIZATION, AND PSYCHOLOGY

## LO 12.1: Describe the ways multicultural interactions are increasing.

This chapter considers ways in which forces of migration and globalization are affecting how people live, think, and behave. As discussed in the Acculturation chapter, people are moving around the globe and interacting internationally at unprecedented rates. Media, economics, climate conditions, military conflict, and other forces exert a cumulative pressure that reshapes our world daily. The resulting changes to identity, livelihood, relationships, and power structure will affect our psyches for the foreseeable future, if not for generations to come. Some of these processes are ancient, others very recent. The massive scale involving eight billion people thrusts humanity into uncharted waters. We will examine some of these forces and highlight some ways that culturally informed psychology may be able to help.

### National Identity and Diversity

Humanity traversed incredible distances in the mere 70,000 years since genetics say we departed the Blombos caves. That ancient community had to stand together to survive in the drastically harsh conditions of the time and cooperate as the earliest groups splintered off to find new opportunity beyond that coast. The migration continues for a variety of economic, environmental, and political reasons (Marsella & Ring, 2003), keeping some identities and relationships while adopting new ones along the way. We now share the globe with 8 billion other people who have innumerable ways of describing their groups and identities, but nearly all of us now live in structured sociopolitical organizations we call nations (e.g., Hatton & Williamson, 2005; Hoerder, 2002).

Borders of modern nation-states have little to do with previous ethnic, linguistic, or religious criteria that usually characterized pre-colonial kingdoms and principalities. Those sociopolitical groups shared history, values, and beliefs that provided common identity, reinforced in ritual and in behavioral norms. These are not necessarily characteristic of modern countries. The nation-state arose in the closing chapters of colonialism, countries separated by lines drawn after wars between European colonial powers, or drawn arbitrarily by those powers for administrative purposes during colonial rule (Kymlicka, 1995). Old regions, like the Manding Empire of

West Africa, are splintered now into multiple countries overlaid with languages from European occupiers. Other autonomous regions have been folded into new political entities, a statement true of the United States, which subsumes the former territories of hundreds of indigenous cultures. Most of these nations are multicultural.

## Research on Diversity

Research shows that diversity in social groups can be a great advantage and/or a great liability, depending on how we deal with the others around us (e.g., Levine & Moreland, 1998; Surowiecki, 2004). Diversity can lead to a greater variety of ideas and potential solutions, on the better end of the spectrum. The collective wisdom of a group can exceed the individual intelligence of members, but *only* when there are diverse and different viewpoints represented and the expression of these opinions is encouraged (Page, 2008). In a diverse group where all can speak freely, erroneous ways of thinking may cancel each other out, allowing the most beneficial answer to emerge, whereas groups of similar people will tend to make the same type of errors and just reinforce each other on the way toward possibly unfortunate outcomes that nobody may anticipate.

On the other hand, diversity in groups can lead to difficulties in understanding each other, interfering with processes of consensus (Levine & Moreland, 1998). Committees are notorious for either mindlessly agreeing with strong leaders or arguing for hours about minor points, and diversity can exacerbate these negative effects. These difficulties are reflected on international levels, too. Certain geopolitical powers have great influence, and the places where countries gather to negotiate solutions (e.g., the United Nations) can only produce effective, enforceable plans when countries reach consensus on a course of action. More powerful countries press their views and interests, but increasingly, smaller countries resist these pressures and create new alliances. All of these possibilities, the advantages and disadvantages of diversity, are in active play as we negotiate our collective global future.

## Diversity in the Real World

Currently, many nations include people from differing, even opposed, ethnocultural groups and religions. In the US, which is relatively stable, many groups coexist with very little common ground. Nations are stable when citizens subscribe to a sense of overarching national identity that is represented by the government, which is what has allowed the US to hold together thus far. Without a perceived legitimate central authority, people seek alternative identification, often going back to historical conflicts, fueling the Shia/Sunni split in some Middle Eastern countries. In the wars that followed the collapse of Yugoslavia in the 1990s, political leaders such as Slobodan Milosevich exploited centuries-old grievances going back to the Ottoman conquest and the Battle of Kosovo in 1389 to stir up ethnic nationalism. These leaders gained brief power through divisiveness but at huge human cost (Cohen & Dragović-Soso, 2008). Countries could prosper more by avoiding expensive militarization and finding cohesion on peaceful grounds such as shared purpose, human rights, and equality. Peace has rarely occurred recently because negotiating commonality requires more skill, effort, and sacrifice than divisively establishing strong political identity based on history, values, and beliefs of one dominant group in opposition to other nations or groups (Kymlicka, 1995; Spinner, 1994).

Humans evolved to make decisions based on social groups we encounter, usually based on membership and some sense of similarity or dissimilarity. Discerning who is friend or foe has allowed us to survive as a species. Globalization and migration make multiculturalism and diversity inevitable in the present day, crossing historic boundaries despite objections of ethnocentric or xenophobic elements in countries. A variety of political and social responses, often extreme, now affect daily life as migrants and refugees attempt relocation and others demand they be kept out.

Leaders in all phases of society from religion to government speak to us in terms of inclusion and exclusion to clarify and promote collective or selective goals. In a positive sense, we can come together despite different heritage to bring about progress toward the greater good. The Civil Rights movement brought about better working conditions and educational access for numerous ethnic groups. In WWII, nations allied to fight fascism and the imperialist aspirations of Japan. We also worked collectively to end polio and other diseases and to improve sanitation and educational access around the world. Societies and cultures are now so complex that small decisions in our intercultural encounters can echo for generations, for good or for ill.

In the negative sense, politicians in multicultural situations may gain support by railing against a foe identified as culturally different. This is currently happening in many countries around the world, including the US. They may place blame on those of other cultures and religions, perhaps by calling them extremists, without considering other historical factors that led to violence, perhaps over hundreds of years. Immigrants and minorities in many countries are targets of polarizing rhetoric blaming them for economic and social issues, despite conclusive evidence they are economic assets rather than drains. Incredibly, a Harvard economist received a doctorate based on his 2009 thesis that Hispanic immigrants will be a constant economic drain because their IQs are naturally lower, an unbelievably prejudiced and inaccurate premise.

In a more benevolent discourse, other politicians court votes from immigrants by easing restrictions or improving community conditions, such as the immigration reform debate in the US following the 2012 elections. The pendulum had swung against immigration by 2018. In a world of changing demographics, politicians and parties vacillate between antagonizing outsiders and courting their support, with policy and social commentary shifting to fit economic perceptions and public opinion. Some societies honor and support cultural differences, embracing multiculturalist policies that accept different ways of being, while others may choose exclusionist strategies promoting homogenized sameness. This may be done by excluding or repressing other groups, rendering them absent or invisible. A more subtle opposite of multiculturalism promotes "colorblindness," in which differences should be glossed over or ignored (Rosenthal et al., 2012). The colorblind society outwardly promotes equality but may actually favor one dominant culture, such as in the former Soviet Union, where Russian was required as the national language despite the presence of dozens of regional and ethnic cultures.

## Multiple Identities and Memberships

*The urban child of today is no longer a "who" in the sense in which the medieval or even frontier child was, with status in his group by virtue of his family. Today the child is a contender for status even in his own group.*

*Murphy, 1947, pp. 523–524*

Today, people in many countries may trace ancestry to a variety of regions and cultures. Such persons may identify, for instance, as African American, Asian American, or Caucasian, or some combination of ethnic identities. A person may choose to identify with a minority group or with a dominant culture, or identification may happen involuntarily, for instance if the person has dark skin in a white-majority region or country. A social identity perspective might focus on issues of political, social, and economic access, and with how a person evaluates in- and out-groups, while a more developmental approach would emphasize what values, behaviors, and beliefs are instilled as the person grows. Rogoff (2016) suggests that the view of culture as a set of unchanging characteristics and individuals as defined by boundaries of ancestral race or ethnicity has passed its usefulness.

In a world of global migration and communication, cultural change has become the constant, and a number of potential identities may be available to individuals. To Rogoff (2016), a transactional approach examining patterns of participation may be more fruitful. Individuals and communities are inseparable, in her view, and people learn, enact, and transmit culture by their daily participation with others around them, without necessarily stopping to examine the origin of a given activity. Rogoff (2011) describes a respected midwife in a Mayan community in Guatemala who speaks Tz'utujil and wears traditional clothing except for her Birkenstocks, uses Western medical techniques along with Mayan birthing practices, and has more European than Mayan ancestry, but there is no identity conflict involved. In Hawai'i, families may include Hawaiian, Filipino, Chinese, European, and Japanese ancestry, celebrating Christmas, Makahiki, Easter, Obon, and Boys' Day each year. A transactional approach may be the only way to understand inhabitants of complex and changing cultural landscapes.

## Demographic Shifts in Population

A number of forces are driving these major shifts in the demographic composition of developed areas. Primary among these is extended lifespan, meaning more and more of the population is older. In 2000, 607 million people over the age of 60 lived on Earth. In 2015, that number swelled to 901 million and is expected to reach 1.4 billion by 2030 and 2.1 billion by 2050. Table 12.1 shows the dramatic rise in percentage of population over the age of 65 (World Bank, 2018). Though this list is not comprehensive, several trends appear. Between 1960 and 2016, the percentage over 65 increased dramatically in most developed nations, led by Japan, which saw the population increase from 6% to 27%. Australia, New Zealand, and the US trail with 15% of their populations over 65. Lifespan has increased somewhat in developing nations, but especially in Africa, lifespan has increased much more slowly.

**Table 12.1  Percentage of Population Over 65 and Average Births per Woman**

| Country | 1960 % > 65 | 1960 Birth Rate | 2016 % > 65 | 2016 Birth Rate | Country | 1960 % > 65 | 1960 Birth Rate | 2016 % > 65 | 2016 Birth Rate |
|---|---|---|---|---|---|---|---|---|---|
| Afghanistan | 3 | 7.5 | 3 | 4.6 | India | 3 | 5.9 | 6 | 2.3 |
| Australia | 9 | 3.5 | 15 | 1.8 | Israel | 5 | 3.9 | 11 | 3.1 |
| Brazil | 3 | 6.1 | 8 | 1.7 | Italy | 9 | 2.4 | 23 | 1.4 |
| Cambodia | 3 | 7.0 | 4 | 2.6 | Japan | 6 | 2.0 | 27 | 1.4 |
| Cameroon | 4 | 5.6 | 3 | 4.7 | S. Korea | 3 | 6.1 | 13 | 1.2 |
| Canada | 8 | 3.8 | 17 | 1.6 | Mexico | 3 | 6.8 | 7 | 2.2 |
| Colombia | 3 | 6.8 | 7 | 1.9 | NZ | 9 | 4.9 | 15 | 1.9 |
| Finland | 7 | 2.7 | 21 | 1.6 | Russia | 6 | 2.5 | 14 | 1.8 |
| France | 12 | 2.9 | 19 | 2.0 | UK | 12 | 2.7 | 18 | 1.8 |
| Germany | 11 | 2.4 | 21 | 1.5 | USA | 9 | 3.7 | 15 | 1.8 |

*Source:* World Bank (2018).

As the number of older people explodes, the fertility rate (average births per woman) is falling markedly worldwide (see Table 12.1). A fertility rate of 2.1 births per woman on average maintains a stable population size. Above that, it grows, and below, it shrinks (Organisation for Economic Co-operation and Development, 2018). This is good news for women's health and family prosperity, because fewer children improve both measures. For overall economies, however, not enough native-born people will be available to fill jobs left vacant through retirement or death, and all developed nations are now below replacement rate without immigration. Aging is predicted to stagnate economies over a long time period (Nagarajan, Teixeira, & Silva, 2016). Farms in particular have suffered as young people leave to get jobs in the cities, and this is as true in Africa as in America.

Healthcare workers should particularly rejoice in the job security this demographic shift will bring, because the over-65 age group utilizes health services at a much higher rate and will need more care for longer than preceding generations. On the other hand, expenditures to pay for their care will be enormous. Further, finding young people to care for them may prove challenging, not only because of the years of training required to expand the pool of doctors, nurses, and other medical specialists, but because lower end support jobs are often unpleasant and difficult to fill. Liu, Goryakin, Maeda, Bruckner, and Scheffler (2017) estimate that based on past trends, 80 million healthcare workers will be needed globally by 2030, with an expected supply of only 65 million, leaving a shortfall of 15 million. These jobs will be concentrated in upper middle-income countries, ironically some of the same ones currently moving to reduce foreign populations and limit immigration.

## REALITY CHECK

*With what ethnicity do you identify? How do you see the role of your group in the future?*

*Are you surprised by the changing percentage of elders in your area?*

*How will the demographics of your area look in a decade? In 30 years?*

## 12.2 APPLIED PSYCHOLOGY: WORKING WITH CULTURE

### LO 12.2: Identify issues that culturally informed psychologists address in the real world.

The following sections highlight areas in which psychology is applied to situations in real life. Whether in communities, business, education, or the military, people in each context face issues of culture due to increasing diversity. Within each are issues of social justice, equity, and inclusion. Voluntary migration between regions and social mobility within regions drive some of these conditions. Warfare and natural disasters push intercultural contact in others. They all share dynamics of cultural process, providing arenas where psychology can contribute insight. All are also areas where psychologists find employment and research opportunities. Disciplines involved include community psychology, cultural and cross-cultural psychology, industrial and organizational psychology, black psychology, Asian social psychology and others.

## Culture in Community

Using the term loosely, community is where culture happens, whether a village, neighborhood, city, or ghetto. Community psychology operates on the principle that healthy, safe communities support healthy residents, and community dysfunction leads to social and psychological ills. Historically, communities tended to be monocultural except in the few large cities that existed before the 19th century. Ancient cities that became Mumbai, Cairo, and Istanbul, along with Paris, Rome, and Beijing drew people from afar for centuries, but most people lived in small villages rarely visited by strangers. Families kept to the same lands and livelihoods for generations with little exposure to other ways of being. Colonialism spurred some migration, with a growing stream of colonists and slaves traversing the Atlantic. East and South Asians moved as workers and merchants in the British Empire. The major shifts began with industrialization, people lured to cities by employment opportunities, farmlands and villages depopulated.

Communities all over the world look very different now. The USA hosts dozens of immigrant groups, whether recent or generations past, African descendants, and surviving Native American groups. The cities of Asia swell with people from various ethnic groups who have left their homelands for work or survival. People from dozens of African tribal groups fill the cities for jobs or to escape war and starvation, sometimes pushed into uneasy community with ancestral foes.

Community-level influences range from destructive, as in drug and gang controlled neighborhoods, to beneficial. This is true in Detroit but also in other cities including Stockholm, where refugees and immigrants experience ghettoized conditions with some degree of drug trade. It is notable, however, that characterizations of African Americans and of Muslim immigrants in Sweden are based more in political expediency than fact (Nordgren, 2017). While lack of educational and economic opportunity are associated with drug abuse, the phenomena are by no means limited to non-Caucasians, and illegal drug use has increased dramatically in white communities in the rural US (e.g., Vickers Smith et al., 2018). Conversely, communities also provide positive and stabilizing influences. For instance, Nasim and colleagues (2011) observed that religious and familial practices moderated drug-use risks among rural African American youths as community disorganization increased. In other words, negative effects of economic recession, job loss, underfunded schools, and ghettoization can be mitigated by positive connections within the community.

Despite public perception, rates of violent crime in the US and internationally fell dramatically over the past quarter century (Kim-Ju, Goodman, & Her, 2018; UN Economic and Social Council, 2017). The reduction is not uniform, however, with violence remaining high in Central America and in areas of armed conflict. Violence also remains high for certain ethnic communities in the US, with youth particularly affected. Homicide remains the second leading cause of death for African American and Hispanic males from age 10 to 24. Community violence exposure (CVE) forms a potent risk to the health and well-being of youth, with a cumulative effect of violent experiences pushing them to internalize and to act out as they experience more exposure (Kim-Ju et al., 2018).

Asians are stereotyped as model immigrants in the developed world. They are perceived to have a strong work ethic, generally do well in school, and avoid criminality. Actually, the term *Asian* covers many ethnic groups and nationalities, and not all individuals fit that model. Like any other group entering a community, new arrivals may enter with language issues, relegated to low-paying jobs and housing in low-SES neighborhoods. Chinatowns, Japantowns, and Koreatowns began as low-income areas, with the immigrant groups struggling to earn enough to move away. The LA Koreatown became famous in the 1992 Rodney King riots, when police cut off exits to limit access to richer neighborhoods beyond. The area burned for three days, as looters rampaged and Korean business owners borrowed guns to defend their stores from rooftops (Lah, 2017).

Many Koreans have long since left the LA Koreatown for more affluent communities. Following behind them came Vietnamese, Cambodians, and Hmong. Kim-Ju et al. (2018) investigated the CVE experience of Hmong youth, many of whom live in low-SES communities rife with violence and drugs. CVE experiences were, indeed, predictive of distress symptoms and behavioral problems including aggression and delinquency. Far from a hopeless situation, however, their results showed a moderating effect of parental support and ethnic identity on negative outcomes. The process is complex, however, and strong ethnic identity combined with identification with the mainstream culture may yield more resilience; connection with both cultures certainly provides more avenues for belonging (Sirikantraporn, 2013).

The success of any immigrant community depends on their interpersonal dynamics, including support from their own ethnic group, if any are present, and how they interact and interface with those around them. As discussed in Chapter 10, New Zealand saw a 20% change in ethnic composition in only two decades. A number of the newly arrived groups formed community organizations called ethnic councils, for economic opportunity and political support. These groups were specific to ethnicity—Filipino, for example—but gradually joined into regional councils and ultimately the New Zealand Federation of Multicultural Councils (NZFMC). The 2017 NZFMC president, Alexis LewGor, herself an immigrant of Chinese, German, and Samoan ancestry from Fiji, posted results of research on challenges faced by immigrants (see Table 12.2). The list is not unique; immigrants face these challenges everywhere, but usually without support of a community-based advocacy organization like NZFMC. The group provides a model for community-based collective support.

## Culture and Organizations

In the boom of internationalized business following WWII, cultural concerns took center-stage in industrial and organizational (IO) psychology as management faced issues and cultural mismatches in running multicultural workforces. Beginning in the

## Table 12.2 Challenges Facing Immigrants to New Zealand

| Challenges faced by immigrants when they first arrive in New Zealand (from most challenging to least) | Challenges faced by immigrants after 1–2 years in New Zealand |
|---|---|
| 1. Employment | 1. Cost of living |
| 2. Cost of living | 2. Housing and accommodation |
| 3. Language and communication | 3. Racism and discrimination |
| 4. Racism and discrimination | 4. Employment |
| 5. Housing and accommodation | 5. Community Support |
| 6. Community support | 6. Government Support |
| 7. Government support | 7. Language and communication |

*Source:* LewGor (2017).

1960s, IO psychologists began trying to tease out factors most relevant to predicting behavior and operating businesses effective across cultural and national situations (Aycan, 2000). It was during this era that Dutch psychologist Geert Hofstede began analysis of IBM data leading to publication of *Culture's Consequences* (1980). Psychology was beginning to become more international, with American and European psychologists taking posts in other countries, and with academics from elsewhere coming to teach in America and Northwestern Europe. IO psychologists increasingly have cultural training or international experience, keeping pace with the continuing expansion of business and manufacturing around the world and accommodating diversity of workforces within countries. Research on these topics reflects the body of knowledge discussed in previous chapters.

Broadly, issues of culture arise due to both internal and external factors. Internal factors include the size and type of business, composition of workforce, the technologies used or produced, and the business' stage of development from new to firmly established. External factors include the surrounding political, legal, and institutional structures, the educational system, and the sociocultural context (Aycan, 2000). These factors bear marked similarity to Bronfenbrenner's (1994) ecocultural model of individual development. The issue is not whether sociocultural factors influence organizations; they do. The issue is what factors are most salient and to what extent do they affect a particular operation? Internal and external factors form a bidirectional relationship between organization and context, each affecting developments in the other.

Also similar to the ecocultural model, Gelfand, Erez, and Aycan (2007) describe organizational behavior (OB) as phenomena on the micro level of individual thoughts and feelings, the mezzo level of organizational leadership, teamwork, and negotiation, and the macro phenomena of organizational culture and structure. Until the 1980s, Americans dominated OB and IO research, operating on melting-pot assumptions that culture takes second position to the organization and leadership. In the intervening decades, the field and its researchers became increasingly diverse, though most journals reflect US-centric perspectives (Allen & Vardaman, 2017). IO psychology also still relies heavily on quantitative methodologies, reflecting the dominant positivistic origins of the field. In actuality, the 2016 Fortune Global 500 list 73% of the companies as based outside the US, and many of the remaining companies have more employees outside than inside the US. Important topics include motivation, values, leadership and management styles, expatriation, and diversity issues (Aycan, 2000).

## Leadership Styles

Leadership obliges a person to define the reality of others who are led. The process is socially constructed by the interactions of both leaders and followers (Smircich & Morgan, 1982). Existing literature on business leadership leans heavily toward individualism and masculinity, a model leader being a "masculine competitive, aggressive, controlling and self-reliant individualist" (Ford, 2010, p. 49). The bulk of this literature originates in America and Europe, primarily in English language. Imagery of that narrative portrays (male) leaders as heroic, tackling challenges, grabbing the bull by the horns, and ruling with an iron fist (Eyong, 2017; Nygaard et al., 2017). Needless to say, the effectiveness of such a monocultural perspective is suspect, and particularly the iron-fist trope has been shown to decrease productivity and increase unethical behavior even in Western contexts (Nygaard et al., 2017).

The Euro-American leadership model most resembles ancient structures of British Isles society, as described Roman writer Tracticus in about 55 BCE. Ultimate authority was held by a king, followed by chieftains and elders, the roles eventually evolving into dukes, lords, and knights. Despite the assumption that European cultural evolved from Greco-Roman sources, this hierarchy differed from the Greeks and pre-imperial Romans. Counsels and senates ruled those cultures. Corporate structure and IO research share more commonality with ancient Briton culture than Greco-Romans.

The dearth of non-male, non-Western leadership research reflects the reality of who actually leads around the world (see Table 12.3). As of 2017, women filled only 3% of CEO positions in large corporations, and only five nations have had a woman in charge for more than 15 of the last 50 years. Of 146 countries reporting, 77 have never had a woman in charge, including the US (Geiger & Kent, 2017). Further down the command chain, only three countries have more than 50% of managerial positions held by women: Jamaica at 59%, Colombia at 53%, and Saint Lucia at 52%. The US ranks 15th at 42.7% (International Labour Organization, 2015). Sixteen Fortune 500 companies shared detailed data including more than 800,000 employees. In their corporate leadership, 72% are white males.

A primary difference affecting leaders of multicultural organizations relates to Hofstede's power distance dimension, and to Triandis's vertical-horizontal axes. Both refer to equality of members in a group or culture. In a situation of high power distance, people higher in authority have greater control, and those below have less right

| Table 12.3 | Ethnic Diversity of Management at 16 Reporting Fortune 500 Companies |
|---|---|
| 21% Asian | |
| 3% Latino | |
| 2% Black | |
| 0.6% two or more races | |
| 0.2% Native American | |
| 0.1% Native Hawaiian or Pacific Islander | |

*Source:* Jones (2017).

to disagree with directives. This describes a vertical social structure. In a horizontal setting, people are more or less equal, as in Sweden where executives are not normally separated on the top floor in a corner office. You might call your professor, boss, or king by his first name. These factors, along with the individualism–collectivism dimension can contribute greatly to understanding of an organization, whether familial, political, or professional.

These cultural factors indicate, to some degree, the type of leadership that will be most effective, or at least what one can expect in an organization. A leadership style can make or break a venture, based on managerial choices. An individualist can easily alienate collectivist employees by pitting them against each other in a competition for rewards, which is a popular method of incentivizing an American sales staff. Workers may resent a manager from a different ethnic origin, and rather than increasing productivity, the manager may unintentionally firm up his status as an outsider by pushing an incongruent agenda, losing rapport with his staff. Conversely, a collectivist may be ill-equipped to deal with dedicated individualists with an every-man-for-himself drive. Assuming the collectivist manager perceives these individualist employees as in-group members, the collectivist may make some unfortunate choices, presuming that the employees will put aside self-interest to work for the good of the company.

## Other Approaches to Leadership

As mentioned, Euro-American models dominate leadership research, but other cultures are gradually appearing in the literature. Edwards (2015) reviewed a small body of anthropological literature on leadership in indigenous cultures. In 1940s Navajo culture, leading was a process rather than a role, emphasizing communal service rather than individual advancement. In earlier times, the logistical leader would likely be different from the war leader, those tasks requiring different skills. In short, leadership is distributed across individuals and situations. Distributed leadership characterized the accounts he reviewed, a concept increasingly discussed in IO research.

# SPOTLIGHT

## MĀORI LEADERSHIP

For the Māori of Aotearoa (NZ), leadership stems from several types of connection. As mentioned earlier, *whakapapa* (recitation of genealogy) forms an important part of introduction, establishing how people are related by family, tribe, land features, or *waka*, canoes on which their people arrived. *Whakapapa* provides evidence of *mana*, a word relating to power, authority, or respect. *Mana atua* comes from spiritual dimensions, including divine beings, but relating on a daily level to sources of wisdom and virtue. *Mana whenua* comes from the land, including mountains and rivers, and providing wisdom by unification with nature over generations. *Mana tupuna* stems from ancestors. *Mana tangata* connects a leader to the people, requiring integrity and continuity across time. The final element is *mana wahine*, leadership of women, associated with the earth (Henry & Wolfgramm, 2018). The word *rangatira* can describe a chief or leader. It derives from *raranga*, to weave, and *tira*, which can be a group or can be rays of light. Metaphorically, the *rangatira* weaves together people of a group.

### Why It Matters

Māori concepts of leadership contrast with the dominant Euro-American narrative of individual advancement and leadership by strong males who dictate to those beneath them. Māori provide an excellent example of distributed leadership in action.

Joseph Eyong (2017) studied African approaches to leadership in a dozen communities in Nigeria and Cameroon, drawing on his lived experience in Africa and African communities in England. Eyong maintains that Sub-Saharan Africans hold a worldview and set of leadership ideals distinct from Anglo-Saxon norms, despite six centuries of colonization and subjugation. He quotes a Bayang language proverb from Cameroon, "An elephant does not become a monkey even when it has learned to climb a tree" (p. 136). Eyong discussed historical records of Europeans describing leadership in Africa, including Mungo Park's 1799 observations that rulers call together a council of respected men before making decisions, and that the king was only distinguished by a leopard skin on his seat. The horizontal social structure and casual conversational style between ruler and subject were deeply disturbing to the British.

To unpack differences between African and British cultures, Eyong (2017) conducted 12 unstructured interviews with knowledgeable people in the different West and Central African communities. Note that Africa holds incredible cultural diversity, so this project does not represent all of Africa, or even of West Africa. Three primary themes emerged in analysis: substitutional leadership and non-linearity, leadership as symbol and mythology, and leadership as nonhuman and metaphysical. In the nonlinear theme, African leaders traditionally ruled in concert with advisers. At times a leader may step aside to allow a qualified person to lead, such as in making offerings to gods. Other respected people of a community may hold more actual power than the appointed leader, who may serve primarily as the public face of the village.

The symbolic level of difference is described in several myths or stories. One regards the community tree, normally at the center of the village. That tree forms the point of connection between the village leaders and external forces. An elder or seer may request help from the tree for health or community needs. Another area of difference involves non-human or metaphysical actors such as ancestors. It would be unimaginable for leaders not to consult these forces. In total, leadership is collective, non-linear, and facilitated by metaphysical forces. While these aspects of leadership may seem strange or unnecessary, one should recall that advanced civilizations in Africa, some the size of the continental US, flourished for centuries prior to European contact.

## Human Resource Management

Human resource management (HRM) professionals form the interface between management and employees, tasked with maintaining an effective workforce within budget constraints. As such, they stand at the front lines of the ongoing negotiation required to operate business and industry in the multicultural world. At this point, American managers may run manufacturing facilities in any of a number of countries, but foreign companies also operate plants on US soil. Toyota, for instance, has large automotive factories in several states, including Alabama, Indiana, and Kentucky. German auto manufacturer Daimler AG makes Mercedes-Benz in Alabama and South Carolina. Establishing and operating these ventures has not been without turmoil.

Oddly, the initial conflict between Japanese management and American workers started from a 1950 talk in Tokyo by an American, William Edwards Deming, a statistician and scholar from the US. Deming believed that the future of success in manufacturing lay in emphasis on quality control, but American companies were not receptive to his ideas. Deming's 1950 audience in Japan embraced his ideas enthusiastically, attempting to save the country from its past.

Japan bet everything on WWII, committing monumental financial and material resources along with people, all irretrievably lost on the way to eventual defeat. By the end, the war demolished Japan's infrastructure, and the country promised hundreds of millions in reparations in treaties ending hostilities (probably trillions in today's dollars). A huge arms manufacturing machine grew during the war, but afterward, they were stuck producing plastic squirt guns and cheap knick-knacks. Recall that Japan adopted psychology within a few years of Wundt's 1879 lab in Germany. They were highly receptive to intelligently designed scientific research. William Deming (1950) offered a solution with his "Statistical Product Quality Administration" system, using scientific method to improve manufacturing from design to client satisfaction. American business dismissed his ideas, but Japan embraced his concepts and quickly transformed into a global leader in manufacture of quality products.

By the 1970s, Japanese cars were taking the world by storm with their performance and reliability. When the first wholly Toyota-owned plant in the US opened in 1986, the company knew it had a winning automotive formula, and the Japanese management felt certain that American workers would share their dedication to such a great company.

This was not the case, though American car manufacturers were already researching Total Quality Management and other offshoots of Deming's concepts.

One approach developed in Japan is the Quality Circle, in which employees work in teams in a process of continuous improvement (M. Ward, 2007). At Toyota, every action of every employee is specified and monitored, whether the time, order, and torque for tightening of the bolts holding a car seat or the activities of office clerks and managers (Spear & Bowen, 1999). If it takes 55 seconds to complete seven tasks installing a seat, it is immediately apparent if the employee has not completed task five by the time 40 seconds pass. For Japanese workers and managers, constant self-improvement fits concepts of honor and obligation to the company collective, and yes, efficiency and profitability improve. It failed miserably in American factories. Eventually, researchers identified a cultural mismatch between Toyota's corporate culture and American workers. With new training approaches, the workers learned to value the deeply cooperative approach (M. Ward, 2007). Since 1992, the company has operated the Toyota Supplier Support Center (TSSC), providing training for hundreds of American companies in the Toyota Production System (Spear & Bowen, 1999), a supply chain for elements of final Toyota products.

### Managing Diversity

Workplace diversity can refer to a number of employee attributes, including educational attainment and focus, motivations and goals, or social identities (Nair & Vohra, 2015). Companies may seek diversity in ethnic or national composition of a workforce or in gender, including LGBTQ+ employees. Companies may be motivated to diversify by legislation, such as the Civil Rights Act in the US or gender equality laws in other countries, or for public relations reasons when consumers expect social justice from companies. Diversity may also be involuntary, driven by an already multicultural population. Despite resistance to affirmative action and gender equity legislation in the US, strong global trends push business to honor diversity, and multinationals have led the trend for decades.

While the business world slowly accepts diversity as a fact of life, at least in espoused attitudes, what that means or how it can be achieved remains surprisingly elusive. Diversity could be defined as inclusion of workers from multiple ethnic or national backgrounds, but should that be achieved by targeted recruitment or by mandated quotas? Should a workforce reflect demographics of the local region, the nation, or some other level of analysis? Ultimately the question is why? Is diversity necessary for some performance goal such as culturally inclusive marketing, for social justice, for public relations, or for some other reason? Diversity initiatives often come from upper management without sufficient explanation or provision of resources for implementation or outcome measurement (Nishii, 2017). Clear expectations create opportunities for goal achievement.

### Staffing: Recruitment and Selection

Recruitment describes processes of attracting and employing human capitol. Recruitment identifies potential employees, informs about jobs and organizations, and attempts to convince desirable workers to join the organization (Allen & Vardaman, 2017). Western companies have long favored impersonal recruitment, going back to the want-ads pages of newspapers, now giving way to online listings. Currently, a number of companies advertise online screening tools in which the candidate fills out a series of question fields with only those meeting automated qualifications passing to a next stage. The idea is that impersonal processes will reduce favoritism and personal interest. US business historically selects employees in a one-way process, employers attempting to determine individual performance factors likely to affect company profitability, then making an offer to the most qualified individual. This may include documentation of education and experience or testing of intelligence and personality traits (Aycan, 2000).

Other national contexts may emphasize agreeableness and interpersonal skills, positive family life, or shared ethnic origin. These factors would indicate whether the prospective employee would blend in harmoniously with other workers in a more collective setting. In areas emphasizing in-group membership in selection, word of mouth may be the favored recruitment strategy, because only those closest to the in-group will hear about the opening. Personal references may be used for a variety of reasons, forming an important factor confirming connections in collectivist cultures at the start of hiring. In individualist settings, personal references are used at the end to confirm expected abilities and performance.

### Prejudice and Discrimination

As discussed earlier, prejudice consists of categorical judgments applied against a type or class of people based on their racial or religious identity or phenological characteristics like skin color or facial shape. **Discrimination** consists of differential treatment of individuals based on categorical memberships in groups described by characteristics such as ethnicity or gender. Prejudice and discrimination both manifest in all phases of business. On the macro organizational level, a business may prefer or reject alliances based on ethnicity or nationality, perhaps with suppliers or distributors. On a mezzo level, team dynamics or negotiation styles may favor one group over another, affecting who participates in any phase of enterprise. On a micro level, individuals within an organization may harbor attitudes favoring one categorical group over another, regardless of a candidate's or organization's inherent characteristics.

In a series of studies in New Zealand, Diego-Mendoza (2010) found surprising examples of discrimination. As mentioned earlier, the country changed its immigration policies because it faced shortages of workers in a number of areas, especially including healthcare. A government agency vets the credentials and qualifications of potential immigrants to establish equivalence with New Zealand requirements. Despite formalized vetting prior to immigration, a common experience on arrival is trouble finding a job matching the qualifications that enabled the person to immigrate. She found that recruiters systematically ignored applications from people with names that sounded non-European. Licensing agencies often required non-European medical personnel to take additional training in New Zealand despite meeting international qualifications. New Zealand is not alone; many countries are restricting immigration.

## GUANXI AND BUSINESS IN CHINA

Dong and Liu (2010) identify the concept of *guanxi* as crucial in understanding how business and business management work in China. The term refers to reciprocal relationships and networks developed via common origins, interests, and experience, nurtured by exchange of favors and consideration. Understanding of *guanxi*, and painstaking development of a *guanxi* network, allows Chinese managers to achieve results more quickly because of their networks of interconnections and collection of favors given and owed (Farh et al., 1998).

A related concept is *xinyong*, or personal trust (Leung et al., 2005). *Xinyong* relates to the Western concept of personal integrity, that a man's word is his bond. Leung and colleagues stress the importance of this concept in doing business in the

People's Republic of China (PRC). *Xinyong* is more important than the wording of any legal document: a contract could be broken, but an agreement with someone who has the quality of *xinyong*, with whom one has developed *guanxi*, forms an agreement that will not be violated. If a person were to violate these relational imperatives, the person would lose face, his socially acknowledged integrity and status, and that is a deeply troubling prospect in China (Hu, 1944), from which one may never recover. The senses of social connection and interpersonal obligation outweigh Western concepts of contract and legal obligation; concrete relations with real people are imminently more important than abstract legal constructs (Lee et al., 2001; Buttery & Wong, 1999).

### Work-Related Values

Say your mother has a brother you have never known well but met at family gatherings as a child. As an adult you get a job as a mid-level manager with a large company. You are at lunch on Friday and get a call from your cousin saying your uncle has died. What you do next will be influenced by your cultural values. Someone of European descent may feel only minimal connection to distant family, and perhaps you feel it is enough to send an e-mail or pick up the phone to send flowers. If you are a Māori in New Zealand, you may drop everything and leave to spend the next several days with the family, participating in a series of *tangihanga* funeral ceremonies. You may not even take a moment to call work because family is the most crucial part of your life, the loss of that relative overwhelming your priorities. Māori novelist Witi Ihimaera describes such a situation in his 1973 debut novel *Tangi*. The protagonist's father dies and he drops everything to meet his familial obligation. His coworkers assume he is just another stereotypically irresponsible Māori, though the protagonist struggled with the certainty that the sudden departure, unexplained on a weekend long before texting or e-mail existed, would endanger his employment. He simply had to do his part for the family collective.

Motivation in the workplace follows the patterns already discussed for dimensions of cultural variation. For instance, Asian Canadians drew motivation from role models conveying a prevention focus to avoid failure, whereas Anglo-Canadians felt more motivated by models promoting strategies for success (Gelfand et al., 2007), reflecting Hofstede's (1980) dimension of uncertainty avoidance. The I-C dimension is associated with preference for team rewards in collectivist settings and for personal recognition and interesting assignments for individualists. Multinational and diverse businesses require managers sensitive to employee response to motivators.

## Motivation and Compensation

Once people become part of a company, they need reasons to behave in desired ways. Eating, drinking, and procreating are primary motivators, those being drives leading to survival. Secondary motivators describe much of modern life: influence, money, power, and other rewards not required for biological existence. Companies must provide the right motivation for employees to perform their duties at a needed level of efficiency. In the most basic terms, employees work to gain resources for physical survival, though material requirements for living vary immensely by context. A garment factory worker in Bangladesh may endure deplorable conditions to ensure the family has a couple of dollars a day to eat. An investment banker in a major city may find conditions unendurable at $250,000 per year. Motivation, however, includes much more than monetary compensation.

Research shows a major area of difference in motivation, as is the case in so much cross-cultural literature, connected to the Individualism–Collectivism spectrum. Rewards can be given to individuals, teams, departments, or entire companies. The type, scope, and targeting of rewards vary somewhat predictably, with collectivists connecting better with group rewards and individualists wanting personal rewards. Individualists also like interesting assignments and professional development opportunities. Providing the proper rewards is crucial in international business, and a major part of diversity management is retaining the best employees in what has been called a "war for talent" (Cooke & Saini, 2010, p. 479).

Compensation and other motivators form factors in overall performance management. A performance management program is designed to monitor and improve employee competence and contributions, normally through cycles of planning, evaluation, and job training/professional development. Planning involves determining dimensions of measurement and setting goals. Emphasis may fall on individual improvement or group benefit, and these goals may be set by management or through a participatory process (Erez, 1997).

Culture affects who is involved in evaluation and how results are used. Power-distance characteristics of a culture influence who performs evaluations. In the US, 360-degree evaluations are popular, in which those above and below a person in hierarchy all submit evaluations. This would cause conflict in high power-distance cultures, where supervisors evaluate those below them and it would be unthinkable for an underling to criticize a superior. Collectivists tend to be uncomfortable with individuals when they are singled out for praise, whereas individualists relish accolades (Aycan, 2000). Further, negative evaluations pose difficulties in some cultures because criticism equals rejection of the person in "associative cultures" (Triandis, 1994, p. 119) and may violate interdependent norms. Increasingly, multi-level performance evaluation is viewed as the most effective path to enhancement, including individual and group levels, and recognizing that group affect and cultural characteristics of the organization all bear on success in business (Allen & Vardaman, 2017; Erez, 1997).

## Equity and Fairness

Equity and fairness require balancing several dimensions including allocation of material resources, but also less tangible elements like respect, voice, and choice. Who is allowed to make decisions and who can advise decision makers? What characteristics are considered in reward and promotion? Who wants and/or receives credit for successes or failures? Factually, compensation is not equitable across any domain. Men are paid more than women everywhere. Males of a dominant ethnicity are paid more than any other demographic. In some cases, the intangible elements may be more important than quantifiable compensations like wages and benefits.

Equity of treatment in a multicultural group can be affected by communication styles. Individualistic tendencies of Westerners lead them to speak up and to speak boldly, whereas East Asians may tend to listen attentively without interrupting (Bazarova & Yuan, 2013). Humility will lead the East Asians to downplay accomplishments and deflect praise to colleagues. Humbleness earns respect in collectivist contexts, but in an individualistic context where it is assumed that people will sing their own praises, could result in promotion of someone less deserving. All involved must be sensitive to the norms of a company's cultural elements.

## Cultural Intelligence

Ang and van Dyne (2008) define cultural intelligence (CQ) as, "the capability of an individual to function effectively in situations characterized by cultural diversity" (p. 3). The concept was described by Early and Ang (2003) in the wake of 9/11, seeking to understand how cultures could harbor such hatred for each other. The concept has enjoyed increasing popularity as researchers attempt to predict sojourner success, but a number of issues have surfaced. The primary quantitative measure of the concept has been the Cultural Intelligence Scale (CQS; Ang et al., 2007). Ward, Fischer, Lam, and Hall (2009) confirmed the factor structure of the scale, but found it correlated strongly with Emotional Intelligence (EQ). To be a legitimate construct, it should be distinct, and a very strong correlation with EQ could indicate that they are not separate concepts. Further, CQ was less predictive of adjustment success than EQ.

The idea of cultural intelligence initially reflected a trait style of concept, suggesting that a person might have or lack an innate ability to perceive and respond appropriately to subtle cultural behavioral cues or norms. By knowing whether a candidate for international assignment possesses this trait, a company could determine likelihood of success in the posting. Subsequent research has demonstrated that CQ can be improved through training, meaning it is more of a skill than a trait, and that is good news for employees and companies alike. CQ correlates positively with cross-cultural adjustment, general psychological adjustment, job satisfaction, and leadership empowerment (Feng, Schei, & Selart, 2018), meaning companies can improve the lives and productivity of employees through CQ training. After several years of development, research connects CQ to a number of practical parameters of employee performance, such as predicting appropriate choice of conflict management style (Gonçalves, Reis, Sousa, Santos, & Orgambidez-Ramos, 2015).

## Sojourners

As discussed in Chapter 10, *sojourner* is a term used to describe people who move temporarily to another region or country for work or school. A great deal of psychological research concerns adaptation of sojourners, both in business and education. When people move for either reason, their success is crucial to the enterprises they enter. If an employer takes on the expense of moving a person from one country to another, that investment needs to pay off. Smoothing of transitions and reducing the difficulties of acculturation can help to insure that an employee fulfills job requirements for long enough to justify the moving and training expenses involved. In education, universities compete for international students. Some will pay much higher tuition rates to attend a respected institution in another country, providing financial support for the institution. Some are exceptionally well qualified, and even if they receive scholarship assistance, they may make significant contribution to a body of knowledge and bring prestige to the institution. In all cases, universities need their students to graduate and go on to succeed if they are to maintain credibility and recruit future students.

Adaptation of expatriates involves comfort with jobs tasks, living conditions, and host culture communication (Allen & Vardaman, 2017). Research in this area has focused primarily on two avenues: measuring readiness for acculturation and enhancing of coping for cultural transition. The former involves testing for concepts like CQ. The latter relates to processes of informing sojourners about the culture to which they will adapt. The idea that training or education can provide sojourners with tools for better outcomes derives from the cultural learning school of thought on acculturation. It forms a very practical avenue to ensure success in both business and education. A long history of research identifies knowledge one needs moving into a new cultural context, including understanding of behavioral and communication norms. Preparation could include language classes, but also information on practical skills like how one shops for food. An acquaintance described her first experience going shopping in an Asian country. Unaware of the variety of meats consumed or that they were purchased in living form, she quickly told her children it was a pet store and never took them shopping for food again during their time overseas.

## Culture and the Military

Culture forms an important consideration for militaries on several levels: the military as an organizational culture, as an organization with diversity in membership, and as an organization that interacts directly with cultures either as allies or opponents or as recipients of aid or assistance. The US military includes about 1.3 million people across five branches, the largest being the army. Ethnic minorities now form about 40% of the force. African Americans form the largest minority in all branches except the Marines, where Hispanics number highest after Caucasians. Males, specifically white males, dominate all branches, though black women outnumber black men (Parker, Cilluffo, & Stepler, 2017; Reynolds & Shendruk, 2018). The military attracts many non-whites because it is relatively easy to join and has mechanisms designed to promote people by merit, though prejudice does exist. The military has recently offered a pathway to US citizenship, for instance under the Obama administration, though rumors circulate that former service people have been deported despite their service. Sweden, on the other hand, specifically encourages jobless immigrants to join ("Swedish Army to Jobless," 2012), providing an enthusiastic path to social inclusion.

In the 1990s, a number of high profile peace-keeping missions required creation of multi-national forces, including the Balkan War, the Tutsi-Hutu conflict in Rwanda, and the ongoing conflicts in Somalia and the Sudan. In the 2000s, response to terrorist attacks, primarily 9/11, placed coalition forces in a conflict zone with a very high degree of cultural distance from the combatants and civilians they met in Afghanistan, Iraq, and other Middle Eastern countries. Research on culture and military increased dramatically at military colleges and other military programs around the world. Syria is a more recent hot spot.

Following the trend of internationalization in business, many countries see international collaboration as a way to increase military efficiency and cut costs, especially in policing and peace-keeping operations (Soeters, 1997). Also as with business, cultural differences have caused turbulence in these efforts. In international military collaboration, problematic national differences emerge in fighting style, war strategy and execution, and occupation (Soeters, Poponete, & Page, 2006). Modern warfare sometimes involves formal rules of engagement, drawn up upon declaration of war or entry into a policing action. These limit actions that may be taken for instance providing protection for civilians and medical personnel. Civil wars, insurgency, and partisan conflicts may lack rules, involving widespread brutality. Rules of engagement attempt to limit humanitarian violations, at least by international forces.

Culture obviously becomes a factor when militaries engage in warfare with members of another culture. After the fall of the Soviet Union, the former Yugoslavia split into several smaller countries, including Serbia, Montenegro, and Bosnia-Herzegovina. Conflict broke out between ethnic Serbs and Muslims, who have cycled between hostility and peaceful coexistence since the Ottomans invaded in the 1300s. The collapse of Yugoslavia placed the Serbs, who were economically favored in the communist government, at risk of losing their authority and financial power. Leaders including Slobodan Milosevic exploited those ancient prejudices and tensions to garner political capital, resulting in several years of civil war. Serbs slaughtered thousands of Muslims, sometimes in the presence of international peacekeepers constrained by rules of engagement that prohibited use of weapons except in self-defense. Peacekeepers sometimes had to watch without reacting as males of whole villages were slaughtered because reaction would have violated the rules.

For many reasons, the military services of many countries routinely hire psychologists. The most infamous cases involve psychologists who monitor and advise interrogators, such as the ones at Abu Ghraib prison in Afghanistan. After years of allegations and denial about members colluding with torture, the American Psychological Association commissioned an independent study, opening all records to a former prosecutor who found definite evidence supporting claims of wrongdoing (Pope, 2016; Hoffman et al., 2015). The APA eventually adopted a policy that forbids members to engage in any activity constituting torture, and a number of members quit.

A more comforting use of psychologists is in reducing intercultural misunderstanding and supporting ethnic and gender equality. The need for intercultural training became obvious in Vietnam and early in the Afghanistan and Iraq conflicts. Cultural misperceptions and violation of norms caused needless suffering and increased hostility on all sides. Misunderstanding of social structures made reorganization and rebuilding more difficult and increased chances of unintended violence. A number of training programs have been implemented to increase cultural sensitivity and awareness of norms. (Abbe & Gouge, 2012; Center for Army Lessons Learned, 2004; Hendrickson & Tucker, 2005; Schnell, 2010).

## Culture and Education

Reshaped by changing demographics and migration, classrooms look very different in many countries, though data are most easily accessed for the US. As of 2014, 50.3 million students attended publicly funded primary and secondary schools in the US, contrasted with 5.3 million in private schools in 2015. Monitoring of student numbers is not consistent across years, and private schools do not have the same reporting requirements as public schools. Several trends do emerge from the available data. Administrators such as principals and district supervisors are overwhelmingly white, at roughly 80%. Teachers are also disproportionately white, and teachers of other ethnicities are underrepresented compared to student demographics in public schools (e.g., Snyder, Brey, & Dikkow, 2016).

### Managing Diverse Schools and Classrooms

Although diversity has increased in schools, the broader world of education has moved toward a homogenized system of operation (Fitzgerald, 2006). Administered in the Western world by white men, primary values for the educational system are affordability, accountability, and uniform measurement. From a universalist perspective, student ethnicity is irrelevant; a student is a student and all should be held to the same standards. On the other hand, we know by now that many culture-related factors shape how people think and react. A single approach may, recalling Einstein's words, require fish to climb trees. The many factors of culture may affect both learning and pedagogy: individualism–collectivism, power distance, vertical–horizontal structure, cognitive styles, communication norms, and other factors included.

A number of projects and studies have established that different cultures learn in different ways. Researchers testing Gardner's theory of multiple intelligences across cultures have found cross-cultural differences in Gardner's domains, with implications for how students might best learn. The many differences we have discussed in socialization and resulting cognitions certainly provide evidence of difference in learning styles. Piaget's error, bringing unfamiliar items to test African children and assuming intellectual deficit when they did not understand instructions, continues in current educational environments.

Using standardized timed tests, every second counts, and unfamiliar ideas or items may slow response time. Questions may contain unintentional bias just by the writer's assumptions of normalcy. Consider a question, "If Santa has 12 elves and each can make 20 toys a day, how long do they need to make toys for 480 children?" For a Hindu child recently immigrated from southern India, these concepts may make sense after some consideration, but the delay trying to remember meanings of Santa, elf, and Christmas loses some amount of time. An entire test of such items could seriously impact a non-Caucasian student, probably resulting in a significant drop in score.

A group of Hawai'i teachers grew concerned at the disparity in scores of their students. They taught at a school on the rural side of Pearl Harbor's military base complexes, where the students were a mix of children from local non-Caucasian agricultural workers and mostly Caucasian military families. The local children consistently underperformed on their standardized tests, though the teachers found them all equivalently bright on a daily basis. Teachers in the US usually work long hours, but this group took the time to rewrite a standardized test using concepts and items from their context. For instance, a question about bass fishing in a lake could be confusing because "bass" could be a fish or a musical instrument and the students would rarely see a lake. "Sally and Susie" were changed to "Lani and Momi," who went to the ocean shore to pick *'opihi*, a common mollusk. On the revised test, the local children outperformed the military migrants, who were confused and delayed by the unfamiliar concepts. The study remains anecdotal, the teachers lacking time to do formal research, but the story has circulated for years in conversations and professional development workshops.

The trick for teachers in any multicultural class is to ascertain the students' strengths and teach to those. In a superb example of intercultural educational research, Roland Tharp (e.g., Tharp, 1982) undertook a project for Kamehameha Schools, a system established by the last of the kingdom's monarchy descendants to benefit "the children of Hawai'i." Hawaiians remain oppressed politically, economically, and judicially, but some of those who go to Kamehameha Schools get into excellent colleges and often do well in life. The administration wanted, at that time, to understand how better to educate Hawaiian students so that all could excel. The trust funding Kamehameha Schools remains one of the largest in the world, and Tharp's budget allowed video cameras in classrooms—unheard of in the late 70s/early 80s—and a constant feedback loop with instructors to find avenues for improvement. Although implementation of Tharp's results was only maintained for a few years, they provide excellent ideas for teaching to a diverse classroom.

Improvements recommended in the Kamehameha project included use of small groups for learning. The most common teaching technique in US schools is whole-class questioning, in which the teacher asks, "Who can tell me ... ?" and waits for a student to speak up. Anyone who teaches in Hawai'i knows a long silence will follow because in a collectivist culture, speaking up makes a person stand out. A common saying is "the nail that sticks up gets hammered down." Tharp and his colleagues found that small groups reduced power distance, and students would actively discuss their lessons.

In multicultural classes, Caucasians/Europeans will often speak up while more collectivist students do not. This creates a false appearance of competence and results in inequitable participation grades. A number of techniques can balance the situation.

One is to use sticks or cards with student names to be drawn during class. All students get to participate actively without having to initiate response themselves.

Two other types of cultural programs should be mentioned: immersion schools and Culture-Based Education (CBE). In the 1970s, the Māori and Hawaiians began efforts to revitalize their cultures. This was an urgent mission; generations had been punished for speaking their languages and engaging in cultural practices, and the cultures were dying. In 1981, Māori educators began establishing Kohanga Reo, Māori language preschools, and later, the Kura Kaupapa Māori primary and secondary schools. Students speak only *te reo Māori* (Māori language) and learn by traditional processes of pedagogy (Hohepa, Smith, Smith, & McNaughton, 1992; Smith, 2012). Punana Leo are the equivalent Hawaiian schools. Similar indigenous programs include Cree Way in Quebec, Canada, and Hualapai in Arizona (Iokepa-Guerrero, 2008; Stiles, 1997).

These programs provide culturally appropriate settings in which students learn their language and traditions. Also highly effective are culture-based education (CBE) programs. In these, cultural activities are used in teaching other subjects like math and engineering. In Hawai'i, classes include astronomy learned through traditional Hawaiian navigation and horticulture learned by tending *lo'i kalo* (taro fields). Other ways of indigenizing curricula include use of story and song, personalizing history to include a class's culture, and having elders come in to teach.

A related approach is called culturally responsive pedagogy (CRP), which was used to adapt a choral program in a Puerto Rican enclave and greatly enriched student experiences (Shaw, 2016). What stories, songs, or elders fit will change depending on the class, and in a multicultural class, inclusiveness can provide opportunities for success by minority students and also for intercultural understanding.

## REALITY CHECK

What is the ethnic composition of your community? Your school? Your workplace?

Do the values of your community match your own?

Have your instructors ever broken your class into small groups for discussions? How did that feel?

## 12.3 CULTURE, COMPETITION, AND CONFLICT

### LO 12.3: Explain how culture shapes conflict and resolution.

Humans share many parameters of existence, an unfortunate one of which is conflict, including competition over resources and control. Other creatures compete for food, territory, and mates. Humans also disagree about belief systems and other intangibles unrelated to survival. Conflict may stimulate growth, as when the US and the Soviet

Union engaged in a mostly peaceful race to land on the moon, eventually cooperating on the International Space Station. Competition is a form of conflict, as when sports teams compete for a championship or companies compete for market share. Of course, the extreme includes violence and open warfare.

Conflict requires interdependence, in that two or more parties share interest in something, whether land, resources, customers, or recognition. Without overlap of interests, there can be no conflict, so conflict and competition requires a relationship of some sort. Human conflict happens in cultural or intercultural contexts, following culturally determined patterns and processes. While psychological study of conflict extends back more than a century, the majority of literature has assumed universals based only on Western cultures (Gelfand et al., 2001). Conflicts may arise over tangible issues, as when a finite resource or location is at stake, or over intangibles like religion. The crucial requirement is that people perceive that a conflict is occurring. At that point, some process happens to resolve the situation, whether via words or violence, and culture plays a major role in the choices conflicting parties make. Certain norms will be preferred in a culture, but people within a culture may engage in many conflict styles, perhaps even within a single conflict. Cultural considerations can, however, guide resolution processes.

## Conflict Styles

People approach conflict with certain ideas about conflict: what it is, how people in conflict should act, and what outcomes are possible. Conflict literature describes several habitual patterns people tend to follow when conflicts come up. Termed *conflict styles*, research settled on five by the 1970s: competing, avoiding, accommodating, collaborating, and compromising (Thomas & Kilmann, 1978). These styles vary on dimensions of assertiveness and cooperation.

The competing style is high in assertiveness and low in cooperation. The accommodation style is low assertiveness and high in cooperation and may be desirable if the other party has greater expertise or resources. The avoiding style is low assertiveness and low in cooperation and may be most difficult to resolve given that the party may not participate. The collaborating style is high in assertiveness *and* high in cooperation. The assertiveness may cause some turmoil, but ultimately this person will express what they want and need so the solution should last. Finally, the compromising style is intermediate in both (see Figure 12.1; Sternberg & Soriano, 1984; Thomas & Kilmann, 1978).

Research into cultural factors in conflict management has blossomed in the past few decades, much of it funded by international business after experiencing cultural miscommunication. This section does not presume to cover all facets, but rather to unpackage some origins of these differences. Connected areas of interest relate to underlying cognitive processes, behavioral norms, and values systems.

All cultures have schema about conflict that we learn as we acculturate. When conflicts arise, certain ways of thinking activate, providing a cultural tendency toward particular conflict styles. Some differences in conflict style are explained by the I-C spectrum. Collectivists prefer indirect critical communication, reflecting the high valuation of interpersonal harmony. Research reveals a preference for an avoiding conflict style among Chinese managers, for example (Morris et al., 1998). Reliance on the

**Figure 12.1   Conflict Management Styles**

High

Assertive

Low

Low

Cooperative

High

Competing

Collaborating

Compromising

Avoiding

Accommodating

*Source:* Adapted from Thomas and Kilmann (1978).

avoiding style has been linked to desire to preserve relationships. Individualists tend to prefer direct communication, leading to a strong association with a competing conflict style. The competing style links to the achievement orientation of Americans and other Westerners. Morris and colleagues (1998) confirmed these connections of values to conflict styles in a survey of 454 MBA students in the US, China, the Philippines, and India, though they acknowledge that such students are arguably among the most Westernized in their countries. Individuals in the same conflict may hold different conflict frames and interpret the conflict differently, and these differences may be amplified by intercultural style norms. Unsurprisingly, this has caused difficulties in negotiation between Americans and East Asians.

## Culture and Negotiation

A basic process for resolution of conflict is **negotiation**, described as "the deliberate interaction of two or more complex social units which are attempting to define or redefine the terms of their interdependence" (Walton & McKersie, 1965, p. 3). Within a culture, people know the rules and norms of the process, at least as happens in daily life. Between cultures, this may not be the case. Negotiations involve moves and counter-moves, expression of interest and intent, and other forms of communication, all of which are cultural in origin.

In traditional Chinese negotiation, opening moves include establishment of intentions and goals. Next is an assessment phase, in which the Chinese historically excel, using indirect and peripheral moves to assess strengths and weaknesses. In the third phase, the process speeds up, with pressure and hard demands. Negotiation may continue after agreement, with further adjustments. More recent observations discuss a pleasant opening phase, intense technical discussions, challenges in setting terms, demands for new concessions before signing, and ongoing negotiations afterward (Stark, Fam, Waller, & Tian, 2005).

China differs from America and Britain in three of Hofstede's dimensions: I-C, plus power distance and long-term orientation (Buttery & Leung, 1998). Chinese negotiators will be very aware of long-range implications of the negotiation, while Westerners are more focused on immediate results. Asians will seek consensus in their team, but in a hierarchic structure. The subtlety of showing respect for that hierarchy may be difficult for Americans, who are accustomed to greater equality at the negotiating table.

In comparing Brazilian and American negotiation styles, Pearson and Stephan (1998) found a slightly different manifestation of I-C difference. Brazilians' normative expressions emphasized concern for the other party's interest. Americans tended to express concern only for their own interests. This does not mean that Brazilians are less focused on their own ultimate outcomes, just that they follow different rules of expression and need for connection to their eventual business partners. Brazilian negotiation may begin with a meal and a lengthy discussion of family, while Americans want to get to the point without delay. When pushed to skip steps of understanding the other party's way of connecting with significant others, a Brazilian business may simply walk away from a negotiating table.

## International and Intercultural Forgiveness and Reconciliation

Unfortunately, the world remains filled with injustice, violence, crime, and misdeeds. Ideally, conflict gives way to peace, and forgiveness follows. Forgiveness appears to be a universal concept, but as discussed in Chapter 9, cultures differ greatly in how and why they conceptualize, seek, and grant it (Ho & Worthington, 2018), and on the larger scale of intercultural forgiveness around the world, much work lies ahead. Group-level process also involves collective interactions, cognitions, and emotions. Entire groups, whether communities, ethnic groups, regions, or nations, must recognize the scope of infraction or injustice, then all sides must feel the need to receive and/or give forgiveness. The offering and acceptance of apology or restitution similarly requires group participation by someone(s) authorized to enter negotiations. For groups to forgive, the perpetrators must collectively acknowledge fault and regret, and they must renounce the thoughts, feelings, and behaviors that caused the situation. Those offended must trust and believe that apology, ultimately renouncing of the right to harbor resentment (Hanke & Fischer, 2013).

Multiple factors may convolute group-level forgiveness. Wrongs may have been committed over a long history and may be ongoing. Members of ethnic groups like African Americans feel wronged by centuries of economic, judicial, and social oppression in the US, as do Native Americans. These situations are complicated by the fact that injustices continue on a daily basis, with African Americans incarcerated at disproportionately higher rates for the same offenses committed by whites. Poverty, substance abuse, and loss or damage of tribal lands additionally faces Native Americans. Forgiveness usually requires that the perpetrator has ceased to cause damage, but these are current conditions of minority life in the US and around the world.

Despite continuing injustice, feelings of forgiveness reduce depressive symptoms among African American men experiencing every-day racial discrimination (Powell, Banks, & Mattis, 2017). At times, forgiveness must be offered to allow progress, even if the situation is still unresolved. Asked by Oprah Winfrey why he harbored no resentment against apartheid in South Africa, despite three decades of imprisonment and abuse, Nelson Mandela said the following:

> Well, I hated oppression. And when I think about the past, the type of things they did, I feel angry. You have a limited time to stay on earth. You must try and use that period for the purpose of transforming your country. (Mandela, 2000)

Understanding forgiveness on international levels requires consideration of historical context and events and cultural norms, along with qualities of previous attempts at apology. Katja Hanke (2009) took on the massive task of examining forgiveness processes for the atrocities of WWII. Aggression by Axis powers, led by Germany and Japan, wrought massive death and destruction across the globe. Millions died in military actions and both Germany and Japan ran brutal concentration camps where torture and death were commonplace. The Germans killed millions in the Holocaust, primarily Jews, along with Roma, gays, and others. Their militaries and police forced thousands of women into prostitution, most notably Koreans by the Japanese and Jews by the Germans. The aggressors seized property and assets, most of which were never returned.

Forgiveness for Germany began in 1970, when Chancellor Willy Brandt went to the Holocaust memorial on the site of Warsaw's Jewish ghetto and broke down in tears during an annual commemoration. He fell to his knees and cried, an action subsequently named *Kniefall von Warschau* by journalists (see Figure 12.2). His act of contrition was accepted as genuine regret on behalf of his country. Generations of Germans born after WWII were raised with strong emphasis on values of nonviolence and tolerance, though increasing immigration has fueled a newly rising nationalism. The horrors of battle and widespread bombing have nearly passed from living memory, bringing concepts of racial purity and authoritarian rule back into mainstream discourse.

Though Americans as a whole are more aware of conditions in the European theater, Japan's actions in WWII were also brutal. In 1937's infamous Rape of Nanking, Japanese soldiers killed an estimated 300,000 civilians and raped literally tens of thousands of women, many of whom were maimed or killed in the process.

**Figure 12.2 Chancellor Willy Brandt's 1970 *Kniefall von Warschau***

*Source:* AFP/Stringer/Getty Images

In a particularly heinous aspect of the atrocity, two Japanese officers had a daily contest to see who could kill 100 people most rapidly using only a sword. The timed results were reported in Japanese newspapers like a sporting event. For the Chinese and Koreans especially, wounds remain unclosed. Despite the many official apologies and a cash settlement paid to the "comfort women" from Korea, Japan's efforts have evidently not restored enough trust for forgiveness. It may not be that the Japanese feel less sincere, but rather that they have somehow not conveyed their regret in a sufficiently effective way to convince the countries and cultures they wronged of their contrition.

### Contemporary Intercultural Issues

The Balkan Wars (1990–1993) claimed hundreds of thousands of lives and pitted neighbors against each other. Three ethnic groups have lived for centuries in what is now the nation of Bosnia and Herzegovina (BIH): Bosniaks, Serbs, and Croats. The region had been tightly controlled as part of Yugoslavia in the Soviet era, effectively eliminating inter-ethnic violence. After the fall, men like Slobodan Milosevic stoked old grievances to gain political capital, eventually resulting in a brutal war during which the men of entire towns were executed in ethnic cleansing actions. Truce ended the armed conflict more than two decades ago, although the groups have now largely segregated into separate regions. Distrust and hatred remain as an intractable barrier to forgiveness.

Cehajic-Clancy and Bilewicz (2017) studied factors that could facilitate sustainable reconciliation. They found that first, all sides need to believe that reconciliation is possible, despite the tendency often engendered during conflict to believe enemies are inhuman and immoral. Three changes they sought were relational, in the form of reduced contact avoidance; belief systems, restoring belief in humanity so shaken by the brutal war; and emotional, in the form of reduced fear and anxiety. Simply increasing contact had increased hatred in some cases, so something else was needed. Bilewicz (2007) had previously shown that the content of interactions was crucial to positive outcomes.

In a study with Poles and Jews in Poland, Bilewicz and Jaworska (2013) had used moral exemplar stories, specifically stories in which people from one group had selflessly helped someone from the other. In two studies with a total of 160 people of all three ethnicities in BIH, they shared and discussed stories of people from each group saving members of another during the war. Both belief in reconciliation and forgiveness increased, and in the second study, negative feelings toward the outgroups were reduced.

### Colonialism and Forgiveness

Colonization provides another source of ongoing sense of grievance. Millions of indigenous people saw their lands stolen and their people killed by outright violence or disease. Settlers remain across the world, in the US, Australia, and many other nations, and while the settler cultures often consider the offenses long past, inequities continue. Indigenous people still hold grievances for their treatment, both historic and current.

Bell (2009) interviewed 16 young adult New Zealanders of European origin. As settlers/colonizers, their identity stems from their ancestral origins in Great Britain or other countries, but also in conjunction with the indigenous Māori. They perceive the Māori as others alien to them, but as the indigenous people of Aotearoa, the actual aliens are the dominant *pakeha*, the white majority. Bell (2009) found that participants' sense of identity was rattled by their awareness of the wrongs done to the indigenous Māori in the colonization process. On the one hand, they identify as New Zealander rather than people of their ancestral countries. On the other hand, they were haunted by a sense of guilt over the injustices of colonization. Despite this unease, however, social, economic, and political oppression of Māori continues, inhibiting forgiveness and resolution. *Tino rangatiratanga*, a Māori concept of political self-determination, was promised in the Māori-language version of the 1840 Treaty of Waitangi but not in the English version. Political voice was quickly suppressed as the number of colonists grew, and old inequities still continue.

The Māori culture itself contains mechanisms for reconciliation, as is common across cultures. In the context of ongoing domination by *pakeha* colonizers, Māori psychologist Arama Rata noticed that forgiveness research was decidedly European in origin, method, and discourse. She undertook a series of structured interviews with Māori participants across a spectrum of ages and experience regarding processes of forgiveness. Results of thematic analysis revealed that, as in other cultures, Māori acknowledge that offenses happen and healing is sometimes required, though application of indigenous techniques is only appropriate when the transgressor(s) are willing to repent and participate fully. Primary concepts in Māori culture included "*Rongo* (demonstration of commitment to restore relationships), *whakapapa* (interconnectedness between people, places, and events overtime forming identity) and *kaupapa* (agenda set based on the costs and benefits of forgiveness)" (Rata et al., 2008, p. 18).

## Ongoing Diversity Issues

Orlando, in the middle of the Sunshine State, conjures images of happy families visiting from the world over, vacationing at massive resort complexes replete with faeries, wizards, orca, and human-sized mice. If you go there, you will traverse Interstate 4 (I-4) and may unknowingly pass very close to sites of an uncomfortably racist past. Downtown, construction of that highway firmly divided the city center from the African American Parramore Avenue district, on one side the City Beautiful, as the official nickname goes, and on the other side poverty. Florida towns typically had sections built by land-owners for the servants and orange grove workers they employed, usually literally on the other side of the railroad tracks from white homes. The current Parramore area is among the poorest in Central Florida (Gama, 2015).

Heading away from Disney and other theme parks, if one drives north on I-4 East (confusing, but true), one will next pass the affluent white enclave of Winter Park, then Eatonville, the oldest chartered African American township in the US and birthplace of Zora Neale Hurston, the famous author of the Harlem Renaissance. Head compass west off the highway to reach Ocoee, site of the 1920 Ocoee Massacre. That event began on November 1, when Ku Klux Klan members paraded through town warning African Americans not to vote the next day. When hopeful voters were blocked from voting, some demonstrably protesting, a mob of about 100 white males began a rampage in which more than 60 African Americans were killed and their homes burned. Entire families abandoned their properties and possessions to survive. Florida ultimately had the highest rate of lynching following the Civil War.

The city is immensely more diverse today. Near the city center is a Vietnamese enclave with several Asian groceries and restaurants. Further out are Indian, Chinese, Japanese, and Brazilian establishments, then a host of Hispanic businesses, grocery stores, and restaurants on the outskirts. Prejudice remains commonplace, but lynching and arson remain in the past, fortunately. A few miles east is Sanford, however, where the unarmed African American teen Trayvon Martin was shot by George Zimmerman in 2012. Atlanta and other southern cities diversified in similar ways, as have cities and towns across America, with similarly mixed results of inclusion and prejudice.

Earth and its inhabitants face an overwhelming array of challenges. The human population expands beyond sustainability, dependent on resources that alter the atmosphere in their use. Cities sprawl across former forests and prairies, while farmers, ranchers, and miners destroy the world's rain forests. Climate effects already bring larger storms and droughts. Water is already a scarce resource in many places. Issues of access to water, housing, and food, along with other social justice issues, increase daily, dividing ethnic groups and economic classes.

Cape Town, South Africa, faces an epic water shortage, nearly running out completely in both 2017 and 2018. The mayor began personally visiting homes violating the severe usage restrictions, and most of those were homes of white families in the wealthiest neighborhoods. In 1994, the country finally rejected apartheid, a system under which white Europeans held economic and political power through brutal repression of the African population. Laws assured fair treatment and more equitable ownership of land, but really, the African townships are filled with shacks while the whites own most of the grand homes. The public water systems never quite reached the African townships, which will be hit hardest as the land becomes drier despite using only 5% of the water (Dawson, 2018). The situation has been described as a water apartheid, a situation likely to spread to the poor worldwide as potable water becomes rare and expensive.

## REALITY CHECK

Has your area experienced intercultural violence recently?

Was your birth area colonized? Are you descended from colonizers or indigenous people?

How do you feel about your country's history?

In your school or workplace, is diversity considered an asset or a liability?

# 12.4 ARTS AND MULTICULTURALISM: HOPE FOR THE FUTURE

## LO 12.4: Discuss ways the arts are a positive factor in this increasingly multicultural world.

How do we conclude this text? Ultimately, a writer hopes for a positive high note. In this case, the text discusses cultural understanding in a world of lethal misunderstandings. Essentially what the world needs is connection. Marilyn Brewer (2000) discusses the need for superordinate commonalities to bridge conflicts and prejudice between groups. The process harkens back to Sharif's (1961) Robbers' Cave experiment in which boys randomly assigned to groups quickly escalated into severe conflict and healed their conflict by uniting to repair (an artificially created loss of) water supply. The greater need provided a larger shared identity in which the boys could unite. Sharing of identity on superordinate levels forms the best path to intercultural connection and reduced hostility. Arts create opportunities for shared understanding and identity.

Our human artistry provides much of what informs and enculturates us into our own cultures, whether through song, story, or dance. That same body of information is available to anyone who cares to read, listen, or move in the same ways. Some cultures restrict expression in public displays of anything called song, poetry, or dance, but these media are widely shared (if not universal). Are these shared processes not superb ways to simultaneously find shared identity and to share our specific culture's understandings?

Works of fiction can provide stunning insight into how people live and think in another culture. The magical realism of Gabriel Garcia Marquez's novels convey the history and lifestyle of Colombia and also the hopes, dreams, and imaginings of the culture—the magical part of his realism. A similar magic fills the work of Chilean author Isabel Allende. Her work *The House of the Spirits* (1985) chronicles two families from the 1920s until the 1973 overthrow of her uncle, Salvador Allende, a democratically elected socialist president, in a brutal coup by Augusto Pinochet with US CIA backing. Chinua Achebe's *Things Fall Apart* (1958) provides an unflinching view of the cultural change wrought by white missionaries in Nigeria, a study in a difficult acculturative process. In *The Tale of Genji* (ca. 1021), credited as the first novel ever written, Lady Murasaki Shikibu's telling of Genji's romantic exploits vividly illustrates the intricacies of life in the courts of Heian Japan a millennium ago. With a great author and some imagination, the reader is transported into the lives and hearts of other times and places. People from these distant cultures now live in our towns, work for the same companies, or fill our earbuds with their music. On American soil, Maya Angelou's *I Know Why the Caged Bird Sings* (1969) conveys an account of African American life unknown to whites at the time and still unfamiliar to the dominant culture as young black men are gunned down by police at inordinate rates.

Arts have always crossed cultures, with textiles, cuisine, and musical instruments traveling the Silk Road for centuries. Balkan soldiers in the Roman legion brought the bagpipe to the British Isles, and timpani drums got to European orchestras via invading Ottoman armies. Benny Goodman fielded the first integrated big band at Carnegie Hall in 1938. From the 1950s, flautist Herbie Mann and other jazz artists travelled to Brazil, collaborating on fusions of jazz and Brazilian styles. The Beatles helped to popularize Indian sitar player Ravi Shankar in the 1960s, and generally the teens and young adults of the counterculture movement embraced the music and arts of other cultures enthusiastically. Arts provided the media to express and endorse concepts of social change and inclusivity.

A new phase of intentionally political intercultural music began around 1980 when Peter Gabriel released Biko, a song eulogizing the death of slain journalist Steven Biko at the hands of South Africa's apartheid regime. It included some elements representing African music, a trend he would amplify in his later work. The same year, Gabriel launched the World of Music, Arts, and Dance (WOMAD) festivals, bringing together artists on a global scale. The intent was to build intercultural bridges through these media. Paul Simon followed suit with his 1985 album *Graceland*, in collaboration with Ladysmith Black Mambazo, a South African a cappella vocal ensemble.

Music has always formed a primary mechanism of social bonding, and this continues both within and between cultures (Boer, 2009). The same can be said of arts more generally, as they are shared in galleries, museums, concert halls, and festivals of multicultural cities around the world. Allport's (1952) contact theory, mentioned in Chapter 10 regarding acculturation, reveals that prejudice is reduced when people from different groups interact and cooperate while holding equal status, shared goals, and shared norms. In 2001, just before the September 11 terror attack, cellist Yo-Yo Ma began a project he called The Silk Road Ensemble, including musicians and instruments from all along that ancient passage. Describing his inspiration, Ma said,

> The music serves to give a different sense of proportion. To bring things that are far away close, and bring things that are closer, not very far away, closer. That's about creating community. It's about creating communities that share and are interested in trying to create a better society.

We can see the visual arts of other cultures, hear their music, see their films. In doing so, we learn their hopes and fears, loves, and aspirations. We can see that these cultural outsiders, however different they may appear, are as human as we are. The world needs understanding. Hopefully these words you have read have given you tools to understand better anyone you meet.

*A hui hou* (until again we gather).

## REFLECTING ON YOUR READING

- Describe the demographic changes in your home town over the past decade.

- If you work, how would you describe your boss's leadership style? If not, describe your instructor's style.

- Is your country's military involved in armed conflict? If so, where and with whom? Is it an intercultural setting? If not, what was the last conflict?

- Have you had difficulty forgiving someone? What would forgiveness take?

# CHAPTER 12 SUMMARY

## 12.1 Multiculturalism, Globalization, and Psychology

Humanity has been fantastically successful as a species, spreading across the globe in only 70,000 years. In that span, an incredible diversity emerged, including thousands of sociopolitical, ethnic, or religious categories. An important structure is the nation-state, a political organization that may group together a variety of ethnic and religious groups. Diversity can strengthen groups and group processes, but only when operating with equity and tolerance.

Prejudice and xenophobia are unfortunately common. Many modern conflicts arise from exploitation of ancient grievances. "Colorblindness" attempts to ignore difference but, in practice, tends to favor a dominant group. People now often identify with multiple cultural groups, either through mixed heritage or by embracing elements of several cultures. Simultaneously, demographics are shifting around the world through changing birth rates, migration, and increased lifespan.

## 12.2 Applied Psychology: Working With Culture

Culture happens in community context, whether traditional or reshaped by migration. Violent crime has declined worldwide over several decades, making this the most peaceful time in human existence, though violence remains common in certain communities, regions, and countries. Immigrant communities face particular challenges and may benefit from internal cooperation.

Since WWII, international business became increasingly multicultural. Cultural psychologists assist in issues of managing diverse workforces. Mismatch of leadership style to employee culture can cause problems, and white males still fill most leadership roles. Colonizers found differing styles disturbing but collective models of leadership survive.

Human resource managers must manage diverse workforces, attempting to provide appropriate environment and compensation while maintaining profitability and equity. Hiring practices also vary by culture. Prejudice and discrimination toward minorities remains a significant problem. Cultural values must be considered to understand employee needs and behavior.

Cultural intelligence (CQ) describes capacity to function in diverse settings. Sojourners travel for work or education and have particular needs when adapting to a new setting.

Military organizations inherently encounter and include diverse cultures. Minorities often turn to the military for work opportunities. International peace-keeping requires cooperation including differing cultures and languages. Many countries now provide cultural training for troops and officers.

Demographic shifts require educators to accommodate diverse cultures, languages, and learning styles. Failure to address difference may cause inadequate or ineffective pedagogy, ultimately yielding inaccurate test results and leading to later socioeconomic disparity.

## 12.3 Culture, Competition, and Conflict

Humans disagree and compete, sometimes in less than peaceful ways. Conflict requires that two or more parties want or claim some shared resource or goal. They differ within and across cultures in how they approach conflict on dimensions of assertiveness and cooperation. Cultures tend toward particular styles in part due to ultimate relational goals and desire for individual or collective benefits.

Forgiveness is a particularly important value and process. Within cultures, people tend to share rationale and procedure for granting forgiveness. Intergroup forgiveness is complicated for a number of reasons including history of conflict, differences in approach, and perceived sincerity of apology.

Colonialism caused much harm around the world and set the stage for on-going inequities between dominant and minority or indigenous groups. Diversity issues continue even as cities diversify.

## 12.4 Arts and Multiculturalism: Hope for the Future

Arts provide opportunities to reduce conflict in diversity. Arts present a safe venue for intercultural contact and understanding. Arts can also encourage superordinate shared identities. Arts can express experiences of diverse lifestyles, unfortunate events, and paths to solution. Arts and music have included multiple cultural elements for millennia. These shared processes and media provide opportunities to bring people together and heal past wrongs.

## GLOSSARY

**Discrimination:** Differential treatment of individuals based on categorical memberships like ethnicity or gender.

**Negotiation:** Deliberate interaction of two or more people or groups attempting to define or redefine terms of their relationship or interdependence.

# REFERENCES

Abbe, A., & Gouge, M. (2012). Cultural training for military personnel. *Military Review*, *92*(4), 9–17.

Abdou, C. M., Dunkel Schetter, C., Campos, B., Hilmert, C. J., Dominguez, T. P., Hobel, C. J., . . . Sandman, C. (2010). Communalism predicts prenatal affect, stress, and physiology better than ethnicity and socioeconomic status. *Cultural Diversity and Ethnic Minority Psychology*, *16*(3), 395–403.

Abel, T. M., & Hsu, F. L. (1949). Some aspects of personality of Chinese as revealed by the Rorschach Test. *Rorschach research exchange and journal of projective techniques*, *13*(3), 285–301.

Abele, F. (2004). Urgent need, serious opportunity: Towards a new social model for Canada's aboriginal peoples. *CPRN Social Architecture Papers Research Report F|39*. Retrieved from http://www.cprn.org/theme.cfm?theme=25&l=en

Aboud, F. K., & Yousafzai, A. K. (2015). Global health and development in early childhood. *Annual Review of Psychology*, *66*(1), 433–457.

Abrams, R. H. (1943). Residential propinquity as a factor in marriage selection: Fifty-year trends in Philadelphia. *American Sociological Review*, 288–294.

Acerbi, A., Tennie, C., & Nunn, C. L. (2011). Modeling imitation and emulation in constrained search spaces. *Learning & Behavior*, *39*(2), 104–114.

Achenbach, J. (2015, Aug, 28). No, science's reproducibility problem is not limited to psychology. *The Washington Post*.

Adams, G. & Plaut, V. C. (2003). The cultural grounding of personal relationship: Friendship in North American and West African worlds. *Personal Relationships*, *10*, 333–347.

Addai, I. (1999) Ethnicity and sexual behavior in Ghana. *Social Biology*, *461*(2), 17–32.

Adekson, M. O. (2003). *The Yoruba traditional healers of Nigeria*. New York: Routledge.

Adelson, N. (1998). Health beliefs and the politics of Cree well-being. *Health*, *2*(1), 5–22.

Ainsworth, M. D. S., Bell, S. M., & Stayton, D. J. (1974). Infant-mother attachment and social development: "Socialization" as a product of reciprocal responsiveness to signals. In P. M. Richards (Ed.), *The integration of a child into a social world* (pp. 99–135). Cambridge, UK: Cambridge University Press.

Ajibade, G. O. (2013). Same-sex relationships in Yorùbá culture and orature. *Journal of Homosexuality*, *60*(7), 965–983.

Akagi, H., & House, A. (2002). The clinical epidemiology of hysteria: Vanishingly rare, or just vanishing? *Psychological Medicine*, *32*, 191–194. doi: 10.1017S0033291701004962

Ali, M., Sugimoto, K., Ramadan, A., & Arimura, G. I. (2013). Memory of plant communications for priming anti-herbivore responses. *Scientific Reports*, *3*, 1872.

Allen, D. G., & Vardaman, J. M. (2017). Recruitment and retention across cultures. *Annual Review of Organizational Psychology and Organizational Behavior*, *8*, 153–181.

Allport, F. H., & Allport, G. W. (1921). Personality traits: Their classification and measurement. *The Journal of Abnormal Psychology and Social Psychology*, *16*(1), 6–40.

Allport, G. W. (1937). *Personality: A psychological interpretation*. New York: Holt, Rinehart & Winston.

Allport, G. W. (1952). *The resolution of intergroup tensions: A critical appraisal of methods*. New York: National Conference of Christians and Jews.

Allport, G. W. (1953). Persistence and change of attitudes. In J. M. Seidman (Ed.), *The adolescent: A book of readings. The Dryden Press publications in interpersonal relations* (pp. 406–411). Ft Worth, TX: Dryden Press. doi: 10.1037/11402-012

Al-Qaradawi, Y., El-Helbawy, K., Shukry, S., Siddiqui, M. M., & Hammad, A. Z. (1985). *The lawful and the prohibited in Islam* (pp. 190–193). Egypt: Shoruuk International.

Altekar, A. S. (2009). *Education in ancient India*. Delhi: Isha Books. (Original work published 1939)

Ambrose, S. H. (2010). Coevolution of composite-tool technology, constructive memory, and language: Implications for the evolution of modern human behavior. *Current Anthropology*, *51*(S1), S135–S147.

American Academy of Orthopedic Surgeons. (2010). *68W advanced field craft: Combat medical skills*. Boston: Jones & Bartlett.

American Psychiatric Association. (2013). *Diagnostic and statistical manual of mental disorders*. New York, NY: Author.

American Psychological Association. (2009). ICD vs. DSM. *Monitor on Psychology*, *40*(9), 63. Retrieved from http://www.apa.org/monitor/2009/10/icd-dsm.aspx

Anderson, C. A., Carnagey, N. L., & Eubanks, J. (2003). Exposure to violent media: The effects of songs with violent lyrics on aggressive thoughts and feelings. *Journal of Personality and Social Psychology 84*(5), 960–971.

Anderson, S. L., Adams, G., & Plaut, V. C. (2008). The cultural grounding of personal relationship: The importance of attractiveness in everyday life. *Journal of Personality and Social Psychology*, *95*(2), 352–368.

Andics, A., Gácsi, M., Faragó, T., Kis, A., & Miklósi, Á. (2014). Voice-sensitive regions in the dog and human brain are revealed by comparative fMRI. *Current Biology*, *24*(5), 574–578.

Andics, A., & Miklósi, Á. (2018). Neural processes of vocal social perception: Dog-human comparative fMRI studies. *Neuroscience & Biobehavioral Reviews*, *85*, 54–64.

Andrade, T. J. (2010). *Ke kānāwai māmalahoe: Equality in our splintered profession*. Honolulu: University of Hawai'i Law Review.

Andreasen, N. C. (1989). The American concept of schizophrenia. *Schizophrenia Bulletin*, *15*(4), 519–531.

Andrzejewski, B. M. (1969). *Somali poetry*. London, UK: Oxford University Press.

Ang, S., & van Dyne, L. (2008). Conceptualization of cultural intelligence: Definition, distinctiveness, and nomological network. In S. Ang & L. van Dyne (Eds.), *Handbook of cultural intelligence: Theory, measurement, and applications* (pp. 3–15). New York, NY: Sharpe.

Ang, S., van Dyne, L., Koh, C., Ng, K. Y., Templer, K. J., Tay, C., & Chandrasekar, N. A. (2007). Cultural intelligence: Its measurement and effects on cultural judgment and decision making, cultural adaptation and task performance. *Management and Organization Review*, *3*(3), 335–371.

Angell, B., Muhunthan, J., Eades, A. M., Cunningham, J., Garvey, G., Cass, A., . . . Jan, S. (2016). The health-related quality of life of indigenous populations: A global systematic review. *Quality of Life Research*, 1–18.

Anton, M., Tedford, R. H., & Wang, X. (2008). *Dogs: Their fossil relatives and evolutionary history*. New York, NY: Columbia University Press.

Anton, S. C. (2003). Natural history of homo erectus. *American Journal of Physical Anthropology*, *37*, 126–170.

Apicella, C. L., & Barrett, H. C. (2016). Cross-cultural evolutionary psychology. *Current Opinion in Psychology*, 7, 92–97. doi:10.1016/j.copsyc.2015.08.015

Arasaratnam, L. A. (2013). A review of articles on multiculturalism in 35 years of IJIR. *International Journal of Intercultural Relations*, *37*(6), 676–685.

Arbib, M. A. (2011). From mirror neurons to complex imitation in the evolution of language and tool use. *Annual Review of Anthropology*, *40*, 257–273.

Arciniega, G. M., Anderson, T. C., Tovar-Blank, Z. G., & Tracey, T. J. G. (2008). Toward a fuller conception of machismo: Development of a traditional machismo and caballerismo scale. *Journal of Counseling Psychology*, *55*(1), 19–33.

Ariyoshi, R. (1998). *Hula is life: The story of halau hula o maiki*. Honolulu: Maiki Aiu Building Corporation.

Armelagos, G. J., & Maes, K. (2006). Revisiting the slavery hypertension hypothesis. *Transforming Anthropology*, *14*(1), 67–76.

Arnett, J. J., & Maynard, A. (2013). *Child development: A cultural approach*. New York, NY: Pearson.

Arnett, J. J., & Maynard, A. (2016). *Child development: A cultural approach*. New York, NY: Pearson.

Arnold, M. D. (2013). Saudade, duende, and feedback: The hybrid voices of twenty-first-century neoflamenco and neofado. *Dissertation Abstracts International Section A: Humanities and Social Sciences*, *76*(8-A(E)).

Arroyo, C. G., & Zigler, E. (1995). Racial identity, academic achievement, and the psychological well-being of economically disadvantaged adolescents. *Journal of Personality and Social Psychology*, *69*(5), 903.

Ashforth, B. E., & Mael, F. (1989). Social identity theory and the organization. *The Academy of Management Review*, *14*(1), 20–39.

Asia New Zealand Foundation. (2018). *Diwali festival of lights*. Retrieved from https://www.asianz.org.nz/arts/2018-diwali-festival-of-lights/

Assad, T., Okasha, T., Ramy, H., Goueli, T., El-Shinnawy, H., Nasr, M.,

. . . Mohsen, N. (2015). Role of traditional healers in the pathway to care of patients with bipolar disorder in Egypt. *International Journal of Social Psychiatry, 61*(6), 583–590.

Atran, S. (2001). The trouble with memes: Inference versus imitation in cultural creation. *Human Nature, 12*(4), 351–381.

Aud, S., Fox, M., & Kewal Ramani, A. (2010). *Status and trends in the education of racial and ethnic groups 2010.* Washington, DC: National Center for Education Statistics Institute of Education Sciences.

Austin, I. (2015). Syrian refugees greeted by Justin Trudeau in Canada. *New York Times.* Retrieved from http://www.nytimes.com/2015/12/12/world/americas/syria-refugees-arrive-in-canada.html?_r=0

Austin Institute for the Study of Family and Culture. (2014). *Divorce in America: Who wants out and why?* Retrieved from http://www.austin-institute.org/research/divorce-in-america/

Awang, S., Maros, M., & Ibrahim, N. (2012). Malay values in intercultural communication. *International Journal of Social Science and Humanity, 2*(3). doi:10.7763/IJSSH.2012.V2.96

Aycan, Z. (2000). Cross-cultural industrial and organizational psychology: Contributions, past developments, and future directions. *Journal of Cross-Cultural Psychology, 31*(1), 110–128.

Ayers, E. L. (1984). *Vengeance and justice: Crime and punishment in the 19th century American South.* London, UK: Oxford University Press.

Ayunerak, P., Alstrom, D., Moses, C., Charlie, J., & Rasmus, S. M. (2014). Yup'ik culture and context in southwest Alaska: Community member perspectives of tradition, social change,

and prevention. *American Journal of Community Psychology, 54*(1–2), 91–99.

Azman, R. L. (2005). The development of the scale of educational attitudes. *Journal of College Teaching and Learning, 2*(4), 51–63.

Azuma, H. (1984). Psychology in a non-Western country. *International Journal of Psychology, 19*(1–2), 45–55.

Bacher, K., Allen, S., Lindholm, A. K., Bejder, L., & Krützen, M. (2010). Genes or culture: Are mitochondrial genes associated with tool use in bottlenose dolphins (Tursiops sp.)? *Behavior Genetics, 40*(5), 706–714.

Bai, X., & Chow, N. (2013). Chinese elders' self-image and their perceived peer image: Possibility of self-enhancement bias. *The International Journal of Aging & Human Development, 77*(1), 1–16.

Bailey, J. (1986). *Sufi music of India and Pakistan: Sound, context and meaning in Qawwali.* Cambridge UK: Cambridge U Press.

Ball, H. L., Hooker, E., & Kelly, P. J. (1999). Where will the baby sleep? Attitudes and practices of new and experienced parents regarding cosleeping with their newborn infants. *American Anthropologist. 101*(1), 143–151.

Baltes, P. B., & Smith, J. (2008). The fascination of wisdom: Its nature, ontogeny, and function. *Perspectives on Psychological Science, 3*(1), 56–64.

Bandura, A. (2009). Social cognitive theory of mass communication. In *Media effects* (pp. 110–140). New York, NY: Routledge.

Banner, L. W. (1983). *American beauty.* New York, NY: Knopf.

Barba, E., & Savarese, N. (2006). *A dictionary of theatre anthropology. The secret*

*art of the performer* (2nd ed.). New York, NY: Routledge.

Barbarossa, C., De Pelsmacker, P., & Moons, I. (2017). Personal values, green self-identity and electric car adoption. *Ecological Economics, 140*(C), 190–200.

Barbato, A. (1998). *Schizophrenia and public health.* Geneva: World Health Organization.

Barber, B. K., & Schluterman, J. M. (2008). Connectedness in the lives of children and adolescents: A call for greater conceptual clarity. *Journal of Adolescent Health, 43*(3), 209–216.

Barclay, B. (2005). *Mana tūturu: Māori treasures and intellectual property rights.* Auckland, NZ: Auckland University Press.

Barclay, L., & Kent, D. (1998). Recent immigration and the misery of motherhood: A discussion of pertinent issues. *Midwifery, 14*(1), 4–9.

Barker, J., & Tietjen, A. M. (1990). Women's facial tattooing among the Maisin of Oro Province, Papua New Guinea: The changing significance of an ancient custom. *Oceania, 60*(3), 217–234.

Barrett, A. E., & Turner, R. J. (2005). Family structure and mental health: The mediating effects of socioeconomic status, family process, and social stress. *Journal of Health and Social Behavior, 46*(2), 156–169.

Barrett, L. F. (2017). Categories and their role in the science of emotion. *Psychological Inquiry, 28*(1), 20–26.

Barrett, L. F., Mesquita, B., Ochsner, K. N., & Gross, J. J. (2007). The experience of emotion. *Annual Review of Psychology, 58,* 373–403.

Barry, C. T., Doucette, H., Loflin, D. C., Rivera-Hudson, N., & Herrington,

L. L. (2015). "Let me take a selfie": Associations between self-photography, narcissism, and self-esteem. *Psychology of Popular Media Culture, 6*(1), 48.

Barry, H., & Paxson, L. M. (1971). Infancy and early childhood: Cross-cultural codes 2. *Ethnology, 10*(4), 466–508.

Baumeister, R. F. (2010). The self. In R. F. Baumeister & E. J. Finkel (Eds.), *Advanced social psychology: The state of the science* (pp. 139–175). New York: Oxford University Press.

Baumeister, R. F. (2016). Toward a general theory of motivation: Problems, challenges, opportunities, and the big picture. *Motivation and Emotion, 40*(1), 1–10.

Baumeister, R. F., & Bushman, B. J. (2010). *Social psychology and human nature* (2nd ed.). Belmont, CA: Thomson/Wadsworth.

Baumeister, R. F., Campbell, J. D., Krueger, J. I., & Vohs, K. D. (2003). Does high self-esteem cause better performance, interpersonal success, happiness or healthier lifestyles? *Psychological Science in the Public Interest, 4*, 1–44.

Baumeister, R. F., & Leary, M. R. (1995). The need to belong: Desire for interpersonal attachments as a fundamental human motivation. *Psychological Bulletin 117*(3), 497–529.

Baumeister, R. F., & Twenge, J. M. (2003). The social self. *Handbook of Psychology, 14*, 327–352.

Baumeister, R. F., & Vonasch, A. J. (2012). Is the essence of morality mind perception, self-regulation, free will, or culture? *Psychological Inquiry, 23*(2), 134–136.

Baumrind, D. (1964). Some thoughts on ethics of research: After reading Milgram's "Behavioral study of obedience." *American Psychologist, 19*(6), 421.

Bax, M., van Heusden, B., & Wildgen, W. (2004). *Semiotic evolution and the dynamics of culture* (Vol. 5). Bern, SZ: Peter Lang.

Baxter, A., Patton, G., Scott, K. M., Degenhardt, L., & Whiteford, H. A. (2013). Global epidemiology of mental disorders: What are we missing? *PLoS One, 8*(6), e65514. doi:10.1371/journal.pone.0065514

Baxter, J., Kani Kingi, T., Tapsell, R., Durie, M., & McGee, M. A. (2006). Prevalence of mental disorders among Māori in Te Rau Hinengaro: The New Zealand Mental Health Survey. *Australian and New Zealand Journal of Psychiatry, 40*(10), 914–923.

Bazarova, N., & Yuan, Y. C. (2013). Expertise recognition and influence in intercultural groups: differences between face-to-face and computer-mediated communication. *Journal of Computer Mediated Communication, 18*(4), 437–453.

Beaglehole, J. C. (1961). *The discovery of New Zealand*. London: Oxford University Press.

Beaman, A. L., Klentz, B., Diener, E., & Svanum, S. (1979). Self-awareness and transgression in children: Two field studies. *Journal of Personality and Social Psychology, 37*(10), 1835–1846.

Beattie, J. (1783). *Dissertations moral and critical: On memory and imagination, on dreaming, the theory of language, on fable and romance, on the attachments of kindred, illustrations on sublimity* (pp. 575–604). Edinburgh: W. Strachen.

Beaupré, M. G., & Hess, U. (2005). Cross-cultural emotion recognition among Canadian ethnic groups. *Journal of Cross-Cultural Psychology, 36*(3), 355–370.

Beauvais, C., & Jenson, J. (2002). *Social cohesion: Updating the state of the research*. Canadian Policy Research Networks Discussion Paper No. F/22. Retrieved from http://www.cprn.org

Bebbington, K., MacLeod, C., Ellison, T. M., & Fay, N. (2017). The sky is falling: Evidence of a negativity bias in the social transmission of information. *Evolution and Human Behavior, 38*(1), 92–101.

Becker, E. (1971). *The birth and death of meaning: An interdisciplinary perspective on the problem of man* (2nd ed.). New York, NY: Free Press.

Becker, E. (1973). *The denial of death*. New York, NY: The Free Press.

Becker, J. (1994). Music and trance. *Leonardo Music Journal, 4*(1), 41–51.

Beggiora, S. (2011). The whisper of the spirits. In F. Ferrari (Ed.), *Health and religious rituals in South Asia: Disease, possession and healing* (p. 129). New York: Taylor & Francis.

Behm-Morawitz, E. (2013). Mirrored selves: The influence of self-presence in a virtual world on health, appearance, and well-being. *Computers in Human Behavior, 29*(1), 119–128.

Bekoff, M. (1977). Social communication in canids: Evidence for the evolution of a stereotyped mammalian display. *Science, 9*, 1097–1099. doi:10.1126/science.197.4308.1097

Belfiore, E. (1985). Pleasure, tragedy and Aristotelian psychology. *The Classical Quarterly, 35*(2), 349–361.

Bell, A. (2009). Dilemmas of settler belonging: Roots, routes and redemption in New Zealand national identity claims. *The Sociological Review, 57*(1), 145–162.

Bell, D. (2002). *Daughters of the dreaming*. Melbourne, Australia: Spinefex Press.

Bemak, F., Chung, R., & Pederson, P. (2003). *Counselling refugees: A psychosocial approach to innovative multicultural interventions*. Westport, CT: Greenwood Press.

Bendjilali, N., Hsueh, W-C., Qimei, H., Wilcox, C., Nevergelt, C., Donlon, T., . . . Willcox, B. (2014). Who are the Okinawans? Ancestry, genome diversity, and implications for the genetic study of human longevity from a geographically isolated population. *The Journals of Gerontology Series A: Biological Sciences and Medical Sciences*. doi:10.1093/gerona/glt203

Bengtson, V. L. (2001). Beyond the nuclear family: The increasing importance of multigenerational bonds. *Journal of Marriage and Family*, *63*(1), 1–16.

Benziman, G., Kannai, R., & Ahmad, A. (2012). The wounded healer as cultural archetype. *Comparative Literature and Culture*, *14*(1), 11.

Berger, L. (2012). Learning possession trance and evaluating oracles' truthfulness in Jinè cults of Bèlèdugu (Mali). *Journal of Cognition and Culture*, *12*(3–4), 163–181. doi:10.1163/15685373-12342071

Berk, L. E., Mann, T. D., & Ogan, A. T. (2006). Make-believe play: Wellspring for development of self-regulation. In D. G. Singer, R. M. Golinkoff, & K. Hirsh-Pasek (Eds.), *Play = learning: How play motivates and enhances children's cognitive and social-emotional growth* (pp. 74–100). New York, NY: Oxford University Press.

Berlin, B., & Berlin, E. A. (1975). Aguaruna color categories. *American Ethnologist*, *2*(1), 61–87.

Berlin, B., & Kay, P. (1969/1991). *Basic color terms: Their universality and evolution*. Los Angeles: University of California Press.

Berman, R. (2015). Donald Trump's call to ban muslim immigrants. *The Atlantic*. Retrieved from http://www.theatlantic.com/politics/archive/2015/12/donald-trumps-call-to-ban-muslim-immigrants/419298/

Bernard, H. R. (2017). *Research methods in anthropology: Qualitative and quantitative approaches*. New York: Rowman & Littlefield.

Bernardi, L., Porta, C., & Sleight, P. (2006). Cardiovascular, cerebrovascular, and respiratory changes induced by different types of music in musicians and non-musicians: The importance of silence. *Heart*, *92*(4), 445–452.

Berndt, R. M., & Berndt, C. H. (1984). *The world of the first Australians*. Sydney: Ure Smith.

Berns-McGown, R. (2007). Redefining "diaspora": The challenge of connection and inclusion. *International Journal*, *63*(1), 3–21.

Berry, J. W. (1969). On cross-cultural comparability. *International Journal of Psychology*, *4*(2), 119–128.

Berry, J. W. (1970). Marginality, stress and ethnic identification in an acculturated Aboriginal community. *Journal of Cross-Cultural Psychology*, *1*(3), 239–252.

Berry, J. W. (1974). Psychological aspects of cultural pluralism: Unity and identity reconsidered. *Topics in Culture Learning*, *2*, 17–22.

Berry, J. W. (1986). The acculturation process and refugee behavior. In C. L. Williams & J. Westermeyer (Eds.), *The series in clinical and community psychology. Refugee mental health in resettlement countries* (pp. 25–37). Washington, DC: Hemisphere.

Berry, J. W. (1990). Psychology of acculturation. In J. Berman (Ed.), *Nebraska symposium on motivation, 1989: Cross-cultural perspectives* (Vol. 37, pp. 201–234). Lincoln: University of Nebraska.

Berry, J. W. (1995). Psychology of acculturation. *The Culture and Psychology Reader*, 457.

Berry, J. W. (1997). Immigration, acculturation, and adaptation. *Applied Psychology: An International Review*, *46*(1), 5–34.

Berry, J. W. (2006). Acculturation: A conceptual overview. In M. H. Bornstein & L. R Cote (Eds.), *Acculturation and parent-child relationships: Measurement and development* (pp. 13–30). Mahwah, NJ: Lawrence Erlbaum.

Berry, J. W., Kim, U., Power, S., Young, M., & Bujaki, M. (1989). Acculturation attitudes in plural societies. *Applied Psychology: An International Review*, *38*(2), 185–206.

Berry, J. W., Phinney, J. S., Sam, D. L., & Vedder, P. (2006a). Immigrant youth: Acculturation, identity, and adaptation. *Applied Psychology: An International Review*, *55*(3), 303–332.

Berry, J. W., Phinney, J. S., Sam, D. L., & Vedder, P. (Eds.) (2006b). *Immigrant youth in cultural transition: Acculturation, identity and adaptation across national contexts*. Mahwah, NJ: Lawrence Erlbaum Associates.

Berry, J. W., Poortinga, Y. H., Segall, M. H., & Dasen, E. R. (1992). *Cross-cultural psychology: Research and applications*. New York, NY: Cambridge University Press.

Berry, J. W., & Sam, D. L. (1997). Acculturation and adaptation. *Handbook of cross-cultural psychology*, *3*(2), 291–326.

Berscheid, E. (2010). Love in the fourth dimension. *Annual Review of Psychology*, *61*, 1–25.

Berscheid, E., & Hatfield, E. (1978). *Interpersonal attraction* (2nd ed.). Reading, MA: Addison-Wesley.

Bhavsar, V., Ventriglio, A., & Bhugra, D. (2016). Dissociative trance and spirit possession: Challenges for cultures in transition. *Psychiatry and Clinical Neurosciences*, *70*(12), 551–559. doi:10.1111/pcn.12425

Bianchi, S. M. (2014). A demographic perspective on family change. *Journal of Family Theory & Review*, *6*(1), 35–44.

Biesele, M., & Howell, N. (1981). "The old people give you life": Aging among !Kung hunter-gatherers. In P. T. Amoss & S. Harrell (Eds.), *Other ways of growing old: Anthropological perspectives* (pp. 77–99). Palo Alto, CA: Stanford University Press.

Bilewicz, M. (2007). History as an obstacle: Impact of temporal-based social categorizations on Polish-Jewish intergroup contact. *Group Processes & Intergroup Relations*, *10*(4), 551–563.

Bilewicz, M., & Jaworska, M. (2013). Reconciliation through the righteous: The narratives of heroic helpers as a fulfillment of emotional needs in Polish-Jewish intergroup contact. *Journal of Social Issues*, *69*(1), 162–179.

Billings, A. (2005). Beyond the ebonics debate: Attitudes about black and standard American English. *Journal of Black Studies*, *36*(1), 68–81.

Bjorklund, D. F., & Pellegrini, A. D. (2002). *The origins of human nature: Evolutionary developmental psychology*. Washington, DC: American Psychological Association.

Black Elk. (1991). *The sacred pipe: Black Elk's account of the seven rites of the Oglala Sioux* (Vol. 36). J. E. Brown (Ed.). New York: HarperCollins. (Original work published 1932)

Blackmon, B. J., Robison, S. B., & Rhodes, J. L. (2016). Examining the influence of risk factors across rural and urban communities. *Journal of the Society for Social Work and Research*, *7*(4), 615–638.

Blackmore, S. (2006). Why we need memetics. *Behavioral and Brain Sciences*, *29*(4), 349–350.

Blanck, G. (1990). Vygotsky: The man and his cause. In L. C. Moll (Ed.), *Vygotsky and education: Instructional implications and applications of sociohistorical psychology* (pp. 31–58). Cambridge, UK: Cambridge University Press.

Bleuler, E. (1987). *The prognosis of dementia praecox: The group of schizophrenias*. Oxford, UK: International Universities Press.

Blome, M. W., Cohen, A. S., Tryon, C. A., Brooks, A. S., & Russell, J. (2012). The environmental context for the origins of modern human diversity: A synthesis of regional variability in African climate 150,000–30,000 years ago. *Journal of Human Evolution*, *62*(5), 563–592.

Boas, F. (1911). *The mind of primitive man: A course of lectures delivered before the Lowell Institute, Boston, Mass., and the National University of Mexico, 1910–1911*. New York, NY: Macmillan.

Boas, F., & Efron, D. F. (1936). A comparative investigation of gestural behavior patterns in "racial" groups living under different as well as similar environmental conditions. *Psychological Bulletin*, *33*, 760.

Bodibe, R. C. (1993). What is the truth? Being more than just a jesting Pilate in South African psychology. *South African Journal of Psychology*, *23*(2), 53–58.

Boehnke, K., Lietz, P., Schreier, M., & Wilhelm, A. (2011). Sampling: The selection of cases for culturally comparative psychological research. In D. Matsumoto & F. J. R. van de Vijver (Eds.), *Culture and psychology. Cross-cultural research methods in psychology* (pp. 101–129). New York, NY: Cambridge University Press.

Boellstorff, T. (2008). *Coming of age in Second Life: An anthropologist explores the virtually human*. Princeton, NJ: Princeton University Press.

Boellstorjf, T. (2009). Virtual worlds and futures of anthropology. *Anthronotes: Museum of Natural History Publication for Educators*, *30*(1), 1–5.

Boer, D. (2009). *Music makes the people come together: Social functions of music listening for young people across cultures* (Unpublished doctoral dissertation). Victoria University of Wellington, New Zealand.

Boer, D., Fischer, R., Strack, M., Bond, M. H., Lo, E., & Lam, J. (2011). How shared preferences in music create bonds between people: Values as the missing link. *Personality and Social Psychology Bulletin*, *37*(9), 1159–1171.

Boer, D., Fischer, R., Tekman, H., Abubakar, A., Njenga, J., & Zenger, M. (2012). Young people's topography of musical functions: Personal, social and cultural experiences with music across genders and six societies, *International Journal of Psychology*, *47*(5), 355–369.

Bolin, A. (2001). French Polynesia (Polynésie Française). *The international encyclopedia of sexuality volume I–IV, 1997–2001*. Retrieved from http://www2.hu-berlin.de/sexology/IES/index.html

Bond, M. H., & van de Vijver, F. J. R. (2011). Making scientific sense of cultural differences in psychological outcomes: Unpackaging the Magnum Mysterium. In D. Matsumoto & F. J. R. van de Vijver (Eds.), *Culture and psychology. Cross-cultural research methods in psychology* (pp. 75–100). New York, NY: Cambridge University Press.

Bonte, M. (1962). The reaction of two African societies to the Müller-Lyer illusion. *The Journal of Social Psychology*, *58*(2), 265–268.

Borisova, I. I., Betancourt, T. S., & Willett, J. B. (2013) Reintegration of former child soldiers in Sierra Leone: The role of caregivers and their awareness of the violence adolescents experienced during the war. *Journal of Aggression, Maltreatment & Trauma*, *22*(8), 803–828.

Bornstein, M. H. (1975). The influence of visual perception on culture. *American Anthropologist*, *77*(4), 774–798.

Bornstein, M. H. (2007). Hue categorization and color naming: Cognition to language to culture. In R. E. MacLaury, G. V. Paramei, & D. Dedrick (Eds.), *Anthropology of color: Interdisciplinary multilevel modeling* (pp. 3–27). Amsterdam, NL: John Benjamins. doi:10.1075/z.137.04bor

Bornstein, M. H., Putnick, D. L., Suwalsky, J. T. D., Venuti, P., de Falco, S., de Galperín, C. Z., . . . Tichovolsky, M. H. (2012). Emotional relationships in mothers and infants: Culture-common and community-specific characteristics of dyads from rural and metropolitan settings in Argentina, Italy, and the United States. *Journal of Cross-Cultural Psychology*, *43*(2), 171–197.

Boroditsky, L. (2001). Does language shape thought? Mandarin and English speakers' conceptions of time. *Cognitive Psychology*, *43*(1), 1–22.

Boroditsky, L. (2010). Remembrances of times east: Absolute spatial representations of time in an Australian Aboriginal community. *Psychological Science*, *21*(11), 1635–1639.

Boroditsky, L., Fuhrman, O., & McCormick, K. (2011). Do English and Mandarin speakers think about time differently? *Cognition*, *118*(1), 123–129.

Bossard, J. H. S. (1932). Residential propinquity in marriage selection. *American Journal of Sociology*, *38*, 219–224.

Boucher, H. C. (2010). Understanding western-east Asian differences and similarities in self-enhancement. *Social and Personality Psychology Compass*, *4*(5), 304–317.

Bowlby, J. (1951). Maternal care and mental health. *Bulletin of the World Health Organization*, *3*, 355–534.

Bowlby, J. (1969). *Attachment and loss*. New York, NY: Basic Books.

Bowman, J. L., & Dollahite, D. C. (2013). "Why would such a person dream about heaven?" Family, faith, and happiness in arranged marriages in India. *Journal of Comparative Family Studies*, *44*(2), 207–225.

Bowring, J. (2008). *A field guide to melancholy*. Harpenden, UK: Oldcastle Books.

Box, H. O., & Gibson, K. R. (Eds.). (1999). *Mammalian social learning*. Oxford, UK: Oxford University Press.

Boyd, R., & Richerson, P. J. (1982). Cultural transmission and the evolution of cooperative behavior. *Human Ecology*, *10*(3), 325–351.

Boyd, R., & Richerson, P. J. (1985). *Culture and the evolutionary process*. Chicago: Chicago University Press.

Boyd, R., & Richerson, P. J. (1996, January). Why culture is common, but cultural evolution is rare. In *Proceedings-British Academy* (vol. 88, pp. 77–94). London: Oxford University Press.

Boyer, P. (1994). *The naturalness of religious ideas: A cognitive theory of religion*. Los Angeles: University of California Press.

Boyer, P. (1998). Cognitive tracks of cultural inheritance: How evolved intuitive ontology governs cultural transmission. *American Anthropologist*, *100*(4), 875–889.

Bradford Brown, B., & Larson, J. (2009). Peer relationships in adolescence. *Handbook of Adolescent Psychology*, *2*. doi:10.1002/9780470479193.adlpsy 002004

Branden, N. (1994). *The six pillars of self-esteem*. New York, NY: Bantam Books.

Brase, G. L., Adair, L., & Monk, K. (2014). Explaining sex differences in reactions to relationship infidelities: Comparisons of the roles of sex, gender, beliefs, attachment, and sociosexual orientation. *Evolutionary Psychology*, *12*(1), 73–96.

Bresler, L. (2006). Toward connectedness: Aesthetically based research. *Studies in Art Education*, *48*(1), 52–69.

Brewer, M. B. (1979). In-group bias in the minimal intergroup situation: A cognitive-motivational analysis. *Psychological Bulletin*, *86*(2), 307–324.

Brewer, M. B. (2000). Superordinate goals versus superordinate identity as bases of intergroup cooperation. In D. Capozza & R. Brown (Eds.), *Social identity processes: Trends in theory and research* (pp. 117–132). Thousand Oaks, CA: SAGE.

Brewer, M. B. (2007). The importance of being we: Human nature and intergroup relations. *American Psychologist*, *62*(8), 728–738.

Brewer, M. B., & Yuki, M. (2007). Culture and social identity. In S. Kitayama & D. Cohen (Eds.), *Handbook of cultural psychology* (pp. 307–322). New York, NY: Guilford Press.

Brinig, M. F. (1990). Rings and promises. *Journal of Law, Economics, and Organization, 6*(1), 203–215.

Brodbeck, J., Bachmann, M. S., Croudace, T. J., & Brown, A. (2013). Comparing growth trajectories of risk behaviors from late adolescence through young adulthood: An accelerated design. *Developmental Psychology, 49*(9), 1732–1738.

Brody, E. (1994). The mental health and well-being of refugees: Issues and directions. In A. J. Marsella, T. Bornemann, S. Ekblad, & J. Orley (Eds.), *Amidst peril and pain: The mental health and well-being of the world's refugees* (pp. 57–68). Washington, DC: American Psychological Association.

Brody, G. H., Stoneman, Z., Flor, D., & McCrary, C. (1994). Religion's role in organizing family relationships: Family process in rural, two-parent African American families. *Journal of Marriage and the Family, 56*, 878–888.

Bronfenbrenner, U. (1979). *The ecology of human development*. Cambridge, MA: Harvard University Press.

Bronfenbrenner, U. (1994). *Ecological models of human development*. In International encyclopedia of education, Vol. 3, 2nd Ed. Oxford: Elsevier. Reprinted in: Gauvain, M. & Cole, M. (Eds.), *Readings on the development of children*, 2nd Ed. New York, NY: Freeman, pp. 37–43.

Bronfenbrenner, U., & Morris, P. A. (2006). The bioecological model of human development. In R. M. Lerner & W. Damon (Eds.), *Handbook of child psychology: Theoretical models of human development* (6th ed., vol. 1, pp. 793–828). Hoboken, NJ: John Wiley.

Broude, G. J. (1975). Norms of premarital sexual behavior. *Ethos, 3*(3), 381–402.

Broude G. J. & Greene, S. J. (1983). Cross-cultural codes on husband-wife relationships. *Ethnology, 22*(3), 263–280.

Brown, B. B., & Larson, J. (2009). Peer relationships in adolescence. In R. M. Lerner & L. Steinberg (Eds.), *Handbook of adolescent psychology: Contextual influences on adolescent development* (pp. 74–103). Hoboken, NJ: John Wiley & Sons.

Brown, J. D., & Kobayashi, C. (2002). Self-enhancement in Japan and America. *Asian Journal of Social Psychology, 5*(3), 145–168.

Brown, J. D., & Kobayashi, C. (2003). Culture and the self-enhancement bias. *Journal of Cross-Cultural Psychology, 34*(5), 492–495.

Brown, J., McDonald, C. A., & Roman, F. (2014). "The dog and the carrot are both useful to me": Functional, self-referent categorization in rural contexts of scarcity in the Dominican Republic. *International Perspectives in Psychology: Research, Practice, Consultation, 3*(2), 63.

Brown, P. J., & Konner, M. (1987). An anthropological perspective on obesity. *Annals of the New York Academy of Sciences, 499*, 29–46.

Brown, R. E. (2016) Hebb and Cattell: The genesis of the theory of fluid and crystallized intelligence. *Frontiers in Human Neuroscience, 10*, 606. doi:10.3389/fnhum.2016.00606

Brown, T. (1827). Of simple suggestion—Mr. Hume's classification of associating principles. In T. Brown & L. Hedge (Ed.), *A treatise on the philosophy of the human mind, being the lectures of the late Thomas Brown* (pp. 239–247). Cambridge, MA: Hilliard and Brown.

Browne, K. (2001). (Ng)amuk revisited: Emotional expression and mental illness in Central Java, Indonesia. *Transcultural Psychiatry, 38*, 147–165.

Browner, T. (2004). *Heartbeat of the people: Music and dance of the northern pow-wow*. Champaign: University of Illinois Press.

Brozman, B. (2009). *The Tau Moe family*. Retrieved from http://www.bobbrozman.com/taumoe.html

Bruner, J. S. (1990). *Acts of meaning* (vol. 3). Cambridge, MA: Harvard University Press.

Bryant, C., & Peck, D. (2009). *Death and the human experience*. Thousand Oaks, CA: SAGE.

Bryant, Y. (2008). Relationships between exposure to rap music videos and attitudes toward relationships among African American youth. *Journal of Black Psychology, 34*, 356–380.

Bryson, B. (2010). *Made in America: An informal history of American English*. New York: Random House.

Buchtel, E. E., Ng, L. C. Y., Norenzayan, A., Heine, S. J., Biesanz, J. C., Chen, S. X., . . . Su, Y. (2018). A sense of obligation: Cultural differences in the experience of obligation. *Personality and Social Psychology Bulletin, 44*(11), 1545–1566.

Bucko, R. A. (1998). *The Lakota ritual of the sweat lodge*. Lincoln: University of Nebraska Press.

Bulbulia, J. A., Xygalatas, D., Schjoedt, U., Fondevila, S., Sibley, C. G., & Konvalinka, I. (2013). Images from a jointly arousing collective ritual reveal affective polarization. *Frontiers in Psychology, 4*, 960.

Burke, K. (1969). *A grammar of motives* (vol. 177). Los Angeles: University of California Press.

Burke, K. (1989). *On symbols and society*. Chicago: University of Chicago Press.

Busby, J. (1837). Letter to the Hon Colonel Secretary of New South Wales. In H. H. Turton (ed.), *An epitome of official documents relative to native affairs and land purchases in the north island of New Zealand*. Wellington: George Didsbury. Retrieved from http://nzetc.victoria.ac.nz/tm/scholarly/tei-TurEpit.html

Buss, D. M. (1988). The evolution of human intrasexual competition: Tactics of mate attraction. *Journal of Personality and Social Psychology*, *54*(4), 616–628.

Buss, D. M. (1989). Sex differences in human mate selection: Evolutionary hypotheses tested in 37 countries. *Behavioral and Brain Sciences*, *12*, 1–49.

Buss, D. M. (1998). The evolutionary psychology of human social strategies. In S. F. D. Gilbert & G. Lindzey (Eds.), *Handbook of social psychology* (pp. 3–38). Chicago, IL: McGraw-Hill.

Buss, D. M. & Schmidt, D. P. (1993). Sexual strategies theory: An evolutionary perspective on human mating. *Psychological Review*, *100*(2), 204–232.

Butler, E. A., Lee, T. L., & Gross, J. J. (2007). Emotion regulation and culture: Are the social consequences of emotion suppression culture-specific? *Emotion*, *7*(1), 30.

Butler, L., & Pilkington, K. (2013). Chinese herbal medicine and depression: The research evidence. *Evidence-based Complementary and Alternative Medicine*. doi:10.1155/2013/739716

Buttery, E. A., & Leung, T. K. P. (1998). The difference between Chinese and Western negotiations. *European Journal of Marketing*, *32*(3–4), 374–389. doi:10.1108/03090569810204652

Buttery, E. A., & Wong, Y. H. (1999). The development of a Guanxi framework. *Marketing Intelligence & Planning*, *17*(3), 147–154.

Byrne, R. W. & Whiten A. (1988). *Machiavellian intelligence*. Oxford, UK: Oxford University Press.

Cacioppo, J. T., & Hawkley, L. C. (2003). Social isolation and health, with an emphasis on underlying mechanisms. *Perspectives in Biology and Medicine*, *46*(3), S39–S52.

Cacioppo, S., Bianchi-Demicheli, F., Hatfield, E., & Rapson, R. L. (2012). Social neuroscience of love. *Clinical Neuropsychiatry*, *9*, 3–13.

Cai, H., Sedikides, C., & Jiang, L. (2013). Familial self as a potent source of affirmation: Evidence from China. *Social Psychological and Personality Science*, *4*(5), 529–537.

Caldwell, C. A., & Millen, A. E. (2009). Social learning mechanisms and cumulative cultural evolution: is imitation necessary?. *Psychological Science*, *20*(12), 1478–1483.

Center for Army Lessons Learned. (2004). *Cultural issues in Iraq. Operation Iraqi Freedom (OIF) CAA T II initial impressions report (IIR)*. Leavenworth, KS: Author.

Call, J., & Tomasello, M. (1995). Use of social information in the problem solving of orangutans (*Pongo pygmaeus*) and human children (*Homo sapiens*). *Journal of Comparative Psychology*, *109*(3), 308–320.

Calverton, V. F. (1928). *The bankruptcy of marriage*. New York, NY: The Macaulay Corporation.

Cameron, M. (2005). Two-spirited aboriginal people: Continuing cultural appropriation by non-aboriginal society. *Canadian Woman Studies*, *24*(2/3), 123–127.

Campbell, A. (2008). Attachment, aggression and affiliation: The role of oxytocin in female social behavior. *Biological Psychology*, *77*(1), 1–10.

Campbell, J. (1973). *The hero with a thousand faces*. Princeton, NJ: Princeton University Press. (Original work published 1949)

Campbell, J. (1986, November). *From ritual to rapture, from Dionysus to the Grateful Dead*. Lecture presented at the Palace of Fine Arts, San Francisco, CA.

Camras, L. A., Bakeman, R., Chen, Y., Norris, K., & Cain, T. R. (2006). Culture, ethnicity, and children's facial expressions: A study of European American, mainland Chinese, Chinese American, and adopted Chinese girls. *Emotion*, *6*(1), 103.

Canadian Council for Refugees. (2000). *Report on systemic racism and discrimination in Canadian refugee and immigration policies*. Quebec, CA: Author. Retrieved from http://www.web.net/ccr/antiracrep.htm

Cannon, W. B. (1927). The James-Lange theory of emotions: A critical examination and an alternative theory. *The American Journal of Psychology*, *39*(1/4), 106–124.

Caporael, L. R. (1997). The evolution of truly social cognition: The core configurations model. *Personality and Social Psychology Review*, *1*(4), 276–298.

Caporael, L. R. (2007). Evolutionary theory for social and cultural psychology. In A. W. Kruglanski & E. T. Higgins (Eds.), *Social psychology: Handbook of basic principles* (pp. 3–18). London: Guilford Press.

Caporael, L. R., & Brewer, M. B. (1995). Hierarchical evolutionary theory: There is an alternative, and it's not creationism. *Psychological Inquiry* 6(1), 31–34.

Carbaugh, D. (1999). Just listen: Listening and landscape among the Blackfeet. *Western Journal of Communication*, 63(3), 250–270.

Carbonell, E., & Mosquera, M. (2006). The emergence of a symbolic behaviour: The sepulchral pit of Sima de los Huesos, Sierra de Atapuerca, Burgos, Spain. *Paleoevol*, 5(1), 155–160.

Carhart-Harris, R. L., Erritzoe, D., Williams, T., Stone, J. M., Reed, L. J., Colasanti, A., . . . Hobden, P. (2012). Neural correlates of the psychedelic state as determined by fMRI studies with psilocybin. *Proceedings of the National Academy of Sciences*, 109, 2138–2143. http://dx.doi.org/10.1073/pnas.1119598109

Carlo, G., Roesch, S. C., Knight, G. P., & Koller, S. H. (2001). Between- or within-culture variation? Culture group as a moderator of the relations between individual differences and resource allocation preferences. *Journal of Applied Developmental Psychology*, 22(6), 559–579.

Carney, J., & Carron, P. M. (2017). Comic-book superheroes and prosocial agency: A large-scale quantitative analysis of the effects of cognitive factors on popular representations. *Journal of Cognition and Culture*, 17(3–4), 306–330.

Carpenter, M. Ahktar, N., & Tomasello, M. (1998) Fourteen-through 18-month-old infants differentially imitate intentional and accidental actions. *Infant Behavior & Development*, 21(2), 315–330.

Carter, C. S. (1998). Neuroendocrine perspectives on social attachment and love. *Psychoneuroendocrinology*, 23(8), 779–818.

Carto, S. L., Weaver, A. J., Hetherington, R., Lam, Y., Wiebe, E. C. (2009). Out of Africa and into an ice age: On the role of global climate change in the late Pleistocene migration of early modern humans out of Africa. *Journal of Human Evolution*, 56(2), 139–151.

Casanave, C. P., & Li, X. (2009). Learning the literacy practices of graduate school: Insiders' reflections on academic enculturation. *Learning*, 13(1), 1–267.

Cattell, R. B. (1943). The measurement of adult intelligence. *Psychological Bulletin*, 40(3), 153–193. doi:10.1037/h0059973

Cattell, R. B. (1950). *Personality: A systematic theoretical and factual study*. New York, NY: McGraw-Hill.

Cavalli-Sforza, L. L., & Feldman, M. W. (1981). *Cultural transmission and evolution: A quantitative approach* (No. 16). Princeton, NJ: Princeton University Press.

Cawley, J., & Choi, A. (2015). Health disparities across education: The role of differential reporting error. *Health Economics*, 27(3), e1–e29. doi:10.1002/hec.3609

Cehajic-Clancy, S., & Bilewicz, M. (2017). Fostering reconciliation through historical moral exemplars in a postconflict society. *Peace and Conflict: Journal of Peace Psychology*, 23(3), 288–296.

Central Intelligence Agency. (2013). *The world factbook 2013–14*. Retrieved from https://www.cia.gov/library/publications/the-world-factbook/index.html

Cerulo, K. A. (1993, June). Symbols and the world system: National anthems and flags. *Sociological Forum*, 8(2), 243–271.

Chagnon, N. (1974). *Studying the Yanomamö*. New York, NY: Holt, Rinehart & Winston.

Chagnon, N. A. (1988a). Life histories, blood revenge, and warfare in a tribal population. *Science*, 239(4843), 985–992.

Chagnon, N. A. (1988b). *Yanomamö: The fierce people*. New York, NY: Holt, Rinehart & Winston.

Chanda, M. L., & Levitin, D. J. (2013). The neurochemistry of music. *Trends in Cognitive Sciences*, 17(4), 179–193.

Chang, C. L.-h., & Chen, J. Q. (2017). The information ethics perception gaps between Chinese and American students: A Chinese guanxi perspective. *Information Technology & People*, 30(2), 473–502.

Chang, L., Wang, Y., Shackelford, T. K., & Buss, D. M. (2011). Chinese mate preferences: Cultural evolution and continuity across a quarter of a century. *Personality and Individual Differences*, 50(5), 678–683.

Chattopadhyay, A., Gorn, G. I., & Darke, P. (2010). Differences and similarities in hue preferences between Chinese and Caucasians. In A. Krishna (Ed.), *Sensory marketing: Research on the sensuality of products* (pp. 219–239). New York, NY: Routledge/Taylor & Francis Group.

Chaves, J. (1976). *Mei Yao-ch'en and the development of early sung poetry* (No. 13). New York, NY: Columbia University Press.

Chen, C., & Jack, R. E. (2017). Discovering cultural differences (and similarities) in facial expressions of emotion. *Current Opinion in Psychology*, *17*, 61–66. doi:10.1016/j.copsyc.2017 .06.010

Chen, F. F. (2008). What happens if we compare chopsticks with forks? The impact of making inappropriate comparisons in cross-cultural research. *Journal of Personality and Social Psychology*, *95*(5), 1005.

Chen, L. F. (1972). *The Confucian way*. Taipei: Commercial Press.

Chen, Y., Nettles, M. E., & Chen, S.-W. (2009). Rethinking dependent personality disorder: Comparing different human relatedness in cultural contexts. *Journal of Nervous and Mental Disease*, *197*(11), 793–800.

Cheng, C., Cheung, S., Chio, J., & Chan, M. (2013). Cultural meaning of perceived control: A meta-analysis of locus of control and psychological symptoms across 18 cultural regions. *Psychological Bulletin*, *139*(1), 152–188.

Cheng, C. Y., & Lee, F. (2013). The malleability of bicultural identity integration (BII). *Journal of Cross-Cultural Psychology*, *44*(8), 1235–1240.

Cheng, C. Y., Lee, F., & Benet-Martínez, V. (2006). Assimilation and contrast effects in cultural frame switching: Bicultural identity integration and valence of cultural cues. *Journal of Cross-Cultural Psychology*, *37*(6), 742–760.

Cheng, G. N., & Christopher, H. K. (2010). The effects of intimacy, passion, and commitment on satisfaction in romantic relationships among Hong Kong Chinese people. *Journal of Psychology in Chinese Societies*, *11*(2), 123–146.

Chengappa, R. (1997, Sep 8). Patents: India wins a victory over turmeric but the war is on. *India Today*. Retrieved from https://www.indiatoday.in/maga zine/science-and-technology/story/ 19970908-patents-india-wins-a-victory-over-turmeric-but-the-war-is-on-832438-1997-09-08

Cheung, F. M., Cheung, S. F., Leung, K., Ward, C., & Leong, F. (2003). The English version of the Chinese Personality Assessment Inventory. *Journal of Cross-Cultural Psychology*, *34*(4), 433–452.

Cheung, F. M., Leung, K., Fan, R. M., Song, W.-Z., Zhang, J.-X., & Zhang, J.-P. (1996). Chinese Personality Assessment Inventory [Database record]. Retrieved from PsycTESTS. doi:10.1037/t27321-000

Chirkov, V. (2009). Summary of the criticism of and potential ways to improve acculturation psychology. *International Journal of Intercultural Relations*, *33*, 177–180.

Chiu, C.-y., Hong, Y.-y., & Dweck, C. S. (1997). Lay dispositionism and implicit theories of personality. *Journal of Personality and Social Psychology*, *73*(1), 19–30.

Chiu, L. H. (1972). A cross-cultural comparison of cognitive styles in Chinese and American children. *International Journal of Psychology*, *7*(4), 235–242.

Choi, C. (2012, Nov. 15). Ancient mariners: Did Neanderthals sail to Mediterranean? *LiveScience.com*. Retrieved from https://www.livescience .com/24810-neanderthals-sailed-mediterranean.html

Choi, I., & Choi, Y. (2002). Culture and self-concept flexibility. *Personality and Social Psychology Bulletin*, *28*(11), 1508–1517.

Choi, K., & Ross, M. (2011). Cultural differences in process and person focus: Congratulations on your hard work versus celebrating your exceptional brain. *Journal of Experimental Social Psychology*, *47*(2), 343–349.

Chomsky, N. (1995). Language and nature. *Mind, New Series*, *104*(413), 1–61.

Chou, K. L., & Chi, I. (2002). Successful aging among the young-old, old-old, and oldest-old Chinese. *The International Journal of Aging and Human Development*, *54*(1), 1–14.

Chou, R. J.-A. (2011). Filial piety by contract? The emergence, implementation, and implications of the "Family Support Agreement" in China. *The Gerontologist*, *51*(1), 3–16. doi:10.1093/ geront/gnq059

Christopher, J. C. (1999). Situating psychological well-being: Exploring the cultural roots of its theory and research. *Journal of Counseling & Development*, *77*(2), 141–152.

Chu, D. (2017). Sex talk: Discourses about female bodies in Hong Kong media. *Sexuality & Culture*, *21*(3), 882–900.

Chua, A. (2011). *Battle hymn of the tiger mother*. London: Bloomsbury.

Chua, H. F., Boland, J. E., & Nisbett, R. E. (2005). Cultural variation in eye movements during scene perception. *Proceedings of the National Academy of Sciences*, *102*(35), 12629–12633.

Chun, M. (2016). *Hooponopono: Traditional ways of healing to make things right again*. Honolulu: University of Hawaiʻi Press.

Chung, R. (2001). Gender, ethnicity, and acculturation in intergenerational conflict of Asian American college students. *Cultural Diversity and Ethnic Minority Psychology*, *7*(4): 376–386.

Church, A. T. (2016). Personality traits across cultures, *Current Opinion in Psychology*, *8*, 22–30.

Church, A. T., & Katigbak, M. S. (1989). Internal, external, and self-report structure of personality in a non-Western culture: An investigation of cross-language and cross-cultural generalizability. *Journal of Personality and Social Psychology, 57*(5), 857–872.

Claidière, N., Trouche, E., & Mercier, H. (2017). Argumentation and the diffusion of counter-intuitive beliefs. *Journal of Experimental Psychology, 146*(7), 1052–1066.

Clark, A. E., & Kashima, Y. (2007). Stereotypes help people connect with others in the community: A situated functional analysis of the stereotype consistency bias in communication. *Journal of Personality and Social Psychology, 93*(6), 1028.

Clayton, M., Sager, R., & Will, U. (2005). In time with the music: The concept of entrainment and its significance for ethnomusicology. *European Meetings in Ethnomusicology, 11*(1), 1–82.

Clegg, J. M., & Legare, C. H. (2016). A cross-cultural comparison of children's imitative flexibility. *Developmental Psychology, 52*(9), 1435–1444.

Cochran, P. A. L., Marshall, C. A., Garcia-Downing, C., Kendall, E., Cook, D., McCubbin, L., & Gover, R. M. S. (2008). Indigenous ways of knowing: Implications for participatory research and community. *American Journal of Public Health, 98*(1), 22–27.

Cocks, M., & Møller, V. (2002). Use of indigenous and indigenised medicines to enhance personal well-being: A South African case study. *Social Science & Medicine, 54*(3), 387–397.

Cocodia, E. (2014). Cultural perceptions of human intelligence. *Journal of Intelligence, 2,* 180–196. doi:10.3390/jintelligence2040180

Coffman, T. (1998). *Nation within.* Honolulu: Koa Books.

Coffman, T. (2002). *Arirang: The Korean American journey.* Honolulu: Arirang Film Project.

Cohen, A. S., Stone, J. R., Beuning, K. R., Park, L. E., Reinthal, P. N., Dettman, D.,...Brown, E. T. (2007). Consequences of early late-pleistocene megadroughts in tropical Africa. *Proceedings of the National Academy of Sciences of the USA, 104*(42), 16422–16427.

Cohen, L. J., & Dragović-Soso, J. (2008). *State collapse in South-Eastern Europe: New perspectives on Yugoslavia's disintegration.* West Lafayette, IN: Purdue University Press.

Colman, M. E. (1998). Obesity in the paleolithic era? The Venus of Willendorf. *Endocrine Practice, 4*(1), 58–59.

Colmant, S. A., & Merta, R. J. (1999). Using the sweat lodge ceremony as group therapy for Navajo youth. *Journal for Specialists in Group Work, 24*(1), 55–73.

Conboy, B. T., & Montanari, S. (2016). Early lexical development in bilingual infants and toddlers. In E. Nicoladis & S. Montanari (Eds.), *Language and the human lifespan series. Bilingualism across the lifespan: Factors moderating language proficiency* (pp. 63–79). Washington, DC: American Psychological Association. http://dx.doi.org.hpu.idm.oclc.org/10.1037/14939-005

Cook, R. S., Kay, P., & Regier, T. (2005). The world color survey database. In *Handbook of categorization in cognitive science* (pp. 223–241). New York, NY: Elsevier Science.

Cooke, F. L., & Saini, D. S. (2010). Diversity management in India: A study of organizations in different ownership forms and industrial sectors. *Human Resource Management, 49*(3), 477–500.

Cooper, J. J. (2010, August 27). Brewer hits U.N. report citing Arizona Law. *The Washington Times.* Retrieved from http://www.washingtontimes.com/news/2010/aug/27/brewer-condemns-un-report-citing-arizona-law/print/

Copen, C. E., Daniels, K., & Mosher, W. D. (2013). First premarital cohabitation in the United States: 2006–2010 National Survey of Family Growth. *National Statistics Health Reports, 4*(64), 1–15.

Copen, C. E., Daniels, K., Vespa, J., & Mosher, W. D. (2012). First marriages in the United States: Data from the 2006–2010 National Survey of Family Growth. *National Statistics Health Reports, 22*(49), 1–21.

Coppens, N. M., Page, R., & Thou, C. T. (2005). Reflections on the evaluation of a Cambodian youth dance program. *American Journal of Community Psychology, 37*(3/4), 321–331.

Correa-Chávez, M., & Rogoff, B. (2009). Children's attention to interactions directed to others: Guatemalan Mayan and European American patterns. *Developmental Psychology, 45*(3), 630–641.

Craft, A. J. (2012). Love 2.0: A quantitative exploration of sex and relationships in the virtual world second life. *Archives of Sexual Behavior, 41*(4), 939–947.

Crespo, C., Jose, P. E., Kielpikowski, M., & Pryor, J. (2013). "On solid ground": Family and school connectedness promotes adolescents' future orientation. *Journal of Adolescence, 36*(5), 993–1002.

Creswell, J. W. (2015). *A concise introduction to mixed methods research*. Thousand Oaks, CA: SAGE.

Crimesider Staff. (2012). Authorities: Texas teen mistakenly deported to Colombia due back in U.S. Friday. *CBS News*. Retrieved from https://www.cbsnews.com/news/authorities-texas-teen-mistakenly-deported-to-colombia-due-back-in-us-friday/

Crocker, J., & Major, B. (2003). The self-protective properties of stigma: Evolution of a modern classic. *Psychological Inquiry 14*(3/4), 232–237.

Cross, I. (2001). Music, mind, and evolution. *Psychology of Music, 29*(1), 95–102.

Cross, I. (2009). The nature of music and its evolution. In S. Hallam, I. Cross, & M. Thaut (Eds.), *The Oxford handbook of music psychology* (pp. 1–13). Oxford: Oxford University Press.

Croucher, S. M., Bruno, A., McGrath, P., Adams, C., McGahan, C., Suits, A., & Huckins, A. (2012). Conflict styles and high–low context cultures: A cross-cultural extension. *Communication Research Reports, 29*(1), 64–73.

Csibra, G., & Gergely, G. (2011). Natural pedagogy as evolutionary adaptation. *Philosophical Transactions of the Royal Society of London B: Biological Sciences, 366*(1567), 1149–1157.

Cunningham, M. R. (1986). Measuring the physical in physical attractiveness: Quasi-experiments on the sociobiology of female facial beauty. *Journal of Personality and Social Psychology, 50*(5), 925.

Cunningham, M. R., Roberts, A. R., Barbee, A. P., Druen, P. B., & Wu, C.-H. (1995). "Their ideas of beauty are, on the whole, the same as ours": Consistency and variability in the cross-cultural perception of female physical attractiveness. *Journal of Personality and Social Psychology, 68*(2), 261–279.

Currie, J. (2008). Healthy, wealthy, and wise: Socioeconomic status, poor health in childhood, and human capital development (NBER Working Paper No. 13987). *Journal of Economic Literature, American Economic Association, 47*(1), 87–122.

Cushner, K., & Brislin, R. W. (1995). *Intercultural interactions: A practical guide* (vol. 9). Thousand Oaks, CA: SAGE.

Cutler, D. M., & Lleras-Muney, A. (2006). *Education and health: Evaluating theories and evidence* (No. w12352). Cambridge, MA: National Bureau of Economic Research.

Cutler, D., & Miller, G. (2005). The role of public health improvements in health advances: The twentieth-century United States. *Demography, 42*(1), 1–22.

Dahl, R. E. (2004). Adolescent brain development: A period of vulnerabilities and opportunities. Keynote address. *Annals of the New York Academy of Sciences, 1021*(1), 1–22.

Dalton, G. (1962). Traditional production in primitive African economies. *The Quarterly Journal of Economics, 76*(3), 360–378.

Dannefer, D. (2003). Cumulative advantage/disadvantage and the life course: Cross-fertilizing age and social science theory. *The Journals of Gerontology Series B: Psychological Sciences and Social Sciences, 58*(6), S327–S337.

Darwin, C. (1851). *The descent of man and selection in relation to sex* (Vol. 2). London: Appleton.

Darwin, C. (1871). *The descent of man, and selection in relation to sex*. London: John Murray.

Das, J. P. (1994). Eastern views on intelligence. In R. J. Sternberg (Ed.), *Encyclopedia of human intelligence* (pp. 387–391). New York: MacMillan.

Dasen, P. R. (1984). The cross-cultural study of intelligence: Piaget and the Baoule. *International Journal of Psychology, 19*(1–4), 407–434.

Dasen, P. R., Lavallée, M., & Retschitzki, J. (1979). Training conservation of quantity (liquids) in West African (Baoulé) children. *International Journal of Psychology, 14*(1), 57–68. doi:10.1080/00207597908246712

Dasen, P. R., et al. (1985). N'glouêlê, l'intelligence chez les Baoulé/N'glouêlê, the Baoulé concept of intelligence. *Archives de Psychologie, 53*(205), 293–324.

Davidson, J. (1983). Māori prehistory: The state of the art. *The Journal of the Polynesian Society, 92*(3), 291–307.

Davies, I., & Corbett, G. (1994). The basic color terms of Russian. *Linguistics, 32*(1), 65–89.

Davies, M. F. (1985). Social roles and social perception biases: The questioner superiority effect revisited. *British Journal of Social Psychology, 24*(4), 239–248.

Davis, B., McGrath, N., Knight, S., Davis, S., Norval, M., Freelander, G., & Hudson, L. (2004). Aminina nud mulumuluna ("You gotta look after yourself"): Evaluation of the use of traditional art in health promotion for Aboriginal people in the Kimberley region of Western Australia. *Australian Psychologist, 39*(2), 107–113.

Dawkins, R. (1976). *The selfish gene*. Oxford, UK: Oxford University Press.

Dawkins, R. (1999). The selfish meme. *Time, 153*(15), 52–53.

Dawson, A. (2018). A water apartheid. *The Washington Post*. Retrieved from https://www.washingtonpost.com/

De Charms, R., Morrison, H. W., Reitman, W., & McClelland, D. C. (1954). *Behavioral correlates of directly and indirectly measured achievement motivation*. Retrieved from http://www.dtic.mil/dtic/tr/fulltext/u2/046311.pdf

Dehaene-Lambertz, G., & Gliga, T. (2004). Common neural basis for phoneme processing in infants and adults. *Journal of Cognitive Neuroscience, 16*(8), 1375–1387.

Delis, I., Chen, C., Jack, R. E., Garrod, O. G. B., Panzeri, S., & Schyns, P. G. (2016). Space-by-time manifold representation of dynamic facial expressions for emotion categorization. *Journal of Vision, 16*(8). doi:10.1167/16.8.14

Deloria, V. (1991). Research, redskins, and reality. *American Indian Quarterly*, 457–468.

D'Emilio, J., & Freedman, E. (1997). *Intimate matters: A history of sexuality in America*. Chicago & London: University of Chicago Press.

Deming, W. E. (1950). *1950 lecture to Japanese management*. Retrieved from http://hclectures.blogspot.com/1970/08/demings-1950-lecture-to-japanese.html

Demoulin, S., Leyens, J-P., Paladino, M-P., Rodriguez-Torres, R., Rodriguea-Perez, A., & Dovivio, J. (2004). Dimensions of uniquely and non-uniquely human emotions. *Cognition & Emotion, 18*(1), 71–96.

De Munck, V. C. (1996). Love and marriage in a Sri Lankan muslim community: Toward a reevaluation of Dravidian marriage practices. *American Ethnologist, 23*(4), 698–716.

Demuru, E., & Palagi, E. (2012). In Bonobos yawn contagion is higher among kin and friends. *PLOS ONE*. doi:10.1371/journal.pone.0049613

den Boer, E. (2012). Spirit conception: Dreams in Aboriginal Australia. *Dreaming, 22*(3), 192.

Denmark, F. L., Eisenberg, K. N., Heitner, E. I., & Holder, N. A. (2003). Immigration to the United States. In L. L. Adler & U. P. Gielen (Eds.), *Migration: Immigration & emigration in international perspective*. Washington, DC: Library of Congress.

Department of Business, Economic Development & Tourism. (2016). *Hawai'i population characteristics 2016*. Retrieved from http://files.hawai'i.gov/dbedt/census/popestimate/2016_county_char_hi_file/Pop_char_hi_2016_final.pdf

d'Errico, F., Henshilwood, C., Lawson, G., Vanhaeren, M., Tillier, A.-M., Soressi, M., ... Julien, M. (2003). Archaeological evidence for the emergence of language, symbolism, and music—An alternative multidisciplinary perspective. *Journal of World Prehistory, 17*(1), 1–70.

Derryberry, D., & Rothbart, M. K. (1988). Arousal, affect, and attention as components of temperament. *Journal of Personality and Social Psychology, 55*(6), 958–966.

De Saussure, F. (1986). *A course in general linguistics* (R. Harris, Trans.). Peru, IL: Open Court. (Original work published 1916)

De Saussure, F., & Baskin, W. (2011). *Course in general linguistics*. London: Duckworth. (Original work published 1916)

de Silva Jayasuriya, S. (2006). Trading on a thalassic network: African migrations across the Indian Ocean. *International Social Science Journal, 58*(2/188), 215–225.

DeSouza, R. (2011). *Doing it for ourselves and our children: Refugee women on their own in New Zealand*. Paper prepared for Refugee Services, Aotearoa New Zealand.

DeSouza, R. (2013). Regulating migrant maternity: Nursing and midwifery's emancipatory aims and assimilatory practices. *Nursing Inquiry, 20*(4), 293–304. doi:10.1111/nin.12020.

Dettwyler, K. A. (1991). Can paleopathology provide evidence for "compassion"? *American Journal of Physical Anthropology, 84*(4), 375–384.

de Waal, F. B. M. (2002). *Tree of origin: What primate behavior can tell us about human social evolution*. Cambridge, MA: Harvard University Press.

de Waal, F. B., & Ferrari, P. F. (Eds.). (2012). *The primate mind*. Cambridge, MA: Harvard University Press.

DeWall, C. N., Pond, R. S., Jr., Campbell, W. K., & Twenge, J. M. (2011). Tuning in to psychological change: Linguistic markers of psychological traits and emotions over time in popular U.S. song lyrics. *Psychology of Aesthetics, Creativity, and the Arts, 5*(3), 200–207. doi:10.1037/a0023195

Diamond, M. (2004). Sexual behavior in precontact Hawai'i: A sexological ethnography. *Revista Española del Pacifico, 16*, 37–58.

Diaz-Guerrero, R. (1991). Historic-sociocultural premises (HSCPs) and global change. *International Journal of Psychology, 26*(5), 665–673.

Diego-Mendoza, S. G. (2010). *An integrative framework on the nature, antecedents and outcomes of perceived discrimination in the workplace*. (Unpublished dissertation). Victoria University of Wellington, NZ.

Dien, D. S. F. (1982). A Chinese perspective on Kohlberg's theory of moral development. *Developmental Review, 2*(4), 331–341.

Diener, E. (1984). Subjective well-being. *Psychological Bulletin, 95*(3), 542.

Diener, E., & Diener, M. (1995). Cross-cultural correlates of life satisfaction and self-esteem. *Journal of Personality and Social Psychology, 68,* 653–663.

Dillon, L. M., Nowak, N., Weisfeld, G. E., Weisfeld, C. C., Shattuck, K. S., Imamoğlu, O. E., . . . Shen, J. (2015). Sources of marital conflict in five cultures. *Evolutionary Psychology, 13*(1), 1–15.

DiMaggio, P., & Ostrower, F. (1990). Participation in the arts by black and white Americans. *Social Forces, 68*(3), 753–778.

Dion, K. K., & Dion, K. L. (1993). Individualistic and collectivistic perspectives on gender and the cultural context of love and intimacy. *Journal of Social Issues, 49,* 53–69.

Dixson, B. J., Vasey, P. L., Sagata, K., Sibanda, N., Linklater, W. L., & Dixson, A. F. (2010). Men's preferences for women's breast morphology in New Zealand, Samoa, and Papua New Guinea. *Archives of Sexual Behavior.* doi:10.1007/s10508-010-9680-6

DiYanni, C. J., Corriveau, K. H., Kurkul, K., Nasrini, J., & Nini, D. (2015). The role of consensus and culture in children's imitation of inefficient actions. *Journal of Experimental Child Psychology, 137,* 99–110.

Dobzhansky, T. (1970). *Genetics of the evolutionary process* (Vol. 139). New York: Columbia University Press.

Doherty, B. (2012). Maldives warns of climate refugees. *Theage.com. au.* Retrieved from http://www .theage.com.au/action/printArticle? id=2878000

Doi, T. (1956). Japanese language as an expression of Japanese psychology. *Western Speech, 20*(2), 90–96.

Doi, T. (1962). Amae: A key concept for understanding Japanese personality structure. In R. J. Smith (Ed.), *Japanese Culture: Its Development and Characteristics.* Chicago: Aldine.

Doi, T. (1988). Dependency in human relationships. In D. I. Okimoto & T. P. Rohlen (Eds.), *Inside the Japanese System: Readings on Contemporary Society and Political Economy* (pp. 20–25). Palo Alto, CA: Stanford University Press.

Doi, T. (1989). The concept of amae and its psychoanalytic implications. *International Review of Psycho-Analysis, 16,* 349–354.

Dole, C., & Csordas, T. (2003). Trials of Navajo youth: Identity, healing, and the struggle for maturity. *Ethos, 31*(3), 357–384.

Donald, M. (2005). Imitation and mimesis. In S. Hurley & N. Chater (Eds.), *Perspectives on imitation: From neuroscience to social science: Vol. 2. Imitation, human development, and culture* (pp. 283–300). Cambridge, MA: MIT Press.

Dong, K. & Liu, Y. (2010). Cross-cultural management in China. *Cross Cultural Management: An International Journal, 17*(3), 223–243.

Donne, J. (1994). Devotions upon emergent occasions and severall steps in my sickness: Meditation XVII. In C. M. Coffin (Ed.). *The complete poetry and selected prose of John Donne.* New York, NY: Modern Library/Random House. (Original work published 1624)

Douvan, E. (1956). Social status and success strivings. *The Journal of Abnormal and Social Psychology, 52*(2), 219.

Drager, K., & Grama, J. (2014). "De tawk dakain ova dea": Mapping language ideologies on Oʻahu. *Dialectologia: Revista Electrònica, 12,* 23–51.

Drake, R. E. (2015). Anthropology and mental health care. *Epidemiology and Psychiatric Sciences, 24,* 283–284. doi:10.1017/S2045796015000402

Du, H., Jonas, E., Klackl, J., Agroskin, D., Hui, E. K. P., & Ma, L. (2013). Cultural influences on terror management: Independent and interdependent self-esteem as anxiety buffers. *Journal of Experimental Social Psychology, 49*(6), 1002–1011.

Dulay, H. C., & Burt, M. K. (1974). Errors and strategies in child second language acquisition. *TESOL Quarterly,* 129–136.

Dunbar, R. I. M. (1992). Neocortex size as a constraint on group size in primates. *Journal of Human Evolution, 20,* 469–493.

Dunbar, R. I. M. (1998). The social brain hypothesis. *Evolutionary Anthropology: Issues, News, and Reviews, 6*(5), 178–190.

Dunbar, R. I. M. (2003). The social brain: Mind, language, and society in evolutionary perspective. *Annual Review of Anthropology, 32,* 163–181.

Dunbar, R. I. M. (2004). Gossip in evolutionary perspective. *Review of General Psychology, 8*(2), 100–110. doi:10.1037/1089-2680.8.2.100

Dunn, A. J., & Berridge, C. W. (1990). Physiological and behavioral responses to corticotropin-releasing factor administration: Is CRF a mediator of anxiety or stress responses? *Brain Research Reviews*, *15*(2), 71–100.

Durant, A., & Shepherd, I. D. H. (2009). "Culture" and "communication" in intercultural communication. *European Journal of English Studies*, *13*(2), 147–162.

Durie, M. (1994). Whaiora. In *Māori Health Development*. Auckland: Oxford University Press.

Durie, M. (1995). Mental health patterns for the New Zealand Māori. In A. Issa (Ed.), *Handbook of culture and mental illness: An international perspective* (pp. 331–345). Madison, CT: International Universities Press.

Durie, M. (2004). Understanding health and illness: Research at the interface between science and indigenous knowledge. *International Journal of Epidemiology*, *33*(5), 1138–1143.

Durojaiye, M. O. A. (1993). Indigenous psychology in Africa: The search for meaning. In U. Kim & J. W. Berry (Eds.), Cross-cultural research and methodology series,. *Indigenous psychologies: Research and experience in cultural context* (Vol. 17, pp. 211–220). Thousand Oaks, CA: SAGE.

Duval, S., & Wicklund, R. A. (1972). *A theory of objective self-awareness*. Oxford, UK: Academic Press.

Duxbury, L., & Dole, G. (2015). Squeezed in the middle: Balancing paid employment, childcare and eldercare. In R. J. Burke, K. M. Page, & C. L. Cooper (Eds.), *Flourishing in life, work and careers: Individual well-being and career experiences* (pp. 141–168). Northampton, MA: Edward Elgar.

Dyer, F. (2002). The biology of the dance language. *Annual Review of Entomology*, *47*, 917–949.

Dzokoto, V. A., & Okazaki, S. (2006). Happiness in the eye and the heart: Somatic referencing in West African emotion lexica. *Journal of Black Psychology*, *32*(2), 117–140. doi:10.1177/009579840628679

Earley, P. C., & Ang, S. (2003). *Cultural intelligence: Individual interactions across cultures*. Palo Alto, CA: Stanford University Press.

Easterbrooks, M. A., Bartlett, J. D., Beeghly, M., & Thompson, R. A. (2013). Social and emotional development in infancy. In R. M. Lerner, M. A. Easterbrooks, J. Mistry, & I. B. Weiner (Eds.), *Handbook of psychology*, *Vol. 6. Developmental psychology* (2nd ed., pp. 91–120). Hoboken, NJ: John Wiley.

Echterhoff, G., Higgins, E. T., & Levine, J. M. (2009). Shared reality: Experiencing commonality with others' inner states about the world. *Perspectives on Psychological Science*, *4*(5), 496–521.

Eckblad, S., Ginsberg, B., Jannson, B., & Levi, L. (1994). Psychosocial and psychiatric aspects of refugee adaptation and care in Sweden. In A. Marsella, T. Bornemann, S. Ekblad, & J. Orley (Eds.), *Amidst peril and pain* (pp. 275–292). Washington, DC: American Psychological Association.

Edwards, G. (2015). *Community as leadership*. Cheltenham, UK: Edward Elgar.

Eerola, T., & Vuoskoski, J. K. (2013). A review of music and emotion studies: Approaches, emotion models, and stimuli. *Music Perception: An Interdisciplinary Journal*, *30*(3), 307–340.

Efron, D. (1941). *Gesture and environment*. Oxford, UK: King's Crown Press.

Eisen, C., Ishii, K., Miyamoto, Y., Ma, X., & Hitokoto, H. (2016). To accept one's fate or be its master: Culture, control, and workplace choice. *Frontiers in Psychology*. doi:10.3389/fpsyg.2016.00936.

Ekman, P. (1992). An argument for basic emotions. *Cognition & Emotion*, *6*(3–4), 169–200.

Ekman, P., & Friesen, W. V. (1969). The repertoire of nonverbal behavior: Categories, origins, usage, and coding. *Semiotica*, *1*(1), 49–98.

Ekman, P., & Friesen, W. V. (1971). Constants across cultures in the face and emotion. *Journal of Personality and Social Psychology*, *17*(2), 124.

Eliade, M. (1978). *A history of religious ideas* (trans. W. R. Trask). Chicago: University of Chicago Press.

Elicker, M. (1997). *Semiotics of popular music: The theme of loneliness in mainstream pop and rock songs*. Tubingen: Gunter Narr.

Emanuele, E., Politi, P., Bianchi, M., Minoretti, P., Bertona, M., & Geroldi, D. (2006). Raised plasma nerve growth factor levels associated with early-stage romantic love. *Psychoneuroendocrinology*, *31*(3), 288–294.

Ember, C. R., & Ember, M. (Eds.). (2003). *Encyclopedia of sex and gender: Men and women in the world's cultures* (Vol. 2). Boston, MA: Springer Science & Business Media.

Engelhardt, G. V., & Gruber, J. (2004). Social Security and the evolution of elderly poverty. *National Bureau of Economic Research*. Retrieved from http://www.nber.org/papers/w10466

Engelmann, J. B., & Pogosyan, M. (2013). Emotion perception across cultures: The role of cognitive mechanisms. *Frontiers in Psychology*, doi:10.3389/fpsyg.2013.00118

English, T., & Chen, S. (2011). Self-concept consistency and culture: The differential impact of two forms of consistency. *Personality and Social Psychology Bulletin*, *37*(6), 838–849.

Engstrom, E. J., & Kendler, K. S. (2015). Emil Kraepelin: Icon and reality. *The American Journal of Psychiatry*, *172*(12), 1190–1196.

Enright, R. D., Bjerstedt, A., Enright, W., Levy, V. Lapsley, D., Buss, R., . . . Zindler, M. (1984). Distributive justice development: Cross-cultural, contextual, and longitudinal evaluations. *Child Development*, *55*, 1737–1751.

Enriquez, V. O. (1977) Filipino psychology in the third world. *Philippine Journal of Psychology*, *10*(1), 3–18.

Enzlin-Dixon, M. (2004). Cultures under threat (Yanomamo, Makuxi). *Faces: People, Places, and Cultures*, *20*(5), 26–29.

Eom, K., & Kim, H. S. (2014). Cultural psychological theory. In B. Garwronski & G. Bodenhausen (Eds.), *Theory and explanation in social psychology* (pp. 328–344). New York: Guilford Press.

Erez, M. (1997). A culture-based model of work motivation. In P. C. Earley & M. Erez (Eds.), *New perspectives on international industrial/organizational psychology* (pp. 193–242). San Francisco, CA: The New Lexington Press.

Erikson, E. H. (Ed.). (1963). *Youth: Change and challenge*. New York: Basic Books.

Espenshade, T. J., Guzman, J. C., & Westoff, C. F. (2003). The surprising global variation in replacement fertility. *Population Research & Policy Review*, *22*(5–6), 575–583. doi:10.1023/B:POPU.0000020882.29684.8e

Espiritu, Y. L. (2001). "We don't sleep around like white girls do": Family, culture, and gender in Filipina American lives. *Signs: Journal of Women in Culture and Society*, *26*(2), 415–440.

Esquirol, É. (1845). *Mental maladies: A treatise on insanity* (trans. E. K. Hunt). Philadelphia: Lea and Blanchard.

Estabrook, E. M., & Yoder, J. I. (1998). Plant-plant communications: Rhizosphere signaling between parasitic angiosperms and their hosts. *Plant Physiology*, *116*(1), 1–7.

Etezadi, S., & Pushkar, D. (2013). Why are wise people happier? An explanatory model of wisdom and emotional well-being in older adults. *Journal of Happiness Studies*, *14*(3), 929–950.

Everett, J. A. C., & Earp, B. D. (2015). A tragedy of the (academic) commons: Interpreting the replication crisis in psychology as a social dilemma for early-career researchers. *Frontiers in Psychology*, *6*, 1152.

Eyong, J. E. (2017). Indigenous African leadership: Key differences from Anglo-centric thinking and writings. *Leadership*, *13*(2), 133–153. doi:10.1177/1742715016663050

Eysenck, H. J. (1967). *The biological basis of personality* (Vol. 689). New York: Transaction.

Eysenck, H. J. (1995). Mind in context: Interaction perspectives in human intelligence. *European Journal of Psychological Assessment*, *12*(1), 83–84.

Ezquiaga, J. M., & Zumalacárregui, M. (2017). Dark energy after GW170817: Dead ends and the road ahead. *Physical Review Letters*, *119*(25), 251–304.

Fachner, J., & Rittner, S. (2011). Ethnotherapy, music and trance: An EEG investigation into a sound-trance induction. In D. Cvetkovic & I. Cosic (Eds.), *States of consciousness: Experimental insights into meditation, waking, sleep and dreams* (pp. 235–256). New York, NY: Springer Verlag.

Fadiman, A. (1998). *The spirit catches you and you fall down*. New York: Farrar, Straus and Giroux.

Falk, C. F., Heine, S. J., & Takemura, K. (2014). Cultural variation in the minimal group effect. *Journal of Cross-Cultural Psychology*, *45*(2), 265–281.

Fang, F., Schei, V., & Selart, M. (2018). Hype or hope? A new look at the research on cultural intelligence. *International Journal of Intercultural Relations*. doi:10.1016/j.ijintrel.2018.04.002

Fang, X., Sauter, D., & van Kleef, G. (2018). Seeing mixed emotions: The specificity of emotion perception from static and dynamic facial expressions across cultures. *Journal of Cross-Cultural Psychology*, *49*(1), 130–148.

Farh, J.-L., Tsui, A. S., Xin, K., & Cheng, B.-S. (1998). The influence of relational demography and Guanxi: The Chinese case. *Organization Science*, *9*(4), 471–488.

Farkas, C., & Vallotton, C. (2016). Differences in infant temperament between Chile and the US. *Infant Behavior & Development*, *44*, 208–218.

Farr, M. (1997). The role of dance/movement therapy in treating at-risk African American adolescents. *The Arts in Psychotherapy*, *24*(2), 183–191.

Farrell, B. (2009). *Pacific islanders face the reality of climate change . . . and of relocation*. UNHCR. Retrieved from http://www.unhcr.org/4b264c836.html

Farrer, J. (2004). A practical approach to diversity. *Industrial and Commercial Training*, *36*(4), 175–177.

Farrer, J., Suo, G., Tsuchiya, H., & Sun, Z. (2012). Re-embedding sexual meanings: A qualitative comparison of the premarital sexual scripts of

Chinese and Japanese young adults. *Sexuality & Culture: An Interdisciplinary Quarterly, 16*(3), 263–286.

Feld, S. (1982). *Sound and sentiment: Birds, weeping, poetics and song in Kaluli expression.* Durham, NC: Duke University Press.

Felmlee, D., Orzechowicz, D., & Fortes, C. (2010). Fairy tales: Attraction and stereotypes in same-gender relationships. *Sex Roles, 62*(3–4), 226–240.

Felsman, J. K., Leong, F. T., Johnson, M. C., & Felsman, I. C. (1990). Estimates of psychological distress among Vietnamese refugees: Adolescents, unaccompanied minors and young adults. *Social Science & Medicine, 31*(11), 1251–1256.

Fenta, H., Hyman, I., Rourke, S. B., Moon, M., & Noh, S. (2010). Somatic symptoms in a community sample of Ethiopian immigrants in Toronto, Canada. *International Journal of Culture and Mental Health, 3*(1), 1–15.

Fernandes, S., Kapoor, H., & Karandikar, S. (2017). Do we gossip for moral reasons? The intersection of moral foundations and gossip. *Basic and Applied Social Psychology, 39*(4), 218–230.

Festinger, L. (1950). Informal social communication. *Psychological Review, 57*(5), 271–282.

Festinger, L. (1957). *A theory of cognitive dissonance.* Palo Alto, CA: Stanford University Press.

Fiaui, P. A., & Hishinuma, E. S. (2009). Samoan adolescents in American Samoa and Hawai'i: Comparison of youth violence and youth development indicators. A study by the Asian/Pacific Islander Youth Violence Prevention Center. *Aggression and Violent Behavior, 14*(6), 478–487.

Field, A. J. (2001). *Altruistically inclined? The behavioral sciences, evolutionary theory, and the origins of reciprocity.* Ann Arbor: University of Michigan Press.

Field, M. J. (1937). *Religion and medicine of the Ga people.* London: Oxford University Press.

Filatova, O. A., Ivkovich, T. V., Guzeev, M. A., Burdin, A. M., & Hoyt, E. (2017). Social complexity and cultural transmission of dialects in killer whales. *Behaviour, 154*(2), 171–194.

Fine, G. (2008). *The Oxford handbook of Plato.* London: Oxford University Press.

Finer, L. (2007). Trends in premarital sex in the United States, 2954–2003. *Public Health Report, 122*(1), 73–78.

Finney, B. (1994). Polynesian voyagers to the new world. *Man and Culture in Oceania, 10,* 1–13.

Fiscella, K., Franks, P., Gold, M. R., & Clancy, C. M. (2000). Inequality in quality: Addressing socioeconomic, racial, and ethnic disparities in health care. *Jama, 283*(19), 2579–2584.

Fischer, J. L. (1961). Art styles as cultural cognitive maps. *American Anthropologist, 63,* 79–93.

Fischer, R., Vauclair, C.-M., Fontaine, J. R. J., & Schwartz, S. H. (2010). Are individual-level and country-level value structures different? Testing Hofstede's legacy with the Schwartz Value Survey. *Journal of Cross-Cultural Psychology, 41*(2), 135–151.

Fischman, J. (1995). Painted puzzles line the walls of an ancient cave. *Science, 267,* 614.

Fiske, A. P., & Fiske, S. T. (2007). Social relationships in our species and cultures. In S. Kitayama & D. Cohen (Eds.), *Handbook of cultural psychology* (pp. 283–306). New York, NY: Guilford Press.

Fiske S. T., & Taylor S. E. (1984). *Social cognition.* Reading, MA: Addison-Wesley.

Fitzgerald, T. (2006). Walking between two worlds: Indigenous women and educational leadership. *Educational Management Administration & Leadership, 34*(2), 201–213.

Fitzpatrick, E. F. M., Martiniuk, A. L. C., D'Antoine, H., Oscar, J., Carter, M., & Elliott, E. J. (2016). Seeking consent for research with indigenous communities: A systematic review. *BMC Medical Ethics.* doi:10.1186/s12910-016-0139-8

Fitzpatrick, S. (2004). Happiness and Toska: An essay in the history of emotions in pre-war Soviet Russia. *Australian Journal of Politics & History, 50*(3), 357–371.

Fitzsimmons, S. R., Lee, Y. T., & Brannen, M. Y. (2013). Demystifying the myth about marginals: Implications for global leadership. *European Journal of International Management, 7*(5), 587–603.

Flanagan, C. A., Cumsille, P., Gill, S., & Gallay, L. S. (2007). School and community climates and civic commitments: Patterns for ethnic minority and majority students. *Journal of Educational Psychology, 99*(2), 421–431.

Flaskerud, J. H. (2012). Case studies in amok? *Issues in Mental Health Nursing, 33*(12), 898–900.

Floccia, C., Sambrook, T. D., Delle Luche, C., Kwok, R., Goslin, J., White, L., . . . Plunkett, K. (2018). Vocabulary of 2-year-olds learning English and an additional language: Norms and effects of linguistic distance: I. Introduction. *Monographs of the Society for Research in Child Development, 83*(1), 7–29.

Florescano, E., & Bork, K. R. (2014). *Memory, myth, and time in Mexico: From the Aztecs to independence*. Houston: University of Texas Press.

Flor-Henry, P., Shapiro, Y., & Sombrun, C. (2017). Brain changes during a shamanic trance: Altered modes of consciousness, hemispheric laterality, and systemic psychobiology. *Cogent Psychology*, *4*(1). doi:10.1080/23 311908.2017.1313522

Fogel, R. W. (1986). Nutrition and the decline in mortality since 1700: Some preliminary findings. In *Long-term factors in American economic growth* (pp. 439–556). Chicago: University of Chicago Press.

Fogel, R. W. (2004). Health, nutrition, and economic growth. *Economic Development and Cultural Change*, *52*(3), 643–658.

Fogel, R. W., & Costa, D. L. (1997). A theory of technophysio evolution, with some implications for forecasting population, health care costs, and pension costs. *Demography*, *34*(1), 49–66.

Folger, J. P., Poole, M. S., & Stutman, R. K. (2016). *Working through conflict: Strategies for relationships, groups, and organizations* (7th ed.). London: Routledge.

Ford, B. Q., Dmitrieva, J. O., Heller, D., Chentsova-Dutton, Y., Grossmann, I., Tamir, M., . . . Mauss, I. B. (2015). Culture shapes whether the pursuit of happiness predicts higher or lower well-being. *Journal of Experimental Psychology: General*, *144*(6), 1053–1062.

Ford, B. Q., Mauss, I. B., & Gruber, J. (2015). Valuing happiness is associated with bipolar disorder. *Emotion*, *15*(2), 211–222.

Ford, J. (2010). Studying leadership critically: A psychosocial lens on leadership identities. *Leadership*, *6*(1), 47–65.

Forman Jr, J. (1991). Driving Dixie down: Removing the confederate flag from southern state capitols. *Yale Law Journal*, 505–526.

Fortes, M. (1936). Ritual festivals and social cohesion in the hinterland of the gold coast. *New Series*, *38*(4), 590–604.

Fortis, P. (2016). Artefacts and bodies among Kuna people from Panama. In *Making and growing* (pp. 103–120). New York: Routledge.

Fox, S. (2001, Aug 21). Jazz legend Bobby Watson. *Honolulu Weekly*, p. 6.

Fox, S. H. (2010). *Ancient ways in current days: Ethno-cultural arts and acculturation* (Unpublished doctoral dissertation). Victoria University of Wellington, NZ.

Fragaszy, D. M., & Perry, S. (Eds.). (2003). *The biology of traditions: Models and evidence*. Cambridge, UK: Cambridge University Press.

Fraley, R. C., Brumbaugh, C. C., & Marks, M. J. (2005). The evolution and function of adult attachment: A comparative and phylogenetic analysis. *Journal of Personality and Social Psychology*, *89*(5), 731–746.

Fraley, R. C., Roisman, G. I., Booth-LaForce, C., Owen, M. T., & Holland, A. S. (2013). Interpersonal and genetic origins of adult attachment styles: A longitudinal study from infancy to early adulthood. *Journal of Personality and Social Psychology*, *104*(5), 817–838.

Freud, S. (1909). *Selected papers on hysteria, and other psychoneuroses* (trans. A. A. Brille). New York: Journal of Nervous & Mental Disorders.

Freud, S. (1920). *A general introduction to psychoanalysis*. New York, NY: Boni and Liveright.

Freud, S. (1961). The ego and the id. In *The standard edition of the complete psychological works of Sigmund Freud, Volume XIX (1923–1925): The ego and the id and other works* (pp. 1–66). London: Hogarth Press.

Freud, S. (1962). *The ego and the id* (trans. J. Riviere). New York: W. W. Norton. (Original work published 1923)

Freud, S. (2015). *Civilization and its discontents*. New York: Broadview Press. (Original work published 1930)

Friedman, H. S., & Schustack, M. W. (2009). *Personality: Classic theories and modern research* (4th ed.). New York: Allen & Bacon.

Frith, S. (1996). Music and identity. In S. Hall & P. duGay (Eds.), *Questions of cultural identity* (pp. 108–127). London: SAGE.

Fu, A. S., & Markus, H. R. (2014). My mother and me: Why tiger mothers motivate Asian Americans but not European Americans. *Personality and Social Psychology Bulletin*, *40*(6), 739–749.

Fuhrman, O., McCormick, K., Chen, E., Jiang, H., Shu, D., Mao, S., & Boroditsky, L. (2011). How linguistic and cultural forces shape conceptions of time: English and Mandarin time in 3D. *Cognitive Science*, *35*(7), 1305–1328.

Fukui, H., & Toyoshima, K. (2014). Music increase altruism through regulating the secretion of steroid hormones and peptides. *Medical Hypotheses*, *83*(6), 706–708.

Furnham, A. (2010). Culture shock: Literature review, personal statement and relevance for the South Pacific. *Journal of Pacific Rim Psychology*, *4*(2), 87–94. doi:10.1375/prp.4.2.87

Furnham, A., McClelland, A., & Omer, L. (2003). A cross-cultural comparison of ratings of perceived fecundity and sexual attractiveness as a function of body weight and waist-to-hip ratio. *Psychology, Health & Medicine, 8*(2), 219–2304.

Gabriels, K., Bauwens, J., & Verstrynge, K. (2012). Second life, second morality? In N. Zagalo, L. Morgado, & A. Boa-Ventura (Eds.), *Virtual worlds and metaverse platforms: New communication and identity paradigms* (pp. 306–320). Hershey, PA: Information Science Reference.

Gabriels, K., & De Backer, C. J. S. (2016). Virtual gossip: How gossip regulates moral life in virtual worlds. *Computers in Human Behavior, 63*, 683–693.

Gaertner, L., Sedikides, C., & Cai, H. (2012). Wanting to be great and better but not average: On the pan-cultural desire for self-enhancing and self-improving feedback. *Journal of Cross-Cultural Psychology, 43*(4), 521–526.

Gailliot, M. T., Stillman, T. F., Schmeichel, B. J., Maner, J. K., & Plant, E. A. (2008). Mortality salience increases adherence to salient norms and values. *Personality and Social Psychology Bulletin, 34*(7), 993–1003.

Gakidou, E., Cowling, K., Lozano, R., & Murray, C. J. (2010). Increased educational attainment and its effect on child mortality in 175 countries between 1970 and 2009: A systematic analysis. *The Lancet, 376*(9745), 959–974.

Gallacher, L. (2005). The terrible twos: Gaining control in the nursery? *Children's Geographies, 3*(2), 243–264.

Gallo, L. C., & Matthews, K. A. (2003). Understanding the association between socioeconomic status and physical health: Do negative emotions play a role? *Psychological Bulletin, 129,* 10–51.

Gallup Healthways. (2014). *2014 country well-being rankings*. Retrieved from http://info.healthways.com/

Gallup International Association. (2015). *Losing our religion? Two thirds of people still claim to be religious*. Retrieved from http://www.wingia.com/web/files/news/290/file/290.pdf

Gama, Y. K. (2015). *Parramore and the interstate 4: A world torn asunder (1880–1980)*. (Unpublished master's thesis). Rollins College, Orlando, FL.

Gangestad, S. W., Haselton, M. G., & Buss, D. M. (2006). Evolutionary foundations of cultural variation: Evoked culture and mate preferences. *Psychological Inquiry, 17*(2), 75–95.

Gann, K. (1997). *American music in the twentieth century*. Independence, KY: Cengage.

García, C., Rivera, N., & Greenfield, P. M. (2015). The decline of cooperation, the rise of competition: Developmental effects of long-term social change in Mexico. *International Journal of Psychology, 50*(1), 6–11.

Gardner, H. (1995). Reflections on multiple intelligences: Myths and messages. *Phi Delta Kappan, 77*(3), 200.

Garland, A., Low, J., & Burns, K. C. (2012). Large quantity discrimination by North Island robins (*Petroica longipes*). *Animal Cognition, 15*, 1129–1140.

Garrett, M. T., Parrish, M., Williams, C., Grayshield, L., Portman, T. A. A., Torres Rivera, E., & Maynard, E. (2014). Invited commentary: Fostering resilience among Native American youth through therapeutic intervention. *Journal of Youth and Adolescence, 43*(3), 470–490.

Gaunt, K. D. (2006). *The games black girls play: Learning the ropes from double-dutch to hip-hop*. New Brunswick, NJ: New York University Press.

Gaw, A. C., & Bernstein, R. L. (1992). Classification of amok in DSM-IV. *Hospital & Community Psychiatry, 43*(8), 789–793.

Geary, D. C., & Bjorklund, D. F. (2000). Evolutionary developmental psychology. *Child Development, 71*(1), 57–65.

Geertz, C. (1964). Ideology as a cultural system. In D. Apter (Ed.), *Ideology and discontent*. Glencoe, IL: The Free Press.

Geertz, C. (1973). *The interpretation of cultures: Selected essays*. New York: Basic Books.

Geertz, C. (1974). "From the native's point of view": On the nature of anthropological understanding. *Bulletin of the American Academy of Arts and Sciences*, 26–45.

Geertz, C. (1975). On the nature of anthropological understanding. *American Scientist, 63*(1), 47–53.

Geertz, C. (2001). Imbalancing act: Jerome Bruner's cultural psychology. In D. Bakhurst & S. Shankar (Eds.), *Jerome Bruner: Language, culture and self* (pp. 19–30). Thousand Oaks, CA: SAGE.

Geiger, A., & Kent, L. (2017). Number of women leaders around the world has grown, but they're still a small group. *Pew Research Center*. Retrieved from http://www.pewresearch.org/fact-tank/2017/03/08/women-leaders-around-the-world/

Gejman, P. V., Sanders, A. R., & Duan, J. (2010). The role of genetics in the etiology of schizophrenia. *Psychiatric Clinics*, *33*(1), 35–66.

Gelfand, M. J., Erez, M., & Aycan, Z. (2007). Cross-cultural organizational behavior. *Annual Review of Psychology*, *58*, 479–514.

Gelfand, M. J., & Kashima, Y. (2016). Culture: Advances in the science of culture and psychology. *Current Opinion in Psychology*, *8*, iv–x.

Gelfand, M. J., Nishii, L. H., Holcombe, K. M., Dyer, N., Ohbuchi, K. I., & Fukuno, M. (2001). Cultural influences on cognitive representations of conflict: Interpretations of conflict episodes in the United States and Japan. *Journal of Applied Psychology*, *86*(6), 1059.

Gentile, B., Twenge, J. M., & Campbell, W. K. (2010). Birth cohort differences in self-esteem, 1988–2008: A cross-temporal meta-analysis. *Review of General Psychology*, *14*(3), 261–268.

Georgas, J. (2003). Family: Variations and changes across cultures. *Online Readings in Psychology and Culture*, *6*(3), 3.

Georgas, J. (2011). Differences and universals in families across cultures. In F. J. R. van de Vijver, A. Chasiotis, & S. M. Breugelmans (Eds.), *Fundamental questions in cross-cultural psychology* (pp. 341–375). New York, NY: Cambridge University Press.

Georgas, J., Mylonas, K., Bafiti, T., Poortinga, Y. H., Christakopoulou, S., Kagitcibasi, C., . . . Kodiç, Y. (2001). Functional relationships in the nuclear and extended family: a 16-culture study. *International Journal of Psychology*, *36*(5), 289–300.

Gergen, K. J., Gulerce, A., Lock, A., & Misra, G. (1996). Psychological science in cultural context. *American Psychologist*, *51*(5), 496.

Gibbs, A., Dawson, J., Forsyth, H., & Mullen, R. (2004). Māori experience of community treatment orders in Otago, New Zealand. *Australian and New Zealand Journal of Psychiatry*, *38*(10), 830–835.

Gibson, E., Futrell, R., Jara-Ettinger, J., Mahowald, K., Bergen, L., Ratnasingam, S., . . . Conway, B. R. (2017). Color naming across languages reflects color use. *PNAS*, *114*(40), 10785–10790.

Gil-da-Costa, R., Martin, A., Lopes, M. A., Munoz, M., Fritz, J. B., & Braun, A. R. (2006). Species-specific calls activate homologs of Broca's and Wernicke's areas in the macaque. *Nature Neuroscience*, *9*, 1064–1070.

Gillett, G., & McKergow, F. (2007). Genes, ownership, and indigenous reality. *Social Science & Medicine*, *65*(10), 2093–2104.

Gilroy, W. G. (2009, June 23). Notre Dame study describes evidence of world's oldest known granaries. *Notre Dame Newswire*. Retrieved from http://newsinfo.nd.edu/news/11901

Gintis, H., Bowles, S., Boyd, R., & Fehr, E. (2008). Gene-culture coevolution and the emergence of altruistic behavior in humans. In C. Crawford & D. Krebs (Eds.), *Foundations of evolutionary psychology* (pp. 313–329). New York, NY: Taylor & Francis.

Glomb, T. M., & Welsh, E. T. (2005). Can opposites attract? Personality heterogeneity in supervisor-subordinate dyads as a predictor of subordinate outcomes. *Journal of Applied Psychology*, *90*(4), 749–757. doi:10.1037/0021-9010.90.4.749

Gogtay, N., Giedd, J. N., Lusk, L., Hayashi, K. M., Greenstein, D., Vaituzis, A. C., . . . Rapoport, J. L. (2004). Dynamic mapping of human cortical development during childhood through early adulthood. *Proceedings of the National Academy of Sciences*, *101*(21), 8174–8179.

Goldenweiser, A. A. (1914). Review of Elemente der Völkerpsychologie: Grundlinien einer Psychologischen Entwicklung der Menschheit. [Review of the book *Elemente der Völkerpsychologie: Grundlinien einer Psychologischen Entwicklung der Menschheit*. W. Wundt]. *Psychological Bulletin*, *11*(10), 387–391.

Gonçalves, G., Reis, M., Sousa, C., Santos, J., & Orgambídez-Ramos, A. (2015). The effect of multicultural experience in conflicts management styles: Mediation of cultural intelligence and self-monitoring. *Journal of Spatial and Organizational Dynamics*, *3*(1), 4–21.

Gonce, L., Upal, M. A., Slone, D. J., & Tweney, D. R. (2006). Role of context in the recall of counterintuitive concepts. *Journal of Cognition and Culture*, *6*(3–4), 521–547.

Gone, J. P. (2006). Mental health, wellness, and the quest for an authentic American Indian identity. In T. M. Witko (Ed.), *Mental health care for urban Indians: Clinical insights from native practitioners* (pp. 55–80). Washington, DC: American Psychological Association.

Gone, J. P. (2008a). Mental health discourse as western cultural proselytization. *Ethos*, *36*(3), 310–315.

Gone, J. P. (2008b). So I can be like a Whiteman: The cultural psychology of space and place in American Indian mental health. *Culture & Psychology*, *14*(3), 369–399.

Gone, J. P. (2013). Redressing first nations historical trauma: Theorizing mechanisms for indigenous culture as mental health treatment. *Transcultural Psychiatry*, *50*(5), 683–706.

Gone, J. P., & Trimble, J. E. (2012). American Indian and Alaska native mental health: Diverse perspectives on enduring disparities. *Annual Review of Clinical Psychology*, *8*, 31–60.

Gonyea, J. G. (2013). Changing family demographics, multigenerational bonds, and care of the oldest old. *Public Policy & Aging Report*, *23*(2), 11–15.

Goodall, J. (1964). Tool-using and aimed throwing in a community of free-living chimpanzees. *Nature*, *201*(4926), 1264–1266.

Goodkind, M., Eickhoff, S. B., Oathes, D. J., Jiang, Y., Chang, A., Jones-Hagata, L. B., . . . Grieve, S. M. (2015). Identification of a common neurobiological substrate for mental illness. *JAMA Psychiatry*, *72*(4), 305–315.

Goodman, J. (2005). *Berber culture on the world stage: From village to video*. Bloomington: Indiana University Press.

Goodman, S., & Greenland, S. (2007). Why most published research findings are false: Problems in the analysis. *PLOS Med*, *4*(4), e168.

Goren, C. C., Sarty, M., & Wu, P. Y. (1975). Visual following and pattern discrimination of face-like stimuli by newborn infants. *Pediatrics*, *56*(4), 544–549.

Goren-Inbar, N., Alperson, N., Kislev, M. E., Simchoni, O., Melamed, Y., Ben-Nun, A., & Werker, E. (2004). Evidence of hominin control of fire at Gesher Benot Ya`aqov, Israel. *Science*, *304*(5671), 725–727.

Goto, S. G., Yee, A., Lowenberg, K., & Lewis, R. S. (2013). Cultural differences in sensitivity to social context: Detecting affective incongruity using the N400. *Social Neuroscience*, *8*(1), 63–74.

Gould, S. J. (1980). Is a new and general theory of evolution emerging? *Paleobiology*, *6*, 119–130.

Gouveia, V. V., Milfont, T. L., & Guerra, V. M. (2014). Functional theory of human values: Testing its content and structure. *Personality and Individual Differences*, *60*, 41–47.

Graburn, N. H. H. (2004). Authentic Inuit art: Creation and exclusion in the Canadian north. *Journal of Material Culture*, *9*(2), 141–159.

Grahame, M. (1998). Material culture and Roman identity. In R. Laurence & J. Berry (Eds.), *Cultural identity in the Roman Empire* (pp. 156–78). New York, NY: Routledge.

Grammer, K., Fink, B., Møller, A. P., & Thornhill, R. (2003). Darwinian aesthetics: Sexual selection and the biology of beauty. *Biological Reviews*, *78*(3), 385–407.

Grandin, T. (2013). My experience with visual thinking and sensory oversensitivity: The need for research on sensory problems. In M. A. Just & K. A. Pelphrey (Eds.), *Carnegie Mellon symposia on cognition. Development and brain systems in autism* (pp. 3–11). New York, NY: Psychology Press.

Graunt, J. (1661). *Natural and political observations mentioned in a following index, and made upon the bills of mortality*. Retrieved from http://www.ac.wwu.edu/~stephan/Graunt/bills.html

Graven, S. N., & Browne, J. V. (2008). Auditory development in the fetus and infant. *Newborn and Infant Nursing Reviews: Brain Development of the Neonate*, *8*(4), 187–193.

Graves, T. D. (1967). Psychological acculturation in a tri-ethnic community. *Southwestern Journal of Anthropology*, *23*(4), 337–350.

Gray, L. E. (2007). Memories of empire, mythologies of the soul: Fado performance and the shaping of saudade. *Ethnomusicology*, *51*(1), 106–130.

Gray, P. (2014). Why is narcissism increasing among young Americans? *Psychology Today*. Retrieved from https://www.psychologytoday.com/blog/freedom-learn/201401/why-is-narcissism-increasing-among-young-americans

Gray-Little, B., & Hafdahl, A. R. (2000). Factors influencing racial comparisons of self-esteem: A quantitative review. *Psychological Bulletin*, *126*(1), 26–54.

Green, E. G. T. (2009). Who can enter? A multilevel analysis on public support for immigration criteria across 20 European countries. *Group Processes & Intergroup Relations*, *12*(1), 41–60.

Greenberg, J., Pyszczynski, X, & Solomon, S. (1986). The causes and consequences of a need for self-esteem: A terror management theory. In R. F. Baumeister (Ed.), *Public self and private self* (pp. 189–212). New York, NY: Springer-Verlag.

Greenberg, J., Schimel, J., Martens, A., Solomon, S., & Pyszczynski, T. (2001). Sympathy for the devil: Evidence that reminding people of their mortality promotes more favorable reactions to white racists. *Motivation and Emotion*, *25*(2), 113–133.

Greene, J. D. (2018). Can we understand moral thinking without understanding thinking? In K. Gray & J. Graham (Eds.), *Atlas of moral psychology* (pp. 3–8). New York, NY: Guilford Press.

Greenfield, P. M. (1972). Cross-cultural studies of mother-infant interaction: Towards a structural-functional approach. *Human Development*, *15*(2), 131–138.

Greenfield, P. M. (1999). Cultural change and human development. In E. Turiel (Ed.), *Development and cultural change: Reciprocal processes* (pp. 37–59). San Francisco: Jossey-Bass.

Greenfield, P. M. (2000). Three approaches to the psychology of culture: Where do they come from? Where can they go? *Asian Journal of Social Psychology*, *3*(3), 223–240.

Greenfield, P. M. (2009). Linking social change and developmental change: Shifting pathways of human development. *Developmental Psychology*, *45*(2), 401–418. doi:10.1037/a00147262

Greenfield, P. M. (2012). Cultural change, human activity, and cognitive development: Commentary on Gauvain and Munroe. *Human Development*, *55*(4), 229–232.

Greenfield, P. M. (2015). Social change, cultural evolution and human development. *International Journal of Psychology*, *50*(1), 4–5.

Greenfield, P. M. (2016). Social change, cultural evolution, and human development. *Current Opinion in Psychology*, *8*, 84–92.

Greenfield, P. M. (2017). Cultural change over time: Why replicability should not be the gold standard in psychological science. *Perspectives on Psychological Science*, *12*(5), 762–771.

Greenfield, P. M., Maynard, A. E., Boehm, C., & Schmidtling, E. Y. (2000). Cultural apprenticeship and cultural change: Tool learning and imitation in chimpanzees and humans. In S. T. Parker, J. Langer, & M. L.

McKinney (Eds.), *Biology, brains, and behavior: The evolution of human development* (pp. 237–277). Santa Fe, NM: School of American Research Press.

Gregory, A. (1923, November). The changing morality of woman. *Current History and Forum*, *19*(2), 295.

Greve, J. (2008). Obesity and labor market outcomes in Denmark. *Economics & Human Biology*, *6*(3), 350–362.

Griesser, M., Wheatcroft, D., & Suzuki, T. N. (2018). From bird calls to human language: Exploring the evolutionary drivers of compositional syntax. *Current Opinion in Behavioral Sciences*, *21*, 6–12.

Grim, J. (2004). Knowing and being known by animals. In P. Waldau & K. Patton (Eds.), *A communion of subjects: Animals in religion, science, and ethics* (pp. 373–390). New York, NY: Columbia University Press.

Grimm, J. (1883). *Teutonic mythology*. London: George Bell & Sons. Retrieved from https://ia700404 .us.archive.org/27/items/teutonicmy tholo02grim/teutonicmytholo02grim .pdf

Groesbeck, C. J. (1975). The archetypal image of the wounded healer. *Journal of Analytical Psychology*, *20*(2), 122–145.

Gross, J. J. (1998). Antecedent- and response-focused emotion regulation: Divergent consequences for experience, expression, and physiology. *Journal of Personality and Social Psychology*, *74*, 224–237.

Gross, J. J. (2014). Emotion regulation: Conceptual and empirical foundations. In J. J. Gross (Ed.), *Handbook of emotion regulation* (pp. 3–20). New York, NY: Guilford Press.

Grossmann, I., Ellsworth, P. C., & Hong, Y.-y. (2012). Culture, attention, and emotion. *Journal of Experimental Psychology*, *141*(1), 31–36. doi:10.1037/ a0023817

Grossmann, I., Huynh, A. C., & Ellsworth, P. C. (2016). Emotional complexity: Clarifying definitions and cultural correlates. *Journal of Personality and Social Psychology*, *111*(6), 895–916.

Grossmann, I., Karasawa, M., Izumi, S., Na, J., Varnum, M. E. W., Kitayama, S., & Nisbett, R. E. (2012). Aging and wisdom: Culture matters. *Psychological Science*, *23*(10), 1059–1066.

Grouzet, F. M. (2013). Self-regulation and autonomy: The dialectic between organismic and sociocognitive valuing processes. In B. W. Sokol, F. M. E. Grouzet, & U. Müller (Eds.), *Self-regulation and autonomy: Social and developmental dimensions of human conduct* (pp. 47–77). New York, NY: Cambridge University Press.

Guerin, P., Fatuma, H. E., & Guerin, B. (2006). Weddings and parties: Cultural healing in one community of Somali women. *Australian e-Journal for the Advancement of Mental Health (AeJAMH)*, *5*(2). Retrieved from http://www.auseinet.com/journal/ vol5iss2/guerin.pdf

Gupta, P. (2013). Ronaiah Tuiasosopo "deeply, romantically in love" with Manti Te'o: The perpetrator of an elaborate online hoax involving the Notre Dame linebacker comes forward on Dr. Phil. *Salon.com*. Retrieved from http://www.salon.com/2013/01/30/ ronaiah_tuiasosopo_deeply_romanti cally_in_love_with_manti_teo/

Gupta, U., & Singh, P. (1982). An exploratory study of love and liking and type of marriages. *Indian Journal of Applied Psychology*, *19*(2), 92–97.

Gureje, O., Nortje, G., Makanjuola, V., Oladeji, B. D., Seedat, S., & Jenkins, R. (2015). The role of global traditional and complementary systems of medicine in the treatment of mental health disorders. *The Lancet Psychiatry, 2*(2), 168–177.

Gurven, M., von Rueden, C., Massenkoff, M., Kaplan, H., & Lero Vie, M. (2013). How universal is the Big Five? Testing the five-factor model of personality variation among forager-farmers in the Bolivian Amazon. *Journal of Personality and Social Psychology, 104*(2), 354–370.

Gusfield, J. R. (1989a). The bridge over separated lands: Kenneth Burke's significance for the study of social action. In H. Simmons & T. Melia (Eds.), *The legacy of Kenneth Burke*, pp. 28–54. Madison: The University of Wisconsin Press.

Gusfield, J. R. (1989b). Introduction. In K. Burke (Ed.), *On symbols and society* (pp. 1–49). Chicago: University of Chicago Press.

Gutmanis, J. (1976). *Hawaiian herbal medicine kahuna la'au lapa'au.* Waipahu: Island Heritage.

Ha, J. Y. (2015). "Lifting up the sound": Ujo Seongeum and performance practice in Pansori tradition. *Journal of the Asian Music Research Institute, 38*, 199–240.

Ha, T., Berg, J. E. M., Engels, R. C. M. E., & Lichtwarck-Aschoff, A. (2012). Effects of attractiveness and status in dating desire in homosexual and heterosexual men and women. *Archives of Sexual Behavior, 41*(3), 673–682.

Hadley, S. & Yancy G. (2012). *Therapeutic uses of rap and hip-hop.* New York, NY: Routledge, Taylor & Francis Group.

Hagan, C. R., Podlogar, M. C., & Joiner, T. E. (2015). Murder-suicide: Bridging the gap between mass murder, amok, and suicide. *Journal of Aggression, Conflict and Peace Research, 7*(3), 179–186.

Hahn, J., & Münzel, S. C. (1995). Knochenflöten aus dem Aurignacien des Geißenklösterle bei Blaubeuren, Alb-Donau-Kreis. *Fundb. aus Baden-Württemberg 20*, 1–12.

Hale, C., Hannum, J., & Espelage, D. (2005). Social support and physical health: The importance of belonging. *Journal of American College Health, 53*(6), 276–284.

Haley, D. (2007). Art, health and well-being. In J. Haworth & G. Hart (Eds.), *Well-being: Individual, community and social perspectives* (pp. 110–119). New York: Palgrave Macmillan.

Hall, E. T. (1976). *Beyond culture.* New York, NY: Doubleday.

Hall, G. C. N., & Barongan, C. (2016). *Multicultural psychology.* New York, NY: Routledge.

Hall, G. C. N., & Yee, A. H. (2012). US mental health policy: Addressing the neglect of Asian Americans. *Asian American Journal of Psychology, 3*(3), 181.

Hamer, F. M. (2012). Anti-black racism and the conception of whiteness. In S. Akhtar (Ed.), *The African American experience: Psychoanalytic perspectives* (pp. 217–227). Lanham, MD: Jason Aronson.

Hamm, J. V. (2000). Do birds of a feather flock together? The variable bases for African American, Asian American, and European American adolescents' selection of similar friends. *Developmental Psychology, 36*(2), 209–219.

Hammack, P. L. (2008), Narrative and the cultural psychology of identity. *Personality and Social Psychology Review, 12*(3), 222–247.

Han, S., & Humphreys, G. (2016). Self-construal: A cultural framework for brain function. *Current Opinion in Psychology, 8*, 10–14.

Han, S., & Ma, Y. (2014). Cultural differences in human brain activity: A quantitative meta-analysis. *NeuroImage, 99*, 293–300.

Haney, C., Banks, C., & Zimbardo, P. (1972). *Interpersonal dynamics in a simulated prison* (No. ONR-TR-Z-09). Washington, DC: Office of Naval Research.

Hanke, K. (2009). *Victim and perpetrator perspectives in post-World War II contexts: Intergroup forgiveness and historical closure in Europe and East Asia.* (Unpublished doctoral dissertation). Victoria University of Wellington.

Hanke, K., & Fischer, R. (2013). Socioeconomical and sociopolitical correlates of interpersonal forgiveness: A three-level meta-analysis of the Enright Forgiveness Inventory across 13 societies. *International Journal of Psychology, 48*(4), 514–526.

Hanke, K., Liu, J. H., Hilton, D. J., Bilewicz, M., Garber, I., Huang, L.-L., . . . Wang, F. (2013). When the past haunts the present: Intergroup forgiveness and historical closure in post–World War II societies in Asia and in Europe. *International Journal of Intercultural Relations, 37*(3), 287–301. doi:10.1016/j.ijintrel.2012.05.003

Hanke, K., & Vauclair, C.-M. (2016). Investigating the human value "forgiveness" across 30 countries: A cross-cultural meta-analytical approach. *Cross-Cultural Research: The Journal of Comparative Social Science, 50*(3), 215–230.

Hanley, J. H. (1999). Beyond the tip of the iceberg. *Reaching Today's Youth: The Community Circle of Caring Journal, 3*(2), 9–12.

Hanson, C. (2010). Documentation for data on maternal mortality. *The Gapminder Foundation*. Retrieved from http://www.gapminder.org/documentation/documentation/gapdoc010.pdf

Hardaway, C., & Fulghini, A. J. (2006). Dimensions of family connectedness among adolescents with Mexican, Chinese, and European backgrounds. *Developmental Psychology*, *42*(6), 1246–1258.

Hargreave, D., & North, A. (1999). The functions of music in everyday life: Redefining the social psychology of music. *Psychology of Music*, *27*, 71–83.

Harkins, J., & Wierzbicka, A. (1997). Language: A key issue in emotion research. *Innovation: The European Journal of Social Science Research*, *10*(4), 319–331.

Harkness, S., Moscardino, U., Bermúdez, M. R., Zylicz, P. O., Welles-Nyström, B., Blom, M., . . . Super, C. M. (2006). Mixed methods in international collaborative research: The experiences of the international study of parents, children, and schools. *Cross-Cultural Research: The Journal of Comparative Social Science*, *40*(1), 65–82.

Harkness, S., & Super, C. M. (1992). The cultural foundations of fathers' roles: Evidence from Kenya and the United States. In B. S. Hewlett (Ed.), *Foundations of human behavior. Father–child relations: Cultural and biosocial contexts* (pp. 191–211). Hawthorne, NY: Aldine de Gruyter.

Harkness, S., Zylicz, P. O., Super, C. M., Welles-Nyström, B., Bermúdez, M. R., Bonichini, S., . . . Mavridis, C. J. (2011). Children's activities and their meanings for parents: A mixed-methods study in six Western cultures. *Journal of Family Psychology*, *25*(6), 799.

Harrington, L., & Liu, J. H. (2002). Self-enhancement and attitudes toward high achievers: A bicultural view of the independent and interdependent self. *Journal of Cross-Cultural Psychology*, *33*, 37–55.

Harris, C. R., & Christenfeld, N. (1996). Jealousy and rational responses to infidelity across gender and culture. *Psychological Science*, *7*(6), 378–379.

Harrison, R. (2009). Excavating second life: Cyber-archaeologies, heritage and virtual communities. *Journal of Material Culture*, *14*(1), 75–106.

Hashimoto, H., & Yamagishi, T. (2016). Duality of independence and interdependence: An adaptationist perspective. *Asian Journal of Social Psychology*, *19*(4), 286–297.

Hassan, I. (1958). The idea of adolescence in American fiction. *American Quarterly*, *10*(3), 312–324.

Hatala, A. (2014). *Narrative structures of Maya mental disorders: An ethnography of Q'eqchi' healing*. (Unpublished doctoral dissertation). University of Saskatchewan.

Hatfield, E., Mo, Y-M., & Rapson, R. L. (2015). Love, sex, and marriage across cultures. In L. Jensen (Ed.), *The Oxford handbook of human development and culture: An interdisciplinary perspective*. London: Oxford University Press.

Hatfield, E., & Rapson, R. L. (1993). *Love, sex, and intimacy: Their psychology, biology, and history*. New York, NY: HarperCollins.

Hatfield, E., & Rapson, R. L. (1996). *Love and sex: Cross-cultural perspectives*. New York, NY: Allyn & Bacon.

Hatfield, E., & Rapson, R. L. (2002). Passionate love and sexual desire: Cross-cultural and historical perspectives. In A. Vangelisti, H. T. Reis,

& M. A. Fitzpatrick (Eds.), *Stability and change in relationships* (pp. 306–324). Cambridge, UK: Cambridge University Press.

Hatfield, E., & Rapson, R. (2005). *Love and sex: Cross-cultural perspectives*. Needham Heights, MA: Allyn & Bacon.

Hatfield, E., & Rapson, R. L. (2006). Passionate love, sexual desire, and mate selection: Cross-cultural and historical perspectives. In P. Noller & J. A. Feeney (Eds.), *Close relationships: Functions, forms and processes* (pp. 227–243). Hove, UK: Psychology Press/Taylor & Francis (UK).

Hatfield, E., & Rapson, R. L. (2010). Love. In I. B. Weiner & W. E. Craighead (Eds.). *The Corsini encyclopedia of psychology* (4th ed., vol. 2., pp. 948–950). Hoboken, NJ: John Wiley and Sons.

Hatfield, E, Rapson, R. L., & Martel, L. D. (2007.) Passionate love and sexual desire. In S. Kitayama & D. Cohen (Eds.), *Handbook of cultural psychology* (pp. 760–779). New York, NY: Guilford Press.

Hatfield, E., & Sprecher, S. (1995). Men's and women's preferences in marital partners in the United States, Russia, and Japan. *Journal of Cross-Cultural Psychology*, *26*(6), 728–750.

Hathaway, S. L., & Kim, D. W. (Eds.). (2012). *Intercultural transmission in the medieval Mediterranean*. London: A&C Black.

Hatta, S. M. (1996). A Malay cross-cultural worldview and forensic review of amok. *Australian and New Zealand Journal of Psychiatry*, *30*(4), 505–510.

Hatton, T. J., & Williamson, J. G. (2005). *Global migration and the world economy: Two centuries of policy and performance*. Cambridge, MA: MIT Press.

Hauser, M. D., Chomsky, N., & Fitch, W. T. (2002). The faculty of language: What is it, who has it, and how did it evolve? *Science*, *298*(5598), 1569–1579.

Haworth, J., & Hart, G. (2007). Introduction. In J. Haworth & G. Hart (Eds.), *Well-being: Individual, community and social perspectives* (pp. 1–24). New York, NY: Palgrave Macmillan.

Haworth, J., & Lewis, S. (2005). Work, leisure and well-being. *British Journal of Guidance & Counselling*, *33*(1), 67–79.

He, J., & van de Vijver, F. (2012). Bias and equivalence in cross-cultural research. *Online Readings in Psychology and Culture*, *2*(2), 8.

Hehman, J. A., & Bugental, D. B. (2013). "Life stage-specific" variations in performance in response to age stereotypes. *Developmental Psychology*, *49*(7), 1396–1406.

Heider, E. R., & Olivier, D. C. (1972). The structure of the color space in naming and memory for two languages. *Cognitive Psychology*, *3*(2), 337–354.

Heine, S. (2013). *Cultural psychology* (3rd ed.). New York, NY: Norton.

Heine, S. J., Kitayama, S., Lehman, D. R., Takata, T., Ide, E., Leung, C., & Matsumoto, H. (2001). Divergent consequences of success and failure in Japan and North America: An investigation of self-improving motivations and malleable selves. *Journal of Personality and Social Psychology*, *81*(4), 599.

Heine, S. J., Lehman, D. R., Markus, H. R., & Kitayama, S. (1999). Is there a universal need for positive self-regard? *Psychological Review*, *106*, 766–794.

Heine, S. J., Takemoto, T., Moskalenko, S., Lasaleta, J., & Henrich, J. (2008). Mirrors in the head: Cultural variation in objective self-awareness. *Personality and Social Psychology Bulletin*, *34*(7), 879–887.

Hendrickson, D., & Tucker, R. (2005). *Revisions in need of revising: What went wrong in Iraq*. Retrieved from http://www.StrategicStudiesInstitute.army.mil

Henn, B. M., Gignoux, C. R., Jobin, M., Granka, J. M., Macpherson, J. M., Kidd, J. M., . . . Feldman, M. W. (2011). Hunter-gatherer genomic diversity suggests a southern African origin for modern humans. *Proceedings of the National Academy of Sciences*, *108*(13), 5154–5162.

Henrich, J. (2004). Demography and cultural evolution: How adaptive cultural processes can produce maladaptive losses—the Tasmanian case. *American Antiquity*, *69*(2), 197–214.

Henrich, J., & Boyd, R. (2001). Why people punish defectors: Weak conformist transmission can stabilize costly enforcement of norms in cooperative dilemmas. *Journal of Theoretical Biology*, *208*(1), 79–89.

Henrich, J., Boyd, R., & Richerson, P. J. (2008). Five misunderstandings about cultural evolution. *Human Nature*, *19*(2), 119–137.

Henrich, J., Heine, S. J., & Norenzayan, A. (2010). The weirdest people in the world? *Behavioral and Brain Sciences*, *33*(2–3), 61–83.

Henry, E., & Wolfgramm, R. (2018). Relational leadership–An indigenous Māori perspective. *Leadership*, *14*(2), 203–219.

Henry, P. J. (2009). Low-status compensation: A theory for understanding the role of status in cultures of honor. *Journal of Personality and Social Psychology*, *97*(3), 451.

Hernandez, A. E. (2009). Language switching in the bilingual brain: What's next? *Brain and Language*, *109*(2–3), 133–140.

Herrmann, E., Call, J., Hernàndez-Lloreda, M. V., Hare, B., & Tomasello, M. (2007). Humans have evolved specialized skills of social cognition: The cultural intelligence hypothesis. *Science*, *317*(5843), 1360–1366.

Herskovits, M. (1938). *Dahomey: An ancient west African kingdom I*. Oxford, UK: Augustin.

Herszenhornoct, D. (2014). Where mud is archaeological gold, Russian history grew on trees. *New York Times*. Retrieved from http://www.nytimes.com/2014/10/19/world/europe/where-mud-is-archaeological-gold-russian-history-grew-on-trees.html

Hewlett, B. S. (1989). Multiple caretaking among African Pygmies. *American Anthropologist*, *91*(1), 186–191.

Hewlett, B. S. (1992). Foundations of human behavior. In *Father–child relations: Cultural and biosocial contexts* (pp. 345–363). Hawthorne, NY: Aldine de Gruyter.

Hewlett, B. S., Berl, R. E. W., & Roulette, C. J. (2016). Teaching and overimitation among Aka hunter-gatherers. In H. Terashima & B. S. Hewlett (Eds.), *Replacement of Neanderthals by modern humans series. Social learning and innovation in contemporary hunter-gatherers: Evolutionary and ethnographic perspectives* (pp. 35–45). New York, NY: Springer.

Hewlett, B. S., Lamb, M. E., Shannon, D., Leyendecker, B., & Schölmerich, A. (1998). Culture and early infancy among central African foragers and farmers. *Developmental Psychology*, *34*(4), 653–661.

Hill, D. L. (2006). Sense of belonging as connectedness, American Indian worldview, and mental health. *Archives of Psychiatric Nursing, 20*(5), 210–216.

Hirata, S., Watanabe, K., & Masao, K. (2008). "Sweet-potato washing" revisited. In *Primate origins of human cognition and behavior* (pp. 487–508). Tokyo: Springer Japan.

Hirst, W. & Echterhoff, G. (2008). Creating shared memories in conversation: Toward a psychology of collective memory. *Social Research, 75*(1), 183–216.

Ho, D. Y.-F. (1976). On the concept of face. *American Journal of Sociology, 81*(4), 867–884.

Ho, M. W. (1991). The role of action in evolution: Evolution by process and the ecological approach to perception. *Cultural Dynamics, 4*(3), 336–354.

Ho, M. Y., & Fung, H. H. (2011). A dynamic process model of forgiveness: A cross-cultural perspective. *Review of General Psychology, 15*(1), 77.

Ho, M. Y., & Worthington, E. L. (2018). Is the concept of forgiveness universal? A cross-cultural perspective comparing Western and Eastern cultures. *Current Psychology*, 1–8.

Hobart, M. (2007). Rethinking Balinese dance. *Indonesia and the Malay World, 35*(101), 107–128.

Hobbs, D. R., & Gallup, G. G., Jr. (2011). Songs as a medium for embedded reproductive messages. *Evolutionary Psychology, 9*(3). doi:147470491100900309.

Hodgson, G. M. (2013). Sex on the brain: Some comments on love, war and cultures: An institutional approach to human evolution. *Journal of Bioeconomics, 15*(1), 91–95. doi:10.1007/s10818-012-9139-z

Hoerder, D. (2002). *Cultures in contact: World migrations in the second millennium*. Durham, NC: Duke University Press.

Hoffman, C. (2014). *Savage harvest: A tale of cannibals, colonialism and Michael Rockefeller's tragic quest for primitive art*. New York, NY: HarperCollins.

Hoffman, D. H., Carter, D. J., Lopez, C. R.V., Benzmiller, H.L., Guo, A. X., Latifi, S. Y., & Craig, D. C. (2015). *Report to the Special Committee of the Board of Directors of the American Psychological Association: Independent review relating to APA ethics guidelines, national security interrogations, and torture (revised)*. Chicago, IL: Sidley Austin LLP. Retrieved from http://www.apa.org/independent-review/revised-report.pdf

Hoffmann, Y. (1986). *Japanese death poems*. N. Clarendon VT: Tuttle.

Hofstede, G. (1980). *Culture's consequences: International differences in work-related values*. Beverly Hills, CA: SAGE.

Hofstede, G. (1984). The cultural relativity of the quality of life concept. *Academy of Management Review, 9*(3), 389–398. doi:10.5465/amr.1984.4279653

Hofstede, G. (1991). Empirical models of cultural differences. In N. Bleichrodt & P. J. D. Drenth (Eds.), *Contemporary issues in cross-cultural psychology* (pp. 4–20). Lisse, NL: Swets & Zeitlinger.

Hofstede, G. (2000). Masculine and feminine cultures. In A. E. Kazdin (Ed.), *Encyclopedia of psychology* (Vol. 5, pp. 115–118). Washington, DC: American Psychological Association.

Hofstede, G. (2003). What is culture? A reply to Baskerville. *Accounting, Organizations and Society, 28*(7–8), 811–813.

Hogbin, H. I. (1945). Marriage in Wogeo, New Guinea. *Oceania*, 324–352.

Hohepa, M., Smith, G. H., Smith, L. T., & McNaughton, S. (1992). Te kohanga reo hei tikango ako i te reo Māori: Te kohanga reo as a context for language learning. *Educational Psychology, 12*(3–4), 333–346. doi:10.1080/0144341920120314

Holbrook, C., & Sousa, P. (2013). Supernatural beliefs, unconscious threat and judgment bias in Tibetan Buddhists. *Journal of Cognition and Culture, 13*(1–2), 33–56.

Holmes, T. A., & Rahe, R. (1967). The social readjustment rating scale. *Journal of Psychosomatic Research, 11*, 213–218.

Holton, K. D. (2006). Fado historiography: Old myths and new frontiers. *Portuguese Cultural Studies, 1*, 1.

Holway, A. R. (1949). Early self-regulation of infants and later behavior in play interviews. *American Journal of Orthopsychiatry, 19*(4), 612–623.

Hong, Y., Morris, M. W., Chiu, C., Benet-Martinez, V. (2000). Multicultural minds: A dynamic constructivist approach to culture and cognition. *American Psychologist, 55*(7), 709–720. doi:10.1037//0003-066X.55.7.709

Hong, Y., Zhan, S., Morris, M. W., and Benet-Martinez, V. (2016). Multicultural identity processes. *Current Opinion in Psychology, 8*, 49–53.

Hopper, L. M., Flynn, E. G., Wood, L. A. N., & Whiten, A. (2010). Observational learning of tool use in children: Investigating cultural spread through diffusion chains and learning mechanisms through ghost displays. *Journal of Experimental Child Psychology, 106*(1), 82–97.

Horner, V., & Whiten, A. (2005). Causal knowledge and imitation/emulation switching in chimpanzees (Pan troglodytes) and children (*Homo sapiens*). *Animal Cognition, 8*(3), 164–181.

Hoshino-Browne, E., Zanna, A. S., Spencer, S. J., Zanna, M. P., Kitayama, S., & Lackenbauer, S. (2005). On the cultural guises of cognitive dissonance: The case of easterners and westerners. *Journal of Personality and Social Psychology, 89*(3), 294–310. doi:10.1037/0022-3514.89.3.294

Hovland, R., McMahan, C., Lee, G., Hwang, J. S., & Kim, J. (2005). Gender role portrayals in American and Korean advertisements. *Sex Roles, 53*(11–12), 887–899.

Howard, J. A., Blumstein, P., & Schwartz, P. (1987). Social or evolutionary theories? Some observations on preferences in human mate selection. *Journal of Personality and Social Psychology, 53*(1), 194–200.

Howard, V. (2003). A "real man's ring": Gender and the invention of tradition. *Journal of Social History, 36*(4), 837–856.

Howe, D. M., & Walker, J. A. (2000). Negation and the creole-origins hypothesis: Evidence from Early African American English. *Language in Society, 28*, 109–140.

Hsu, C. Y., O'Connor, M., & Lee, S. (2013). The difficulties of recruiting participants from a non-dominant culture into palliative care research. *Progress in Palliative Care, 21*(1), 1–6.

Hu, H. C. (1944). The Chinese concept of face. *American Anthropologist, 46*(1), 45–64.

Hublin, J.-J. (2009). The prehistory of compassion. *Proceedings of the National Academy of Sciences of the USA, 106*(16), 6429–6430.

Huddle, D. (1987). Salad bowl or melting pot? *National Review, 39*(19), 56–58.

Hudson, A. E. (1938). *Kazak social structure*. New York, NY: Yale University Press.

Hug, L., Sharrow, D., & You, D. (2017). *Levels & trends in child mortality: Report 2017*. New York, NY: UNICEF.

Hui, C. H., & Triandis, H. C. (1985). Measurement in cross-cultural psychology: A review and comparison of strategies. *Journal of Cross-Cultural Psychology, 16*(2), 131–152.

Hull, D. L. (1988). *Science as a process: An evolutionary account of the social and conceptual development of science*. Chicago: University of Chicago Press.

Human Rights Watch. (2001). *Indonesia: The violence in central Kalimantan (Borneo)*. Retrieved from http://www.hrw.org/legacy/backgrounder/asia/borneo0228.htm

Human Rights Watch. (2012). *January 2012 country summary: European Union*. Retrieved from http://www.hrw.org/sites/default/files/related_material/eu_2012.pdf

Hurd, N. M., Sánchez, B., Zimmerman, M. A., & Caldwell, C. H. (2012). Natural mentors, racial identity, and educational attainment among African American adolescents: Exploring pathways to success. *Child Development, 83*(4), 1196–1212.

Huyge, D. (1991). The Venus of Laussel in the light of ethnomusicology. *Archeologie in Vlanderen, 1*, 11–18.

Hwang, K. K. (2017). The rise of indigenous psychologies: In response to Jahoda's criticism. *Culture & Psychology, 23*(4), 551–565.

Hynie, M., Lalonde, R. N., & Lee, N. (2006). Parent-child value transmission among Chinese immigrants to North America: The case of traditional mate preferences. *Cultural Diversity and Ethnic Minority Psychology, 12*(2), 230–244.

Iacoboni, M. (2009). Imitation, empathy, and mirror neurons. *Annual Review of Psychology, 60*, 653–670.

Imada, T., & Ellsworth, P. (2011). Proud Americans and lucky Japanese: Cultural differences in appraisal and corresponding emotion. *Emotion, 11*(2), 329–345.

Imai, M., Kanero, J., & Masuda, T. (2016). The relation between language, culture, and thought. *Current Opinion in Psychology, 8*, 70–77.

Inglehart, R. et al. (2000). World values surveys and European values surveys, 1981–1984, 1990–1993, and 1995–1997. Inter-university Consortium for Political and Social Research http://faith-health.org/wordpress/wp-content/uploads/wvs.pdf

Insko, C. A., Worchel, S., Songer, E., & Arnold, S. E. (1973). Effort, objective self-awareness, choice, and dissonance. *Journal of Personality and Social Psychology, 28*(2), 262–269.

International Labour Organization. (2015). *A global snapshot: Women leaders and managers in employers' organizations*. Retrieved from http://www.ilo.org

International Phonic Alphabet (IPA) (2014). Homepage. http://www.internationalphoneticalphabet.org/

Ioannidis, J. (2005). Why most published research findings are false. *PLOS Medicine, 2*(8), 696–701.

Iokepa-Guerrero, N. (2008). Raising a child in the Punana Leo. *Exchange*.

Ishak, M. (2019). Testing general relativity in cosmology. *Living Reviews in Relativity*, *22*(1), 1.

Ishii, K. (2013). Culture and the mode of thought: A review. *Asian Journal of Social Psychology*, *16*(2), 123–132. doi:10.1111/ajsp.12011

Ishii, K., Miyamoto, Y., Rule, N. O., & Toriyama, R. (2014). Physical objects as vehicles of cultural transmission: Maintaining harmony and uniqueness through colored geometric patterns. *Personality and Social Psychology Bulletin*, *40*(2), 175–188.

Iverson, J. M., Capirci, O., Volterra, V., & Goldin-Meadow, S. (2008). Learning to talk in a gesture-rich world: Early communication in Italian vs. American children. *First Language*, *28*(2), 164–181.

Jablensky, A. (1997). The 100-year epidemiology of schizophrenia. *Schizophrenia Research*, *28*(2), 111–125.

Jablensky, A. (2000). Epidemiology of schizophrenia: The global burden of disease and disability. *European Archives of Psychiatry and Clinical Neuroscience*, *250*(6), 274–285.

Jablensky, A., Marsella, A., Ekblad, S., Jannsonn, B., Levi, L., & Bornemann, T. (1994). Refugee mental health and well-being: Conclusions and recommendations. In A. Marsella, T. Bornemann, S. Ekblad, & J. Orley (Eds.), *Amidst peril and pain* (pp. 327–39). Washington, DC: American Psychological Association.

Jablensky, A., Sartorius, N., Ernberg, G., Anker, M., Korten, A., Cooper, J. E., . . . Bertelsen, A. (1992). Schizophrenia: Manifestations, incidence and course in different cultures. *Psychological Medicine*, *20*, 1–97.

Jack, R. E. (2013). Culture and facial expressions of emotion. *Visual Cognition*, *21*(9–10), 1248–1286.

Jackman, M. (2015). Understanding the cheating heart: What determines infidelity intentions? *Sexuality & Culture: An Interdisciplinary Quarterly*, *19*(1), 72–84.

Jahoda, G. (2016). On the rise and decline of "indigenous psychology." *Culture & Psychology*, *22*(2), 169–181.

James, D. (1999). *Songs of the women migrants: Performance and identity in South Africa* (Vol. 22). Edinburgh: Edinburgh University Press.

James, J. A. (1829). The duties of children to their parents. In J. A. James, *The family monitor, or, A help to domestic happiness* (pp. 149–178). doi:10.1037/11838-005

James, T. E. (1960). The age of majority. *The American Journal of Legal History 4*(1), 22–33.

James, W. (1884). What is an emotion? *Mind*, *9*(34), 188–205.

James, W. (1890). Association. In W. James, *The principles of psychology* (Vol. 1, pp. 550–604). New York, NY: Henry Holt and Co. doi:10.1037/10538-014

Jameson, K. A. (2005). Introductory remarks on cognition, culture, and color experience. *Cross-Cultural Research: The Journal of Comparative Social Science*, *39*(1), 5–9. doi:10.1177/1069397104267885

Jankowiak, W. (1992). Father–child relations in urban China. In B. S. Hewlett (Ed.), *Foundations of human behavior. Father–child relations: Cultural and biosocial contexts* (pp. 345–363). Hawthorne, NY: Aldine de Gruyter.

Jankowiak, W. R., & Fischer, E. F. (1992). A cross-cultural perspective on romantic love. *Ethnology*, 149–155.

Jankowiak, W., & Gerth, H. (2012). Can you love more than one person at the same time? A research report. *Anthropologica*, *54*(1), 95–105.

Jankowiak, W., Nell, M. D., & Buckmaster, A. (2002). Managing infidelity: A cross-cultural perspective. *Ethnology*, *41*(1), 85.

Japanese Cultural Center of Hawai'i. (2018). *Okage Sama De: I am what I am because of you*. Retrieved from https://www.jcch.com/okage-sama-de-i-am-what-i-am-because-you.

Jaramillo, J. A. (1996). Vygotsky's sociocultural theory and contributions to the development of constructivist curricula. *Education*, *117*(1), 133–141.

Jellema, T., Baker, C. I., Wicker, B., & Perrett, D. I. (2000). Neural representation for the perception of the intentionality of actions. *Brain and Cognition*, *44*(2), 280–302.

Jenkins, K. E., & Marti, G. (2012). Warrior chicks: Youthful aging in a postfeminist prosperity discourse. *Journal for the Scientific Study of Religion*, *51*(2), 241–256. doi:10.1111/j.1468-5906.2012.01651.x

Jerison, H. J. (1955). Brain to body ratios and the evolution of intelligence. *Science New Series*, *121*(3144), 447–449.

Jerison, H. J. (1973). *Evolution of the brain and intelligence*. New York, NY: Academic Press.

Jerison, H. J. (1975). Fossil evidence of the evolution of the human brain. *Annual Review of Anthropology*, *4*(1), 27–58.

Jerison, H. J. (1976). Evolution of the brain and intelligence: Comment on

Radinsky's review. *Evolution, 30*(1), 186–187.

Ji, L.-J., Peng, K., & Nisbett, R. E. (2000). Culture, control, and perception of relationships in the environment. *Journal of Personality and Social Psychology, 78*(5), 943–955.

Jin, M. K., Jacobvitz, D., Hazen, N., & Jung, S. H. (2012). Maternal sensitivity and infant attachment security in Korea: Cross-cultural validation of the Strange Situation. *Attachment & Human Development, 14*(1), 33–44.

John F. Kennedy and PT 109. (n.d.). Retrieved from https://www.jfklibrary.org/JFK/JFK-in-History/John-F-Kennedy-and-PT109.aspx

Johnson, M. H., Dziurawiec, S., Ellis, H., & Morton, J. (1991). Newborns' preferential tracking of face-like stimuli and its subsequent decline. *Cognition, 40*(1–2), 1–19.

Johnson-Hanks, J. (2002). On the limits of life stages in ethnography: Toward a theory of vital conjunctures. *American Anthropologist, 104*(3), 865–880.

Join the military. (2019). *USA.gov.* Retrieved from https://www.usa.gov/join-military

Joint Economic Committee. (2016). *Gender pay inequality.* Washington, DC: US Senate.

Jolly, M. (1994). Hierarchy and encompassment: Rank gender, and place in Vanuatu and Fiji. *History and Anthropology, 7*(1–4), 137–167.

Jones, C. P. (2002). Confronting institutionalized racism. *Phylon,* 7–22.

Jones, H., Cross, W., & Defour, D. (2007). Race-related stress, racial identity attitudes, and mental health among black women. *Journal of Black Psychology, 33,* 208–231.

Jones, S. (2017). White men account for 72% of corporate leadership at 16 of the Fortune 500 companies. *Fortune.* Retrieved http://fortune.com/2017/06/09/white-men-senior-executives-fortune-500-companies-diversity-data/

Jordan, B. (1978). *Birth in four cultures: A cross-cultural investigation of childbirth in Yucatan, Holland, Sweden, and the United States.* Montreal: Eden Press.

Jouili, J. S., & Moors, A. (2014). Introduction: Islamic sounds and the politics of listening. *Anthropological Quarterly, 87*(4), 977–988.

Józsa, L. G. (2011). Obesity in the paleolithic era. *Hormones, 10*(3), 241–244.

Julia, C., & Valleron, A. J. (2011). Louis-René Villermé (1782–1863), a pioneer in social epidemiology: Re-analysis of his data on comparative mortality in Paris in the early 19th century. *Journal of Epidemiology & Community Health, 65*(8), 666–670.

Jung, C. G. (1936). Über den Archetypus [The archetype]. *Zentralblatt für Psychotherapie, 9,* 259–274.

Jung, R. S., & Jason, L. A. (1998). Job interview social skills training for Asian-American immigrants. *Journal of Human Behavior in the Social Environment, 1*(4), 11–25.

Juslin, P. N., & Västfjäll, D. (2008). Emotional responses to music: The need to consider underlying mechanisms. *Behavioral and Brain Sciences, 31*(5), 559–575.

Kagan, C., & Kilroy, A. (2007). Psychology in the community. In J. Haworth & G. Hart (Eds.), *Well-being: Individual, community, and social perspectives* (pp. 93–109). London: Palgrave Macmillan.

Kağıtçıbaşı, Ç. (1984). Socialization in traditional society: A challenge to psychology. *International Journal of Psychology, 19*(1–2), 145–157.

Kağıtçıbaşı, Ç. (2007). *Family, self and human development across cultures.* Mahwah, NJ: Lawrence Erlbaum and Associates.

Kahlenberg, S. M., & Wrangham, R. W. (2010). Sex differences in chimpanzees' use of sticks as play objects resemble those of children. *Current Biology, 20,* R1067–R1068.

Kahn, R. L., & Antonucci, T. C. (1980). Convoys over the life course: Attachment, roles, and social support. *Life-Span Development and Behavior, 3,* 253–286.

Kakabadse, N., Kouzmin, A., Korac-Kakabadse, A., & Savery, L. (2001). Low- and high-context communication patterns: Towards mapping cross-cultural encounters. *Cross Cultural Management An International Journal, 8*(2), 3–24.

Kamble, S., Shackelford, T. K., Pham, M., & Buss, D. M. (2014). Indian mate preferences: Continuity, sex differences, and cultural change across a quarter of a century. *Personality and Individual Differences, 70,* 150–155.

Kameʻeleihiwa, L. (2009). Hawaiʻi-nui-akea cousins: Ancestral gods and bodies of knowledge are treasures for the descendants. *Te Kaharoa, 2,* 42–63.

Kammann, R., & Flett, R. (1986). *Structure and measurement of psychological well-being: A report to the New Zealand Social Sciences Research Fund Committee.* Wellington, NZ: Social Sciences Research Fund Committee.

Kann, L., Kinchen, S., Shanklin, S. L., Flint, K. H., Hawkins, J., Harris, W. A., . . . Whittle, L. (2014). Youth risk behavior surveillance—United States, 2013. *Morbidity and Mortality Weekly Report: Surveillance Summaries, 63*(4), 1–168.

Kann, L., McManus, T., Harris, W. A., Shanklin, S. L., Flint, K. H., Hawkins, J. . . . Zaza, S. (2016). Youth risk behavior surveillance—United States, 2015. *Morbidity and Mortality Weekly Report: Surveillance Summaries, 65*(6), 1–174.

Kann, L., McManus, T., Harris, W. A., Shanklin, S. L., Flint, K. H., Queen, B., . . . Lim, C. (2018). Youth risk behavior surveillance—United States, 2017. *Morbidity and Mortality Weekly Report: Surveillance Summaries, 67*(8), 1.

Kantner, L. A. (1968). The influence of culture on visual perception. In H. Toch & C. Smith, *Social perception*. New York, NY: Van Nostrand Reinhold.

Kanuha, V. K. (2005). 'Ohana: Native Hawaiian families. In M. McGoldrick, J. Giordano, & N. G. Preto. (Eds.), *Ethnicity and family therapy* (3rd ed., pp. 64–74). New York, NY: Guilford Press.

Kaomea, J. (2004). Dilemmas of an indigenous academic: A native Hawaiian story. In K. Mutua & Swadener, B. B. (Eds.), *Decolonizing research in cross-cultural contexts: Critical personal narratives* (pp. 27–44). Albany: SUNY Press.

Kara, M. A. (2007). Applicability of the principle of respect for autonomy: The perspective of Turkey. *Journal of Medical Ethics, 33,* 627–630.

Kashima, E. S., & Kashima, Y. (1998). Culture and language: The case of cultural dimensions and personal pronoun use. *Journal of Cross-Cultural Psychology, 29*(3), 461–486.

Kashima, Y. (2000). Conceptions of culture and person for psychology.

*Journal of Cross-Cultural Psychology, 31*(1), 14–32.

Kashima, Y. (2005). Is culture a problem for social psychology? *Asian Journal of Social Psychology, 8*(1), 19–38.

Kashima, Y. (2008). A social psychology of cultural dynamics: Examining how cultures are formed, maintained, and transformed. *Social and Personality Psychology Compass, 2*(1), 107–120.

Kashima, Y. & Gelfand, M. J. (2012). A history of culture in psychology. In A. W. Kruglanski & W. Stroebe (Eds.), *Handbook of the history of social psychology* (pp. 499–520). New York, NY: Psychology Press.

Kashima, Y., Koval, P., & Kashima, E. S. (2011). Reconsidering culture and self. *Psychological Studies, 56*(1), 12–22. doi:10.1007/s12646-011-0071-4

Kashima, Y., Siegal, M., Tanaka, K., & Kashima, E. S. (1992). Do people believe behaviours are consistent with attitudes? Towards a cultural psychology of attribution processes. *British Journal of Social Psychology, 31*(2), 111–124.

Kashima, Y., Yamaguchi, S., Kim, U., Choi, S.-C., Gelfand, M. J.; Yuki, M. (1995). Culture, gender, and self: A perspective from individualism-collectivism research. *Journal of Personality and Social Psychology, 69*(5), 925–937.

Kay, P., & Kempton, W. (1984). What is the Sapir-Whorf hypothesis? *American Anthropologist, 86*(1), 65–79.

Kay, P., & Regier, T. (2006). Language, thought and color: Recent developments. *Trends in Cognitive Sciences, 10*(2), 51–54.

Keefe, S. E. (1992). Ethnic identity: The domain of perceptions of and attachment to ethnic groups and cultures. *Human Organization, 51*(1), 35.

Keeler, J. R., Roth, E. A., Neuser, B. L., Spitsbergen, J. M., Waters, D. J. M., & Vianney, J. M. (2015). The neurochemistry and social flow of singing: Bonding and oxytocin. *Frontiers in Human Neuroscience, 9,* 518.

Keightley, R. (2005). *Ancient and modern history*. Retrieved June 21, 2009, from http://www.enzed.com/hist.html

Keller, H. (2013). Attachment and culture. *Journal of Cross-Cultural Psychology, 44*(2), 175–194.

Keller, H. (2016). Attachment: A pan-cultural need but a cultural construct. *Current Opinion in Psychology, 8,* 59–63.

Keller, H., Borke, J., Lamm, B., Lohaus, A., & Dzeaye Yovsi, R. (2011). Developing patterns of parenting in two cultural communities. *International Journal of Behavioral Development, 35*(3), 233–245.

Keller, H., & Greenfield, P. M. (2000). History and future of development in cross-cultural psychology. *Journal of Cross-Cultural Psychology, 31*(1), 52–62.

Kerckhoff, A. C. (1958). Anomie and achievement motivation: A study of personality development within cultural disorganization. *Social Forces, 37,* 196.

Keupp, S., Behne, T., & Rakoczy, H. (2013). Why do children overimitate? Normativity is crucial. *Journal of Experimental Child Psychology, 116*(2), 392–406.

Khalaila, R., & Litwin, H. (2012). Modernisation and filial piety among traditional family care-givers: A study of Arab-Israelis in cultural transition. *Ageing & Society, 32*(5), 769–789.

Khan, S. S., Hopkins, N., Tewari, S., Srinivasan, N., Reicher, S. D., & Ozakinci, G. (2014). Efficacy and well-being in rural north India: The role of social identification with a large-scale community identity. *European Journal of Social Psychology*. Advance online publication.

Kiang, L., Yip, T., Gonzales-Backen, M., Witkow, M., & Fuligni, A. J. (2006). Ethnic identity and the daily psychological well-being of adolescents from Mexican and Chinese backgrounds. *Child Development*, 77(5), 1338–1350.

Killawi, A., Khidir, A., Elnashar, M., Abdelrahim, H., Hammoud, M., Elliot, H., . . . Fetters, M. D. (2014). Procedures of recruiting, obtaining informed consent, and compensating research participants in Qatar: Findings from a qualitative investigation. *BMC Medical Ethics*, 15(9). Retrieved from http://www.biomedcentral.com/1472-6939/15/9

Killen, M., & Dahl, A. (2018). Moral judgment. In K. Gray & J. Graham (Eds.), *Atlas of moral psychology* (p. 20). New York: Guilford Press.

Kim, E., Bhave, D. P., & Glomb, T. M. (2013). Emotion regulation in workgroups: The roles of demographic diversity and relational work context. *Personnel Psychology*, 66(3), 613–644.

Kim, H., & Markus, H. R. (1999). Deviance or uniqueness, harmony or conformity? A cultural analysis. *Journal of Personality and Social Psychology*, 77(4), 785.

Kim, H., Schimmack, U., & Oishi, S. (2012). Cultural differences in self- and other-evaluations and well-being: A study of European and Asian Canadians. *Journal of Personality and Social Psychology*, 102(4), 856–873.

Kim, M.-H., & Cha, K.-H. (2008). Traveling with MI education in a turbulent sea: Stories of South Korea. *International Journal of Qualitative Studies in Education*, 21(4), 389–405. doi:10.1080/09518390701701386

Kim-Ju, G. M., Goodman, Z. T., & Her, S. (2018). Community violence exposure and internalizing and externalizing behaviors among Hmong Americans. *Asian American Journal of Psychology*, 9(2), 87–97. doi:10.1037/aap0000089

King, J. E. & Figueredo, A. J. (1997). The five-factor model plus dominance in chimpanzee personality. *Journal of Research in Personality*, 31(2), 257–271.

King, M. (Ed.). (1992). *Te Ao Hurihuri: The world moves on*. Auckland: Reed.

King, M. (2001). *Nga iwi o te motu: 1000 years of Māori history*. Auckland: Reed Books.

King, R. B., McInerney, D. M., & Nasser, R. (2017). Different goals for different folks: A cross-cultural study of achievement goals across nine cultures. *Social Psychology of Education*, 20(3), 619–642.

Kingi, Te K. R. (2006). *Culture, health, and Māori development*. Paper presented at Te Mata o te Tau Lecture Series, Palmerston North, NZ, 14 June, 2006.

Kinney, D. K., Miller, A. M., Crowley, D. J., Huang, E., & Gerber, E. (2008). Autism prevalence following prenatal exposure to hurricanes and tropical storms in Louisiana. *Journal of Autism and Developmental Disorders*, 38(3), 481–488.

Kirch, P. (2000). *On the road of the winds: An archaeological history of the Pacific Islands before European contact*. Berkeley: University of California Press.

Kirmayer, L. J. (2003). Asklepian dreams: The ethos of the wounded-healer in the clinical encounter. *Transcultural Psychiatry*, 40(2), 248–277.

Kirmayer, L. J., & Ryder, A. G. (2016). Culture and psychopathology. *Current Opinion in Psychology*, 8, 143–148.

Kita, S. (2009) Cross-cultural variation of speech-accompanying gesture: A review. *Language and Cognitive Processes*, 24(2), 145–167.

Kitayama, S., & Marcus, H. (1991). Culture and the self: Implications for cognition, emotion, and motivation. *Psychological Review*, 98(2), 224–253.

Kitayama, S., & Park, J. (2010). Cultural neuroscience of the self: Understanding the social grounding of the brain. *Social Cognitive and Affective Neuroscience*, 5(2–3), 111–129. doi:10.1093/scan/nsq052

Kivisto, P. (2012). We really are all multiculturalists now. *The Sociological Quarterly*, 53(1), 1–24.

Klein, R. E., Freeman, H. E., Spring, B., Nerlove, S. B., & Yarbrough, C. (1976). Cognitive test performance and indigenous conceptions of intelligence. *The Journal of Psychology: Interdisciplinary and Applied*, 93(2), 273–279. doi:10.108 0/00223980.1976.9915823

Kleinman, A. (1977). Depression, somatization and the new cross-cultural psychiatry. *Social Science & Medicine*, 11(1), 3–10.

Kleinman, A. (1987). Anthropology and psychiatry: The role of culture in cross-cultural research on illness. *British Journal of Psychiatry*, 151(4), 447–454.

Klineberg, O. (1938). Emotional expression in Chinese literature. *The Journal of Abnormal and Social Psychology*, 33(4), 517.

Kluckhohn, C. (1951). An anthropological approach to the study of values. *Bulletin of the American Academy of Arts and Sciences*, 4(6), 2–3.

Kluckhohn, C. E., Murray, H. A., & Schneider, D. M. (1953). *Personality in nature, society, and culture*. New York: Knopf.

Kluckhohn, F. R., & Strodtbeck, F. L. (1961). *Variations in value orientations*. Oxford, England: Row, Peterson.

Knight, M. M. (1924). The companionate and the family. *Journal of Social Hygiene*, 10, 257–267.

Knutzen, K. B., & Kennedy, D. M. (2012). Designing the self: The transformation of the relational self-concept through social encounters in a virtual immersive environment. *Interactive Learning Environments*, 20(3), 271–292.

Ko, E., Cho, S., Perez, R., Yeo, Y., Palomino, H. (2013). Good and bad death: Exploring the perspectives of older Mexican Americans. *Journal of Gerontological Social Work*, 56(1), 6–25.

Koburger, N., Mergl, R., Rummel-Kluge, C., Ibelshäuser, A., Meise, U., Postuvan, V., . . . Hegerl, U. (2015). Celebrity suicide on the railway network: Can one case trigger international effects? *Journal of Affective Disorders*, 185, 38–46.

Koch, S. (2014). *Louis Jordan: Son of Arkansas, Father of R&B*. Charleston, SC: The History Press.

Kohlberg, L. (1958). *The development of modes of thinking and choice in the years 10 to 16*. (Unpublished doctoral dissertation). University of Chicago.

Kohlberg, L. (1971). From is to ought: How to commit the naturalistic fallacy and get away with it in the study of moral development. In L. Mischel (Ed.), *Cognitive development and epistemology* (pp. 151–284). New York: Academic Press.

Kohlberg, L. (1975). The cognitive-developmental approach to moral education. *The Phi Delta Kappan*, 56(10), 670–677.

Kohlberg, L., & Hersh, R. H. (1977). Moral development: A review of the theory. *Theory Into Practice*, 16(2), 53–59.

Köhler, W. (1927). *The mentality of apes* (E. Winter, trans.). New York: Harcourt, Brace, & Co.

Kohnstamm, G. A. (1989). Temperament in childhood: Cross-cultural and sex differences. In G. A. Kohnstamm, J. E. Bates, & M. K. Rothbart (Eds.), *Temperament in childhood* (pp. 483–508). Oxford, UK: John Wiley.

Kopano, B. N. (2002). Rap music as an extension of the black rhetorical tradition: Keepin' it real. *Western Journal of Black Studies*, 26(4), 204–214.

Korson, J. H. (1968). Residential propinquity as a factor in mate selection in an urban Muslin society. *Journal of Marriage and the Family*, 30(3), 518–527.

Kosonogov, V., & Titova, A. (2018). Recognition of all basic emotions varies in accuracy and reaction time: A new verbal method of measurement. *International Journal of Psychology*. doi:10.1002/ijop.12512

Koss-Chioino, J. D. (2006). Spiritual transformation, relation and radical empathy: Core components of the ritual healing process. *Transcultural Psychiatry*, 43(4), 652–670.

Kramer, J. (2004). Figurative repatriation: First nations "artist-warriors" recover, reclaim, and return cultural property through self-definition. *Journal of Material Culture*, 9(2), 161–182.

Krassner, A. M., Gartstein, M. A., Park, C., Dragan, W. Ł., Lecannelier, F., & Putnam, S. P. (2017). East–west, collectivist-individualist: A cross-cultural examination of temperament in toddlers from Chile, Poland, South Korea, and the U.S. *European Journal of Developmental Psychology*, 14(4), 449–464.

Kreutz, G. (2014). Does singing facilitate social bonding? *Music and Medicine*, 6(2), 51–60.

Krippner, S. (2009). Indigenous healing practitioners and their use of hypnotic-like procedures. *Activitas Nervosa Superior*, 51(1), 51–63.

Kroeber, A. L. (1940). Stimulus diffusion. *American Anthropologist*, 42(1), 1–20.

KRTV. (2013). *Blackfeet, Conrad basketball video clip goes viral*. Retrieved from http://www.krtv.com/news/black feet-conrad-basketball-video-clip-goes-viral/

Kua, E. H. (1991). Amok in nineteenth-century British Malaya history. *History of Psychiatry*, 2(8), 429–436.

Kuijt, I., & Finlayson, B. (2009). Evidence for food storage and predomestication granaries 11,000 years ago in the Jordan Valley. *Proceedings of the National Academy of Sciences*, 106(27), 10966–10970.

Kumari, H., & Nishteshwar, K. (2013). A pilot study on Rasa (taste quality) determination of an extra ayurvedic pharmacopoeial drug Bulbophyllum neilgherrense Wight. *Annals of Ayurvedic Medicine*, 2(3), 72–79.

Kuo, B. C., & Roysircar, G. (2006). An exploratory study of cross-cultural adaptation of adolescent Taiwanese unaccompanied sojourners in Canada. *International Journal of Intercultural Relations*, 30(2), 159–183.

Kurman, J. (2001). Is self-enhancement related to modesty or to individualism-collectivism? A test with four Israeli groups. *Asian Journal of Social Psychology*, *4*(3), 225–237.

Kus-Harbord, L., & Ward, C. (2015). Ethnic Russians in post-Soviet Estonia: Perceived devaluation, acculturation, well-being, and ethnic attitudes. *International Perspectives in Psychology: Research, Practice, Consultation*, *4*(1), 66–81. http://dx.doi.org.hpu.idm.oclc.org/10.1037/ipp0000025

Kwan, V., Bond, M., & Singelis, T. (1997). Pancultural explanations for life satisfaction: Adding relationship harmony to self-esteem. *Journal of Personality and Social Psychology*, *73*(5), 1O3S–1O5I.

Kyler, J. & Munz, R. (1993). Infant mortality in Austria, 1820–1950. In C. A. Corsini & P. P. Viazzo (Eds.), *The decline of infant mortality in Europe 1800–1950*. Florence, Italy: UNICEF.

Kymlicka, W. (1995). *Multicultural citizenship : A liberal theory of minority rights*. New York, NY: Oxford University Press.

Kyselka, W. (1987). *An ocean in mind*. Honolulu: University of Hawaiʻi Press.

Lachman, M. E. (2004). Development in midlife. *Annual Review of Psychology*, *55*, 305–331.

LaFrance, J. (2004). Culturally competent evaluation in Indian country. *New Directions for Evaluation*, *102*, 39–50.

Lah, K. (2017). The LA riots were a rude awakening for Korean-Americans. *CNN*. Retrieved from https://www.cnn.com/2017/04/28/us/la-riots-korean-americans/index.html

Lamont, A. (2009). Music in the school years. In S. Hallam, I. Cross, & M. Thaut (Eds.), *The Oxford handbook of music psychology* (pp. 235–243). Oxford, UK: Oxford University Press.

Lancy, D. F. (2010). Learning from nobody: The limited role of teaching in folk models of children's development. *Childhood in the Past 3*, 79–106.

Lancy, D. F. (2012). Why anthropology of childhood? A short history of an emerging discipline. *AnthropoChildren*, *1*(1). Retrieved from http://popups.ulg.ac.be/AnthropoChildren/document.php?id=918

Lang, P. J., & Greenwald, M. K. (1988). *The international affective picture system standardization procedure and initial group results for affective judgments: Technical report 1A*. Tampa: The Center for Research in Psychophysiology, University of Florida.

Lange, C. G. (1885). The mechanism of the emotions. *The Classical Psychologists*, 672–684.

Langfur, S. (2013). The you-I event: On the genesis of self-awareness. *Phenomenology and the Cognitive Sciences*, *12*(4), 769–790.

Langlois, J. H., & Roggman, L. A. (1990). Attractive faces are only average. *Psychological Science*, *1*(2), 115–121.

Laouira, O. (1999). Schools as agents of cultural transmission and social control. *Sciences Humaines*, *12*, 41–51.

Lasser, J., & Gottlieb, M. (2017). Facilitating informed consent: A multicultural perspective. *Ethics & Behavior*, *27*(2), 106–117.

Lau, B., Blackwell, B. A., Schwarcz, H. P., Turk, I., & Blickstein, J. I. (1997). Dating a flautist? Using ESR (electron spin resonance) in the Mousterian cave deposits at Divje Babe I, Slovenia. *Geoarchaeology: An International Journal*, *12*(6), 507–536.

Laurentini, A., & Bottino, A. (2014). Computer analysis of face beauty: A survey. *Computer Vision and Image Understanding*, *125*, 184–199.

Lazarus, R. S., & Folkman, S. (1984). *Appraisal, stress, and coping*. New York, NY: Springer.

Leach, C. W., Spears, R., Branscombe, N. R., & Doosje, B. (2003). Malicious pleasure: Schadenfreude at the suffering of another group. *Journal of Personality and Social Psychology*, *84*(5), 932–943. doi:10.1037/0022-3514.84.5.932

Leach, M. A. (2014). A burden of support? Household structure and economic resources among Mexican immigrant families. *Journal of Family Issues*, *35*(1), 28–53.

Ledoux, J. (2012). Rethinking the emotional brain. *Neuron*, *73*(4), 653–676.

Lee, D.-J., Pae, J. H., & Wong, Y.H. (2001). A model of close business relationships in China (guanxi). *European Journal of Marketing*, *35*(1–2), 51–69.

Lee, H. I., Leung, A. K-y., & Kim, Y.-H. (2014). Unpacking East–West differences in the extent of self-enhancement from the perspective of face versus dignity culture. *Social and Personality Psychology Compass*, *8*(7), 314–327.

Lee, S. (1995). Reconsidering the status of anorexia nervosa as a western culture-bound syndrome. *Social Science & Medicine*, *42*(1), 21–34.

Lee, T. L., Fiske, S. T., & Glick, P. (2010). Next gen ambivalent sexism: Converging correlates, causality in context, and converse causality, an introduction to the special issue. *Sex Roles*, *62*(7–8), 395–404.

Legge, J. (1965). *A record of Buddhistic kingdoms: Being an account by the Chinese monk Fa-Hien of his travels in India and Ceylon (A.D. 399–414) in search of the Buddhist Books of Discipline*. Oxford, UK: Clarendon Press. (Original work published 1886)

Legge, J. (Trans.). (2014). *The analects of Confucius*. Adelaide, SA: University of Adelaide. (Original work published 1861)

Le Mesurier, S. (2012). *Violence against migrants, migrant workers and their families: How the IFRC is ensuring access, dignity, respect for diversity and social inclusion*. Retrieved from http://www.ifrc.org/en/news-and-media/opinions-and-positions/speeches/2012/violence-against-migrants-migrant-workers-and-their-families/

Lenski, G., & Lenski, J. (1987). *Human societies: An introduction to macrosociology* (5th ed.). New York, NY: McGraw-Hill.

Leung, A. K.-Y., & Cohen, D. (2011). Within- and between-culture variation: Individual differences and the cultural logics of honor, face, and dignity cultures. *Journal of Personality and Social Psychology*, *100*(3), 507–526.

Leung, K., & Bond, M. H. (1984). The impact of cultural collectivism on reward allocation. *Journal of Personality and Social Psychology*, *47*(4), 793.

Leung, T. K. P., Lai, K.-h., Chan, R. Y. K., & Wong, Y. H. (2005). The roles of xinyong and guanxi in Chinese relationship marketing. *European Journal of Marketing*, *39*(5–6), 528–559.

Levenstein, H. A. (2003). *Paradox of plenty: A social history of eating in modern America* (Vol. 8). Los Angeles: University of California Press.

Levine, J. M., & Moreland, R. L. (1998). Small groups. In D. Gilbert, S. Fiske, & G. Lindzey (Eds.), *Handbook of social psychology* (4th. ed., Vol. 2, pp. 415–469). Boston: McGraw-Hill.

Levine, N. (1980). Nyinba polyandry and the allocation of paternity. *Journal of Comparative Family Studies*, *XI*(3), 283–298.

Levine, N. E. & Silk, J. B. (1997). Why polyandry fails: Sources of instability in polyandrous marriages. *Current Anthropology*, *38*(3), 375–398.

Levine, T. R., Bresnahan, M. J., Park, H. S., Lapinsky, M. K., Wittenbaum, G. M., Shearman, S. M., ... Ohashi, R. (2003). Self-construal scales lack validity. *Human Communication Research*, *29*(2), 210–252.

Levinson, S. C. (2016). Turn-taking in human communication–origins and implications for language processing. *Trends in Cognitive Sciences*, *20*(1), 6–14.

LewGor, A. (2017). *What data can tell us about the challenges faced by migrants in Aotearoa, New Zealand*. Retrieved from https://multiculturalnz.org.nz

Li, L. (2000). Ancestor worship: An archaeological investigation of ritual activities in Neolithic north China. *Journal of East Asian archaeology*, *2*(1–2), 129–164.

Liebkind, K. (1996). Acculturation and stress. *Journal of Cross-Cultural Psychology*, *27*(2), 161–180.

Lin, T. Y. (1983). Psychiatry and Chinese culture. *Western Journal of Medicine*, *139*(6), 862.

Linguistic Data Consortium. (2018). *Languages West Africa*. Retrieved from https://www.ldc.upenn.edu/sites/www.ldc.upenn.edu/files/west-african-languages.pdf

Little, J. F. (1961). The social architect. *American Psychologist*, *16*(9), 602b.

Liu, J. H., & Khan, S. S. (2014). Nation building through historical narratives in pre-independence India: Gandhi, Nehru, Savarkar, and Golwalkar as entrepreneurs of identity. In M. Hanne (Ed.), *Warring with words: Narrative and metaphor in domestic and international politics* (pp. 211–237). New York, NY: Psychology Press.

Liu, J. H., Wilson, M. S., McClure, J., & Higgins, T. R. (1999). Social identity and the perception of history: Cultural representations of Aotearoa/New Zealand. *European Journal of Social Psychology*, *29*(8), 1021–1047.

Liu, J. X., Goryakin, Y., Maeda, A., Bruckner, T., & Scheffler, R. (2017). Global health workforce labor market projections for 2030. *Human Resources for Health*, *15*(1), 11.

Locke, D., & Pennington, D. (1982). Reasons and other causes: Their role in attribution processes. *Journal of Personality and Social Psychology*, *42*(2), 212–223.

Locke, J. (1836). *An essay concerning human understanding*. London: T. Tegg & Son. (Original work published 1690)

Locke, J. (2007). *Some thoughts concerning education*. New York, NY: Dover. (Original work published 1693)

Lohndorf, R. T., Vermeer, H. J., Cárcamo, R. A., & Mesman, J. (2018). Preschoolers' vocabulary acquisition in Chile: The roles of socioeconomic status and quality of home environment. *Journal of Child Language*, *45*(3), 559–580. doi:10.1017/S0305000917000332

Lomas, T. (2016). Towards a positive cross-cultural lexicography: Enriching our emotional landscape through 216 "untranslatable" words pertaining to well-being. *The Journal of Positive Psychology*, *11*(5), 546–558.

Lombardo, N. E. (2017). Boredom and modern culture. *Logos: A Journal of Catholic Thought and Culture*, *20*(2), 36–59.

Long, H. (2016). Female CEOs are at record level in 2016, but it's still only 5%. *CNN Money*. Retrieved from http://money.cnn.com/2016/09/29/investing/female-ceos-record-high/

Long, M. H. (1990). Maturational constraints on language development. *Studies in Second Language Acquisition*, *12*(3), 251–285.

Lopez, S. J., Pedrotti, J. T., & Snyder, C. R. (2018). *Positive psychology: The scientific and practical explorations of human strengths*. Thousand Oaks, CA: SAGE.

Lotem, A., Halpern, J. Y., Edelman, S., & Kolodny, O. (2017). The evolution of cognitive mechanisms in response to cultural innovations. *Proceedings of the National Academy of Sciences*, *114*(30), 7915–7922.

Love, P., Moore, M., & Warburton, J. (2016). Nurturing spiritual well-being among older people in Australia: Drawing on Indigenous and non-Indigenous way of knowing. *Australasian Journal on Ageing*. doi:10.1111/ajag.12284

Luijk, M. P. C. M., Mileva-Seitz, V. R., Jansen, P. W., van IJzendoorn, M. H., Jaddoe, V. W. V., Raat, H., . . . Tiemeier, H. (2013). Ethnic differences in prevalence and determinants of mother–child bed-sharing in early childhood. *Sleep Medicine*, *14*(11), 1092–1099.

Lupyan, G. (2016). The centrality of language in human cognition. *Language Learning*, *66*(3), 516–553.

Luu, T. D., & Bartsch, R. A. (2011). Relationship between acculturation and attitudes toward gay men and lesbians in the Vietnamese American community. *Journal of Applied Social Psychology*, *41*(11), 2621–2633.

Lyons, D. E., & Keil, F. C. (2013). Overimitation and the development of causal understanding. In M. R. Banaji & S. A. Gelman (Eds.), *Oxford series in social cognition and social neuroscience. Navigating the social world: What infants, children, and other species can teach us* (pp. 145–149). New York, NY: Oxford University Press.

Ma, X., Tamir, M., & Miyamoto, Y. (2018). A socio-cultural instrumental approach to emotion regulation: Culture and the regulation of positive emotions. *Emotion*, *18*(1), 138–152.

Ma, Y., Wang, C., Li, B., Zhang, W., Rao, Y., & Han, S. (2014). Does self-construal predict activity in the social brain network? A genetic moderation effect. *Social Cognitive and Affective Neuroscience*, *9*(9), 1360–1367.

Machluf, K., Liddle, J. R., & Bjorklund, D. F. (2014). An introduction to evolutionary developmental psychology. *Evolutionary Psychology*, *12*(1), 264–272.

MacKenzie, M. K. (2010). Ka lama ku o ka noʻeau: The standing torch of wisdom. *University of Hawaiʻi Law Review*, *33*, 3.

Madathil, J., & Benshoff, J. M. (2008). Importance of marital characteristics and marital satisfaction: A comparison of Asian Indians in arranged marriages and Americans in marriages of choice. *The Family Journal*, *16*(3), 222–230.

Madsen, M. C. (1970). *Developmental and cross-cultural differences in the cooperative and competitive behavior of young children*. Washington, DC: Office of Economic Opportunity.

Maguire, E. A., Woollett, K., & Spiers, H. J. (2006). London taxi drivers and bus drivers: A structural MRI and neuropsychological analysis. *Hippocampus*, *16*(12), 1091–1101. doi:10.1002/hipo.20233

Mahalingam, R. (2007). Beliefs about chastity, machismo, and caste identity: A cultural psychology of gender. *Sex Roles*, *56*(3–4), 239–249.

Mahalingam, R., & Jackson, B. B. (2007). Idealized cultural beliefs about gender: Implications for mental health. *Social Psychiatry and Psychiatric Epidemiology*, *42*(12), 1012–1023.

Mahmoudzadeh, M., Dehaene-Lambertz, G., Fournier, M., Kongolo, G., Goudjil, S., Dubois, J., . . . Wallois, F. (2013). Syllabic discrimination in premature human infants prior to complete formation of cortical layers. *Proceedings of the National Academy of Sciences*, *110*(12), 4846–4851.

Main, M., & Goldwyn, R. (1995). Interview-based adult attachment classifications: Related to infant-mother and infant-father attachment. *Developmental Psychology*, *19*, 227–239.

Maira, S. (1999). Identity dub: The paradoxes of an Indian American youth subculture (New York mix). *Cultural Anthropology*, *14*(l), 29–60.

Ma-Kellams, C., & Blascovich, J. (2012). Enjoying life in the face of death: East-west differences in responses to mortality salience. *Journal of Personality and Social Psychology*, *103*(5), 773–786.

Makkai, A. (Ed.). (2000). *In quest of the miracle stag: The poetry of Hungary*. New York, NY: Atlantis-Centaur.

Malinowski, B. (2002). *The father in primitive psychology*. New York, NY: Routledge. (Original work published 1927)

Mandela, N. (2000). Interview [Television series episode]. *The Oprah Winfrey Show*. Chicago, IL: ABC Network.

Markovitzky, G., & Mosek, A. (2005). The role of symbolic resources in coping with immigration. *Journal of Ethnic and Cultural Diversity in Social*

*Work, 14*(1–2), 145–158. doi:10.1300/J051v14n01_07

Markus, H. R. (2004). Culture and personality: Brief for an arranged marriage. *Journal of Research in Personality, 38*(1), 75–83.

Markus, H. R., & Kitayama, S. (1991). Culture and the self: Implications for cognition, emotion and motivation. *Psychological Review, 98*(2), 224–253.

Markus, H. R., & Kitayama, S. (1994). The cultural shaping of emotion: A conceptual framework. In S. Kitayama & H. R. Markus (Eds.), *Emotion and culture: Empirical studies of mutual influence* (pp. 339–351). Washington, DC: American Psychological Association.

Markus, H. R., & Kitayama, S. (2010). Cultures and selves: A cycle of mutual constitution. *Perspectives on Psychological Science, 5*(4), 420–430.

Marlow, M. L., & Giles, H. (2006). From the roots to the shoots: A Hawaiian case study of language revitalization and modes of communication. *Annals of the International Communication Association, 30*(1), 343–385.

Marsella, A. J. (1993). Sociocultural foundations of psychopathology: An historical overview of concepts, events and pioneers prior to 1970. *Transcultural Psychiatric Research Review, 30*(2), 97–142.

Marsella, A. J. (1994). Ethnocultural diversity and international refugees. In A. Marsella, T. Bornemann, S. Ekblad, & J. Orley (Eds.), *Amidst peril and pain* (pp. 341–364). Washington, DC: American Psychological Association.

Marsella, A. J. (1999). *Internationalizing the psychology curriculum: Toward a new psychology.* Paper presented at 107th Annual Convention of American Psychological Association, Boston, MA.

Marsella, A. J. (2009). Diversity in a global era: The context and consequences of differences. *Counselling Psychology Quarterly, 22*(1), 119–135.

Marsella, A. J., & Pedersen, P. (2004). Internationalizing the counselling psychology curriculum: Toward new values, competencies, and directions. *Counselling Psychology Quarterly, 17*(4), 413–423.

Marsella, A. J., & Ring, E. (2003). Human migration and immigration. In L. Adler & U. Gielen (Eds.), *Migration: Immigrants and emigration in international perspective* (pp. 3–22). Westport, CT: Greenwood Press.

Marsella, A. J., & Yamada, M. (2000). Culture and mental health: An introduction and overview of foundation, concepts, and issues. In I. Cuelar & F. A. Panagua (Eds.), *Handbook of multicultural mental health* (pp. 3–24). San Diego, CA: Academic Press.

Marsella, A. J., & Yamada, A. M. (2010). Culture and psychopathology: Foundations, issues, directions. *Journal of Pacific Rim Psychology, 4*, 103–115.

Marsh, A., Elfenbein, H., & Ambady, N. (2003). Nonverbal "accents": Cultural differences in facial expressions of emotion. *Psychological Science, 14*(4), 373–376.

Martinez, R., & Dukes, R. L. (1997). The effects of ethnic identity, ethnicity, and gender on adolescent well-being. *Journal of Youth and Adolescence, 26*(5), 503–516.

Mashhour, A. (2005). Islamic law and gender equality: Could there be a common ground? *Human Rights Quarterly, 27*(2), 562–596.

Maslow, A. H. (1943). A theory of human motivation. *Psychological Review, 50*(4), 370–396.

Maslow, A. H. (1948). "Higher" and "lower" needs. *The Journal of Psychology, 25*(2), 433–436.

Masuda, T., Gonzalez, R., Kwan, L., & Nisbett, R. E. (2008). Culture and aesthetic preference: Comparing the attention to context of East Asians and Americans. *Personality and Social Psychology Bulletin, 34*(9), 1260–1275.

Masuda, T., & Nisbett, R. E. (2001). Attending holistically versus analytically: Comparing the context sensitivity of Japanese and Americans. *Journal of Personality and Social Psychology, 81*(5), 922.

Masuda, T., & Nisbett, R. E. (2006). Culture and change blindness. *Cognitive Science, 30*(2), 381–399. doi:10.1207/s15516709cog0000_63

Mataragnon, R. H. (1979). The case for an indigenous psychology. *Philippine Journal of Psychology, 12*(1), 3–8.

Matsumoto, D. (2006). The cultural bases of nonverbal communication. In D. E. Matsumoto, H. C. Hwang, & M. G. Frank (Eds.), *APA handbook of nonverbal communication.* New York: American Psychological Association.

Matsumoto, D., & van de Vijver, F. J. (Eds.). (2010). *Cross-cultural research methods in psychology.* New York: Cambridge University Press.

Matsumoto, D., Weissmann, M. D., Preston, K., Brown, B. R., & Kuppersbusch, C. (1997). Context specific measurement of individualism-collectivism on the individual level: The individualism-collectivism interpersonal assessment inventory. *Journal of Cross-Cultural Psychology, 28*(6), 743–767.

Matsumoto, D., & Yoo, S. H. (2006). Toward a new generation of cross-cultural research. *Perspectives on Psychological Science, 1*(3), 234–250.

Matsumoto, D., Yoo, S., & Fontaine, J. (2008). Mapping expressive differences around the world: The relationship between emotional display rules and individualism versus collectivism. *Journal of Cross-Cultural Psychology*, *39*(1), 55–74.

Matthews, T. J., & Ventura, S. J. (1994). *Mother's educational level influences birth rate*. Washington, DC: Government Printing Office.

May-Collado, L. J., Agnarsson, I., & Wartzok, D. (2007). Phylogenetic review of tonal sound production in whales in relation to sociality. *BMC Evolutionary Biology*, *7*, 136.

Maynard, A. E., & Greenfield, P. M. (2005). An ethnomodel of teaching and learning: Apprenticeship of Zinacantec Maya women's tasks. In A. E. Maynard & M. I. Martini (Eds.), *International and cultural psychology series. Learning in cultural context: Family, peers, and school* (pp. 75–103). doi:10.1007/0-387-27550-9_4

Maynard, A. E., & Greenfield, P. M. (2006). Cultural teaching and learning: Processes, effects, and development of apprenticeship skills. In Z. Bekerman, N. C. Burbules, & D. Silberman-Keller (Eds.), *Counterpoints: Studies in the postmodern theory of education: Vol. 249. Learning in places: The informal education reader* (pp. 139–162). New York: Peter Lang.

Maynard, A. E., Greenfield, P. M., & Childs, C. P. (1999). Culture, history, biology, and body: Native and non-native acquisition of technological skill. *Ethos*, *27*(3), 379–402.

Maynard, A. E., Greenfield, P. M., & Childs, C. P. (2015). Developmental effects of economic and educational change: Cognitive representation in three generations across 43 years in a Maya community. *International Journal of Psychology*, *50*(1), 12–19.

McAdams, D. P. (2013). *The redemptive self: Stories Americans live by*. New York: Oxford University Press.

McClelland, D. C. (1987). *Human motivation*. New York: Cambridge University Press.

McClelland, D. C., Atkinson, J. W., Clark, R. A., & Lowell, E. L. (1958). *A scoring manual for the achievement motive*. Princeton, NJ: Van Nostrand.

McCrae, R. R. (2002). NEO-PI-R data from 36 cultures. In *The five-factor model of personality across cultures* (pp. 105–125). Boston, MA: Springer.

McCrae, R. R., & Costa, P. T., Jr. (1987). Validation of the five-factor model of personality across instruments and observers. *Journal of Personality and Social Psychology*, *52*(1), 81–90.

McDermott, R. C., & Schwartz, J. P. (2013). Toward a better understanding of emerging adult men's gender role journeys: Differences in age, education, race, relationship status, and sexual orientation. *Psychology of Men & Masculinity*, *14*(2), 202.

McDevitt, S. C., & Carey, W. B. (1978). The measurement of temperament in 3–7 year old children. *Child Psychology & Psychiatry & Allied Disciplines*, *19*(3), 245–253.

McElhinny, B. (2005). "Kissing a baby is not at all good for him": Infant mortality, medicine, and colonial modernity in the U.S.-occupied Philippines. *American Anthropologist, New Series*, *107*(2), 183–194.

McElroy, A., & Townshend, P. (2004). *Medical anthropology in ecological context*. Oxford: Westview Press.

McGerty, L.-J. (2000). "Nobody lives only in cyberspace": Gendered subjectivities and domestic use of the internet. *CyberPsychology & Behavior*, *3*(5), 895–899.

McGrath, J. J. (2006). Variations in the incidence of schizophrenia: Data versus dogma. *Schizophrenia Bulletin*, *32*(1), 195–197.

McGrath, R. E., Mitchell, M., Kim, B. H., & Hough, L. (2010). Evidence for response bias as a source of error variance in applied assessment. *Psychological Bulletin*, *136*(3), 450–470.

McKenna, K. Y. A., & Bargh, J. A. (1998). Coming out in the age of the internet: Identity "demarginalization" through virtual group participation. *Journal of Personality and Social Psychology*, *75*(3), 681–694.

McKennell, A. (1974). Surveying subjective welfare: Strategies and methodological considerations. In B. Strumpel (Ed.), *Subjective elements of well-being* (pp. 45–72). Paris: OEDC.

McLaren, S., & Challis, C. (2009). Resilience among men farmers: The protective roles of social support and sense of belonging in the depression-suicidal ideation relation. *Death Studies*, *33*(3), 262.

Mead, M. (1961). *Coming of age in Samoa: A psychological study of primitive youth for Western civilization*. New York, NY: Morrow.

Medin, D. L., & Atran, S. (2004). The native mind: Biological categorization and reasoning in development and across cultures. *Psychological Review*, *111*(4), 960–983. doi:10.1037/0033-295X.111.4.960

Meltzer, D. (2008). *Sexual states of mind* (No. 2). New York, NY: Karnac Books.

Menon, T., Morris, M. W., Chiu, C. Y., & Hong, Y. Y. (1999). Culture and the construal of agency: Attribution to individual versus group dispositions. *Journal of Personality and Social Psychology, 76*(5), 701.

Menon, U. (2011). The three selves of adulthood: Cultural conceptions of self among Oriya Hindu women. *Psychological Studies, 56*(1), 23–35.

Menon, U. (2012). Hinduism, happiness and well-being: A case study of adulthood in an Oriya Hindu Temple Town. In H. Selin & G. Davey (Eds.), *Science across cultures: Vol. 6. Happiness across cultures: Views of happiness and quality of life in non-Western cultures* (pp. 417–434). New York, NY: Springer Science + Business Media.

Merriam, A. P. (1964). *The anthropology of music.* Seattle, WA: Northwestern University Press.

Merrie Monarch Festival. (2012). Retrieved from http://www.merriemonarch.com

Mesoudi, A. (2009). How cultural evolutionary theory can inform social psychology and vice versa. *Psychological Review, 116*(4), 929–952. doi:10.1037/a0017062

Mesoudi, A., Whiten, A., & Dunbar, R. (2006). A bias for social information in human cultural transmission. *British Journal of Psychology, 97*(3), 405–423. doi:10.1348/000712605X858713.

Mesquita, B., & Markus, H. R. (2004). Culture and emotion: Models of agency as sources of cultural variation in emotion. In A. S. R. Manstead, N. Frijda, & A. Fischer (Eds.), *Studies in emotion and social interaction. Feelings and emotions: The Amsterdam symposium* (pp. 341–358). New York, NY: Cambridge University Press.

Migrant crisis: Migration to Europe explained in seven charts. (2016, March 4). *BBC News.* Retrieved from http://www.bbc.com/news/world-europe-34131911

Mihai, A., Jordanova, V., Volpe, U., & Sartorius, N. (2016). Evaluating mental healthcare systems by studying pathways to care. In A. Fiorillo, U. Volpe, & D. Bhugra (Eds.), *Psychiatry in practice: Education, experience, and expertise* (pp. 23–31). New York, NY: Oxford University Press.

Mileva-Seitz, V. R., Bakermans-Kranenburg, M. J., Battaini, C., & Luijk, M. P. C. M. (2017). Parent-child bed-sharing: The good, the bad, and the burden of evidence. *Sleep Medicine Reviews, 32,* 4–27.

Milgram, S. (1963). Behavioral study of obedience. *Journal of Abnormal and Social Psychology, 67*(4), 371–378.

Military.com (2014). *Are you eligible to join the military?* Retrieved from http://www.military.com/join-armed-forces/join-the-military-basic-eligibility.html

Mill, J. (1878). *Analysis of the phenomena of the human mind* (2nd ed.). London: Longmans, Green, Reader, & Dyer. (Original work published 1829)

Mill, J. S. (1884). How Sir W. Hamilton and Mr. Mansel dispose of the law of inseparable association. In J. S. Mill, *An examination of Sir William Hamilton's philosophy and of the principal philosophical questions discussed in his writings* (pp. 307–330). New York, NY: Henry Holt and Company.

Miller, J. G. (1999). Cultural psychology: Implications for basic psychological theory. *Psychological Science, 10*(2), 85–91.

Miller, J. G. (2003). Culture and agency: Implications for psychological theories of motivation and social development. In V. Murphy-Berman & J. J. Berman (Eds.), *Vol. 49 of the Nebraska symposium on motivation. Cross-cultural differences in perspectives on the self* (pp. 76–116). Lincoln: University of Nebraska Press.

Miller, J. G., Das, R., & Chakravarthy, S. (2011). Culture and the role of choice in agency. *Journal of Personality and Social Psychology, 101*(1), 46–61.

Miller, K., & Rasco, L. (2004). *The mental health of refugees: Ecological approaches to healing and adaptation.* Mahwah, NJ: Lawrence Erlbaum Associates.

Minagawa-Kawai, Y., Mori, K., Naoi, N., & Kojima, S. (2007). Neural attunement processes in infants during the acquisition of a language-specific phonemic contrast. *Journal of Neuroscience, 27*(2), 315–321.

Mingione, A. D. (1968). Need for achievement in negro, white, and Puerto Rican children. *Journal of Consulting and Clinical Psychology, 32*(1), 94.

Ministry of Social Development. (2008). *Diverse communities: Exploring the refugee and migrant experience in New Zealand.* Wellington, NZ: Author.

Mintz, S. (2012). The jazz age: The American 1920s. *Digital History.* Retrieved from http://www.digitalhistory.uh.edu

Mio, J. S., Barker, L. A., & Tumambing, J. S. (2012). *Multicultural psychology: Understanding our diverse communities* (3rd ed.). New York, NY: Oxford University Press.

Misra, G., & Gergen, K. J. (1993). On the place of culture in psychological science. *International Journal of Psychology, 28*(2), 225–243.

Mitchell, B. A. (2010). Midlife marital happiness and ethnic culture: A life course perspective. *Journal of Comparative Family Studies, 41*(1), 167–183.

Miyagawa, S., Berwick, R. C., & Okanoya, K. (2013). The emergence of hierarchical structure in human language. *Frontiers in Psychology*, *4*. doi:10.3389/fpsyg.2013.00071.

Miyamoto, Y. (2013). Culture and analytic versus holistic cognition: Toward multilevel analyses of cultural influences. In *Advances in Experimental Social Psychology* (Vol. 47, pp. 131–188). New York: Academic Press.

Miyamoto, Y., & Ji, L. J. (2011). Power fosters context-independent, analytic cognition. *Personality and Social Psychology Bulletin*, *37*(11), 1449–1458.

Miyamoto, Y., Nisbett, R. E., & Masuda, T. (2006). Culture and the physical environment: Holistic versus analytic perceptual affordances. *Psychological Science*, *17*(2), 113–119.

Moffett, M. W. (2013). Human identity and the evolution of societies. *Human Nature*, *24*(3), 219–267. doi:10.1007/s12110-013-9170-3

Mok, A. O. (2014). East meets west: Learning-practices and attitudes towards music-making of popular musicians. *British Journal of Music Education*, *31*(2), 179–194.

Mok, A., & Morris, M. W. (2012). Managing two cultural identities: The malleability of bicultural identity integration as a function of induced global or local processing. *Personality and Social Psychology Bulletin*, *38*(2), 233–246.

Moore, S. E., Leslie, H. Y., & Lavis, C. A. (2005). Subjective well-being and life satisfaction in the Kingdom of Tonga. *Social Indicators Research*, *70*(3), 287–211. http://dx.doi.org.hpu.idm.oclc.org/10.1007/s11205-004-1541-z

Moorfield, J. C. (2019). *Te aka online Māori dictionary*. Retrieved from https://maoridictionary.co.nz/

Morelli, G. A., Rogoff, B., Oppenheim, D., & Goldsmith, D. (1992). Cultural variation in infants' sleeping arrangements: Questions of independence. *Developmental Psychology*, *28*(4), 604–613. doi:10.1037/0012-1649.28.4.604

Morelli, G. A., & Rothbaum, F. (2007). Situating the person in relationships: Attachment relationships and self-regulation in young children. *Handbook of Cultural Psychology*, 500–527.

Morgan, T. J., Uomini, N. T., Rendell, L. E., Chouinard-Thuly, L., Street, S. E., Lewis, H. M., . . . Whiten, A. (2015). Experimental evidence for the co-evolution of hominin tool-making teaching and language. *Nature Communications*, *6*, 6029.

Morie, J. F., Antonisse, J., Bouchard, S., & Chance, E. (2009). Virtual worlds as a healing modality for returning soldiers and veterans. *Annual Review of CyberTherapy and Telemedicine*, *7*, 273–276.

Morley, I. (2003). *The evolutionary origins and archaeology of music* (Unpublished doctoral dissertation). Darwin College Cambridge University, Oxford.

Morris, M. W., Chiu, C.-y., & Liu, Z. (2015). Polycultural psychology. *Annual Review of Psychology*, *66*, 631–659.

Morris, M. W., Williams, K. Y., Leung, K., Larrick, R., Mendoza, M. T., Bhatnagar, D., . . . Hu, J. C. (1998). Conflict management style: Accounting for cross-national differences. *Journal of International Business Studies*, *29*(4), 729–747.

Mulla, Z. R., & Krishnan, V. R. (2014). Karma-yoga: The Indian model of moral development. *Journal of Business Ethics*, *123*(2), 339–351.

Munsell, A. H. (1912). A pigment color system and notation. *The American Journal of Psychology*, *23*(2), 236–244.

Murdock, G. P. (1949). *Social structure*. Retrieved from https://archive.org/details/socialstructurem00murd

Murdock, G. P., & White, D. R. (1969). Standard cross-cultural sample. *Ethnology*, *8*(4), 329–369.

Murphy, G. (1947). Enhancement and defense of the self. In G. Murphy (Ed.), *Personality: A biosocial approach to origins and structure* (pp. 523–539). New York: Harper.

Murray, L. M. A., Byrne, K., & D'Eath, R. B. (2013). Pair-bonding and companion recognition in domestic donkeys, *Equus asinus*. *Applied Animal Behaviour Science*, *143*(1), 67–74.

Murray, T. (2004). Introduction. In T. Murray (Ed.), *The archaeology of contact in settler societies* (pp. 1–18). Cambridge, UK: Cambridge University Press.

Mussell, B. (2008). Cultural pathways for decolonization. *Visions: BC's Mental Health and Addictions Journal*, *5*(1), 4–5. Retrieved from http://www.heretohelp.bc.ca/publications/aboriginal-people/bck/2

Musu-Gillette, L., de Brey, C., McFarland, J., Hussar, W., Sonnenberg, W., & Wilkinson-Flicker, S. (2017). *Status and trends in the education of racial and ethnic groups*. Washington, DC: National Center for Education Statistics Institute of Education Sciences.

Myers, J. E., Madathil, J., & Tingle, L. R. (2005). Marriage satisfaction and wellness in India and the United States: A preliminary comparison of arranged marriages and marriages of choice. *Journal of Counseling & Development*, *83*(2), 183–190.

Na, J., Choi, I., & Sul, S. (2013). I like you because you think in the "right" way: Culture and ideal thinking. *Social Cognition*, *31*(3), 390–404.

Na, J., & Kitayama, S. (2011). Spontaneous trait inference is culture-specific: Behavioral and neural evidence. *Psychological Science*, *22*(8), 1025–1032.

Nagarajan, N. R., Teixeira, A. A., & Silva, S. T. (2016). The impact of an ageing population on economic growth: An exploratory review of the main mechanisms. *Análise Social*, 4–35.

Nagell, K., Olguin, R. S., & Tomasello, M. (1993). Processes of social learning in the tool use of chimpanzees (Pan troglodytes) and human children (Homo sapiens). *Journal of Comparative Psychology*, *107*(2), 174–186.

Nagpal, R., & Sell, H. (1985). *SEARS regional health papers: Subjective well-being*. New Delhi: World Health Organization.

Nahemow, L., & Lawton, M. P. (1975). Similarity and propinquity in friendship formation. *Journal of Personality and Social Psychology*, *32*(2), 205–213. http://dx.doi.org.hpu.idm.oclc.org/10.1037/0022-3514.32.2.205

Naidoo, J. C., & Mahabeer, M. (2006). Acculturation and integration patterns among Indian and African university students in South Africa: Implications for ethno-gender relations in the "rainbow" nation. *Psychology and Developing Societies*, *18*(1), 115–132.

Nair, N., & Vohra, N. (2015). *Diversity and inclusion at the workplace: A review of research and perspectives*. Working Paper No. 2015-03-34. Ahmedabad, India: Indian Institute of Management.

Nand, K., Masuda, T., Senzaki, S., & Ishii, K. (2014). Examining cultural drifts in artworks through history and development: Cultural comparisons between Japanese and Western landscape paintings and drawings. *Frontiers in Psychology*, *5*, 1041.

Nasim, A., Fernandez, A., Townsend, T. G., Corona, R., & Belgrave, F. Z. (2011). Cultural protective factors for community risks and substance use among rural African American adolescents. *Journal of Ethnicity in Substance Abuse*, *10*(4), 316–336.

National Center for Health Statistics. (2015). *Health United States, 2014: With special feature on adults aged 55–64*. Hyattsville, MD: Department of Health and Human Services.

Native Hawaiian Hospitality Association. (2013). *Hawaiian values*. Honolulu: Author.

Nattiez, J.-J. (1990). *Music and discourse: Toward a semiology of music* (C. Abbate, Trans.). Princeton, NJ: Princeton University Press.

Nayar, S. C. (2009). *The everyday occupations of Indian migrant women: A process of navigating cultural spaces* (Unpublished doctoral dissertation). Auckland University of Technology, Auckland, New Zealand.

Ndetei, D. M., Mbwayo, A. W., Mutiso, V. N., Khasakhala, L. I., & Chege, P. M. (2013). Traditional healers and their provision of mental health services in cosmopolitan informal settlements in Nairobi, Kenya. *African Journal of Psychiatry*, *16*(2), 134–140.

Neki, J. S. (1973). Gurū-Chelā relationship: The possibility of a therapeutic paradigm. *American Journal of Orthopsychiatry*, *43*(5), 755–766.

Neki, J. S. (1976). An examination of the cultural relativism of dependence as a dynamic of social and therapeutic relationships: I. Socio-developmental. *British Journal of Medical Psychology*, *49*(1), 1–10.

Nelson, C. A., Thomas, K. M., & de Haan, M. (2006). Neural bases of cognitive development. In D. Kuhn, R. S. Siegler, W. Damon, & R. M. Lerner (Eds.), *Handbook of child psychology: Cognition, perception, and language* (pp. 3–57). Hoboken, NJ: John Wiley & Sons.

Nelson Mandela Foundation. (2015). Retrieved from https://www.nelson-mandela.org/content/page/biography.

Neto, F., Barros, J., & Schmitz, P. G. (2005). Acculturation attitudes and adaptation among Portuguese immigrants in Germany: Integration or separation. *Psychology & Developing Societies*, *17*, 19–32.

Neville, H. A., Oyama, K. E., Odunewu, L. O., & Huggins, J. G. (2014). Dimensions of belonging as an aspect of racial-ethnic-cultural identity: An exploration of indigenous Australians. *Journal of Counseling Psychology*, *61*(3), 414–426. doi:10.1037/a0037115

Nevo, B., & Bin Khader, A. M. (1995). Cross-cultural, gender, and age differences in Singaporean mothers' conceptions of children's intelligence. *The Journal of Social Psychology*, *135*(4), 509–517. doi:10.1080/00224545.1995.9712219

Newcomb, T. M. (1956). The prediction of interpersonal attraction. *American Psychologist*, *11*(11), 575–586. http://dx.doi.org.hpu.idm.oclc.org/10.1037/h0046141

Ng, S. H., Han, S., Mao, L., & Lai, J. C. (2010). Dynamic bicultural brains: fMRI study of their flexible neural representation of self and significant others in response to culture primes. *Asian Journal of Social Psychology*, *13*, 83–91.

Nguyen, H., Messe, L., & Stollack, G. (1999). Toward a more complex understanding of adjustment and acculturation. *Journal of Cross-Cultural Psychology*, *30*(1), 5–31.

Nicholas, J. L. (1817). *Narrative of a voyage to New Zealand*. London: James Black and Son. Retrieved from https://archive.org/details/narrativeavoyag00nichgoog

Nicole, P. (1696). *Moral essays contain'd in several treatises on many important duties, Vol 3 and Vol 4 contained in two treatises* (pp. 78–112). London, UK: Samuel Manship.

Niederkrotenthaler, T. King-Wa, F. Yip, P., Fong, D. Y., Stack, S., Qijin, C., & Pirkis, J. (2012). Changes in suicide rates following media reports on celebrity suicide: A meta-analysis. *Journal of Epidemiology and Community Health*, 66(11), 1037–1042.

Nielsen, M. (2006). Copying actions and copying outcomes: Social learning through the second year. *Developmental Psychology*, 42(3), 555–565.

Nielsen, M., Fischer, R., & Kashima, Y. (2018). Shamanism and the social nature of cumulative culture. *Behavioral and Brain Sciences*, 41. https://doi.org/10.1017/S0140525X17002126

Nielsen, M., Mushin, I., Tomaselli, K., & Whiten, A. (2016). Imitation, collaboration, and their interaction among Western and Indigenous Australian preschool children. *Child Development*, 87(3), 795–806.

Nielsen, M., & Tomaselli, K. (2010). Overimitation in Kalahari bushman children and the origins of human cultural cognition. *Psychological Science*, 21(5), 729–736.

Nikora, L. W., Rua, M., & Te Awekotuku, N. (2004). Wearing moko: Māori facial marking in today's world. In N. Thomas, A. Cole & B. Douglas (Eds.), *Tattoo: Bodies, art and exchange in the Pacific and the West* (pp. 191–203). London: Reaktion Books.

Nisbett, R. E., & Cohen, D. (2018). *Culture of honor*. New York, NY: Routledge.

Nisbett, R., Peng, K., Choi, I., & Norenzayan, A. (2001). Culture and systems of thought: Holistic versus analytic cognition. *Psychological Review*, 108(2), 291–310.

Nishii, L. N. (2017, July). *A multilevel process model for understanding diversity practice effectiveness (CAHRS ResearchLink No. 5)*. Ithaca, NY: Cornell University.

Nishimura, S., Nevgi, A., & Tella, S. (2008). Communication style and cultural features in high/low context communication cultures: A case study of Finland, Japan and India. *Teoksessa A. Kallioniemi (toim.), Uudistuva ja kehittyvä ainedidaktiikka. Ainedidaktinen symposiumi*, 8, 783–796.

Nittle, N. K. (2017). *Introduction to cultural appropriation*. Retrieved from https://www.thoughtco.com/cultural-appropriation-and-why-iits-wrong-2834561

Nitz, K., Lerner, R. M., Lerner, J. V., & Talwar, R. (1988). Parental and peer ethnotheory demands, temperament, and early adolescent adjustment. *The Journal of Early Adolescence*, 8(3), 243–263.

Noh, S., Beiser, M., Kaspar, V., Hou, F., & Rummens, J. (1999). Perceived racial discrimination, depression, and coping: A study of Southeast Asian refugees in Canada. *Journal of Health and Social Behavior*, 40(3), 193–207.

Nordgren, J. (2017). Making up the "drug-abusing immigrant": Knowledge production in Swedish social work and drug treatment contexts, 1960s–2011. *Contemporary Drug Problems 2017*, 44(1), 49–68.

Norenzayan, A., Atran, S., Faulkner, J., & Schaller, M. (2006). Memory and mystery: The cultural selection of minimally counterintuitive narratives. *Cognitive Science*, 30(3), 531–553.

Norenzayan, A., & Nisbett, R. E. (2000). Culture and causal cognition. *Current Directions in Psychological Science*, 9(4), 132–135. doi:10.1111/1467-8721.00077

Novin, S., Banerjee, R., & Rieffe, C. (2012). Bicultural adolescents' anger regulation: In between two cultures? *Cognition & Emotion*, 26(4), 577–586.

Nsamenang, A. B. (1995). Factors influencing the development of psychology in sub-Saharan Africa. *International Journal of Psychology*, 30(6), 729–739.

Nsamenang, A. B. (2006). Human ontogenesis: An indigenous African view on development and intelligence. *International Journal of Psychology*, 41(4), 293–297. doi:10.1080/00207590544000077

Nsamenang, A. B. (2011). The culturalization of developmental trajectories. *Bridging cultural and developmental approaches to psychology: New syntheses in theory, research, and policy* (pp. 235–254). New York, NY: Oxford University Press.

Núñez, R., Cooperrider, K., Doan, D., & Wassmann, J. (2012). Contours of time: Topographic construals of past, present, and future in the Yupno valley of Papua New Guinea. *Cognition*, 124(1), 25–35.

Núñez, R., & Sweetser, E. (2006). With the future behind them: Convergent evidence from Aymara language and gesture in the crosslinguistic comparison of spatial construals of time. *Cognitive Science*, 30, 401–450.

Nwoye, A. (2015). What is African psychology the psychology of? *Theory & Psychology*, 25(1), 96–116.

Nygaard, A., Biong, H., Silkoset, R., & Kidwell, R. E. (2017). Leading by example: Values-based strategy to instill ethical conduct. *Journal of Business Ethics*, *145*(1), 133–139.

Obeng, P. (1998). Re-membering through oath: Installation of African kings and queens. *Journal of Black Studies*, *28*(3), 334–356.

Oberg, K. (1960). Culture shock: Adjustment to new cultural environments. *Practical Anthropology*, *7*, 177–182.

Oetzel, J. G. (1998). Explaining individual communication processes in homogeneous and heterogeneous groups through individualism-collectivism and self-construal. *Human Communication Research*, *25*(2), 202–224.

O'Gorman, R., Sheldon, K. M., & Wilson, D. S. (2008). For the good of the group? Exploring group-level evolutionary adaptations using multilevel selection theory. *Group Dynamics: Theory, Research, and Practice*, *12*(1), 17–26.

O'Hagin, I. B., & Harnish, D. (2006). Music as cultural identity. *International Journal of Music Education*, *24*(1), 56–70.

Ohama, M. L. F., Gotay, C. C., Pagano, I. S., Boles, L., & Craven, D. D. (2000). Evaluations of Hawaii creole English and standard English. *Journal of Language and Social Psychology*, *19*(3), 357–377.

ojalehto, B. L., & Medin, D. L. (2015). Perspectives on culture and concepts. *Annual Review of Psychology*, *66*, 249–275.

Okimoto, J. T. (2001). The appeal cycle in three cultures: an exploratory comparison of child development. *J Am Psychoanal Assoc*, *49*, 187.

Oohashi, T., Nishina, E., Kawai, N., Fuwamoto, Y., & Imai, H. (1991, October). High-frequency sound above the audible range affects brain electric activity and sound perception. In *Audio Engineering Society Convention 91*. Audio Engineering Society.

Oppedal, B. (2006). Development and acculturation. In D. L. Sam & J. W. Berry (Eds.), *The Cambridge handbook of acculturation psychology*. Cambridge: Cambridge University Press.

Organisation for Economic Co-operation and Development. (2018). *Data*. Retrieved from https://data.oecd.org/chart/5cJl

Ossorio, P. G. (1983). A multicultural psychology. *Advances in Descriptive Psychology*, *3*, 13–44.

Ostrosky-Solís, F. (2004). Can literacy change brain anatomy? *International Journal of Psychology*, *39*(1), 1–4.

O'Sullivan, J. L. (1845). Annexation. *United States Magazine and Democratic Review*, *17*(1), 5–10.

Otterbeck, J. (2004). Music as a useless activity: Conservative interpretations of music in Islam. In M. Korpe (Ed.), *Shoot the singer* (pp. 11–16). New York, NY: Zed Books.

Otters, R. V., & Hollander, J. F. (2015). Leaving home and boomerang decisions: A family simulation protocol. *Marriage & Family Review*, *51*(1), 39–58.

Over, H., & Carpenter, M. (2013). The social side of imitation. *Child Development Perspectives*, *7*(1), 6–11.

Oyebode, O., Kandala, N. B., Chilton, P. J., & Lilford, R. J. (2016). Use of traditional medicine in middle-income countries: a WHO-SAGE study. *Health Policy and Planning*, *31*, 984–991.

Page, S. (2008). *The difference: How the power of diversity creates better groups, firms, schools, and societies*. Princeton, NJ: Princeton University Press.

Pandey, J. (2004). Psychology in India enters the twenty-first century: Movement toward an indigenous discipline. In J. Pandey (Ed.), *Psychology in India revisited: Developments in the discipline, Vol. 3. Applied social and organisational psychology* (pp. 342–370). Thousand Oaks, CA: SAGE.

Pandit, S. A. (2011). The concept of "rasa" in Indian psychology: A preliminary qualitative study. *Journal of Psychosocial Research*, *6*(1), 139–148.

Papp, Z. (2010). *Traditional monster imagery in manga, anime and Japanese cinema*. New York, NY: Global Oriental.

Paranjpe, A. C. (2009). In defence of an Indian approach to the psychology of emotion. *Psychological Studies*, *54*(1), 3–22.

Park, C. E. (2006). *Voices from the straw mat: Toward an ethnography of Korean story singing*. Honolulu: University of Hawai'i Press.

Park, J. E. (2016). Turn-taking in Korean conversation. *Journal of Pragmatics*, *99*, 62–77.

Park, R. E. (1928). Human migrations and the marginal man. *American Journal of Sociology*, *33*, 881–893.

Parker, K., Cilluffo, A., & Stepler, R. (2017). 6 facts about the U.S. military and its changing demographics. *Pew Research*. Retrieved from http://www.pewresearch.org/fact-tank/2017/04/13/6-facts-about-the-u-s-military-and-its-changing-demographics/

Patkowski, M. S. (1990). Age and accent in a second language: A reply to James Emil Flege. *Applied Linguistics*, *11*(1), 73–89.

Peace, R., Spoonley, P., Butcher, A., O'Neill, D. (2005). *Immigration and social cohesion: Developing an indicator framework for measuring the impact of settlement policies in New Zealand*.

Wellington, NZ: Centre for Social Research and Evaluation.

Pearce, J., & Bidder, J. (1999). *Baby and toddler sleep program*. Tucson, AZ: Fisher Books.

Pearson, V. M. S., & Stephan, W. G. (1998). Preferences for styles of negotiation: A comparison of Brazil and the U.S. *International Journal of Intercultural Relations*, 22(1), 67–83. doi:10.1016/S0147-1767(97)00036-9

Pedersen, D. M., & Wheeler, J. (1983). The Müller-Lyer illusion among Navajos. *The Journal of Social Psychology*, 121(1), 3–6.

Pedersen, P. B., Crethar, H. C., & Carlson, J. (2008). Intellectual understanding: Race, gender, religion, and spirituality. In P. B. Pedersen, H. C. Crethar, & J. Carlson (Eds.), *Inclusive cultural empathy: Making relationships central in counseling and psychotherapy* (pp. 115–134). Washington, DC: American Psychological Association.

Peng, K., & Nisbett, R. E. (1999). Culture, dialectics, and reasoning about contradiction. *American Psychologist*, 54(9), 741–754. doi:10.1037/0003-066X.54.9.741

Penn, D. C., Holyoak, K. J., & Povinelli, D. J. (2008). Darwin's mistake: Explaining the discontinuity between human and nonhuman minds. *Behavioral and Brain Sciences*, 31(2), 109–178.

Peregrine, P. N. (2007). Cultural correlates of ceramic styles. *Cross-Cultural Research*, 41(3), 223–235.

Petchkovsky, L., & Cawte, J. (1986). The dreams of the Yolngu aborigines of Australia. *Journal of Analytical Psychology*, 31(4), 357–375.

Peters, K., Jetten, J., Radova, D., & Austin, K. (2017). Gossiping about deviance: Evidence that deviance spurs the gossip that builds bonds. *Psychological Science*, 28(11), 1610–1619.

Peters, K., & Kashima, Y. (2015). A multimodal theory of affect diffusion. *Psychological Bulletin*, 141(5), 966.

Pettigrew, T. F., & Tropp, L. R. (2006). A meta-analytic test of intergroup contact theory. *Journal of Personality and Social Psychology*, 90(5), 751–783.

Phillips, J. (2008). History of immigration. *Te Ara: The encyclopedia of New Zealand*. Retrieved from http://www .TeAra.govt.nz

Phinney, J. S. (1990). Ethnic identity in adolescents and adults: Review of research. *Psychological Bulletin*, 10(3), 499–514.

Phinney, J. S. (1992). The multigroup ethnic identity measure: A new scale for use with diverse groups. *Journal of Adolescent Research*, 7, 156–176.

Phinney, J. S. (1996). Understanding ethnic diversity. *The American Behavioral Scientist*, 40(2) 143–152.

Phinney, J. S., Kim-Jo, T., Osorio, S., & Vilhjalmsdottir, P. (2005). Autonomy and relatedness in adolescent-parent disagreements: Ethnic and developmental factors. *Journal of Adolescent Research*, 20, 8–37.

Phinney, J., & Ong, A. (2002). Adolescent-parent disagreements and life satisfaction in families from Vietnamese and European American backgrounds. *International Journal of Behavioral Development*, 26(6), 556–561.

Piaget, J. (2005). *The psychology of intelligence*. New York, NY: Routledge. (Original work published 1947)

Pilling, M., & Davies, I. R. L. (2004). Linguistic relativism and colour cognition. *British Journal of Psychology*, 95(4), 429–455.

Piske, T., MacKay, I. R. A., & Flege, J. E. (2001). Factors affecting degree of foreign accent in an L2: A review. *Journal of Phonetics*, 29(2), 191–215.

Planalp, E. M., van Hulle, C., Lemery-Chalfant, K., & Goldsmith, H. H. (2017). Genetic and environmental contributions to the development of positive affect in infancy. *Emotion*, 17(3), 412–420.

Po'A-Kekuawela, K.'O., Okamoto, S. K., Nebre, L. R. H., Helm, S., & Chin, C. I. H. (2009). 'A'ole drugs! Cultural practices and drug resistance of rural Hawai'ian youths. *Journal of Ethnic & Cultural Diversity in Social Work: Innovation in Theory, Research & Practice*, 18(3), 242–258.

Podsiadlowski, A., & Fox, S. (2011). Collectivist value orientations among four ethnic groups: Collectivism in the New Zealand context. *New Zealand Journal of Psychology*, 40(1), 5–18.

Polanczyk, G. V., Salum, G. A., Sugaya, L. S., Caye, A., & Rohde, L. A. (2015). Annual research review: A meta-analysis of the worldwide prevalence of mental disorders in children and adolescents. *Journal of Child Psychology and Psychiatry*, 56(3), 345–365.

Polk, T. A., & Hamilton, J. P. (2006). Reading, writing, and arithmetic in the brain: Neural specialization for acquired functions. In P. B. Baltes, P. A. Reuter-Lorenz, & F. Rösler (Eds.), *Lifespan development and the brain: The perspective of biocultural co-constructivism* (pp. 183–199). New York, NY: Cambridge University Press.

Polka, L., & Werker, J. F. (1994). Developmental changes in perception of nonnative vowel contrasts. *Journal of Experimental Psychology: Human Perception and Performance*, 20, 42–435.

Pollet, T. V., Roberts, S. G. B., & Dunbar, R. I. M. (2011). Extraverts have larger social network layers: But do not feel emotionally closer to individuals at any layer. *Journal of Individual Differences*, *32*(3), 161–169.

Pontzer, H. (2012) Overview of hominin evolution. *Nature Education Knowledge*, *3*(10), 8–14.

Poortinga, Y. H. (1989). Equivalence of cross-cultural data: An overview of basic issues. *International Journal of Psychology*, *24*(6), 737–756.

Poortinga, Y. H. (2016). Integration of basic controversies in cross-cultural psychology. *Psychology and Developing Societies*, *28*(2), 161–182.

Poortinga, Y. H., & van Hemert, D. A. (2001). Personality and culture demarcating between the common and the unique. *Journal of Personality*, *69*, 1033–1060.

Pope, K. (2016). *The Hoffman report and the American psychological association: Meeting the challenge of change.* Retrieved from https://kspope.com/kpope/Hoffman.php

Popenoe, R. (2012). *Feeding desire: Fatness, beauty and sexuality among a Saharan people.* New York: Routledge.

Poroch, N., Arabena, K., Tongs, J., Larkin, S., Fisher, J., & Henderson, G. (2009). Spirituality and aboriginal people's social and emotional well-being: A review. Cooperative Research Centre for Aboriginal Health Discussion Paper Series: No. 11. Casuarina, Australia: Cooperative Research Centre for Aboriginal Health. Retrieved from https://www.lowitja.org.au/sites/default/files/docs/DP_11_spirituality_review.pdf

Posada, G., Gao, Y., Wu, F., Posada, R., Tascon, M., Schöelmerich, A., . . . Synnevaag, B. (1995). The secure base phenomenon across cultures: Children's behavior, mothers' preferences, and experts' concepts. *Monographs of the Society for Research in Child Development*, *60*(2–3), 27–48.

Powell, J. W. (1881). *On the evolution of language.* First Annual Report of the Bureau of Ethnology to the Secretary of the Smithsonian Institution, 1879–80. Washington, DC: Government Printing Office.

Powell, W., Banks, K. H., & Mattis, J. S. (2017). Buried hatchets, marked locations: Forgiveness, everyday racial discrimination, and African American men's depressive symptomatology. *American Journal of Orthopsychiatry*, *87*(6), 646–662.

Price, L. J., & Briley, D. (1999). *A review and discussion of Chinese versus American cognitive styles.* HKUST archives.

Price-Williams, D., & Gaines, R. (1994), The dreamtime and dreams of northern Australian aboriginal artists. *Ethos*, 373–388.

Prilleltensky, I. (2008). Migrant well-being is a multilevel, dynamic, value-dependent phenomenon. *American Journal of Community Psychology*, *42* (3–4),359–364.

Prilleltensky, I., & Prilleltensky, O. (2007). Organizational and communal well-being. In J. Haworth & G. Hart (Eds.), *Well-being: Individual, community and social perspectives* (pp. 57–74). New York: Palgrave Macmillan.

Prince, R. (1985). The concept of culture-bound syndromes: Anorexia nervosa and brain-fag. *Social Science & Medicine*, *21*(2), 197–203.

Pryor, T. (2004). Fado: The soul of Portugal sing out! *The Folk Song Magazine*, *48*(3), 27–32.

Pukui, M. K., & Elbert, S. H. (2019). *Hawaiian dictionary.* Retrieved from http://wehewehe.org/

Punathamberkar, A. (2005). Bollywood in the Indian-American diaspora: Mediating a transitive logic of cultural citizenship. *International Journal of Cultural Studies 8*, 151–173. doi:10.1177/1367877905052415

Putnam, J. J. (1906). Recent experiences in the study and treatment of hysteria at the Massachusetts General Hospital; with remarks on Freud's method of treatment by "Psychoanalysis". *The Journal of Abnormal Psychology*, *1*(1), 26–41.

Quek, K. M. T., & Fitzpatrick, J. (2013). Cultural values, self-disclosure, and conflict tactics as predictors of marital satisfaction among Singaporean husbands and wives. *The Family Journal*, *21*(2), 208–216.

Ramirez-Christiansen, E. (1994). *Heart's flower: The life and poetry of Shinkei.* Palo Alto, CA: Stanford University Press.

Rampell, C. (2016, May 7). Ivy league economist ethnically profiled, interrogated for doing math on American Airlines flight. *Washington Post.* Retrieved from https://www.washingtonpost.com/news/rampage/wp/2016/05/07/ivy-league-economist-interrogated-for-doing-math-on-american-airlines-flight/

Rapp-Paglicci, L. A., Rowe, W., & Ersing, R. L. (2006). The effects of cultural arts programs on at-risk youth: Are there more than anecdotes and promises? *Journal of Social Service Research*, *33*(2), 51–56.

Rapson, R. L. (2007). *Magical thinking and the decline of America.* New York: Xlibris.

Rata, A., Liu, J. H., & Hanke, K. (2008). Te ara hohou rongo (The path to peace): Māori conceptualisations of inter-group forgiveness. *New Zealand Journal of Psychology*, *37*(2), 18–30.

Rata, E. (2013). The unintended outcomes of institutionalizing ethnicity: Lessons in Māori education from New Zealand. In F. Widdowson, F. & A. Howard (Eds.), *Approaches to aboriginal education in Canada: Searching for solutions* (pp. 318–339). Calgary, Alberta: Brush Education.

Rath, F. H., Jr., & Okum, M. E. (2006). Parents and children sleeping together: Cosleeping prevalence and concerns. *American Journal of Orthopsychiatry*, *65*(3), 411–418.

Rauscher, F. H. (2009). The impact of music instruction on other skills. In S. Hallam, I. Cross, & M. Thaut (Eds.), *The Oxford handbook of music psychology* (pp. 244–252). Oxford: Oxford University Press.

Ray, S. (2017, May 9). India 3rd most porn watching country in the world, up from 4th last year. *India Times*. Retrieved from https://www.indiatimes.com/news/world/india-3rd-most-porn-watching-country-in-the-world-up-from-4th-last-year-249212.html

Rayson, A. (2004). *Modern history of Hawaii*. Honolulu: Bess Press.

Reddish, P., Fischer, R., & Bulbulia, J. (2013). Let's dance together: Synchrony, shared intentionality and cooperation. *PLOS One*, *8*(8), e71182. https://doi.org/10.1371/journal.pone.0071182

Redfield, A., & Thouin-Savard, M. (2017). Electronic dance music events as modern-day ritual. *International Journal of Transpersonal Studies*, *36*(1). https://doi.org/10.24972/ijts.2017.36.1.52

Redfield, R., Linton, R., & Herskovits, M. J. (1936). Memorandum for the study of acculturation. *American Anthropologist, New Series*, *38*(1), 149–152.

Regan, D. (1988). *For the record: From Wall Street to Washington*. San Diego: Harcourt.

Regan, P. C., Lakhanpal, S., & Anguiano, C. (2012). Relationship outcomes in Indian-American love-based and arranged marriages. *Psychological Reports*, *110*(3), 915–924.

Regier, T., & Kay, P. (2009). Language, thought, and color: Whorf was half right. *Trends in Cognitive Sciences*, *13*(10), 439–446.

Reilly, D. (2012). Gender, culture, and sex-typed cognitive abilities. *PLOS One*, *7*(7). doi:10.1371/journal.pone.0039904

Reitz, J. G., Breton, R., Dion, K. K., & Dion, K. L. (2009). *Multiculturalism and social cohesion: Potentials and challenges of diversity*. New York: Springer Science & Business Media.

Reynolds, G. & Shendruk, A. (2018). *Demographics of the US military*. Council on Foreign Relations.

Rheinstein, M. (1953). Trends in marriage and divorce law of Western countries. *Law and Contemporary Problems*, 3–19.

Rhodes, J. E. (2004). The critical ingredient: Caring youth-staff relationships in after-school settings. *New Directions for Youth Development*, *101*, 145–161.

Rhodes, G., Yoshikawa, S., Clark, A., Lee, K., McKay, R., & Akamatsu, S. (2001). Attractiveness of facial averageness and symmetry in non-Western cultures: In search of biologically based standards of beauty. *Perception*, *30*(5), 611–625.

Richerson, P. J., & Boyd, R. (2008). *Not by genes alone: How culture transformed human evolution*. Chicago: University of Chicago Press.

Richter, R., & Pflegerl, J. (2001). Living in migration in Austria. *Journal of Comparative Family Studies*, *32*(4), 517–531.

Richwine, J. (2009). *IQ and immigration policy* (Unpublished doctoral dissertation). Harvard University.

Robbins, B. (2012). Confronting the cadaver: The denial of death in modern medicine. *Janus Head*, *12*(2), 131–140.

Robbins, R. L. (2000). Vocal communication in free-ranging African wild dogs (Lycaonpictus). *Behaviour*, *137*, 1271–1298.

Roberson, D. (2005). Color categories are culturally diverse in cognition as well as in language. *Cross-Cultural Research: The Journal of Comparative Social Science*, *39*(1), 56–71.

Roberson, D., Davies, I., & Davidoff, J. (2000). Color categories are not universal: Replications and new evidence from a stone-age culture. *Journal of Experimental Psychology*, *129*(3), 369–398.

Roberts, S. (1988). White House confirms Reagans follow astrology, up to a point. *New York Times*. Retrieved from http://www.nytimes.com/1988/05/04/us/white-house-confirms-reagans-follow-astrology-up-to-a-point.html

Roberts, S. G. B. & Dunbar, R. I. M. (2011). Communication in social networks: Effects of kinship, network size and emotional closeness. *Personal Relationships*, *18*, 439–452.

Roberts, S. G. B., & Roberts, A. I. (2018, August 16). Visual attention, indicative gestures, and calls accompanying gestural communication are associated with sociality in wild chimpanzees (*Pan troglodytes schweinfurthii*). *Journal of Comparative Psychology*. Advance online publication.

Rodriguez-Fornells, A., De Diego Balaguer, R., & Münte, T. F. (2006). Executive control in bilingual language processing. *Language Learning*, *56*, 133–190.

Rogers, R. A. (2006). From cultural exchange to transculturation: A review and reconceptualization of cultural appropriation. *Communication Theory*, *16*(4), 474–503.

Rogoff, B. (1996). Developmental transitions in children's participation in sociocultural activities. In A. J. Sameroff & M. M. Haith (Eds.), *The John D. and Catherine T. MacArthur Foundation series on mental heath and development. The five to seven year shift: The age of reason and responsibility* (pp. 273–294). Chicago, IL: University of Chicago Press.

Rogoff, B. (2003). *The cultural nature of human development*. Oxford, UK: Oxford University Press.

Rogoff, B. (2011). *Developing destinies: A Mayan midwife and town*. New York: Oxford University Press.

Rogoff, B. (2013). The joint socialization of development by young. *Social Influences and Socialization in Infancy*, *6*, 253.

Rogoff, B. (2016). Culture and participation: A paradigm shift. *Current Opinion in Psychology*, *8*, 182–189.

Rogoff, B., & Morelli, G. (1989). Perspectives on children's development from cultural psychology. *American Psychologist*, *44*(2), 343.

Rohlof, H. G., Knipscheer, J. W., & Kleber, R. J. (2014). Somatization in refugees: A review. *Social Psychiatry and Psychiatric Epidemiology*, *49*(11), 1793–1804.

Rokeach, M. (1973). *The nature of human values*. New York: Free Press.

Rokeach, M. (1974). Change and stability in American value systems, 1968–1971. *Public Opinion Quarterly*, *38*(2), 222–238. doi:10.1086/268153

Roland, A. (2006). Across civilizations: Psychoanalytic therapy with Asians and Asian Americans. *Psychotherapy: Theory, Research, Practice, Training*, *43*(4), 454.

Rollet, C. & Bordelais, P. (1993). Infant mortality in France, 1750–1950. In C. A. Corsini & P. P. Viazzo (Eds.), *The decline of infant mortality in Europe 1800–1950*. Florence, Italy: UNICEF.

Rosch Heider, E. (1971). "Focal" color areas and the development of color names. *Developmental Psychology*, *4*(3), 447–455. doi:10.1037/h0030955

Rosch Heider, E. (1972). Universals in color naming and memory. *Journal of Experimental Psychology*, *93*(1), 10–20.

Rosch Heider, E., & Olivier, D. C. (1972). The structure of the color space in naming and memory for two languages. *Cognitive Psychology*, *3*(2), 337–354.

Rosenblatt, A., Greenberg, J., Solomon, S., Pyszczynski, T., & Lyon, D. (1989). Evidence for terror management theory: I. The effects of mortality salience on reactions to those who violate or uphold cultural values. *Journal of Personality and Social Psychology*, *57*(4), 681.

Rosenthal, L., Levy, S. R., & Moss, I. (2012). Polyculturalism and openness about criticizing one's culture: Implications for sexual prejudice. *Group Processes & Intergroup Relations*, *15*(2), 149–165. doi:10.1177/1368430211412801

Rossier, J., Ouedraogo, A., Dahourou, D., Verardi, S., & de Stadelhofen, F. M. (2013). Personality and personality disorders in urban and rural Africa: Results from a field trial in Burkina Faso. *Frontiers in Psychology*, *4*. doi:10.3389/fpsyg.2013.00079

Rothbaum, F., Weisz, J., Pott, M., Miyake, K., & Morelli, G. (2000). Attachment and culture: Security in the United States and Japan. *American Psychologist*, *55*(10), 1093–1104.

Rotter, J. B. (1966). Generalized expectancies for internal versus external control of reinforcement. *Psychological Monographs: General and Applied*, *80*(1), 1–28.

Rotter, J. B. (1975). Some problems and misconceptions related to the construct of internal versus external control of reinforcement. *Journal of Consulting and Clinical Psychology*, *43*(1), 56–67.

Roughton, R. (2014). The significance of Brokeback Mountain. *Journal of Gay & Lesbian Mental Health*, *18*(1), 83–94.

Routledge, C., Juhl, J., Vess, M., Cathey, C., & Liao, J. (2013). Who uses groups to transcend the limits of the individual self? Exploring the effects of interdependent self-construal and mortality salience on investment in social groups. *Social Psychological and Personality Science*, *4*(4), 483–491.

Rowley, S. J., Sellers, R. M., Chavous, T. M., & Smith, M. A. (1998). The relationship between racial identity and self-esteem in African American college and high school students. *Journal of Personality and Social Psychology*, *74*(3), 715–724.

Royal, T. A. C. (2008). Hawaiki. *Te Ara — the Encyclopedia of New Zealand*. Retrieved from http://www.TeAra .govt.nz

Rubel, A. J., O'Nell, C. W., & Collado, R. (1985). The folk illness called susto. In *The culture-bound syndromes* (pp. 333–350). Amsterdam: Springer Netherlands.

Ruby, M. B., Falk, C. F., Heine, S. J., Villa, C., & Silberstein, O. (2012). Not all collectivisms are equal: Opposing preferences for ideal affect between East Asians and Mexicans. *Emotion*, *12*(6), 1206–1209.

Rudmin, F. W. (2006). Debate in science: The case of acculturation. *AnthroGlobe Journal*. Retrieved from http://www.anthroglobe.ca/docs/rudminf_acculturation_061204.pdf

Rudmin, F. W. (2010). Steps towards the renovation of acculturation research paradigms: What scientists' personal experiences of migration might tell science. *Culture & Psychology*, *16*(3). https://doi.org/10.1177/1354067X10371140

Ruggles, S. (2012). The future of historical family demography. *Annual Review of Sociology*, *38*, 423.

Ruiz-Alfaro, S. (2012). From Chavela to Frida: Loving from the margins. *Journal of Homosexuality*, *59*(8), 1131–1144.

Runde, C., & Armon, B. K. (2016). Conflict competence in a multicultural world. In J. L. Wildman, R. L. Griffith, & B. K. Armon (Eds.), *Critical issues in cross cultural management* (pp. 61–72). Cham, Switzerland: Springer International.

Russell, J. A. (1991). In defense of a prototype approach to emotion concepts. *Journal of Personality and Social Psychology*, *60*(1), 37.

Russock, H. I. (2011). An evolutionary interpretation of the effect of gender and sexual orientation on human mate selection preferences, as indicated by an analysis of personal advertisements. *Behaviour*, *148*(3), 307–323.

Ryan, R. M., & Deci, E. L. (2000). Self-determination theory and the facilitation of intrinsic motivation, social development, and well-being. *American Psychologist*, *55*(1), 68.

Rybak, C., & Decker-Fitts, A. (2009). Theory and practice: Understanding Native American healing practices. *Counseling Psychology Quarterly*, *22*, 333–342.

Ryder, A. G., & Chentsova-Dutton, Y. E. (2012). Depression in cultural context: "Chinese somatization," revisited. *Psychiatric Clinics of North America*, *35*(1), 15–36.

Ryff, C. D., & Keyes, C. L. M. (1995). The structure of psychological well-being revisited. *Journal of Personality and Social Psychology*, *69*(4), 719–727.

Sabatier, C. (2008). Ethnic and national identity among second-generation immigrant adolescents in France: The role of social context and family. *Journal of Adolescence*, *31*(2), 185–205.

Sabatini, F. (2014). The relationship between happiness and health: Evidence from Italy. *Social Science & Medicine*, *114*, 178–187.

Sacks, H., Schegloff, E. A., & Jefferson, G. (1974). A simplest systematics for the organization of turn-taking for conversation. *Language*, *50*(4–1), 696–735.

Sakashita, J. (2006). Yakudoshi marks our peak year. *Honolulu Advertiser*. Retrieved from http://the.honolulu advertiser.com/article/2006/Mar/18/il/FP603180319.html

Sam, D. L. (2006). Acculturation: Conceptual background and core components. In D. L. Sam & J. W. Berry (Eds.), *The Cambridge handbook of acculturation psychology* (pp. 11–26). New York, NY: Cambridge University Press.

Samuels, N., Gropp, C., Singer, S. R., & Oberbaum, M. (2008). Acupuncture for psychiatric illness: A literature review. *Behavioral Medicine*, *34*(2), 55–62.

Sanderson, C. A. (2010). *Social psychology*. Danvers, MA: John Wiley & Sons.

Sapir, E. (1929). The status of linguistics as a science. *Language*, *5*(4), 207–214.

Sarapin, S. H., Christy, K., Lareau, L., Krakow, M., & Jensen, J. D. (2014). Identifying admired models to increase emulation: Development of a multidimensional admiration scale. *Measurement and Evaluation in Counseling and Development*, *48*(2), 95–108.

Sargent, C., & Bascope, G. (1996). Ways of knowing about birth in three cultures. *Medical Anthropology Quarterly*, *10*(2), 213–236.

Saucier, G. (2009). Recurrent personality dimensions in inclusive lexical studies: Indications for a big six structure. *Journal of Personality*, *77*(5), 1577–1614.

Saucier, G., Thalmayer, A. G., & Bel-Bahar, T. S. (2014). Human attribute concepts: Relative ubiquity across twelve mutually isolated languages. *Journal of Personality and Social Psychology*, *107*(1), 199–216.

Savage, J. (2007). *Teenage: The creation of youth culture*. New York: Viking.

Save the Children. (2015). *State of the world's mothers*. Fairfield, CT: Author.

Saylor, E. S., & Aries, E. (1999). Ethnic identity and change in social context. *The Journal of Social Psychology*, *139*(5), 549–566.

Scales, C. (2007). Powwows, intertribalism, and the value of competition. *Ethnomusicology*, *51*(1), 1–29.

Scarantino, A. (2012). Discrete emotions: From folk psychology to causal mechanisms. In P. Zachar & R. D. Ellis (Eds.), *Consciousness and emotion book series: Vol. 7. Categorical versus dimensional models of affect: A seminar on the theories of Panksepp and Russell* (pp. 135–154). Amsterdam, NL: John Benjamins.

Schaller, M., Conway, L. G., & Crandall, C. S. (2004). The psychological foundations of culture: An introduction. In M. Schaller & C. S. Crandall (Eds.), *The psychological foundations of culture* (pp. 1–12). Mahwah, NJ: Lawrence Erlbaum Associates.

Schechner, R. (1985). *Between theatre and performance*. Philadelphia: University of Pennsylvania Press.

Schechner, R. (1988). *Performance theory* (2nd ed.). New York: Routledge.

Scheffey, K. L., Ogden, S. N., & Dichter, M. E. (2019). "The idea of categorizing makes me feel uncomfortable": University student perspectives on sexual orientation and gender identity labeling in the healthcare setting. *Archives of Sexual Behavior, 48*(5), 1555–1562.

Scheib, J. E., Gangestad, S. W., & Thornhill, R. (1999). Facial attractiveness, symmetry and cues of good genes. *Proceedings of the Royal Society of London. Series B: Biological Sciences, 266*(1431), 1913–1917.

Schiff, J. W., & Moore, K. (2006). The impact of the sweat lodge ceremony on dimensions of well-being. *American Indian and Alaska Native Mental Health Research: The Journal of the National Center, 13*(3), 48–69.

Schlaug, G. (2009). Music, musicians, and brain plasticity. In S. Hallam, I. Cross, & M. Thaut (Eds.), *The Oxford handbook of music psychology* (pp. 197–207). Oxford: Oxford University Press.

Schmidt, K., Dietrich, O., & Notroff, J. (2012). Turkey: Göbekli Tepe. *World Archaeology, 53*. Retrieved from http://www.world-archaeology.com/features/turkey-gobekli-tepe/

Schmitt, D., & Allik, J. (2005). Simultaneous administration of the Rosenberg Self-Esteem Scale in 53 nations: Exploring the universal and culture-specific features of global self-esteem. *Journal of Personality and Social Psychology, 89*(4), 623–642.

Schmitt, D. P., Allik, J., McCrae, R. R., Benet-Martínez, V., Alcalay, L., & Ault, L. (2007). The geographic distribution of Big Five personality traits: Patterns and profiles of human self-description across 56 nations. *Journal of Cross-Cultural Psychology, 38*, 173–212.

Schnarch, B. (2004). Ownership, control, access, and possession (OCAP) or self-determination applied to research: A critical analysis of contemporary First Nations research and some options for First Nations communities. *International Journal of Indigenous Health, 1*(1), 80.

Schneiderman, I., Zagoory-Sharon, O., Leckman, J. F., & Feldman, R. (2012). Oxytocin during the initial stages of romantic attachment: relations to couples' interactive reciprocity. *Psychoneuroendocrinology, 37*(8), 1277–1285.

Schnell, J. (2010) Perspective on the Iraq War: Mass media implications, U.S. military policy, and cross-cultural communication. *Media Psychology Review, 3*(1).

Schniter, E. (2010). *Why old age: Non-material contributions and patterns of aging among older adult tsimané*. Dissertation Abstracts International Section A: Humanities and Social Sciences, 71(2–A), 611. (UMI No. AAI3390774)

Scholz, C. A., Johnson, T. C., Cohen, A. S., King, J. W., Peck, J. A., Overpeck, J. T., . . . Lyons, R. P. (2007). East African megadroughts between 135 and 75 thousand years ago and bearing on early-modern human origins. *Proceedings of the National Academy of Sciences, 104*(42), 16416–16421.

Schuck, P. (1993). The new immigration and the old civil rights. *The American Prospect, 15*, 102–111.

Schug, J., Yuki, M., & Maddux, W. (2010). Relational mobility explains between- and within-culture differences in self-disclosure to close friends. *Psychological Science, 21*(10), 1471–1478.

Schwartz, S. (2001). Extending the cross-cultural validity of the theory of basic human values with a different method of measurement. *Journal of Cross-Cultural Psychology, 32*(5), 519–542.

Schwartz, S. (2006). A theory of cultural value orientations: Explication and applications. *Comparative Sociology, 5*(2–3), 137–192.

Schwartz, S. (2007). The relationship between love and marital satisfaction in arranged and romantic Jewish couples. *Dissertation Abstracts International: Section B: The Sciences and Engineering, 68*(4–B), 2716.

Schwartz, S. & Boehnke, K. (2004). Evaluating the structure of human values with confirmatory factor analysis. *Journal of Research in Personality, 38*(3), 230–255.

Schwartz, S. H. (1992). Universals in the content and structure of values: Theoretical advances and empirical tests in 20 countries. In M. P. Zanna

(Ed.), *Advances in experimental social psychology* (Vol. 25, pp. 1–65). San Diego, CA: Academic Press.

Schwartz, S. H. (1994). Are there universal aspects in the structure and contents of human values? *Journal of Social Issues, 50*(4), 19–45.

Schwartz, S. H. (2008). *Cultural value orientations: Nature and implications of national differences.* Moscow: Higher School of Education.

Schwartz, S. H. (2014). Functional theories of human values: Comment on Gouveia, Milfont, and Guerra. *Personality and Individual Differences, 68*, 247–249.

Schwartz, S. H., & Bardi, A. (2001). Value hierarchies across cultures: Taking a similarities perspective. *Journal of Cross-Cultural Psychology, 32*(3), 268–290.

Schwartz, S. H., & Bilsky, W. (1987). Toward a universal psychological structure of human values. *Journal of Personality and Social Psychology, 53*(3), 550–562.

Schwartz, S. H., & Bilsky, W. (1990). Toward a theory of the universal content and structure of values: Extensions and cross-cultural replications. *Journal of Personality and Social Psychology, 58*(5), 878–891.

Schwartz, S. H., & Boehnke, K. (2004). Evaluating the structure of human values with confirmatory factor analysis. *Journal of Research in Personality, 38*(3), 230–255.

Schweigman, K., Soto, C., Wright, S., & Unger, J. (2011). The relevance of cultural activities in ethnic identity among California Native American youth. *Journal of Psychoactive Drugs, 43*(4), 343–348.

Scott, S. (1982). Grannies, mothers and babies: An examination of traditional southern Appalachian midwifery. *Central Issues in Anthropology, 4*(2), 17–30.

Scovel, T. (1988). *A time to speak: A psycholinguistic inquiry into the critical period for human speech.* New York, NY: Newbury House.

Sedikides, C., Gaertner, L., & Vevea, J. L. (2005). Pancultural self-enhancement reloaded: A meta-analytic reply to Heine (2005). *Journal of Personality and Social Psychology, 89*(4), 539–551.

Segall, M. H., Campbell, D. T., & Herskovits, M. J. (1966). *The influence of culture on visual perception.* Indianapolis, IN: Bobbs-Merrill.

Segall, M. H., Lonner, W. J., & Berry, J. W. (1998). Cross-cultural psychology as a scholarly discipline: On the flowering of culture in behavioral research. *American Psychologist, 53*(10), 1101–1110.

Sekiguchi, R. (2006). *10,000 shovels: China's urbanization and economic development.* Palo Alto, CA: Stanford Program on International and Cross-Cultural Education (SPICE).

Seligman, M. E. P., & Csikszentmihalyi, M. (2000). Positive psychology: An introduction. *American Psychologist, 55*(1), 5–14. http://dx .doi.org.eres.library.manoa.hawaii .edu/10.1037/0003-066X.55.1.5

Sell, H., & Nagpal, R. (1992). *Assessment of subjective well-being: The subjective well-being inventory (SUBI).* Geneva: World Health Organization, Regional Office for South-East Asia.

Selnick, C. N. (2012). *White sow, white stag, and white buffalo: The evolution of white animal myths from personal belief to public policy* (Unpublished doctoral dissertation).

Semin, G. R. (2011). Culturally situated linguistic ecologies and language use: Cultural tools at the service of representing and shaping situated realities. In M. J. Gelfand, C.-y. Chiu, & Y.-y. Hong (Eds.), *Advances in culture and psychology* (Vol. 1, pp. 217–249). New York, NY: Oxford University Press.

Senturia, K. D. (1997). A woman's work is never done: Women's work and pregnancy outcome in Albania. *Medical Anthropology Quarterly, 11*(3), 375–395.

Sered, S. S. (1994). Husbands, wives, and childbirth rituals. *Ethos, 22*(2), 187–208.

Serpell, R., Mumba, P., & Chansa-Kabali, T. (2011). Early educational foundations for the development of civic responsibility: An African experience. *New Directions for Child and Adolescent Development, 134*, 77–93.

Servaes, J. (1989). Cultural identity and modes of communication. *Annals of the International Communication Association, 12*(1), 283–416.

Sessarego, S. (2013). Some remarks on the origin of Chota Valley Spanish. In A. M. Carvalho & S. Beaudrie (Eds), *Selected proceedings of the 6th workshop on Spanish sociolinguistics* (pp. 87–96). Somerville, MA: Cascadilla Proceedings Project.

Seyle, H. (1956). *The stress of life.* New York, NY: McGraw-Hill.

Seymour, H. N., Bland-Stewart, L., & Green, L. J. (1998). Difference versus deficit in child African American English. *Language, Speech, and Hearing Services in Schools, 29*(2), 96–108.

Shafa, S., Harinck, F., & Ellemers, N. (2017). Sorry seems to be the hardest word: Cultural differences in apologizing effectively. *Journal of Applied Social Psychology, 47*(10), 553–567.

Shafer, M. (2004). Havasupai blood samples misused. *Indian Country Today, 10*. Retrieved from https://indiancountrymedianetwork.com/news/havasupai-blood-samples-misused/

Shamsui, A. B. (2001). A history of an identity, an identity of a history: The idea and practice of Malayness in Malaysia reconsidered. *Journal of Southeast Asian Studies, 32*(3), 355–366. Retrieved from http://www.jstor.org/stable/20072352

Shand, N. & Kosawa, Y. (1985). Culture transmission: Caudill's model and alternative hypotheses. *American Anthropologist, 87*(4), 862–871.

Sharma, M. N. (2016). Catharsis and rasa: The intersecting theories. *Research Scholar, 4*(1). Retrieved from http://www.researchscholar.co.in

Shattuck, R. M., & Kreider, R. M. (2013). Social and economic characteristics of currently unmarried women with a recent birth: 2011. *US Census Bureau*. Retrieved from https://www.census.gov/prod/2013pubs/acs-21.pdf

Shaw, J. T. (2016). "The music I was meant to sing": Adolescent choral students' perceptions of culturally responsive pedagogy. *Journal of Research in Music Education, 64*(1), 45–70. doi:10.1177/0022429415627989

Shek, D. T. (2001). Paternal and maternal influences on family functioning among Hong Kong Chinese families. *The Journal of Genetic Psychology, 162*(1), 56–74.

Shen, X. B., Wu, Q., & Fu, X. L. (2012). Effects of the duration of expressions on the recognition of microexpressions. *Journal of Zhejiang University Science B, 13*(3), 221–230.

Shennan, S. J., & Steele, J. (1999). Cultural learning in hominids: A behavioral ecological approach. In H. O. Box and K. R. Gibson (Eds.), *Mamalian social learning* (pp. 367–389). Oxford: Oxford University Press.

Sherif, M. (1961). *Intergroup conflict and cooperation: The robbers' cave experiment* (Vol. 10, pp. 150–198). Norman, OK: University Book Exchange.

Sherif, M., Harvey, O. J., White, B. J., Hood, W., & Sherif, C. W. (1961). *Intergroup conflict and cooperation: The robbers cave experiment*. Norman, OK: The University Book Exchange.

Sherman, M., Berrang-Ford, L., Ford, J., Lardeau, M-P., Hofmeijer, I., & Cortijo, C. (2012). Balancing indigenous principles and institutional research guidelines for informed consent: A case study from the Peruvian Amazon. *AJOB Primary Research, 3*(4), 53–68.

Shiota, M. N., & Keltner, D. (2005). What do emotion words represent? *Psychological Inquiry, 16*(1), 32–37.

Shipton, C., & Nielsen, M. (2015). Before cumulative culture: The evolutionary origins of overimitation and shared intentionality. *Human Nature, 26*(3), 331–345.

Shirov, A. A., & Gordon, R. (2013). Life before earth. *MIT Technology Review*. doi:10.1037/1304.3381

Shteynberg, G. (2010). A silent emergence of culture: The social tuning effect. *Journal of Personality and Social Psychology, 99*(4), 683–689. doi:10.1037/a0019573

Shweder, R. (1995). Cultural psychology: What is it? In N. R. Goldberger & J. B. Veroff (Eds.), *The culture and psychology reader* (pp. 41–86). New York: New York University Press.

Shweder, R. (1999). Why cultural psychology? *Ethos 27*(1), 62–73.

Shweder, R. A. (2000). The psychology of practice and the practice of the three psychologies. *Asian Journal of Social Psychology, 3*(3), 207–222.

Shweder, R. A. (2004, April). Deconstructing the emotions for the sake of comparative research. In *Feelings and emotions: The Amsterdam symposium* (pp. 81–97). Cambridge, UK: Cambridge University Press.

Shweder, R. A., & Haidt, J. (1994). The future of moral psychology: Truth, intuition, and the pluralist way. In B. Puka (Ed.), *Moral development: A compendium, Vol. 7. Reaching out: Caring, altruism, and prosocial behavior* (pp. 336–341). New York, NY: Garland.

Shweder, R. A., Haidt, J., Horton, R., & Joseph, C. (2008). The cultural psychology of the emotions: Ancient and renewed. In M. Lewis, J. M. Haviland-Jones & L. F. Barrett (Eds.), *Handbook of emotions* (3rd ed., pp. 409–427). New York, NY: Guilford Press.

Shweder, R. A., Much, N. C., Mahapatra, M., & Park, L. (1997). The "big three" of morality (autonomy, community, divinity) and the "big three" explanations of suffering. In A. M. Brandt & P. Rozin (Eds.), *Morality and health* (pp. 119–169). Florence, KY: Taylor & Frances/Routledge.

Shweder, R. A., & Sullivan, M. A. (1990). The semiotic subject of cultural psychology. *Handbook of personality: Theory and research* (pp. 399–416). New York, NY: Guilford Press.

Shweder, R. A., & Sullivan, M. A. (1993). Cultural psychology: Who needs it? *Annual Review of Psychology, 44*(1), 497–523.

Silles, M. A. (2009). The causal effect of education on health: Evidence from the United Kingdom. *Economics of Education Review, 28*(1), 122–128.

Silva, P. A., & Stanton, W. R. (Eds.). (1996). *From child to adult. The Dunedin Multidisciplinary Health and Development Study*. Auckland, NZ: Oxford University Press.

Silver, A. (1989). Sentiments moraux, effets sociaux: Friendship and trust as moral ideals: an historical approach. *European Journal of Sociology, 30*(2), 274–297.

Silvia, P. J., & Duval, T. S. (2001). Objective self-awareness theory: Recent progress and enduring problems. *Personality and Social Psychology Review, 5*, 230–241.

Sims, T., Koopmann-Holm, B., Young, H. R., Jiang, D., Fung, H., & Tsai, J. L. (2018). Asian Americans respond less favorably to excitement (vs. calm)-focused physicians compared to European Americans. *Cultural Diversity and Ethnic Minority Psychology, 24*(1), 1.

Singelis, T. M., Bond, M. H., Sharkey, W. F., & Lai, S. Y. (1999). Unpacking culture's influence on self-esteem and embarrassability: The role of self-construals. *Journal of Cross-Cultural Psychology, 30*, 315–341.

Singer, I. (1987). *The nature of love*. Chicago, IL: University of Chicago Press.

Singh, A. (2012). *Indian perspectives on intelligence: Some psychological and philosophical evidences*. Conference: 5th International Conference on Cognitive Science, at Immanuel Kant Baltic Federal University, Kaliningrad Russia.

Singh, D. (1993). Adaptive significance of female physical attractiveness: Role of waist-to-hip ratio. *Journal of Personality and Social Psychology, 65*(2), 293.

Singh, D., Dixson, B. J., Jessop, T. S., Morgan, B., & Dixson, A. F. (2010). Cross-cultural consensus for waist–hip ratio and

women's attractiveness. *Evolution and Human Behavior, 31*(3), 176–181.

Singleton, J. (1998). *Learning in likely places: Varieties of apprenticeship in Japan*. Cambridge: Cambridge University Press.

Sirikantraporn, S. (2013). Biculturalism as a protective factor: An exploratory study on resilience and the bicultural level of acculturation among Southeast Asian American youth who have witnessed domestic violence. *Asian American Journal of Psychology, 4*, 109–115.

Slobodskaya, H. R., Gartstein, M. A., Nakagawa, A., & Putnam, S. P. (2013). Early temperament in Japan, the United States, and Russia: Do cross-cultural differences decrease with age? *Journal of Cross-Cultural Psychology, 44*(3), 438–460.

Slone, D. J., Gonce, L., Upal, A., Edwards, K., & Tweeny, R. (2007). Imagery effects on recall of minimally counterintuitive concepts. *Journal of Cognition and Culture, 7*, 355–367.

Slot, B. J. (1992). *Abel Tasman and the discovery of New Zealand*. Amsterdam: Otto Cramwinckel.

Smircich, L., & Morgan, G. (1982). Leadership: The management of meaning. *Journal of Applied Behavioral Science, 18*(3), 257–273.

Smith, G. E. (1933). *The diffusion of culture*. London: Watts.

Smith, G. H. (2012). The politics of reforming Māori education: The transforming potential of Kura Kaupapa Māori. *Towards Successful Schooling*, 73–87.

Smith, L. T. (1999). *Decolonizing methodologies: Research and indigenous peoples*. London: Zed Books.

Smith, L. T. (2013). *Decolonizing methodologies: Research and indigenous peoples*. London: Zed Books.

Smith-Oka, V. (2008). Plants used for reproductive health by Nahua women in northern Veracruz, Mexico. *Journal of Economic Botany 62*(4), 604–614.

Smuts, B. B., & Gubernick, D. J. (1992). Male-infant relationships in nonhuman primates. In B. S. Hewlett (Ed.), *Foundations of human behavior. Father–child relations: Cultural and biosocial contexts* (pp. 1–30). Hawthorne, NY: Aldine de Gruyter.

Snarey, J. R. (1985). Cross-cultural universality of social-moral development: A critical review of Kohlbergian research. *Psychological Bulletin, 97*(2), 202.

Snyder, T. D., de Brey, C., & Dillow, S. A. (2016). *Digest of education statistics 2015* (NCES 2016-014). Washington, DC: National Center for Education Statistics.

Soares, P., Alshamali, F., Pereira, J. B., Fernandes, V., Silva, N. M., Afonso, C., . . . Pereira, L. (2011). The expansion of mtDNA haplogroup L3 within and out of Africa. *Molecular Biology and Evolution*, 245.

Soares, R. R. (2007). On the determinants of mortality reductions in the developing world. *Population and Development Review, 33*(2), 247–287.

Sobal, J., & Hanson, K. L. (2011). Marital status, marital history, body weight, and obesity. *Marriage & Family Review, 47*(7), 474–504.

Sobal, J., & Stunkard, A. J. (1989). Socioeconomic status and obesity: A review of the literature. *Psychological Bulletin, 105*(2), 260–275.

Sobeck J., Chapleski E., & Fisher, C. (2003) Conducting research with American Indians. *Journal of Ethnic and Cultural Diversity in Social Work, 12*(1), 69–84.

Soeters, J. (1997). Culture and conflict: An application of Hofstede's theory to the conflict in the former Yugoslavia. *Peace and Conflict: Journal of Peace Psychology*, *2*(3), 233–244.

Soeters, J. L., Poponete, C.-R., & Page, J. T., Jr. (2006). Culture's consequences in the military. In T. W. Britt, A. B. Adler, & C. A. Castro (Eds.), *Military life: The psychology of serving in peace and combat* (pp. 13–34). Westport, CT: Praeger.

Son, G., & Kim, H. (2006). Culturally familiar environment among Korean elders. *Research and Theory for Nursing Practice*, *20*(2), 159–172.

Sorokowski, P., Kościński, K., & Sorokowska, A. (2013). Is beauty in the eye of the beholder but ugliness culturally universal? Facial preferences of Polish and Yali (Papua) people. *Evolutionary Psychology*, *11*(4), 907–925.

Sousa, M. D. R., Neto, F., & Mullet, F. N. E. (2005). Can music change ethnic attitudes among children? *Psychology of Music*, *33*(3), 304–316.

Southard, E. E. (1912). On the somatic sources of somatic delusions. *The Journal of Abnormal Psychology*, *7*(5), 326–339. doi:10.1037/h0070895

Soysal, Y. N. (1994). *Limits of citizenship: Migrants and postnational membership in Europe*. Chicago: University of Chicago Press.

Spear, S., & Bowen, H. K. (1999). Decoding the DNA of the Toyota production system. *Harvard Business Review*, *77*(5), 96–106.

Spearman, C. (1904). "General intelligence," objectively determined and measured. *The American Journal of Psychology*, *15*(2), 201–292.

Spinner, J. (1994). *The boundaries of citizenship: Race, ethnicity, and nationality in the liberal state*. Baltimore, MD: Johns Hopkins University Press.

Spitz, R. A., & Wolf, K. M. (1946). Anaclitic depression: an inquiry into the genesis of psychiatric conditions in early childhood, II. *The Psychoanalytic Study of the Child*, *2*(1), 313–342.

Spivey, M. J., & Marian, V. (1999). Cross talk between native and second languages: Partial activation of an irrelevant lexicon. *Psychological Science*, *10*(3), 281–284.

St. John de Crèvecoeur, J. H. (1782). *Letters from an American farmer; by J. Hector St. John Crevecoeur, reprinted from the original ed., with a prefatory note by W. P. Trent and an introduction by Ludwig Lewisohn*. New York: Fox, Duffield. Retrieved from http://xroads.virginia.edu/~hyper/CREV/letter03.html

Stack, S. (2003). Media coverage as a risk factor in suicide. *Journal of Epidemiology and Community Health*, *57*(4), 238–240.

Staes, N., Bradley, B., Hopkins, W., & Sherwood, C. (2018). Genetic signatures of socio-communicative abilities in primates. *Current Opinion in Behavioral Sciences*, *21*, 33–38.

Stankov, L. (2010). Unforgiving Confucian culture: A breeding ground for high academic achievement, test anxiety and self-doubt? *Learning and Individual Differences*, *20*(6), 555–563.

Stanton, W. R., & Silva, P. A. (1992). A longitudinal study of the influence of parents and friends on children's initiation of smoking. *Journal of Applied Developmental Psychology*, *13*, 423–434.

Stark, A., Fam, K., Waller, D., & Tian, Z. (2005). Chinese negotiation practice: A perspective from New Zealand exporters. *Cross Cultural Management*, *12*(3), 85–102.

Statistics NZ. (2012). New Zealand's prison population. *New Zealand Official Yearbook, 2012*. Retrieved from http://www.stats.govt.nz/browse_for_stats/snapshots-of-nz/yearbook/society/crime/corrections.aspx

Stearns, P. N. (2002). *Fat history: Bodies and beauty in the modern west*. New York: NYU Press.

Steel, Z., Marnane, C., Iranpour, C., Chey, T., Jackson, J. W., Patel, V., & Silove, D. (2014). The global prevalence of common mental disorders: A systematic review and metaanalysis 1980–2013. *International Journal of Epidemiology 43*, 476–493.

Steele, C. J., Bailey, J. A., Zatorre, R. J., & Penhune, V. B. (2013). Early musical training and white-matter plasticity in the corpus callosum: Evidence for a sensitive period. *The Journal of Neuroscience*, *33*(3), 1282–1290.

Stein, B. D., Jaycox, L. H., Kataoka, S., Rhodes, H. J., & Vestal, K. D. (2003). Prevalence of child and adolescent exposure to community violence. *Clinical Child and Family Psychology Review*, *6*(4), 247–264.

Steinberg, H. (2015). Emil Kraepelin's ideas on transcultural psychiatry. *Australasian Psychiatry*, *23*(5), 531–535.

Steinthal, H., & Lazarus, M. (1860). Einleitende Gedanken über Völkerpsychologie als Einladung zu einer Zeitschrift für Völkerpsychologie und Sprachwissenschaft. Olms.

Stephen, M., & Suryani, L. K. (2000). Shamanism, psychosis and autonomous imagination. *Culture, Medicine and Psychiatry*, *24*(1), 5–40. doi:10.1023/A:1005528028869

Stephens, D. P., & Few, A. L. (2007). Hip hop honey or video ho: African American preadolescents' understanding of female sexual scripts in hip hop culture. *Sexuality & Culture*, *11*(4), 48–69.

Stern, F. (2004). Bridging two cultures. *The World & I, 19*(3), 96–102.

Sternberg, R. J. (1986). A triangular theory of love. *Psychological Review, 93*(2), 119–135.

Sternberg, R. J. (2004). Culture and intelligence. *American Psychologist, 59*(5), 325.

Sternberg, R. J., & Soriano, L. J. (1984). Styles of conflict resolution. *Journal of Personality and Social Psychology, 47*(1), 115–126.

Stewart, S. M., Bond, M. H., Deeds, O., & Chung, S. F. (1999). Intergenerational patterns of values and autonomy expectations in cultures of relatedness and separateness. *Journal of Cross-Cultural Psychology, 30*(5), 575–593.

Stiles, D. (1997). Four successful indigenous language programs. In J. Reyhner (Ed.), *Teaching indigenous languages*. Flagstaff, AZ: Northern Arizona University. Retrieved from http://jan.ucc.nau.edu/~jar/TIL_Contents.html

Stone, V. E. (2006). Theory of mind and the evolution of social intelligence. In J. T. Cacioppo, P. S. Visser, & C. L. Pickett (Eds.), *Social neuroscience: People thinking about thinking people* (pp. 103–129). Cambridge, MA: MIT Press.

Stout, D., Toth, N., Schick, K., & Chaminade, T. (2008). Neural correlates of early stone age toolmaking: Technology, language and cognition in human evolution. *Philosophical Transactions of the Royal Society of London B: Biological Sciences, 363*(1499), 1939–1949.

Strous, R. D., Opler, A. A., & Opler, L. A. (2016). Reflections on "Emil Kraepelin: Icon and reality". *The American Journal of Psychiatry, 173*(3), 300–301.

Stuart, J., & Ward, C. (2015). The ecology of acculturation. *Counselling Across Cultures, 7*, 383–405.

Stuart, J., Ward, C., Jose, P., & Narayanan, P. (2010). Working with and for communities: A collaborative study of harmony and conflict in well-functioning, acculturating families. *International Journal of Intercultural Relations, 34*, 114–126.

Stuart, J., Ward, C., & Robinson, L. (2016). The influence of family climate on stress and adaptation for Muslim immigrant young adults in two Western countries. *International Perspectives in Psychology: Research, Practice, Consultation, 5*(1), 1–17.

Sue, D. W. (2001). Multidimensional facets of cultural competence. *The Counseling Psychologist, 29*, 790–821.

Sue, D. W., & Sue, D. (2008). *Counseling the culturally diverse* (6th ed.). Hoboken, NJ: John Wiley & Sons.

Suen, H. K., & Yu, L. (2006). Chronic consequences of high-stakes testing? Lessons from the Chinese Civil Service Exam. *Comparative Education Review, 50*(1), 46–55.

Sugiyama, M. S. (2017). Oral storytelling as evidence of pedagogy in forager societies. *Frontiers in Psychology, 8*, Article ID 471.

Sumner, W. S. (1906). *Folkways: A study of the sociological importance of usages, manners, customs, mores, and morals*. Boston: Ginn & Co.

Sundararajan, L. (2009). The painted dragons in affective science: Can the Chinese notion of ganlei add a transformative detail? *Journal of Theoretical and Philosophical Psychology, 29*(2), 114.

Sundararajan, L. (2016). *Rebuttal to Jahoda on IP*. Retrieved from http://indigenouspsych.org/Discussion/forum/PDF/Rebuttal%20to%20Jahoda%20on%20IP.pdf

Super, C. M. (1981). Behavioral development in infancy. *Handbook of Cross-Cultural Human Development*, 181–270.

Super, C. M., & Harkness, S. (1986). The developmental niche: A conceptualization at the interface of child and culture. *International Journal of Behavioral Development, 9*(4), 545–569.

Super, C. M., & Harkness, S. (1991). The development of affect in infancy and early childhood. *Becoming a Person*, 56–73.

Suprakash, C., Kumar, S., Kumar, S., & Kiran, C. (2013). Dissociative trance disorder: A clinical enigma. *Unique Journal of Medical and Dental Sciences, 1*(1), 12–22.

Suprapto, N., Liu, W-L., & Ku, C-H. (2017). The implementation of multiple intelligence in (science) classroom: From empirical into critical. *Pedagogika/Pedagogy 126*(2), 214–227.

Surowiecki, J. (2004). *The wisdom of crowds*. Garden City: Doubleday.

Sussman, N. M. (2010). *Return migration and identity: A global phenomenon, a Hong Kong case* (Vol. 1). Hong Kong: Hong Kong University Press.

Suzuki, T. N. (2014). Communication about predator type by a bird using discrete, graded and combinatorial variation in alarm calls. *Animal Behaviour, 87*, 59–65. doi:10.1016/j.anbehav.2013.10.009

Swartz, L. (1985). Anorexia nervosa as a culture-bound syndrome. *Social Science & Medicine, 20*(7), 725–730.

Swedish army to jobless immigrants: We want you. (2012). *The Local SE*. Retrieved from https://www.thelocal.se/20120530/41148

Szucs, D., & Ioannidis, J. P. A. (2017). When null hypothesis significance testing is unsuitable for research: A reassessment. *Frontiers in Human Neuroscience, 11*. doi:10.3389/fnhum.2017.00390

Tadmor, C. T., Tetlock, P. E., & Peng, K. (2009). Acculturation strategies and integrative complexity: The cognitive implications of biculturalism. *Journal of Cross-Cultural Psychology, 40*(1), 105–139.

Tafoya, T. (2003). Embracing the shadow: Dancing with Dashkayah. In A. Cox & D. H. Albert (Eds.), *The healing heart: Storytelling to build strong communities* (pp. 89–92). Gabriola Island, BC: New Society.

Tafreshi, D., Slaney, K. L., & Neufeld, S. D. (2016). Quantification in psychology: Critical analysis of an unreflective practice. *Journal of Theoretical and Philosophical Psychology, 36*(4), 233–249.

Tajfel, H. E. (1978). *Differentiation between social groups: Studies in the social psychology of intergroup relations*. New York, NY: Academic Press.

Tajfel, H. (1981). *Human groups and social categories*. Cambridge: Cambridge University Press.

Tajfel, H. (2010). Social categorization, social identity and social comparison. Rediscovering social identity. In T. Postmes & N. Branscombe (Eds.), *Rediscovering social identity: Key readings in social psychology* (pp. 119–128). New York, NY: Psychology Press.

Tajfel, H., & Turner, J. C. (1979). An integrative theory of intergroup conflict. *The Social Psychology of Intergroup Relations*, 33–47.

Tajfel, H., & Turner, J. C. (1986). The social identity theory of intergroup behaviour. In S. Worchel & W. G. Austin (Eds.), *Psychology of intergroup relations*. Chicago: Nelson Hall.

Takata, T. (2003). Self-enhancement and self-criticism in Japanese culture. An experimental analysis. *Journal of Cross-Cultural Psychology, 34*(5), 542–551.

Tamariz, M., & Kirby, S. (2014). Culture: Copying, compression and conventionality. In E. Cartmill, S. Roberts, H. Lyn, & H. Cornish (Eds.), *Proceedings of the 10th international conference on the evolution of language*. Singapore: World Scientific.

Tan, J., & Hare, B. (2013). Bonobos share with strangers. *PLOS One, 8*(1), e51922.

Tanaka, H. (2000). Turn projection in Japanese talk-in-interaction. *Research on Language and Social Interaction, 33*(1), 1–38.

Taonui, R. (2012). The meaning of canoe traditions. In *Te Ara: The encyclopedia of New Zealand*. Retrieved from http://www.TeAra.govt.nz/en/photograph/2294/te-tumu-herenga-waka-marae-victoria-university-of-wellington

Tappan, M. B. B. (1997). Language, culture, and moral development: A Vygotskian perspective. *Developmental Review, 17*(1), 78–100.

Tasca, C., Rapetti, M., Carta, M. G., & Fadda, B. (2012). Women and hysteria in the history of mental health. *Clinical Practice and Epidemiology in Mental Health, 8*, 110–119.

Taylor, R. J., Chatters, L. M., Woodward, A. T., & Brown, E. (2013). Racial and ethnic differences in extended family, friendship, fictive kin, and congregational informal support networks. *Family Relations: An Interdisciplinary Journal of Applied Family Studies, 62*(4), 609–624.

Terman, L. M. (1921). Mental growth and the IQ. *Journal of Educational Psychology, 12*(7), 401–407. doi:10.1037/h0069457

Terman, L. M., & Childs, H. G. (1912). A tentative revision and extension of the Binet-Simon measuring scale of intelligence. *Journal of Educational Psychology, 3*(2), 61–74. doi:10.1037/h0075624

Thai, H. C. (2002). Formation of ethnic identity among second-generation Vietnamese Americans. In P. G. Min (Ed.), *The second generation: Ethnic identity among Asian Americans* (pp. 53–83). New York, NY: Rowman & Littlefield.

Tharp, R. (1982). The effective instruction of comprehension: Results and description of the Kamehameha Early Education Program. *Reading Research Quarterly, 17*(4), 503–527.

Tharp, T. G., Jordan, C., Speidel, G. E., Au, K. H-P., Klein, T. W., Calkins, R. P., . . . Gallimore, R. (2007). Education and native Hawaiian children: Revisiting KEEP. *Hūlili, 4*(1).

Thelen, M. H., Miller, D. J., Fehrenbach, P. A., Frautschi, N. M., & Fishbein, M. D. (1980). Imitation during play as a means of social influence. *Child Development, 51*, 918–920.

Thoits, P. A. (2010). Stress and health major findings and policy implications. *Journal of Health and Social Behavior, 51*(1), S41–S53.

Thomas, E. R., & Carter, P. M. (2006). Prosodic rhythm and African American English. *English World-Wide, 27*(3), 331–355.

Thomas, K. (1991). Introduction. In J. N. Bremmer & H. Roodenburg (Eds.), *A cultural history of gesture* (pp. 1–14). Ithaca, NY: Cornell University Press.

Thomas, K. W., & Kilmann, R. H. (1978). Comparison of four instruments measuring conflict behavior. *Psychological Reports, 42*(3), 1139–1145.

Thomas, S. B., & Quinn, S. C. (1991). The Tuskegee Syphilis Study, 1932 to 1972: Implications for HIV education and AIDS risk education programs in the black community. *American Journal of Public Health, 81*(11), 1498–1505.

Thornhill, R., & Gangestad, S. W. (1993). Human facial beauty: Averageness, symmetry and parasite resistance. *Human Nature, 4*, 237–269.

Thornton, A., & McAuliffe, K. (2006). Teaching in wild meerkats. *Science, 313*(5784), 227–229.

Tietjen, A. M., & Walker, L. J. (1985). Moral reasoning and leadership among men in a Papua New Guinea society. *Developmental Psychology, 21*(6), 982.

Times Higher Education. (2018). *World university rankings 2018 by subject: Psychology*. Retrieved from https://www.timeshighereducation.com/world-university-rankings/2018/subject-ranking/psychology#!/page/1/length/25/sort_by/rank/sort_order/asc/cols/stats

Tomasello, M. (1990). Cultural transmission in the tool use and communicatory signaling of chimpanzees? In S. T. Parker & K. R. Gibson (Eds.), *"Language" and intelligence in monkeys and apes: Comparative developmental perspectives* (pp. 274–311). New York, NY: Cambridge University Press.

Tomasello, M. (1999). The human adaptation for culture. *Annual Review of Anthropology, 28*(1), 509–529.

Tomasello, M., Davis-Dasilva, M., Cama, K. L., & Bard, K. (1987). Observational learning of tool-use by young chimpanzees. *Human Evolution, 2*(2), 175–183.

Tomasello, M., & Rakoczy, H. (2003). What makes human cognition unique? From individual to shared to collective

intentionality. *Mind & Language, 18*(2), 121–147. doi:10.1111/1468-0017.00217

Tönnies, F. (1957). Gemeinschaft und gesellschaft. *Theories of Society, 1*.

Tooby, J., & Cosmides, L. (1992). The psychological foundations of culture. In J. H. Barkow, L. Cosmides, & J. Tooby (Eds.), *The adapted mind: Evolutionary psychology and the generation of culture* (pp. 19–136). New York, NY: Oxford University Press.

Townsend, K. C., & McWhirter, B. T. (2005). Connectedness: A review of the literature with implications for counseling, assessment, and research. *Journal of Counseling & Development, 83*(2), 191–201.

Trapnell, P. D., & Wiggins, J. S. (1990). Extension of the interpersonal adjective scales to include the Big Five dimensions of personality. *Journal of Personality and Social Psychology, 59*(4), 781–790.

Travis, R., Jr. (2013). Rap music and the empowerment of today's youth: Evidence in everyday music listening, music therapy, and commercial rap music. *Child & Adolescent Social Work Journal, 30*(2), 139–167.

Trehub, S. E. (2009). Music lessons from infants. In S. Hallam, I. Cross, & M. Thaut (Eds.), *The Oxford handbook of music psychology* (pp. 229–234). Oxford: Oxford University Press.

Trevathan, W. R. (1987). *Foundations of human behavior. Human birth: An evolutionary perspective*. Hawthorne, NY: Aldine de Gruyter.

Triandis, H. C. (1967). Welcome message. *Cross-Cultural Social Psychology Newsletter, 1*.

Triandis, H. C. (1972). *The analysis of culture*. New York, NY: Wiley.

Triandis, H. C. (1980). Introduction to handbook of cross-cultural psychology. In H. C. Triandis et al. (Eds.), *Handbook of cross-cultural psychology* (pp. 1–14). New York, NY: Wiley.

Triandis, H. C. (1989). The self and social behavior in differing cultural contexts. *Psychological Review, 96*(3), 506–520.

Triandis, H. C. (1994). Cross-cultural industrial and organizational psychology. In H. C. Triandis, M. D. Dunnette, & L. M. Hough (Eds.), *Handbook of industrial and organizational psychology* (Vol. 4, 2nd ed., pp. 103–172). Palo Alto, CA: Consulting Psychologists Press.

Triandis, H. C., Bontempo, R., Villareal, M. J., Asai, M., & Lucca, N. (1988). Individualism and collectivism: Cross-cultural perspectives on self-ingroup relationships. *Journal of Personality and Social Psychology, 54*(2), 323–338.

Trinkaus, E. (1982). Artificial cranial deformation in the Shanidar 1 and 5 Neandertals. *Current Anthropology, 23*(2), 198–199.

Trommsdorff, G. (2012). Development of "agentic" regulation in cultural context: The role of self and world views. *Child Development Perspectives, 6*(1), 19–26. doi:10.1111/j.1750-8606.2011.00224.x

Trope, Y. (1980). Self-assessment, self-enhancement, and task preference. *Journal of Experimental Social Psychology, 16*(2), 116–129.

Trudeau welcomes Syrian refugees but Canada may not reach target. (2015, December 23). *The Guardian*. Retrieved from http://www.theguardian.com/world/2015/dec/23/justin-trudeau-welcome-syrian-refugees-christmas-address

Trujillo, L. T., Jankowitsch, J. M., & Langlois, J. H. (2014). Beauty is in the ease of the beholding: A neurophysiological test of the averageness theory of facial attractiveness. *Cognitive, Affective & Behavioral Neuroscience, 14*(3), 1061–1076.

Tsai, J. L., Ying, Y.-W., & Lee, P. A. (2001). Cultural predictors of self-esteem: A study of Chinese American female and male young adults [Special Issue]. *Cultural Diversity and Ethnic Minority Psychology, 7*(3), 284–297.

Tsai, W., Lau, A. S., Niles, A. N., Coello, J., Lieberman, M. D., Ko, A. C., . . . Stanton, A. L. (2015). Ethnicity moderates the outcomes of self-enhancement and self-improvement themes in expressive writing. *Cultural Diversity and Ethnic Minority Psychology, 21*(4), 584–592.

Tsethlikai, M., & Rogoff, B. (2013). Involvement in traditional cultural practices and American Indian children's incidental recall of a folktale. *Developmental Psychology, 49*(3), 568–578.

Turino, T. (1999). Signs of imagination, identity and experience: A Peircian semiotic theory for music. *Ethnomusicology, 43*(2), 221–255.

Turk, I., Dirjec, J., & Kavur, B. (1995). *The oldest musical instrument in Europe discovered in Slovenia.* Retrieved from http://www.zrc-sazu.si/www/iza/pis cal.html

Turkle, S. (1994). Constructions and reconstructions of self in virtual reality: Playing in the MUDs. *Mind, Culture, and Activity, 1*(3), 158–167.

Turkle, S. (1997). Constructions and reconstructions of self in virtual reality: Playing in the MUDs. In S. Kiesler (Ed.), *Culture of the internet* (pp. 143–155). Mahwah, NJ: Lawrence Erlbaum Associates.

Turner, J. (1982). Towards a cognitive redefinition of the social group. In H. Tajfel (Ed.), *Social identity and intergroup relations* (pp. 15–40). Cambridge, UK: Cambridge University Press.

Turner, J. (1999). Some current issues in research on social identity and self-categorization theories. In N. Ellemers, R. Spears, & B. Doosje (Eds.), *Social identity: Context, commitment, content* (pp. 6–34). Oxford, UK: Blackwell Science.

Turner, R. J., & Avison, W. R. (2003). Status variations in stress exposure: Implications for the interpretation of research on race, socioeconomic status, and gender. *Journal of Health and Social Behavior,* 488–505.

Turner, V. (1967). Betwixt and between: Liminal period. In V. Turner, *The forest of symbols: Aspects of Ndembu ritual* (pp. 93–111). Ithaca, NY: Cornell University Press.

Turner, V. (1982a). *Celebration, studies in festivity and ritual.* Washington, DC: Smithsonian Institution Press.

Turner, V. (1982b). *From ritual to theatre: The human seriousness of play.* New York, NY: Performing Arts Journal.

Turner, V. (1986). *The anthropology of performance.* New York, NY: PAJ.

Tweney, D. R., Upal, M. A., Slone, D. J., & Gonce, L. (2006). Role of context in the recall of counterintuitive concepts. *Journal of Cognition and Culture, 6*(3–4), 521–547.

Twenge, J. M., & Campbell, W. K. (2001). Age and birth cohort differences in self-esteem: A cross-temporal meta-analysis. *Personality and Social Psychology Review, 5,* 321–344.

Twenge, J. M., & Campbell, W. K. (2002). Self-esteem and socioeconomic status: A meta-analytic review. *Personality and Social Psychology Review, 6*(1), 59–71.

Tyack, P. 1981. Interactions between singing Hawaiian humpback whales and conspecifics nearby. *Behavioral Ecology and Sociobiology, 8*(2), 105–116.

Tylor, E. B. (1861). Anahuac or, Mexico and the Mexicans, ancient and modern. London: Longman, Green, Longman and Roberts. Retrieved from http://www.gutenberg.org/ebooks/13115

Uchida, Y., & Kitayama, S. (2009). Happiness and unhappiness in east and west: Themes and variations. *Emotion, 9*(4), 441–456.

Uchida, Y., Townsend, S. S., Rose Markus, H., & Bergsieker, H. B. (2009). Emotions as within or between people? Cultural variation in lay theories of emotion expression and inference. *Personality and Social Psychology Bulletin, 35*(11), 1427–1439.

Ueda, Y., & Komiya, A. (2012). Cultural adaptation of visual attention: Calibration of the oculomotor control system in accordance with cultural scenes. *PLOS One, 7*(11), e50282. doi:10.1371/journal.pone.0050282

Umaña-Taylor, A. J. (2004). Ethnic identity and self-esteem: Examining the role of social context. *Journal of Adolescence, 27,* 139–146.

Umaña-Taylor, A. J., Diversi, M., & Fine, M. A. (2002). Ethnic identity and self-esteem of Latino adolescents: Distinctions among the Latino populations. *Journal of Adolescent Research, 17*(3), 303–327.

Umberson, D., Williams, K., Powers, D. A., Liu, H., & Needham, B. (2006).

You make me sick: Marital quality and health over the life course. *Journal of Health and Social Behavior* 47, 1–16.

UN Economic and Social Council. (2017). *World crime trends and emerging issues and responses in the field of crime prevention and criminal justice.* Retrieved from http://www.unodc .org/documents/data-and-analysis/ statistics/crime/ccpj/World_crime_ trends_emerging_issues_E.pdf

Underhill, P. A., Shen, P., Lin, A. A., Jin, L., Passarino, G., Yang, W. H., ... Oefner, P. J. (2000). Y-chromosome sequence variation and the history of human populations. *Nature Genetics*, 26(3), 358–361.

UNICEF Innocenti Research Centre. (2012). *Measuring child poverty: New league tables of child poverty in the world's rich countries. Innocenti Report Card 10.* Florence, Italy: Author. Retrieved from http://www.unicef-irc.org/publi cations/pdf/rc10_eng.pdf.

United Nations Department of Economic and Social Affairs Population Division (UNDESAPD). (2011). *Population distribution, urbanization, internal migration and development: An international perspective.* Retrieved from http://www.un.org/esa/population/ publications/PopDistribUrbanization/ PopulationDistributionUrbanization.pdf

United Nations High Commissioner for Refugees. (2018). *Report of the United Nations High Commissioner for Refugees.* New York: Author.

Usher, E. L. (2018). Acknowledging the whiteness of motivation research: Seeking cultural relevance. *Educational Psychologist*, 53(2), 131–144.

Utsey, S. O., Chae, M. H., Brown, C. F., & Kelly, D. (2002). Effect of ethnic group membership on ethnic identity, race-related stress and quality of life.

*Cultural Diversity and Ethnic Minority Psychology*, 8(4), 366–377.

Utter, J., Denny, S., Peiris-John, R., Moselen, E., Dyson, B., & Clark, T. (2017). Family meals and adolescent emotional well-being: Findings from a national study. *Journal of Nutrition Education and Behavior*, 49(1), 67–72.

Vaillant, G. E. (2000). Adaptive mental mechanisms: Their role in a positive psychology. *American Psychologist*, 55(1), 89.

Vaioleti, T. (2006). Talanoa research methodology: A developing position on Pacific research. *Waikato Journal of Education*, 12, 21–34.

Valdez, A., & Halley, J. A. (1996). Gender in the culture of Mexican American conjunto music. *Gender and Society*, 10(2), 148–167.

Vale, G. L., Flynn, E. G., & Kendal, R. L. (2012). Cumulative culture and future thinking: Is mental time travel a prerequisite to cumulative cultural evolution? *Learning and Motivation*, 43(4), 220–230.

Valladas, H., Clottes, J., Geneste, J.-M., Garcia, M. A., Arnold, M., Cachier, H., & Tisnérat-Laborde, N. (2001). Evolution of prehistoric cave art. *Nature*, 413(4), 479.

van de Vijver, F. J. R. (2000). Research methods. In D. Matsumoto (Ed.), *Handbook of culture and psychology*. New York, NY: Oxford University Press.

van de Vijver, F. J., & Leung, K. (2000). Methodological issues in psychological research on culture. *Journal of Cross-Cultural Psychology*, 31(1), 33–51.

van Duijl, M. (2014). *Spirits, devils and trauma. Dissociation in south-west Uganda.* Masstricht, NL: Boekenplan.

van Duijl, M., Kleijn, W., & de Jong, J. (2013). Are symptoms of

spirit possessed patients covered by the DSM-IV or DSM-5 criteria for possession trance disorder? A mixed-method explorative study in Uganda. *Social Psychiatry and Psychiatric Epidemiology*, 48(9), 1417–1430.

van Gennep, A. (2004). *The rites of passage.* London: Routledge. (Original work published 1909)

van Hemert, D. A., Poortinga, Y. H., & van de Vijver, F. J. (2007). Emotion and culture: A meta-analysis. *Cognition and Emotion*, 21(5), 913–943.

van Ijzendoorn, M. H., & Kroonenberg, P. M. (1988). Cross-cultural patterns of attachment: A meta-analysis of the strange situation. *Child Development*, 147–156.

van Leeuwen, E. J. C., Cronin, K. A., & Haun, D. B. M. (2014). A group-specific arbitrary tradition in chimpanzees (*Pan troglodytes*). *Animal Cognition*, 17(6), 1421–1425.

van Oudenhoven, J. P., Ward, C., & Masgoret, A.-M. (2006). Patterns of relations between immigrants and host societies. *International Journal of Intercultural Relations*, 30(6), 637–651.

van Schaik, C. (2004). *Among orangutans: Red apes and the rise of human culture.* Cambridge, MA: Belknap Press.

van Tubergen, F. (2006). *Immigrant integration: A cross-national study.* New York: LFB Scholarly.

van Wilgenburg, E., Sulc, R., Shea, K. J., & Tsutsui, N. D. (2010). Deciphering the chemical basis of nestmate recognition. *Journal of Chemical Ecology*, 36(7), 751–758 doi:10.1007/s10886-010-9812-4

van Willigen, J., Chada, N., & McDonald, J. (1999). Culture and aging. *Social Change*, 29(1), 21–31.

Vannoy, D. (2000). Roles in the divorce process and identity strength. *Journal of Divorce & Remarriage, 32*(3–4), 101–118.

Varnum, M. E. W., Grossmann, I., Kitayama, S., & Nisbett, R. E. (2010). The origin of cultural differences in cognition: The social orientation hypothesis. *Current Directions in Psychological Science, 19*(1), 9–13.

Vauclair, C.-M., Fischer, R., Ferreira, M. C., Guerra, V., Hößler, U., Karabati, S., . . . Spieß, E. (2015). What kinds of value motives guide people in their moral attitudes? The role of personal and prescriptive values at the culture level and individual level. *Journal of Cross-Cultural Psychology, 46*(2), 211–228.

Vauclair, C.-M., Hanke, K., Fischer, R., & Fontaine, J. (2011). The structure of human values at the culture level: A meta-analytical replication of Schwartz's value orientations using the Rokeach Value Survey. *Journal of Cross-Cultural Psychology, 42*(2), 186–205.

Velleman, J. D. (2008). Bodies, selves. *American Imago, 65*(3), 405–426.

Venkataramaiah, V., Mallikarjunaiah, M., Chandrasekhar, C. R., Rao, C. V., & Reddy, G. N. (1981). Possession syndrome: An epidemiological study in West Karnataka. *Indian Journal of Psychiatry, 23*(3), 213.

Verma, S., & Saraswati, T. S. (2002). *Adolescence in India: An annotated bibliography*. New Delhi: Rawat.

Vespa, J., Lewis, J. M., & Kreider, R. M. (2013). America's families and living arrangements: 2012. *Current Population Reports*, 20–570.

Vickers Smith, R., Boland, E. M., Young, A. M., Lofwall, M. R., Quiroz,

A., Staton, M., & Havens, J. R. (2018). A qualitative analysis of gabapentin misuse and diversion among people who use drugs in Appalachian Kentucky. *Psychology of Addictive Behaviors, 32*(1), 115–121. doi:10.1037/adb0000337

Vigilant, L., Stoneking, M., Harpending, H., Hawkes, K., & Wilson, A. C. (1991). African populations and the evolution of human mitochondrial DNA. *Science, 253*(5027), 1503–1507.

Vignoles, V. L., Owe, E., Becker, M., Smith, P. B., Easterbrook, M. J., Brown, R., . . . Bond, M. H. (2016). Beyond the "east–west" dichotomy: Global variation in cultural models of selfhood. *Journal of Experimental Psychology: General, 145*(8), 966–1000.

Viladrich, A. (2005). Tango immigrants in New York City: The value of social reciprocities. *Journal of Contemporary Ethnography, 34*(5), 533–559.

Virgil. (2004). *The Aeneid of Virgil*. New York, NY: Bantam Classics.

Vitebsky, P. (2008). Loving and forgetting: Moments of inarticulacy in tribal India. *Journal of the Royal Anthropological Institute, 14*(2), 243–261.

Vivona, J. M. (2000). Parental attachment styles of late adolescents: Qualities of attachment relationships and consequences for adjustment. *Journal of Counseling Psychology. 47*(3), 316–329.

von Frisch, K. (1953). *The dancing bees: An account of the life and senses of the honey bee*. New York, NY: Harcourt, Brace.

Vygotsky, L. S. (1978). *Mind in society: The development of higher psychological processes*. Cambridge, MA: Harvard University Press.

Walker, R. (2004). *Ka whawhai tonu matou: Struggle without end*. Auckland, NZ: Penguin.

Wallen, K. (1989). Mate selection: Economics and affection. *Behavioral and Brain Sciences, 12*, 37–38.

Walsh, J. J. (1912). *Psychotherapy: Including the history of the use of mental influence, directly and indirectly in healing and the principles for the application of energies derived from the mind to the treatment of disease*. New York, NY: D Appleton & Company. doi:10.1037/10544-030

Walsh, R. (2011). The varieties of wisdom: Contemplative, cross-cultural, and integral contributions. *Research in Human Development, 8*(2), 109–127. doi:10.1080/15427609.2011.568866

Walters, R., & Spitzer, J. (2003). Making sense of American popular song. *History Matters: The U.S. Survey Course on the Web*. Retrieved from http://historymatters.gmu.edu/mse/Songs/.

Walton, R. E., & McKersie, R. B. (1965). *A behavioral theory of labor negotiations*. New York, NY: McGraw-Hill.

Wang, D., Laidlaw, K., Power, M. J., & Shen, J. (2010). Older people's belief of filial piety in China: Expectation and non-expectation. *Clinical Gerontologist: The Journal of Aging and Mental Health, 33*(1), 21–38.

Wang, W., & Vallotton, C. (2016). Cultural transmission through infant signs: Objects and actions in U.S. And Taiwan. *Infant Behavior & Development, 44*, 98–109. doi:10.1016/j.infbeh.2016.06.003

Ward, C. (1980). Spirit possession and mental health: A psycho-anthropological perspective. *Human Relations, 33*(3), 149–163.

Ward, C. (2001). The ABC's of acculturation. In D. Matsumoto (Ed.), *The handbook of culture and psychology (pp. 411–416). New York, NY: Oxford University Press.

Ward, C. A., & Beaubrun, M. H. (1980). The psychodynamics of demon possession. *Journal for the Scientific Study of Religion*, 201–207.

Ward, C., Bochner, S., & Furnham, A. (2001). *The psychology of culture shock* (2nd ed.). New York, NY: Routledge.

Ward, C., Fischer, R., Lam, F. S. Z., & Hall, L. (2009). The convergent, discriminant, and incremental validity of scores on a self-report measure of cultural intelligence. *Educational and Psychological Measurement*, *69*(1), 85–105. doi:10.1177/0013164408322001

Ward, C., Fox, S., Wilson, J., Stuart, J., & Kus, L. (2010). Contextual influences on acculturation processes: The roles of family, community and society. *Psychological Studies*, *55*(1), 26–34.

Ward, C., & Geeraert, N. (2016). Advancing acculturation theory and research: The acculturation process in its ecological context. *Current Opinion in Psychology*, *8*, 98–104.

Ward, C., & Kennedy, A. (1994). Acculturation strategies, psychological adjustment, and sociocultural competence during cross-cultural transitions. *International Journal of Intercultural Relations*, *18*(3), 329–343.

Ward, C., & Masgoret, A.-M. (2006). An integrative model of attitudes toward immigrants. *International Journal of Intercultural Relations*, *30*(6), 671–682.

Ward, C., & Masgoret, A.-M. (2007). Immigrant entry into the workforce: A research note from New Zealand. *International Journal of Intercultural Relations*, *31*(4), 525–530.

Ward, C., & Rana-Deuba, A. (1999). Acculturation and adaptation revisited. *Journal of Cross-Cultural Psychology*, *30*(4), 422–442.

Ward, M. S. (2007). Omoshiroi: An appreciative narrative about Quality Circles in the Toyota Production System. *Dissertation Abstracts International Section A: Humanities and Social Sciences*, *68* (5–A), 1734.

Warren, H. C. (1921). *A history of the association psychology*. London: C. Scribner's Sons.

Waseda, M. (2005). Extraordinary circumstances, exceptional practices: Music in Japanese American concentration camps. *Journal of Asian American Studies*, *8*(2), 171–209.

Washington, J., & Thomas-Tate, S. (2009). How research informs cultural-linguistic differences in the classroom: The bi-dialectal African American child. In S. A. Rosenfield & V. W. Berninger (Eds.), *Implementing evidence-based academic interventions in school settings* (pp. 147–163). New York, NY: Oxford University Press.

Wassink, A. B., & Curzan, A. (2004). Addressing ideologies around African American English. *Journal of English Linguistics*, *32*(3), 171–185.

Wassmann, J., & Dasen, P. R. (1994). "Hot" and "Cold": Classification and sorting among the Yupno of Papua New Guinea. *International Journal of Psychology*, *29*(1), 19–38.

Watson, B. (1958). *Ssu-ma Ch'ien: Grand historian of China*. New York, NY: Columbia University Press.

Watson, J. B. (1913). Psychology as the behaviorist views it. *Psychological Review*, *20*(2), 158.

Watson, J. B. (1924/1925). *Behaviorism*. New York, NY: People's Institute.

Waugh, E., & Mackenzie, L. (2011). Ageing well from an urban Indigenous Australian perspective. *Australian Occupational Therapy Journal*, *58*(1), 25–33.

Wechsler, D. (1944). The nature of intelligence. In D. Wechsler (Ed.), *The measurement of adult intelligence* (3rd ed., pp. 3–12). Baltimore, MD: Williams & Wilkins.

Wegman, M. E. (2001). Infant mortality in the 20th century, dramatic but uneven progress. *Journal of Nutrition*, *131*(2), 401S–408S.

Weisner, T. S., Gallimore, R., Bacon, M. Barry, H., Bell, C., Novaes, S., . . . Ritchie, P. (1977). My brother's keeper: Child and sibling caretaking. *Current Anthropology*, *18*(2), 169–190.

Weiss, A., King, J. E., Inoue-Murayama, M., Matsuzawa, T., & Oswald, A. J. (2012). Evidence for a midlife crisis in great apes consistent with the U-shape in human well-being. *Proceedings of the National Academy of Sciences of the United States of America*, *109*(49), 19949–19952.

Welles-Nyström, B. (2005). Co-sleeping as a window into Swedish culture: Considerations of gender and health. *Scandinavian Journal of Caring Sciences*, *19*(4), 354–360.

Welsh, T. (2006). Do neonates display innate self-awareness? Why neonatal imitation fails to provide sufficient grounds for innate self-and other-awareness. *Philosophical Psychology*, *19*(2), 221–238.

Wendt, D. C., & Gone, J. P. (2012). Rethinking cultural competence: Insights from indigenous community treatment settings. *Transcultural Psychiatry*, 49(2), 206–222.

Werker, J. F., & Desjardins, R. N. (1995). Listening to speech in the 1st year of life: Experiential influences on phoneme perception. *Current Directions in Psychological Science*, 4(3), 76–81.

West, B. A. (2000). Segments of self and other: The Magyar Hungarian case. *National Identities*, 2(1), 49–64.

West, T. V., Popp, D., & Kenny, D. A. (2008). A guide for the estimation of gender and sexual orientation effects in dyadic data: An actor-partner interdependence model approach. *Personality and Social Psychology Bulletin*, 34(3), 321–336.

Westermeyer, J., Vang, T. F., & Neider, J. (1984). Symptom change over time among Hmong refugees: Psychiatric patients versus nonpatients. *Psychopathology* 17, 168–177.

Westermeyer, P. (1998). *Te Deum: The church and music: A textbook, a reference, a history, an essay*. Minneapolis, MN: Fortress Press.

Western, B., & Pettit, B. (2010). Incarceration and social inequality. *Daedalus*, 8–19.

Wethington, E., Kessler, R. C., & Pixley, J. E. (2004). Turning points in adulthood. In O. G. Brim, C. D. Ryff, & R. C. Kessler (Eds.), *How healthy are we? A national study of well-being at midlife* (pp. 586–613). Chicago: University of Chicago Press.

Wheeler, L., Reis, H. T., & Bond, M. H. (1989). Collectivism-individualism in everyday social life: The middle kingdom and the melting pot. *Journal of Personality and Social Psychology*, 57(1), 79–86.

White, J. (2001). *The ancient history of the Māori* (Vols. 1–13). Retrieved from http://www.nzetc.org/tm/scholarly/tei-corpus-WhiAnci.html

White, L. (1985). Is there a "logical problem" of second language acquisition? *TESL Canada Journal/Revue TESL du Canada*, 2(2).

White, W. (1916). *Mechanisms of character formation*. New York: The MacMillan Co.

Whiten, A. (2005). The second inheritance system of chimpanzees and humans. *Nature*, 437(7055), 52–55. doi:10.1038/nature04023

Whiten, A., & van de Waal, E. (2016). Social learning, culture and the "socio-cultural brain" of human and non-human primates. *Neuroscience & Biobehavioral Reviews*. doi:10.1016/j.neubiorev.2016.12.018

Whiten, A., & van Schaik, C. P. (2007). The evolution of animal "cultures" and social intelligence. *Philosophical Transactions of the Royal Society of London B: Biological Sciences*, 362(1480), 603–620.

Whorf, B. L. (1956). *Language, thought, and reality: Selected writings*. Cambridge, MA: MIT Press.

Widdowson, F., & Howard, A. (2013). Introduction. In F. Widdowson & A. Howard (Eds.), *Approaches to aboriginal education in Canada: Searching for solutions* (pp. xi–xxix). Calgary, Alberta: Brush Education.

Wierzbicka, A. (2009). Overcoming Anglocentrism in emotion research. *Emotion Review*, 1(1), 21–23.

Williams, K. (2003). Has the future of marriage arrived? A contemporary examination of gender, marriage, and psychological well-being. *Journal of Health and Social Behavior*, 44, 470–487.

Willott, S., & Lyons, A. C. (2012). Consuming male identities: Masculinities, gender relations and alcohol consumption in Aotearoa New Zealand. *Journal of Community & Applied Social Psychology*, 22(4), 330–345.

Wilson, D. S., & Sober, E. (1994). Reintroducing group selection to the human behavioral sciences. *Behavioral and Brain Sciences*, 17(4), 585–608.

Wilson, K. (2003). Therapeutic landscapes and First Nations peoples: An exploration of culture, health and place. *Health & Place*, 9(2), 83–93.

Wilton, J. (2005). Identity, racism, and multiculturalism : Chinese-Australian responses. In R. Benmayor & A. Skotnes (Eds.), *Migration & identity* (pp. 85–100). New Brunswick, NJ: Transaction.

Witkin, H. A., & Asch, S. E. (1948). Studies in space orientation. III. Perception of the upright in the absence of a visual field. *Journal of Experimental Psychology*, 38(5), 603.

Witkin, H. A., & Berry, J. W. (1975). Psychological differentiation in cross-cultural perspective. *ETS Research Bulletin Series*, 1975(1), 1–100.

Witkin, H. A., Moore, C. A., Goodenough, D. R., & Cox, P. W. (1977). Field-dependent and field-independent cognitive styles and their educational implications. *Review of Educational Research*, 47(1), 1–64.

Wlodarski, R., & Dunbar, R. I. M. (2014). The effects of romantic love on mentalizing abilities. *Review of General Psychology*, 18(4), 313–321.

Wolf, N. (2013). *The beauty myth: How images of beauty are used against women*. New York: Random House.

Wong, L. P., Awang, H., & Jani, R. (2012). Midlife crisis perceptions, experiences, help-seeking, and needs among multi-ethnic Malaysian women. *Women & Health*, *52*(8), 804–819.

Wood, M. (2017). Cultural appropriation and the plains Indian headdress. *Auctus: The Journal of Undergraduate Research and Creative Scholarship*. Retrieved from https://scholars compass.vcu.edu/cgi/viewcontent .cgi?article=1042&context=auctus

Woodworth, R. S. (1917). Some criticisms of the Freudian psychology. *The Journal of Abnormal Psychology*, *12*(3), 174–194.

Woodworth, R. S. (1921). Native and acquired traits. In R. S. Woodworth (Ed.), *Psychology: A study of mental life* (pp. 89–104). New York, NY: Henry Holt.

Woollett, K., Glensman, J., & Maguire, E. A. (2008). Non-spatial expertise and hippocampal gray matter in humans. *Hippocampus*, *18*(10), 981–984. doi:10.1002/hipo.20465

World Bank. (2013). *Mortality rate, infant (per 1,000 live births)*. Retrieved from http://data.world bank.org/indicator/SP.DYN.IMRT .IN?order=wbapi_data_value_1998%20 wbapi_data_value%20wbapi_data_ value-first&sort=asc

World Bank. (2018). *Population ages 65 and above (% of total)*. Retrieved from https://data.worldbank.org/indicator/ SP.POP.65UP.TO.ZS

World Bank Group. (2015). *Life expectancy at birth, total (years)*. Retrieved from http://data.worldbank.org/indi cator/SP.DYN.LE00.IN

World Health Organization. (2002). *Traditional medicine: Growing needs and potential* (No. WHO/EDM/2002.4). Geneva: Author.

World Health Organization. (2004). *Gender in mental health research*. Geneva: Author.

World Health Organization. (2006). *History of the development of the ICD*. Geneva: Author.

Wright, A. C. (2017). Access to justice in indigenous communities: An intercultural strategy to improve access to justice. *Canadian Research Institute for Law and the Family*. http://dx.doi .org/10.11575/PRISM/32752

Wright, D. (2011). *Classical Indian love poetry*. Retrieved from http:// deniswright.blogspot.com/2011/07/ classical-indian-love-poetry.html

Wu, S.-h., & Alrabah, S. (2009). A cross-cultural study of Taiwanese and Kuwaiti EFL students' learning styles and multiple intelligences. *Innovations in Education and Teaching International*, *46*(4), 393–403.

Wundt, W. (1900–1920). Völkerpsychologie. Eine Untersuchung der Entwicklungsgesetze von Sprache, Mythos und Sitte (Cultural Psychology. An investigation into developmental laws of language, myth, and conduct), 10 Vols.

Wundt, W. (1913). *Elemente der Völkerpsychologie: Grundlinien einer Psychologischen Entwicklung der Menschheit*. Leipzig: Andrew Kroner Verlag.

Würtz, E. (2006). Intercultural communication on web sites: A cross-cultural analysis of web sites from high-context cultures and low-context cultures. *Journal of Computer-Mediated Communication*, *11*(1), 274–299.

Xu, X., & Whyte, M. K. (1990). Love matches and arranged marriages: A Chinese replication. *Journal of Marriage and the Family*, *52*(3), 709–722.

Yamagishi, T. (2011). Micro-macro dynamics of the cultural construction of reality: A niche construction approach to culture. In M. J. Gelfand, C.-y. Chiu, & Y.-y. Hong (Eds.), *Advances in culture and psychology: Advances in culture and psychology* (Vol. 1, pp. 251–308). New York, NY: Oxford University Press.

Yamagishi, T., & Hashimoto, H. (2016). Social niche construction. *Current Opinion in Psychology*, *8*, 119–124.

Yan, X., Young, A. W., & Andrews, T. J. (2017). Differences in holistic processing do not explain cultural differences in the recognition of facial expression. *The Quarterly Journal of Experimental Psychology*, *70*(12), 2445–2459.

Yang, S. Y. (2001). Conceptions of wisdom among Taiwanese Chinese. *Journal of Cross-Cultural Psychology*, *32*(6), 662–680.

Yen, C.-L. (2013). It is our destiny to die: The effects of mortality salience and culture-priming on fatalism and karma belief. *International Journal of Psychology*, *48*(5), 818–828.

Yeung, W.-F., Chung, K.-F., Ng, K.-Y., Yu, Y.-M., Ziea, E. T.-C., & Ng, B. F.-L. (2014). A systematic review on the efficacy, safety and types of Chinese herbal medicine for depression. *Journal of Psychiatric Research*, *57*, 165–175.

Younes, M. N. (2007). The resilience of families in Israel: Understanding their struggles and appreciating their strengths. *Marriage & Family Review*, *41*(1–2), 101–117.

Young-Leslie, H. (2002). Producing what in the transition? Health messaging and cultural constructions of health in Tonga. *Pacific Health Dialog*, *9*(2), 296–302. Retrieved from https://

heatheryoungleslie.files.wordpress
.com/2007/03/producingwhatintransi
tion-pacifichealthdialog02.pdf

Yousafzai, M. (2013). *I am Malala*.
New York: Back Bay Books.

Yu, E. S. (1985). Studying Vietnamese
refugees: Methodological lessons in
transcultural research. In T. Owan
(Ed.), *Southeast Asian mental health:
Treatment, prevention, services, training and research* (pp. 517–541).
Washington, DC: DHHS.

Yuen, E. K., Herbert, J. D., Forman,
E. M., Goetter, E. M., Comer, R., &
Bradley, J.-C. (2013). Treatment of
social anxiety disorder using online
virtual environments in Second Life.
*Behavior Therapy*, *44*(1), 51–61.

Zandbergen, D. L., & Brown, S.
G. (2015). Culture and gender
differences in romantic jealousy.
*Personality and Individual Differences*,
*72*, 122–127.

Zangwill, I. (1908/1909). *The melting-
pot*. Baltimore, MD: The Lord
Baltimore Press. Retrieved from http://
www.gutenberg.org/files/23893/23893-
h/23893-h.htm

Zarkov, D., & Davis, K. (2018).
Ambiguities and dilemmas around
#MeToo: #ForHow Long and
#WhereTo? *European Journal of
Women's Studies*, *25*(1), 3–9.

Zeidler, H., Hermann, E., Haun, D.,
& Tomasello, M. (2016). Taking turns
or not? Children's approach to limited
resource problems in three different
cultures. *Child Development*, *87*(3),
677–688.

Zhang, J., Xiao, X., & Lee, Y. K.
(2004). The early development of
music. Analysis of the Jiahu bone
flutes. *Antiquity*, *78*(302), 769–778.

Zhou, X., Min, S., Sun, J., Kim, S.
J., Ahn, J.-s., Peng, Y., . . . Ryder, A.
G. (2015). Extending a structural

model of somatization to South
Koreans: Cultural values, somatization tendency, and the presentation
of depressive symptoms. *Journal of
Affective Disorders*, *176*, 151–154.

Zilhao, J. (2012). Personal ornaments and symbolism among the
Neanderthals. *Developments in Quater-
nary Sciences*, *16*, 35–49.

Zimbardo, P. G. (1973). On the ethics
of intervention in human psychological research: With special reference
to the Stanford prison experiment.
*Cognition*, *2*, 243–256.

Zimmer, B. (2013). Catfish: How
Manti Te'o's imaginary romance got
its name. *Boston Globe*. Retrieved from
https://www.bostonglobe.com

Zusho, A., & Clayton, K. (2011).
Culturalizing achievement goal theory
and research. *Educational Psychologist*,
*46*(4), 239–260.

# NAME INDEX

Chang, A., 402
Chang, C. L.-h., 314
Chang, L., 214
Chansa-Kabali, T., 255
Chapleski, E., 101
Charlie, J., 69
Chatters, L. M., 203
Chattopadhyay, A., 250
Chaves, J., 229
Chavez, E., 96
Chavous, T. M., 147
Chege, P. M., 412
Chen, C., 285
Chen, E., 274
Chen, F. F., 104
Chen, J. Q., 314
Chen, L. F., 253
Chen, S., 139
Chen, S.-W., 140, 403
Chen, S. X., 309, 311, 326
Chen, Y., 140, 282, 403
Cheng, B.-S., 63, 438
Cheng, C., 140
Cheng, C. Y., 354
Cheng, G. N., 219
Chengappa, R., 100
Chentsova-Dutton, E., 404
Chentsova-Dutton, Y., 402
Cheung, F. M., 91, 107,
   121, 122
Cheung, S. F., 122, 140
Chey, T., 401
Chi, I., 162
Childs, C. P., 67, 164, 173
Childs, H. G., 251
Chilton, P. J., 401
Chin, C. I. H., 179
Chio, J., 140
Chirkov, V., 355
Chiu, C., 353
Chiu, C.-y., 97, 138, 290, 356
Chiu, L. H., 239, 240
Cho, S., 187
Choi, A., 386
Choi, C., 20
Choi, I., 60, 61, 138, 238, 239
Choi, K., 137
Choi, S.-C., 139, 144
Choi, Y., 138

Chomsky, N., 256, 267, 269,
   270, 272
Chou, K. L., 162
Chou, R. J.-A., 184
Chouinard-Thuly, L., 269
Chow, N., 308
Christakopoulou, S., 205, 206
Christenfeld, N., 225
Christopher, H. K., 219
Christopher, J. C., 398
Christy, K., 46
Chu, D., 311
Chua, A., 309
Chua, H. F., 246
Chun, M., 413
Chung, K.-F., 415
Chung, R., 343, 361
Chung, S. F., 166
Church, A. T., 90, 119, 120,
   121, 123
Cilluffo, A., 442
Clancy, C. M., 410
Clark, A., 213, 213 (figure)
Clark, A. E., 55
Clark, R. A., 305
Clark, T., 82
Clayton, K., 306
Clayton, M., 75
Clegg, J. M., 46
Clottes, J., 27
Cochran, P. A. L., 99, 100
Cocks, M., 413
Cocodia, E., 253
Coello, J., 307
Coffman, T., 352, 368
Cohen, A. S., 49
Cohen, D., 308
Cohen, L. J., 424
Colasanti, A., 257
Coleman, M. E., 210
Collado, R., 409
Colmant, S. A., 413
Comer, R., 145
Conboy, B. T., 167
Conway, B. R., 250
Conway, L. G., 6
Cook, D., 99, 100
Cook, R. S., 250
Cooke, F. L., 439

Cooper, J. E., 402
Cooper, J. J., 339, 357
Cooperrider, K., 241, 242
Copen, C. E., 224
Coppens, N. M., 363, 368, 369
Corbett, G., 249
Corona, R., 429
Correa-Chávez, M., 173
Corriveau, K. H., 46
Cortijo, C., 101–102
Cosmides, L., 49
Costa, D. L., 384
Costa, P. T., Jr., 120
Cowling, K., 385, 386
Cox, P. W., 247
Craft, A. J., 145
Craig, D. C., 443
Crandall, C. S., 6
Craven, D. D., 279
Crespo, C., 5
Creswell, J. W., 106
Crethar, H. C., 126, 127
Crimesider Staff, 334
Crocker, J., 349
Cronin, K. A., 40 (figure)
Cross, I., 25, 194
Cross, W., 145
Croucher, S. M., 279, 280
Croudace, T. J., 181
Crowley, D. J., 164
Csibra, G., 52
Csikszentmihalyi, M., 394, 395
Csordas, T., 368
Cumsille, P., 395
Cunningham, J., 398
Cunningham, M. R., 210, 212
Currie, J., 386
Curzan, A., 276
Cushner, K., 350
Cutler, D. M., 384, 386

Dahl, A., 310
Dahl, R. E., 273
Dahourou, G., 121
Dalton, G., 322
Daniels, K., 224
Dannefer, D., 387
D'Antoine, H., 101
Darke, P., 250

Fukui, H., 75
Fukuno, M., 446
Fulghini, A. J., 395
Fuligni, A. J., 147
Fung, H., 287
Fung, H. H., 325
Furman, O., 242–243
Furnham, A., 211, 347, 349, 350, 351
Futrell, R., 250
Fuwamoto, Y., 262

Gabriels, K., 312
Gácsi, M., 16, 24, 267, 268 (figure)
Gaertner, L., 135, 137, 138
Gailliot, M. T., 186
Gaines, R., 256
Gakidou, E., 385, 386
Gallacher, L., 171
Gallay, L. S., 395
Gallimore, R., 136, 171
Gallo, L. C., 363
Gallup, G. G., Jr., 230
Gallup Healthways, 391 (table), 392 (table)
Gallup International Association, 220, 390
Gama, Y. K., 451
Gangestad, S. W., 49, 212
Gangestad, W., 212
Gann, K., 370
Gao, Y., 170
Garber, I., 324
García, C., 67, 323
Garcia, M. A., 27
Garcia-Downing, C., 99, 100
Gardner, H., 252, 253
Garland, A., 13
Garrett, M. T., 179, 184
Garrod, O. G. B., 285
Gartstein, M. A., 119, 172
Garvey, G., 398
Gaunt, K. D., 194, 365, 366
Gaw, A. C., 408
Geary, D. C., 47
Geeraert, N., 355
Geertz, C., 31, 83, 103, 123–124, 132, 157, 416
Geiger, A., 432

Gejman, P. V., 402
Gelfand, M. J., 6, 8, 10, 83, 139, 144, 431, 439, 446
Geneste, J.-M., 27
Gentile, B., 135
Georgas, J., 205, 206
Gerber, E., 164
Gergely, G., 52
Gergen, K. J., 88, 90, 92, 95
Geroldi, D., 217, 218
Gerth, H., 215
Gibbs, A., 410
Gibran, K., 191
Gibson, E., 250
Gibson, K. R., 42
Giedd, J. N., 178, 180
Gignoux, C. R., 11
Gil-da-Costa, R., 24
Giles, H., 279
Gill, S., 395
Gillett, G., 102
Gilroy, W. G., 27
Ginsberg, B., 362
Gintis, H., 48
Glensmen, J., 242
Glick, P., 142
Gliga, T., 167
Glomb, T. M., 210, 288
Goetter, E. M., 145
Gogtay, N., 178, 180
Gold, M. R., 410
Golden-Meadow, S., 278
Goldenweiser, A. A., 400
Goldsmith, D., 168
Goldsmith, H. H., 119
Goldwyn, R., 171
Gonçalves, G., 441
Gonce, L., 56
Gone, J. P., 146, 179, 204, 398, 410, 411
Gonyea, J. G., 182
Gonzales-Bracken, M., 147
Gonzalez, R., 261
Goodall, J., 43
Goodenough, D. R., 247
Goodkind, M., 402
Goodman, J., 368
Goodman, S., 108
Goodman, Z. T., 429, 430

Gordon, R., 12
Goren, C. C., 166
Goren-lnbar, N., 19
Gorn, G. I., 250
Goryakin, Y., 428
Goslin, J., 272, 274
Gotay, C. C., 279
Goto, S. G., 246
Gottlieb, M., 102
Goudjil, S., 164
Goueli, T., 401
Gouge, M., 443
Gould, S. J., 48
Gouveia, V. V., 320
Graburn, N. H. H., 368
Grahame, M., 117
Grama, J., 279
Grammer, K., 212
Grandin, T., 248
Granka, J. M., 11
Graunt, J., 384
Graven, S. N., 164
Graves, T. D., 340
Gray, L. E., 295
Gray, P., 403
Gray-Little, B., 147
Grayshield, L., 179, 184
Green, E. G. T., 345, 348
Green, L. J., 276
Greenberg, J., 186–187
Greene, J. D., 310
Greene, S. J., 222, 223 (table), 226, 226 (table)
Greenfield, P. M., 53, 67, 68 (figure), 90, 91, 92, 94, 110, 164, 166, 168, 171, 172, 173, 175, 176, 179, 323
Greenland, S., 108
Greenstein, D., 178, 180
Greenwald, M. K., 289
Gregory, A., 143
Greve, J., 389
Griesser, M., 270
Grieve, S. M., 402
Grim, J., 102
Grimm, J., 184
Groesbeck, C. J., 380
Gropp, C., 415
Gross, J. J., 281, 286, 286 (figure), 287, 325

Grossmann, I., 185, 238, 289, 402
Group for Child Mortality Estimation, 166
Grouzet, F. M., 305
Grover, R., 99, 100
Gruber, J., 183, 402
Gubernick, D. J., 206
Guerin, B., 369
Guerin, P., 369
Guerra, V. M., 320, 322
Gulerce, A., 92, 95
Guo, A. X., 443
Gupta, P., 145
Gupta, U., 223
Gureje, O., 412
Gurven, M., 121
Gusfield, J. R., 84, 201, 222
Gutmanis, J., 412, 413
Guzeev, M. A., 41
Guzman, J. C., 335, 336

Ha, J. Y., 57
Ha, T., 214
Hadley, S., 193
Hafdahl, A. R., 147
Hagan, C. R., 408
Hahn, J., 27
Haidt, J., 289, 292
Hale, C., 58
Haley, G., 27, 396
Hall, E. T., 278
Hall, G. C. N., 96, 97
Hall, L., 440
Halley, J. A., 366
Halpern, J. Y., 269
Hamer, F. M., 60
Hamilton, J. P., 47
Hamm, J. V., 210
Hammack, P. L., 124
Hammad, A. Z., 75
Hammoud, M., 101
Han, S., 110, 129, 353
Haney, C., 101
Hanke, K., 322, 324, 448, 449, 451
Hanley, J. H., 7
Hannum, J., 58
Hansen, C., 385
Hanson, K. L., 211
Hardaway, C., 395

Hare, B., 19, 49
Hargreave, D., 31, 75, 76, 192, 366
Harinck, F., 324
Harkins, J., 290
Harkness, S., 106, 163, 169, 172, 208–209
Harnish, D., 357, 369
Harpending, H., 11
Harrington, L., 307
Harris, C. R., 225
Harris, W. A., 60, 220, 388
Harrison, R., 145
Hart, G., 382, 389, 395, 396
Harvey, O. J., 87
Haselton, M. G., 49
Hashimoto, H., 124, 132, 137, 138
Hassan, I., 178
Hatala, A., 381
Hatfield, E., 111, 214, 217, 218, 221 (table), 223 (table), 225
Hathaway, S. L., 70
Hatta, S. M., 408
Hatton, T. J., 423
Haun, D., 40 (figure), 323
Hauser, M. D., 267, 269
Havens, J. R., 429
Hawkes, K., 11
Hawkins, J., 60, 220, 388
Hawkley, L. C., 58
Haworth, J., 382, 389, 395, 396
Hayashi, K. M., 178, 180
Hazen, N., 170
He, J., 104
Hegerl, U., 46
Hehman, J. A., 184
Heider, E. R., 249
Heine, S. J., 19, 84, 88, 134, 135, 136, 172, 307, 309, 311, 326
Heitner, E. I., 362
Heller, D., 402
Helm, S., 179
Hemera, R., 31
Henderson, G., 398
Hendrickson, D., 443
Henn, B. M., 11
Henrich, J., 52, 54, 66–67, 88, 134, 135
Henry, E., 434
Henry, P. J., 308

Henshilwood, C., 185
Her, S., 429, 430
Herbert, J. D., 145
Hermann, E., 323
Hernandez, A. E., 275
Hernàndez-Lloreda, M. V., 49
Herrington, L. L., 403
Herrmann, E., 49
Hersch, R. H., 313
Herskovits, M. J., 220, 244, 339
Herszenhornoct, D., 215
Hess, U., 285
Hetherington, R., 49
Hewlett, B. S., 46, 168, 169, 207, 208
Higgins, E. T., 61
Higgins, T. R., 358
Hill, D. L., 145
Hilmert, C. J., 164
Hilton, D. J., 324
Hirata, S., 41
Hirst, W., 60, 61
Hishinuma, E. S., 178
Hitokoto, H., 309
Ho, D. Y.-F., 139
Ho, M. W., 48
Ho, M. Y., 324, 325, 448
Hobart, M., 263
Hobbs, D. R., 230
Hobden, P., 257
Hobel, C. J., 164
Hößler, U., 322
Hodgson, G. M., 16
Hoerder, D., 178, 336, 338, 343, 423
Hoffman, C., 87
Hoffman, D. H., 443
Hoffmann, Y., 188
Hofmeijer, I., 101–102
Hofstede, G., 8, 29, 62–63, 83, 88, 91, 93, 99, 132, 235, 240, 255, 271, 274, 337, 394, 431, 439
Hogbin, H. I., 220
Hohepa, M., 445
Holbrook, C., 186
Holcombe, K. M., 446
Holder, N. A., 362
Holland, A. S., 203
Hollander, J. F., 205, 206
Holmes, T. A., 387
Holton, K. D., 294, 295

Kreutz, G., 76
Krippner, S., 262
Krishnan, V. R., 314
Kroeber, A. L., 53
Kroonenberg, P. M., 170
KRTV, 156
Krueger, J. I., 135
Krützen, M., 41
Ku, C-H., 253
Kua, E. H., 408
Kuijt, I., 27
Kumar, S., 414
Kumari, H., 292
Kuo, B. C., 341, 345
Kupperbusch, C., 30
Kurkul, K., 46
Kurman, J., 307
Kus, L., 355–356, 360, 361
Kus-Harbord, L., 357
Kwan, L., 261
Kwan, V., 122
Kwok, R., 272, 274
Kyler, J., 166
Kymlicka, W., 423, 425
Kyselka, W., 27

Lachman, M. E., 182
Lackenbauer, S., 138
LaFrance, J., 100
Lah, K., 430
Lai, J., 110, 353
Lai, K.-h., 63, 438
Lai, S. Y., 104
Laidlaw, K., 183
Lakhanpal, S., 223
Lalonde, R. N., 395
Lam, F. S. Z., 440
Lam, J., 76, 193, 416
Lam, Y., 49
Lamb, M. E., 168
Lamm, B., 166
Lamont, A., 194
Lancy, D. F., 173, 175, 176
Lang, P. J., 289
Lange, C. G., 281
Langfur, S., 124
Langlois, J. H., 212, 213
Laouira, O., 52
Lapinsky, M. K., 132

Lapsley, D., 322
Lardeau, M-P., 101–102
Lareau, L., 46
Larkin, S., 398
Larrick, R., 446, 447
Larson, J., 178
Lasaleta, J., 134, 135
Lasser, J., 102
Latifi, S. Y., 443
Lau, A. S., 307
Lau, B., 25
Laurentini, A., 212
Lavallée, M., 254
Lavis, C. A., 393, 394
Lawson, G., 185
Lawton, M. P., 222
Lazarus, M., 85
Lazarus, R. S., 347
Leach, C. W., 291
Leach, M. A., 206
Leary, M. R., 48, 303–304, 305, 360, 398
Lecannelier, F., 119
Leckman, J. F., 217
Ledoux, J., 281
Lee, D.-J., 63, 438
Lee, F., 354
Lee, G., 142
Lee, H. I., 307, 308
Lee, K., 213, 213 (figure)
Lee, N., 395
Lee, P. A., 147
Lee, S., 188, 408
Lee, T. L., 142, 286
Lee, Y. K., 27
Lee, Y. T., 354
Legare, C. H., 46
Legge, J., 85, 207
Lehman, D. R., 307
Lehman, H. R., 136
Lemery-Chalfant, K., 119
Le Mesurier, S., 340, 344–345, 363
Lenski, G., 12, 19
Lenski, J., 12, 19
Leong, F., 122
Leong, F. T., 344
Lerner, J. V., 163
Lerner, R. M., 163
Lero Vie, M., 121

Leslie, H. Y., 393, 394
Leung, A. K-y., 307, 308
Leung, C., 307
Leung, K., 91, 104, 107, 121, 122, 322, 446, 447
Leung, T. K. P., 63, 438, 447
Levenstein, H. A., 211
Levi, L., 343, 362, 363, 369
Levine, J. M., 61, 424
Levine, N. E., 205
Levine, T. R., 132
Levinson, S. C., 271
Levitin, D. J., 76
Levy, S. R., 362, 425
Levy, V., 322
LewGor, A., 430, 431 (table)
Lewis, J. M., 206
Lewis, R. S., 246
Lewis, S., 395
Leyendecker, B., 168
Leyens, J-P., 281, 282
Li, L., 189
Li, X., 52
Liao, J., 186
Lichtwarck-Aschoff, A., 214
Liddle, J. R., 48
Lieberman, M. D., 307
Liebkind, K., 343, 348, 360
Lietz, P., 99
Lilford, R. J., 401
Lim, C., 388
Lin, A. A., 11
Lin, T. Y., 414
Lindholm, A. K., 41
Linguistic Data Consortium, 254
Linton, R., 339
Little, J. F., 396
Litwin, H., 183
Liu, H., 222
Liu, J. H., 111, 307, 324, 358, 451
Liu, J. X., 428
Liu, Y., 63, 438
Liu, Z., 97, 356
Lleras-Muney, A., 386
Lo, E., 76, 193, 416
Lock, A., 92, 95
Locke, D., 135
Locke, J., 85, 236
Lofall, M. R., 429

Loflin, D., 403
Lohaus, A., 166
Lohndorf, R. T., 272–273
Lomas, T., 296
Lombardo, N. E., 291
Long, H., 142
Long, M. H., 273
Lonner, W. J., 87, 88, 90
Lopes, M. A., 24
Lopez, C. R. V., 443
Lopez, S. J., 394
Lotem, A., 269
Louis, H. M., 269
Love, P., 398
Low, J., 13
Lowell, E. L., 305
Lowenberg, K., 246
Lozano, R., 385, 386
Lu, W-L., 253
Lucca, N., 203, 204
Luijk, M. P. C. M., 168
Lupyan, G., 248
Lusk, E., 178, 180
Luu, T. D., 362
Lyon, D., 186
Lyons, A. C., 143
Lyons, D. F., 46
Lyons, R. P., 49

Ma, L., 186
Ma, X., 129, 289, 309
Ma, Y., 110, 129
Machluf, K., 48
MacKay, I. R. A., 167, 273
MacKenzie, M. K., 301
MacLeod, C., 46, 55
Macpherson, J. M., 11
Madathil, J., 223
Maddux, W., 204, 223
Madsen, M. C., 67
Maeda, A., 428
Mael, F., 60
Maes, K., 164
Maguire, E. A., 242
Mahabeer, M., 143
Mahalingam, R., 143
Mahapatra, M., 316, 342
Mahmoudzadeh, M., 164
Mahowald, K., 250

Main, M., 171
Maira, S., 359
Major, B., 349
Makanjuola, V., 412
Ma-Kellams, C., 188, 244
Makkai, A., 366
Malinowski, B., 163
Mallikarjunaiah, M., 257
Mandela, N., 449
Maner, J. K., 186
Mann, T. D., 159
Mao, L., 110, 353
Mao, S., 274
Marcus, H., 118
Marian, V., 275
Markovitzky, G., 94, 179, 369
Marks, M. J., 207
Markus, H. R., 90, 124, 129, 130
    (figure), 131 (figure), 132, 136,
    138, 139, 239, 240, 261, 290,
    291, 308, 309, 348, 360
Marlow, M. L., 279
Marnane, C., 401
Maros, M., 293
Marsella, A. J., 30, 85, 88, 343, 348,
    363, 369, 400, 423
Marsh, A., 284
Marshall, C. A., 99, 100
Martel, L. D., 111, 217
Martens, A., 187
Marti, G., 184
Martin, A., 24
Martinez, R., 144
Martiniuk, A. L. C., 101
Masao, K., 41
Masgoret, A.-M., 348
Mashhour, A., 226
Maslow, A. H., 304, 394, 395
    (figure)
Massenkoff, M., 121
Masuda, T., 246, 247, 250, 261
Mataragnon, R. H., 94
Matsumoto, D., 30, 98, 104, 105,
    267, 277, 283, 286
Matsumoto, H., 307
Matsuzawa, T., 182
Matthews, K. A., 363
Matthews, T. J., 336
Mattis, J. S., 448

Mauss, I. B., 402
May-Collado, L. J., 13
Maynard, A. E., 53, 67, 164, 170,
    171, 173, 175, 176
Maynard, E., 179, 184
Mbwayo, A. W., 412
McAdams, D. P., 57
McAuliffe, K., 52
McClelland, A., 211
McClelland, D. C., 303, 305, 306
McClure, J., 358
McCormick, K., 242–243, 274
McCrae, R. R., 120
McCrary, C., 338
McCubbin, L., 99, 100
McDermott, R. C., 181
McDevitt, S. C., 107
McDonald, C. A., 239, 240, 240
    (figure), 241 (table)
McDonald, J., 242
McElhinny, B., 166
McElroy, A., 408, 409, 410, 412
McGahan, C., 279, 280
McGee, M. A., 410
McGerty, L.-J., 145
McGrath, J. J., 402
McGrath, N., 416
McGrath, P., 279, 280
McGrath, R. E., 105
McGuire, E. A., 242
McInerney, D. M., 306
McKay, R., 213, 213 (figure)
McKenna, K. Y. A., 145
McKennell, A., 389
McKenzie, L., 183
McKergow, F., 102
McKersie, R. B., 447
McLaren, S., 58
McMahan, C., 142
McManus, T., 388
McNaughton, S., 445
McWirter, B. T., 395, 398
Mead, M., 132
Medin, D. L., 236, 241
Mei, Y., 229
Meise, U., 46
Melamed, Y., 19
Meltzer, D., 178
Mendoza, M. T., 446, 447

Menon, T., 290
Menon, U., 180, 181, 183
Mergl, R., 46
Merriam, A. P., 75
Merrie Monarch Festival, 352
Merta, R. J., 413
Mesman, J., 272–273
Mesoudi, A., 10, 51, 55, 312
Mesquita, B., 281, 308
Messe, L., 343, 345, 368
Mihai, A., 401
Miklósi, Á., 16, 24, 267, 268 (figure)
Mileva-Seitz, V. R., 168
Milfont, T. L., 320
Milgram, S., 87, 101
Mill, J. S., 235, 236
Millen, A. E., 49
Miller, A. M., 164
Miller, D. J., 46–47
Miller, G., 384
Miller, J. G., 92, 309
Miller, J. H., 224 (figure)
Miller, K., 343, 368
Min, S., 404
Minagawa-Kawai, Y., 167
Mingione, A. D., 305, 306
Ministry of Social Development, 358
Minoretti, P., 217, 218
Mintz, S., 370
Mio, J. S., 96–97
Misra, G., 88, 90, 92, 95
Mitchell, B. A., 181
Mitchell, M., 105
Miyagawa, S., 271
Miyake, K., 171
Miyamoto, Y., 129, 237, 238, 240, 247, 261, 289, 309
Mo, Y.-M., 218
Moffett, M. W., 201
Mohsen, N., 401
Mok, A. O., 326, 354
Møller, A. P., 212
Møller, V., 413
Monk, K., 226
Montanari, S., 167
Moon, M., 404
Moons, I., 305
Moore, C. A., 247
Moore, K., 413, 415

Moore, M., 398
Moore, S. E., 393, 394
Moorfield, J. C., 396
Moors, A., 75
Moreland, R. L., 424
Morelli, G. A., 159, 168, 170, 171
Morgan, B., 211
Morgan, G., 432
Morgan, T. J., 269
Mori, K., 167
Morie, J. F., 145
Morley, I., 27
Morris, M. W., 97, 290, 353–357, 446, 447
Morris, P. A., 162
Morrison, H. W., 305
Morton, J., 166, 167
Moscardino, U., 106
Mosek, A., 94, 179, 369
Moselen, E., 82
Moses, C., 69
Mosher, W. D., 224
Moskalenko, S., 134, 135
Mosquera, M., 19, 185
Moss, I., 362, 425
Motley, W., 185
Much, N. C., 316, 342
Muhunthan, J., 398
Mulla, Z. R., 314
Mullen, R., 410
Mullet, F. N. E., 357, 369
Mumba, P., 255
Munoz, M., 24
Munsell, A. H., 249
Münte, T. F., 275
Munz, R., 166
Münzel, S. C., 27
Murasaki Shikibu, 228–229
Murdock, G. P., 171, 205
Murphy, G., 426
Murray, C. J., 385, 386
Murray, H. A., 117
Murray, L. M. A., 203
Murray, T., 345
Mushin, I., 46
Mussell, B., 352
Mutiso, V. N., 412
Myers, J. E., 223
Mylonas, K., 205, 206

Na, J., 60, 138, 185
Nagarajan, N. R., 428
Nagell, K., 44
Nagpal, R., 389, 390, 393, 393 (table)
Nahemow, L., 222
Naidoo, J. C., 143
Nair, N., 436
Nakagawa, A., 172
Nand, K., 261
Naoi, N., 167
Narayanan, P., 361
Nasim, A., 429
Nasr, M., 401
Nasrini, J., 46
Nassar, R., 306
National Center for Health Statistics, 220, 382
Native Hawaiian Hospitality Association, 3
Nattiez, J.-J., 76
Nayar, S. C., 343, 356
Ndetei, D. M., 412
Nebre, L. R. H., 179
Needham, B., 222
Neider, J., 357
Neki, J. S., 95
Nell, M. D., 225
Nelson, C. A., 167
Nelson Mandela Foundation, 395
Nerlove, S. B., 254
Neto, F., 345, 357, 369
Nettles, M. E., 140, 403
Neufeld, S. D., 103
Neuser, B. L., 261
Nevergelt, C., 182
Nevgi, A., 278
Neville, H. A., 65
Nevo, B., 253
Newcomb, T. M., 222
Ng, B. F.-L., 415
Ng, K.-Y., 415, 440
Ng, L. C. Y., 309, 311, 326
Ng, S. H., 110, 353
Nguyen, H., 343, 345, 368
Nhat Hanh, T., 123
Nicholas, J. L., 9, 396
Nicole, P., 135
Niederkrotenthaler, T., 46

Nielsen, M., 43, 45, 46, 49, 259
Nikora, L. W., 214
Niles, A. N., 307
Nini, D., 46
Nisbett, R. E., 60, 61, 185, 237, 238, 239, 243, 244, 246, 247, 261, 289, 308
Nishii, L. H., 446
Nishii, L. N., 436
Nishimura, S., 278
Nishina, E., 262
Nishteshwar, K., 292
Nittel, N. K., 70
Nitz, K., 163
Njenga, J., 142
Noh, S., 147, 404
Nordgren, J., 429
Norenzayan, A., 56, 60, 61, 88, 237, 238, 239, 309, 311, 326
Norris, K., 282
North, A., 31, 75, 76, 192, 366
Nortje, G., 412
Norval, M., 416
Notroff, J., 27
Novaes, S., 171
Novin, S., 287–288
Nowak, N., 225, 226
Nsamenang, A. B., 93–94, 96, 178, 255
Núñez, R., 241, 242
Nunn, C. L., 44, 49
Nwoye, A., 96
Nygaard, A., 432

Oathes, D. J., 402
Obeng, P., 366
Oberaum, M., 415
Oberg, K., 347
Ochsner, K. N., 281
O'Connor, M., 188
Odunewu, L. O., 65
Oefner, P. J., 11
Oetzel, J. G., 280
Ogan, A. T., 159
Ogden, S. N., 215
O'Gorman, R., 61
O'Hagin, I. B., 357, 369
Ohama, M. L. F., 279
Ohashi, R., 132

Ohbuchi, K. I., 446
Oishi, S., 137
ojalehto, B. L., 236
Okamoto, S. K., 179
Okanoya, K., 271
Okasha, T., 401
Okazaki, S., 290, 291, 292
Okimoto, J. T., 169
Okum, M. E., 168
Oladeji, B. D., 412
Olguin, R.S., 44
Olivier, D. C., 249
Omer, L., 211
O'Neill, D., 356, 364, 365
O'Nell, C. W., 409
Ong, A., 361
Oohashi, T., 262
Opler, A. A., 400
Opler, L. A., 400
Oppedal, B., 361
Oppenheim, D., 168
Orgambídez-Ramos, A., 441
Organisation for Economic Co-operation and Development, 428
Orzechowicz, D., 215
Oscar, J., 101
Osorio, S., 361
Ossorio, P. G., 96
Ostrosky-Solís, F., 47
Ostrower, F., 345
O'Sullivan, J. L., 339
Oswald, A. J., 182
Otterbeck, J., 75
Otters, R. V., 205, 206
Ouedraogo, A., 121
Over, H., 46
Overpeck, J. T., 49
Owe, E., 132, 133
Owen, M. T., 203
Oyama, K. E., 65
Oyebode, O., 401
Ozakinci, G., 60

Pae, J. H., 63, 438
Pagano, I. S., 279
Page, J. T., Jr., 442
Page, R., 363, 368, 369
Page, S., 424
Paladino, M-P., 281, 282

Palagi, E., 203
Palomino, H., 187
Pandey, J., 95
Pandit, S. A., 292
Panzeri, S., 285
Papp, Z., 296
Paranjpe, A. C., 294
Park, C., 119
Park, C. E., 57, 339
Park, H. S., 132
Park, J., 242
Park, J. E., 271
Park, L., 316, 342
Park, L. E., 49
Park, R. E., 346
Parker, D., 141
Parker, K., 442
Parrish, M., 179, 184
Passarino, G., 11
Patel, V., 401
Patkoski, M. S., 273
Patton, G., 401
Paxson, L. M., 171
Peace, R., 356, 364, 365
Pearce, J., 168
Pearson, V. M. S., 448
Peck, D., 187
Peck, J. A., 49
Pedersen, D. M., 173, 245
Pedersen, P. B., 126, 127
Pederson, P., 30, 88, 343, 361
Pedrotti, J. T., 394
Peiris-John, R., 82
Pelligrini, A. D., 47
Peng, K., 60, 61, 238, 239, 243, 244, 247, 289, 348, 360
Peng, Y., 404
Penhune, V. B., 194
Penn, D. C., 24
Pennington, D., 135
Percy, W. E., 31
Peregrine, P. N., 73–74
Pereira, J. B., 11
Pereira, L., 11
Perez, R., 187
Perrett, D. I., 17
Perry, S., 47
Petchovsky, L., 256
Peters, K., 53, 280

Petit, B., 357
Pettigrew, T. F., 359, 370
Pflegerl, J., 206
Pham, M., 214
Phillips, J., 358
Phinney, J. S., 8, 145, 146, 349, 352, 353, 361
Piaget, J., 93, 158, 161 (table), 251
Pilkington, K., 414
Pilling, M., 250
Pirkis, J., 46
Piske, T., 167, 273
Pixley, J. E., 182
Planalp, E. M., 119
Plant, E. A., 186
Plaut, V. C., 204, 210
Plunkett, K., 272, 274
Po'A-Kekuawela, K.'O., 179
Podlogar, M. C., 408
Podsiadlowski, A., 346
Pogosyan, M., 172
Polanczyk, G. V., 401
Politi, P., 217, 218
Polk, T. A., 47
Polka, L., 167
Pollet, T. V., 16
Pond, R. S., Jr., 111
Pontzer, H., 19, 25
Poole, M. S., 288
Poortinga, Y. H., 90, 91, 104, 105–106, 122, 205, 206, 282, 283
Pope, K., 443
Popenoe, R., 210
Poponete, C.-R., 442
Popp, D., 215
Poroch, N., 398
Porta, C., 75
Portman, T. A. A., 179, 184
Posada, G., 170
Posada, R., 170
Postuvan, V., 46
Pott, M., 171
Povinelli, D. J., 24
Powell, J. W., 99, 338, 339, 352
Powell, W., 448
Power, M. J., 183
Power, S., 351

Powers, D. A., 222
Preston, K., 30
Price, L. J., 240
Price-Williams, D., 256
Prilleltensky, I., 359, 395
Prilleltensky, O., 395
Prince, R., 408
Pryor, J., 5
Pryor, T., 295
Pukui, M. K., 65 (table), 412
Pumam, S. P., 119
Punathamberkar, A., 369
Pushkar, G., 184
Putnam, J. J., 407
Putnam, S. P., 172
Putnick, D. L., 207
Pyszczynski, T., 186–187
Pyszezynski, X., 186

Qijin, C., 46
Qimei, H., 182
Queen, B., 388
Quek, K. M. T., 223
Quinn, S. C., 101
Quiroz, A., 429

Raat, H., 168
Radova, D., 53
Rahe, R., 387
Rakoczy, H., 47, 235
Ramadan, A., 267
Ramirez-Christiansen, E., 295, 296
Rampell, C., 346
Ramy, H., 401
Rana-Deuba, A., 341, 345
Rao, C. V., 257
Rapetti, M., 407
Rapoport, J. L., 178, 180
Rapp-Paglicci, L. A., 194
Rapson, R. L., 111, 217, 218, 221 (table), 223 (table), 225
Rasco, L., 343, 368
Rasmus, S. M., 69
Rata, A., 324, 451
Rata, E., 179
Rath, F. H., Jr., 168
Ratnasingam, S., 250
Rauscher, F. H., 194
Ray, S., 312

Raymond, K., 64
Rayson, A., 352
Reddish, P., 259
Reddy, G. N., 257
Redfield, A., 263
Redfield, R., 339
Reed, L. J., 257
Regan, D., 379
Regan, P. C., 223
Regier, T., 250
Régio, J., 294–295
Reicher, S. D., 60
Reilly, D., 142
Reinthal, P. N., 49
Reis, H. T., 204
Reis, M., 441
Reitmen, W., 305
Reitz, J. G., 356
Rendell, L. F., 269
Retschitzki, J., 254
Reynolds, G., 442
Rheinstein, M., 226
Rhodes, G., 213, 213 (figure)
Rhodes, H. J., 178
Rhodes, J. E., 178
Rhodes, J. L., 178
Richardson, P. J., 4
Richerson, P. J., 48, 51, 54
Richter, R., 206
Richwine, J., 425
Rieffe, C., 287–288
Ring, E., 343, 363, 369, 423
Ritchie, P., 171
Rittner, S., 262
Rivera, N., 67, 323
Rivera-Hudson, N., 403
Rivers, W., 244
Robbins, B., 187
Robbins, R. L., 13
Roberson, D., 249, 250
Roberts, A. I., 269
Roberts, A. R., 212
Roberts, S., 379
Roberts, S. G. B., 16, 25, 269
Robinson, L., 359
Robinson, S. B., 178
Rodriguea-Perez, A., 281, 282
Rodriguez-Fornells, A., 275
Rodriguez-Torres, R., 281, 282

Roesch, S. C., 322, 323
Rogers, R. A., 70, 71
Roggman, L. A., 212, 213
Rogoff, B., 93, 157, 159, 162, 168, 173, 174, 175, 354, 426
Rohde, L. A., 401
Rohlof, H. G., 404
Roisman, G. I., 203
Rokeach, M., 318, 319, 324
Roland, A., 89
Rollet, C., 166
Roman, S., 239, 240, 240 (figure), 241 (table)
Rosch Heider, E., 249
Rosenblatt, A., 186
Rosenthal, L., 362, 425
Ross, M., 137
Rossier, J., 121
Roth, E. A., 261
Rothbart, M. K., 119
Rothbaum, F., 170, 171
Rotter, J. B., 140
Roughton, R., 215
Roulette, C. J., 46
Rourke, S. B., 404
Routledge, C., 186
Rowe, W., 194
Rowley, S. J., 147
Royal, T. A. C., 147
Roysircar, G., 341, 345
Rua, M., 214
Rubel, A. J., 409
Ruby, M. B., 172
Rudmin, F. W., 352, 365
Rueden, C., 121
Ruggles, S., 205
Ruiz-Alfaro, S., 215
Rule, N. O., 261
Rumi, 216
Rummel-Kluge, C., 46
Rummens, J., 147
Runde, C., 288
Russell, J., 49
Russell, J. A., 291
Russock, H. I., 214
Ryan, R. M., 309
Ryback, C., 413
Ryder, A. G., 402, 404
Ryff, C. D., 147

Sabatier, C., 166, 359
Sabatini, F., 387
Sacks, H., 271
Sager, R., 75
Saini, D. S., 439
Sakashita, J., 182
Salum, G. A., 401
Salum, L. S., 401
Sam, D. L., 341, 347, 352, 353
Sambrook, T. D., 272, 274
Samuels, N., 415
Sánchez, B., 181
Sander, A. R., 402
Sanderson, C. A., 135, 136 (table)
Sandman, C., 164
Santos, J., 441
Sapir, E., 248
Sarapin, S. H., 46
Saraswati, T. S., 178
Sargent, C., 165, 166
Sartorius, N., 401, 402
Sarty, M., 166
Saucier, G., 119, 121, 122, 124
Sauter, D., 99
Savage, J., 178
Savarese, N., 148
Savery, L., 278
Save the Children, 385
Saylor, E. S., 145
Scales, C., 416
Scarantino, A., 290
Schaller, M., 6, 56
Schechner, R., 149
Scheffey, K. L., 215
Scheffler, R., 428
Schegloff, E. A., 271
Schei, V., 440
Scheib, J. E., 212
Schick, K., 269
Schieider, D. M., 117
Schiff, J. W., 413, 415
Schimel, J., 187
Schimmack, U., 137
Schjoedt, U., 259
Schlaug, G., 194
Schluterman, J. M., 360, 398
Schmeichel, B. J., 186
Schmidt, D. P., 120
Schmidt, K., 27

Schmidtling, E. Y., 53
Schmitt, D. P., 135, 214
Schmitz, P. G., 345
Schnarch, B., 102
Schneiderman, I., 217
Schnell, J., 443
Schniter, E., 182
Schöelmerich, A., 170
Schölmerich, A., 168
Scholz, C. A., 49
Schreier, M., 99
Schuck, P., 364
Schug, J., 204, 223
Schustak, M. W., 118, 121 (table)
Schwarez, H. P., 25
Schwartz, J. P., 181
Schwartz, P., 214
Schwartz, S. H., 90, 223, 305, 318, 320, 321, 321 (figure), 326
Schweigman, K., 53
Schyns, P. G., 285
Scott, K. M., 401
Scott, S., 166
Scovel, T., 273
Sedikides, C., 135, 137, 138, 186
Seedat, S., 412
Segall, M. H., 87, 88, 90, 91, 244
Sejong Cultural Society, 368
Sekiguchi, R., 66
Selart, M., 440
Seligman, M. E. P., 394, 395
Sell, H., 389, 390, 393, 393 (table)
Sellers, R. M., 147
Selnick, C. N., 366
Semin, G. R., 61
Senturia, K. D., 164
Senzaki, S., 261
Sered, S. S., 165
Serpell, R., 255
Servaes, J., 278
Sessarego, S., 276
Seyle, H., 386
Seymour, H. N., 276
Shackelford, T. K., 214
Shafa, S., 324
Shafer, M., 100
Shakespeare, W., 117
Shamsui, A. B., 357
Shand, N., 207

Shanklin, S. L., 60, 220, 388
Shannon, D., 168
Shapiro, Y., 257
Sharkey, W. F., 104
Sharma, M. N., 294
Sharrow, D., 166
Shattuck, K. S., 225, 226
Shattuck, R. M., 221
Shaw, J. T., 445
Shea, K., 13
Shearman, S.M., 132
Shek, D. T., 223
Sheldon, K. M., 61
Shen, J., 183, 225, 226
Shen, P., 11
Shen, X. B., 285
Shendruk, A., 442
Shennan, S. J., 174
Shepard, I. D. H., 293
Sherif, C. W., 87
Sherif, M., 87
Sherman, M., 101–102
Sherwood, C., 268–269
Shinkei, 295–296
Shinnō, M-Y., 228
Shiota, M. N., 290
Shipton, C., 49
Shirov, A. A., 12
Shteynberg, G., 8
Shu, D., 274
Shukry, S., 75
Shweder, R. A., 91, 92, 93, 281, 289, 292, 316, 317, 317 (table), 342
Sibley, C. G., 259
Siddiqui, M. M., 75
Siegal, M., 138
Silberstein, O., 172
Silk, J. B., 205
Silkoset, R., 432
Silles, M. A., 386
Silove, D., 401
Silva, N. M., 11
Silva, P. A., 119
Silva, S. T., 428
Silver, A., 203
Silvia, P. J., 134
Simchoni, O., 19
Sims, T., 287
Singelis, T. M., 104, 122

Singer, I., 216
Singer, S. R., 415
Singh, A., 253
Singh, D., 211
Singh, P., 223
Singleton, J., 176
Sirikantraporn, S., 430
Slaney, K. L., 103
Sleight, P., 75
Slobodskaya, H. R., 172
Slone, D. J., 56
Slot, B. J., 358
Smircich, L., 432
Smith, G. F., 53
Smith, G. H., 445
Smith, J., 184
Smith, L. T., 99, 100, 445
Smith, M. A., 147
Smith, P. B., 132, 133
Smith-Oka, V., 413
Smuts, B. B., 206
Snarey, J. R., 313, 314, 315
Snyder, C. R., 394
Snyder, T. D., 443
Soares, P., 11
Soares, R. R., 382, 384
Sobeck, J., 101
Sober, E., 48
Sobol, J., 211
Soeters, J. L., 442
Solomon, S., 186–187
Sombrun, C., 257
Son, G., 363, 366
Song, W.-Z., 91, 107, 121, 122
Songer, E., 134
Soriano, L. J., 446
Sorokowska, A., 212
Sorokowski, P., 212
Soto, C., 53
Sousa, C., 441
Sousa, M. D. R., 357, 369
Sousa, P., 186
Southard, E. E., 363
Soysal, Y. N., 364
Spear, S., 436
Spearman, C., 251
Spears, R., 291
Speidel, G. E., 136
Spencer, S. J., 138

Spieß, E., 322
Spiers, H. J., 242
Spinner, J., 425
Spitz, R. A., 170
Spitzbergen, J. M., 261
Spitzer, J., 230
Spivey, M. J., 275
Spoonley, P., 356, 364, 365
Sprecher, S., 214
Spring, B., 254
Srinivasan, N., 60
Stack, S., 46
Staes, N., 268–269
Stankov, L., 324
Stanton, W. R., 119
Stark, A., 447
Statistics NZ, 359
Staton, M., 429
Stayton, D. J., 170
Stearns, P. N., 211
Steel, Z., 401
Steele, C. J., 194
Steele, J., 174
Stein, B. D., 178
Steinberg, H., 400
Steinthal, H., 85
Stephan, W., 448
Stephen, M., 258
Stephens, D. P., 311
Stepler, R., 442
Stern, F., 366
Sternberg, R. J., 219, 252, 446
Stewart, J., 355–356, 360, 361
Stewart, S. M., 166
Stiles, D., 179, 445
Stillman, T. F., 186
St. John de Crèvecoeur, J. H., 339, 364
Stollack, G., 343, 345, 368
Stone, J. M., 257
Stone, J. R., 49
Stone, V. E., 13, 16–17, 18
Stoneking, M., 11
Stoneman, Z., 338
Stout, D., 269
Strack, M., 76, 193, 416
Street, S. E., 269
Strodtbeck, F. L., 319
Strous, R. D., 400

Stuart, J., 354–355, 359, 361
Stunkard, A. J., 211
Stutman, R. K., 288
Su, Y., 309, 311, 326
Sue, D., 126 (table), 148
Sue, D. W., 125 (figure), 126, 126 (table), 148
Suen, H. K., 174
Sugaya, L. S., 401
Sugimoto, K., 267
Sugiyama, M. S., 52, 57
Suits, A., 279, 280
Sul, S., 60
Sule, R., 13
Sullivan, M. A., 92
Sumner, W. S., 42
Sun, J., 404
Sun, Z., 139
Sundararjan, L., 96, 291, 292
Suo, G., 139
Super, C. M., 106, 163, 168, 169, 172, 208–209
Suprakash, C., 414
Suprapto, N., 253
Surowiecki, J., 424
Suryani, L. K., 258
Sussman, N. M., 366
Suwalsky, J. T. D., 207
Suzuki, T. N., 270
Svanum, S., 134
Swartz, L., 408
Sweetser, E., 241
Synnevaag, B., 170
Szucs, D., 108

Tadmor, C. T., 348, 360
Tafoye, T., 57
Tafreshi, D., 103
Tajfel, H. E., 60, 146
Takata, T., 137, 307
Takemoto, E., 134, 135
Takemura, K., 84
Talwar, R., 163
Tamariz, M., 42, 51, 55
Tamir, M., 129, 289, 402
Tan, J., 19
Tanaka, H., 271
Tanaka, K., 138
Taonui, R., 33

Tappan, M. B. B., 316
Tapsell, R., 410
Tasca, C., 407
Tascon, M., 170
Tay, C., 440
Taylor, E. B., 99
Taylor, R. J., 203
Taylor, S. E., 32
Te Awekotuku, N., 214
Tedford, R. H., 13
Teixeira, A. A., 428
Tekman, H., 142
Tella, S., 278
Templer, K. J., 440
Tennie, C., 44, 49
Terman, L. M., 251
Tetlock, P. E., 348, 360
Tewari, S., 60
Thai, H. C., 344
Thalmeyer, A. G., 122
Tharp, R., 444
Tharp, T. G., 136
Thelen, M. H., 46–47
Thoits, P. A., 387
Thomas, D., 187
Thomas, E. R., 276
Thomas, K., 277
Thomas, K. M., 167
Thomas, K. W., 446, 447 (figure)
Thomas, S. B., 101
Thomas-Tate, S., 275, 276
Thompson, R. A., 167
Thornhill, R., 212
Thornton, A., 52
Thou, C., 363, 368, 369
Thouin-Savard, M., 263
Tian, Z., 447
Tichovolsky, M. H., 207
Tiemeier, H., 168
Tietjen, A. M., 214, 314
Tiller, A.-M., 185
Times Higher Education, 88
Tingle, L. R., 223
Tisnérat-Laborde, N., 27
Titova, A., 284
Tomaselli, K., 45, 46
Tomasello, M., 43, 44, 48, 49, 175, 235, 323
Tongs, J., 398

Tönnies, F., 67
Tooby, J., 49
Toriyama, R., 261
Torres Rivera, E., 179, 184
Toth, N., 269
Tovar-Blank, Z. G., 143
Townsend, K. C., 395, 398
Townsend, S. S., 291
Townsend, T. G., 429
Townshend, P., 408, 409, 410, 412
Toyoshima, K., 75
Tracey, T. J. G., 143
Trapnell, P. D., 120
Travis, R., Jr., 193
Trehub, S. E., 192
Trevathan, W. R., 165
Triandis, H. C., 90, 94, 105, 125 (figure), 126, 132, 203, 204, 322, 439
Trimble, J. E., 146
Trinkaus, E., 410
Trommsdorf, G., 139
Trope, Y., 135
Tropp, L. R., 359, 370
Trujillo, L. T., 212, 213
Tryon, C. A., 49
Tsai, J. L., 147, 287
Tsai, W., 307
Tsethlikai, M., 174, 175
Tsuchiya, H., 139
Tsui, A. S., 63, 438
Tsutsui, N. D., 13
Tucker, R., 443
Tumambing, J. S., 96–97
Turino, T., 31, 192
Turk, I., 25
Turkle, S., 145
Turner, J., 58, 75, 349
Turner, J. C., 60
Turner, R. J., 387
Turner, V., 94, 148, 158, 177, 194, 416
Tweeny, D. R., 56
Tweeny, R., 56
Twenge, J. M., 58, 111, 135
Tyack, P., 13
Tylor, E. B., 8

Uchida, Y., 137, 291, 308
Ueda, Y., 247

Umaña-Taylor, A. J., 145, 147
Umberson, D., 222
Underhill, P., 11
UN Economic and Social
    Council, 429
Unger, J., 53
UN High Commissioner For
    Refugees, 390
UNICEF Innocenti Research
    Centre, 385
United Nations Department
    of Economic and Social
    Affairs Population Division
    (UNDESAPD), 345, 348
Uomini, N. T., 269
Upal, A., 56
Upal, M. A., 56
Usher, E. L., 305
Utsey, S. O., 147
Utter, J., 82

Vaillant, G. E., 395
Vaioleti, T., 106
Vaituzis, A. C., 178, 180
Valdez, A., 366
Vale, G. L., 66
Valladas, H., 27
Valleron, A. J., 384
Vallotton, C., 119, 277
van de Vijver, F. J. R., 98, 104, 282,
    283
van de Waal, E., 44, 45
van Duijl, M., 257, 258
van Dyne, L., 440
van Gennep, A., 158
van Hemert, D. A., 122, 282, 283
van Heusden, B., 235
van Hulle, C., 119
van Ijzendoorn, M. H., 168, 170
van Kleef, G., 99
van Leeuwen, E. J. C., 40 (figure)
van Oudenhoven, J. P., 348
van Schaik, C. P., 19, 47, 48
van Tubergen, F., 348, 360
van Wilgenburg, E., 13
van Willigen, J., 242
Vandaire, C.-M., 324
Vang, T. F., 357
Vanhaeren, M., 185

Vannoy, D., 226
Vardaman, J. M., 432, 437, 440, 441
Varnum, M. E. W., 185, 238
Västfjäll, D., 110
Vauclair, C.-M., 321, 322
Vedder, P., 352, 353
Velleman, J. D., 145
Venkataramaiah, V., 257
Ventriglio, A., 257, 258
Ventura, S. J., 336
Venuti, P., 207
Verardi, S., 121
Verma, S., 178
Vermeer, H. J., 272–273
Verstrynge, K., 312
Vespa, J., 206, 224
Vess, M., 186
Vestal, K. D., 178
Vevea, J. L., 135, 137
Vianney, J. M., 261
Vickers Smith, R., 429
Vigilant, L., 11
Vignoles, V. L., 132, 133
Viladrich, A., 369
Vilhjalmsdottir, P., 361
Villa, C., 172
Villareal, M. J., 203, 204
Virgil, 84–85, 366
Vitebsky, P., 414
Vivona, J. M., 171
Vohra, N., 436
Vohs, K. D., 135
Volpe, U., 401
Volterra, V., 278
Vonasch, A. J., 310, 311
von Frisch, K., 13
Vuoskoski, J. K., 110–111
Vygotsky, L. S., 23, 58, 87, 159, 173,
    316, 355

Walker, J. A., 276
Walker, L. J., 314
Walker, R., 148, 358
Wallen, K., 214
Waller, D., 447
Wallois, F., 164
Walsh, J. J., 363
Walsh, R., 184
Walters, R., 230

Walton, R. E., 447
Wang, D., 183
Wang, F., 324
Wang, W., 277
Wang, X., 13
Wang, Y., 214
Warburton, J., 398
Ward, C., 122, 146, 258, 259, 338,
    340, 341, 345, 347, 348, 349,
    350, 351, 354–355, 355–356,
    357, 359, 360, 361, 440
Ward, M. S., 436
Warner, L., 158
Warren, H. C., 236
Wartzok, D., 13
Waseda, M., 366
Washington, J., 275, 276
Wassink, A. B., 276
Wassmann, J., 241, 242
Watanabe, K., 41
Waters, D. J. M., 261
Watson, B., 85
Watson, J. B., 6, 158
Waugh, E., 183
Weaver, A. J., 49
Wechsler, D., 251
Wegman, M. E., 166
Weisfeld, C. C., 225, 226
Weisfeld, Q. R., 225, 226
Weisner, T. S., 171
Weiss, A., 182
Weissmann, M. D., 30
Weisz, J., 171
Welles-Nyström, B., 106, 168
Welsh, F. T., 210
Welsh, T., 124
Wendt, D. C., 146
Werker, E., 19
Werker, J. F., 167
West, B. A., 366
West, T. V., 215
Westermeyer, J., 357
Westermeyer, P., 75
Western, B., 357
Westoff, C. F., 335, 336
Wethington, E., 182
Wheatcroft, D., 270
Wheeler, J., 173, 245
Wheeler, L., 204

# SUBJECT INDEX

altered states in performance,
262–263
cognition, perception, and, 260–263
culture and, 71–77, 72 (figure),
73 (figure), 74 (figure)
emotion and, 294–296
intergroup relations and,
369–370, 370 (figure)
lifespan development,
socialization, and, 192–194
morals and, 327–330, 328 (figure)
motivation and, 326–327
multiculturalism and, 453–454
in psychological research,
110–111
relationships and, 227–230
self and, 147–149
as theme in this book, 33–34
well-being and, 415–418, 417
(figure)
*See also specific arts*
ASC. *See* Altered states of
consciousness
Asia:
agency and control, 308–309
attribution, 237
cognition and perception, 244,
261
death, 187–186
shoe removal indoors, 9–10, 9
(figure)
*See also* East Asia; *specific countries*
Asian Americans, 246, 287, 309
Asian immigrants, 430
Assimilation, 351, 373
Associationism, 235–236
Associative learning, 48
Asylum seekers, 341, 373
*As You Like It* (Shakespeare), 117
*Ataque de nervios*, 406 (table)
Attachment, 170–172
Attention, 17–18, 37, 246–247
Attraction:
about, 209–210
facial aesthetics, 211–214, 213
(figure)
female body attractiveness,
210–214, 210 (figure)
gender and, 214–215

Attributions:
defined, 135, 152
dispositional, 237
fundamental attribution error,
135, 153, 237, 306–307
self-serving, 136 (table)
situational, 237
Australia, 45, 65, 183, 256, 398
Authority, abuse of, 87, 101, 110
Autonomy, 317 (table), 321

Bali, Indonesia, 262–263
Balkan Wars, 450
Bands, 22
Baoulé, 254
Bard, Phillip, 281
Basic emotions, 282–283, 298
Basket weaving, 53
*Battle Hymn of the Tiger Mother*
(Chua), 309
Beethoven, Ludwig van,
76–77, 193
Behavioral Styles Questionnaire,
107–108
Behaviorism, 86
Beliefs, 62, 136 (table)
Belongingness, 304, 305
Bias:
about, 104–105
acquiescence, 104, 112
administration, 104, 112
construct, 104, 112
content information, 55–57
defined, 104
extremity, 105, 112
instrument, 104, 113
method, 104
moderacy, 105, 113
prestige, 51–52
sample, 104, 113
self-enhancement, 307
self-esteem, 307
self-improvement, 307
self-serving, 136 (table)
social desirability, 104–105, 113
success, 51–52
Bicultural, defined, 351, 373
Bicultural identity integration,
354, 373

Bicultural system, New Zealand, 358
Big 3 ethics, 316–318, 317 (table)
Big 5, 120–121, 121 (table), 122,
124, 153
Big 6, 121, 124
Bilingual brain, 275
Bioecological model of
development, 58–60, 59
(figure), 125, 159, 162
Biosocial, defined, 157, 197
Birds, 200–201, 267, 270–271
Birth, 165–166, 427 (table), 428
Black Elk, 380
Blacks. *See* African Americans
Blombos Caves, 11, 25–26
Body and emotions, 281, 292
Body attractiveness, female,
210–214, 210 (figure)
Bollywood, 76, 369
Bonobos, 18–19, 203, 423
Borneo, 9, 9 (figure), 342, 342
(figure)
Bosnia and Herzegovina, 450
Boston fathers, 208–209
Boundaries of self and others,
130–132
Brain research, 218
Brain size, 14–16, 14 (figure)
Brandt, Willy, 449, 449 (figure)
Brazil, 323, 370 (figure), 448
Bridge of birds tale, 200–201
Brisbane, Australia, 45
Britain, 358, 386
Buddhism, 188–189, 329
Bushmen, 45–46

California, 309
Cameroon, 255, 434
Canada, 102, 307, 360
Cannon-Bard Theory, 281
Canoes, 2–3, 2 (figure)
Cape Town, South Africa, 452
Caribou Eskimos, 52
Carter, Jimmy, 364
Castes, 202 (table)
Categorization styles, 239–241,
240 (figure), 241 (table)
Catfishing, 145
Cause, perceived, 406

Centers for Disease Control and
Prevention, 388
Change, cultural, 66–69, 68 (figure),
71, 79
Chastity, 143
Chelā, 95
Chen, Edison, 311
Childbirth, 165–166, 427 (table), 428
Childhood:
early, 172
health, physical, 384–386
middle, 172–176
theory of mind and, 16–18
toddlers, 169–172
Child poverty, 385
Chile, 272–273
Chimpanzees, 18–19, 40–41, 40
(figure), 43, 44
China:
ancestors, 189–190
bridge of birds tale, 200–201
cognition, 239, 243, 244
elder care, 183, 184
emotions, 283, 292
forgiveness, 324
group interaction concepts, 63
love, 219
mental health practice, 414–415
morality, 314
motivation, 326–327
negotiation, 447–448
self-enhancement, 308
self-improvement, 137–138
social orientation, 238
Chinese Americans, 283
Chinese herbal medicine, 414–415
Chinese language, 324
Chinese Personality Assessment
Inventory (CPAI), 91, 107, 122
Chiron, 380
Christianity, 329
Civil war, 341, 373
Climate, 49, 282
Co-ethnics, 348, 373
Cognition:
about, 234–235, 235–237
arts and, 260–263
categorization styles, 239–241,
240 (figure), 241 (table)

defined, 373
holistic and analytic thought,
238–239
human versus animal, 13
intelligence, 250–255
reasoning and contradiction,
243–244
social orientation, 238–239
time, 241–243
*See also* Consciousness;
Perception
Cognitive, defined, 157, 197
Cognitive development, 93, 158,
159, 161 (table)
Cognitive dissonance, 138, 153
Cognitive reframing, 287, 298
Cohly, Hari, 100
Cohorts, 157, 197
Collectivism, 63–64, 65 (table), 140,
153, 373
*See also* Individualism-
collectivism dimension
Colonialism, 336, 373, 450–451
Color, language of, 249–250
*Comedia dell'arte*, 118, 118 (figure)
Communication:
about, 266–267
context dependence and,
278–280
cultural patterns in, 277–280
difficulties in, 28
evolution of human, 267–271
innovation and, 23–24
language acquisition, 272–276
linguistic, 270–271
nonverbal, 277–278
*Communitas*, 75, 94, 416
Communities:
acculturation and, 359–360
defined, 374
ethics of, 317 (table)
ethnic, 99–100
Indian, 358–359, 369, 370
(figure)
multiculturalism and, 429–430,
431 (table)
well-being and, 391 (table)
Community violence exposure, 430
*Compadrazgo*, 202 (table)

Companionate love, 218–219
Compensation, 439–440
Competition, 51
*See also* Conflict and competition
Concepts, generally, 236–237, 264
Conceptual equivalence, 105
Concubinage, 202 (table)
Confederate Flag, 72–73
Conflict and competition:
about, 445–446
conflict styles, 446–447, 447
(figure)
diversity issues, ongoing,
451–452
forgiveness and reconciliation,
448–451, 449 (figure)
negotiation, 447–448
Conflict styles, 446–447, 447
(figure)
Conformist transmission, 51–52
Connectedness, 322, 395–396, 420
Conscientiousness, 121 (table)
Consciousness:
about, 255–256
altered states of, 257–259, 259
(figure), 262–263, 264
dreaming, 256–257
Consensus effects, false, 136 (table)
Consent, informed, 100–102
Consistency, 138
Constancy, 138
Construal, 129, 153
*See also* Self-construal
Construct bias, 104, 112
Contact theory, 357, 359, 370, 451
Content information, 54, 55–57, 79
Contextual information, 237
Contradiction, 243–244
Control, 136 (table), 140, 153,
308–309
Conventional level of moral
development, 313, 313 (table),
315
Conventional wisdom, 32, 36
Cooperation, 16
Cortez, Tika Lanay, 334
Co-sleeping, 168
Côte d'Ivoire, 254
Country and western music, 70

*Djeli*, 174
Dogs, 14, 14 (figure), 267–268, 268 (figure)
Dominican Republic, 240, 241 (table)
*Dosha*, 413
DPD. *See* Dependent personality disorder
Drama, 294, 327, 328 (figure)
Dramatistic pentad, 327, 328 (figure)
Dreaming, 256–257
Dreamtime, 256, 398
DSM-5. *See* Diagnostic and Statistical Manual of Mental Disorders
Dugum Dani, 249
Dunbar's number, 21–22
Dunedin Multidisciplinary Health and Development Study, 119
Dyads, 22
Dynamic expression, 285, 298

Ear adornment, 40–41, 40 (figure), 41 (figure)
Early childhood, 172
East Asia:
    cognition and perception, 261
    emotional regulation, 287
    equity, 440
    intelligence, conceptualizations of, 253
    mortality salience, 188
    self-construal, 129
    somatization, 404
    *See also* Asia; *specific countries*
Eating disorders, 407–408
EC. *See* Emotional complexity
Ecocultural model, 407–409, 431
Ecological niche, 124
Ecological systems model, 58–60, 59 (figure), 125, 159, 162
Education, 173–174, 385–386, 443–445
Efficacy/entertainment braid, 149
Egalitarianism, 321
Egypt, 227–228
Elder care, 183–184
Electronic dance music, 263
Electronic self, 144–145
*Elegant Gathering in the Apricot*

*Garden* (Xie Huan), 73, 74 (figure)
Embeddedness, 321
Emerging adulthood, 180–181
Emic, defined, 91, 112
Emotional complexity (EC), 289, 298
Emotional intelligence, 440
Emotional regulation (ER), 286–288, 286 (figure), 298
Emotions:
    about, 266, 267, 280–281
    arts and, 294–296
    basic, 282–283, 298
    body and, 281, 292
    cultural understandings of, 291–293
    emotional regulation, 286–288, 286 (figure)
    experience and expression of, 289–293
    facial expression, 283–285, 284 (figure), 285 (table)
    folk concepts, 290–291
    socially engaged, 325
Emulation, 43, 79
Enculturation:
    about, 52–53
    cultural learning, 173
    defined, 79, 197, 338, 374
Endo, Kenny, 367
Endorsement, perceived, 54
Engagement, 223, 225
Engagement rings, 215–216, 225
Ennui, 290–291
Entitativity, 140, 222, 223 (table)
Entity theory of self, 133, 153
Environmental change, 66
Epidemiology, 402–403
Epigenetic, defined, 164, 197
Epistemic drive, 61
Epistemology, 12, 36, 103, 236–237
Equity, 440
Equivalence, 105–106
ER. *See* Emotional regulation
Erikson, Erik, 158, 159, 179
Ethics of
    autonomy, 316–318, 317 (table)
    community, 316–318, 317 (table)
    divinity, 316–318, 317 (table)

Ethnic diversity, 432, 433 (table)
Ethnic enclaves, 360, 374
Ethnic identity, 145–147
Ethnography, 106
Ethnotheory, 163, 197
Etic:
    defined, 91, 112
    derived, 91, 112
    imposed, 91, 113
Euro-American classical music, 326
European Americans:
    agency and control, 309
    attention, 246
    emotions, 283
    leadership, 432
    mortality salience, 188
    resource distribution, 323
    sleeping practices, 168
Evoked culture, 49, 79
Evolutionary perspective of parental investment theory, 214
Executive function. *See* Agentic self
Experience, openness to, 121 (table)
Extraversion, 121 (table)
Extremity bias, 105, 112
Extrinsic factors, 29, 36
Eyebrows, raised, 266

Face, 139, 153, 307–308
Facial aesthetics, 211–214, 213 (figure)
Facial expression, 283–285, 284 (figure), 285 (table)
*Fado*, 295
Fairey, Shepard, 72, 72 (figure)
Fairness, 440
False consensus effects, 136 (table)
False uniqueness, 136 (table)
Family, 204–209, 360–361
Family Investment Model, 272–273
Fante language, 292
Fathers, 207–209
Fechner, Gustav, 103
Female body attractiveness, 210–214, 210 (figure)
Feminism, 143
Fertility rate, 427 (table), 428
Festival of Lights, 358–359, 369

Hmong immigrants, 430
Holistic thought, 238–239, 264
Holland, 287–288
Holmes-Rahe Life Stress Inventory, 362–363
Hominids, 18–21, 20 (figure)
*Homo erectus*, 19, 20
*Homo habilis*, 19
*Homo heidelbergensis*, 19
Homology, 13, 37
*Homo sapiens neaderthalensis*, 19–20, 20 (figure)
Hong Kong, 311, 326–327
Honor cultures, 308, 324
Horizontal transmission, 51, 53
Horizontal-vertical social structures, 432–433
*Hula*, 352, 367
Human groups, 21–23, 22 (figure)
Human nature orientation, 319, 319 (table)
Human resource management, 435–437
Human thought, 14–18, 14 (figure), 238–239, 264

ICD-10. *See International Statistical Classification of Diseases and Related Health Problems*
ICE. *See* Inclusive Cultural Empathy
*I Ching (Book of Changes)*, 243
Ideas, minimally counterintuitive, 56
Identity:
    defined, 117
    ethnic, 145–147
    multicultural, 354
    multiple, 426
    national, 423–425
    social, 60, 80, 146, 349–350, 426
    *See also* Identity information
Identity information:
    about, 58
    defined, 54, 79
    dimensions of cultural variability, 62–63

layers of groups, 58–60, 59 (figure)
reality, shared, 60–61
social identity theory, 60
values and beliefs, shared, 62
Illness:
    about, 410–411, 411 (table)
    alternative medicine, 411 (table)
    as gift, 380–381, 381 (figure)
    indigenous, traditional, and alternative treatment, 412–414
    practitioners and treatment, 412
    traditional/alternative mental health practice, 414–415
    traditional medicine, 411–412, 411 (table)
Imitation, 43, 44, 175
Immersion schools, 445
Immigrants:
    defined, 335, 374
    New Zealand, 430, 431 (table)
    stress and health, 387
    *See also* Migration
Imposed etic, 91, 113
"In Broad Daylight I Dream" (Mei), 229
Inclusive Cultural Empathy (ICE), 126–127
Income, 383 (figure), 384
Incremental theory of self, 133, 153
Independent, defined, 129, 153
Independent self-construal, 129, 130 (figure), 132
India:
    agency and control, 309
    emotions, 292–293, 294
    ethics, 316–317
    eyebrows, raised, 266
    indigenous psychology, 95
    shamans, 413–414
Indian communities across world, 358–359, 369, 370 (figure)
Indigenization, 100
Indigenous, defined, 374

Indigenous groups:
    Australia, 65, 183, 256, 398
    Big 5, 121
    illness treatment, 410–411, 412–414
    mental health and substance abuse treatment, 179
    migration, 335
    research issues, 99–100, 101–102
    well-being, 396–398
Indigenous psychology, 93–96
Indirect paternal activities, 208
Individualism, 126, 153
    *See also* Individualism-collectivism dimension
Individualism-collectivism dimension:
    about, 62
    agency and control, 309
    cognition, 239, 240, 241 (table)
    communication, 274–275, 278
    education, 444–445
    emotions, 283, 289
    equity, 440
    ethics, 318–319
    forgiveness, 325
    leadership styles, 433
    motivation, 439
    negotiation, 448
    New Zealand, 345–346
    relationships, 203–204
    resource distribution, 322–323
    self-enhancement and self-improvement, 307
    self-esteem, 136–137
Individuality, 117, 153
Indonesia, 262–263, 408, 409
Indonesian language, 248, 274
Industrial-organizational psychology, 62–63, 430–431
Inequality in health, 388
Infancy, 166–169
Infant attachment, 170–171
Infant care, 167–169
Infant mortality, 166, 384
Inferring goals and intentions, 17, 37
Infidelity, 225–226, 228

second language acquisition, 273–274

skills, 24

tools and, 269–270

as a universal, 270

*Latah*, 408

Latin America, 408–409

Latin music, 369

Law of the Splintered Paddle, 301

Layers of groups, 58–60, 59 (figure)

Leadership styles, 432–435, 433 (table)

Learning:

associative, 48

social, 42–47

ways of, 173–175

*See also* Cultural learning and transmission

Leontiev, Alexsei, 86

Levels of analysis, 29, 37, 98, 113

LGBTQ individuals, 362

Life expectancy, 382, 383 (figure), 384

Lifespan development and socialization:

about, 156

adolescence, 177–179

adulthood, 179–185

arts and, 192–194

birth and infancy, 162–169

childhood, 169–176

death and dying, 185–190, 189 (figure), 190 (figure), 191 (figure)

lifespan emphasis in development, 162

perspectives on, 157–159, 160–161 (table), 162

stages in development, 158–159, 160–161 (table), 162

Lili'uokalani (Queen), 422

Limina, 158–159, 177, 197

Linguistic communication, 270–271

Linguistic equivalence, 105

Linguistic relativity, 274–276

Lisbon, Portugal, 295

*Listura*, 254

Locus of control, 140, 153

*Lōkahi*, 64, 65 (table)

London taxi drivers, 242

Los Angeles, 98, 430

Love:

about, 216–217

companionate, 218–219

historical changes and, 224–225

in media, 224–225

music and, 229–230

passionate, 217–218

physiology of, 217–218

triangular theory of, 219

Love poetry, 227–229

"Love the One You're With" (Stills), 328

Low-context cultures, 278–280

Luria, Alexander, 86

Ma, Yo-Yo, 454

Macaques, 17, 18, 41

MacArthur, Douglas, 71

Machiavellian Intelligence Hypothesis, 48

*Machismo*, 143

Macrobands, 22

Macrodemes, 23

Madsen Marble Pull Game, 67, 323

*Maladi moun*, 406 (table)

Malaysia, 9, 9 (figure), 205, 342, 342 (figure)

*Mana*, 434

Mandarin language, 242–243

Mandela, Nelson, 394–395

Manet, Edouard, 73, 73 (figure)

Man-nature orientation, 319, 319 (table)

Māori:

colonialism and forgiveness, 451

creativity, 27

education, 445

individualism-collectivism, 345–346

leadership, 434

*marae*, 33, 117, 147–148, 397

multiculturalism and, 358, 359

relationships, 201

self, 116–117, 116 (table)

shoe removal indoors, 9–10

*tapu* system, 9–10, 396–397

values, 438

well-being, 396–397

*whakapapa*, 116–117, 147–148, 434

*whare tapa wha*, 116, 116 (table), 124, 397

Mapuche, 273

*Marae*, 33, 117, 147–148, 396

Marble Pull Game, 67, 323

Marginalization, 346–347, 351, 374

Marriage and intimacy:

about, 202 (table)

engagement, 223, 225

mating, 222–223, 223 (table), 225

problems in relationships, 225–226, 226 (table)

types of mating/marital arrangements, 205, 221, 221 (table)

Masculinity–femininity dimension, 63

Masks, 118, 118 (figure), 148

Maslow's hierarchy of needs, 304, 394–395, 395 (figure)

Mastery, 306, 321

Maternal mortality, 385

Mating, 222–223, 223 (table), 225

Mayans:

cognitive skills, 92

identity/memberships, multiple, 426

modernization, effects of, 67

prenatal development, 164–165

wounded healer, 380, 380 (figure)

Mealtime, 5, 5 (figure)

Measurement equivalence, 105

Media, love in, 224–225

Medically directed birth, 166

Melting pot, 339, 364, 374

Memberships, multiple, 426

Memes, 53, 80, 236

Mental development, 385, 420

Mental illness. *See* Psychopathology

Mentalism, 18

Mentality, 92

Menzo, Guido, 346

Merrie Monarch Festival, 352, 367

Metarepresentation, 18, 37

Method bias, 104

Methodological considerations:
about, 103
bias and equivalence, 104–106
mixed methods studies, 106–108
qualitative studies, 106
quantitative studies, 103–104
Mexican Americans, 187
Microexpressions, 285
Middle adulthood, 181–182
Middle childhood, 172–176
Midlife crisis, 182
Midwives, 165
Migration:
adaptation and acculturation, 335–337, 335 (figure), 337 (figure), 341–343
defined, 374
Great Pacific Migration, 2–3
*See also* Acculturation; Immigrants
Military, 441–443
Milk-kinship, 202 (table)
Mimesis, 44, 80
Minimally counterintuitive ideas, 56
Minorities and health, 387, 388, 410–411
Mirror neurons, 44, 80
Misremembering, 136 (table)
Mixed methods studies, 106–108
Moderacy bias, 105, 113
Modernization, effects of, 67–69, 68 (figure)
*Monet Family in Their Garden at Argenteuil, The* (Manet), 73, 73 (figure)
Monogamy, 221 (table)
*Mono no aware*, 228, 229, 295–296, 298
Moore's Law, 12, 37
Moral development, 312–316, 313 (table)
Morals:
about, 300–302, 310–311
arts and, 327–330, 328 (figure)
cross-cultural theories, 312–316, 313 (table)
defined, 302, 331
gossip, 53, 55, 312

moral development, 312–316, 313 (table)
religious, 311, 329
semiotics of, 329–330
sex and sexuality, 311–312
Shweder's systems of ethics, 316–318, 317 (table)
*See also* Motivation
Morocco, 287–288
Mortality:
death and dying, 186–187
infant, 166, 384
maternal, 385
Mortality salience, 185–186, 188, 197
Mothers, 207, 309, 384–386
Motivation:
about, 302–304
achievement, 305–306
agency and goals, 305–309
arts and, 326–327
compensation and, 439–440
defined, 302, 331
fundamental, 303–304
migration, 341–343
self-enhancement and self-improvement, 306–308
work-related values, 439–440
*See also* Morals
Movies, 77, 224–225, 369
MUDs. *See* Multi-user domains
Müller-Lyer illusion, 173, 192, 244–246, 245 (figure), 249
Multicultural identity, 354
Multiculturalism:
adaptation and acculturation, 335–337, 335 (figure), 337 (figure)
arts and, 453–454
community, 429–430, 431 (table)
conflict and competition, 445–452, 447 (figure), 449 (figure)
defined, 335, 374
demographic shifts, 426, 427 (table), 428
education, 443–445
globalization, 423–426, 427 (table), 428

Hawai'i, 422–423
human resource management, 435–437
identity/memberships, multiple, 426
leadership styles, 432–435, 433 (table)
military, 441–443
national identity and, 423–425
as national-level factor, 356–357
New Zealand, 358–359
organizations, 430–432
sojourners, 441
values, work-related, 438–441
Multicultural psychology, 96–97
Multigenerational households, 205, 206
Multi-layered self, 124–127, 125 (figure), 126 (figure)
Multiple identities/memberships, 426
Multiple intelligences, 252–253
Multi-user domains (MUDs), 145
Music:
acculturation and, 368–369, 370
Bollywood, 76, 369
cognition and perception, 261–262
country and western, 70
culture and, 74–77
Divje Babe flute, 25, 26 (figure)
electronic dance, 263
emotion in, 295
Euro-American classical, 326
Hawaiian steel guitars, 70
hip-hop, 193
history of, 25, 26 (figure), 27
Latin, 369
learning in *djeli* tradition, 174
lifespan development/socialization and, 192, 193–194
love and, 229–230
motivation and, 326–327
multiculturalism and, 453–454
rap, 193, 368
religious, 75

rock and roll, 74–75, 230
songs, 57, 227, 328–329
as stimulus, 110–111
Mysore, India, 309

Nanahuatzin, 380, 380 (figure)
National anthems, 75
National Family Growth Survey, 311
National identity, 423–425
National-level factors in
acculturation, 356–357, 359
Nation-states, 336, 374
Native Americans, 70, 411, 413, 448
See also specific tribes
Natural pedagogy, 52, 57, 80
Nature versus nurture, 157, 197, 282
Nātyaśāstra, 292
Navajo, 179, 245, 433
Navigation, 2–3
Neanderthals, 19–20, 20 (figure)
Needs, hierarchy of, 304, 394–395,
395 (figure)
Negative information, 55–56
Negotiation, 447–448, 456
Nervios, 406 (table)
Neural specialization, 167
Neurology, 242
Neuroscience, cultural, 242
Neuroticism, 121 (table)
New Guinea:
categorization styles, 241
color, language of, 249
facial attractiveness, 212
facial expression, 284, 285 (table)
morality, 314
New York City, 309
New Zealand:
acculturation strategies, 353, 353
(figure)
bicultural system, 358
colonialism and forgiveness, 451
creativity, 27
gender and self, 141
immigrants, 430, 431 (table)
Indian community, 358–359
individualism-collectivism,
345–346
multiculturalism, 358–359

shoe removal indoors, 9
See also Māori
New Zealand Europeans, 345–346,
358
New Zealand Federation of
Multicultural Councils, 430
Nigeria, 434
"1999" (Prince), 329
Ninth Symphony (Beethoven),
76–77
Noa, 396–397
Nonverbal accents, 284–285
Nonverbal communication,
277–278
Nosology, 399, 420
Numerism, 13, 37
Nutrition, 210–211

Obama, Barack, 72, 72 (figure)
Obedience, 87, 101, 110
Objective self-awareness, 133–135,
134 (figure), 153
Obligatory interdependence, 4, 37
Obon festival, 22, 22 (figure), 190,
190 (figure), 191 (figure)
Ocoee Massacre, 451–452
"Ode to Joy" (Beethoven), 76–77
"Ode to Joy" (Schiller), 76–77
'Ohana, 65 (table)
Ojibway, 397–398
Older people, 426, 427 (table), 428
Openness to experience, 121 (table)
Operational definitions, 8, 10, 37
Optimism, unrealistic, 136 (table)
Organizational behavior, 431–432
Organizations, 288, 430–432
See also specific organizations
Oriya, 181, 183, 316–317
Orlando, Florida, 451–452
Orthogonal, defined, 351, 374
Other, 25
Others and self, 128–133, 130
(figure), 131 (figure)
Overconfident judgments, 136
(table)
Overimitation, 45–47, 80
Overtone series, 261–262
Ownership, 102

Pakistan, 222
Pansori singers, 57
Papua New Guinea, 314
Parental attachment style, 171
Parental roles, 163, 206–209
Participant considerations in
cultural research:
about, 97–98
ethnic communities, issues for,
99–100
informed consent issues, 100–102
levels of analysis, 98
representativeness, 98–99
Participation, guided, 173
Passionate love, 217–218
Passive paternal involvement, 208
Paternal investment, 207, 208
Paternal involvement, 207, 208
Peanuts, 345, 345 (figure)
Pedagogy, 52, 57, 80, 445
People's Republic of China. See
China
Perceived cause, 406
Perceived control, 136 (table)
Perceived endorsement, 54
Perceived sharedness, 54
Perception:
about, 234–235, 244–246, 245
(figure)
arts and, 260–263
attention, 246–247
field dependence/independence,
247–248
language and, 248–250
See also Cognition; Consciousness
Performance, altered states in,
262–263
Peripheral possession, 258
Perry, Katy, 70
Perry, Matthew, 95
Persistence, 307
Persona:
about, 117–118
personality theories, 119–123
temperament, 118–119
Personality, defined, 118, 153
Personality theories, 119–123
Personhood, concepts of, 102

Relationships:
  arts and, 227–230
  attraction, 209–215, 210 (figure),
    213 (figure)
  bridge of birds tale, 200–201
  couples, 215–221
  family, 204–209
  friendships, 203–204
  love, 216–219
  marriage and intimacy, 221–226,
    221 (table), 223 (table),
    226 (table)
  problems in, 225–226, 226 (table)
  roles, 201–209, 202 (table)
  sex, 219–221
Relativism, 90–91, 113, 249
Religious complexes, 27
Religious moralities, 311, 329
Religious music, 75
*Ren qing*, 122
Replicability, 108–110, 113
Representativeness, 98–99, 113
Research considerations:
  about, 82
  approaches to studying psychology
    and culture, 89–97
  arts, in psychological research,
    110–111
  history of culture and psychology,
    84–89
  issues in psychological study of
    culture, 83–84
  methodological considerations,
    103–108
  participant considerations,
    97–102
  replicability issues, 108–110
Resilience, 178–179
Resource distribution, 322–323
Revitalization, cultural, 179
Rings, engagement, 215–216, 225
Ritual, 416
Ritual covenant, 202 (table)
Ritual possession, 258
Robbers' Cave experiment, 453
Rock and roll, 74–75, 230
Rokeach Values Survey, 320
Role conflict, 408–409
Role models, overimitation of, 46

Roles:
  about, 201, 202 (table), 203
  defined, 201
  family, 204–209
  friendships, 203–204
  parental, 163, 206–209
Romance:
  love, 216–219, 224–225
  sex, 219–221
"Rosie the Riveter," 224, 224
  (figure)
Rotating credit associations, 202
  (table)
Russia, 289–290

Salad bowl, 364–365, 375
Samburu, 323
Samoa, 106, 192
Sample bias, 104, 113
Sampling, 126
Sanskrit language, 292–293
Sapir-Whorf hypothesis, 248–249,
  274
*Saudade*, 294–295, 298
Scapegoating, 346
Schachter-Singer two-factor model,
  281
*Schadenfreude*, 291, 298
Schiller, Fredrich, 76–77
Schizophrenia, 401–402
Schwartz's theory of basic values,
  320–322, 321 (figure)
Second language acquisition,
  273–274
Second Life, 145
*Second Symphony* (Beethoven), 193
Secret societies, 202 (table)
Self:
  agentic, 128, 139–140, 152
  arts and, 147–149
  electronic, 144–145
  ethnic identity and, 145–147
  gender and, 141–144
  incremental theory of, 133, 153
  as individual, 117–123
  interpersonal, 128, 153
  Māori, 116–117, 116 (table)
  multi-layered, 124–127, 125
    (figure), 126 (figure)

others and, 128–133, 130 (figure),
    131 (figure)
  persona, 117–123
  perspectives on, 123–127
  public, 153
  self-awareness, perception,
    and choice, 133–140, 134
    (figure), 136 (table)
  tripartite model of, 126, 126
    (table), 148
Self-actualization, 304
Self-awareness:
  defined, 153
  objective, 133–135, 134
    (figure), 153
  subjective, 134, 153
Self-concept, 153
Self-construal:
  defined, 129, 153
  identifying self and others,
    128–129, 130 (figure), 131
    (figure), 132–133
  independent, 129, 130 (figure), 132
  interdependent, 129, 131
    (figure), 132
  unpackaging studies, 104
Self-determination theory, 309
Self-enhancement, 135–136, 136
    (table), 137, 153, 306–308
Self-esteem, 135, 136–138, 153, 306
Self-fulfilled connectedness, 322
Self-improvement, 137–138,
    306–308
Self-knowledge, 128, 153
Self-regulation, 172
Self-serving attributions, 136 (table)
Self-serving beliefs, 136 (table)
Self-serving biases, 136 (table)
Semiology, 92
Semiotics, 92, 236, 329–330
"Semiotic Subject of Cultural
  Psychology, The" (Shweder &
  Sullivan), 92
Senior citizens, 426, 427 (table), 428
Sensitive periods, 162, 167, 197
Separation, 351, 375
Sequence time, 241, 264
SES. *See* Socioeconomic status
Sex and sexuality, 219–221, 311–312

Toddlers, 169–172
*Toi*, 27
Tonga, 393–394
Tonoho O'odham, 174
Tools, 15, 43, 44, 269–270
Torture, 442–443
Totemic relationships, 202 (table)
Toyota, 435–436
Trade routes, 71
Tradition, 47–48
Traditional medicine, 411–415, 411 (table)
Traits, defined, 153
Trait theories of personality, 119–123
Trance and possession phenomena, 257–259
Transculturation, 70–71, 80
Transmitted culture, 49, 80
Traveling Thunder, 411
*Treatise on Insanity* (Esquirol), 85, 85 (figure)
Triangular theory of love, 219
Tricksters, 329–330
Tripartite model of self, 126, 126 (table), 148
Trudeau, Justin, 360
Trust, personal, 63, 80, 438
Tsimane', 183
Tuiasosopo, Ronaiah, 145
Turmeric, 100
Turn constructional units (TCUs), 271, 298
Turner, Jakadrien Lorece, 334
Tuskegee Syphilis Study, 101
*Twelfth Night* (Shakespeare), 229

UN Declaration of Human Rights, 382, 389
Uniqueness, false, 136 (table)
United Kingdom, 358, 386
United States:
  agency and control, 309
  beauty norms, 211
  cognition and perception, 239, 246–247, 261
  emotions, 283, 291
  fathers, 208–209

forgiveness, 324
gestures, 278
human resource management, 435–436
immigration, 339, 340 (figure), 430
life expectancy, 382
as melting pot, 364
military, 441–442
negotiation, 448
relationships, 204
self-enhancement and self-improvement, 307
Southern, 308
Vietnamese refugees, 344, 357
Universal grammar, 270
Universalism, 91, 113, 249
University of Alaska Fairbanks, 68–69
University of Mississippi, 100
Unpackaging studies, 104, 113
Unrealistic optimism, 136 (table)

Value, 302, 331
Values:
  basic, 320–322, 321 (figure)
  defined, 302, 320
  forgiveness, 323–325, 448–451, 449 (figure)
  resource distribution, 322–323
  Schwartz's theory, 320–322, 321 (figure)
  shared, 62
  theoretical models, 318–322, 319 (table), 321 (figure)
  values orientation model, 318–320, 319 (table)
  work-related, 438–441
  *See also specific values*
Values orientation model, 318–320, 319 (table)
Variation, 51
Vertical-horizontal social structures, 432–433
Vertical transmission, 51, 53
Veterans, 387
Victoria University of Wellington, 33
Vietnamese refugees, 344, 357
Villermé, René Louis, 382, 384

Violence, 4, 25, 28, 178, 429–430
*Vismaya*, 292, 293
Visual arts:
  cognition and perception, 260–261
  culture and, 72–74, 72 (figure), 73 (figure), 74 (figure)
  history, 27
  moral values, 329
  as stimuli, 110
*Völkerpsychologie*, 85–86
Voluntary acculturation, 341–343
Vygotsky, Lev, 52, 86–87, 159

Waist to hip ratio, 211
*Waka*, 2–3, 2 (figure)
War survivors, 387
Water apartheid, 452
Watson, Bobby, 326
"We Can Do It!" (Miller), 224 (figure)
Well-being:
  about, 378–379
  arts and, 415–418, 417 (figure)
  context, connectedness, and, 395–396
  defined, 389, 420
  global, 390–391, 390–391 (table), 392 (table), 393–394, 393 (table)
  indigenous views of, 396–398
  measuring, 389–390
  physical, 391 (table)
  positive psychology, 394–395, 395 (figure)
  self-esteem and, 306
  social, 390 (table)
  *See also* Health
West Africa, 254–255
  *See also* Africa
Western cultures:
  adolescent rebellion, 178
  cognition and perception, 237, 243, 244, 261
  family structure, 205, 206
  intelligence, 250–253
  self-construal, 129
*Whakapapa*, 116–117, 147–148, 434